The Civil War Era

For our students

The Civil War Era:

An Anthology of Sources

Edited by

Lyde Cullen Sizer *and* Jim Cullen

Blackwell
Publishing

Editorial material and organization © 2005 by Blackwell Publishing Ltd

BLACKWELL PUBLISHING
350 Main Street, Malden, MA 02148-5020, USA
108 Cowley Road, Oxford OX4 1JF, UK
550 Swanston Street, Carlton, Victoria 3053, Australia

First published 2005 by Blackwell Publishing Ltd

Library of Congress Cataloging-in-Publication Data

The Civil War era: an anthology of sources / edited by Lyde Cullen Sizer and Jim Cullen.
    p. cm.
  Includes bibliographical references and index.
  ISBN 1-4051-0690-5 (alk. paper) — ISBN 1-4051-0691-3 (pbk. : alk. paper)
    1. United States—History—Civil War, 1861–1865—Sources. I. Sizer, Lyde Cullen. II.
Cullen, Jim, 1962–

E464.C47 2004
973.7—dc22   2004056041

A catalogue record for this title is available from the British Library.

Set in 10/12pt Sabon
by Kolam Information Services Pvt. Ltd, Pondicherry, India

For further information on
Blackwell Publishing, visit our website:
www.blackwellpublishing.com

Contents

List of Plates

Acknowledgments

Connections made this book, even as this book is about connections. Historian Jacqueline Jones initially enlisted me to do this project, as part of a series in cultural and social history. If it morphed since then, becoming the larger book now in your hands, it was first an idea I adopted in order to work with her. Originally, also, this was a book I took on alone. Only after one of our sons was diagnosed, last summer, with an autistic spectrum disorder did I draw Jim in to help me finish: I will never forget his intellectual and emotional generosity, in putting aside his own work to help me with mine during a time of mutual pain and bewilderment. As the book has come together our son has also come, gradually and tentatively, out of his shell of silence and reserve. Both have been labors of love.

This book also came together on the porch of Jack Thomas's Maine camp house, as all Sizer–Cullen scholarship produced in the last ten years has tended to do. To him goes, as always, our deepest admiration and respect; he remains a mentor, colleague, and dear friend years after graduate school. The Civil War scholars at the Huntington, last fall, were also part of the community that helped this volume along: although the sources had been chosen beforehand, their laughter, vibrant scholarship, and scholarly camaraderie encouraged me on at a faltering moment. Both Catherine Clinton and David Blight, in particular, have reached out to Jim and me on numerous occasions, modeling the best in collegiality. I remain as always very glad to have met Alice Fahs at a Berks conference when still graduate students; she's been a marvelous fellow traveler throughout the strains and successes of our early careers.

Sarah Lawrence College has been a fruitful place to work, in all kinds of ways. Thanks, as always, go to our marvelous librarians, particularly dear friends Judy Kicinski and Jenni MacSpadden, and wonderful computer guru Jenn Reshen. Historian Priscilla Murolo remains one of the best of colleagues, in her acute and decided way, and the Faculty Writing Group has helped my thinking on the Civil War era along throughout the past ten years. Research assistants Emily Park, Kristen Kuriga, and Marguerite Avery have been invaluable resources for this volume over the past years: Thank you.

With a family as large and busy as mine only a strong infrastructure could make writing and assembling a book possible. For Jan Drucker, maybe the strongest thread in my safety net of the last year, my gratitude knows no bounds. Without Jan, and the many caregivers who tended my children so lovingly and so well, there would be no book. And without my running partners Alexandra Soiseth, Patricia Dunn, and now Elizabeth Haase, there would be no sanity, without which there might as well be no book. My loving, generous family, in their own ways scholars all, also made this possible. And for Jim, Jay (budding historian of his own), Grayson, Ryland, and Nancy, powerful and beloved distractions, there are no words.

Finally, this book is for our students. Buoyed by their energy, challenged by their insight, tickled by their enthusiasm, inspired by their passion for truth and social justice, they remind us again and again of the immense humanity, intelligence, and decency possible in a world today – as in the mid-nineteenth century – full of unnecessary suffering.

Lyde Cullen Sizer
Yonkers, NY, May 2004

Besides seconding the thanks cited above, it is essential to add, on behalf of Lyde and myself, special thanks to Ken Provencher of Blackwell, who has shown extraordinary patience and generosity in bringing this project to fruition. Thanks are also due to Kelvin Matthews, Linda Auld, Louise Spencely, and Mervyn Thomas for their skills and advice during production.

J.C.

The editors and publisher gratefully acknowledge the permission granted to reproduce the copyright material in this book:

Bruce Catton, "A House Divided," in *The American Heritage Picture History of the Civil War* (New York: American Heritage Publishing, 1960), pp. 9–13. Reprinted by permission of American Heritage.

William W. Freehling, "The Divided South, Democracy's Limitations, and the Causes of the Peculiarly North American Civil War," in *Why the Civil War Came*, ed. Gabor S. Boritt (New York: Oxford University Press, 1996), pp. 127–37, 167–75. Copyright © 1996 by Gabor S. Boritt. Used by permission of Oxford University Press, Inc.

Louisa S. McCord, "Uncle Tom's Cabin," in *Southern Quarterly Review* 7, 13 (January 7, 1853), 81–120 in *Louisa S. McCord: Political and Social Essays*, ed. Richard C. Lounsbury (Charlottesville: University Press of Virginia, 1995), *pp.* 245–80. Reprinted with permission of the University of Virginia Press.

George M. Fredrickson, "The Spirit of '61," in *The Inner Civil War: Northern Intellectuals and the Crisis of the Union* (New York: Harper & Row, 1965), pp. 65–78.

Keziah Goodwyn Hopkins Brevard, "Diary of Keziah Hopkins Brevard" 1860, South Caroliniana Library, University of South Carolina, in *Our Common Affairs: Texts from Women in the Old South*, ed. Joan E. Cashin (Baltimore: Johns Hopkins University Press, 1996), p. 263. Reprinted by permission of the South Caroliniana Library.

Eric T. Dean, Jr., " 'Dangled over Hell': The Trauma of the Civil War," in *Shook Over Hell: Post-Traumatic Stress, Vietnam, and the Civil War* (Cambridge, MA: Harvard University Press, 1997), pp. 46–69. Copyright © 1997 by Eric T. Dean, Jr. Reprinted by permission of the publisher.

Wilbur Fisk, "Letter to Family, Camp near Harrison's Landing, Virginia" (July 15, 1862), in *Hard Marching Every Day: The Civil War Letters of Private Wilbur Fisk, 1861–1865*, ed. Emil and Ruth Rosenblatt (Lawrence: University Press of Kansas, 1988), pp. 36–40. Copyright © University Press of Kansas 1988. Reprinted by permission of the University Press of Kansas.

Reid Mitchell, "The War at Home," in *Civil War Soldiers* (New York: Simon & Schuster, 1988), pp. 64–75. Copyright © 1988 by Reid Mitchell. Used by permission of Viking Penguin, a division of Penguin Group (USA) Inc.

Jeanie Attie, " 'For the Boys in Blue': Organizing the Home Front," in *Patriotic Toil: Northern Women and the American Civil War* (Ithaca, NY: Cornell University Press, 1998), pp. 87–91; 99–104. Copyright © by Cornell University. Used by permission of the publisher, Cornell University Press.

Fanny Perry, "Letter to Norfleet Perry, Spring Hill, Texas" (December 28, 1862), in *We Are Your Sisters: Black Women in the Nineteenth Century*, ed. Dorothy Sterling (New York: Norton, 1984), p. 240. From *The Journal of Negro History*, vol. 65, no. 4, (Autumn 1980), 363–4. Reprinted by permission of the Association for the Study of African American Life and History.

Phillip Shaw Paludan, "Industrial Workers and the Costs of War", in *"A People's Contest": The Union and Civil War, 1861–1865* (New York: Harper & Row, 1988), pp. 170–97.

W. J. Cash, *The Mind of the South* (New York: Knopf, 1941), pp. 15–17. Copyright © 1941 by Alfred A. Knopf, Inc. and renewed 1969 by Mary R. Maury. Used by permission of Alfred A. Knopf, a division of Random House, Inc.

Mary Herrick, "Letters to Edwin Stanton, Nunda, NY" (May 30, 1863), in *Root of Bitterness: Documents of the Social History of American Women Second Edition*, eds. Nancy F. Cott, Jeanne Boydston, Ann Braude, Lori Ginzberg, and Molly Ladd-Taylor (Boston, MA: Northeastern University Press, 1996) pp. 268–9. Copyright ©1996 by Nancy F. Cott. Reprinted with the permission of Northeastern University Press.

James L. Roark, "A Loss of Mastery," in *Masters Without Slaves: Southern Planters in the Civil War and Reconstruction* (New York: Norton, 1977), pp. 68–91. Copyright © 1977 by W. W. Norton & Company, Inc. Used by permission of W. W. Norton & Company, Inc.

Tera W. Hunter, "Answering Bells is Played Out," in *To 'Joy My Freedom: Southern Black Women's Lives and Labors after the Civil War* (Cambridge, MA: Harvard University Press, 1997), pp. 4–20. Copyright © 1997 by the President and Fellows of Harvard College. Reprinted by permission of the publisher.

G. W. Hatton, "Letter, Wilson's Landing, Virginia" (May 28, 1864), in *A Grand Army of Black Men: Letters from African-American Soldiers in the Union Army, 1861–1865*, ed. Edwin S. Redkey (New York: Cambridge University Press, 1992), pp. 95–6. Reprinted by permission of Cambridge University Press.

Eric Foner, "The Meaning of Freedom in the Age of Emancipation," *The Journal of American History*, vol. 81, no. 2 (Sept 1994) 435–60. Copyright © 1994 Organization of American Historians. Reprinted with permission.

L. Maria Child, "Mrs L. Maria Child to the President of the United States," in *A Lydia Maria Child Reader* ed. Carolyn L. Karcher (Durham, NC: Duke University Press, 1997), pp. 254–61. Copyright © 1997 Duke University Press. All rights reserved. Used by permission of the publisher.

Frederick Douglass, "Emancipation Proclaimed," in *Douglass' Monthly* (October 1862), in *Frederick Douglass: Selected Writings and Speeches,* ed. Philip S. Foner, abridged and adapted by Yuval Taylor (1950; Chicago: Lawrence Hill Books, 1999), pp. 517–20. Reprinted by permission of the publisher.

Iver Bernstein, "A Multiplicity of Grievances," in *The New York City Draft Riots: Their Significance for American Society and Politics in the Age of the Civil War* (New York: Oxford University Press, 1990), pp. 17–42. Copyright © 1990 by Iver Bernstein. Used by permission of Oxford University Press, Inc.

Adelaide Fowler, "Letter to Henry Fowler" (July 1863, Daversport, MA), in *Yankee Correspondence: Civil War Letters Between New England Soldiers and the Home Front*, eds. Nina Silber and Mary Beth Sievens (Charlottesville: University of Virginia Press, 1996), p. 120 Reprinted by permission of The Phillips Library at the Peabody Essex Museum.

Alvin Josephy, Jr., "The Way to Pea Ridge," in *The Civil War in the American West* (New York: Alfred A. Knopf, 1991), pp. 319–30. Copyright © 1991 by Alvin M. Josephy, Jr. Used by permission of Alfred A. Knopf, a division of Random House, Inc.

Emory M. Thomas, *The Confederate Nation, 1861–1865* (New York: Harper & Row, 1979), pp. 190–9. Copyright ©1979 by Emory M. Thomas. All rights reserved. Reprinted by arrangement with HarperCollins Publishers, Inc.

William E. Gienapp, *Abraham Lincoln and Civil War American: A Biography* (New York: Oxford University Press, 2002), pp. 165–76. Copyright © 2002 by William E. Gienapp. Used by permission of Oxford University Press, Inc.

Drew Gilpin Faust, "What Shall We Do?," in *Mothers of Invention: Women of the Slaveholding South in the American Civil War* (Chapel Hill: University of North Carolina Press, 1996), pp. 9–19. Copyright © 1996 by the University of North Carolina Press. Used by permission of the publisher.

Jim Cullen, "I's a Man Now: Gender and African-American Men," in *Divided Houses: Gender and the Civil War*, eds. Catherine Clinton and Nina Silber (New York: Oxford University Press, 1992), pp. 76–91. Copyright © 1992 by Catherine Clinton and Nina Silber. Used by permission of Oxford University Press, Inc.

Alice Fahs, "Popular Literary Culture in Wartime," in *The Imagined Civil War: Popular Literature of the North & South, 1861–1865* (Chapel Hill: University of North Carolina, 2001), pp. 17–41. Copyright © 2001 by the University of North Carolina Press. Used by permission of the publisher.

James McPherson, "The Same Holy Cause," in *For Causes and Comrades: Why Men Fought in the Civil War* (New York: Oxford University Press, 1997), pp. 167–79. Copyright © 1997 by Oxford University Press, Inc. Used by permission of Oxford University Press, Inc.

Garland H. White, (April 12, 1865), in *A Grand Army of Black Men: Letters from African-American Soldiers in the Union Army, 1861–1865*, ed. Edwin S. Redkey (New York: Cambridge University Press, 1992), pp. 175–8. Reprinted by permission of Cambridge University Press.

Laura Edwards, " 'Privilege' and 'Protection': Civil and Political Rights during Reconstruction," in *Gendered Strife and Confusion: The Political Culture of Reconstruction* (Urbana: University of Illinois Press, 1997), pp. 184–98.

David Blight, "Quarrel Forgotten or Revolution Remembered? Reunion and Race in the Memory of the Civil War, 1875–1913," in *Union and Emancipation: Essays on Politics and Race in the Civil War Era* (Kent, OH: Kent State University Press, 1997), pp. 151–79. With permission of The Kent State University Press.

Every effort has been made to trace copyright holders and to obtain their permission for the use of copyright material. The publisher apologizes for any errors or omissions in the above list and would be grateful if notified of any corrections that should be incorporated in future reprints or editions of this book.

Plate 1 Picturing the Battle: Photographer Timothy O'Sullivan took this picture of artist Alfred R. Waud making a sketch of the Battle of Gettysburg in the summer of 1863. What any of us know about the Civil War is mediated in the most literal sense of the term – sometimes many times over. (Selected Civil War photographs, Library of Congress)

Introduction: The American Civil War in the Twenty-first Century

The Civil War Ain't What it Used to Be

In some sense, of course, this is nonsense. After all, the Civil War is history, and history is a record of past events, events whose outcome is known and unchanging. Read any account of the Civil War – and as the most popular subject in American history, there are a great many of them – and nowhere will you learn that General Grant surrendered to General Lee, that South Carolina chose to remain in the Union, or that Abraham Lincoln lived until his sixty-fifth birthday. The facts don't change, and for all the what-if speculation on the part of war-gaming enthusiasts or the academic theorizing of college professors, the fact remains that facts remain the core of history, Civil War or any other kind.

But then the question becomes: *which* facts? Depending on who is recording them, where the recorder happens to be in time or space, and to what end – for history without an end, moral or temporal, is finally pointless – very different, even conflicting, true stories can be told. Yes, Lee (or, more accurately, the thousands of men who followed his orders) lost at Gettysburg. No one disputes that fact. But facts are meaningless unless they're interpreted, and interpretation is inherently subjective. So, why does it *matter* that Lee lost? Is it because Gettysburg shows that Lee, for all his brilliance – and you're going to have a hard time finding accounts that say Lee wasn't brilliant – overreached militarily on the outskirts of a small Pennsylvania town on July 3, 1863? Or is it because Gettysburg shows the inherent limits of outmanned Confederate armies? Or perhaps it was simply that Lee's soldiers were simply unlucky that day (after all, they came *so* close during Pickett's Charge!). Anyone who reads multiple accounts of the Civil War will find it hard to escape the conclusion that when it comes to the Battle of Gettysburg, among others, the past keeps changing.

You might say that there are as many Civil Wars as there are people willing to narrate or to receive them. But between the two extremes – one fixed war and countless unique ones – there are some relatively stable, albeit overlapping, categories of interpretation. This is worth keeping in mind: the past may keep changing, but it doesn't necessarily change all that much.

The first of these broad, widely shared categories is generational. Just as people who come of age at a particular time tend to have similar taste in music – how many people born before 1965 do you know who like hip-hop? – so too do they often have a similar take on what constitutes common sense. For example, somebody who lived through the Great Depression, whatever one's income, tends to think about money differently than someone who lived through the Internet boom of the 1990s. And the experiences of *their* lifetimes tend to affect the way they view the experiences of *other* ones. Of no event is this more true than the Civil War. At different times in the last hundred years, the Civil War has been viewed as a tragic mistake (as old enemies embraced, and died, in the early twentieth century); an inevitable conflict between capitalism and feudalism (in the wake of Progressive era modernization); the product of blundering politicians (when ominous dictatorships waxed and passive democracies waned between World Wars); a moral crusade against slavery (when the Civil Rights movement was seen as the Civil War of the 1960s); and so on. Not everybody felt the same way at a given time, of course. But enough people did for a particular view to become the dominant one, the standard against which other views were measured.

This brings us to another lens through which people view the past: ideology. People with a general political outlook on matters that affect their lives often apply that outlook more broadly. So, for example, someone angry about the ravages of capitalism in the twenty-first century may well cast a skeptical eye on the triumph of the industrial North in the Civil War. So might someone who feels that national government tends not to be as responsive to peoples' needs as local government. On the other hand, someone who thinks of race as the most important organizing principle in American life is likely to regard these issues as secondary at best. The views of any of these people may correspond to a generational view of history, or may lead them to reject such conventional wisdom. History, you might say, is the story of how conventional wisdom changes.

Perhaps the most striking divide of the past century in Civil War history has been between so-called "professional" and "popular" historians and their followers. Professional historians have formal academic training; the PhD is in effect a membership card in a guild that values shared criteria for research, writing, and teaching. This guild first formed in the late nineteenth century amid the growth of large research universities in Europe and the United States, and while there have been important shifts in emphasis or demographic priorities, the parameters of historical scholarship have been quite stable. No one *has* to follow rules about bibliographies, footnotes, and publication by a prestigious scholarly press, but no one who fails to follow such rules is likely to be taken seriously by other members of the guild. Professional academics covet, and occasionally even win, large general audiences for their work. But their primary loyalty (in terms of their salaries, if not their hearts) is to each other.

Popular historians, by contrast, are a much more motley lot, consisting of novelists, filmmakers, re-enactors and other enthusiasts, along with writers of non-fiction articles and books. They have little allegiance to – and often some scorn for – academic historians. Popular historians see themselves, often correctly, as cultural democrats, people whose primary allegiance is to the People. The impact of popular history on the Civil War is especially significant, because it is an event that has inspired some of the most famous and beloved works of popular culture in American history. Though there are some exceptions to the rule, it may be safely said that while academics have class appeal, popular historians have mass appeal.

It is widely believed that professional and popular versions of the Civil War diverge greatly in terms of topic and temperament. In many cases, this is true. Nowadays, the typical work of Civil War academic history will be a short, tightly focused monograph on a particular wartime movement or development (like, say, the passage and impact of the Thirteenth Amendment to the Constitution), whereas a reader of a magazine like *Civil War Times* is likely to read a reassessment of a lesser-known general or an account of a particular regiment in a major battle.

Academic historians tend to highlight, even insist, on the centrality of slavery; popular historians tend to resist, even deny, its importance. Yet it would be an oversimplification to consider such characterizations fixed, or to deny the influence these factions have on each other. The most famous – and notorious – film of the early twentieth century, D. W. Griffith's *Birth of a Nation* (1915), offered viewers a scathing view of the post-Civil War period of Reconstruction consonant with most professional scholarship of the time. Three Civil War films from the turn of the current century – Ang Lee's *Ride with the Devil* (1999), Martin Scorsese's *Gangs of New York* (2002), and Anthony Minghella's *Cold Mountain* (2003) – depict people on the fringes of the fighting to raise compelling questions about how much sense it makes to make clear distinctions between North and South, Union and Confederate, even freedom and slavery. So do many scholarly books.

This book is avowedly academic. As editors of this volume, both of whom hold PhDs, we welcome readers of all kinds. But we're assuming this is something you're reading because a teacher in a college course assigned it, not because that teacher assumes you're going to become a professional historian (a real danger for a few of you, perhaps). We're hoping that the practice of thinking, reading, and writing like a historian will foster analytic skills that can help you improve your judgment so that you can both hold a good conversation with your roommate about what the Civil War was *really* about, and take those skills with you into the voting booth.

This may be an academic book, but it's a particular *kind* of academic book. *The American Civil War* is a textbook anthology of sources. Let's break that down into its component parts.

- *Textbook*: Among other things, to say this is a textbook is to say what it's *not*: a trade book, something you typically read for fun. You're reading this book as part of an attempt to master some material and develop good habits of thought. Also, this is a textbook because its primary purpose is pedagogical: it's more about learning new information than about participating in a professional scholarly discourse. Many of the people in this book are distinguished academics, chosen so you can listen in on their conversation with relative ease – and start a few conversations of your own. But although the material here is challenging, this is meant to be an introduction to the Civil War for intelligent beginners, not the Civil War for seasoned experts.
- *Anthology*: As you've probably already noticed, this is not a typical textbook that covers a topic A–Z – or, as one might expect of a history text, a volume that describes the Civil War in a chronological fashion. Instead, it's a collection of pieces, mostly excerpts from longer works, that have been arranged thematically. We imagined this book to be a companion volume, something to accompany a standard textbook history or a professor's lectures. The essays and documents in this book can add color and texture to other material – a movie you've been assigned *for* class, or a discussion you're going to have *in* class. They may also serve as a point of departure for an essay you might write.
- *Sources*: To call this book an anthology of sources is redundant – what anthology isn't? But it nevertheless seems useful to do so because the word "sources" helps emphasize just what kind of anthology this is – an academic one, and, more specifically, a historical one. Sources are the very tissue of historical scholarship. While a novelist or poet can at least theoretically invent from imagination, any kind of history – even the most imaginative kind – must rely on some kind of previously recorded information. This book is a big repository of such information: *primary* sources produced during the war, and *secondary* sources about the war written in its aftermath. It's meant to be a point of departure for any number of journeys into Civil War history.

Having explained what the book is, perhaps it would now be useful to explain how it's organized. The heart of the volume comprises 15 Parts, each divided into two main sections. The first of these consists of one or two essays by a noted historian on the topic in question. The second consists of documents that relate to the topic of the essay. All of these pieces begin with headnotes that put them in context, and all of them include topics for discussion (short pieces have a question or two in the headnote; longer ones in a "Questions to Consider" box at the end). You might think of this book as a freezer full of easy-to-cook classes; just heat with intellectual energy and serve.

We've tried to provide a tasty mix of entrées here, but inevitably there are limits, limits that reflect our expertise and priorities as well as that of a publisher that wanted us to come up with a book that came in under 500 pages. There are all kinds of Civil War topics not covered here. Here are some important examples:

- *Foreign policy*: To a great degree, the success of the Confederate cause hinged on official recognition from a major European power, particularly Britain, and even presumably domestic initiatives like the Emancipation Proclamation were implemented with foreign policy considerations in mind (something that is touched on in the section on Emancipation). International disputes over damaged property, as well as incidents like the Trent Affair of 1861, in which the Lincoln administration backed down and released Confederate agents who had been traveling on a British vessel, loomed large in the war years.
- *Technology*: The Civil War was in many ways the first modern war in the history of the world: railroads, repeating rifles, and early experimentation with ironclad ships and submarines are among the innovations that came out of, or were greatly accelerated by, the war. Foreign governments sent military observers to monitor these developments. As many historians have noted, the trench warfare style of fighting that had evolved on the eastern front in particular anticipated that of the First World War by half a century.
- *The naval war*: The Union's grand strategy of the Civil War, ultimately realized, consisted of three parts: dividing the Confederacy in half by gaining control of the Mississippi River; dividing again by slicing diagonally from down the Tennessee River to the Atlantic seaboard; and encircling its circumference with a naval blockade that stretched from Virginia to Texas. This was known as the "Anaconda plan," after the snake that chokes its prey. Of the three components, the blockade is typically the least remembered and arguably the most decisive. Moreover, other aspects of the naval war are very much bound up in others like technology (those ironclads) and foreign policy (the Trent Affair).

So why aren't these topics covered in depth in this book? We've already given some reasons, like space and our expertise. But there are others that reflect what kind of book – what kind of *academic* book – this is.

For most of the past 150 years, a book about the Civil War has generally involved some very traditional topics: politics, military affairs, and every once in a while, economic and social issues (slavery figuring prominently among these). These are important matters, and they're discussed here. But this book also reflects some of the more recent trends in academic scholarship in the past three decades, and those trends involve inquiries into sub-disciplines like social history, which focuses on everyday life rather than that of leading political figures, and cultural history, which focuses more on widely shared ideas rather than exclusively those of major intellectuals. We have also tried to reconceptualize some of the most basic assumptions surrounding Civil War history – like the simple division, questioned in movies like *Ride with the Devil* and *Gangs of New York*, between North and South. In fact, there were many sides in the Civil War: Union and Confederate; white and black; east and west; rich and poor, country and city, male and female, and so on. We have also tried to highlight the significant points of overlap, like the aspects of military service (mud, sweat, tears) that were common to veterans of both sides. Again, the point here is not to be comprehensive – a truly hopeless goal – but to stimulate, provoke, and maybe even annoy you enough to articulate your own ideas through the process of sorting through those of others.

In all these ways, then, this book about a long-ago event known as the Civil War is inevitably a book of its time, i.e. the early twenty-first century. But we feel compelled to end this introduction by asking: is the Civil War really a long-ago event? In what sense is it actually over? Have slavery and its legacy ceased to be an issue in American life? Has the relationship between states and the federal government been settled? Consider the electoral map of the United States today, when most of the old Confederacy continues to vote as a bloc (once Democratic, now Republican) as does New England (same story, inverted – how the inversion took place is the subject for another book). Newer states largely settled by northerners, like Oregon, are inhabited by people who tend to think and act differently than those largely settled by southerners, like Oklahoma, and not even large waves of immigration have made much difference. Then as now, national elections tend to be decided by Border States like Ohio and Pennsylvania, whose heritage was shaped by both regions. A great deal has changed. But a great deal has not.

Let's end with a conclusion not just about Civil War history, but about the study of history generally. Here it is – There are really only two moments in time: *now* and *not now*. "Now" may be defined as this morning, or the epoch that began when Columbus arrived, or when Christ was born, or when humans acquired opposable thumbs. "Not now," by contrast, might be that moment when you were still getting along with your boyfriend, or before September 11, or, yes, before the Civil War – a "not now" so widely used in American life that it has its very own (Latin) adjective: "antebellum." Like a binary code of ones and zeroes that creates an endless strand of possibilities, history, a complex strand of "now" and "not now," is finally an unfinished journey in search of the truth.

And so it is that when you turn the page the war will begin again.

Questions to consider

- What are some of the ways "the past keeps changing"?

- How would you describe the difference between "professional" and "popular" history?

- What kinds of things should you – and shouldn't you – expect to learn about the Civil War from this book?

Plate 2 Serpentine Approach: An 1861 cartoon map by J. B. Elliott of Cincinnati illustrating Gen. Winfield Scott's plan to crush the Confederacy economically via naval blockade. This "Anaconda plan," as it was known in honor of the snake of the same name, did indeed choke the rebels and played a major role in their ultimate defeat. (Geography and Map Division, Library of Congress)

A Civil War Chronology

The Antebellum Era

1607: Virginia Company founds first permanent English settlement in North America.

1619: First slaves imported into North America through Virginia.

1620: Mayflower passengers, bound for Virginia, settle instead on Cape Cod.

1630: Massachusetts Bay Company founders settle in Boston.

1682: Pennsylvania settled by anti-slavery Quakers.

1754–63: Seven Years' War marks British triumph over French in North America.

1765–75: Amid tensions with Britain, inter-colonial cooperation grows in form of Stamp Act Congress, Committees of Correspondence, and Continental Congress.

1775–83: American Revolution.

1781: Mason–Dixon line marks commonly accepted boundary between North and South.

1785–6: Northwest Ordinances bar slavery from new states of upper Midwest.

1787: Constitutional Convention works out sectional tensions via three-fifths Compromise, ending of the international slave trade in 1808, and Fugitive Slave provision, convincing Southern states to ratify the agreement.

1793: Eli Whitney invents cotton gin, intensifying demand for slave labor.

1797: Responding to the Alien & Sedition Acts, Virginia and Kentucky legislatures pass resolutions that assert states' right to void national measures.

1803: Louisiana Purchase more than doubles the territory of United States.

1804: Essex Junto plans northern confederacy of New England, New York, and New Jersey opposed to policies of the Thomas Jefferson administration.

1812–14: War of 1812 with Britain.

1814: Hartford Convention denounces federal actions in the War of 1812, leading to accusations of disloyalty to the Union. Treaty of Ghent resolves the War (December).

1816: American Colonization Society founded to buy freedom for slaves and send them to Liberia.

1819–20: Missouri Compromise (also known as the Compromise of 1820). Missouri admitted to union as slave state, Maine as free state, and 36'30' line going west to henceforth demarcate boundary between future free and slave states.

1828–32: Nullification Controversy. South Carolina threatens to leave Union over tariff policy, then relents in the face of possible military retaliation by President Andrew Jackson's administration.

1831: First abolitionist newspaper, *The Liberator*, founded.

Nat Turner slave insurrection.

Virginia legislature debates, and rejects, emancipation proposals.

1836–44: US House imposes "gag rule" forbidding discussion of slavery.

1844–5: Texas annexation debate.

1846: Wilmot Proviso, proposing that any territory acquired from Mexico be designated as non-slavery.

Mexican War begins.

1848: Treaty of Guadelope–Hildago ends Mexican War.

1850: Compromise of 1850. Among its provisions: California enters Union as free state; slave trade abolished in Washington DC; stronger Fugitive Slave Act.

1851: *Uncle Tom's Cabin* begins serial publication as response to the Fugitive Slave Act.

1854: Kansas–Nebraska Act replaces Missouri Compromise by having territories vote to decide for themselves whether to allow slavery.

1856–7: Pro- and anti-slavery forces fight for control over Kansas government.

1857: US Supreme Court *Scott v. Sandford* decision rules that slaves have no rights under federal law and that property rights trump state laws regarding slavery.

Kansas adopts pro-slavery constitution in election marked by widespread fraud.

1858: Lincoln–Douglas debates galvanize national conversation about slavery.

1859: John Brown leads failed abolitionist insurrection on Federal armory in Virginia.

1860: Abraham Lincoln elected president.

South Carolina becomes first state to leave the Union (December).

The American Civil War, 1861–5

1861: A total of ten more states leave the Union (January–May).

Confederate constitution written and adopted; capital moves from Montgomery, AL to Richmond, VA (February–May).

Fort Sumter, SC attacked and taken by Confederate forces (April).

Confederates win decisive victory in First Battle of Bull Run, VA (July).

Abraham Lincoln capitulates to British demands and releases Confederate agents captured aboard British ship in the *Trent* Affair (December).

1862: Union launches unsuccessful Peninsular Campaign in the East to capture Richmond (March–July).

Confederates fail to stop Union advance down the Mississippi at the Battle of Shiloh, TN (April).

Union amphibious force captures New Orleans (April).

Confederates relieve pressure on Richmond from Peninsular Campaign with victory in the Second Battle of Bull Run (August).

First major Confederate invasion of Northern-held territory at Battle of Antietam, MD, is a draw militarily, but becomes pretext for Preliminary Emancipation Proclamation (September).

Confederates win decisive victory at Fredericksburg (December).

1863: Emancipation Proclamation officially takes effect (January).

Union forces approach and lay siege to Vicksburg, MS, the last Confederate stronghold on the Mississippi River (March–July).

Confederates confound Union advance at the Battle of Chancellorsville (May).

Confederates advance into Pennsylvania but are defeated at the Battle of Gettysburg (July).

Vicksburg falls into Union hands; Confederacy split (July).

Confederate counterattack in the West pushes Union forces back on Tennessee River at Chickamauga (September).

Union line solidifies despite Confederate assault on the Tennessee at Chattanooga (November).

1864: Fierce fighting with massive casualties marks Wilderness Campaign in the east; Union and Confederate forces wheel around Richmond and stalemate at Petersburg, south of the Confederate capital (March–December).

Atlanta campaign commences on the Tennessee and culminates with capture of the city (May–September).

Abraham Lincoln re-elected to second term as president (November).

"Sherman's March to the Sea" results in scorched earth policy from Atlanta to Savanna (November–December).

1865: Congress passes and Abraham Lincoln signs the Thirteenth Amendment to the Constitution ending slavery everywhere in the United States; 27 states ratify it (February–December).

Under threat of complete encirclement, Confederate forces withdraw from Richmond, culminating in their surrender at Appomattox Court House (April).

Lincoln assassinated in Washington (April).

Remaining major Confederate forces surrender in Louisiana and North Carolina (April–May).

Reconstruction, 1863–77

1863: Lincoln administration announces plan for Reconstruction whereby a seceded state would return to the Union when 10 percent of its citizens swear loyalty to the Union.

1864: Congress responds to Lincoln plan with Wade–Davis bill requiring 50 percent of a state's citizens to give loyalty the Union; Lincoln vetoes it.

1865: Lincoln's successor, Andrew Johnson, tries to continue Lincoln's approach amid growing Congressional resistance. Johnson gives amnesty to most Confederates, some of whom are then elected to Congress. Republican majority in Congress refuses to seat them.

1866: Johnson vetoes bill to extend Freedmen's Bureau created during the war to help newly emancipated slaves; "Black Codes" passed in Southern states restrict their freedom. Ku Klux Klan formed in Tennessee.

1867: Republican-led Congress passes Tenure of Office Act requiring Senate review of Cabinet dismissals, as well as Reconstruction Act dividing Southern into military districts and imposing more stringent rules for readmission.

1868: Johnson impeached for violating Tenure of Office Act, but acquitted in the Senate. Ratification of Fourteenth Amendment guarantees Civil Rights on the federal level. Ulysses S. Grant elected president.

1870: Fifteenth Amendment gives African American men the right to vote.

1877: Last occupying US troops leave the South in aftermath of the presidential election of 1876. "Redemption" of former Confederate states complete. South will be "solid" for Democrats for next century. Jim Crow laws go on books, modeled on antebellum northern statutes.

Part I

The Impending Crisis

Plate 3 Little Big Man: Confederate Vice-President Alexander Stephens, in a photograph taken some time between 1860 and 1865. Stephens, a former US Congressman (where he had been friendly with the obscure – and considerably taller – Abraham Lincoln) described slavery as the "cornerstone" of Southern life in 1861, but later emphasized the constitutional basis for secession in his postwar writings. (Selected Civil War photographs, Library of Congress)

Chapter 1

A House Divided

Bruce Catton

Where to begin: This crucial question confronts any storyteller, whether that storyteller is a reporter describing a traffic accident, a student writing a term paper, or a historian narrating a battle. Very often, the task of providing an answer is more complex than it initially appears. Does the story of the accident begin at the scene of the crash, for example, or at the bar where the driver had too much to drink? And if, upon establishing the story really does begin with the drinking, should it be the first thing the storyteller says? How much does a reader need to know to understand an event, and how much of the importance of an account depends on the person who narrates it? These are issues that almost instantly confront any writer – and, for that matter, any attentive reader. (Speaking of which: are you awake, dear reader? Rub your eyes or get some coffee. We're in the nineteenth century now, and you never know when writers are going to address you directly.)

For few events is the question of beginnings more complicated than the American Civil War. On the surface, it seems straightforward: the war began when shots were first fired at Fort Sumter, South Carolina, on April 12, 1861. Not a bad place to start, except that there were no casualties there, and one generally expects wars to involve people who get hurt or killed. By that definition, you might say, the war really began with the First Battle of Bull Run – known as "First Manassas" by Confederates – in July of that year. (The Union tended to name battles after the nearest major geographical feature – in this case, a creek – while the Confederacy did so on the basis of the nearest town.) People were certainly shot, wounded, and killed there. But then plenty of shots had been fired in Kansas in the mid-1850s: although it's not usually customary to say so, one could make a case that the fighting began there.

But then we get into the notion of how you define "fighting" – is it all about bullets? – and whether one should really have such a narrow definition of warfare, which involves social and political conflict as well as military engagement. One can clearly see the roots of the Civil War in the struggle between Northern and Southern states in the ratification of US Constitution, for example, and sectional tensions were apparent long before that.

For those who regard slavery as the core issue, one could point to the arrival of the first slave in Virginia in 1619 as a pivotal turning point. (This is what film director D. W. Griffith did in his legendary – and notorious – 1915 film *Birth of a Nation*.) But now we've gone back 242 years from Fort Sumter, which is a little impractical for our purposes.

So we're going to have to be pragmatic about this, to begin this book with as much simplicity and clarity as possible. And when it comes to sparse clarity there have been few Civil War writers who can match Bruce Catton. Catton (1899–1978) informed and enthralled generations of students in his many books on the subject. In this excerpt, from his now-classic centennial history of the Civil War, he provides an overview of the conflict that touches on some of the most important events leading up to the conflict. Subsequent generations of historians may question his emphasis or sense of balance, but none have exceeded his gracefulness. Catton should not be considered the last word on the Civil War. But one could do worse than make him the first.

Bruce Catton, "A House Divided," in *The American Heritage Picture History of the Civil War* (New York: American Heritage Publishing, 1960), pp. 9–13. Reprinted by permission of American Heritage.

The American people in 1860 believed that they were the happiest and luckiest people in all the world, and in a way they were right. Most of them lived on farms or in very small towns, they lived better than their fathers had lived, and they knew that their children would do still better. The landscape was predominantly rural, with unending sandy roads winding leisurely across a country which was both drowsy with enjoyment of the present and vibrant with eagerness to get into the future. The average American then was in fact what he has been since only in legend, an independent small farmer, and in 1860 – for the last time in American history – the products of the nation's farms were worth more than the output of its factories.

This may or may not have been the end of America's golden age, but it was at least the final, haunted moment of its age of innocence. Most Americans then, difficult as the future might appear, supposed that this or something like it would go on and on, perhaps forever. Yet infinite change was beginning, and problems left unsolved too long would presently make the change explosive, so that the old landscape would be blown to bits forever, with a bewildered people left to salvage what they could. Six hundred thousand young Americans, alive when 1860 ended, would die of this explosion in the next four years.

At bottom the coming change simply meant that the infinite ferment of the industrial revolution was about to work its way with a tremendously energetic and restless people who had a virgin continent to exploit. One difficulty was that two very different societies had developed in America, one in the North and the other in the South, which would adjust themselves to the industrial age in very different ways. Another difficulty was that the differences between these two societies were most infernally complicated by the existence in the South of the institution of chattel slavery. Without slavery, the problems between the sections could probably have been worked out by the ordinary give-and-take of politics; with slavery, they became insoluble. So in 1861 the North and the South went to war, destroying one America and beginning the building of another which is not even yet complete.

In the beginning slavery was no great problem. It had existed all across colonial America, it died out in the North simply because it did not pay, and at the turn of the century most

Americans, North and South alike, considered that eventually it would go out of existence everywhere. But in 1793 Yankee Eli Whitney had invented the cotton gin – a simple device which made it possible for textile mills to use the short-staple cotton which the Southern states could grow so abundantly – and in a very short time the whole picture changed. The world just then was developing an almost limitless appetite for cotton, and in the deep South enormous quantities of cotton could be raised cheaply with slave labor. Export figures show what happened. In 1800 the United States had exported $5,000,000 worth of cotton – 7 per cent of the nation's total exports. By 1810 this figure had tripled, by 1840 it had risen to $63,000,000, and by 1860 cotton exports were worth $191,000,000 – 57 per cent of the value of all American exports. The South had become a cotton empire, nearly four million slaves were employed, and slavery looked like an absolutely essential element in Southern prosperity.

But if slavery paid, it left men with uneasy consciences. This unease became most obvious in the North, where a man who demanded the abolition of slavery could comfort himself with the reflection that the financial loss which abolition would entail would, after all, be borne by somebody else – his neighbor to the south. In New England the fanatic William Lloyd Garrison opened a crusade, denouncing slavery as a sin and slaveowners as sinners. More effective work to organize antislavery sentiment was probably done by such Westerners as James G. Birney and Theodore Weld, but Garrison made the most noise – and, making it, helped to arouse most intense resentment in the South. Southerners liked being called sinners no better than anyone else. Also, they undeniably had a bear by the tail. By 1860 slave property was worth at least two billion dollars, and the abolitionists who insisted that this property be outlawed were not especially helpful in showing how this could be done without collapsing the whole Southern economy. In a natural reaction to all of this, Southerners closed ranks. It became first unhealthy and then impossible for anyone in the South to argue for the end of slavery; instead, the institution was increasingly justified as a positive good. Partly from economic pressure and partly in response to the shrill outcries of men like Garrison, the South bound itself emotionally to the institution of slavery.

Yet slavery (to repeat) was not the only source of discord. The two sections were very different, and they wanted different things from their national government.

In the North society was passing more rapidly than most men realized to an industrial base. Immigrants were arriving by the tens of thousands, there were vast areas in the West to be opened, men who were developing new industries demanded protection from cheap European imports, systems of transportation and finance were mushrooming in a fantastic manner – and, in short, this dynamic society was beginning to clamor for all sorts of aid and protection from the Federal government at Washington.

In the South, by contrast, society was much more static. There was little immigration, there were not many cities, the factory system showed few signs of growth, and this cotton empire which sold in the world market wanted as many cheap European imports as it could get. To please the South, the national government must keep its hands off as many things as possible; for many years Southerners had feared that if the North ever won control in Washington it would pass legislation ruinous to Southern interests.

John C. Calhoun of South Carolina had seen this first and most clearly. Opposing secession, he argued that any state could protect its interests by nullifying, within its own borders, any act by the Federal government which it considered unconstitutional and oppressive. Always aware that the North was the faster-growing section, the South foresaw the day when the North would control the government. Then, Southerners believed, there would be legislation – a stiff high-tariff law, for instance – that would ruin the South. More and more, they developed the theory of states' rights as a matter of self-protection.

Although there were serious differences between the sections, all of them except slavery could have been settled through the democratic process. Slavery poisoned the whole situation. It was the issue that could not be compromised, the issue that made men so angry they did not want to compromise. It put a cutting edge on all arguments. It was not the only cause of the Civil War, but it was unquestionably the one cause without which the war would not have taken place. The antagonism between the sections came finally, and tragically, to express itself through the slavery issue.

Many attempts to compromise this issue had been made. All of them worked for a while; none of them lasted. Perhaps the most that can be said is that they postponed the conflict until the nation was strong enough – just barely so – to survive the shock of civil war.

There had been the Missouri Compromise, in 1820, when North and South argued whether slavery should be permitted in the land acquired by the Louisiana Purchase. Missouri was admitted as a slave state, but it was decreed that thereafter there should be no new slave states north of the parallel that marked Missouri's southern boundary. Men hoped that this would end the whole argument, although dour John Quincy Adams wrote that he considered the debate over the compromise nothing less than "a title-page to a great, tragic volume."

Then there was the Compromise of 1850, which followed the war with Mexico. Immense new territory had been acquired, and Congressman David Wilmot of Pennsylvania introduced legislation stipulating that slavery would never be permitted in any of these lands. The Wilmot Proviso failed to pass, but it was argued furiously, in Congress and out of it, for years, and immense heat was generated. In the end the aging Henry Clay engineered a new compromise. California was to be admitted as a free state, the territories of New Mexico and Utah were created without reference to the Wilmot Proviso, the slave trade in the District of Columbia was abolished, and a much stiffer act to govern the return of fugitive slaves was adopted. Neither North nor South was entirely happy with this program, but both sections accepted it in the hope that the slavery issue was now settled for good.

This hope promptly exploded. Probably nothing did more to create anti-Southern, antislavery sentiment in the North than the Fugitive Slave Act. It had an effect precisely opposite to the intent of its backers: it aroused Northern sentiment in favor of the runaway slave, and probably caused a vast expansion in the activities of the Underground Railroad, the informal and all but unorganized system whereby Northern citizens helped Negro fugitives escape across the Canadian border. With this excitement at a high pitch, Harriet Beecher Stowe in 1852 brought out her novel *Uncle Tom's Cabin*, which sold three hundred thousand copies in its first year, won many converts to the antislavery position in the North, and, by contrast, aroused intense new resentment in the South.

On the heels of all of this, in 1854 Senator Stephen A. Douglas of Illinois introduced the fateful Kansas–Nebraska Act, which helped to put the whole controversy beyond hope of settlement.

Douglas was a Democrat, friendly to the South and well liked there. He cared little about slavery, one way or the other; what he wanted was to see the long argument settled so that the country could go about its business, which, as he saw it, included the development of the new Western country between the Missouri River and California. Specifically, Douglas wanted a transcontinental railroad, and he wanted its eastern terminus to be Chicago. Out of this desire came the Kansas–Nebraska Act.

Building the road would involve grants of public land. If the northerly route were adopted the country west of Iowa and Missouri must be surveyed and platted, and for this a proper territorial organization of the area was needed. But the South wanted the road to go to the

Pacific coast by way of Texas and New Mexico. To get Southern support for his plan, the Illinois Senator had to find powerful bait.

He found it. When he brought in a bill to create the territories of Kansas and Nebraska he put in two special provisions. One embodied the idea of "popular sovereignty" – the concept that the people of each territory would decide for themselves, when time for statehood came, whether to permit or exclude slavery – and the other specifically repealed the Missouri Compromise. The South took the bait, the bill was passed – and the country moved a long stride nearer to war.

For the Kansas–Nebraska Act raised the argument over slavery to a desperate new intensity. The moderates could no longer be heard; the stage was set for the extremists, the fire-eaters, the men who invited violence with violent words. Many Northerners, previously friendly to the South, now came to feel that the "slave power" was dangerously aggressive, trying not merely to defend slavery where it already existed but to extend it all across the national domain. Worse yet, Kansas was thrown open for settlement under conditions which practically guaranteed bloodshed.

Settlers from the North were grimly determined to make Kansas free soil: Southern settlers were equally determined to win Kansas for slavery. Missouri sent over its Border Ruffians – hardfisted drifters who crossed the line to cast illegal votes, to intimidate free-soil settlers, now and then to raid an abolitionist town. New England shipped in boxes of rifles, known as Beecher's Bibles in derisive reference to the Reverend Henry Ward Beecher, the Brooklyn clergyman whose antislavery fervor had led him to say that there might be spots where a gun was more useful than a Bible. The North also sent down certain free-lance fanatics, among them a lantern jawed character named John Brown.

By 1855 all of this was causing a great deal of trouble. Proslavery patrols clashed with antislavery patrols, and there were barn-burnings, horse-stealings, and sporadic shootings. The free-soil settlement of Lawrence was sacked by a proslavery mob; in retaliation, John Brown and his followers murdered five Southern settlers near Pottawatomie Creek. When elections were held, one side or the other would complain that the polls were unfairly rigged, would put on a boycott, and then would hold an election of its own; presently there were two territorial legislatures, of clouded legality, and when the question of a constitution arose there were more boycotts, so that no one was quite sure what the voters had done.

Far from Kansas, extremists on both sides whipped up fresh tensions. Senator Charles Sumner, the humorless, self-righteous abolitionist from Massachusetts, addressed the Senate on "the crime against Kansas," loosing such unmeasured invective on the head of Senator Andrew Butler of South Carolina that Congressman Preston Brooks, also of South Carolina, a relative of Senator Butler, caned him into insensibility on the Senate floor a few days afterward. Senator William H. Seward of New York spoke vaguely but ominously of an "irrepressible conflict" that was germinating. Senator Robert Toombs of Georgia predicted a vast extension of slavery and said that he would one day auction slaves on Boston Common itself. In Alabama the eloquent William Lowndes Yancey argued hotly that the South would never find happiness except by leaving the Union and setting up an independent nation.

Now the Supreme Court added its bit. It had before it the case of Dred Scott, a Negro slave whose master, an army surgeon, had kept him for some years in Illinois and Wisconsin, where there was no slavery. Scott sued for his freedom, and in 1857 Chief Justice Roger Taney delivered the Court's opinion. That Scott's plea for freedom was denied was no particular surprise, but the grounds on which the denial was based stirred the North afresh. A Negro of slave descent, said Taney, was an inferior sort of person who could not be a citizen of any state and hence could not sue anyone; furthermore, the act by which Congress had forbidden slavery in the Northern territories was invalid because the Constitution gave slavery ironclad protection. There was no legal way in which slavery could be excluded from any territory.

An intense political ferment was working. The old Whig Party had collapsed utterly, and the Democratic Party was showing signs of breaking into sectional wings. In the North there had risen the new Republican Party, an amalgamation of former Whigs, free-soilers, business leaders who wanted a central government that would protect industry, and ordinary folk who wanted a homestead act that would provide free farms in the West. The party had already polled an impressive number of votes in the Presidential campaign of 1856, and it was likely to do better in 1860. Seward of New York hoped to be its next Presidential nominee; so did Salmon P. Chase, prominent antislavery leader from Ohio; and so, also, did a lawyer and former congressman who was not nearly so well known as these two, Abraham Lincoln of Illinois.

In 1858 Lincoln ran for the Senate against Douglas. In a series of famous debates which drew national attention, the two argued the Kansas–Nebraska Act and the slavery issue up and down the state of Illinois. In the end Douglas won re-election, but he won on terms that may have cost him the Presidency two years later. Lincoln had pinned him down: Was there any lawful way in which the people of a territory could exclude slavery? (In other words, could Douglas' "popular sovereignty" be made to jibe with the Supreme Court's finding in the Dred Scott case?) Douglas replied that the thing was easy. Slavery could not live a day unless it were supported by protective local legislation. In fact, if a territorial legislature simply refused to enact such legislation, slavery would not exist regardless of what the Supreme Court had said. The answer helped Douglas win re-election, but it mortally offended the South. The threatened split in the Democratic Party came measurably nearer, and such a split could mean nothing except victory for the Republicans.

The 1850s were the tormented decade in American history. Always the tension mounted, and no one seemed able to provide an easement. The Panic of 1857 left a severe business depression, and Northern pressure for higher tariff rates and a homestead act became stronger than ever. The depression had hardly touched the South, since world demand for cotton was unabated, and Southern leaders became more than ever convinced that their society and their economy were sounder and stronger than anything the North could show. There would be no tariff revision, and although Congress did pass a homestead act President James Buchanan, a Pennsylvanian but a strong friend of the South, promptly vetoed it. The administration, indeed, seemed unable to do anything. It could not even make a state out of Kansas, in which territory it was clear, by now, that a strong majority opposed slavery. The rising antagonism between the sections had almost brought paralysis to the Federal government.

And then old John Brown came out of the shadows to add the final touch.

With a mere handful of followers, Brown undertook, on the night of October 16, 1859, to seize the Federal arsenal at Harpers Ferry and with the weapons thus obtained to start a slave insurrection in the South. He managed to get possession of an enginehouse, which he held until the morning of the eighteenth; then a detachment of US marines – temporarily led by Colonel Robert E. Lee of the US Army – overpowered him and snuffed out his crack-brained conspiracy with bayonets and clubbed muskets. Brown was quickly tried, was convicted of treason, and early in December he was hanged. But what he had done had a most disastrous effect on men's minds. To people in the South, it seemed that Brown confirmed their worst fears: this was what the Yankee abolitionists really wanted – a servile insurrection, with unlimited bloodshed and pillage, from one end of the South to the other! The fact that some vocal persons in the North persisted in regarding Brown as a martyr simply made matters worse. After the John Brown raid the chance that the bitter sectional argument could be harmonized faded close to the vanishing point.

It was in this atmosphere that the 1860 election was held. The Republicans nominated Lincoln, partly because he was considered less of an extremist than either Seward or Chase; he was moderate on the slavery question, and agreed that the Federal government lacked power to interfere with the peculiar institution in the states. The Republican platform, however, did represent a threat to Southern interests. It embodied the political and economic program of the North – upward revision of the tariff, free farms in the West, railroad subsidies, and all the rest.

But by now a singular fatalism gripped the nation. The campaign could not be fought on the basis of these issues; men could talk only about slavery, and on that subject they could neither talk nor, for the most part, even think, with moderation. Although it faced a purely sectional opposition, the Democratic Party promptly split into halves. The Northern wing nominated Douglas, but the Southern wing flatly refused to accept the man because of his heresy in regard to slavery in the territories; it named John C. Breckinridge of Kentucky, while a fourth party, hoping desperately for compromise and conciliation, put forward John Bell of Tennessee.

The road led steadily downhill after this. The Republicans won the election, as they were bound to do under the circumstances. Lincoln got less than a majority of the popular votes, but a solid majority in the electoral college, and on March 4, 1861, he would become President of the United States ... but not, it quickly developed, of all of the states. Fearing the worst, the legislature of South Carolina had remained in session until after the election had been held. Once it saw the returns it summoned a state convention, and this convention, in Charleston on December 20, voted unanimously that South Carolina should secede from the Union.

This was the final catalytic agent. It was obvious that one small state could not maintain its independence; equally obvious that if South Carolina should now be forced back into the Union no one in the South ever need talk again about secession. The cotton states, accordingly, followed suit. By February, South Carolina had been joined by Mississippi, Alabama, Georgia, Florida, Louisiana, and Texas, and on February 8 delegates from the seceding states met at Montgomery, Alabama, and set up a new nation, the Confederate States of America. A provisional constitution was adopted (to be replaced in due time by a permanent document, very much like the Constitution of the United States), and Jefferson Davis of Mississippi was elected President, with Alexander Stephens of Georgia as Vice-President.

Perhaps it still was not too late for an adjustment. A new nation had come into being, but its creation might simply be a means of forcing concessions from the Northern majority; no blood had been shed, and states which voluntarily left the old Union might voluntarily return if their terms were met. Leaders in Congress worked hard, that winter of 1861, to perfect a last-minute compromise, and a committee led by Senator John J. Crittenden of Kentucky worked one out. In effect, it would re-establish the old line of the Missouri Compromise, banning slavery in territories north of the line and protecting it south; it would let future states enter the Union on a popular sovereignty basis; it called for enforcement of the fugitive slave law, with Federal funds to compensate slaveowners whose slaves got away; and it provided that the Constitution could never be amended in such a way as to give Congress power over slavery in any of the states.

The Crittenden Compromise hung in the balance, and then collapsed when Lincoln refused to accept it. The sticking point with him was the inclusion of slavery in the territories; the rest of the program he could accept, but he wrote to a Republican associate to "entertain no proposition for a compromise in regard to the extension of slavery."

So the last chance to settle the business had gone, except for the things that might happen in the minds of two men – Abraham Lincoln and Jefferson Davis. They were strangers, very unlike each other, and yet there was an odd linkage. They were born not far apart in time or space; both came from Kentucky, near the Ohio River, and one man went south to become spokesman for the planter aristocracy, while the other went north to become representative of the best the frontier Northwest could produce. In the haunted decade that had just ended, neither man had been known as a radical. Abolitionists considered Lincoln too conservative, and Southern fire-eaters like South Carolina's Robert B. Rhett felt that Davis had been cold and unenthusiastic in regard to secession.

Now these two men faced one another, figuratively, across an ever-widening gulf, and between them they would say whether a nation already divided by mutual misunderstanding would be torn apart physically by war.

Questions to consider

- What are some of the broad social differences Catton identifies between the North and South in the decades preceding the Civil War? Which do you think are the most important?

- Catton identifies a number of important events – the Wilmot Proviso; the Kansas–Nebraska Act; the Dred Scott Decision; John Brown's Raid; the election of Abraham Lincoln – that greatly heightened the tension between North and South. Which of these do you think was the turning point?

- What role did the growth of the nation play in heightening sectional tension?

- At a number of points in the nineteenth century, politicians were able to settle their differences, notably the Compromise of 1820 and again in 1850. Yet by 1860, with the failure of the Crittenden Compromise, this became impossible. Why? Who do you blame?

Chapter 2

The Divided South, Democracy's Limitations, and the Causes of the Peculiarly North American Civil War

William W. Freehling

One perennial issue for historians of Southern history is that of difference. So, for example, they have debated questions like whether the South was a feudal society in contrast to the industrial North, or whether its slave economy was in essence capitalistic, just like that of the rest of the country. They've also asked if the South was like other slave societies of its time in Latin America (or earlier ones in other parts of the world), or whether it was unique.

For the distinguished American historian William W. Freehling, there is little doubt that the South was a place apart – distinct from the lands to the south, distinct from the territory to the north. And yet at the very time it was unique it was also divided from within, shaped by a powerful minority that was itself separate from the population, black as well as white, that surrounded it. These realities shaped the development of the region in the decades that led up to the Civil War. The power of this minority, Freehling says, goes a long way toward explaining "Why the War Came" – the title of the book from which this essay was adapted.

William W. Freehling, "The Divided South, Democracy's Limitations, and the Causes of the Peculiarly North American Civil War," in *Why the Civil War Came*, ed. Gabor S. Boritt (New York: Oxford University Press, 1996), pp. 127–37, 167–75. Copyright © 1996 by Gabor S. Boritt. Used by permission of Oxford University Press, Inc.

Democracy has become the most coveted American export. The cold war has been won; the democratic way vindicated. Throughout yesterday's totalitarian half of the globe, long-repressed voices demand freedom of speech, free elections, and majority rule. As the twenty-first century approaches, Americans have seemingly lived up to their seventeenth-century forebears' ambition: to become a City Upon a Hill for all the world to emulate.

Such ideological imperialism, however, has sometimes ill-served this nation. In striving to spread their supposedly ideal political system, Americans on occasion have generated foreign policy disasters, especially in Vietnam. So now more than ever, historians must remind their fellow citizens that democracy, like all things human, is no universal panacea. American democracy indeed could not peacefully resolve our own gravest social problem, slavery. It is a telling historical irony that of all the New World slavocracies, only slaveholders in the United States lived in an advanced republic, and only the United States required a civil war between whites to abolish slavery for blacks.

Despite that singularity of the American Civil War, violence sometimes accompanied emancipation in less republican New World regimes. Abolition in Haiti evolved out of an equally singular civil war, in that case between slaves and slaveholders. Agitation over emancipation also led to some bloodshed in Cuba. So too, slaveholders' rage at not receiving recompense for their slaves helped inspire a revolution in Brazil after emancipation. But nowhere else in the Americas did slaveholders rise in revolution before emancipation, accepting the risks of a military showdown with nonslaveholders.

The southern slaveholders' unique acceptance of trial by warfare demanded unique self-confidence. Secession required both nerve and the perception of power. The Brazilian and Cuban slavocracies could have no such nerve in the 1870s and 1880s, after watching US slaveholders go down in flames in the 1860s. Nor did their nondominant position in their respective political power structures embolden Cuban or Brazilian slaveholders with the illusion that they could win a civil war.

Latin American slaveholders also lacked illusions about their worldwide economic power. No Caribbean or South American planter imagined that his European customers would intervene on his side in a New World civil war. Fantasies that European customers would bolster King Cotton's army, however, rarely dominated the secessionists' thinking. Rather, US slaveholders' unique political power inside a peculiarly advanced republic above all else instilled in them the illusion – and for a long while the reality – that they could control slavery's fate.[1]

Or to be more accurate, the minority of slaveholders inside the US majoritarian republic swung between feelings of infuriating powerlessness and perceptions of imperial powerfulness, as they exerted their unusual leverage over slavery's destiny. On the one hand, some ideological and institutional aspects of US republicanism empowered nonslaveholding majorities to assault the slaveholding minority. Because of the possibility of majority control, US slaveholders were potentially as much at the mercy of outside forces as were Latin American slaveholders, who could only postpone their less democratic governments' emancipation decrees. On the other hand, some aspects of the US republican system, as embedded in the Constitution, empowered the slaveholder minority to resist emancipation in a manner impossible elsewhere in the Americas. The southern minority's power over the northern majority inspired a new northern word, the most charged in the antebellum political vocabulary: *Slavepower*. The term connoted the driving force of the US sectional controversy: the slaveholders' arguably undemocratic power over northern white citizens no less than over southern black slaves.

All of the resulting thrusts for power – the northern majority's disavowal of the Slavepower's dominion over whites, the southern minority's secession from the Union after the northern majority rejected Slavepower rule, fugitive slaves' escape from their masters, the Border South's defiance of Deep South disunionism, the North's reversal of slaveholders' secession from the Union – all this unraveling of a republic and coercive reconsolidation stemmed from the foundations of American democratic practice and belief. But America had become an ugly City Upon a Hill, demonstrating that the world's most advanced republic could end slavery only by one of the bloodiest fratricides in human history.

I

The divergent US and Latin American roads toward emancipation began with dissimilar colonial settlements. During the seventeenth century, England, the most republican of the European colonizing nations, sent to the North American mainland by far the largest percentage of nonslaveholding settlers to be found in any New World area containing large numbers of slaves.[2] Because of that comparatively huge white republican population, the thirteen colonies had special leverage to resist English metropolitan impositions on colonial republicanism; and out of that resistance came the American Revolution and the first New World liberation from Old World control. With the establishment of the federal Union, the Revolutionaries encased one of the most extensive slaveholder regimes in the Americas inside the most republican nation in the New World.

Within the republican Union, advanced Anglo-American anti-slavery ideas could especially flourish – if abolitionists could mobilize the majority of nonslaveholders. Yet within the Union, the minority of slaveholders had a special New World power to protect themselves – if they could mobilize the masses. Nowhere else in the New World did slavery's fate hang on popular mobilization.

A second peculiarity in colonial settlement of the future United States ultimately threatened slaveholder mobilization of southern public opinion. Just as a higher proportion of nonslaveholding whites peopled the original thirteen colonies than could be found in other New World locales with large numbers of slaves, so only North American colonists planted slavery primarily in nontropical areas. Anglo-American economists have always echoed the Latin American colonials' conventional wisdom that tropical climates spawned the largest plantation profits. Seventeenth- and eighteenth-century English settlers, however, considered the climate of the most tropical part of North America, the Lower South, too cool for sugar and coffee, Latin America's profitable plantation products. North American colonists turned to other tropical crops for the Georgian and South Carolinian swamplands and Sea Islands on the Atlantic coast. In these Lower South tropics, huge slave gangs grew rice, indigo, and Sea Island cotton.

Nowhere west of the Lower South's coastal swamps, however, could these crops be lucratively extended. The most farflung North American eighteenth-century slaveholder enterprises instead thrived northward, still farther from the sugar- and coffee-producing tropics. North of South Carolina – in Middle South latitudes – North Carolina and especially Virginia planters raised primarily tobacco. North of the Middle South – in Border South latitudes – Delaware and especially Maryland planters raised less tobacco and more grains. Farther yet from the tropics – in the most southern part of the eventually free-labor North – Pennsylvania, New Jersey, and New York grain farmers used some slaves; and in New England, a few Puritans utilized house slaves. In late-eighteenth-century North America, the coolest locale of New World slaveholders, almost four slaves out of five lived north of the more tropical Lower South.

As the eighteenth century gave way to the nineteenth, an invention and a law pressed US slavery toward tropical habitats. Eli Whitney's invention of the cotton gin in 1793 impelled the movement of slaveholders toward Lower South frontiers. Fourteen years later, in 1807, the federal government's closure of the African slave trade contracted the Cotton Kingdom's source of slaves. Unlike mid-nineteenth-century tropical developers in Cuba and Brazil, the two other large New World slavocracies, cotton planters could not legally buy slaves from Africa. But only US slaveholders could purchase slaves from their own northerly, relatively nontropical areas, which had concurrently fallen into chronic economic recession.

A slave drain ensued, especially from the more northern South to the more southern South. Between 1790 and 1860, some 750,000 Middle and Border South slaves traveled downriver to the Cotton Kingdom. The Lower South, which had had 21 percent of US slaves in 1790, had 59 percent in 1860. Maryland and Virginia, with 60 percent in 1790, had 18 percent in 1860. Some 37 percent of Lower South white families owned slaves in 1860, compared with only 12 percent in the Border South, down from 20 percent in 1790.[3]

At the same time that the more southerly US slaveholders expanded toward Latin American-style tropical locations, the more northerly US slavocracy contracted toward Latin American-style antislavery ideas. The Latin American slavocracies lacked the power to defy worldwide antislavery currents in the manner of Lower South slaveholders. Latin slaveholders instead gave ground grudgingly, stalling for more time to reap profits, mostly through the passage of so-called free-womb laws. These edicts freed only slaves born after a given law's enactment and only after they reached a distant target age, usually eighteen or twenty-one. These laws set a clock ticking toward the end of slavery.

The clock ran slowly, satisfyingly so from Latin American slaveholders' perspective. A slave born even a day before a law was passed would never be freed, which meant that slavery could profitably persist for at least fifty years. As for lucky slaves born at the right time, they were lucklessly doomed to involuntary servitude throughout their youth; and by the time they were twelve years old, black children toiled hard in the fields. A series of Latin American regimes with relatively few slaves, including Chile, Peru, and Venezuela, first tried delaying emancipation through free-womb laws. Then in the two Latin American countries with large slave populations, Cuba's Moret Law (1870) and Brazil's Rio Branco Law (1871) brought the free-womb tradition to climax.

Nowhere did free-womb emancipation work as slowly as entrepreneurs had hoped. Abolitionists and slaves pressed for a faster end to the system. Slaves born only a short time before passage of a free-womb law deployed especially angry resistance. In response, slaveholders often bargained individually with their slaves, scheduling freedom for each before the law freed any. Slaves, in return, promised to labor willingly during the interim.

These bargains drew on older Latin American manumission traditions. Latins had long liberated favorite slaves under certain conditions: when a master and a cherished black woman had a sexual relationship; when beloved mulatto offspring had resulted from such a union; or when a slave had given especially valued economic service. The combination of free-womb laws, expanded manumissions, intensified abolitionist attacks, and more widespread slave resistance finally toppled the regimes in Cuba in 1886 and Brazil in 1888 – or before these slavocracies' respective free-womb laws had freed any slave.

These Latin American patterns, shunned in US tropical areas where slavery was concentrating, had originated in US temperate areas where the institution was dwindling. Freewomb emancipation bore a different title in the United States – post-nati emancipation – but only the name was different. In 1780, Pennsylvania enacted the hemisphere's first post-nati law. In 1799, New York followed suit, as did New Jersey in 1804. In 1817, New York followed up its preliminary post-nati law in the later Cuba/Brazil manner, declaring an end to the institution ten years hence.

South of these belatedly emancipated Middle Atlantic states, slaveholding states never passed a post-nati law. The Border South, however, emulated another aspect of Latin American gradualism: individual manumissions. Different nations took censuses of their populations in different years, which makes comparisons imprecise. Still, a similar pattern of manumission is clear enough. In 1830, 19.5 percent of black residents of the Border South were free, compared with 23 percent in Brazil (in 1817–18) and 46 percent in Cuba (in 1846). Two Border South states manumitted their slaves at rates faster than the Latin American norm. By 1830 in Maryland, 34 percent of the resident blacks were free, as were 83 percent of Delaware's blacks.[4]

But just as post-nati laws penetrated no farther south than the Middle Atlantic states, so manumissions flourished no farther south than the Border South. While 21 percent of Border South blacks were free in 1860, the percentage sank to 7 percent in the Middle South and 1.5 percent in the Lower South. The Border South manumission story was a subplot of the larger tale: that US slavery was incremently waning in northern nontropical habitats but rapidly strengthening in southwestern tropical locales.

With slavery swiftly concentrating southward and slowly fading northward, different social attitudes and political priorities developed. Lower South slaveholders came to call slavery a probably perpetual blessing, while Border South masters persistently called the institution a hopefully temporary evil. So too Lower South political warriors cared more about perpetuating slavery than the Union, while Border South leaders would compromise on slavery in order to save the Union. Still, even in Delaware, where over 15,000 slaves in 1790 had shrunk to under 2,000 in 1860, slaveholders resisted final emancipation. In Maryland, where manumissions plus slave sales to the Lower South had halved the percentage of white slaveholding families, the increasingly outnumbered slavocracy counterattacked desperately in the mid-1850s, futilely seeking to re-enslave the freed blacks. Concurrently, in Missouri, the state's even faster declining fraction of slaveholders counterattacked still more desperately, unsuccessfully seeking to establish slavery in neighboring Kansas.

In the mid-nineteenth century, then, slaveholders overwhelmingly controlled the Lower South, which had been belatedly but massively developed. The slavocracy somewhat less solidly controlled the Middle and Border South, where percentages of slave owners were slowly dropping. But even in the Border South, vestiges (and sometimes defiant concentrations) of the old relatively nontropical slavocracy occasionally fought to salvage a fading system. The mature Slave South had a tropical base of states, containing large slave populations, and several layers of buffer zones to the north, with less tropical conditions and less proslavery commitments and fewer slaves in each successive tier above.

Yet despite this degree of geographic disunity, no other New World slavocracy could muster as united a front against world-wide antislavery currents. The difference between slaveholders' unity, albeit incomplete, in the United States and their utter disarray in Brazil is especially revealing, for similar experiences yielded dissimilar outcomes. In both countries, a once flourishing northerly slaveholding region fell into decline and sold many of its slaves to a newly flourishing southerly region. In the United States, the Upper South Tobacco Kingdom sold hundreds of thousands of slaves to the Lower South Cotton Kingdom. In Brazil, the Northeastern Sugar Kingdom, which in 1822 had held almost 70 percent of the country's slaves, transferred equally huge numbers of blacks to the South Central Coffee Kingdom, which by the early 1880s owned 65 percent of Brazil's slaves.[5]

There the similarity ended. In Brazil, the old sugar provinces, despite a population still 15 percent enslaved, led the movement for free-womb abolition, with the Ceará region in the vanguard. When the national Chamber of Delegates voted on the Rio Branco free-womb bill in 1871, the Northeastern sugar provinces favored gradual emancipation, 39–6, thus canceling out the South Central coffee provinces' 30–12 vote against.[6] The Border South, in contrast, usually voted with the Lower South on slavery propositions in Congress and never enacted a post-nati law.

A more intense racism fueled the US slaveholders' greater capacity to mobilize a united front. Because Latin American racial attitudes toward blacks were less hidebound than in the United States, greater tolerance for free-womb emancipation, for mulattoes, and for individual manumissions – and less willingness to fight a civil war over the issue – pervaded Latin American slavocracies. Because US racism was so extreme, a more unified slaveholding class and more support from white nonslaveholders – and thus a greater capacity to fight a civil war – infused the Slave South.

Behind the more severe US racism lay in part a different heterosexual situation, itself another result of the largest white migration to an important New World slavocracy. English colonists to the future United States migrated far more often in family groups and/or with equal numbers of unmarried males and females in the entourage than did colonists headed farther south, who more often sought their fortunes as unattached males, with only slaves available for sexual liaisons. More frequent and less taboo interracial sexual intimacies resulted south of British North America, which led to more mulattoes and less insistence that the world be rigidly separated into black and white.

Politically no less than biologically, US slaveholders preferred nothing between black and white. The very basis of black slavery, in so republican a regime for whites, had to be a rigid color line. The Old South had to cleave advanced republicanism for whites totally from abject slavery for blacks. That black and white separation mystified Brazilian quasi-republicans, to say nothing of Latin American nonrepublicans. Only US slaveholders, in short, considered *free black* an oxymoron.

Some historians doubt that racism was more culturally deep-seated in the United States than south of the border. That position founders before the greater US taboo surrounding miscegenation and the far greater desire to deport blacks from antebellum America than from any other New World slavocracy. But the comparative power of cultural racism *before* slaveholders politically mobilized is unimportant to the comparative history of emancipation, for uniquely in the United States, slaveholders had to mobilize nonslaveholders, and racism was their most potent weapon. After southern slaveholders had used the distinction between equality for all whites and inequality for all blacks to rally the nonslaveholders, southern racism inarguably had become an especially powerful idea.

The racial foundation of Southwide unity, however, was a two-edged sword. For racism to unite nonslaveholders and slaveholders, the black race had to be significantly present. With the slave drain to the Lower South and the movement of European whites to such northerly slave states as Maryland and Missouri, Border South blacks became steadily less visible. As for that highly visible group of blacks in northern Maryland and Delaware, the free blacks, their energetic labor and law-abiding deportment demonstrated that racial control hardly required slavery.

That conclusion had proved fatal to slavery in northern states, where percentages of blacks had declined. In the colonial period, New York had had slave proportions in the 1860 Border South's range, about 15 percent of the total population. As New York's slave percentage had dwindled toward 5 percent, sentiment for post-nati emancipation had grown. Mid-nineteenth-century Border South states were in no immediate danger of becoming a New York, much less a Brazilian Ceará. But given the Border South's waning percentage of blacks, its Latin American-style manumissions, its propensity for thinking of slavery as a temporary evil, and its commitment to Union-saving compromises on the institution, could the Lower South rely on its northern hinterlands' future loyalty?

On the answer hung the Slave South's capacity to be that unique New World slave regime: the one that could defy an emancipating century rather than settle for a few more decades of slaveholder profits. Latin American slavocracies lacked not only the South's intensely racist reasons to stonewall antislavery but also its political basis for confidence that emancipation could be routed. The Latin American slavocracies were either too vulnerable to black insurrection (as in Haiti), too much under the power of European empires (as in the French and British West Indies and in Spanish-owned Cuba), or too small a minority (as in Venezuela and Peru) to command their fate inside a government that could abolish slavery. True, the Latin American regime closest in type to the southern slaveholders, the Brazilian slavocracy, also possessed a powerful minority in a partly parliament-ruled (and partly monarchical) nation. But Brazilian slaveholders, compared with their more intransigent US counterparts, were too divided against each other over slavery's future, too lacking in a rigid racism that might control the nonslaveholders, and too fond of a *regime des notables* to risk enfranchising and mobilizing the "nonnotables." Unable to mount a united front, in or out of parliament, the Brazilian slavocracy could only postpone emancipation with Rio Branco laws. The Old South, in contrast, had various powers to command a majoritarian democracy despite its minority status – *if* all fifteen slave states hung together and the Border South did not go the way of New York, or worse, Ceará.

Numbers indicate how much was at stake in that *if*. The seven Lower South states of 1860 (South Carolina, Georgia, Florida, Alabama, Mississippi, Louisiana, and Texas, with 47 percent of their population enslaved) could not fight off the eighteen northern states (containing 61 percent of the American population) without the enthusiastic support of the four Middle South states (Virginia, North Carolina, Tennessee, and Arkansas, with 32 percent of their population enslaved) and the four Border South states (Maryland, Delaware, Kentucky, and Missouri, with 13 percent of their population enslaved). Those buffer areas above the Lower South could come under siege – the siege of democratic public opinion. Would the Border South remain foursquare behind slavery and the Lower South, even if the slavocracy's northern hinterlands came to possess scantier and scantier percentages of blacks?

That question transcended the Border South. The slaveholders' worst internal problem involved not a single localized place but a regionwide lopsided distribution of blacks. While the Border South was the most widespread locale with a relatively low percentage of slaves, some areas farther south also contained few blacks; and everywhere a paucity of slaves allowed more nonslaveholder hostility toward slaveholders. Wherever blacks were concentrated, whites drew together, however much the poor resented the rich, for lowly whites despised lowlier blacks even more than they resented lordly masters. But whenever blacks were scarce, race hatred intensified class hatred, for nonslaveholders preferred to have neither autocrats nor blacks around. A relatively slaveless situation, while most prevalent in the Border South, also predominated in western Virginia, in eastern Tennessee, and in piney woods and semimountainous areas of the Lower South. Here the Border South predicament came closer to home to worried Lower and Middle South slavocrats. Could upper-class ideology command lower-class loyalties in areas where no racial tensions united the whites?

[...]

II

Before Southern secessionists could escape the northern majority, they had to win over their own majority. If some Southwide Gallup poll had inquired whether Southerners wished to secede immediately after Lincoln's election, the secessionists' vote likely would have been down in the 25 percent range. In the Border South, where secessionists lost even after civil war began, 37 percent of all southern whites resided. Another 31 percent lived in the Middle South, where secessionists lost until civil war began. Even in the Lower South, a slim majority might have voted against secession had a Southwide referendum occurred immediately after

Lincoln's election. In late November 1860, only Mississippi and Florida probably would have affirmed the expediency of secession, and only South Carolina assuredly would have done so.

The Southwide majority against disunion in November 1860 fed on conservatives' dread of revolution, on Southerners' patriotism as Americans, and on moderates' doubts that Lincoln could or would threaten slavery. Southern Unionists denounced the president-elect for declaring slavery immoral, for calling its spread to new territory unacceptable, and for terming its ultimate extinction desirable. But Lincoln conceded, Unionists pointed out, that the Constitution barred federal intervention in the South to force slavery's extinction. To re-emphasize this federal powerlessness, Lincoln in his inaugural address supported an unamendable constitutional amendment, already passed by Congress, that would have forever banned federal antislavery coercion in the South. But no constitutional amendment was needed, Unionists added. Lincoln's party did not have a majority in the Senate or in the House or on the Supreme Court. If Lincoln nevertheless managed to act against slavery, the South could *then* secede. Why secede now over an uncertain northern menace, thereby subjecting slavery to certain menace in a civil war?

Secessionists retorted that a stealthy northern majority would initially let Southerners do the menacing. Southern politicians would form a wing of the Black Republican party, dedicated to agitating against slavery, especially in the Border South. South Carolina patricians, the most avid secessionists, considered all agitating parties dangerous. These aristocratic republicans had long taken the proslavery rationale beyond a vision of whites directing blacks. Theirs was a more universal paternalistic conception: The best men should direct lesser humans of all races. To them all national parties portended mobocratic republicanism. Patronage-hungry demagogues would stir up the masses and thus overwhelm disinterested paternalists.

In contrast, Lower South mainstream politicians beyond crusty South Carolina, having long happily participated in national parties, feared not democratic parties in general but a prospective Southern Republican party in particular. They uneasily recalled Frank Blair's delivery of 10 percent of Missourians to Lincoln in the election of 1860, Delaware's 24 percent vote for Lincoln, the more northern South's Opposition party's recent overtures to the Republicans, and Northern Republicans' publication of Helper's call for nonslaveholder war against slaveholders. They knew that Lincoln had patronage jobs at his disposal and that Border South leaders wanted them. They understood that Lincoln, like the Border South's hero, Henry Clay, carried on Thomas Jefferson's vision of emancipation with freedmen's removal financed by the federal government. Lincoln, in short, need not force abolition on the most northern South. He could instead encourage and bribe Border Southerners to agitate for their misty hope of, and his nebulous plan for, removing blacks from a whitened republic.

Nor, warned the secessionists, would Republican efforts for black removal be restricted to rallying a Border South *white* majority. Republicans would encourage slaves to flee the Border South. With white support melting away and black slaves running away, border slaveholders would dispatch their human property to Lower South slave markets. Then nothing could deter a Border South Republican party. The Slave South, shrunk to 11 states or less and prevented from expanding into new territories, could only watch while northern free-labor states swelled from 18 to 33. In that 44-state Union, concluded secessionists, Republican emancipators would have the three-fourths majority to abolish slavery in 11 states by constitutional amendment.

Southern extremists meant to cancel that democratic drama before the staging began. They would not let northern-style republicanism, with all issues open for discussion, replace southern-style republicanism, in which debate about slavery was impermissible. They would not sit back and watch while a new president used patronage to forge a new centrist position on the forbidden subject. They would not allow Lincoln's method of antislavery, the slow transformation of public opinion, to operate within the South. They had long especially feared democratic agitation in the Border South, that nontropical vestige of seventeenth-century slaveholders' effort to defy tropical geography. Many of the Slavepower's aggressive defenses, including the Fugitive Slave Law and the Kansas-Nebraska Act, had sought to keep Border South whites and Border South blacks separated from contamination by freedom.

Now Lincoln's and the Border South's favorite national solution to slavery – compensated emancipation conditional on federally financed black removal – might establish the most contaminating and indestructible vital center yet. Since gag rule times, southern and northern extremists had unintentionally collaborated to destroy centrist ideological positions and centrist national parties. After twenty years of slavery crises, the Democratic party could no longer find a middle position between that of southern moderates, enraged by Yankee insults, and that of northern moderates, enraged by proslavery ultimatums. But no extremist tactic in the Union might deter a new centrist program, institutionalized in a newly national Republican party. Cries of "traitor" would not deter Border South Republicans, for the region's numerous advocates of black removal thought an all-white Border South exceedingly patriotic. Fear of losing southern elections would not deter conditional antislavery moderates, for Henry Clay Whiggery had done well in the Border South, and Lincoln's party figured to be a rebuilt Whiggish coalition. Furthermore, Border South demagogues could not feast on Lincoln's national patronage. After well-fed politicians started agitating, wouldn't Border South inhabitants agree to remove blacks at federal expense, or Border South masters sell out at Lower South purchasers' expense, especially if more and more of the region's slaves ran away?

For the first time, many Lower South slaveholders felt powerless to answer such questions. Their feeling of impotence rivaled that of Latin American colonists when European metropolitan centers abolished slavery and that of Brazilian coffee planters when sugar planters assaulted the institution. But if Lincoln's election seemed to revoke a democracy's unique invitation for slaveholders to control their fate, the US republican system offered a final invitation for minority self-protection, unavailable in less democratic Latin America. The people of a single colony, the American Revolutionaries had declared, had a right to withdraw their consent to be governed. It was as if the Brazilian coffee provinces had a *right* to secede, which the sugar provinces might feel an obligation to defend.

A *right* of secession, held by a single one of the South's fifteen states! That right did empower a secessionist minority to force the southern majority's hand on the expediency of secession. But to force-feed secession to the antisecessionist majority, secessionists had to abort the southern Unionists' favorite idea: a regionwide southern convention, where a Southwide majority would veto immediate secession. Secessionists instead wanted the most secessionist state to call a convention to consider disunion. If the most secessionist state seceded, other southern state conventions would have to decide not whether secession was *expedient* but whether a seceded state could be denied its *right* of secession. Furthermore, other slave states might discern less expediency in remaining in the Union after several states with large slave populations had departed to form a proslavery confederacy.

The single-state secession strategy neatly countered Lincoln's supposed fusion strategy. Instead of the Union's president building a Republican party in southern buffer zones and drawing the Upper South away from slavery's Lower South base, secessionists would build a southern nation in the Lower South and drag the Upper South beyond Lincoln's patronage bribes. Or to use the modern metaphor, instead of slavery falling like the top row of a pile of dominoes, with the Border South and then the Middle South collapsing onto the Lower South, the Union would fall by secessionists' pulling out the lower row, with the Lower South and then the Middle South leaving the Border South no foundation for staying in the Union.

That was the secessionists' master plan, devised in private correspondence and carried out in public lockstep. On December 20, 1860, the secessionists' stronghold, South Carolina, withdrew its consent to Union. South Carolina's neighbor, Georgia, was wary of secession. But with its neighbor out, could Georgia stay in? After a brilliant internal debate, Georgia decided, narrowly, to join South Carolina. And so it went, neighbor following neighbor, throughout the Cotton South. By the time Lincoln was inaugurated on March 4, 1861, the seven Lower South states had left the Union. But the eight Upper South states, containing the majority of southern whites, still opposed secession.

The balance of power changed in mid-April after the Civil War started. Now the more northern South had to decide not on secession per se but on whether to join a northern or a southern army. In making that decision, the Middle South affirmed that each state had the American right to withdraw its consent to be governed. These southern men in the middle also reaffirmed that Yankee extremists were more hateful than secessionist extremists. The Garrisonian insult, encompassing all southerners who would not unconditionally and immediately emancipate, had long infuriated most Southerners. The Republican insult, encompassing all southerners who sought to dominate or depart the Union, was equally enraging. To protect their self-respect and honor, Southerners usually felt compelled to unite against taunting Yankees. That duty had so often drawn together a region otherwise partially disunited. In April 1861, when Lincoln sent reinforcements to federal troops in Charleston's harbor, the old tribal fury swept the Middle South. By May 1861, eleven angry southern states had departed the Union. In that fury, parallel to Republican rage over an allegedly anti-republican Slavepower, lies the solution to the largest apparent puzzle about secession: why 260,000 men, whatever their initial preference for Union, died for the Confederacy.

III

Thus did the secessionist minority of the no-longer-ruling southern minority escape the at-last-ruling northern majority. Thus did southern extremists move to abort the expected Republican attempt to rally a new Border South-northern national majority, with Lincoln's patronage supplying the organizational basis, with race removal providing the ideological basis, and with an ultimate constitutional amendment auguring the worst danger. But by moving outside a majoritarian Union's sway, the secessionist minority of the southern minority moved toward a more perilous rendezvous with majoritarianism's own requirement: the need to win men's minds and hearts. Considering the free-labor states' somewhat greater predominance of military power and considering northern determination to save majoritarian government from the southern minority, secession, to be effective, would have to sweep farther than the Middle South. Border Southerners would have to make common cause with secessionists rather than with Republicans.

Or to put the Confederacy's problem in the most revealing way, the secessionists, having secured a southern numerical majority, now had to rally a Calhoun-style concurrent majority: a concurrence of everyone. Now more than ever, the margin of error was thin for the only slaveholders in the New World who defied worldwide antislavery currents. The US slavocracy, to prevail in its extraordinary Civil War gamble, had to control all southerners, black and white. Several southern minorities could nullify the white majority in the eleven Confederate states, for the North was passionately united in its eighteen free-labor states. Let the four Border South states refuse to secede from the Union; let western Virginia nonslaveholders secede from Virginia; let eastern Tennessee nonslaveholders desert Tennessee; let the slaves depart from the slaveholders and . . .

The sequels would fill the rest. Slave runaways, having initiated the fugitive slave controversies that helped lead to civil war, would join northern armies and help secure an emancipating triumph. So too Border Southerners, whose possible fusion with Yankees had helped fuel disunion, would unite with Black Republicans on the battlefields. But though much is fittingly democratic about fugitive slaves doing in slaveholders and about the conditional antislavery Border South doing in the unconditional proslavery Lower South, democrats can hardly cheer the spectacle. The coming of the American Civil War is a case study in democracy's limitations.

Only an especially convulsive internal issue could expose those limits. As the American antebellum experience shows, a democratic system can survive a very large degree of divisiveness. Such national issues as nativism, temperance, national banks, protective tariffs, women's rights, and religious freedom were settled peaceably. Nor did some singular aspects of US culture, peculiar among the world's republics to these North Americans, destroy this democracy. The unusually constant stream of US localistic elections, for example, did not lead to more electioneering agitation than a stable governing system could handle. Those localistic elections usually focused on resolvable local issues. In contrast, national presidential campaigns, occurring only every four years, focused increasingly on the only unresolvable issue, slavery. Nor did America's unusually strong encouragement of individualistic eccentricity destroy nationalizing institutions. The national political parties found a peaceable common ground on every issue involving white individuals' opportunities except slavery – and for a long while on that issue too.

The point is that agitation over slavery ultimately superseded all other agitations and alone could expose a democratic system's most deep-seated, most universal limits. Despite its cult of majority rule, democracy is very susceptible to minority control. A minority that knows what it wants and knows how to manipulate the system will defeat a less determined majority every time. The impasse comes when a majority grows equally determined and the minority cannot accept defeat. The problem is particularly explosive when the minority is a powerful ruling class and the dogma of government by consent permits imperious rulers to withdraw from the republic. In the United States, only the slavery issue called forth this sort of inflexible minority, determined to use every available power to rule supposedly barbaric blacks, assuredly infuriating outsiders, and uncertainly softhearted insiders. And in the New World, only the US republican system swelled intransigent slaveholders with the illusion that they could command their own fate, whether by dominating or by departing a republic.

Lower South slaveholders exhausted all means of dominating before they departed. They tried ideological persuasion. That partly failing, they tried lynchings. That partly failing, they tried shaming dissenters into loyalty. Fearing verbal coercion would fail, they tried protective laws that might consolidate vulnerable outposts. When the northern majority finally found minority governance intolerable, the southern minority (or rather, initially, the secessionist minority of the southern minority) withdrew its consent to be ruled.

Two democratic imperatives clashed here: the majority's right to govern, Lincoln's favorite wartime slogan, and the minority's right to withdraw consent to be governed, Jefferson Davis's favorite patriotic emblem. The ideological clash would blur in the second half of the Civil War, after Lincoln's Union came to fight for slaves' right to withdraw their consent to be ruled by slaveholders. But in the first half of the Civil War, when Lincoln rejected black troops and repudiated his generals' emancipation initiatives, the issue was stark. Lincoln's Union initially fought to contain a minority that had controlled and now would revoke majority rule. The slaveholders fought to establish a Confederacy that would save a minority's consent to be governed and prevent the minority's property from becoming a discussable issue. Latin American slavery controversies never carried the added burden of these showdowns over republicanism. And so in all the Americas after the Haitian slave revolt, only in the United States did the final fate of slavery hang on the verdict supposedly reserved for undemocratic governments: Whose regime can rally the largest and most sustained commitment on the battlefields?

Notes

1   The most important published secondary sources for this essay are discussed in the bibliography below. To avoid repetition, these notes will be restricted to sources of quotations, statistics, etc., to occasional comments on primary sources, and to acknowledgment of unpublished insights of fellow historians.
2   A point forcefully made in Seymour Drescher, "The Long Goodbye: Dutch Capitalism and Antislavery in Comparative Perspective," *American Historical Review*, 99 (Feb. 1994), 44–69.
3   All US demographic statistics in this essay are drawn from *The Statistics of the Population of the United States*, Francis A. Walker, comp. (Washington, 1872), 11–74, and from US Bureau of the Census, *A Century of Population Growth: From the First Census of the United States to the Twelfth, 1790–1900* (Washington, 1909).
4   For the Brazilian/Cuban figures, see Robert Conrad, *The Destruction of Brazilian Slavery, 1850–1888* (Berkeley, 1972), 283, and Rebecca J. Scott, *Slave Emancipation in Cuba: The Transition to Free Labor, 1860–1899* (Princeton, 1985), 7.
5   David Brion Davis, *Slavery and Human Progress* (New York, 1984), 291.
6   Conrad, *Destruction of Brazilian Slavery*, 301.

Questions to consider

- In what ways was the American South different from its Latin American neighbors?

- In what ways was it divided from within?

- How, according to Freehling, did rich slaveholders convince poor white Southerners to side with them against a rising Republican party that had at least theoretical political appeal?

- To a great extent, this essay is about the role of minorities in American history. Can you think of other examples of powerful minorities who were able to exert an influence disproportionate to their size? (You might consider the role of abolitionists here.) Do you tend to see their influence as positive or negative?

Chapter 3

The Impending Crisis: Primary Sources

Speech on the Compromise of 1850

John C. Calhoun

For decades, the principal spokesman for the planter class – and in the minds of many
Southerners, the region generally – was John C. Calhoun. Over the course of his long
career, Calhoun served as secretary of war, vice-president, senator, secretary of state,
and political philosopher, evolving from a staunch nationalist at the time of the War of
1812 into a committed sectionalist by the time of the Compromise of 1850, which he
adamantly opposed before his death that year. In this speech, Senator Calhoun urges his
colleagues to reject the measure. Ask yourself: in what ways does, and doesn't, this
excerpt correspond to the themes in William Freehling's essay?

John C. Calhoun's speech to the United States Senate against the Compromise of 1850 (March
4, 1850), in *John C. Calhoun Papers* in the American Memory, Historical Collections for the
National Digital Library, Library of Congress.

[...]

What has caused this widely diffused and almost universal discontent? ...

One of the causes is, undoubtedly, to be traced to the long-continued agitation of the slave
question on the part of the North, and the many aggressions which they have made on the
rights of the South during the time. . . .

There is another lying back of it – with which this is intimately connected – that may be
regarded as the great and primary cause. This is to be found in the fact that the equilibrium
between the two sections, in the Government as it stood when the constitution was ratified and
the Government put in action, has been destroyed. At that time there was nearly a perfect
equilibrium between the two, which afforded ample means of each to protect itself against the
aggression of the other; but, as it now stands, one section has the exclusive power of controlling

the Government, which leaves the other without any adequate means of protecting itself against its encroachment and oppression . . .

As, then, the North has the absolute control over the Government, it is manifest, that on all questions between it and the South, where there is a diversity of interests, the interests of the latter will be sacrificed to the former, however oppressive the effects may be; as the South possesses no means by which it can resist, through the action of the Government. But if there was no question of vital importance to the South, in reference to which there was a diversity of views between the two sections, this state of things might be endured, without the hazard of destruction to the South. But such is not the fact. There is a question of vital importance to the Southern section, in reference to which the views and feelings of the two sections are as opposite and hostile as they can possibly be.

I refer to the relation between the two races in the Southern section, which constitutes a vital portion of her social organization. Every portion of the North entertains views and feelings more or less hostile to it. . . . On the contrary, the Southern section regards the relation as one which cannot be destroyed without subjecting the two races to the greatest calamity, and the section to poverty, desolation, and wretchedness; and accordingly they feel bound, by every consideration of interest and safety, to defend it.

This hostile feeling on the part of the North towards the social organization of the South long lay dormant, but it only required some cause to act on those who felt most intensely that they were responsible for its continuance, to call it into action. The increasing power of this Government, and of the control of the Northern section over all its departments, furnished the cause. It was this which made an impression on the minds of many, that there was little or no restraint to prevent the Government from doing whatever it might choose to do. This was sufficient of itself to put the most fanatical portion of the North in action, for the purpose of destroying the existing relation between the two races in the South.

In Which the Reader is Introduced to a Man of Humanity

Harriet Beecher Stowe

"So this is the little lady that made this great war," Abraham Lincoln was reputed to have said upon meeting Harriet Beecher Stowe in 1862. If the story happened as told, Lincoln was undoubtedly joking – to a point. No one person "made" the Civil War (not even the president himself, who no doubt took solace reminding himself of this amid the ordeal). To many Americans, however, even the millions who never read her book but nevertheless regarded her and her characters as household names, Stowe was the woman who for better or worse crystallized the argument as it raged in culture and politics and crested on battlefields.

The daughter, wife, and mother of ministers, Stowe was a native New Englander who saw slavery first-hand as a young woman living near the Ohio River in the 1830s and 1840s. Like many Northerners, she was enraged by the passage of the Fugitive Slave Act as part of the Compromise of 1850 – she, like Calhoun, but for very different reasons, opposed the Compromise – and when her sister-in-law encouraged her to use that rage to change the hearts and minds of others she took up that challenge. The story she was inspired to write appeared in monthly segments in 1851–2, and was published in book form shortly afterward. It became one of the best-selling books of all time, and the most famous book written by an American in the nineteenth century.

This opening chapter gives a flavor of Stowe's writing – and the fierce, as well as clever and even amusing, strategies she used to attack the great social evil of her time. It also reflects the romantic racism of even the most well-intentioned Northerners.

Harriet Beecher Stowe, "In Which the Reader is Introduced to a Man of Humanity," in *Uncle Tom's Cabin* (1851), pp. 1–10.

Late in the afternoon of a chilly day in February, two gentlemen were sitting alone over their wine, in a well-furnished dining-parlor, in the town of P–, in Kentucky. There were no servants present, and the gentlemen, with chairs closely approaching, seemed to be discussing some subject with great earnestness.

For convenience' sake, we have said, hitherto, two *gentlemen*. One of the parties, however, when critically examined, did not seem, strictly speaking, to come under the species. He was a short, thick-set man, with coarse, common-place features, and that swaggering air of pretension which marks a low man who is trying to elbow his way upward in the world. He was much over-dressed, in a gaudy vest of many colors, a blue neckerchief, bedropped gayly with yellow spots, and arranged with a flaunting tie, quite in keeping with the general air of the man. His hands, large and coarse, were plentifully bedecked with rings; and he wore a heavy gold watch-chain, with a bundle of seals of portentous size, and a great variety of colors, attached to it, – which, in the ardor of conversation, he was in the habit of flourishing and jingling with evident satisfaction. His conversation was in free and easy defiance of Murray's Grammar, and was garnished at convenient intervals with various profane expressions, which not even the desire to be graphic in our account shall induce us to transcribe.

His companion, Mr. Shelby, had the appearance of a gentleman; and the arrangements of the house, and the general air of the housekeeping, indicated easy, and even opulent circumstances. As we before stated, the two were in the midst of an earnest conversation.

"That is the way I should arrange the matter," said Mr. Shelby.

"I can't make trade that way – I positively can't, Mr. Shelby," said the other, holding up a glass of wine between his eye and the light.

"Why, the fact is, Haley, Tom is an uncommon fellow; he is certainly worth that sum anywhere, – steady, honest, capable, manages my whole farm like a clock."

"You mean honest, as niggers go," said Haley, helping himself to a glass of brandy.

"No; I mean, really, Tom is a good, steady, sensible, pious fellow. He got religion at a camp-meeting, four years ago; and I believe he really *did* get it. I've trusted him, since then, with everything I have, – money, house, horses, – and let him come and go round the country; and I always found him true and square in everything."

"Some folks don't believe there is pious niggers, Shelby," said Haley, with a candid flourish of his hand, "but *I do*. I had a fellow, now, in this yer last lot I took to Orleans – it was as good as a meetin' now, really, to hear that critter pray; and he was quite gentle and quiet like. He fetched me a good sum, too, for I bought him cheap of a man that was 'bliged to sell out; so I realized six hundred on him. Yes, I consider religion a valeyable thing in a nigger, when it's the genuine article, and no mistake."

"Well, Tom's got the real article, if ever a fellow had," rejoined the other. "Why, last fall, I let him go to Cincinnati alone, to do business for me, and bring home five hundred dollars. 'Tom,' says I to him, 'I trust you, because I think you're a Christian – I know you wouldn't cheat.' Tom comes back, sure enough; I knew he would. Some low fellows, they say, said to him – 'Tom, why don't you make tracks for Canada?' 'Ah, master trusted me, and I couldn't,' – they told me about it. I am sorry to part with Tom, I must say. You ought to let him cover the whole balance of the debt; and you would, Haley, if you had any conscience."

"Well, I've got just as much conscience as any man in business can afford to keep, – just a little, you know, to swear by, as 'twere," said the trader, jocularly; "and, then, I'm ready to do anything in reason to 'blige friends: but this yer, you see, is a leetle too hard on a fellow – a leetle too hard." The trader sighed contemplatively, and poured out some more brandy.

"Well, then, Haley, how will you trade?" said Mr. Shelby, after an uneasy interval of silence.

"Well, haven't you a boy or gal that you could throw in with Tom?"

"Hum! – none that I could well spare; to tell the truth, it's only hard necessity makes me willing to sell at all. I don't like parting with any of my hands, that's a fact."

Here the door opened, and a small quadroon boy, between four and five years of age, entered the room. There was something in his appearance remarkably beautiful and engaging. His black hair, fine as floss silk, hung in glossy curls about his round, dimpled face, while a pair of large dark eyes, full of fire and softness, looked out from beneath the rich, long lashes, as he peered curiously into the apartment. A gay robe of scarlet and yellow plaid, carefully made and neatly fitted, set off to advantage the dark and rich style of his beauty; and a certain comic air of assurance, blended with bashfulness, showed that he had been not unused to being petted and noticed by his master.

"Hulloa, Jim Crow!" said Mr. Shelby, whistling, and snapping a bunch of raisins towards him, "pick that up, now!"

The child scampered, with all his little strength, after the prize, while his master laughed.

"Come here, Jim Crow," said he. The child came up, and the master patted the curly head, and chucked him under the chin.

"Now, Jim, show this gentleman how you can dance and sing." The boy commenced one of those wild, grotesque songs common among the negroes, in a rich, clear voice, accompanying his singing with many comic evolutions of the hands, feet, and whole body, all in perfect time to the music.

"Bravo!" said Haley, throwing him a quarter of an orange.

"Now, Jim, walk like old Uncle Cudjoe, when he has the rheumatism," said his master.

Instantly the flexible limbs of the child assumed the appearance of deformity and distortion, as, with his back humped up, and his master's stick in his hand, he hobbled about the room, his childish face drawn into a doleful pucker, and spitting from right to left, in imitation of an old man.

Both gentlemen laughed uproariously.

"Now, Jim," said his master, "show us how old Elder Robbins leads the psalm." The boy drew his chubby face down to a formidable length, and commenced toning a psalm tune through his nose, with imperturbable gravity.

"Hurrah! bravo! what a young 'un!" said Haley; "that chap's a case, I'll promise. Tell you what," said he, suddenly clapping his hand on Mr. Shelby's shoulder, "fling in that chap, and I'll settle the business – I will. Come, now, if that ain't doing the thing up about the rightest!"

At this moment, the door was pushed gently open, and a young quadroon woman, apparently about twenty-five, entered the room.

There needed only a glance from the child to her, to identify her as its mother. There was the same rich, full, dark eye, with its long lashes; the same ripples of silky black hair. The brown of her complexion gave way on the cheek to a perceptible flush, which deepened as she saw the gaze of the strange man fixed upon her in bold and undisguised admiration. Her dress was of the neatest possible fit, and set off to advantage her finely moulded shape; – a delicately formed hand and a trim foot and ankle were items of appearance that did not escape the quick eye of the trader, well used to run up at a glance the points of a fine female article.

"Well, Eliza?" said her master, as she stopped and looked hesitatingly at him.

"I was looking for Harry, please, sir;" and the boy bounded toward her, showing his spoils, which he had gathered in the skirt of his robe.

"Well, take him away, then," said Mr. Shelby; and hastily she withdrew, carrying the child on her arm.

"By Jupiter," said the trader, turning to him in admiration, "there's an article, now! You might make your fortune on that ar gal in Orleans, any day. I've seen over a thousand, in my day, paid down for gals not a bit handsomer."

"I don't want to make my fortune on her," said Mr. Shelby, dryly; and, seeking to turn the conversation, he uncorked a bottle of fresh wine, and asked his companion's opinion of it.

"Capital, sir, – first chop!" said the trader; then turning, and slapping his hand familiarly on Shelby's shoulder, he added –

"Come, how will you trade about the gal? – what shall I say for her – what'll you take?"

"Mr. Haley, she is not to be sold," said Shelby. "My wife would not part with her for her weight in gold."

"Ay, ay! women always say such things, 'cause they ha'n't no sort of calculation. Just show 'em how many watches, feathers, and trinkets, one's weight in gold would buy, and that alters the case *I* reckon."

"I tell you, Haley, this must not be spoken of; I say no, and I mean no," said Shelby, decidedly.

"Well, you'll let me have the boy, though," said the trader; "you must own I've come down pretty handsomely for him."

"What on earth can you want with the child?" said Shelby.

"Why, I've got a friend that's going into this yer branch of the business – wants to buy up handsome boys to raise for the market. Fancy articles entirely – sell for waiters, and so on, to rich 'uns, that can pay for handsome 'uns. It sets off one of yer great places – a real handsome boy to open door, wait, and tend. They fetch a good sum; and this little devil is such a comical, musical concern, he's just the article."

"I would rather not sell him," said Mr. Shelby, thoughtfully; "the fact is, sir, I'm a humane man, and I hate to take the boy from his mother, sir."

"O, you do? – La! yes – something of that ar natur. I understand, perfectly. It is mighty onpleasant getting on with women, sometimes. I al'ays hate these yer screechin' screamin' times. They are *mighty* onpleasant; but, as I manages business, I generally avoids 'em, sir. Now, what if you get the girl off for a day, or a week, or so; then the thing's done quietly, – all over before she comes home. Your wife might get her some earrings, or a new gown, or some such truck, to make up with her."

"I'm afraid not."

"Lor bless ye, yes! These critters an't like white folks, you know; they gets over things, only manage right. Now, they say," said Haley, assuming a candid and confidential air, "that this kind o' trade is hardening to the feelings; but I never found it so. Fact is, I never could do things up the way some fellers manage the business. I've seen 'em as would pull a woman's child out her arms, and set him up to sell, and she screechin' like mad all the time; – very bad policy – damages the article – makes 'em quite unfit for service sometimes. I knew a real handsome gal once, in Orleans, as was entirely ruined by this sort o' handling. The fellow that was trading for her didn't want her baby; and she was one of your real high sort, when her blood was up. I tell you, she squeezed up her child in her arms, and talked, and went on real awful. It kinder makes my blood run cold to think on't; and when they carried off the child, and locked her up, she jest went ravin' mad, and died in a week. Clear waste, sir, of a thousand dollars, just for want of management, – there's where 'tis. It's always best to do the humane thing, sir; that's been *my* experience." And the trader leaned back in his chair, and folded his arms, with an air of virtuous decision, apparently considering himself a second Wilberforce.

The subject appeared to interest the gentleman deeply; for while Mr. Shelby was thoughtfully peeling an orange, Haley broke out afresh, with becoming diffidence, but as if actually driven by the force of truth to say a few words more.

"It don't look well, now, for a feller to be praisin' himself; but I say it jest because it's the truth. I believe I'm reckoned to bring in about the finest droves of niggers that is brought in, – at least, I've been told so; if I have once, I reckon I have a hundred times, – all in good case, – fat and likely, and I lose as few as any man in the business. And I lays it all to my management, sir; and humanity, sir, I may say, is the great pillar of *my* management."

Mr. Shelby did not know what to say, and so he said, "Indeed!"

"Now, I've been laughed at for my notions, sir, and I've been talked to. They an't pop'lar, and they an't common; but I stuck to 'em, sir; I've stuck to 'em, and realized well on 'em; yes, sir, they have paid their passage, I may say," and the trader laughed at his joke.

There was something so piquant and original in these elucidations of humanity, that Mr. Shelby could not help laughing in company. Perhaps you laugh, too, dear reader; but you know humanity comes out in a variety of strange forms nowadays, and there is no end to the odd things that humane people will say and do.

Mr. Shelby's laugh encouraged the trader to proceed.

"It's strange, now, but I never could beat this into people's heads. Now, there was Tom Loker, my old partner, down in Natchez; he was a clever fellow, Tom was, only the very devil with niggers, – on principal 'twas, you see, for a better hearted feller never broke bread; 'twas his *system*, sir. I used to talk to Tom. 'Why, Tom,' I used to say, 'when your gals takes on and cry, what's the use o' crackin' on 'em over the head, and knockin' on 'em round? It's ridiculous,' says I, 'and don't do no sort o' good. Why, I don't see no harm in their cryin',' says I; 'it's natur,' says I, 'and if natur can't blow off one way, it will another. Besides, Tom,' says I, 'it jest spiles your gals; they get sickly, and down in the mouth, and sometimes they gets ugly, – particular yellow gals do, – and it's the devil and all gettin' on 'em broke in. Now,' says I, 'why can't you kinder coax 'em up, and speak 'em fair? Depend on it, Tom, a little humanity, thrown in along, goes a heap further than all your jawin' and crackin'; and it pays better,' says I, 'depend on't.' But Tom couldn't get the hang on't; and he spiled so many for me, that I had to break off with him, though he was a good-hearted fellow, and as fair a business hand as is goin'."

"And do you find your ways of managing do the business better than Tom's?" said Mr. Shelby.

"Why, yes, sir, I may say so. You see, when I anyways can, I takes a leetle care about the onpleasant parts like selling young'uns and that, – get the gals out of the way – out of sight, out of mind, you know, – and when it's clean done and can't be helped, they naturally gets used to it. 'Tan't, you know, as if it was white folks, that's brought up in the way of 'spectin' to keep their children and wives, and all that. Niggers, you know, that's fetched up properly, ha'n't no kind of 'spectations of no kind; so all these things comes easier."

"I'm afraid mine are not properly brought up, then," said Mr. Shelby.

"S'pose not; you Kentucky folks spile your niggers. You mean well by 'em, but 'tan't no real kindness, arter all. Now, a nigger, you see, what's got to be hacked and tumbled round the world, and sold to Tom, and Dick, and the Lord knows who, 'tan't no kindness to be givin' on him notions and expectations, and bringin' on him up too well, for the rough and tumble comes all the harder on him arter. Now, I venture to say, your niggers would be quite chop-fallen in a place where some of your plantation niggers would be singing and whooping like all possessed. Every man, you know, Mr. Shelby, naturally thinks well of his own ways; and I think I treat niggers just about as well as it's ever worth while to treat 'em."

"It's a happy thing to be satisfied," said Mr. Shelby, with a slight shrug, and some perceptible feelings of a disagreeable nature.

"Well," said Haley, after they had both silently picked their nuts for a season, "what do you say?"

"I'll think the matter over, and talk with my wife," said Mr. Shelby. "Meantime, Haley, if you want the matter carried on in the quiet way you speak of, you'd best not let your business in this neighborhood be known. It will get out among my boys, and it will not be a particularly quiet business getting away any of my fellows, if they know it, I'll promise you."

"O! certainly, by all means, mum! of course. But I'll tell you, I'm in a devil of a hurry, and shall want to know, as soon as possible, what I may depend on," said he, rising and putting on his overcoat.

"Well, call up this evening, between six and seven, and you shall have my answer," said Mr. Shelby, and the trader bowed himself out of the apartment.

"I'd like to have been able to kick the fellow down the steps," said he to himself, as he saw the door fairly closed, "with his impudent assurance; but he knows how much he has me at advantage. If anybody had ever said to me that I should sell Tom down south to one of those rascally traders, I should have said, 'Is thy servant a dog that he should do this thing?' And now it must come, for aught I see. And Eliza's child, too! I know that I shall have some fuss with my wife about that; and, for that matter, about Tom, too. So much for being in debt, – heigho! The fellow sees his advantage, and means to push it."

Perhaps the mildest form of the system of slavery is to be seen in the State of Kentucky. The general prevalence of agricultural pursuits of a quiet and gradual nature, not requiring those periodic seasons of hurry and pressure that are called for in the business of more southern districts, makes the task of the negro a more healthful and reasonable one; while the master, content with a more gradual style of acquisition, has not those temptations to hardheartedness which always overcome frail human nature when the prospect of sudden and rapid gain is weighed in the balance, with no heavier counterpoise than the interests of the helpless and unprotected.

Whoever visits some estates there, and witnesses the good-humored indulgence of some masters and mistresses, and the affectionate loyalty of some slaves, might be tempted to dream the oft-fabled poetic legend of a patriarchal institution, and all that; but over and above the scene there broods a portentous shadow – the shadow of *law*. So long as the law considers all these human beings, with beating hearts and living affections, only as so many *things* belonging to a master, – so long as the failure, or misfortune, or imprudence, or death of the kindest owner, may cause them any day to exchange a life of kind protection and indulgence for one of hopeless misery and toil, – so long it is impossible to make anything beautiful or desirable in the best-regulated administration of slavery.

Mr. Shelby was a fair average kind of man, good-natured and kindly, and disposed to easy indulgence of those around him, and there had never been a lack of anything which might contribute to the physical comfort of the negroes on his estate. He had, however, speculated largely and quite loosely; had involved himself deeply, and his notes to a large amount had come into the hands of Haley, and this small piece of information is the key to the preceding conversation.

Now, it had so happened that, in approaching the door, Eliza had caught enough of the conversation to know that a trader was making offers to her master for somebody.

She would gladly have stopped at the door to listen, as she came out; but her mistress just then calling, she was obliged to hasten away.

Still she thought she heard the trader make an offer for her boy; – could she be mistaken? Her heart swelled and throbbed, and she involuntarily strained him so tight that the little fellow looked up into her face in astonishment.

"Eliza, girl, what ails you to-day?" said her mistress, when Eliza had upset the wash-pitcher, knocked down the work-stand, and finally was abstractedly offering her mistress a long night-gown in place of the silk dress she had ordered her to bring from the wardrobe.

Eliza started. "O missis!" she said, raising her eyes; then bursting into tears, she sat down in a chair and began sobbing.

"Why, Eliza, child! what ails you?" said her mistress.

"O! missis, missis," said Eliza, "there's been a trader talking with master in the parlor! I heard him."

"Well, silly child, suppose there has."

"O, missis, *do* you suppose mas'r would sell my Harry?" And the poor creature threw herself into a chair, and sobbed convulsively.

"Sell him! No, you foolish girl! You know your master never deals with those southern traders, and never means to sell any of his servants, as long as they behave well. Why, you silly child, who do you think would want to buy your Harry? Do you think all the world are set on him as you are, you goosie? Come, cheer up, and hook my dress. There now, put my back hair up in that pretty braid you learnt the other day, and don't go listening at doors any more."

"Well, but, missis, you never would give your consent – to – to –"

"Nonsense, child! to be sure, I shouldn't. What do you talk so for? I would as soon have one of my own children sold. But really, Eliza, you are getting altogether too proud of that little fellow. A man can't put his nose into the door, but you think he must be coming to buy him."

Reassured by her mistress' confident tone, Eliza proceeded nimbly and adroitly with her toilet, laughing at her own fears, as she proceeded.

Mrs. Shelby was a woman of high class, both intellectually and morally. To that natural magnanimity and generosity of mind which one often marks as characteristic of the women of Kentucky, she added high moral and religious sensibility and principal, carried out with great energy and ability into practical results. Her husband, who made no professions to any particular religious character, nevertheless reverenced and respected the consistency of hers, and stood, perhaps, a little in awe of her opinion. Certain it was that he gave her unlimited scope in all her benevolent efforts for the comfort, instruction, and improvement of her servants, though he never took any decided part in them himself. In fact, if not exactly a believer in the doctrine of the efficiency of the extra good works of saints, he really seemed somehow or other to fancy that his wife had piety and benevolence enough for two – to indulge a shadowy expectation of getting into heaven through her superabundance of qualities to which he made no particular pretension.

The heaviest load on his mind, after his coversation with the trader, lay in the foreseen necessity of breaking to his wife the arrangement contemplated, – meeting the importunities and opposition which he knew he should have reason to encounter.

Mrs. Shelby, being entirely ignorant of her husband's embarrassments, and knowing only the general kindliness of his temper, had been quite sincere in the entire incredulity with which she had met Eliza's suspicions. In fact, she dismissed the matter from her mind, without a second thought; and being occupied in preparations for an evening visit, it passed out of her thoughts entirely.

Questions to consider

- What are some of the reasons you imagine might lead slaveholders to sell slaves? How realistic is the scenario depicted here?

- How does Stowe depict Haley the slave trader? Mr Shelby? How important are the distinctions between them?

- What are the strengths and weaknesses of Stowe's depiction of slaves?

- Stowe's novel went on to become a best-seller: what, do you believe, was the nature of its great appeal?

Uncle Tom's Cabin

Louisa S. McCord

Uncle Tom's Cabin generated a fierce backlash in the South. A series of "Anti-Tom" novels followed in its wake with titles like *Aunt Phillis's Cabin* (1852); *The Cabin and the Parlor* (1852); *Uncle Robin in His Cabin in Virginia* (1853); *The Planter's Northern Bride* (1854); and so on. There were dozens, each trying to refute various aspects of Stowe's depiction of slavery, all – often unwillingly – flattering her through imitation.

The book also provoked a strong critical response to the South on the part of reviewers who challenged Stowe's depiction of an institution she did not know intimately. Among the most important of these responses came from essayist Louisa McCord, whose review of the book for *The Southern Quarterly Review* in January 1853 is excerpted here. Note that this selection includes an analysis of Chapter 1 of the novel, included above. McCord was a slave-owner, and had run a plantation on her own previous to her marriage; at the time that this review was written she was well known and respected North and South for her translations, reviews, and political essays.

Louisa S. McCord, "Uncle Tom's Cabin," in *Southern Quarterly Review* vol. 7, no. 13 (January 7, 1853), 81–120 in *Louisa S. McCord: Political and Social Essays*, ed. Richard C. Lounsbury (Charlottesville: University Press of Virginia, 1995), pp. 245–80. Reprinted with permission of the University of Virginia Press.

Truly it would seem that the labour of Sisyphus is laid upon us, the slaveholders of these southern United States. Again and again have we, with all the power and talent of our clearest heads and strongest intellects, forced aside the foul load of slander and villainous aspersion so often hurled against us, and still, again and again, the unsightly mass rolls back, and, heavily as ever, fall the old refuted libels, vamped, remodelled, and lumbering down upon us with all the force, or at least impudent assumption, of new argument. We anticipate here the answer and application of our charitable opponents. We, too, have studied our mythology, and remember well, that the aforesaid Sisyphus was condemned to his torment for the sins of injustice, oppression, and tyranny.[1] Like punishment to like sin will, no doubt, be their corollary. Boldly, however, before God and man, we dare hold up our hand and plead "not guilty." Clearly enough do we see through the juggle of this game. It is no hand of destiny, no fiat of Jove, which rolls back upon us the labouring bulk. There is an agent behind the curtain, vulnerable at least as ourselves; and the day may yet come when, if this unlucky game cease not, the destructive mass shall find another impetus, and crush beneath its unexpected weight the hand which now directs it, we scarce know whether in idle wantonness or diabolic malice.

Among the revelations of this passing year, stand prominent the volumes we are about to review. In the midst of political turmoil, Mrs. Harriet Beecher Stowe has determined to put *her* finger in the pot, and has, it would seem, made quite a successful dip. Wordy philanthropy – which blows the bellows for discontent, and sends poor fools wandering through the clouds upon its treacherous breezes, yet finds no crumb of bread for one hungry stomach – is at a high premium nowadays. Ten thousand dollars (the amount, it is said, of the sales of her work) was, we presume, in the lady's opinion, worth risking a little scalding for. We wish her joy of her ten thousand thus easily gained, but would be loath to take with it the foul imagination which could invent such scenes, and the malignant bitterness (we had almost said ferocity) which, under the veil of christian charity, could find the conscience to publish them. Over this, their new-laid egg, the abolitionists, of all colours – black, white, and yellow – foreign and domestic – have set up so astounding a cackle, it is very evident, that (labouring, perhaps, under some mesmeric biologic influence) they think the goose has laid its golden egg at last. They must wake up from their dream, to the sad disappointment of finding their fancied treasure an old addle thing, whose touch contaminates with its filth.

There is nothing new in these volumes. They are, as we have said, only the old Sisyphus rock, which we have so often tumbled over, tinkered up, with considerable talent and cunning, into a new shape, and rolled back upon us. One step, indeed, we do seem to have gained. One accusation at least, which, in bygone times, used to have its changes rung among the charges brought against us, is here forgotten. We see no reference to the old habit, so generally (according to some veracious travellers) indulged in these Southern States, of fattening negro babies for the use of the soup-pot. This, it would appear, is a species of black broth which cannot be swallowed any longer. If, however, Mrs. Stowe has spared us the story of this delectable soup, with the small *nigger paws* floating in it by way of garnish, truly it is all that she *has* spared us. Libels almost as shocking to humanity she not only indulges herself in detailing, but dwells upon with a gusto and a relish quite edifying to us benighted heathen, who, constantly surrounded (as according to her statements we are) by such moving scenes and crying iniquities, yet, having ears, hear not, and having eyes, see not[2] those horrors whose stench become[s] an offence to the nostrils of our sensitive and self-constituted directors.
[...]

But let us look a little into the drama of our romance. The book opens with the introduction of "*two gentlemen*," seated at a table in a house, of which the general style "indicated easy, and even opulent circumstances." The master of the house is one of the "gentlemen." The other, "when *critically* examined, did not seem, *strictly* speaking, to come under the species." [LSM's italics] This gentleman, who proves to be a slave-trader, but who must be so *critically* examined to discover that he is not *strictly a gentleman*, seems, however, quite at his ease, and rattles his watch-seals like a man of consequence, hale fellow well met with the opulent signor, whom he constantly and familiarly terms Shelby (leaving off the form of Mr.) and occasionally slaps on the back, to make his conversation more impressive. Into what society can Mrs. Stowe have been admitted, to see slave-traders so much at their ease in gentlemen's houses? We have lived at the South, in the very heart of a slave country, for thirty years out of forty of our lives, and have never seen a slavetrader set foot in a gentleman's house. Such a début argues somewhat queerly for the society with which madame and her clerk-brother have associated, and prepares us for some singular scenes in the elegant circles to which she introduces us.[3]

To give some idea of the style of these volumes, we will presently quote a page from the conversation of these two *gentlemen*. Mr. Shelby, the opulent owner of the house, is, it appears, in debt to an amount not stated, but, as he proposes paying his debt by the transfer of *one* negro, we are to presume that it does not exceed a thousand dollars. Strange to say, this opulent Kentucky gentleman has no resource in so pressing a difficulty but the sale of a favourite negro, the manager of his farm and his companion from childhood. There are, apparently, neither banks nor friends who could loan so enormous a sum as one thousand dollars to rescue the opulent gentleman from this difficulty, or Mr. Shelby is of the same opinion, perhaps, as our little girl of six years old, who shakes her head gravely and exclaims, "One thousand dollars! Why, there is not so much money in this world, I think." At any rate it is so insurmountable a difficulty that, for this one thousand dollars, our opulent gentleman forgets that he is a gentleman – forgets that he is a man – forgets honour, principle, gratitude, and common sense, and offers his old black friend, his father's slave, his childhood's companion and guardian, the manager of his farm, the husband and father of a whole family of attached servants, to this brute of a slave-dealer, with decidedly more coolness than we could command in ordering the whipping of a thievish cur. To heighten the value of the commodity offered, this gentleman is praising his wares in rather singular language, by the way, for an educated man: "Tom is a good, steady, sensible, pious fellow. He *got religion* at a camp-meeting, four years ago" [LSM's italics]. To which remark the gentleman negro trader, who must be so *critically* examined to discover that he is not *strictly* of the first stamp, responds (we beg our readers to notice the elegant familiarity of his style):

> Some folks don't believe there is pious niggers, Shelby, [. . .] but *I do*. I had a fellow, now, in this yer last lot I took to Orleans – 'twas as good as a meetin', now, really, to hear that critter pray; and he was quite gentle and quiet like. He fetched me a good sum, too, for I bought him cheap of a man that was 'bliged to sell out; so I realized six hundred on him. Yes, I consider religion a valeyable thing in a nigger, when it's the genuine article, and no mistake.

To this, instead of kicking the scoundrel out of doors, our opulent gentleman answers, politely falling into the tone of his companion:

> "Well, Tom's got the real article, if ever fellow had, [. . .] You ought to let him cover the whole balance of the debt; and you would, Haley, if you had any conscience."
> "Well, I've got just as much conscience as any man in business can afford to keep – just a little, you know, to swear by, as 'twere," said the trader, jocularly; "and, then, I'm ready to do anything in reason to 'blige friends; but this yer, you see, is a leetle too hard on a fellow – a leetle too hard."

O tempora! O mores! This is a *leetle* too hard to swallow. But let us go on. After a little more conversation of the same kind, "a small quadroon boy, four or five <between four and five> years of age," makes his appearance. Evidently this "small quadroon" is a gentleman at large, and a pet in the family, for he enters unsummoned, is patted on his "curly head," and "chucked [...] under the chin" by his master, who receives him in whistling and "*snapping* a bunch of raisins at <towards> him." The gentleman master then, for the amusement of his gentleman visitor, causes his "small quadroon" to go through sundry funny exhibitions, such as imitating "Uncle Cudjoe when he has the rheumatism," showing "how old Elder Robbins leads the psalm," etc., during which exhibitions "both the gentlemen laughed *uproariously*." [LSM's italics] On their termination, the gentleman visitor bursts out anew:

> "Hurrah! bravo! what a young 'un! [...] that chap's a case, I'll promise. Tell you what," said he, suddenly clapping his hand on Mr. Shelby's shoulder, "fling in that chap, and I'll settle the business – I will. Come, now, if that ain't doing the thing up about the rightest!"

The mother of the child, at that moment making her appearance, carries him off; and as soon as she leaves the room, our facetious and gentlemanly trader, struck with *her* saleable qualities, takes a new start.

> "By Jupiter! [...] there's an article now! You might make your fortune on that ar gal in Orleans, any day. I've seen over a thousand, in my day, paid down for gals not a bit handsomer."

The *Westminster* finds no vulgarity nor exaggeration in these volumes! In answer to this vulgar insolence, the master of the house can apparently find no better way of showing his disapprobation than by uncorking a fresh bottle of wine, of which he politely asks the opinion of his polished guest.

> "Capital, sir – first chop!" said the trader; then turning, and slapping his hand familiarly on Shelby's shoulder, he added: "Come, how will you trade about the gal?"

But enough of this disgusting vulgarity. Need we say to any reader who has ever associated with decent society anywhere, that Mrs. Stowe evidently does not know what "a gentleman" is. We will pass over the one who, upon *critical* examination, shows that he is somewhat deficient; but what will any gentleman or lady say to Mr. Shelby? Mrs. Stowe has associated much, it would appear, with negroes, mulattoes, and abolitionists; possibly, in her exalted dreams for the perfection of the race, she has forgotten the small punctilios of what, in the ordinary parlance of the world, is called decent society. She will, therefore, perhaps, excuse a hint from us, that her next dramatic sketch would be much improved by a somewhat increased decency of deportment in her performers. Whatever may be the faults, the vices, or the crimes of any man holding the position of gentleman (at least we vouch for a southern community), he would be above such coarse vulgarity. We would suggest, too – as she, no doubt taken up with her glorious aspirations and high and *uncommon* feelings, has forgotten what portion of *common* ones more ordinary creatures have – that it would be well to allow the appearance of the shadow of such even to us wretched slaveholders. If we are brutes, we usually try to appear a little more like human beings; and it would decidedly look more "nateral like" so to represent us. She describes this Mr. Shelby as "a fair average kind of man, good-natured and kindly" [19]; and yet, after the above scene, and a great deal more of discussion as to how a mother bears to have her children taken from her, in which the negrotrading gentleman, Haley, edifies the opulent gentleman, Shelby, with sundry descriptions in the taste and tone of the following:

> "I've seen 'em as would pull a woman's child out of her arms, and set him up to sell, and she screechin' like mad all the time – very bad policy – damages the article – makes 'em quite unfit for

service sometimes. I knew a real handsome gal once, in Orleans, as was entirely ruined by this sort
o' handling. The fellow that was tradin' <trading> for her didn't want her baby; and she was one of
your real high sort, when her blood was up. I tell you, she squeezed up her child in her arms, and
talked, and went on real awful. It kinder makes my blood [run] cold to think on't; and when they
carried off the child, and locked her up, she jest went ravin' mad, and died in a week. Clear waste,
sir, of a thousand dollars, just for want of management."

After this, we say, the "good-natured and kindly" Mr. Shelby determines to sell the child in a
quiet way, to avoid the *screechin'*, by stealing it away from its mother. Upon this very probable
and natural incident, as Mrs. Stowe and the *Westminster* pronounce it, turns the principal
romance of the story. The woman runs away with her child, and after adventures infinite,
finally arrives among the Quakers and in Canada, etc.
[...]
   To conclude. We have undertaken the defence of slavery in no temporizing vein. We do *not*
say it is a necessary evil. We do *not* allow that it is a temporary makeshift to choke the course of
Providence for man's convenience. It is *not* "a sorrow and a wrong to be lived down." We
proclaim it, on the contrary, a Godlike dispensation, a providential caring for the weak, and a
refuge for the portionless. Nature's outcast, as for centuries he appeared to be, he – even from
the dawning of tradition, the homeless, houseless, useless negro – suddenly assumes a place,
suddenly becomes one of the great levers of civilization. At length the path marked out for him
by Omniscience becomes plain. Unfit for all progress, so long as left to himself, the negro has
hitherto appeared simply as a blot upon creation, and already the stronger races are, even in his
own land, threatening him with extinction. Civilization must spread. Nature seems to require
this, by a law as stringent as that through which water seeks its level. The poor negro,
astounded by the torrent of progress which, bursting over the world, now hangs menacingly
(for to the wild man is not civilization always menacing?) above him, would vainly follow with
the stream, and is swept away in the current. Slavery, even in his own land, is his destiny and
his refuge from extinction. Beautifully has the system begun to expand itself among us. Shorn
of the barbarities with which a slavery established by conquest and maintained by brute force is
always accompanied, we have begun to mingle with it the graces and amenities of the highest
Christian civilization. Have begun, we say, for the work is but begun. The system is far from its
perfection, and at every step of its progress is retarded by a meddling fanaticism, which has in
it, to borrow a quotation from Mrs. Stowe herself, "a dread, unhallowed necromancy of evil,
that turns things sweetest and holiest to phantoms of horror and affright". Our system of
slavery, left to itself, would rapidly develop its higher features, softening at once to servant and
to master. The satanic school of arguers are far too much inclined to make capital of man's
original sin, and to build upon this foundation a perfect tower of iniquitous possibilities,
frightful even to imagine. Men are by no means as hopelessly wicked as Mrs. Stowe and others
of this school would argue; and these would do well to remember, that when God created man,
"in the image of God created he him;" and though "sin came into the world and death by sin,"[4]
yet is the glorious, though clouded, image still there, and erring man is still a man, and
not a devil.
   We, too, could speculate upon the possibilities of this system, and present a picture in
beautiful contrast with Mrs. Stowe's, as purely bright as hers is foully dark; but, as we
remarked earlier in our argument, the fairest reasoning is not from what a system might be, but
from what it is. We grant that there is crime, there is sin, there is abuse of power under our
laws; but let the abolitionist show us any rule where these are not. Utopias have been vainly
dreamed. That system is the best which, not in theory, but in practice, brings the greatest sum

of good to the greatest number. We challenge history, present and past, to show any system of government which, judged by this test, will be found superior to the one we defend.

"Oh liberté!" exclaimed Mme. Roland, when led to the scaffold, "que de crimes a-t-on commis en ton nom!"[5] *Theoretic* virtues are more dangerous than open vice. Cloaks for every crime, they are pushed boldly forward, stifling our natural sense of practical right, and blinding men with the appearance of a righteousness, which dazzles like the meteor, but warms not like the sun. Theoretic liberty and theoretic bread satisfy neither the hungry soul nor the hungry stomach, and many a poor fugitive to the land of freedom, sated full with both, has wept to return to the indulgent master and the well filled corncrib. The negro, left to himself, does not dream of liberty. He cannot indeed grasp a conception which belongs so naturally to the brain of the white man. In his natural condition, he is, by turns, tyrant and slave, but never the free man. You may talk to the blind man of light, until he fancies that he understands you, and begins to wish for that bright thing which you tell him he has not; but vainly he rolls his sightless orbs, unhappy that he cannot see the brightness of that beam whose warmth before sufficed to make him happy. Thus it is with the moral sunbeam of the poor negro. He cannot see nor conceive the "liberty" which you would thrust upon him, and it is a cruel task to disturb him in the enjoyment of that life to which God has destined him. He basks in his sunshine, and is happy. Christian slavery, in its full development, free from the fretting annoyance and galling bitterness of abolition interference, is the brightest sunbeam which Omniscience has destined for his existence.

L. S. M.

Questions to consider

- McCord begins her excerpt by citing the Greek myth of Sisyphus, who was forced by Hades, the god of the Underworld, to perpetually roll a boulder up a hill, only to have it roll down again when it reaches the top. How is this metaphor relevant to her understanding of the South's image regarding slavery?

- How does McCord attack the scenario in the first chapter of *Uncle Tom's Cabin*? How compelling do you find her critique?

- Juxtapose McCord's ideas about race with Stowe's: how does each understand the proper relationship between whites and blacks?

Escaped Slave Advertisements from *The Key to Uncle Tom's Cabin*

Harriet Beecher Stowe

The critical attacks on *Uncle Tom's Cabin* led Stowe to respond with a rejoinder: a huge compendium of facts she called *The Key to Uncle Tom's Cabin* (1853). The *Key* was designed to refute criticism of her understanding of slavery, and to show that her portrayal was, if anything, too mild. To that end, she included a series of advertisements for runaway slaves. As you read them, ask yourself: how effectively do these function as evidence of the evils of slavery? What are their limits? What are their strengths as pieces of primary evidence?

Harriet Beecher Stowe, "Slaves as They Are, On Testimony of Owners," in *The Key to Uncle Tom's Cabin* (Salem, NH: Ayer Co., 1987; reprint of 1854 edn), pp. 346–9.

SLAVES AS THEY ARE, ON TESTIMONY OF OWNERS

The investigation into the actual condition of the slave population at the South is beset with many difficulties. So many things are said *pro* and *con* – so many said in one connexion and denied in another – that the effect is very confusing.

Thus we are told that the state of the slaves is one of blissful contentment; that they would not take freedom as a gift; that their family relations are only now and then invaded; that they are a stupid race, almost sunk to the condition of animals; that generally they are kindly treated, &c.

In reading over some two hundred Southern newspapers this fall, the author has been struck with the very graphic and circumstantial pictures, which occur in all of them, describing fugitive slaves. From these descriptions one may learn a vast many things. The author will here give an assortment of them, taken at random. It is a commentary on the contented state of the slave population that the writer finds two or three always, and often many more, in every one of the hundreds of Southern papers examined.

In reading the following little sketches of "slaves as they are," let the reader notice:

1 The colour and complexion of the majority of them.
2 That it is customary either to describe slaves by some *scar*, or to say, "*No scars recollected.*"
3 The *intelligence* of the parties advertised.
4 The number that *say they are free* that are to be *sold to pay jail fees.*

Every one of these slaves has a history – a history of woe and crime, degradation, endurance, and wrong. Let us open the chapter.

South-side Democrat, October 28, 1852. Petersburgh, Virginia:

REWARD

Twenty-five dollars, with the payment of all necessary expenses, will be given for the apprehension and delivery of my man CHARLES, if taken on the Appomattox river, or within the precincts of Petersburgh. He ran off about a week ago, and if he leaves the neighbourhood, will no doubt make for Farmville and Petersburgh. He is a mulatto, rather below the medium height and size, but well proportioned, and very active and sensible. He is aged about 27 years, has a mild, submissive look, and will, no doubt, show the marks of a recent whipping if taken, He must be delivered to the care of Peebles, White, Davis, & Co.

Oct. 25.–3t.   R. H. DE JARNETT, LUNENBURGH.

Poor Charles! – *mulatto!* – has a mild, submissive look, and will probably show marks of a recent whipping!

Kosciusko Chronicle, November 24, 1852:

COMMITTED

To the Jail of Attila County, on the 8th instant, a negro boy, who calls his name GREEN, and says he belongs to James Gray, of Winston County. Said boy is about 20 years old, yellow complexion, round face, has a scar on his face, one on his left thigh, and one in his left hand: is about 5 feet 6 inches high. Had on when taken up a cotton check shirt, Linsey pants, new cloth cap, and was riding a large roan horse about 12 or 14 years old, and thin in order. The owner is requested to come forward, prove property, pay charges, and take him away, or he will be sold to pay charges.

Oct. 12, 1852.   E. B. SANDERS, JAILER A. C.
                                                                              n12tf.

Capitolian Vis-à-Vis, West Baton Rouge, Nov. 1, 1852.

ONE HUNDRED DOLLARS REWARD.

RUNAWAY from the subscriber, in Randolph County, on the 18th of October, a yellow boy, named JIM. This boy is 19 years old, a light mulatto with dirty sunburnt hair inclined to be straight; he is just 5 feet 7 inches high, and slightly made. He had on when he left a black cloth cap, black cloth pantaloons, a plaided sack coat, a fine shirt, and brogan shoes. One hundred dollars will be paid for the recovery of the above-described boy, if taken out of the State, or fifty dollars if taken in the State.

                                                                      MRS. S. P. HALL,
Nov. 4, 1852.   Huntsville, Mo.

American Baptist, Dec. 20, 1852:

TWENTY DOLLARS REWARD FOR A PREACHER.

The following paragraph, headed "Twenty Dollars Reward," appeared in a recent number of the *New Orleans Picayune:*

"Runaway from the plantation of the undersigned the negro man Shedrick, a preacher, 5 feet 9 inches high, about 40 years old, but looking not over 23, stamped N. E. on the breast, and having both small toes cut off. He is of a very dark complexion, with eyes small but bright, and a look quite insolent. He dresses good, and was arrested as a runaway at Donaldsonville, some three years ago. The above reward will be paid for his arrest, by addressing Messrs. Armant Brothers, St. James parish, or A. Miltenberger & Co., 30, Carondelet-street."

Here is a preacher who is branded on the breast and has two toes cut off – and *will* look insolent yet! There's depravity for you!

Jefferson Inquirer, Nov. 27, 1852:

ONE HUNDRED DOLLARS REWARD.

RANAWAY from my plantation, in Bolivar County, Miss., a negro man named MAY, aged 40 years, 5 feet 10 or 11 inches high, copper coloured, and very straight; his front teeth are good and stand a little open; stout through the shoulders, and has some scars on his back that show above the skin plain, caused by the whip; he frequently hiccups when eating, if he has not got water handy;

he was pursued into Ozark County, Mo, and there left. I will give the above reward for his confinement in jail, so that I can get him.

JAMES H. COUSAR,

Nov. 13, lm.   Victoria, Bolivar County, Mississippi.

Delightful master to go back to, this man must be!

————

The Alabama Standard has for its motto, "RESISTANCE TO TYRANTS IS OBEDIENCE TO GOD." Date of Nov. 29th, this advertisement:

COMMITTED

To the Jail of Choctaw County, by Judge Young, of Marengo County, a RUNAWAY SLAVE, who calls his name BILLY, and says he belongs to the late William Johnson, and was in the employment of John Jones, near Alexandria, La. He is about 5 feet 10 inches high, black, about 40 years old, much scarred on the face and head, and quite intelligent.

The owner is requested to come forward, prove his property, and take him from jail, or he will be disposed of according to law.

S. S. HOUSTON, Jailer, C. C.

Dec. 1, 1852.   tf.

Query: whether this "quite intelligent" Billy hadn't been corrupted by hearing this incendiary motto of the *Standard?*

————

Knoxville (Tennessee) *Register*, Nov. 3rd:

LOOK OUT FOR RUNAWAYS! TWENTY-FIVE DOLLARS REWARD!

RANAWAY from the subscriber, on the night of the 26th July last, a negro woman named HARRIET. Said woman is about 5 feet 5 inchcs high, has prominent cheek-bones, large mouth and good front teeth, tolerably spare built, about 26 years old. We think it probable she is harboured by some negroes not far from John Mynatt's in Knox County, where she and they are likely making some arrangements to get to a free State: or she may be concealed by some negroes (her connexions) in Anderson County, near Clinton. I will give the above reward for her apprehension and confinement in any prison in this State, or I will give fifty dollars for her confinement in any jail out of this State, so that I get her.

Nov. 3. 4m.   H. B. GOENS, Clinton, Tenn.

————

The *Alexandria Gazette*, November 29, 1852, under the device of Liberty trampling on a tyrant, motto, *Sic "semper tyrannis,"* has the following:

˙TWENTY-FIVE DOLLARS REWARD.

Ranaway from the subscriber, living in the County of Rappahannock, on Tuesday last, DANIEL, a bright mulatto, about 5 feet 8 inches high, about 35 years old, very intelligent, has been a waggoner for several years, and is pretty well acquainted from Richmond to Alexandria. He calls himself DANIEL TURNER; his hair curls without showing black blood, or wool; he has a scar on one cheek, and his left hand has been seriously injured by a pistol-shot, and he was shabbily dressed when last seen. I will give the above reward if taken out of the county, and secured in jail, so that I get him again, or ten dollars if taken in the county.   A. M. WILLIS.

Rappahannock Co., Va, Nov. 29.—eo 1m.

Another "very intelligent," straight-haired man. Who was his father?

———

The *New Orleans Daily Crescent*, office, No. 93, St. Charlesstreet; Tuesday morning, December 13, 1852:

BROUGHT TO THE FIRST DISTRICT POLICE PRISON.

NANCY, a griffe, about 34 years old, 5 feet $1\frac{3}{4}$ inch high, a scar on left wrist; says she belongs to Madame Wolf.

CHARLES HALL, a black, about 18 years old, 5 feet 6 inches high; says he is free, but supposed to be a slave.

PHILOMONIA, a mulattress, about 10 years old, 4 feet 3 inches high; says she is free, but supposed to be a slave.

COLUMBUS, a griffe, about 21 years old, 5 feet $5\frac{3}{4}$ inches high; says he is free, but supposed to be a slave.

SEYMOUR, a black, about 21 years old, 5 feet $1\frac{3}{4}$ inch high; says he is free, but supposed to be a slave.

The owners will please to comply with the law respecting them.

J. WORRALL, Warden.

New Orleans, Dec. 14, 1852.

What chance for any of these poor fellows who *say they are free?*

Notes

1   More precisely, Sisyphus, king of Corinth, suffered for insulting the gods (*hubris*). Sentenced to die for betraying one of Zeus' love affairs, Sisyphus instructed his wife Merope to refuse his body proper burial. In the Underworld he persuaded Hades to permit him to visit earth, so that he might punish Merope for her impiety before returning to the Under-world. Hades agreed; Sisyphus then was careful never to punish Merope. But when he came to die of old age, Hades had not forgotten the trick and sentenced Sisyphus eternally to roll up a hill a boulder which, at the summit, eternally rolls back down again.
2   Ps. 115:5–6; Jer. 5:21.
3   "In no State in the Union is a negro-trader less respected, than in South Carolina. It has always been so within the recollection of the writer, which extends to more than half a century. Familiar with most of the Southern States, he believes the same feeling of dislike exists everywhere in the slaveholding country. They are always contemptuously called by the negroes, 'speculators'; and it would astonish Cuffee to see 'a speculator' at a gentleman's table, no less than to see a black face like his own taking wine with 'mauser.' " David James McCord, "Life of a Negro Slave," *Southern Quarterly Review*, n.s., 7 (Jan. 1853): 206–27; 209.
4   Gen. 1:27; Rom. 5:12.
5   Jeanne-Marie Philipon Roland de La Platière (1754–93), French revolutionary; her husband was a Girondin leader, her salon a center of Girondin activity; guillotined with other Girondins.

Part II

Justifying the War

Plate 4 Snappy Shot: Portrait of an enlisted man, 23rd Massachusetts Volunteers, Company A, taken some time between 1860 and 1865. Soldiers departing for the front often had formal portraits made for family and friends as keepsakes.

Chapter 4

The Spirit of '61

George M. Fredrickson

Wars are never merely fought: they are always explained – before, during, and after the event. Moreover, wars almost always have more than one explanation, explanations that may differ even among people on the same side, and which may shift in emphasis or appear or disappear entirely. The recent Iraq War, for example, was discussed in terms of weapons of mass destruction, overthrowing a brutal regime, and protecting important strategic interests in a volatile part of the world. Each of these explanations was embraced by some – and questioned, if not outrightly rejected, by others. For if wars always have their supporters, they always have their critics (even if those supporters and critics deem it politic to be silent at times).

Few American wars have been more complex, even elusive, in their justification than the Civil War. On the surface at least, the cause(s) may seem simple enough: ending slavery/protecting slavery; saving the Union/preserving the Southern way of life; an opportunity for adventure/an imperative to defend home and family. Yet the closer some historians look at such explanations, the more mysterious they become. Why did the South, which controlled so many key government offices in the Federal government, take such a risk in attempting to leave the Union? Why did Northern boys, most of whom were indifferent at best about slavery, feel compelled to leave their homes and risk death, disease and even financial disaster? Very often, there are no single answers to such questions. Indeed it finally seems impossible to truly understand the Civil War by viewing it in terms of a single cause, because any cause consists of a variety of people, each of whom may be inspired by a variety of motivations, experiences, and structural imperatives.

One group of people who pay a lot of attention to justifications is intellectuals. Justifications are ideas, and ideas – articulating them, attacking them, defending or revising them – are intellectuals' stock-in-trade. While they typically cultivate an air of detachment and reflection, dramatic events often led writers and artists to think of themselves, whether rightly or with an exaggerated sense of their own importance, as crucial figures in helping society respond. In this chapter from his classic

1965 book *The Inner Civil War*, George M. Fredrickson, an eminent historian on race relations, traces the varied responses to the outbreak of the Civil War among Northern intellectuals.

George M. Fredrickson, "The Spirit of '61," in *The Inner Civil War: Northern Intellectuals and the Crisis of the Union* (New York: Harper & Row, 1965), pp. 65–78.

The South's attack on Fort Sumter, wrote the *New York Times* three days after the event, has made the North "a unit"; for "one intense, inspiring sentiment of patriotism has fused all other passions in its fiery heat." Two weeks later, another paper described the "wonderful transformation which has taken place in the public mind since the fall of Fort Sumter," and called the enthusiastic response to the President's call for volunteers "the most remarkable event of this and probably of any age."[1] As a group, the intellectuals participated fully in the public enthusiasm. Unlike more unreflective patriots, however, they sought to explain and justify their passion, and, as might be expected, the explanations and justifications were various and contradictory.

Emerson, who only a few days earlier had been willing to see the Union go to pieces in the hope that "adult individualism" could now replace formal institutions of government, rejoiced in the post-Sumter "whirlwind of patriotism" which was "magnetizing all discordant masses under its terrific unity." What impressed him most about the public reaction was its spontaneity. "It is an affair of instincts," he told his lecture audience; "we did not know we had them; we valued ourselves as cool calculators; we were very fine with our learning and culture, with our science that was of no country, and our religion of peace; – and now a sentiment mightier than logic, wide as light, strong as gravity, reaches into the college, the bank, the farmhouse, and the church. It is the day of the populace; they are wiser than their teachers. . . . I will never again speak lightly of a crowd."[2] Emerson, who had always been an admirer of "noble passions" but had heretofore considered them the prerogative of isolated genius, had now lost his contempt for the masses and for crowds of all kinds and seemed willing to accept collective feeling as the equivalent of individual intuition. The war spirit was inspiring because there seemed to be nothing formal or institutional about it; it was "a sentiment mightier than logic" which was reaching into dead institutions and bringing forth live men.

If the opening of the war had apparently converted Emerson to the Whitmanic faith that divine human nature could be expressed by mass democracy, it had made Whitman himself more optimistic than ever about the capabilities of the people en masse. Up to this time, Whitman had never really found an answer to the question of what would hold together the unorganized populace, if one dispensed, as he desired, with all institutions; but the spirit of 1861 suggested that the ideological fervor of a people at war for the democratic idea could be the cohesive force; and Whitman celebrated this fervor in his early war poems.

From the beginning Whitman, like President Lincoln, regarded the slavery question as secondary. "The negro was not the chief thing," he recalled in later years; "the chief thing was to stick together."[3] Yet, even though he was not an abolitionist, his Unionism (again like Lincoln's) derived in no essential way from the rights-of-authority school. It was based squarely on the idea of an American mission – the belief that the advance of democracy in the world depended on the preservation of the American nation. Whitman and Lincoln were almost alone among the philosophers of Unionism in giving a strong democratic meaning to the conflict.[4]

One way in which the war would realize the promise of American democracy, according to Whitman, was by raising men's sights from material interests. Whitman, who before the war had described his disgust with American materialism, as reflected in "the shallowness and miserable selfism of these crowds of men, with all their minds so blank of high humanity and aspiration," had come to recognize that the great danger of democracy was the opening it gave for the wrong kind of individualism – the pursuit of personal advantage.[5] As a result, he was quick to hail the new patriotic spirit as an antidote to materialism.

Long, too long, O land,
Traveling roads all even and peaceful, you learn'd from joys and prosperity only;
But now, ah now, to learn from crisis of anguish – advancing, grappling with direst fate, and recoiling not;
And now to conceive and show to the world, what your children en-masse really are;
(For who except myself has yet conceived what your children en-masse really are?)[6]

In addition to being tested by adversity, Americans were also being saved from an excessive attachment to institutions. In "Beat! Beat! Drums!" Whitman rejoiced in the manner of Emerson at the way the war spirit would go "Into the solemn church and scatter the congregation" and "Into the school where the scholar was studying." It would not even leave "the bridegroom quiet with his bride." In another poem, he expressed genuine pleasure at the disruption of ordinary institutional life that preceded the creation of a mass army. Describing the "torrents of men" going to war as representing "DEMOCRACY" breaking forth with thunder and lightning, Whitman indicated that his hunger for "primal energies," for "Nature's dauntlessness" was finally satisfied. "I am glutted," he wrote;

I have witness'd the true lightning – I have witness'd my cities electric;
I have lived to behold man burst forth, and warlike America rise.[7]

Since Whitman's "DEMOCRACY" was an irrational, quasinatural force, or a collective emotion, he could easily lead himself to think that all war patriotism was enthusiasm for liberty, equality, and fraternity. For him, as for Emerson, all large passions seemed to come from the cosmic spirit.

Other believers in a cosmic spirit, however, were not satisfied with patriotic or even ideological enthusiasm as the expression of the divine energy. They hoped that the spirit of 1861 could be deepened and transformed into an explicitly religious feeling, a burning millennial faith.

One such millennialist was Henry James, Sr., a Swedenborgian philosopher, who had often sounded like Emerson. In a lecture of 1849, James had proclaimed that "society affords no succor to the divine life in man," – "there exists no tie either natural or social, as society is now constituted, which does not tend to slavery, which does not cheat man's soul of its fair proportions." But he had rejected Emersonian individualism as an end in itself. Existing society, he felt, should be replaced by a communal order based on love – what he called the reign of "divine-natural humanity."[8] In this aspiration, James was in complete agreement with "fraternity" transcendentalists like Parker and Conway. In the Fourth of July oration he gave in Newport in 1861, James described the war as a great step in the progress of mankind toward "divine-natural humanity." The American idea of liberty, for which he believed the North was fighting, was not simply liberty under a constitution, it was that transcendental liberty "which is identical with the God-made constitution of the human mind itself, and which consists in the inalienable rights of every man to believe according to the unbridled inspiration of his own heart, and to act according to the unperverted dictates of his own understanding."[9]

Unlike Whitman, and more emphatically than Emerson, however, James made his national fulfillment dependent upon a conscious repudiation of slavery. Without this change of heart, there was no value in patriotic or Unionist fervor. He spoke for the abolitionists in considering it essential that the war be turned into an antislavery crusade, that it be fought for universal and religious rather than national and political concerns. With such a righteous aim, American society would, in James' Swedenborgian terms, pass "from appearance to reality, from passing shadow to deathless substance." For it was "the hour of our endless rise into all beautiful human proportions, into all celestial vigor and beatitude, or [in the unlikely event that slavery was not abolished and as a result of the war] of our endless decline into all infernality and uncleanness."[10] The Jamesian vocabulary was unique, but his millennial expectation, his belief that an affectionate society of free individuals would somehow emerge out of the bloodshed and hatred of war, was characteristic of the thinking of many abolitionists in 1861.

There were others who thought, in the late spring and early summer of 1861, that the war, rather than encouraging anti-institutional or transcendental ideas, would have the opposite tendency. Charles Eliot Norton, for example, interpreted the unity of the North as being the product of no "contagion of a short-lived popular excitement," but a result of the people's "conservative love of order, government, and law."[11]

Norton apparently felt that these conservative instincts needed some encouragement, for he quickly turned to the writing of patriotic tracts. His first effort, *The Soldier of the Good Cause*, was directed at the man in the field. In it, Norton tried to impress on the new recruits the value of discipline. "Enthusiasm will not supply the place of discipline," he wrote, "and there is need of more than a good cause when it comes to the push." One thing that was needed was the professional military attitude – the conviction that "the first duty of a soldier is obedience." The volunteer should also understand that motives such as "enthusiasm for the flag, devotion to the Union, indignation against traitors, patriotic pride, an honest love of liberty, and hate of slavery . . . are of too external a character to form a safe and sufficient reliance in this great contest." Norton then described in a vague way "motives of deeper and more spiritual origin." Since the war was "a religious war . . . a man must carry with him the assurance that he is acting in the immediate presence and as the commissioned soldier of God."[12]

Norton did not explain further what he meant by the "religious" motive, but the fact that it could be separated from hatred of slavery showed that he was not speaking the language of the abolitionists. Whatever he meant, his use of Cromwellian rhetoric gave him the momentary sense that he was playing the role of his Puritan clerical ancestors, that people were listening to him as the preacher of a stern faith. It is curious to see emancipated Unitarians, of rationalistic, almost positivistic beliefs, like Norton and the elder Oliver Wendell Holmes, writing in 1861 like seventeenth century Puritans. Holmes, whose urbane and amusing "One Horse Shay" had put forth the claim that Calvinism was dead, was now writing poems like the "Army Hymn," a fervent appeal to the Puritan God of battles.

It was left to Henry W. Bellows to work out with clarity and consistency the meaning of the "religious" impulse in the war. Preaching as the news of Fort Sumter was still coming in, Bellows told his congregation that he wished "to know nothing of that kind of religion which will not defend the sacred interests of society, with all the power, physical and moral, which God and nature have supplied."[13] A week later, he further developed his analysis of the close connection of religion and defense of the Union. Deploring "the unhappy alienation of church and state" in America, he argued that the state should be "the body of the church . . . as essentially and vitally connected with the prosperity and life of the church as the health of our bodies with the welfare of our spirits." He then went on to define "*the state*" in a way that put to good use his "doctrine of institutions" of 1859. It was nothing less than "the great common life of a nation, organized in laws, customs, institutions; its total social being incarnate in a political unit, having common organs and functions; a living body, with a head and a heart . . . with a common consciousness. . . . The state is indeed divine, as being the great incarnation of a nation's rights, privileges, honor and life. . . . "[14] Here was one of the ablest statements of the organic social theory to come out of nineteenth century America. Because he could argue that the war was being fought for the maintenance of order and in defense of an inherited way of life, Bellows had a strong position from which to attack all varieties of anti-institutionalism.

He even found the courage to hint at the supreme heresy – the idea that all recognized nationalities and established governments rest on the same solid religious basis as that of the United States. He spoke of nationalism as "sublimely . . . exhibiting itself" in Czarist Russia. He praised Napoleon III, although "a despot," as being "true to [France's] national instincts and aspirations. . . . "[15] Whether Bellows realized it or not, this kind of reasoning could lead to a repudiation of the doctrines of the Declaration of Independence.

Orestes Brownson in the July issue of his review echoed Bellows in giving a conservative meaning to the struggle. Incredibly exuberant about the war for a man who a few years previously had espoused the theories of Calhoun, Brownson called the conflict "the thunderstorm that purifies the moral and political atmosphere." Like almost everyone else, he foresaw salvation of the national character from materialism – its principal vice. A people which had "seemed to be wholly engrossed in trade and speculation, selfish, and incapable of any disinterested, heroic or patriotic effort" had responded magnificently to the call for self-sacrifice. War thus seemed an excellent means of bridling the economic individualism which had always been Brownson's major complaint about American life. In addition, the war might teach another lesson. "In asserting popular sovereignty, in appealing to the people, and exaggerating both their wisdom and their virtue," Brownson complained, "we have overlooked the necessity and authority of government. . . . " He implied, however, that the war would reveal to all the limitations of the democratic philosophy and wean the American people from their absurd political notions.[16]

With such varying views as those of James and Brownson being enunciated in July 1861, it would appear that the first three months of the war had brought no consensus on the meaning of the conflict. The most diverse conclusions had been drawn as to what was signified by the fact that the American people had divided into two warring nations. There was agreement only on the fact that the conflict would have a salutary effect on the country, and that pecuniary selfishness, for one thing, would be cured by the stern purgative of battle. Beyond that, intellectuals looked either for a closer approximation of the utopia which they saw foreshadowed in the national creed, or for a society which would reject the more "dangerous" aspects of that creed and return to the "sound" principles of conservative government. Both parties could not be satisfied.

II

For young men of military age, sharing in the patriotic outburst meant volunteering to fight, rather than speculating on the meaning of the new Unionist spirit. Personal commitments, however, could speak louder and more eloquently of the concerns of the upper-class intellectuals of the North than all the sermons, articles, and pamphlets. Many of the younger generation of

New England Brahmins, for example, rallied to the colors with an enthusiasm which revealed not only a desire to regenerate the nation but also a hope for personal salvation. Like Charles Eliot Norton, these grandsons of the old Federalist elite had been seeking something worth doing, and the opportunity for a commission in the army seemed an answer to their prayers.

The Brahmin response to the call for volunteers was seen by Oliver Wendell Holmes, Sr., as the answer to his plea for a military experience to stiffen the backbone of America's "chryso-aristocracy." Noting happily that "the war fever" which had seized the North had infected "our poor 'Brahmins'," and brought many of them into the army, he suggested that the time had come at last for the testing of the American aristocrat.[17]

Some young patricians were especially eager to get into the fray. Scarcely a week after the firing on Fort Sumter, Charles Russell Lowell, aroused because the first contingent of Massachusetts volunteers had been attacked by a mob while passing through Baltimore, set off for Washington to join up. Since rail transportation to the capital was cut off, he had to travel on foot. The young Emersonian, who had spent so many years in search of a profession which would satisfy his ideal aspirations, had at last found a vocation. He wrote to his mother from Washington, after gaining a commission in the regular army, that " . . . the Army is to assume a new position among us – it will again become a profession."[18] Fighting in such a glorious war seemed the way to combine the highest idealism with practical activity. Lowell's friend Henry Lee Higginson was another who found going to war a release from the anxiety of being unable to enter any of the acceptable professions. Higginson was mustered in as a second lieutenant on May 11, 1861. As he observed later, "I always did long for some such war, and it came in the nick of time for me."[19]

Another well-born wanderer who found a home in one of the first regiments was Theodore Winthrop. This young novelist, who, like Parkman, had found his only prewar fulfillment in the thrill of remote travels and explorations, thought he had now discovered a more fruitful way to spend his time. After enlisting in the first regiment raised in New York, he wrote to a friend that he had undertaken a life's task. Since he believed that the South would have to be occupied after the war, that the North "must hold the South as the Metropolitan police holds New York," he wished to enroll himself "in the *Police of the Nation*. And for life, if the Nation will take me. I do not see that I can put myself, – experience and character – to any more useful use."[20] Winthrop's lifetime service was tragically short. He was killed in June – one of the first "martyrs" of the war.

III

The death of Theodore Winthrop and a few others may have given the North some preview of what was to come; but it was the unexpected defeat of the Union forces at the First Battle of Bull Run on July 21 which gave both soldiers and civilians their first real sense of what the war would be like. Strangely enough, this disaster was greeted by some of the intellectuals with even greater joy than they had shown after Sumter. Moncure Conway reported after a visit to Concord that Thoreau was "in a state of exultation about the moral regeneration of the nation." Wendell Phillips, according to the recollections of one observer, described the defeat as exactly what was needed and the best thing that could have happened to the North. Henry W. Bellows agreed; he wrote to the *Christian Inquirer* on the "moral necessity of the late defeat," claiming that "nothing but the disaster could thoroughly arouse the country to the efforts, the reforms, and the spirit essential to the proper and vigorous conduct of this war." For Thomas Wentworth Higginson, the defeat was valuable for a more specific reason; it forced Congress to pass a stern confiscation law which, on paper at least, freed those slaves directly employed in the rebellion. In this action, Higginson saw the first signs of "a war of emancipation." Since all these men hoped for a long war which would give free rein to the favorable impulses they observed, Bull Run was welcome proof that peace would not come too soon.[21] A review of the fuller comments on the new picture of the war suggests, however, that the greatest encouragement was given to those who sought a reversal of the democratic and humanitarian tendencies of American thought.

Charles Eliot Norton, to take one exuberant conservative, waxed lyrical over "the advantages of defeat" in the September *Atlantic*. Norton, who had long feared that prosperity would lead to national decadence, could now exult in the fact that "we are not to expect or hope for a speedy return of what is called prosperity." How fortunate it was that "we, who have so long been eager in the pursuit and accumulation of riches, are now to show more generous energies in the free spending of our means to gain the valuable object for which we have gone to war." But Norton hoped for more than just the expenditure of wealth by a people grown too fond of luxury. Striking at the humanitarian reformers, especially the nonresistants who had believed in the inviolability of human life, Norton argued boldly that human life had been overvalued in America: "We have thought it braver to save it than to spend it; and a questionable humanity has undoubtedly led us sometimes into feeble sentimentalities, and false estimates of its value." Now, however, "the first sacrifice for which war calls is life; and we must revise our estimates of its value, if we would conduct our war to a happy end." There should be no flinching at "the prospect of the death of our soldiers," not even at the prospect "that a million men should die on the battlefield."[22]

In his assault on the "feeble sentimentalities" of an age which had devoted itself to alleviating suffering rather than justifying it, Norton not only spoke to the necessities of the hour, but marshaled a powerful new argument which was destined to become a formidable weapon against philanthropy and reform. Norton had been much impressed with Darwin's *Origin of Species* when it appeared in 1859, and he now presented his tough-minded view of war as a new and profound application of Darwin's theories. "Nature is careless of the single life," he wrote. "Her processes seem wasteful, but out of seeming waste, she produces her great and durable results. Everywhere in her works are the signs of life cut short for the sake of some effect more permanent. . . ."[23] In what may have been the first use of Darwinism to justify war, Norton argued from the premise that human progress, like that of the animal kingdom, was built on pain and loss of life. Invoking such a concept of evolution was one way to give meaning to the suffering of the Civil War.

Francis Parkman, in a long letter to the *Boston Advertiser* which appeared about the same time as Norton's article, also described the post-Bull Run situation as favorable to national progress. Parkman, however, had a clearer idea of what form the regeneration of America would take. "Our position," he wrote, "is a solemn, a critical, but not a melancholy one." If American society had heretofore been "cramped and vitiated" by a "too exclusive pursuit of material success," there were signs of a change. If, "in the absence of an exigency to urge or any great reward to tempt it, the best character and culture of the nation has remained for the most part in privacy, while a scum of reckless politicians has choked all the avenues of power," it was evident already that, "like a keen fresh breeze, the war has stirred our clogged and humid atmosphere." "The time may come," he concluded, "when, upheaved from its depths, fermenting and purging itself, the nation will stand at length clarified and pure in a renewed and strengthened life."[24] Parkman, the most pessimistic of the deprived aristocrats of the ante-bellum period, was thus awakening to the prospect that "the best character and culture" had a new chance to regain national leadership. In a desperate situation, the nation might scorn the "scum of reckless politicians" and turn to its "natural leaders" – the heirs of the old Federalist elite.

Parkman's optimism was undoubtedly buttressed by the fact that Lowells and Higginsons had found in the army the positions of prestige and authority that peacetime society had denied them.

Horace Bushnell, in a sermon delivered on the Sunday after the Bull Run disaster, went even further than Parkman in heralding the return to an earlier social ideal. Bushnell, who up to now had lacked an occasion to express his profound hatred of the enlightenment basis of American politics, seized on Bull Run as evidence that the nation was being punished for the heinous sin of disregarding God's own idea of human government. For Bushnell, the origin of the national troubles lay in the faulty philosophy of the Declaration of Independence. The American government, he asserted, had been founded "without moral and religious ideas; in one view merely a man-made compact...." The dangerous, atheistic doctrines of natural rights and government by consent had been a poison in the national life: "... we have been gradually wearing our nature down to the level of our doctrines; breeding out, so to speak, the sentiments in it that took hold of authority, till at last, we have brought ourselves down as closely as may be, to the dissolution of all nationality and all ties of order. Hence the war."[25]

Bushnell could not completely repudiate the American Revolution, so he alleged that there was also present in the beginning of the nation an "historic element," opposed to the visionary speculations of men like Jefferson and based on those inherited political ideas of New England which had been "shaped by religion." The New England way, which specified that government, rather than being based on consent of the governed, was an ordinance of God, had been overwhelmed by the democratic impulse set in motion by the Jeffersonian heresies. To Bushnell's Old Testament way of thinking, the secular eighteenth century ideology had thereafter functioned as an American golden calf which had smiled down on the most licentious behavior. Now, however, the wrath of God could be seen in a disaster like Bull Run, punishing the people for their idolatry and sinfulness and recalling them to proper respect for traditional authority. "Peace will do for angels," he proclaimed fiercely, "but war is God's ordinance for sinners, and they want the schooling of it often. In a time of war, what a sense of discipline is forced. Here, at least, there must and will be obedience; and the people, outside, get the sense of it about as truly as the army itself...."[26]

Sermons like those of Bushnell signified a revival of the spirit of New England Federalism, with its abhorrence of the religious and political views of Jefferson and its passion for order and popular "obedience" to ministers and others in authority. It was at this time that the *Anarchiad*, an almost forgotten collection of virulent attacks on democratic ideas by Federalist poets of the eighteenth century, was republished, to the great joy of the conservative *North American Review*. "The publication is well timed," announced the journal, "at an epoch when we are again threatened with disintegration and anarchy."[27]

By December 1861, Wendell Phillips thought he observed some signs of this recrudescent Federalism in the policy of the government, particularly in its suspension of the writ of habeas corpus. Phillips himself had fully repudiated his Federalist ancestors. In his "Disunion" lecture of the previous January, he had noted with pleasure that Federalism seemed safely dead. "Our theological aristocracy," he claimed, "went down before the stalwart blows of Baptist, Unitarian and Freethinker," and "theoretical democracy" had "conquered the Federal Government, and emancipated the working-classes of New England. Bitter was the cup to honest Federalism and the Essex Junto." Phillips even saw the abolition movement as the culmination of the "Democratic principle," which, "crumbling classes into men," had "reached the negro at last."[28] But now, eleven months later, he was afraid that the "democratic principle" was, for the moment at least, in some danger.

He pointed to the fact that the government was following a dangerous course in regard to civil liberties, that each of the three essential rights – "*habeas corpus*, the right of free meeting, and a free press – is annihilated in every square mile of the Republic." He concluded that "we are tending toward that strong government which frightened Jefferson; toward that unlimited debt, that endless army. We have already those alien and sedition laws which, in 1798, wrecked the Federal Party, and summoned the Democratic into existence."[29] Phillips did not realize it, but even as he spoke, Horace Binney, one of the last of the Federalists, was completing a pamphlet which would provide an elaborate legal defense for the government's suspension of habeas corpus. For Binney, as for Phillips, the time of the Alien and Sedition Acts had returned, but for Binney it was an occasion for rejoicing.[30]

Despite all his misgivings, however, Phillips was not giving up his hope that the war would contribute to national salvation. "...I do not complain of this state of things; but it is momentous" was the conclusion of his catalogue of evils.[31] The moral was that the people should make certain that the price in bad precedents was worth paying by insisting that the conflict be transformed from a war for the Union into a crusade against slavery.

The abolitionists were beginning to realize in late 1861 that the war was a complex affair. It was not a short and easy road to emancipation. It had released forces which threatened the kind of America that the abolitionists hoped to bring into being. It had provided an occasion for the open expression of a form of conservative thinking that had been underground since the victory of Jefferson in 1800. It had led to thoughts of a revival of the elitism of the Federalist era in the minds of those who had quietly cherished the Federalist tradition. The situation was truly "momentous."

Notes

1   *New York Times*, April 15, 1861, *Erie Weekly Gazette*, May 2, 1861, in *Northern Editorials on Secession*, ed. Howard C. Perkins (New York and London, 1942), II, 735, 756.

2   Quoted from an unpublished lecture of Emerson, given soon after Fort Sumter, in James E. Cabot, *A Memoir of Ralph Waldo Emerson* (Boston and New York, 1887), II, 600.

3   Horace Traubel, *With Walt Whitman in Camden* (New York, 1906–1914), I, 13.

4   See Herbert W. Schneider, *A History of American Philosophy* (New York, 1946), pp. 161–5.

5   *Walt Whitman's Workshop: A Collection of Unpublished Manuscripts*, ed. Clifton Joseph Furness (Cambridge, MA., 1928), p. 57.

6   Walt Whitman, "Long, Too Long, O Land," *Drum Taps* (New York, 1865), p. 45.

7   "Rise Oh Days From Your Fathomless Depths," *Drum Taps*, pp. 35–7.

8   F. O. Matthiessen, *The James Family* (New York, 1947), pp. 12–13, 50, 55.

9   Henry James, Sr., *The Social Significance of Our Institutions, an Oration Delivered at Newport, R.I., July 4, 1861* (Boston, 1861), p. 27.

10 Ibid., pp. 33–4.

11 Letter of Norton to A. H. Clough, May 27, 1861, *Letters of Charles Eliot Norton*, ed. Sara Norton and M. A. De Wolfe Howe (Boston and New York, 1913), I, 234.

12 Charles Eliot Norton, *The Soldier of the Good Cause* (Boston, 1861), pp. 5–6, 12–13. Pamphlet in the Harvard University Library.

13 Henry W. Bellows, *Duty and Interest Identical in the Present Crisis, Sermon of April 14, 1861* (New York, 1861), p. 16. Sermon in the Harvard University Library.

14 Henry W. Bellows, *The State and the Nation – Sacred to Christian Citizens, Sermon of April 21, 1861* (New York, 1861), pp. 6, 7. Sermon in the Harvard University Library.

15 *Ibid.*, p. 8.

16   *The Works of Orestes Brownson*, ed. Henry F. Brownson (Detroit, 1882–7), XVII, 121, 139.

17   Oliver Wendell Holmes, "Bread and Newspapers," in *Pages from an Old Volume of Life*, The Writings of Oliver Wendell Holmes, VIII (Boston and New York, 1895), pp. 3, 9.

18   *Harvard Memorial Biographies* (Cambridge, MA, 1866), I, 306; Edward W. Emerson, *The Life and Letters of Charles Russell Lowell* (Boston and New York, 1907), p. 19; Letter of Lowell to his mother, May 13, 1861, ibid., pp. 207–208.

19   Bliss Perry, *The Life and Letters of Henry Lee Higginson* (Boston, 1921), pp. 183–4.

20   Letter of Theodore Winthrop to George W. Curtis, May 5, 1861, quoted in Ellsworth Eliot, Jr., *Theodore Winthrop* (New Haven, 1938), p. 24.

21   Moncure Conway, *Autobiography, Memories, and Experiences* (Boston and New York, 1904), I, 335; John Murray Forbes, *Letters and Recollections*, ed. Sarah Forbes Hughes (Boston and New York, 1900), I, 227; *Christian Inquirer*, Aug. 10, 1861, clipping in the Charles Eliot Norton Papers, Harvard University Library. *Letters and Journals of Thomas Wentworth Higginson*, ed. Mary Thacher Higginson (Boston and New York, 1921), p. 156.

22   Charles Eliot Norton, "The Advantages of Defeat," *Atlantic*, VIII (September 1861), pp. 361–3.

23   Ibid., p. 364.

24   Letter to *Boston Daily Advertiser*, Sept. 4, 1861, in *Letters of Francis Parkman*, ed. W. R. Jacobs (Norman, OK, 1960), I, 142–3.

25   Horace Bushnell, *Reverses Needed: A Discourse Delivered on the Sunday after the Disaster at Bull Run in the North Church, Hartford* (Hartford, 1861), pp. 9–10.

26   Ibid., pp. 10–11, 24.

27   *North American Review*, XCIII (October 1861), p. 588.

28   Wendell Phillips, *Speeches, Lectures, and Letters, First Series* (Boston, 1902), p. 348.

29   Ibid., pp. 422–3.

30   Charles Chauncey Binney, *The Life of Horace Binney with Selections from His Letters* (Philadelphia and London, 1903), pp. 346–7; Horace Binney, *The Privilege of the Writ of Habeas Corpus under the Constitution* (Philadelphia, 1862).

31   Wendell Phillips, *Speeches, Lectures and Letters, First Series* (Boston, 1882), p. 424.

Questions to consider

- What are some of the hopes Northern intellectuals had for what the Civil War could do for American society in 1861?

- Do you see any similarities in the disparate views of Transcendentalists like Ralph Waldo Emerson, conservatives like Orestes Brownson, or abolitionist activists like Wendell Phillips?

- Knowing what you do about how the War turned out, whose views do you think proved most justified?

- Do you think some of the justifications described here – like the opportunity to be tested through adversity, or rededicating individuals to religion – have relevance for other wars?

Chapter 5

Justifying the War: Primary Sources

The Confederate Cornerstone

Alexander H. Stephens

A former prominent US Congressman (where he was friendly with the good deal less prominent Abraham Lincoln), Alexander H. Stephens of Georgia was elected vice-president of the Confederacy in February of 1861. That March, he gave a famous speech in which he explained the basis of the Confederate nation. What was that basis? How did Stephens choose to frame it? How compelling do you think it is today as an explanation for the Civil War?

Alexander H. Stephens, "The Confederate Cornerstone," March 21, 1861.

[The Confederate] Constitution has put at rest forever all the agitating questions relating to our peculiar institution – African slavery as it exists among us – the proper status of the negro in our form of civilization. This was the immediate cause of the late rupture and present revolution. Jefferson, in his forecast, had anticipated this, as the "rock upon which the old Union would split." He was right. What was conjecture with him, is now a realized fact. But whether he fully comprehended the great truth upon which that rock stood and stands, may be doubted. The prevailing ideas entertained by him and most of the leading statesmen at the time of the formation of the old Constitution were, that the enslavement of the African was in violation of the laws of nature; that it was wrong in principle, socially, morally, and politically. It was an evil they knew not well how to deal with; but the general opinion of the men of that day was, that, somehow or other, in the order of Providence, the institution would be evanescent and pass away.... Those ideas, however, were fundamentally wrong. They rested upon the assumption of the equality of races. This was an error. It was a sandy foundation, and the idea of a Government built upon it – when the "storm came and the wind blew, it fell."

Our new Government is founded upon exactly the opposite ideas; its foundations are laid, its cornerstone rests, upon the great truth that the negro is not equal to the white man; that slavery, subordination to the superior race, is his natural and moral condition. This, our new Government, is the first, in the history of the world, based upon this great physical, philosophical, and moral truth....

...It is the first Government ever instituted upon principles in strict conformity to nature, and the ordination of Providence, in furnishing the materials of human society. Many Governments have been founded upon the principles of certain classes; but the classes thus enslaved, were of the same race, and in violation of the laws of nature. Our system commits no such violation of nature's laws. The negro by nature, or by the curse against Canaan, is fitted for that condition which he occupies in our system. The architect, in the construction of buildings, lays the foundation with the proper material – the granite – then comes the brick or the marble. The substratum of our society is made of the material fitted by nature for it, and by experience we know that it is the best, not only for the superior but for the inferior race, that it should be so. It is, indeed, in conformity with the Creator. It is not for us to inquire into the wisdom of His ordinances or to question them.

Diary Entry

Keziah Goodwyn Hopkins Brevard

Alexander Stephens was a prominent Confederate whose words were read and evaluated by a large number of people. Keziah Goodwyn Hopkins Brevard, by contrast, was a white South Carolina widow living on a plantation when Abraham Lincoln was elected president. As you read this entry from her diary, ask yourself in what ways her views accord with those of Stephens – and in what ways her particular circumstances may have shaped her understanding of events and support for the Southern cause. To what degree do those circumstances limit the broader validity of her reasoning? To what degree do those circumstances make her position all the more compelling?

Keziah Goodwyn Hopkins Brevard, "Diary of Keziah Hopkins Brevard" 1860, South Caroliniana Library, University of South Carolina, in *Our Common Affairs: Texts from Women in the Old South*, ed. Joan E. Cashin (Baltimore: Johns Hopkins University Press, 1996), p. 263. Reprinted by permission of the South Caroliniana Library.

Friday Morning the 9th [1860]. Oh my God!!! This morning heard that Lincoln was elected – I had prayed that God would thwart his election in some way & I prayed for my Country – Lord we [know?] not what is to be the result of this – but I do pray if there is to be a crisis that we all [word missing; lay?] down our lives sooner than free our slaves in our midst – No soul on this earth is more willing for justice than I am but the idea of being mixed up with free blacks is horrid!! I must trust in God that he will not forget us as unworthy as we are – Lord save us – I would give my life to save my Country. I have never been opposed to giveing up slavery if we could send them out of our Country – I have often wished I had been born in just such a country – with all our religious privileges & liberties with none of them in our midst – if the

North had let us alone – the Master & the servant were happy with our advatages – but we had had vile wretches ever making the restless worse[1] than they would have been & from my experience my own negroes are as happy as I am – happier[2] – I never am cross to my servants without cause & they give me impudence, if I find the least fault, this is of the women the men are not half as impudent as the women are. I have left a serious & what has been an <u>all absorbing</u> theme to a common one – but the die is cast – "Caesar has past the Rubicon."[3] We now have to act, God be with us is my prayer & let us all be willing to die rather than free our slaves in their present uncivilized state.

Disunion for Existing Causes

North Carolina Standard

Not all Southerners supported the Civil War. Indeed, internal dissent was a major complication for Confederates in regions like eastern Tennessee and western Virginia. Even before the war broke out, skeptical voices warned that the reasons for war being offered by Southern leaders did not necessarily justify it. This editorial from the *North Carolina Standard*, published three weeks after Lincoln's election in a state whose loyalty would sometimes be questioned by Confederate politicians, offers a revealing glimpse of incipient dissent.

North Carolina Standard, "Disunion for Existing Causes" (December 1, 1860), in *Southern Editorials on Secession*, ed. Dwight L. Dumond (Gloucester, MA: Smith, 1964), pp. 284–6.

A Confederacy or Union composed of the fifteen slaveholding States would, after a while, encounter some of the same difficulties which now beset the existing Union. The States south of us would produce and export cotton, while the middle or bread-stuff States would become deeply interested in manufactures. Foreigners from Europe and the North would pour into the latter, and push the slave population farther south. Manufacturers would demand and obtain protection, and free labor would contend with and root out slave labor in the middle States, until at length the latter could commence to agitate against the cotton States as the North is now agitating against us. As new regions towards the tropics should be acquired by the Southern Confederacy, and as the demand for cotton increased, the policy of re-opening the African slave trade would gain ground, and ultimately that trade would be established, and would be carried on openly under the Southern flag. This would be a death-blow to slavery in the middle States. It would at once reduce the price of our best slaves from twelve hundred to four hundred dollars, for the Southern planter would much prefer a barbarian at two hundred dollars to a civilized negro at five hundred. In addition to this, such a policy would expose the Southern Confederacy to the hazards of war with the Northern Confederacy and with European powers.

The two Confederacies, the Northern and the Southern, would meet as rivals at foreign courts and in foreign markets. Their ministers and merchants would partake of the spirit of the people at home, and they would cripple each other and involve themselves in endless and most injurious complications in their intercourse with foreign powers – These foreign powers, stimulated by the hope of gain, and disliking us for our popular forms of government, would insinuate themselves into the very heart of our system – would foment jealousies between the two Confederacies, and lay one or the other under obligations to them for aid or mediation in the midst of strifes and wars; and the end would be *foreign influence* in all our councils, foreign manners in all our social walks, and *foreign gold* in the hands of unscrupulous demagogues as the price of some portion of their country's liberties.

In case of separation party spirit, the excesses of which are now so obvious and injurious, would rage with tenfold heat. There would be parties in each Confederacy against each; there would be parties opposed to and in favor of foreign influence; there would be parties advocating dictatorial powers in the central governments and parties advocating the largest liberty or least restraint; there would be parties advocating and parties opposing the acquisition of more territory; there would be parties siding with the great body of people, and parties endeavoring to grasp exclusive privileges for the few at the expense of the many. In the midst of all this war would most probably be waged along the lines of the two Confederacies – war interrupted only by hollow truces, or by compromises made but never intended to be observed, or by mediations at the hands of foreign powers. Of course as the result of all this industry would languish, trade would be obstructed, education would be neglected, internal improvements of all kinds would be arrested, and the morals of society would be injured. War would raise up standing armies, which would obstruct civil rule and eat out the substance of the people. This would be the case especially in the Southern States, where large armies would be necessary not only for defensive operations against the foreign Northern States, but to keep the slave population in subjection. The result would be *military despotism*. The Legislatures of the Southern States would have to sit perpetually or clothe their Governors with large discretionary powers. These powers would be abused, and the voice of law and the claims of justice would be unheard amid the alarms of war. – *Constitutional* liberty would no longer be the birthright of our people, but instead thereof we would have discretionary powers, martial law, military rule, oppressive taxation, perpetual contentions, and civil and servile war.

Such are some of the evils which would most probably result from disunion for existing causes. Disunion at this time will certainly occasion war. If a peaceful separation in the last resort could be effected, the two Confederacies, or any number of Confederacies *might* tread their respective paths without engaging in mortal conflict. They *might* at length re-unite in a new union on foundations more lasting than the present; but if any one State shall secede, with the expectation of drawing other States after her, and if blood shall be shed, the beginning, the middle, and the end will be civil war. The States thus forced out, though they will sympathize with the State which committed them to disunion against their will, and though they may stand by her and defend her in her extremity, yet they will dislike her and watch her as an evil star in the new constellation. A violent separation would, therefore, sow the seeds of discord in the new Confederacy. It would commence its career with growing antagonisms in its members. It would be a *forced* union which time would dissolve or passion fret to pieces.

There is only one evil greater than disunion, and that is the loss of honor and Constitutional right. *That evil the people of the South will never submit to.* Sooner than submit to it they would put their shoulders to the pillars, as Samson did, and tear down the temple, though they themselves should perish in the ruins. But our honor as a people is still untarnished – our Constitutional rights, so far as the federal government is concerned, are still untouched. If the federal government should *attempt* even to tarnish the one or to deprive us of the other, we for one would be ready to resist, and ready to dissolve the Union without regard to consequences. *But not now!* – the non-slaveholder says *not now!* – the slaveholder, whose property civil war would involve in imminent peril, says *not now!* – millions of our friends in the free States say *not now!* If we *must* dissolve the Union, let us do it as one people, and not by a bare majority. Let us wait until the people of the State are more united on the subject than they are now. Depend upon it our people are not submissionists. If their rights should be assailed they will defend them. But if they should not be assailed, and if we *can* preserve the government with safety and honor to ourselves, in the name of all that is sacred let us do so.

Questions to consider

- What reasons does the newspaper give for questioning whether a separate Southern nation would achieve desired objectives? How compelling is the logic of the editorial?

- Does the newspaper refuse to support secession? How would you describe its stance? What would the editorial staff regard as the best way to take North Carolina out of the Union?

A Constitutional View of the Late War Between the States

Alexander H. Stephens

Disgraced by defeat in 1865, denied a seat in the Senate by Radical Republicans in 1866, Alexander Stephens temporarily left politics in the late 1860s to write a two-volume treatment of the Civil War published in 1868 and 1870. In the first volume, he offered readers an introductory overview of the South's justification for secession. How do you compare the excerpt below to that of the "Cornerstone" speech? What threads of logic connect them? How is the emphasis different? What factors might explain the difference?

Alexander H. Stephens, "Introduction," in *A Constitutional View of the Late War Between the States* (Philadelphia: The National Publishing Co., 1868–70), p. 13.

It is a postulate, with many writers of this day, that the late War was the result of two opposing ideas, or principles, upon the subject of African Slavery. Between these, according to their theory, sprung the "irrepressible conflict," in principle, which ended in the terrible conflict of arms. Those who assume this postulate, and so theorize upon it, are but superficial observers.

That the War had its origin in *opposing principles*, which, in their action upon the *conduct of men*, produced the ultimate collision of arms, may be assumed as an unquestionable fact. But the opposing principles which produced these results in physical action were of a very different character from those assumed in the postulate. They lay in the organic Structure of the Government of the States. The conflict in principle arose from different and opposing ideas as to the nature of what is known as the General Government. The contest was between those who held it to be strictly Federal in its character, and those who maintained that it was thoroughly National. It was a strife between the principles of Federation, on the one side, and Centralism, or Consolidation, on the other.

Slavery, so called, was but *the question* on which these antagonistic principles, which had been in conflict, from the beginning, on diverse *other questions*, were finally brought into actual and active collision with each other on the field of battle.

Notes

1 Brevard seems to believe that some slaves deliberately stirred up discontent among other bondsmen.
2 She was actually not very happy. In other entries she regrets that she did not have children, laments her bad education, and wishes she had more friends.
3 In 49 BC Julius Caesar defied an order from the Roman senate and crossed this small river in central Italy, thus precipitating a civil war.

Part III

The Battle Front

Plate 5 Blood Brothers? Confederate wounded near Keedysville, MD, in the aftermath of the Battle of Antietam, September 1862. A Union medical officer, Dr. Anson Hurd of the 14th Indiana Volunteers, attends to them. Civil War combatants, enemies or not, shared experiences most civilians could never understand. (Photo by Alexander Gardner; Selected Civil War photographs, Library of Congress)

Chapter 6

"Dangled Over Hell": The Trauma of the Civil War

Eric T. Dean, Jr.

Although we customarily think of the Civil War as a struggle between North and South, it was in fact a many-sided engagement that involved a series of divisions, among them black and white, male and female, slaveholder and non-slaveholder, rich and poor, neutral and partisan. This book is to a great degree premised on exploring such divisions: real, perceived, and even mistaken. But in the minds of many who fought in the war, no divide was finally more decisive than this one: soldier and civilian. Diverse observers of the Civil War have agreed that by the end of the war the experience of belonging to the military – and, in particular, the experience of combat – gave soldiers of Blue and Gray a shared experience, even a kinship, that transcended the causes they fought for. This may be why in subsequent decades they so often literally and figuratively embraced at reunions in places like Gettysburg, much to the chagrin of those who feel that their decision to do so overlooked or even belittled such causes (like those of African Americans that some Confederates enslaved).

It is a truism that no one who does not actually participate in a war can ever really understand what it was like. And yet if history is finally an act of imagination, we all have the right – we may all even have the obligation – to try to understand for the sake of those who have borne the battle, their widows, and their orphans. We may also come to see that the experience of war is in some ways truly shared – not only among people at a given time and place, but for those of other times and places. Psychologists have recognized, for example, that the symptoms of the First World War-era syndrome known as "Shell Shock" has clear parallels in other conflicts, and even among people who have experienced catastrophes in non-military situations. In his 1997 book *Shook Over Hell: Post-Traumatic Stress, Vietnam, and the Civil War*, Eric T. Dean, a practicing attorney, compared the medical records of 291 Indiana Civil War veterans admitted to insane asylums between 1861 and 1919, and saw obvious similarities in their cases with those of Vietnam veterans suffering what is now called post-traumatic stress disorder (PTSD). In this chapter from his book, he looks at various aspects of the Civil War soldier's experience in ways that allow us a glimpse of the realities – sometimes boring, sometimes harrowing – that defined military life.

Eric T. Dean, Jr., " 'Dangled over Hell': The Trauma of the Civil War," in *Shook Over Hell: Post-Traumatic Stress, Vietnam, and the Civil War* (Cambridge, MA: Harvard University Press, 1997), pp. 46–69. Copyright © 1997 by Eric T. Dean, Jr. Reprinted by permission of the publisher.

In post-Vietnam America, the key word in considering the psychological state of returning veterans is "trauma." Specifically, what hardships and trials did the veteran undergo during his service in the military? Was he placed in situations in which he experienced anxiety and fear? Was he exposed to combat, to the death and mutilation of his fellow warriors, or to the spectacle of enemy soldiers being slaughtered in battle or, as prisoners, being summarily executed? Did he encounter disease or discomforts that might have weakened his psychic defenses or exacerbated his sense of alienation and unease about being sent far from home and given the anomalous task of killing other human beings? Did his bonds to fellow soldiers or to civilians at home somehow ameliorate his problems and prevent psychological breakdown? Did an eventual warm homecoming "wash away" disturbing memories of pain and death?

In comparing the trauma experienced by the Civil War soldier with that of the Vietnam veteran or any combatant in modern twentieth-century armies, one is struck first of all by the physical hardships that soldiers encountered in what one man characterized as a "destroying manner of living." Although the Civil War has been portrayed as the first modern or industrial war in which machinery such as locomotives and rifled muskets or ironclad warships and naval torpedoes were engaged, the infantryman in this war moved from one place to another mainly on foot. He sometimes covered ten and twenty miles a day, or even more in the case of a forced march when troops had to be maneuvered quickly to come to the aid of embattled and endangered comrades or to defend or seize key positions. During the Civil War, the 11th Indiana Infantry marched a total of 9,318 miles; during a key three-and-a-half-month period, the 44th Indiana Infantry marched over 725 miles, an average march of 10 miles per day when on the move. One Northerner noted in a letter home: "Walking ten or twelve miles a day will hurt no one, but walking 12 miles and carrying a knapsack full of clothing, a blanket, half tent, several days rations, gun, ammunition, &c, is the hardest kind of work, and makes many a man wish he was not a soldier." Civil War soldiers quickly learned to jettison everything from their packs that was not absolutely essential, and still the task of marching over long distances could be crushing.[1]

Men were frequently marched through suffocating dust and under the blazing sun throughout the day, with minimal and sometimes seemingly no breaks allowed. A New York volunteer remembered that on a forced march of thirty miles in the fierce heat of summer, the men had thrown away overcoats, blankets, and even their knapsacks. Nonetheless many became violently ill from the exertion, some having convulsions and others dying from heatstroke. Another soldier recalled that during such a forced march he had to stop and vomit "every once in a while and my head ached dreadful." He vomited eight or ten times during the day, and the last time threw up blood. An overcome Indiana volunteer fell unconscious, with his eyes jerking and his tongue protruding out of his mouth in a type of epileptic fit induced by the heat. Nor were these torturous marches necessarily merely one- or two-day ordeals; an Alabama infantryman wrote to his mother: "I am not very well at this time. We have been on a march for about nine-teen days. . . . I am so near marched to death that I cannot write with any degree of intelligence, and having lost so much sleep too." The scenery on these marches was not always calculated to lighten the mental burden consequent to such physical exertion, as is demonstrated by the letter of one Rebel soldier to his wife: "i am well as common except for a bad cold and march most to death. . . . Mi dear wife i want you to pray for me i hop i will se you agin. . . . I have walked over more ded yankes than i ever want to do agin." Within two weeks this man was killed at the Battle of Antietam.[2]

Confederate troops in particular also had to deal with the problem of inadequate (or no) footwear. One Rebel surgeon lamented in a letter to his wife that she could hardly believe what the army had recently endured: "Most of our marches were on graveled turnpike roads, which were very severe on the barefooted men and cut up their feet horribly. When the poor fellows could get rags they would tie them around their feet for protection." Sometimes these forced marches lasted into or throughout the night, and soldiers literally learned to walk while asleep or would sometimes collapse from fatigue and sleep at that spot for hours, oblivious to all attempts to rouse them and force them to continue. A Massachusetts volunteer wrote: "I doubt if our ancestors at Valley Forge suffered more from cold than we did. . . . [I] often found that I had been sound asleep while my legs were trudging along."[3] Accounts of marching three hundred miles in the rain and mud, with inadequate rations and rest, only to be thrown immediately into a deadly battle are not at all unusual in Civil War letters and diaries. When the health of the Civil War soldier deteriorated to the point that he could no longer keep up with the unit on the march, he might become part of a pack of what became known as "stragglers." One account of such men described the following:

We met hundreds of stragglers in squads of from two to fifty – indeed enough to make in themselves, if consolidated, a large army. The majority of them were sick, however, or miserably worn. Their countenances are sunken and melancholy and indifferent almost to stolidity. When left to themselves they progress very slowly, cooking their own food and sleeping upon the ground. . . . They are all thoroughly disgusted with the life they lead and swear that if ever they get out of the army they will commit suicide almost before entering it again.[4]

Such was the centrality of marching to the experience of the Civil War soldier that when some men were eventually issued disability discharges, it was not uncommon for the examining surgeon to give as the reason for such separation the fact that the man was no longer able to carry a knapsack or keep up with the army on the march. In the years following the war, Union veterans frequently claimed "sun-stroke" and "hard marching" as the basis for military disability pensions – and these claims were often granted. All who had been through the experience knew exactly how trying and destructive it could be.[5]

When the hard-marching Civil War soldier reached his destination, conditions did not improve, for a constant fact of life in the Civil War era was that all soldiers, Northerners as well as Southerners, were routinely exposed to the elements. These men were expected to sleep out in the open on the ground in the middle of winter or in the midst of a driving rainstorm, oftentimes with only one blanket or the equivalent of a pup tent to fend off the damp and cold or the frost and snow. One Indiana soldier wrote in his diary: "Rained nearly all last night, woke up two or three times before day, the water was running under us so that we had to get up and sit shivering around the fire until morning." Another Hoosier volunteer's diary revealed similar circumstances: "Last night very cold, did not sleep well . . . woke from a dream crying. . . . Day rainy and gloomy. . . . Have the blues." As a Michigan volunteer reflected: "We had atuf time Last night. it rained all night and when I got up this morning my bed was wet thru this is what a soldier has got to stand." Regarding winter conditions, in letters and diaries,

Civil War soldiers frequently mention waking up covered with frost or snow, and with both their boots and clothes, and even their very bodies, seeming to be frozen, requiring several hours to thaw out. Under such circumstances, a Confederate who was called to fall out in the middle of the night recalled: "I had gotten chilled and my teeth were glued together and a feeling of complete wretchedness came over me as I took my place in the ranks to march to the front." One irony was that when railroad cars were made available to transport Civil War troops, the conditions could be all the more difficult, as when men were transported on open cars throughout the night in a driving rainstorm: "We have bin shiped several hundard miles and we have done the most of it of nights right through the rain and cold on top of freitcars I have bin allmost chilled to death & have shook for hours & worse than if I had ague... then when we got to lay down we had to lay down wet through and cover up with a wet blanket." In pension claims after the war, one frequently encounters the expression "exposure in the army" as the claimed basis of a disability such as rheumatism or mental prostration. In reviewing the conditions that these men had to endure, one begins to understand exactly what this "exposure" was and how it shattered men's constitutions and health – a situation from which many never recovered.[6]

Soldiers shivering in the rain or snow had the added anxiety, of course, resulting from the ever-present danger of being killed by the enemy. One Confederate assigned to protect Missionary Ridge as Federal troops massed for an attack in the vicinity of Chattanooga during the winter of 1863 recalled later that he would never be able to forget the hard fight itself or the suffering endured by his comrades in the three or four weeks preceding the battle. Because the men had no tents, they had to use their blankets stretched on poles to keep the rain off; since few had more than one blanket, this left the Confederate soldiers nothing with which to cover themselves or to place over the freezing ground. They suffered intensely: "You could hear the boys praying and wishing for the fight to come if it was coming, anything to get out of the suspense and suffering caused by lack of rations and shelter." He noted that at night the only fire allowed was a few coals over which the men would warm their fingers and toes, because the light from any more substantial fire would inevitably attract the attention of enemy snipers. Undergoing a similar experience, a Union soldier wrote home to his wife that civilians could never imagine the suffering and hardships that had to be endured by the men in the ranks: "All last night they lay right out in the rain in line of battle without even their rubber blankets. May this cruel rebellion soon be crushed is the wish of every soldier."[7]

In light of the frequent rain, mud was another of the elements with which Civil War soldiers had to contend, and memoirs and letters are filled with depressing accounts of men, animals, and equipment mired in the muck. On occasion the situation was so bad that equipment sank halfway into the ooze, and had to be abandoned. One Hoosier infantryman characterized camp at Cheat Mountain in West Virginia as "this infernal mountain which is the meanest camping ground that I have ever seen," noting that the mud was not less than shoe-top deep. Another Hoosier volunteer, sent to the front shortly after the Battle of Shiloh in April of 1862, was appalled by the stench of dead bodies, and struggled with his comrades to move an artillery piece up to a bluff. The men were literally masses of sticky mud moving around, and were so tired that they were ready to lie down in the mud to sleep, which they had to do eventually anyway: "There was not a dry spot in the Country about to make camp on. Mud mud *every* where." A Confederate reminisced: "Space forbids my describing the length, depth and breadth of the mud." It seemed that both armies were usually foundering in the mud to some degree, and that the discomfort associated with wet feet was the usual state of affairs for Civil War soldiers. Sherman's men during the Carolinas campaign late in the war were described as follows: "Uniforms, worn threadbare and in rags, from head to foot were covered with mud.

Their shoes were in the last stage of existence, many being held together with strings tied around them."[8]

Although the marching, rain, snow, damp, and mud clearly had a depressing effect on the spirits and health of men in Civil War armies, the psychological and physical effect of these conditions probably did not compare with the impact of infectious disease. Paul Steiner has noted that the Civil War was a form of "biological warfare" in which several hundred thousand men died of disease; because accounts of the Civil War often focus on the dash and verve of famous commanders, it is easy to forget the basic pedestrian fact that for every battle death, two men died of disease in the Civil War. Exact statistics are not available, but by most estimates about 164,000 Confederates and 250,000 Federals died of disease during the war. In the absence of a sound understanding of public health or effective medical therapies, diseases such as cholera, typhoid, malaria, smallpox, measles, mumps, scurvy, and tuberculosis, in addition to a variety of "camp fevers" and chronic diarrhea, were prevalent, frequently spread without restraint, and took a substantial toll. Although diseases such as typhoid and smallpox killed large numbers of men, dysentery and diarrhea were the great nuisance, affecting 78 percent of the soldiers annually. At times, up to two-thirds of a regiment might be on sick call at the same time, and historians have estimated that there were approximately 10 million cases of sickness (6 million for the Union Army and 4 million for the Confederates) during the Civil War, with every participant falling ill an average of four to six times.[9]

Medicine was still in its dark ages during the Civil War era, and the great advances in sanitation, germ theory, medical education and medical training, as well as the emergence of the hospital as the modern technological palace of healing, were all in the future. Of all the great advances of the nineteenth century, only anesthesia was available at this time; Koch and Pasteur were still conducting experiments in their laboratories, and Lister's precepts regarding the use of disinfectants were not yet established. Asepsis was almost half a century away, meaning that Civil War surgeons operated with germ-infested instruments; the infectious agents of disease were unknown, with the result that there was no conception that certain diseases could be communicated by air, water, or in the case of inadequate cleanliness, by touch. Moreover, tragically, the Civil War was marked by an almost total absence of any significant medical discovery or addition to existing knowledge. Civil War medical men operated in ignorance, and continued to make the same mistakes throughout the war, which often led to unnecessary suffering and death. Writing in 1905, a Civil War veteran recalled that in his youth a doctor had – astonishingly – denied him any water during his bout with typhoid; of this ignorant and dangerous treatment, the veteran observed: "Darkness & fog surrounded the medical profession. The doctors were then feeling their way thru their duties, as a blind man gropes his way along a strange street." Confidence in the medical profession was not great in the Civil War era, as indicated by the comment of one soldier: "Dr. seems to have been the executioner indirectly."[10]

Civil War doctors' ministrations to their troops consisted mainly of dispensing drugs such as opium to kill pain or control chronic diarrhea, or calomel and other purgatives to purge the system when deemed appropriate. One physician recalled of his work in the Civil War: "In one pocket of my trousers I had a ball of blue mass [mercurial ointment], in another a ball of opium. All complaints were asked the same question, 'How are your bowels?' If they were open, I administered a plug of opium; if they were shut I gave a plug of blue mass." The common soldier's lack of understanding concerning the risk of infectious disease is demonstrated by one man's account of filling his canteen: "Nearby was a ditch that had some stagnate water in it we poaked the Skum one side with our cups then gave the water a spat to scare the bugs and wiglers to the bottom then filled our canteens and returned to our Regiment."[11]

It is no shock, then, that Civil War letters and diaries report the frequent deaths in camp of soldiers from disease (in one man's words, the "fangs of disease") and the depressing effects of illness and death on the troops. One soldier wrote home: "Sickness causes more deaths in the army than Rebel lead. . . . A man here gets sick and unless he has a strong constitution he sinks rapidly to the grave." A typical diary of a Union soldier reported: "June 1, 1862: Sunday, On guard. Had the tooth ache. Thomas Shepherd died. June 2, 1862: In camp. very warm. Harry Arnold died." Another Federal noted that the unit was losing a man a day on average, and that the roll of the muffled drum and the blank discharge of a dozen muskets served as a solemn reminder to the entire camp that another soldier had gone to his last bivouac. Civil War soldiers could be haunted by the deaths of comrades, especially when they died far from home and did not receive decent burials. Years after the war, Ben R. Johnson of the 6th Michigan Infantry wrote of the disease and death he had witnessed in the swamps of Louisiana, something that he would never forget:

> The enemy [was swamp fever]. . . . His slimy, cold, and merciless hand bore down upon us until we moaned in our anguish and prayed for mercy . . . many comrades were stricken down in the midst of life and laid away under the accursed soil of the swamp. . . . Ask any living member of the old 6th if they remember Camp Death, and ten chances to one he will tell you its fearful perils are engraved upon memory's tablet as with a pen of iron. I wonder when I look back how any of us boys from the clime of Michigan ever escaped from the doom that hung over us in that hades of the swamp.[12]

Also hardly calculated to ease the mental stress and anxiety of Civil War soldiers was the fact that pay was often in arrears, and that, especially for Confederate soldiers, food was chronically in short supply. As one Southerner wrote his wife: "The main topic of conversation among the men is what they could eat if they had it."[13]

As devastating as marching, exposure to the elements, and disease could be, the major psychological trauma that Civil War soldiers encountered related to the terror of battle. One of the ironies of the experience of fighting men in the Civil War was that green recruits were often terribly worried that the war would end before they had a chance to experience combat; as one Confederate recalled: "I was tormented by feverish anxiety before I joined my regiment for fear the fighting would all be over before I got into it." In a similar vein, a Hoosier volunteer reminisced: "We really conceived the idea that if we could only get to the front with our six guns the whole affair would soon be settled to the entire satisfaction of our side. . . . A horrible fear took possession of all of us that the war would be over before we got to the front." Veterans, however, assured one Union Army novice that there would be sufficient action ahead: "They always advised us not to worry about not having plenty of chances to meet the enemy as we would soon get enough and plenty when spring came."[14]

Indeed, the glories of war regarded from afar were one thing, but as troops were assembled and moved to the front to enter combat, men began to experience the worst sort of nerve-wracking anxiety, fear, and tension imaginable. It was particularly difficult for men – especially new recruits – to be within earshot of the battlefield, to hear the bullets, exploding shells, and screams of the combatants, without yet being engaged. One Union man commented: "The real test comes before the battle." Rice Bull depicted the terrific anxiety of the moment as his unit awaited the order to move forward at the Battle of Chancellorsville and, while waiting, witnessed terror-stricken Union troops fleeing from the battlefield for the rear. These men had thrown away everything that was loose – guns, knapsacks, caps, and coats: "Nothing could stop them. They were crazed and would fight to escape as though the enemy were close to them. We were ordered to stop them but we might as well have tried to stop a cyclone, . . . One can hardly conceive of the terror that possessed them . . . their panic was nerve-wracking to troops new to the service." An Ohio veteran recalled his experience directly before the Battle of Winchester in 1864:

> [O]ne second you want to dash forward; the next, you want a rock or a tree to dash behind; men think by seconds and part of a second; minutes are too long to dwell on; . . . One second you are filled with anxiety; the next with fear; one second you want to, and the next you dont. At times your heart is jumping a thousand times a minute; at other times it dont seem to move at all; your knees begin to tremble; your hair to stand up so stiff that you are unable to tell if you have hair or hazel brush on your head . . . the suspense is awful . . . you have no conception of time under such conditions. You are chained; riveted to the spot; . . . we waited on and on; every minute appeared to be a full century.[15]

Some men on the line before battle could look merely solemn or even calm, but the reaction of another Union soldier seemed more typical when he recalled that a feeling of horror, dread, and fear came over him: "I was faint. . . . A glance along the line satisfied me that I was not alone in my terror; many a face had a pale, livid expression of fear." A Michigan volunteer remembered: "Some may say they never had any fear that may be true but it was not so with me I was scared . . . I was scared good and sure." Sometimes this fear was so intense that men would fall to the ground paralyzed with terror, bury their face in the grass, grasp at the earth, and refuse to move. Officers would scream and cajole and beat on these men, even striking them with bayonets, or, in extreme instances, resort to shooting them – but with no effect. Before one battle, a Union soldier noticed one man who was trembling so badly that he could not stay on his feet or hold his gun, and another who had great beads of sweat on his forehead and a fixed stare on his face. A third man threw his head back and, with mouth wide open, sang a hymn at the top of his lungs; it was understood that he was simply trying to steady himself under the well-nigh unendurable strain. Instances of men being so terrified before a battle that they lost control of their bowels were not unknown.[16]

Once men actually entered combat and began to fire their weapons, however, there was a radical transformation as fear and anxiety evaporated and gave way to rage, anger, and a sense of disembodiment. One Federal soldier recalled: "As soon as the first volley was fired all dread and sense of personal danger was gone." As the line surged forward in one assault, a Union officer noted great hysterical excitement, the eagerness to go forward, and a reckless disregard of life: "The soldier who is shooting is furious in his energy. . . . The men are loading and firing with demoniacal fury and shouting and laughing hysterically." Another Union soldier participating in such an attack heard his comrades shrieking like demons. Standing on a defensive line, Rice Bull of the 123rd NY Infantry recalled that a feeling of fearlessness and rage took the place of nervousness and timidity; as the Rebel attackers approached to within twenty yards of the Union line, one soldier accidentally fired his ramrod: "He looked a good deal surprised, and shaking his fist in the direction of the Johnnies yelled, 'Take that you —— and see how you like it.' " Another Northerner observed a hellish scene: "Some of the men, with faces blackened by the powder from the tearing open of cartridges with the teeth in the act of loading their rifles, looked like demons rather than men, loading their guns and firing with a fearful, fiend-like intensity; while others, under an intense, insane excitement, would load and fire without aim." Seeing one of his comrades killed, one Union soldier remembered that a savage desire for revenge and retaliation drowned out the finer emotions, and he was eager to put this new desire into execution.

Commenting on this rage as well as an obliviousness to personal danger, Franklin H. Bailey of the 12th Michigan Infantry wrote to his parents: "Strange it may seam to you, but the more men I saw kiled the more reckless I became; when George Gates . . . was shot *I was so enraged*

I could have tore the heart out of the rebel could I have reached him."[17] These wild emotional extremes could push some men to the breaking point on the battlefield itself, as in the case of one young Confederate: "I witnessed a sight I have never forgotten a member of the 14 Miss, a young boy looked to be about 15 was calling on his regt for Gods sake to reform and charge the Yankees again the tears were rolling down his face and I think he would have gone alone if an officer had not taken him to the rear."[18]

Numerous Civil War soldiers testified to the sense of disembodiment they felt during battle: when the firing began, they became oblivious of their own bodies and needs, and focused entirely on the action at hand in the battle. The matters of food, water, and comfort were forgotten, and one Northerner described what almost appeared to be an out-of-body experience. He seemed to be living out of and beyond himself, with all sympathy for suffering, all sense of bereavement having been obliterated: "Through all this din of danger I was both spectator and actor . . . there was steadily with me another feeling – a sort of double self-consciousness. This new and higher self was watching the old one I had known so long, criticising its thoughts and acts, and expressing one continual astonishment that this enthusiastic fellow, fond of ease, of home and all its peaceful joys, should be found an active participant in any deadly strife." When men were wounded, it frequently came as a complete surprise: in memoirs or letters they would describe the feeling of a sting, a "strange sensation," a feeling of being struck with an axe or a board, or of being inexplicably whirled around or knocked off their feet; sometimes the realization of having been hit came only when a soldier was no longer able to lift an arm, or when his vision was suddenly blurred by his own blood flowing into his eyes from a head wound:

> By far the larger number felt, when shot, as though some one had struck them sharply with a stick, and one or two were so possessed with this idea at the time, that they turned to accuse a comrade of the act, and were unpleasantly surprised to discover, from the flow of blood, that they had been wounded. About one-third experienced no pain nor local shock when the ball entered. A few felt as though stung by a whip at the point injured. More rarely, the pain of the wound was dagger-like and intense; while a few, one in ten, were convinced for a moment that the injured limb had been shot away.[19]

Such shell or gunshot wounds could quickly bring a man back to the reality of his own body and a sense of vulnerability, leading in some cases to panic, terror, and the fear of dying: "When hit, he thought his arm was shot off. It dropped, the gun fell, and, screaming that he was murdered, he staggered, bleeding freely, and soon fell unconscious." Those who fought on rarely experienced such vulnerability, however, and in some cases, men became so engrossed in the action that they refused to leave the front when their unit was relieved. A Confederate soldier recalled the scene after one battle: "[O]n every living face was seen the impress of an excitement which has no equal here on earth."[20]

The demoniacal appearance of the men – enraged, blackened faces, screaming, firing their rifles in a frenzy, grappling in hand-to-hand combat – was matched by the surreal aspect of the battlefield, its smoke, smell, noise, confusion, and havoc. Smokeless gunpowder had not yet been developed, so after the firing began, the Civil War battlefield was frequently enshrouded in a pall of smoke and sulphurous vapor, which severely limited one's field of vision and added to one's sense of confusion and disorientation. Appalling sounds assaulted one's senses from all directions in what one man described as the "awful shock and rage of battle," and others characterized as "that howling acre," a "portrait of hell," or a "rumbling, grinding sound that cannot be described." One veteran recalled pandemonium, and another that his ears were deafened by noise from the "crash of worlds," the "dreadful, tremendous cannonading," often compared to the sound of an earthquake or being engulfed in and having one's life threatened every moment by the most fearsome storm one could imagine. The Battle of Chancellorsville "was like two wrathful clouds had come down on the plains, rushing together in hideous battle with all their thunders and lightnings. . . . The timber was literally torn to pieces . . . with grape, canister, shot and shell." The dreadful pounding and concussion from the cannonading was such that blood gushed out of the nose and ears of one Indiana infantryman at the Battle of New Hope Church in Georgia, and numerous Civil War soldiers were permanently deafened from exposure to the concussion of cannon fire.[21]

At Chickamauga, the "rattle of musketry was dreadful and to see the men lying dead and dying on the field and being run over by artillery and lines of men it was perfectly appalling." At Spotsylvania Court House, "it was an awful din. The air seemed full of bullets." The cacophony of zipping bullets and bursting shells created such a maelstrom that it was impossible to shout orders so that one could be heard. An Ohio soldier recalled an atmosphere hideous with the shrieks of the messengers of death at the Battle of Franklin: "The booming of cannon, the bursting of bombs, the rattle of musketry, the shrieking of shells, the whizzing of bullets, . . . the falling of men in their struggle for victory, all made a scene of surpassing terror and awful grandeur." Of the sights and sounds of battle, one Northerner concluded: "The half can never be told – language is all too tame to convey the horror and the meaning of it all."[22]

Nor should one overrate the ability of men infuriated and obsessed with battle to screen out all horror of death. Although men concentrated on the task at hand and put personal safety aside, they still witnessed and reacted to – even if belatedly – horrific scenes of slaughter, and these sights and memories took an eventual toll. In the Civil War, innovations in weapons (particularly the rifled musket and an array of antipersonnel artillery charges) had extended the range of deadly fire on the battlefield and allowed defenders, ensconced in trenches or behind abatis and breastworks, to mercilessly shred the ranks of assaulting troops; in spite of this, however, Civil War commanders still frequently attempted to storm enemy fortifications by means of frontal assaults. The results could be deadly as attacking columns were torn and blasted by the defenders: "Brains, fractured skulls, broken arms and legs, and the human form mangled in every conceivable and inconceivable manner. . . . At every step they take they see the piles of wounded and slain and their feet are slipping in the blood and brains of their comrades."[23] Soldiers who participated in these scenes of slaughter would never be able to forget what they had seen. Elbridge Copp recalled that at the Battle of Deep Bottom a man standing near him was struck by a piece of a shell: "The sickening thud as it entered his body, sent a chill of horror through me, such as those only who have heard can know." In a similar vein, another soldier recalled seeing a man in the ranks in front cut down by rifle fire: "I heard the bullets chug into his body; it seemed half a dozen struck him. I shall never forget the look on his face as he turned over and died." At times the horror and shock overwhelmed men, who would flee from the battlefield in terror, for sights of the wounded could be devastating:

> A wounded man begged piteously for us to take him to the rear; he was wounded in the neck, or head, and the blood flowed freely; everytime he tried to speak the blood would fill his mouth and he would blow it out in all directions; he was all blood, and at the time I thought he was the most dreadfull sight I ever saw. We could not help him, for it was of no use, for he could not live long by the way he was bleeding.[24]

The Civil War has sometimes been portrayed as almost gentlemanly, an unfortunate war between brothers in which Union and Confederate soldiers routinely chatted with each other and exchanged newspapers or tobacco for coffee. Such incidents surely did take place, but not on the battlefield. There frenzy drove and impelled soldiers to commit acts of violence and cruelty toward their fellow men. Participating in the assault on Confederate positions at Spotsylvania Courthouse on May 12, 1864, Robert S. Robertson of the 93rd New York Infantry recalled a scene of violent chaos when the Rebel line was finally broken:

> The 26th Mich. was the first to reach the breastworks, and as the line scaled the bank it was met by a volley from close quarters & recoiled with fearful loss, but only for an instant, for we pushed on, and the works were ours. The men, infuriated and wild with excitement, went to work with bayonets and clubbed muskets, and a scene of horror ensued for a few moments. It was the first time I had been in the midst of a hand to hand fight, and seen men bayonetted, or their brains dashed out with the butt of a musket, & I never wish to see another scene.[25]

On another occasion a Confederate fleeing before a Union attack at the Battle of Antietam was frantically trying to climb over a fence to escape when he was brought down by rifle fire; so infuriated were the pursuing Northerners that numerous men in their band continued to shoot or bayonet the body of the doomed Rebel, even after he was already dead.[26]

In other recorded incidents, Confederates took aim at a Federal running for his life on a battlefield several hundred yards away, and shot the man in the back, watching calmly as the stricken soldier stopped in his tracks and dropped to his knees. In another such episode, a Confederate trapped an unarmed Union soldier, who, with tears running down his cheeks, pleaded for his life while attempting to hide behind a tree; the Rebel calmly took aim and prepared to shoot and kill the Union man until he was restrained by a comrade. And, of course, once battle lines were established – whether in campaigns in Georgia or in siege warfare in the vicinity of Richmond and Petersburg, Virginia – snipers from both sides would shoot and kill any soldier who was careless enough to expose his head above the parapet: "As soon as a man showed himself during daylight a bullet would come. Not more than one shot in fifty hit its mark, but it was nerve-wracking. . . . Every day someone in the Regiment was hit."

Cases of atrocities in which prisoners of war were killed in cold blood, furthermore, were certainly not unknown in the Civil War: in some instances, the motivation was racial as Confederates killed captured African-Americans, or Northerners retaliated by killing captured Rebels. In one such instance, Union men took a Confederate prisoner only to notice a "Fort Pillow" tattoo – Fort Pillow having been the scene of the Confederate massacre of dozens of Union troops, who had surrendered, but were nonetheless slaughtered: "As soon as the boys saw the letters on his arm, they yelled, 'No quarter for you,' and a dozen bayonets went into him and a dozen bullets were shot into him. I shall never forget his look of fear." In describing the Battle of Gettysburg, Wladimir Krzyzanowski wrote that the men with their powder-blackened faces and fierce expressions looked more like animals than human beings and that they indeed had an animal-like eagerness for blood and the need for revenge. He concluded that this "portrait of battle was a portrait of hell. This, indeed, must weigh heavily on the consciences of those who started it. Terrible, indeed, was the curse that hung over their heads."[27]

The vicious disregard for human life evident at pitched battles such as Shiloh, Gettysburg, and Spotsylvania Courthouse was particularly pronounced in the guerrilla warfare that raged constantly behind the lines in Tennessee, Kentucky, Missouri, and Kansas; this guerrilla warfare is particularly relevant in assessing the claims of some that the Vietnam War was singular in the history of American warfare. Rebel guerrillas routinely blew up trains and destroyed Union property throughout the war, and in early 1865, Franklin H. Bailey of the 4th Michigan Cavalry wrote to his mother that "bushwhackers" would kill any Union soldier who strayed from his unit. Another Michigan man observed that his camp – despite being "behind the lines" – was every bit as dangerous as a battlefield: "Our lives are in danger every moment without having the satisfaction of even defending ourselves. Those Bushwhackers fire on you as they would on sparrows." In innumerable incidents, guerrillas would single out and murder African-American soldiers or shoot and kill Union troopers out foraging; they would place dead animals in ponds to poison the water and then threaten to kill anyone who removed the carcasses; utilizing their spies, they would take care not to attack an adequately guarded train, but would strike and kill unsuspecting Union soldiers and civilians on trains, boats, and elsewhere when the opportunity permitted. In Missouri and Kansas, atrocities were all too common, such as the incident in Lawrence, Kansas, in August of 1863, when marauding Rebels under the leadership of William C. Quantrill shot and killed over 150 civilian Union men and boys in cold blood. The legendary James brothers, Frank and Jesse, got their start as Confederate "raiders" or guerrillas – "murderers" in the Union Army's lexicon – in the Civil War.[28]

Under such circumstances, reprisals were common in which entire towns were shelled and destroyed or plundered in retaliation for guerrilla activity. As was the case in Vietnam, Union soldiers were frequently fired upon, but the guerrillas would scatter before they could be engaged; in these cases, Northern infantrymen would burn and pillage all houses and towns within reach: "[W]e burned all their houses & everything they had & we boys hooked everything we could carry & some things we could not." When Union soldiers found army mail in a house, they burned down the house in which they found the mail in addition to adjacent houses, and "throwd women and childern out of dores and plaid hell Generaly." In other instances, when the Union Army determined that a house had been used to harbor guerrillas or if Union men were killed in the vicinity, these houses, or even all houses within a certain radius, would be torched and the occupants ordered to leave the district. Union retaliation went beyond the destruction of property; when guerrillas were captured, they were frequently hanged with or without a trial. In some cases there would be some measure of due process, as was the case in one instance when seven Rebels were caught and held under guard pending a trial: "i think we will see them shot i could shoot them myself and would like to have the chanse." In other instances, Union men did not bother with judicial forms: "Yesterday morning a citizen came in & Sayed he had just cut the ropes & let down 3 rebles that he found hanging by the neck about one mile out of town on the Shelbyville Pike. You see our 4th Tenn boys take no prisoners, but when they come acrost the rebs they make a clean job of it." A Confederate soldier commented on the Union Army's employment of such drastic measures: "That was their way!"[29]

Did Union soldiers feel guilt over such acts of violence committed during the war? Regarding the mere observation of these executions, one notes occasional comments in letters and diaries such as "entirely beyond the pale of civilization" or "awful." Regarding the feelings of Union men who actually did the hanging or shooting, the case of John A. Cundiff of the 99th Indiana Infantry is suggestive of an answer. Cundiff had apparently been detailed to shoot a Confederate prisoner during the war, and in the years after the war, he was convinced that Rebel spies or relatives of the dead Confederate were after him. Affidavits taken by Pension Bureau officials in 1893 and 1894 revealed the following behavior:

> He has always claimed that the rebels had spies out to kill him, and would take his gun and blanket and stay in the woods for days and nights at a time, and would leave the house at night and sleep in the fence corners. . . . He told me one day that two or three of his neighbors were rebels from the south (there were some new people came in then) & that they were going to kill him but that he put his axe under his bed at night to defend himself.[30]

Cundiff's troubling memories of having shot Rebel prisoners calls to mind the atrocities and "abusive violence" that psychologists frequently discuss in reference to Vietnam veterans.

In addition to the adverse impact on soldiers, civilians were also affected by guerrilla violence. In Ohio, George W. Campbell was committed to the insane asylum because of fright over Morgan's Raid; the asylum ledger noted: "When Morgan in his raid passed through Harrison this patient was found in an upper room of his house 'wringing his hands and crying, and saying that the soldiers were going to take and kill him. Since then most of the time he has been indisposed to talk. He says little on any subject. The supposed exciting cause is fright.' " In Illinois, Emma D. Lawrence, a teenager, was committed to the Jacksonville asylum in 1863 with the following notation: "Caused by a severe fright in Sept 1861. Was in a house in Morristown Cass Co., Mo., which was attacked by Guerrillas. A nervous fever followed & insanity soon began to show itself." In addition, in considering the psychological impact of the war on civilians, one should not overlook what foraging meant in reality, for when Union or Confederate troops went out to collect supplies, they frequently for all intents and purposes took all a family's available food and livestock, with or without compensation:

> I have just returned from a forage expedition across the Cumberland.... Our labors lasted three nights and days and resulted in the capture of one hundred and fifty loads of corn and oats. I'm afraid you wouldn't be so fierce if you could see us taking all the property in the world from heartbroken women whose husbands have been forced by circumstances into the Secesh Army. A man had been taken from his bed three weeks ago and carried South leaving a beautiful woman, looking very much like Aunt Catharine twenty years ago, and five children under ten years old to our mercy. Of course we took her food and horses and left her weeping over coming starvation.[31]

Historians have often claimed that World War I was the watershed in psychological casualties during warfare, that such casualties were minimal before 1914 and epidemic in numbers thereafter. This argument is based on two assertions. First, soldiers of World War I, compared with soldiers from the nineteenth century, had less training and regimentation to shield them from the horrors of war: they are viewed as industrial, "deskilled" workers/soldiers. Second, and more important, the advent of high-powered explosives shifted the nature of warfare to a situation in which as many as 70 percent of casualties resulted from artillery fire, and this killing occurred at long range, leading to a sense of dread and helplessness in infantrymen subjected to this type of bombardment. An army surgeon commented on the eve of World War I: "[T]he mysterious and widely destructive effects of modern artillery fire will test men as they have never been tested before. We can surely count then on a larger percentage of mental diseases, requiring our attention in a future war." In considering the experience of soldiers in the Civil War era, attention must therefore be paid to the attitude of infantrymen to artillery fire. A review of the evidence quickly reveals that Civil War soldiers were indeed terrified at the prospect and actuality of such bombardment, and experienced considerable psychological fear and anxiety as a result.[32]

In his first exposure to combat, Rice Bull noted the terrifying noise of a shell overhead, which, "hissing and shrieking," tore through the branches and leaves of a tree; Bull noted that the shell made everyone jump and duck. This was a nervous habit few ever fully overcame, and perhaps the basis of what may have become startle reactions, a classic symptom of PTSD, in some of these men. Other Union soldiers who witnessed artillery duels wrote of "screaming metal," which made the earth groan and tremble; one recalled that through the murk, he heard hoarse commands, the bursting of shells, and cries of agony:

We saw caissons hit and blown up, splinters flying, men flung to the ground, horses torn and shrieking. Solid shot hit the hill in our front, sprayed battalions with fountains of dirt, and went plunging into the ranks, crushing flesh and bone.... The shock from a bursting shell will scatter a man's thoughts as the iron fragments will scatter the leaves overhead.[33]

The Union cannonading at Fredericksburg was so awful that the ground shook and even rabbits left their dens in the earth and came into the camps, trembling with fright. A Federal at the Battle of Chickamauga was stunned at the carnage wreaked by Union artillery on Confederate ranks, as a cannonball wiped out four lines of Rebels, making a space large enough to drive and turn around a six-mule team: "It was terrible to behold. It seemed like they had almost annihilated them." Predictably, a Confederate wrote that men subjected to artillery bombardment never forgot how to hug the ground. In addition to solid shot, Civil War soldiers particularly feared what was called canister, a load of antipersonnel shrapnel (three-quarter-inch iron balls) fired from cannons at close range on charging infantry; these projectiles frequently dismembered or disemboweled attacking soldiers.[34]

Men subjected to long-range bombardment lost the ability to calculate time objectively. Recalling a seemingly interminable Rebel artillery bombardment at Gettysburg, one Northerner commented that the thunder of the guns was incessant as the whole air seemed to be filled with rushing, screaming, and bursting shells: "Of course, it would be absurd to say we were not scared.... How long did this pandemonium last? Measured by our feelings it might have been an age. In point of fact it may have been an hour or three or five. The measurement of time under such circumstances, regular as it is by the watch, is exceedingly uncertain by the watchers." Another Union soldier reflected that in the space of a mere two seconds on the approach of a shell, thoughts and images of all types of possible mutilation and death occupied the minds of men, and that if one wrote for an entire day afterward, one could not completely express these myriad fears and terrors as they had run through the mind the instant before impact.

These horrific scenes and emotions were forever burned into the memories of the men who huddled in their trenches or "bomb-proofs" praying that they would not be annihilated by a direct hit. During Sherman's Atlanta Campaign, one Northerner commented that if he lived a hundred years, he would never forget the fearful night in which "all the earth and sky semed on fire and in a struggle for life or death.... The earth seems crashing into ten thousand atoms ... the world about us seem[ed] like a very hell.... The cries of the wounded and dying murdered all sleep for me that night." Terrified men wrote of the "death dealing cannon," of cannons "belching forth their deadly contents," of "villainous" artillery, of artillery as a "messenger of death." As happens with men subjected to such terror (and is perhaps instructive regarding the attitude toward Vietnam), some soldiers were convinced that what they were experiencing was completely unprecedented. They claimed, for instance, that the barrage at Gettysburg surpassed anything in ancient or modern history. A Rebel subjected to artillery bombardment during the siege of Vicksburg characterized the situation as desperate and talked of certain death. He noted that the troops had behaved nobly, but couldn't stand it much longer: "Night is almost as bad as day. The air is filled with missiles of destruction." Of a Union artillery barrage, another Rebel wrote: "O Sister I can not pertend to discribe it."[35]

Aside from dead soldiers or mangled bodies, what were the psychological repercussions of this horrific cannon fire? Artillery and high explosives produced a number of psychiatric casualties in the Civil War that seemed at times almost identical to the hysterias, mutism, and uncontrollable shaking produced by the barrages on the Western Front in World War I. One nurse recounted the case of a man buried alive in the terrific explosion of a Union mine at

Petersburg in 1864, when Union sappers had attempted to breach the Confederate defenses by placing a huge load of high explosives in a mine shaft under the Rebel lines: "[He] was buried alive in the explosion of the mine at Petersburg and has lost hearing, speech and almost all sensation. He has a piteous expression of face and makes signs, as best he can, of gratitude for even a look of sympathy." Another man almost struck by a shell fragment which narrowly missed his head "went all to pieces, instantly" and was described as completely "demoralized, panic-stricken and frantic with terror." In a similar incident, a man who had been chattering away before a shell shrieked overhead and landed nearby was left completely speechless. When shelling began in another instance, an officer begged a companion: "For Gods sake dont leave me."

Perhaps the most striking case, however, is that of Albert Frank. Sitting in a trench near Bermuda Hundred in the vicinity of Richmond, Virginia, Frank offered a drink from his canteen to a man sitting next to him. Frank kept the strap around his own neck and extended the canteen to the other man's mouth for him to take a drink, but at just this moment a shell decapitated the other man, splattering blood and brain fragments on Frank. The shell continued on, exploded to the rear of the trench, and in no way directly injured Frank. That evening, Albert Frank began to act strangely, and a fellow soldier advised that he go to the bomb shelter; once there Frank began screaming, ran out the other door, and went over the top of the breastworks toward the enemy. His fellow soldiers, alarmed, went looking for him, and eventually found him huddled in fear. On the way back to Union lines, he seemed to go mad: "[H]e would drop his gun, and make a noise like the whiz of a shell, and blast and say 'Frank is killed.' " Because he had completely lost control, his comrades tied him up that night to restrain him and took him to the doctor the next day. There he was declared insane, and sent to the Government Hospital for the Insane in Washington, DC.[36]

Also deeply affected after artillery fire was John Bumgardner of the 26th Indiana Light Artillery. At Dalton Hill, Kentucky, he was knocked down by the concussion of an exploding shell, and other soldiers at the scene noticed that he was shaken and pale; after returning to camp, he was morose and sullen and continued to tremble for weeks. He talked constantly about fighting when there was no enemy in sight, and would suddenly start yelling: "There they come men run boys run they are after us." He was eventually sent to the insane asylum at Lexington, Kentucky.[37] The Civil War experience seems to confirm the theory that soldiers in a passive position of helplessness – such as those subjected to artillery bombardments – feel intense terror and anxiety, and may be at great risk for psychological breakdown. Although the experience of World War I might have intensified this phenomenon, it certainly did not originate it.

While exposure to artillery fire and the sights and sounds of a battle in progress could be unnerving in the extreme, perhaps the most horrific aspect of the Civil War experience was the scene of the battlefield after the firing had subsided. Mangled men, dead and dying, littered the landscape; the wounded would frequently plead for water and medical attention, and an occasional man, terminally wounded, would beg to be shot and put out of his misery. One North Carolina soldier wrote that after the heat and excitement of the battle ended and the smoke cleared away, the battlefield presented a harrowing scene that beggared description: "The grim monster death having done its terrible work leaves its impress on the faces of its unfortunate victims... now wrapt in the cold embrace of death." A Confederate described the scene at Chickamauga as ghastly, with hundreds of dead on the field, their faces upward and some with their arms sticking up as if reaching for something. According to a Maine volunteer, the dead were lying about as thickly as if they were slumbering in camp: "[T]he sight was most appalling... the horror of such a picture can never be penned." A Rebel recalled that after the

Battle of Seven Pines in 1862 many Union wounded were too weak to pull themselves out of ditches, which were full of water because of inordinately heavy rains; judging by the sounds he heard, these men seemed to be drowning and strangling to death: "The cries of the wounded Yankees sound in my ears yet."[38]

After fierce fighting in Georgia in 1864, a Rebel walked over the field and saw the dead piled four deep. Some guns were still standing on end, their bayonets having been driven through the bodies of victims, giving ample evidence of the awful conflict that had gone before. Of the field at Shiloh, a Hoosier noted that dead men seemed to be everywhere: "You could find them in every hollow, by every tree and stump – in open field and under copse – Union and Rebel, side by side – in life foes, in death, of one family." The psychological effect of these scenes could be devastating, as evidenced by one Confederate, who characterized the battlefield at Franklin, Tennessee, as one vast slaughter pen: "After gazing on it I felt sick at heart for days afterwards. . . . The men were so disheartened by gazing on that scene of slaughter that they had not the nerve for the work before them." In a similar vein, a Northerner wrote: "It was a scene that I wish never again to behold. I have had enough of War." Nor did these impressions fade with time; a Union soldier wrote decades after the war that the Shiloh battlefield had shocked and disheartened him: "Tho it now lacks but two days of forty two years since that morning, the picture has not faded in the least . . . it was a rude awakening to the realities of an active War Service." He characterized this scene as the "real stuff good & strong." After attempting to describe such a scene, a Michigan volunteer ended a letter to his sister: "I cannot comment more, nor dwell on the subject. *I am so unwell.*"[39]

As with recruits aching for a fight, Civil War soldiers had a great curiosity to see what a battlefield looked like. One such experience was usually satisfactory, as indicated by the account of Calvin Ainsworth of the 25th Iowa Infantry:

> I went over the field of battle as soon as possible after the surrender. At some points it was terrible. My eyes never beheld such a sight before. I hope they may never again. In some places the dead lay very thick, not more than 3–5–10 feet apart; some were shot in the head, others in the breast and lungs, some through the neck, and I saw 3 or 4 torn all to pieces by cannon balls; their innards lying by their side, ... It is indeed a sickening sight, . . . I had often wished that I could be in one battle and go over a battle field. My curiosity has been gratified. I never wish to see another.[40]

Twentieth-century research into psychiatric disorders associated with military service has indicated that soldiers attached to the Graves Registration Detail (that is, those who handle dead bodies) often experience psychological problems related to this work, and, in the Civil War era, duty with burial details could indeed produce psychological distress. One man noted that he helped to bury the dead after a battle, and it was, to say the least, a disagreeable job: "i helped to bury Some that was tore in pieces and throwed in every direction one leg here and another there wee Just had to gather up the pieces and fix them away the best wee could wee caried a hundred and fifty together and dug a big ditch. . . . i never want to See another battle field." The bodies of the dead would sometimes lie on the field for several days before they were buried, creating an unbearable stench. Particularly during the summer, this would result in scenes of sunbaked and putrefied bodies: "These corpses were so black that we, at first glance, thought they were negroes; but they had lain in the hot August sun all the day before and all this day and had been burned black and were in a state of loathsome corruption and covered with living vermin. . . . Our task of burying these poor fellows was loathsome and disgusting."[41] The attempts of Civil War soldiers to describe the carnage of the battlefield seemed time and again to end with phrases such as "pen cannot properly describe this valley of death, it was too horrible"; "the horrors of a battle field cannot be described, they must be seen"; "[t]he most shocking sight I ever saw"; "ghastly"; "O what a sight, it almost makes me shudder to think of it"; "I am shure I would not want you to witness the sight I did."[42]

Last of all, in assessing the psychological trauma to which Civil War soldiers were exposed, one should consider the ritual execution of deserters. In the Vietnam era, executing deserters would have been an utter impossibility – completely unthinkable. In the Civil War, however, hundreds of such men were shot to death by the military, and these executions were staged in ceremonies calculated to terrify the men remaining in the ranks, so as to discourage others from engaging in such behavior. The temptation to desert did, of course, exist, as one might imagine after considering the situation regarding marching, exposure to the elements, lack of adequate clothing and food, the prevalence of disease, and the horrors of battle.[43]

When executions were staged, the men in the regiment were lined up on three sides, and the condemned man was placed on top of his coffin and brought to the grounds by wagon; after the man was shot to death by the firing squad, the entire company of men was paraded by the bullet-riddled body. At times, the man executed would then be buried on the spot and the ground above smoothed over with no marker, to further terrify onlookers with the prospect not only of death, but eternal oblivion. On most occasions, men who were forced to witness these executions were appalled and deeply disturbed. One Confederate soldier witnessed an execution at which the condemned man begged piteously for his life, but was nonetheless tied to a stake and shot; the Rebel observer called it "one of the most sickening scenes I ever witnessed . . . [it] looked more like some tragedy of the dark ages, than the civilization of the nineteenth century." A Union soldier who witnessed such an execution wrote in his diary: "I call it murder in the first degree in taking his life. I don't think I will ever witness another such a horror if I can get away from it. I have seen men shot in battle but never in cold blood before." A New Hampshire volunteer was equally stunned: "I venture to say it was [a scene] never to be forgotten while life lasted, with any who witnessed it. There the body lay, the clothing stripped from the breast revealing it perforated with bullets." Writing forty years after the end of the war, a Hoosier veteran remembered that it had taken him a long time to mentally recover from the shocking sight of an execution he had witnessed so many years before: "To me it was a dreadful thing to see a human being sat on a box, blindfold & his life taken in such a savage barbarous manner. I have long since disbelieved in capital punishment, & this affair was, I think, the forerunner of this disbelief." Another Civil War soldier summed up the entire experience: "War is horrid beyond the conception of man."[44]

Notes

1   Francis Wayland Dunn, diary entry of October 30, 1862, Bentley Historical Library, University of Michigan, Ann Arbor ["destroying manner of living"]; W. H. H. Terrell, *Report of the Adjutant General of the State of Indiana*, vol. II (Indianapolis: W. R. Holloway, 1865), pp. 85 [11th Ind. Inf.], 439 [44th Ind. Inf.]; Dwight Fraser to his sister Lizzie, April 11, 1864, Fraser Papers, Indiana Historical Society ["walking"]; Rice C. Bull, *Soldiering: The Civil War Diary of Rice C. Bull, 123rd New York Volunteer Infantry*, ed. K. Jack Bauer (San Rafael, Calif.: Presidio Press, 1977), p. 38 [jettisoning items].

2   C. Macfarlane, *Reminiscences of an Army Surgeon* (Oswego, NY: Lake City Print Shop, 1912), p. 55 [forced march]; Robert Watson memoirs, entry of July 4, 1863, Florida State Archives, Tallahassee [vomiting]; federal pension record of John C. Martin [F 42 Ind. Inf.], National Archives [epileptic fit]; David Ballenger to his mother, September 7, 1862, and May 8, 1863, South Caroliniana Library

[continuous marches]; Thomas Clark to his wife, Martha Ann, September 7, 1862, Florida State Archives, Tallahassee [killed at Antietam].

3   Spencer Glasgow Welch, *A Confederate Surgeon's Letters to His Wife* (Marietta, GA.: Continental Book Co., 1954; originally published in 1911), p. 31; John G. Perry, *Letters from a Surgeon of the Civil War*, ed. Martha Derby Perry (Boston: Little, Brown and Co., 1906), p. 144.

4   Edward G. Longacre, ed., *From Antietam to Fort Fisher: The Civil War Letters of Edward King Wightman, 1862–1865* (Cranbury, NJ: Associated University Presses, 1985), p. 32.

5   Disability discharge papers, September 10, 1862, federal pension file of Wesley Lynch [A 35 Ind. Inf.], National Archives.

6   Aurelius Lyman Voorhis journal, entry for December 5, 1862, Indiana Historical Society [shivering]; Andrew Jackson Smith diary, entries for January 2, December 19, and December 25, 1864, Indiana Historical Society [blues]; David R. Trego to his brother, October 3, 1863, Bentley Historical Library [wet bed]; Wash Vosburgh to Ella, January 30, 1863, Nina L. Ness Collection, Bentley Historical Library [covered with snow]; John Johnston memoirs, p. 29, Confederate Collection, Tennessee State Archives [wretched feeling]; James N. Wright to his brother, Squire, November 17, 1864, John Johnson Papers, Indiana Historical Society [freight cars].

7   Henry W. Reddick, *Seventy-Seven Years in Dixie: The Boys in Gray of 61–65* (Santa Rosa, Fla.: H. W. Reddick, 1910), p. 21; Wash Vosburgh to Ella, May 13, 1864, Nina L. Ness Collection, Bentley Historical Library.

8   Carroll Henderson Clark memoirs, p. 9, Confederate Collection, Tennessee State Archives [equipment abandoned; breadth of mud]; Augustus M. Van Dyke to his parents, August 12, 1861, Indiana Historical Society [Cheat Mountain]; DeWitt C. Goodrich memoirs, p. 114, Indiana Historical Society [at Shiloh]; Bull, *Soldiering*, p. 123 [wet feet], 234 [Sherman's men].

9   Paul E. Steiner, *Disease in the Civil War: Natural Biological Warfare in 1861–1865* (Springfield, Ill.: Charles C. Thomas, 1968). The *Medical and Surgical History of the War of the Rebellion*, Medical History, pt. I, vol. I (Washington, D.C.: U.S. Government Printing Office, 1870), indicates that for Union troops (white and black), there were 6,454,834 cases of disease, with 195,627 deaths from disease. In general, see Courtney Robert Hall, "Confederate Medicine: Caring for the Confederate Soldier," *Medical Life*, 42 (1935): 445–508; William M. Straight, "Florida Medicine and the War between the States," *Journal of the Florida Medical Association*, 67 (8) (August 1980): 748–60; Alfred Jay Bollet, "To Care for Him That Has Borne the Battle: A Medical History of the Civil War," *Resident and Staff Physician*, 35 (November 1989): 121–9; James O. Breeden, "Confederate Medicine: The View from Virginia," *Virginia Medical Quarterly*, 118 (4) (Fall 1991): 222–31; and John Ochsner, "The Genuine Southern Surgeon," *Annals of Surgery*, 215 (5) (May 1992): 397–408.

10 In general, see George W. Adams, *Doctors in Blue: The Medical History of the Union Army in the Civil War* (Dayton, Ohio: Morningside Press, 1985), and Horace H. Cunningham, *Doctors in Gray: The Confederate Medical Service* (Cloucester, MA.: Peter Smith, 1970). DeWitt C. Goodrich memoirs, pp. 9–10, Indiana Historical Society [primitive state of medicine]; Andrew Newton Buck to Myron and Susan, January 28, 1862, Buck Family Papers, Bentley Historical Library [executioner].

11 R. Maurice Hood, "Medicine in the Civil War," *Texas Medicine*, 63 (March 1967): 53–5, 53, 54; W. H. Taylor, "Some Experiences of a Confederate Assistant Surgeon," *Trans. Coll. Phys. Phila.*, 28 (1906): 104, 105 [standard practice]; James Houghton diary, entry from July 1863, Bentley Historical Library [canteen].

12 Roderick Gospero Shaw to his sister, October 8, 1863, Florida State Archives, Tallahassee [fangs of disease]; Henry G. Noble to Ruth, February 26, 1863, Bentley Historical Library [Rebel lead]; Chauncey H. Cooke, *Soldier Boy's Letters to His Father and Mother, 1861–5* (privately published, 1915), p. 23 [muffled drum]; Ben C. Johnson, *Soldier's Life: Civil War Experiences of Ben C. Johnson*, ed. Alan S. Brown, Faculty Contributions, ser. VI, no. 2 (Kalamazoo, MI.: Western Michigan University Press, 1962), pp. 48–9.

13 James J. Nixon to his wife, May 11, 1864, P. K. Yonge Library of Florida History, University of Florida, Gainesville.

14 Col. James L. Cooper memoirs, p. 4, Confederate Collection, Tennessee State Archives; DeWitt Goodrich memoirs, p. 106, Indiana Historical Society; Rice C. Bull, *Soldiering*, p. 36.

15   Abner R. Small, *The Road to Richmond: The Civil War Memoirs of Major Abner R. Small of the Sixteenth Maine Volunteers, Together with the Diary Which He Kept When He Was a Prisoner of War*, ed. Harold Adams Small (Berkeley: University of California Press, 1939), p. 185 [real test]; Bull, *Soldiering*, p. 51; William Henry Younts memoirs, pp. 51–3, Indiana Historical Society [Ohio soldier].

16   Elbridge J. Copp, *Reminiscences of the War of the Rebellion, 1861–1865* (Nashua, NH: Telegraph Publishing Co., 1911), pp. 134–5 [horror and dread]; William Baird memoirs, p. 16, Bentley Historical Library [Michigan volunteer]; Perry, *Letters from a Surgeon*, p. 168 [screaming officers; singing soldier]; Small, *The Road to Richmond*, p. 71 [trembling soldier]; Major and Surgeon S. C. Gordon, "Reminiscences of the Civil War from a Surgeon's Point of View," in Military Order of the Loyal Legion of the United States, Maine Commandery, *War Papers* (Portland, ME: Lefavor-Tower, 1898–1919), p. 143 [trembling soldiers]; George T. Ulmer, *Adventures and Reminiscences of a Volunteer, or a Drummer Boy from Maine* (1892), p. 28 [loss of control of bowels].

17   Charles A. Fuller, *Personal Recollections of the War of 1861* (Sherburne, NY: News Job Printing House, 1906), p. 20 [first volley]; Major Rufus R. Dawes [*Service with the Sixth Wisconsin Volunteers*], quoted in Henry Steele Commager, ed., *The Blue and the Gray: The Story of the Civil War as Told by Participants* (New York: Bobbs-Merrill, 1950), p. 213 [demoniacal fury]; Robert S. Robertson, *Diary of the War*, ed. Charles N. Walker and Rosemary Walker (Fort Wayne, IN: Allen County-Fort Wayne Historical Society, 1965), pp. 181–2 [shouts which startle the dead]; Bull, *Soldiering*, p. 149; Copp, *Reminiscences of the War of the Rebellion*, p. 142 [hellish scene]; Washington Davis, *Camp-Fire Chats of the Civil War: Being the Incident, Adventure and Wayside Exploit of the Bivouac and Battle Field, as Related by Veteran Soldiers Themselves. Embracing the Tragedy, Romance, Comedy, Humor, and Pathos in the Varied Experiences of Army Life* (Lansing, MI: P. A. Stone, 1889), pp. 302–3 [revenge]; Franklin H. Bailey to his parents, April 8, 1862, Bentley Historical Library.

18   William Lewis McKay memoirs, p. 37, Confederate Collection, Tennessee State Archives.

19   William A. Ketcham memoirs, p. 4, Indiana Historical Society [forgot personal needs]; B.S.P., "Battle Impressions," in *The Soldier's Friend*, July 1867, p. 1 [sense of disembodiment]; Bull, *Soldiering*, p. 57 [sharp sting]; Copp, *Reminiscences of the War of the Rebellion*, p. 377 [blow from club]; Fuller, *Personal Recollections of the War of 1861*, p. 95 [arm ceased to function]; William E. Sloan diary, September 19, 1863, Confederate Collection, Tennessee State Archives [terror of the wounded]; Robertson, *Diary of the War*, p. 183 [legs knocked out]; James L. Cooper memoirs, p. 39 [felt like struck with board], Confederate Collection, Tennessee State Archives; S. Weir Mitchell, George R. Morehouse, and William W. Keen, *Gunshot Wounds and Other Injuries of Nerves* (Philadelphia: J. B. Lippincott & Co., 1864), p. 14 [by far].

20   Mitchell et al., *Gunshot Wounds*, p. 87 [case study of David Schively, E 114 Pa. Inf.; staggered]; James L. Cooper memoirs, p. 22 [excitement], Confederate Collection, Tennessee State Archives.

21   George E. Ranney, "Reminiscences of an Army Surgeon," in *War Papers Read before the Michigan Commandery of the Military Order of the Loyal Legion of the United States*, vol. 2 (Detroit: James H. Stone & Co., 1898), p. 189 [awful shock and rage of battle]; Small, *The Road to Richmond*, p. 133 [the Battle of the Wilderness as "that howling acre"]; Alfred A. Atkins to parents, February 11, 1864, Georgia State Archives [rumbling, grinding noise]; David Ballenger to his mother, May 8, 1863, South Caroliniana Library [Chancellorsville]; declaration of January 2, 1900 [blood gushing], federal pension file of Thomas B. Hornaday [E 70 Ind. Inf.], National Archives. For a typical pension claim for deafness induced by cannonading, see federal pension file of Elijah Wingert [D 118 Pa. Inf.], National Archives.

22   William B. Miller diary, entry for September 19, 1863 [Chickamauga]; Robertson, *Diary of the War*, p. 182 [Spotsylvania]; Gus F. Smith, "Battle of Franklin," in *War Papers Read before the Michigan Commandery of the Military Order of the Loyal Legion of the United States*, p. 262 [awful grandeur]; Copp, *Reminiscences of the War of the Rebellion*, p. 242 [the half].

23   *John Dooley War Journal* (Washington, DC, 1945), p. 23, quoted in Horace H. Cunningham, *Field Medical Services at the Battles of Manassas (Bull Run)*, University of Georgia Monographs, no. 16 (Athens, GA: University of Georgia Press, 1968), p. 87.

24 Copp, *Reminiscences of the War of the Rebellion*, pp. 143, 447 [chill of horror]; George F. D. Paine, *How I Left Bull Run Battlefield*, p. 31, quoted in Cunningham, *Field Medical Services* [bullets chug]; Austin C. Stearns, *Three Years with Company K: Sergt. Austin C. Stearns, Company K, 13th Mass. Infantry (Deceased)*, ed. Arthur A. Kent (Rutherford, NJ: Fairleigh Dickinson University Press, 1976), p. 109 [wounded man].

25 Robertson, *Diary of the War*, p. 182.

26 From Thomas L. Livermore, *Days and Events*, quoted in Commager, ed., *The Blue and the Gray*, p. 222; for a similar incident, see Fuller, *Personal Recollections of the War of 1861*, p. 60.

27 John Johnston memoirs, pp. 30, 74, 138, Confederate Collection, Tennessee State Archives [running man shot down]; Joseph T. Glatthaar, *Forged in Battle: The Civil War Alliance of Black Soldiers and White Officers* (New York: Meridian Books, 1991), pp. 155–8 [racially motivated atrocities]; Robert Hale Strong, *A Yankee Private's Civil War* (Chicago: Henry Regnery Co., 1961), p. 16 [Fort Pillow]; Bull, *Soldiering*, pp. 155, 136 [deadly sniper fire]; Wladimir Krzyzanowski, *The Memoirs of Wladimir Krzyzanowski*, trans. by Stanley J. Pula, ed. James S. Pula (San Francisco: R & E Research Associates, 1978), p. 49.

28 Franklin H. Bailey to his mother, January 3, 1865, Bentley Historical Library; Victor E. Comte to wife Elise, May 12, 1863, Bentley Historical Library [sparrows]; Elvira J. Powers, *Hospital Pencillings: Being a Diary while in Jefferson General Hospital, Jeffersonville, Ind., and Others at Nashville Tennessee, as Matron and Visitor* (Boston: Edward L. Mitchell, 1866), p. 107 [Negro soldiers killed]; Elijah P. Burton, *Diary of E. P. Burton, Surgeon 7th Reg. Ill. 3rd Brig. 2nd Div. 16 A.C.* (Des Moines, IA: Historical Records Survey, 1939), p. 26 [forager killed]; David Wiltsee diary, February 28, 1862, Indiana Historical Society [dead animals]; Michael Fellman, *Inside War: The Guerrilla Conflict in Missouri during the American Civil War* (New York: Oxford University Press, 1989), p. 25 [Quantrill raid]. See also Stephen V. Ash, "Sharks in an Angry Sea: Civilian Resistance and Guerrilla Warfare in Occupied Middle Tennessee, 1862–1865," *Tennessee Historical Quarterly*, 45 (3) (Fall 1986): 217–29; and Gary L. Cheatham, " 'Desperate Characters': The Development and Impact of the Confederate Guerrillas in Kansas," *Kansas History*, 14 (3) (Autumn 1991): 144–61.

29 Horace Charles to unknown, October 23, 1862, Bentley Historical Library [burned houses]; Victor E. Comte to Elise, May 12, 1863, Bentley Historical Library [burning and plundering in retaliation]; William R. Stuckey to unknown, December 19, 1861 [could shoot guerrillas himself], April 27, 1863 [captured mail], Indiana Historical Society; Russell F. Weigley, *Quartermaster General of the Union Army: A Biography of M. C. Meigs* (New York: Columbia University Press, 1959), pp. 307–8 [retribution after Union soldier killed]; Judson L. Austin to wife, Sarah, July 11, 1863, Nina L. Ness Collection, Bentley Historical Library [summary execution]; Reddick, *Seventy-Seven Years in Dixie*, p. 35 [six bushwackers executed]; John Johnston memoirs, p. 39, Confederate Collection, Tennessee State Archives [Union ways].

30 Joseph Dill Alison diary, entry for May 19, 1861, P. K. Yonge Library of Florida History, University of Florida, Gainesville [pale]; John H. Sammons, *Personal Recollections of the Civil War* (Greensburg, IN.: Montgomery & Son, n.d.), p. 13 [awful]; for the Cundiff case, see affidavits of Henry C. Coffin, May 8, 1893, Harrison Walters, May 8, 1893, Harvey R. Benshan (guardian), June 5, 1894, John A. Jordan, June 6, 1894, James H. Pebworth, June 6, 1894, and L. B. Ashby, June 6, 1894, federal pension file of John A. Cundiff [H 99 Ind. Inf.], National Archives.

31 George W. Campbell case records, Longview Hospital (Cincinnati), Ohio State Archives, Columbus, Ohio. For others adversely affected by Morgan's Raid, see cases 4125 (Lydia M. Shaw) and 4156 (James Johnson), from Case Records, Columbus Hospital for the Insane, Ohio State Archives, Columbus, Ohio. Case no. 1913, Emma D. Lawrence, Case Records, Illinois State Asylum (Jacksonville State Hospital), Illinois State Archives, Springfield; A. T. Volwiler, "Letters from a Civil War Officer," *Mississippi Valley Historical Review*, 14 (4) (March 1928): 510–521, 512.

32 See Edward A. Strecker, "II. Military Psychiatry: World War I, 1917–1918," in J. Hall, G. Zilboorg, and H. Bunker, eds., *One Hundred Years of American Psychiatry* (New York: Columbia University Press, 1944), pp. 385–416, 385; Harold Wiltshire, "A Contribution to the Etiology of Shell Shock," *Lancet, 1* (June 17, 1916): 1207–1212; and Eric J. Leed, *No Man's Land; Combat and Identity in World*

War I (New York: Cambridge University Press, 1979), pp. 163–92; R. L. Richards, "Mental and Nervous Disease in the Russo-Japanese War," *Military Surgeon*, 26 (1910): 177–93, 179 [mysterious].

33 Bull, *Soldiering*, p. 41; Small, *The Road to Richmond*, pp. 105, 185 ["screaming metal"].

34 Robertson, *Diary of the War*, p. 73 [rabbits]; William B. Miller diary, September 19, 1863 [Chickamauga]; William Lewis McKay memoirs, p. 37, Confederate Collection, Tennessee State Archives ["hugging the ground"]; Calvin Ainsworth diary, p. 42, Bentley Historical Library [canister]. For an explanation of varieties of Civil War artillery, see Wayne Austerman, "Case Shot and Canister: Field Artillery in the Civil War," *Civil War Times Illustrated*, 26 (5) (September 1987): 16–48.

35 John Gibbon, *Personal Recollections of the Civil War* (New York: G. P. Putnam's Sons, 1928), pp. 147–9 [sense of time]; Charles B. Haydon, *For Country, Cause, and Leader: The Civil War Journal of Charles B. Haydon*, ed. Stephen W. Sears (New York: Ticknor & Fields, 1993), p. 306 [two seconds]; Cooke, *Soldier Boy's Letters to His Father and Mother*, p. 75 [bombardment in May, 1864]; Richard Harwell, ed., *A Confederate Marine: A Sketch of Henry Lea Graves with Excerpts from the Graves Family Correspondence, 1861–1865*, Confederate Centennial Studies (Tuscaloosa, AL.: Confederate Publishing Company, 1963), p. 63 ["death dealing cannon"]; James Garvin Crawford, *"Dear Lizzie*," ed. Elizabeth Ethel Parker Bascom (privately published, 1978), p. 75 ["belching cannons"]; James L. Cooper memoirs, p. 58, Confederate Collection, Tennessee State Archives ["villainous" artillery]; John Francis Lanneau, "Remembrances of the Civil War," p. 26, South Caroliniana Library ["messenger of death"]; Robert Richardson to his sister, July 7, 1863, Richardson Collection, Georgia State Archives [unprecedented]; Joseph Dill Alison Diary, June 10, 1863, P. K. Yonge Library, University of Florida, Gainesville [Vicksburg]; Abram Hayne Young to sister, May 13, 1862, South Caroliniana Library [can't describe].

36 Jane S. Woolsey, *Hospital Days* (New York: D. Van Nostrand, 1970), p. 112 [man buried at Petersburg]; William Meade Dame, *From the Rapidan to Richmond and the Spottsylvania Campaign* (Baltimore: Green-Lucas Co., 1920), p. 122 [demoralized man]; Ferdinand Davis memoirs, pp. 127–8, 141, Bentley Historical Library [man rendered speechless; terrified officer]; declaration of Albert Frank, June 7, 1884, and affidavit of Henry Moody, October 15, 1884, federal pension file of Albert Frank [B 8 Conn. Inf.], National Archives. For Frank's admission to the Government Hospital for the Insane, see admission number 1707, November 17, 1864, National Archives. For a case of aphonia, see William W. Keen, S. Weir Mitchell, and George R. Morehouse, "On Malingering, Especially in Regard to Simulation of Diseases of the Nervous System," *American Journal of Medical Sciences* 48 (July–October 1864): 367–94, 383.

37 Affidavits of Allen M. Bridges, February 3, 1888, and Thomas McMahon, February 1, 1888, federal pension file of John Bumgardner [26 Ind. L.A.], National Archives.

38 P. L. Ledford, *Reminiscences of the Civil War, 1861–1865* (Thomasville, NC: News Printing House, 1909), p. 67 [grim monster death]; Washington Ives, *Civil War Journal and Letters of Serg. Washington Ives, 4th Florida C.S.A.* (Jim R. Cabanniss, privately published, 1987), p. 44; Ulmer, *Adventures and Reminiscences of a Volunteer*, pp. 40–1 [slumbering camp]; Samuel Elias Mays, *Genealogical Notes on the Family of Mays and Reminiscences of the War between the States* (Plant City, FL.: Plant City Enterprise, 1927), p. 65 [drowning Yankees].

39 Gervis D. Grainger, *Four Years with the Boys in Gray* (Dayton, OH: Morningside Press, 1972; originally published in 1902), p. 21 [bayonets]; Jesse B. Connelly diary, p. 33, Indiana Historical Society [one family]; James L. Cooper, pp. 50–1, Confederate Collection, Tennessee State Archives [Franklin]; J. M. Coleman to Mrs. R. B. Hanna, April 29, 1862, Robert B. Hanna Papers, Indiana Historical Society [enough of war]; DeWitt C. Goodrich memoirs, pp. 113–15, Indiana Historical Society [Shiloh]; Stephen Lampman Lowing to sister, Mary, May 17, 1862, Bentley Historical Library [unwell].

40 Calvin Ainsworth diary, pp. 23–4, Bentley Historical Library.

41 Samuel Futterman and Eugene Pumpian-Mindlin, "Traumatic War Neuroses Five Years Later," *American Journal of Psychiatry*, 108 (1951–1952): 417 [soldiers in graves registration units at risk for

traumatic war neuroses]; James E. McCarroll et al., "Symptoms of Posttraumatic Stress Disorder Following Recovery of War Dead," *American Journal of Psychiatry* 150 (12) (December 1993): 1875–7; Patricia B. Sutker et al., "Psychopathology in War-Zone Deployed and Nondeployed Operation Desert Storm Troops Assigned Graves Registration Duties," *Journal of Abnormal Psychology*, 103 (2) (1994): 383–90 [psychological aftermath of war-zone participation involving the task of handling human remains was profound]; James H. Jones to his parents, January 9, 1863, Indiana Historical Society [pieces of bodies]; William G. Le Duc, *Recollections of a Civil War Quartermaster: The Autobiography of William G. Le Duc* (St. Paul, Minn.: North Central Publishing Company, 1963), p. 77 [unendurable stench]; John Johnston, p. 99, Confederate Collection, Tennessee State Archives [loathsome task].

42 Rufus W. Jacklin, Records of the Military Order of the Loyal Legion of the United States, Michigan Commandery, 1885–1937, p. 14 [valley of death]; Robertson, *Diary of the War*, pp. 23–4 [horrors]; Curtis Buck to unknown, May 23, 1864, Buck Family Papers, Bentley Historical Library [shocking sight]; Eli Augustus Griffin diary, entry of May 3, 1864, Bentley Historical Library [ghastly]; Franklin H. Bailey to parents, April 8, 1862, Bentley Historical Library [shudder]; Judson L. Austin to wife, September 12, 1863, Nina L. Ness Collection, Bentley Historical Library [you would not want to witness].

43 In *Desertion during the Civil War* (Gloucester, Mass.: Peter Smith, 1966), Ella Lonn estimates that there were 103,400 Confederate deserters and 278,644 Union deserters from 1863 to 1865. In *Stop the Evil: A Civil War History of Desertion and Murder* (San Rafael, Calif.: Presidio Press, 1978), p. 77, Robert I. Alotta concludes that nearly 60,000 Union deserters returned to duty, and that the actual number of deserters apprehended and brought to trial is unknown.

44 Joshua Hoyet Frier memoirs, Florida State Archives, Tallahassee [dark ages]; William B. Miller diary, pp. 320–1, Indiana Historical Society [murder]; Ferdinand Davis memoirs, pp. 63–4, Bentley Historical Library [shock]; George M. Fredrickson, *The Inner Civil War: Northern Intellectuals and the Crisis of the Union* (New York: Harper and Row, 1965), p. 85.

Questions to consider

- What are some of the challenges that Civil War soldiers faced in common with those of other wars?

- How would you describe the relationship between physical and psychological stress?

- One of the major points Eric T. Dean makes in his book is that for all their similarities, there were also crucial differences in the experiences of Civil War and Vietnam veterans. The latter, he argues, benefited from the insights of modern psychiatry, and from the large government bureaucracy that existed to ease their transition to civilian life in ways that ranged from medical care to a college education. While the Vietnam War was widely unpopular, he notes, there was significant dissent during the Civil War as well – and many Southern veterans returned to homes and livelihoods that had been destroyed. "Contrary to what has become the conventional wisdom in the United States," he asserts, "the Vietnam veteran – in the larger scheme of things – may not have fared so badly." In what other ways might you make this comparison? Do you think Dean is right?

Chapter 7

The Battle Front: Primary Sources

The Red Badge of Courage

Stephen Crane

Soldiers and students alike have marveled that Stephen Crane, the son of a minister with no military experience, could have written a novel like *The Red Badge of Courage*. Born the son of a New Jersey Methodist, Crane (1871–1900) lived a short, meteoric life that included stints of war reporting, investigative journalism, and a small but deeply influential body of fiction. The *Red Badge of Courage* (written in 1895, before he had become a war correspondent) is a fictionalized account of the 1863 Battle of Chancellorsville. The novel tells the story of Henry Fleming, a callow Union soldier anxious to prove to himself and his comrades that he will show courage in combat. In this chapter, Fleming approaches his moment of truth – or, at any rate, what he believes will be his moment of truth. Consider, as you read it, how Crane's account of combat compares with that described by Eric T. Dean.

Stephen Crane, *The Red Badge of Courage* (New York: D. Appleton & Co., 1895), pp. 36–43.

There were moments of waiting. The youth thought of the village street at home before the arrival of the circus parade on a day in the spring. He remembered how he had stood, a small, thrillful boy, prepared to follow the dingy lady upon the white horse, or the band in its faded chariot. He saw the yellow road, the lines of expectant people, and the sober houses. He particularly remembered an old fellow who used to sit upon a cracker box in front of the store and feign to despise such exhibitions. A thousand details of color and form surged in his mind. The old fellow upon the cracker box appeared in middle prominence.

Some one cried, "Here they come!"

There was rustling and muttering among the men. They displayed a feverish desire to have every possible cartridge ready to their hands. The boxes were pulled around into various positions, and adjusted with great care. It was as if seven hundred new bonnets were being tried on.

The tall soldier, having prepared his rifle, produced a red handkerchief of some kind. He was engaged in knitting it about his throat with exquisite attention to its position, when the cry was repeated up and down the line in a muffled roar of sound.

"Here they come! Here they come!" Gun locks clicked.

Across the smoke-infested fields came a brown swarm of running men who were giving shrill yells. They came on, stooping and swinging their rifles at all angles. A flag, tilted forward, sped near the front.

As he caught sight of them the youth was momentarily startled by a thought that perhaps his gun was not loaded. He stood trying to rally his faltering intellect so that he might recollect the moment when he had loaded, but he could not.

A hatless general pulled his dripping horse to a stand near the colonel of the 304th. He shook his fist in the other's face. "You've got to hold 'em back!" he shouted, savagely; "you've got to hold 'em back!"

In his agitation the colonel began to stammer. "A-all r-right, General, all right, by Gawd! We-we'll do our – we-we'll d-d-do – do our best, General." The general made a passionate gesture and galloped away. The colonel, perchance to relieve his feelings, began to scold like a wet parrot. The youth, turning swiftly to make sure that the rear was unmolested, saw the commander regarding his men in a highly resentful manner, as if he regretted above everything his association with them.

The man at the youth's elbow was mumbling, as if to himself: "Oh, we're in for it now! oh, we're in for it now!"

The captain of the company had been pacing excitedly to and fro in the rear. He coaxed in schoolmistress fashion, as to a congregation of boys with primers. His talk was an endless repetition. "Reserve your fire, boys – don't shoot till I tell you – save your fire – wait till they get close up – don't be damned fools –"

Perspiration streamed down the youth's face, which was soiled like that of a weeping urchin. He frequently, with a nervous movement, wiped his eyes with his coat sleeve. His mouth was still a little ways open.

He got the one glance at the foe-swarming field in front of him, and instantly ceased to debate the question of his piece being loaded. Before he was ready to begin – before he had announced to himself that he was about to fight – he threw the obedient, well-balanced, rifle into position and fired a first wild shot. Directly he was working at his weapon like an automatic affair.

He suddenly lost concern for himself, and forgot to look at a menacing fate. He became not a man but a member. He felt that something of which he was a part – a regiment, an army, a cause, or a country – was in a crisis. He was welded into a common personality which was dominated by a single desire. For some moments he could not flee no more than a little finger can commit a revolution from a hand.

If he had thought the regiment was about to be annihilated perhaps he could have amputated himself from it. But its noise gave him assurance. The regiment was like a firework that, once ignited, proceeds superior to circumstances until its blazing vitality fades. It wheezed and banged with a mighty power. He pictured the ground before it as strewn with the discomfited.

There was a consciousness always of the presence of his comrades about him. He felt the subtle battle brotherhood more potent even than the cause for which they were fighting. It was a mysterious fraternity born of the smoke and danger of death.

He was at a task. He was like a carpenter who has made many boxes, making still another box, only there was furious haste in his movements. He, in his thought, was careering off in other places, even as the carpenter who as he works whistles and thinks of his friend or his enemy, his home or a saloon. And these jolted dreams were never perfect to him afterward, but remained a mass of blurred shapes.

Presently he began to feel the effects of the war atmosphere – a blistering sweat, a sensation that his eyeballs were about to crack like hot stones. A burning roar filled his ears.

Following this came a red rage. He developed the acute exasperation of a pestered animal, a well-meaning cow worried by dogs. He had a mad feeling against his rifle, which could only be used against one life at a time. He wished to rush forward and strangle with his fingers. He craved a power that would enable him to make a world-sweeping gesture and brush all back. His impotency appeared to him, and made his rage into that of a driven beast.

Buried in the smoke of many rifles his anger was directed not so much against the men whom he knew were rushing toward him as against the swirling battle phantoms which were choking him, stuffing their smoke robes down his parched throat. He fought frantically for respite for his senses, for air, as a babe being smothered attacks the deadly blankets.

There was a blare of heated rage mingled with a certain expression of intentness on all faces. Many of the men were making low-toned noises with their mouths, and these subdued cheers, snarls, imprecations, prayers, made a wild, barbaric song that went as an undercurrent of sound, strange and chant-like with the resounding chords of the war march. The man at the youth's elbow was babbling. In it there was something soft and tender like the monologue of a babe. The tall soldier was swearing in a loud voice. From his lips came a black procession of curious oaths. Of a sudden another broke out in a querulous way like a man who has mislaid his hat. "Well, why don't they support us? Why don't they send supports? Do they think –"

The youth in his battle sleep heard this as one who dozes hears.

There was a singular absence of heroic poses. The men bending and surging in their haste and rage were in every impossible attitude. The steel ramrods clanked and clanged with incessant din as the men pounded them furiously into the hot rifle barrels. The flaps of the cartridge boxes were all unfastened, and bobbed idiotically with each movement. The rifles, once loaded, were jerked to the shoulder and fired without apparent aim into the smoke or at one of the blurred and shifting forms which, upon the field before the regiment, had been growing larger and larger like puppets under a magician's hand.

The officers, at their intervals, rearward, neglected to stand in picturesque attitudes. They were bobbing to and fro roaring directions and encouragements. The dimensions of their howls were extraordinary. They expended their lungs with prodigal wills. And often they nearly stood upon their heads in their anxiety to observe the enemy on the other side of the tumbling smoke.

The lieutenant of the youth's company had encountered a soldier who had fled screaming at the first volley of his comrades. Behind the lines these two were acting a little isolated scene. The man was blubbering and staring with sheeplike eyes at the lieutenant, who had seized him by the collar and was pommeling him. He drove him back into the ranks with many blows. The soldier went mechanically, dully, with his animal-like eyes upon the officer. Perhaps there was to him a divinity expressed in the voice of the other – stern, hard, with no reflection of fear in it. He tried to reload his gun, but his shaking hands prevented. The lieutenant was obliged to assist him.

The men dropped here and there like bundles. The captain of the youth's company had been killed in an early part of the action. His body lay stretched out in the position of a tired man resting, but upon his face there was an astonished and sorrowful look, as if he thought some friend had done him an ill turn. The babbling man was grazed by a shot that made the blood stream widely down his face. He clapped both hands to his head. "Oh!" he said, and ran. Another grunted suddenly as if he had been struck by a club in the stomach. He sat down and gazed ruefully. In his eyes there was mute, indefinite reproach. Farther up the line a man standing behind a tree, had had his knee joint splintered by a ball. Immediately he had dropped his rifle and gripped the tree with both arms. And there he remained, clinging desperately and crying for assistance that he might withdraw his hold upon the tree.

At last an exultant yell went along the quivering line. The firing dwindled from an uproar to a last vindictive popping. As the smoke slowly eddied away, the youth saw that the charge had been repulsed. The enemy were scattered into reluctant groups. He saw a man climb to the top of the fence, straddle the rail, and fire a parting shot. The waves had receded, leaving bits of dark *débris* upon the ground.

Some in the regiment began to whoop frenziedly. Many were silent. Apparently they were trying to contemplate themselves.

After the fever had left his veins, the youth thought that at last he was going to suffocate. He became aware of the foul atmosphere in which he had been struggling. He was grimy and dripping like a laborer in a foundry. He grasped his canteen and took a long swallow of the warmed water.

A sentence with variations went up and down the line. "Well, we've helt 'em back. We've helt 'em back; derned if we haven't." The men said it blissfully, leering at each other with dirty smiles.

The youth turned to look behind him and off to the right and off to the left. He experienced the joy of a man who at last finds leisure in which to look about him.

Under foot there were a few ghastly forms motionless. They lay twisted in fantastic contortions. Arms were bent and heads were turned in incredible ways. It seemed that the dead men must have fallen from some great height to get into such positions. They looked to be dumped out upon the ground from the sky.

From a position in the rear of the grove a battery was throwing shells over it. The flash of the guns startled the youth at first. He thought they were aimed directly at him. Through the trees he watched the black figures of the gunners as they worked swiftly and intently. Their labor seemed a complicated thing. He wondered how they could remember its formula in the midst of confusion.

The guns squatted in a row like savage chiefs. They argued with abrupt violence. It was a grim pow-wow. Their busy servants ran hither and thither.

A small procession of wounded men were going drearily toward the rear. It was a flow of blood from the torn body of the brigade.

To the right and to the left were the dark lines of other troops. Far in front he thought he could see lighter masses protruding in points from the forest. They were suggestive of unnumbered thousands.

Once he saw a tiny battery go dashing along the line of the horizon. The tiny riders were beating the tiny horses.

From a sloping hill came the sound of cheerings and clashes. Smoke welled slowly through the leaves.

Batteries were speaking with thunderous oratorical effort. Here and there were flags, the red in the stripes dominating. They splashed bits of warm color upon the dark lines of troops.

The youth felt the old thrill at the sight of the emblem. They were like beautiful birds strangely undaunted in a storm.

As he listened to the din from the hillside, to a deep pulsating thunder that came from afar to the left, and to the lesser clamors which came from many directions, it occurred to him that they were fighting, too, over there, and over there, and over there. Heretofore he had supposed that all the battle was directly under his nose.

As he gazed around him the youth felt a flash of astonishment at the blue, pure sky and the sun-gleamings on the trees and fields. It was surprising that Nature had gone tranquilly on with her golden process in the midst of so much devilment.

Letter from the Peninsula Campaign

Wilbur Fisk

A scholarly account of combat is one thing; a fictionalized version is another. Still another is the recollection – subjective, incomplete, and yet nevertheless important – of a direct participant. This one comes from Wilbur Fisk, a private in the Second Vermont Volunteers. Fisk participated in the so-called Peninsula Campaign of 1862, in which Union General George McClellan made an amphibious landing in Virginia as part of an effort to take Richmond. A series of engagements that have come to be known as the "Seven Days Battles" culminated at Malvern Hill, in which McClellan got quite close, and – as was typical of him – backed away from the goal. Fisk gives his version of events to the folks back home.

Wilbur Fisk, "Letter to Family, Camp near Harrison's Landing, Virginia" (July 15, 1862), in *Hard Marching Every Day: The Civil War Letters of Private Wilbur Fisk, 1861–1865*, ed. Emil and Ruth Rosenblatt (Lawrence: University Press of Kansas, 1988), pp. 36–40. Copyright © University Press of Kansas 1988. Reprinted by permission of the University Press of Kansas.

[. . .]

The ball opened Thursday, June 26, in the afternoon, and till nine o'clock that evening there was the most rapid firing of artillery I have heard during the war. That night there was a detail of picked men sent to dig a rifle-pit close up to the rebel line. This was rather delicate and dangerous business; the men selected were those that could work rapidly, keep quiet, and fight if necessary. The rest of the regiment – and I don't know but that other regiments were sent out on the same business – went as guard. Very cautiously we crept up to the place we were to occupy, as a hunter would approach a sleeping lion, and all night we lay there giving the officers all the annoyance imaginable to keep us from falling asleep. The muffled sound of the picks, spades and shovels was all that disturbed the silence of the night. At the first appearance of daylight, the guard withdrew and were relieved by the regiments. It was now expected that we should make another step in our journey toward Richmond; we had secured a good position, but alas it was destined to be of no benefit to us. We went back to our tents, but not to sleep, for we were continually being ordered under arms and into line to repel attacks that the rebels persisted in making on our front and just to the left. All day long the battle raged on the opposite side of the Chickahominy, and its progress could be distinctly seen from our camping ground. We could see that our men were apparently driven back. In fact nothing could have been more apparent. It was all a trap of Gen. McClellan to catch the enemy, so the officers said, and this served to allay apprehensions which might otherwise have produced serious evil. The Generals and their aids appeared remarkably tickled with the progress of events, and the course things were taking, and they even proclaimed that twenty-four hours more of such prosperous and successful strategy would open to us the way to Richmond.

Near sundown the rebels commenced to compliment ourselves by throwing shot and shell with remarkable precision directly into our camp. We couldn't stand this and accordingly skedaddled. I suppose we retreated in "good order" though we did it as fast as we comfortably could. Just over a steep bank to the right of our camp, we were comparatively safe. Here we came to a halt and listened to the music of the enemy's shells as they whistled over our heads and plowed up the dirt just beyond us. All at once the artillery stopped firing, and for a moment there was an ominous silence, but it was soon broken by a volley of musketry directly in our front. In an instant every man was on his feet, for we knew that here was a chance for us. Double quick we went out there, and found the Fourth Regiment engaged with the foe, and they appeared abundantly able to give the rebels all they were capable of bargaining for. It seemed they had attempted to storm our position but found a serious impediment in the Fourth, who were already there. Darkness soon closed the struggle and we returned to camp to get a little rest which we very much needed. Thus ended the first day's "strategy."

The next morning we were ordered to pack up and fall in, two orders which the soldier very well knows how to comprehend. We were only going to move our camp to a safer place they told us, which was strictly true, though in a much different sense from what we expected. We marched a short distance to the left when we were set to falling timber. About noon we were compelled to submit to another shelling. We threw ourselves on our faces and every shell that passed a foot above the ground passed harmlessly over our heads. Only one or two were hit, and these were mangled horribly. Our batteries, as soon as they opened made warm work for the rebels so that the enjoyment was not all on one side. The enemy were soon effectually silenced. We laid that night in the woods near by, and in the morning we started on our backward march. We passed through the camp of the 4th New Jersey, which came so near being annihilated in the fight on the right of the Chickahominy, stopping only long enough to destroy a few boxes of hard crackers to prevent them from furnishing the rebels a feast. This was the first time I had seen our own subsistence destroyed, and it was difficult to believe that the necessity for it was wholly premeditated. A little farther along and skirmishers were thrown out of our regiment to the rear, which opened our eyes to the fact that we were not only retreating but we were to act as rear guard. At Savage Station we halted in the woods after crossing the railroad, and rested there a short time. Meanwhile the troops from the entrance, left of the line belonging to Heintzelman, Keyes and Sumner's army corps, came pouring down the road past us. Large piles of subsistence stores and ammunition were burned here. At length when all the rest of the troops had passed we had orders to move on too. We had marched less than two miles when a brisk cannonading was heard back at the Station, and our brigade was immediately ordered to about face – an order that savored unmistakably of a collision. We returned, formed in battle array, the Fifth taking the lead in line of battle, followed by the Second in close column ready to support it on the right or left as the exigencies of the case might require. We charged up hill through the woods bordering on the Williamsburg road where we had stopped to rest. With a yell the Fifth bounded forward for the rebels were retreating. Without stopping to get into a more fighting shape our regiment followed them making the woods fairly ring with their shouts. At the farther verge of the woods the tug of war commenced. The rebels had some pieces of artillery which sifted the grape through our ranks like hail stones making huge openings at every discharge. The Fifth manfully stood their ground, though their loss was terrible. We drove the rebels from the ground and had clear possession of the field when night closed the contest. We took what care of the wounded we could which was but very little for we were soon ordered forward. All night we plodded our weary way, halting just at break of day. After crossing the creek at White Oak Swamp on a small eminence well calculated for defense, we threw down our blankets and assumed a horizontal position without stopping to calculate our proximity to the enemy or our chances of being awakened by a compliment of shells.

Our slumber was short. In the morning we reconnoitered our position to the right and left, to assure ourselves that all was right; then stacked arms and sat down to rest. While quietly sitting here discussing the peculiarity of our position and freely expressing opinions pro and con relative to the wisdom of the strategy which made such mysterious movements necessary, and inwardly doubting whether it was not forced on us instead of being planned at leisure by our Generals, – for the rank and file are by no means indifferent to these important matters – we were suddenly startled by a perfect storm of shells, which the rebels threw simultaneously from perhaps a dozen pieces of artillery which they had shrewdly got into position unperceived. It was as if a nest of earthquakes had suddenly exploded under our feet. Cavalry and artillery horses, some with riders and some without, rushed helter skelter through our ranks, – if ranks there were – frightened almost to death. We repaired to the woods and there formed into line, and each took a position best calculated for defence. Here we endured another shelling similar to that we were compelled to submit to the Saturday previous. A cannon ball passed close by a friend's ear, near me, brushed his knapsack and lodged just to our rear. An inclination of his head – he was lying on his breast – to one side, if not more than two inches, would have secured to him an eternal discharge from all terrestrial warfare.

It was nearly midnight before we were ready to leave. Tired and exhausted as we all still were, we were impatient to get to a place of safety, where we would not be in constant danger of being attacked with a superior force at every disadvantage. As long as I have been in the service I have not yet become educated up to that degree of bravery, that makes the shriek of a shell music in my ears, and I fear I never shall. I ought to have said the rebels' guns were effectually silenced on this occasion, by our artillery without the aid of infantry. They could not cross the creek in the face of such a fire as Captain Ayer dealt them.

Once on our journey again we marched with all possible speed till sunrise when we halted in an open field near the James river. Here within sight of the naked masts of the gunboats we felt that a brief respite of rest could now be enjoyed free from the turmoil of war. Alas, before we had hardly eaten our breakfast we were ordered back into the woods for it was reported that the enemy were advancing. All day we remained in the woods in line, but no enemy appeared. There was, however, fierce fighting on our left during the day, as there had been the day before.

At two o'clock in the morning, we were aroused. The enemy were advancing in three directions. We had got pretty thoroughly rested and began to feel our courage revive in consequence. Doubtless we should have made a tolerably effective show of resistance if they had pressed us to it but they did not. It began to rain early in the morning and till noon it poured as if the windows of the heavens were opened. We were ordered to march, which we had not the slightest reluctance in doing, stormy as it then was. Through the mud and slosh we tramped till we reached Harrison's Landing. We put up our tents on the liquid soil and forthwith repaired to an extensive wheat field where the grain had been cut and bound and probably we cleared that field of every vestige of straw or grain in as short a space of time as it was ever done before. This made us excellent bedding. In the morning we moved our camp back from the river a mile or so to the place we now occupy. It is a pleasant position with plenty of water, and probably much more healthy than the one we occupied on the Chickahominy. The brigade has been terribly thinned, but is now improving in health, if not in numbers. There are many incidents connected with this retreat or "strategical movement," worthy of mention which I leave to those better acquainted with the facts to relate.

Questions to consider

- What do you make of the tone of this letter – opening with a comparison between a battle and a ball, or the description of the Confederate decision "to compliment ourselves by throwing shot and shell with remarkable precision"? What does this say about Fisk – and his assessment of his audience?

- What things do – and don't – you learn about the Battle of Malvern Hill from this account?

- How does Fisk's letter complement or complicate the picture of combat you see in the Dean or Crane accounts?

J. C. R., The Battle of Fredericksburg

Charleston Daily Courier

Not all Civil War battles took place on remote fields. Occasionally, the struggle was waged through towns and even cities, creating an intersection between soldiers' and civilians' lives. This letter, published in a Southern newspaper, offers a vivid description of what happened when the war came to Fredericksburg, Virginia, in 1862. The battle was a resounding Confederate victory – but as this letter suggests, it may not have felt that way to people who lived and fought there.

Charleston Daily Courier (January 17, 1863), "The Battle of Fredericksburg," in *The Civil War: Ironweed American Newspapers and Periodicals Project*, ed. Brayton Harris (Forest Hills, NY: Ironweed Press, 1999), pp. 299–301.

THE BATTLE OF FREDERICKSBURG
Camp near Fredericksburg, Virginia

Dear Uncle: – Today gives me an opportunity of writing the third letter since I received one from you. I wish to know what is the matter with you, if you have run out of something to write. I thought a few days ago we would have a dull time about Christmas, but I think the Yankees have quite enough of us to do them until we can spend Christmas, anyway. I wish you could only see the battlefield. On the morning of the 11th, before day, the signal guns were fired; and by daylight we were under arms and took our position in line of battle, and laid out six days in sight of nearly all the fighting that was done, but did not get a chance to fire a gun during the fight. This was the first time we were ever held in reserve.

I have never seen men lie so thick as they did on the outskirts of the city. In one little garden, not more than two thirds of an acre, there were one hundred forty-seven lying dead, and all over the city they were lying dead, where it seemed that balls could not have gotten to them. The city is torn to pieces, houses plundered, furniture destroyed, books torn from the libraries and scattered over the floor; even ladies' dresses were taken from their wardrobes and packed in Yankee knapsacks. The houses that were on our line of breastworks were torn to pieces by their balls. I think there is a bullet hole for every four inches in the houses. Our men let them come up within thirty paces of them, and then would fire into them, and would sweep them off as far as the balls could reach for the houses. There was a plank fence they would dodge behind that was shot entirely away by our riflemen. The planks were torn in splinters. We had four 32-pound rifle cannons that did great execution. I saw some of the best shots made by them I ever saw in my life. There was one company of Yankees that would come up in a railroad car and fire at our men, and I saw a shell from a 32-pound ball fall among them and explode, killing several. On the right of our line, where General Hill's division fought them, we could see their line advancing on ours, but they would not stand long before they would break and run like frightened sheep. There is scarcely a house in Fredericksburg but has the mark of cannonballs – many of them torn to pieces and some burned. We had but one man from our regiment wounded, and he belonged to our company. The Yankees are said to be leaving and going back toward the Potomac, where they will go into winter quarters. The river is our picket line. Our sentinels and theirs are close enough to each other to talk. We were on picket day before yesterday, and relieved the 11th Virginia Regiment. They informed us that the Yankees had been making inquiries about our regiment, and Sergeant McKinstry asked one of the Yankees why he was making inquiries about the 6th South Carolina Regiment. His reply was that they were such d – d fools they were afraid they would shoot at them. It is an understanding between Generals Lee and Burnside that the pickets shall not fire on each other unless one or the other advances. The river is about one hundred yards wide. Some of the Yankees came over and traded coffee for tobacco the day before we went down. Thus you will perceive that they are deprived of some of the pleasures of the earth as well as we are.

General Lee, however, has ordered all talking and passing to be stopped; but we were compelled to talk a little on the sly with them anyhow. We took one of the Bucktail Rifles a prisoner. He asked for our regiment and said it was the first fight he had ever been in, that he didn't want to fight our regiment. We have six regiments in our brigade, and the Hampton Legion, which has been recently attached to it. Our regiment has nearly armed itself with Enfield rifles; got most of them at Manassas. Our army is in better spirits than I have ever seen it. We commenced, as soon as we got here, to fortifying and are now well fortified. You must write me all the news from the coast, and if there are any Yankees about there. If there are not, I expect there will be soon, as General Lee has made Burnside *take water*. I am afraid, however, the next time we fight the Yankees that McClellan will be at their head. We have had some of the coldest days I ever felt – wood being scarce and no prospect of moving from here very soon. Our general is a strong believer in drilling his men. When we are not marching, we are drilling twice a day: regimental in the forenoon and brigade in the afternoon. This consumes the greater part of the day. We drill in an old field about one mile square and run all over it twice a day. A gun in hand on a cold day is not pleasant, as you are aware. But we should not murmur, but take it all in that way in which Southerners should do. I trust the day is not far distant when I shall meet you in a home of peace and a land of independence.

Your nephew,
J. C. R.

Questions to consider

- How would you describe this soldier's attitude toward his Union opponents? What about his perception of the two sides generally (consider the policy on pickets)?

- What do you make of the way this letter ends? What does it suggest about the relationship between soldier and civilian?

Letter from the Red River

Sarah Rosetta Wakeman

It is generally assumed that the Civil War was fought by men. But this was not always the case. Although it is difficult to assess with any precision – how many secrets hide in soldiers' graves? – scholars estimate that hundreds of women cross-dressed and fought as men. One such person was Sarah Rosetta Wakeman. A member of the 153rd New York State volunteers, Wakeman – who refers to herself here as Edwin R. Wakeman – was stationed in Louisiana, where she saw combat near the Red River. Wakeman died of disease shortly after writing this letter. Consider how her experiences, and the way she discussed them, compares with other accounts you have read.

Sarah Rosetta Wakeman, "Letter to Family" (April 14, 1864), in *An Uncommon Soldier: The Civil War Letters of Sarah Rosetta Wakeman, alias Private Lyons Wakeman 153rd Regiment, New York State Volunteers*, ed. Lauren Cook Burgess (New York: Oxford University Press, 1995), pp. 71–2.

Grand Ecore Landing, LA[1]
on the Red River
April the 14/64

Dear Mother and Father, Brothers and Sisters,

I take my time to write a few lines to you. I am well and in good spirit and I hope those few lines will find you all the same.

Our army made an advance up the river to pleasant hill about 40 miles. There we had a fight. The first day of the fight our army got whip[ped] and we had to retreat back about ten miles.

The next day the fight was renewed and the firing took place about eight o'Clock in the morning. There was a heavy Cannonading all day and a Sharp firing of infantry. I was not in the first day's fight but the next day I had to face the enemy bullets with my regiment. I was under fire about four hours and laid on the field of battle all night. There was three wounded in my Co. and one killed.[2]

Albert Weathermax wounded in the head. Ranson Conklin wounded through the hip. Edwin West had one of his fingers shot off.[3] Joseph Blanchard killed. That is all that was hurt in my Co.

I feel thankful to God that he spared my life and I pray to him that he will lead me safe through the field of battle and that I may return safe home.

I receive you kind and welcome letter the other day. I was glad to learn that you was agoing to work the Ham farm this summer and milk twenty cows. I would advise you to buy the farm and if you will, I will Come home and help you pay for it, if I live to get out of the army. By that time Robert will be big enough to do a good days work and he and my Self can work both of them farm like everything.

I can't think of any more to write at present. So good-by from you Affectionate,

Edwin R. Wakeman

Notes

1   Banks' command spent the days of April 11 through 21 at Grand Ecore Landing, above Natchitoches on the Red River. Rosetta spelled words as she heard them, and in the case of "Grand Ecore," she heard "Brandycore," which is the heading that appears on her original letter.

2   Here Rosetta describes the part taken by the 153rd in the Union loss at Sabine Cross Roads on April 8 and in the Batle of Pleasant Hill, which occurred the next day on April 9. Reports of Maj. Gen. William B. Franklin of operations on April 6–25, *The War of Rebellion: A Compilation of Official Records of the Union and Confederate Armies*, Series I, Vol. 34, Part 1, Reports, (Washington: Government Printing Office 1880–1901), pp. 256–62. Also, Report of Edwin P. Davis, Colonel commanding the 153rd New York, pp. 425–6.

3   Medical records for these men confirm Rosetta's report of their injuries. Surprisingly, Weathermax recovered from a severe head wound and returned to duty with the 153rd in July. Conklin and West spent over a month in USA General Hospital in New Orleans before being furloughed in mid-May, just before Rosetta arrived there on May 22. RG 94, Carded Medical Records, Volunteers, Mexican & Civil Wars, 1846–1865, 153rd New York Infantry, National Archives.

Part IV

The Home Front

Plate 6 Home Work: Nurses and officers of the US Sanitary Commission in Fredericksburg, VA, during the Wilderness Campaign of spring 1864. The Civil War mobilized civilians in unprecedented ways, creating new opportunities – and new tensions – for women in particular. (Photo by James Gardner; Selected Civil War photographs, Library of Congress)

Chapter 8

The War at Home

Reid Mitchell

The military experience may have been a world unto itself for the Union and Confederate soldiers, but the meaning of that experience was measured in terms of another one: the world of home. Every soldier came to the war by leaving behind a life that may have been left reluctantly, or fled in desperation. That life – a home, a barn, a town, a family, some neighbors – was something a soldier carried with him. For Confederates, especially, who could find themselves fighting on home turf, defending that home was the very essence of what the Civil War was all about.

And yet the reality of home as it was experienced by soldiers – returning for visits on furloughs, returning to recuperate from injuries, or returning when an enlistment ended – was often a complex experience riddled with ambivalence and ambiguity. Some civilians reacted to veterans with indifference, even hostility; others, however well-intentioned or sympathetic, were unable to connect emotionally with those they loved. Many soldiers returned joyfully to their homes, which became safe sites from which to remember their military experiences (which, of course, ranged from pleasure to horror, often in the life of the same veteran).

In this excerpt from his 1988 book *Civil War Soldiers*, Reid Mitchell, a historian who has specialized in documenting the experience of the rank-and-file veteran, outlines the complexities in one of the most powerful relationship in a soldier's life: that between the battlefront and the home front.

Reid Mitchell, "The War at Home," in *Civil War Soldiers* (New York: Simon & Schuster, 1988), pp. 64–75. Copyright © 1988 by Reid Mitchell. Used by permission of Viking Penguin, a division of Penguin Group (USA) Inc.

[. . .]

One thing that helped a soldier bear the hardships of his life was the respect of his fellow citizens. Men who had made considerable sacrifices and who were risking their lives expected a certain amount of adulation from those who had not joined them in service. If army life degraded him, acclaim could exalt the soldier to the status of a hero. The dehumanization of military service could be offset by the gratitude of one's country. Respect provided a salutory context for soldiering – a means to resist degradation.

Early in the war their fellow citizens willingly gave the soldiers the respect they demanded. The passage of volunteers through a town was a cause of celebration. Just as their hometowns had sent the troops to war with lavish public ceremony, other communities welcomed their patriotic defenders. For example, the Oglethorpe Light Infantry received the warmest greetings as they proceeded from Savannah to the Virginia war front. They marched through the streets of Petersburg to the tunes of brass bands, with the eyes of lovely women on them, and banners waving over their heads. The ladies called them the "company of bachelors" – the soldiers were sixteen to twenty-five, without a married man among them. "... indeed, we looked like boys," one wrote his mother, "with our handsome blue uniforms & smooth faces." They were great favorites everywhere they went.[1]

Occasionally civilian response was overenthusiastic. When the 5th New Jersey passed through Philadelphia in August 1861, citizens came to the train station to see them off. Young ladies freely distributed cigars, tobacco, handkerchiefs, and flowers to the soldiers. The train left the station "amid the crack of firearms and the cheers from thousands of throats." One soldier of the 5th New Jersey was shot in the arm during this patriotic demonstration, and later discharged from service.[2]

Such accidents aside, these receptions cheered the volunteers – who felt they deserved them. The public placed the value on the soldier that military life threatened to deny them. As the war continued, however, the sight of a soldier became commonplace. Civilians no longer thronged to meet the soldiers. In fact, as civilians went about their daily pursuits, they did not simply take soldiers for granted – they looked down on them. Or so the soldiers came to feel.[3]

Soldiers began to hear stories of civilian disdain; they began to complain of their treatment on their furloughs home. Cpl. Rudolphe Rey of the 102nd New York Volunteers received a discouraging letter from a fellow soldier who had lost a leg. Upon his return home, the crippled soldier reported that all his friends acted as if they could not remember him; he swore he would be able to support himself without their aid. He warned Rey that if he wore his uniform home while on leave, he could travel with a railroad car to himself. Another New York soldier said much the same thing: at home, "Soldiers and dogs go together."[4]

It might be thought that indifference toward soldiers was characteristic of a money-grubbing, unchivalrous North and not the militaristic South. As early as 1862, however, a Virginia Confederate observed that "six months ago a soldier was the greatest thing in the world but now they are worse than the devil not countenanced by nobody at all but the soldiers." Confederate soldiers, campaigning near Jackson, Mississippi, in June 1863, heard rumors that "The City Council in compliance with the solicitations of many citizens attempted some time since to pass an ordinance forbidding *soldiers the use of the pavement* and *sidewalks* and forcing them to walk in the middle of the streets. The motion was defeated by a majority of *only Three* votes." When the soldiers marched through the city, they would cry out, "Boys, don't get on the sidewalk!" and "Corporal of the Guard, here's a soldier on the sidewalk!" and the citizens nervously assured them, "Yes, you *can* walk on the sidewalks." "The Boys would frequently ask them 'where the Yankees walked while they were here'? They would cry out good-humoredly while passing a crowd of Ladies and Gentlemen, 'Here's the boys that cant walk on the pavements.' *We* can fight for you though.' " Whether the proposed civic ordinance existed or not, it is significant that the soldiers so readily believed that it did.[5]

Whatever the indifference or contempt of the civilian population at large, soldiers felt a particularly acute grievance when it seemed that the members of their own local communities did not respect their efforts. It violated the very notion that the soldier who had gone to war was an extension of that community. As the war went on, soldiers found it difficult not to see themselves as distinct from the folks back home. Instead of representing his community he began to feel alienated from it – another way in which the volunteer became a soldier.

One source of discontent was the soldiers' feeling that the people did not understand how difficult their job was. Both sides went to war expecting a quick victory; both sides were quickly, but not thoroughly, disillusioned. Soldiers who were themselves reluctant to admit that the war would not end with the next big battle were likely to be sensitive to accusations that victory could easily be achieved with different strategy, different commanders, and different armies. Even though all soldiers reserved the right to grumble about the mistakes of their superior officers, most resented it when home folks judged the operations of the army in the field unfavorably. In part, of course, such judgments were felt to reflect not only on the commanders but on the men as well. Furthermore, the soldier felt that civilian judgments were made in ignorance. The folks at home had no concept of the difficulties experienced by the soldiers in the field. A Pennsylvania lieutenant wrote home testily, when civilians were complaining that McClellan allowed Lee to escape after Antietam, that if men there "think the Rebble army can be Bagged let them come & bagg them.... Bagging an army is easy to talk about." The men who remained at home had forfeited their right to criticize those who had marched away to war.[6]

A Confederate wrote his cousin on the subject of civilian military expertise thus: "I saw a gentleman who left DeSoto Parish about two weeks since. He says the old men at home are all generals now – gather in groups in the little towns over there and talk about the war and discuss the abilities of our Generals – Know more than any of them – Except General Lee only – They admit him to be a great man, but all the others do wrong all the time. Our soldiers have all come to the conclusion that they have no friends out of the army except the ladies." And Lee himself, admitting that "the movements of our armies cannot keep pace with the expectations of the editors of papers," said he would like to see them exercise their abilities in the field.[7]

Another, more onerous grievance was the difference between the economic positions of the soldier and the civilian. Many civilians did well during the war, particularly in the North. Soldiers and their families, conversely, often suffered. With furloughs home and the surprisingly frequent exchange of mail between the front and home, soldiers were perfectly well informed as to the economic success of those they had left behind.[8]

A particular problem arose when the soldier thought that the people at home were not fair to his family or were grasping and picayune in money matters while he risked his life for the cause. John Pierson, a Union officer, reacted angrily when he learned that one of his creditors in Pontiac, Michigan, dunned his wife. "Those left at home in the quiet pursuit of their business," he told his daughter, "can well aford to wait. The business I am engaged in is a game of heads and I may loose mine and his is in no danger unless they chose to get up a war at home...."[9]

When the man continued to hound his wife, Pierson wrote her "any man that is so avaricious as to dun a woman for a small demand he may have against her Husband while he is in the Army helping to Suppress this Monstrous Rebelion is mean enough to make a false bill and ought to lose and honest one." He assured her, "If I get home Pontiac will not suffer much on my account if I get killed they may come where I am and collect...."[10]

The issue was not simply one of personal debts. It was also one of forgone opportunities for profit in the wartime economy. Henry Seys, the Union abolitionist, summed up the soldiers' fears and pride well when he wrote his wife from Chattanooga: "True I sometimes think why should *I* care so much of what is my duty to my country? Why not do as others, stay at home and fatten in purse on the blood of the land?" In ten years, he predicted, "the parvenu, made rich by lucky speculation, or some swindling contract" would "elbow from place the soldier broken down or maimed, by long exposure or ghastly wound received on some battle field or lonely picket post...." But he answered his question by saying that he served because his childhood education and his concern for the respect of his own children made him patriotic both "in *deed* as well as word." He asked his wife to teach their children that "their duty to the land of their birth is next to their duty to God."[11]

Those soldiers who believed that their immediate family had become indifferent to them probably felt the most wretched sense of abandonment. In May 1862 an officer in the Army of the Potomac, then located near Richmond, complained, "I am tired of soldiering and were it not for us being just where we are, I would not stay a day longer not careing whether you wanted me home or not. I cannot understand why you deserve [desire?] me to stay I see other letters to young men from their parents, begging and imploring of them to come home this makes me feel sad and sometimes I think I am not wanted at home by my parents[.]" He was killed not long after, at the battle of Seven Pines.[12]

Civilian disdain was as potent a source of degradation as military life. Still, the soldiers' resentment of civilian contempt and indifference was not always unambiguous. Sometimes they feared it was deserved. Soldiers knew that military life might indeed transform men into beasts and this could inform a soldier's reactions to civilians. For example, in the fall of 1862 a Union soldier in Illinois suffered from the usual camp diseases and decided to treat himself with "some fresh air and a good bed to sleep in...." He went to a farm near camp to request a place to stay for the night; the "old lady" was obviously suspicious and reluctant to shelter him but the soldier persuaded her to relent. When he wrote his parents, he explained, "The people here are suspicious of soldiers just as Ma is of pedlars and dont like to put them into their beds and I cannot blame them either some of the soldiers have not pride enough to keep themselves halfway decent. Some of them seem to think that being a soldier is a license for a man to make a brute of himself."[13]

In 1863 a Mississippi Confederate heard that a military hospital was planned for his hometown. The idea depressed him. "It seems to me that wherever soldiery predominate decay and scarcity follow, and a certain appearance of cheerlessness (as far as the inhabitants are concerned) seems to exist in proportion as the number of soldiers (locusts) increase." Charity compelled him to add, "Anyway, as they are stationed upon you, you do the best you can for poor fellows! they have a hard time even when not sick."[14]

So while men sometimes prided themselves on their patriotism and soldierly qualities, they also worried about the changes military service had made in their fellows when they compared the men around them to their families back home. The psychological transformation caused by war sometimes upset men more than anything else. Lyman C. Holford, a Wisconsin soldier, wrote in his diary, "a little after dark I saw something which was a little the worst of any thing I have yet seen in the army. Some of the boys of the 24th Mich (a new Regt lately attached to our Brigade) found a cow which had been dead for several days and being a little meat hungry they went to work and cut meat from the cow and carried it to camp and ate it." It was not just the spectacle of dead animals and rotten meat that disgusted Holford; as a veteran of battle he had seen far worse. What disgusted Holford was seeing men reduce themselves to hyenas. Somehow the dehumanization implicit in that selfish and sickening act was greater than that of killing and wounding in battle, for it showed men turned into beasts.[15]

Dehumanizing treatment was inflicted from outside; it might be resisted. Psychological transformation was more insidious. The changes that soldiering made in men might be impossible to eradicate. The Assistant Surgeon of the 12th Michigan observed, "Soldiering is certainly not beneficial to the mind, and the large lists of sick do not look as if it improved the bodily health much. I think it certainly engenders laziness." He attributed this laziness to "the alternation of very hard work, which is compulsory, and nothing at all to do, with very few resources for amusement." Laziness, unfortunately, might become a permanent part of the volunteer's personality. The surgeon feared, "When the war is over if that happy time ever comes, I believe the greater part of them will join the regular service, from sheer unfittness for anything else."[16]

The Union surgeon was echoed by Confederate soldiers. Henry Greer wrote his mother from the lines near Petersburg, "If I stay much longer in service I fear that I will never be fit for anything but the army." Richard Webb, a regimental chaplain, may have been more worried about the changes he detected in himself. "This is a very demoralized kind of life. So hardening to human feelings. I can now walk over a battlefield and see the ground strewed with dead bodies, or see a man's lim amputated without any of that tendency of fainting that the sight of blood used to cause." The irony was that serving as chaplain hardened Webb's feelings at a time when a chaplain was particularly valued by other frightened men for his sensitivity.[17]

In some cases, men were surprised by the direction of the moral transformation engendered by war. One Confederate soon learned that "War is a strange scale for measuring men." He described a fellow soldier, from whom nobody expected very much, who "made as good a soldier as there was in the Regiment. Cool and brave in battle and always on hand and never shirking duty in camp." This man proved a far better soldier than "others who occupied honorable positions in society." A New York regiment enlisted one of its soldiers after finding him sleeping drunkenly in a lumberyard. "He was dirty filthy and covered with vermin." They exchanged his rags for a new uniform. John Fleming remembered that "Strange as it may appear, that man became very steady, and one of the cleanest men and best soldiers we had." While such improvements in character were no doubt welcome, they also served to reinforce the distance felt between civilian life and the life of the soldier. These reformations were only extreme examples of how little one's peacetime identity seemed to relate to one's soldiering.[18]

The families back home shared the fears that the Civil War experience would change men beyond recognition. Soldiers frequently reassured wives and parents in their letters that they would not change or that their love was constant, apparently responding to the distressed queries of their loved ones. Such fears found their expression whether those they possessed wanted to admit them or not. A dream about her husband terrified one Georgia woman. She dreamed he had gone mad and had to be brought home. "I thought you would not speak to me. I thought all you wanted to do was to fill up the roads with logs and brush so that Lincoln's Army could not pass through the country. it pestered me worse than any dream I ever dreamed before but I hope there is nothing of it." Such a dream revealed the fear on the woman's part that the war, which ironically was often cast as a defense of the home, would alienate husbands and fathers from their families.[19]

In most cases the transformation experienced by Civil War soldiers was not as dramatic or as clear-cut as that from drunkard to model soldier, devoted husband to madman, or man to beast. Men found that the war called forth a broad array of emotional responses. One of the most perceptive analysts of the psychology of soldiering was a Union soldier, James T. Miller. While Miller's letters home reveal him to be a man particularly concerned with the ways war was influencing his character, his observations probably applied to men less articulate and introspective.

The battle of Chancellorsville sparked Miller's self-scrutiny. In May 1863 he wrote home, "i can hardly make it seem possible that three short weeks ago that i was rite in the thickest of a terrible battle but such is a soldiers life. . . . " Miller confessed that such a life had its appeal "for a brave reckless man who has no family even in war times it has a good many charms and i think i can begin to understand something of the love an old sailor has for his ship and dangers of the Ocean." The appeal, in part, may have been aesthetic. A month after Chancellorsville, Miller explained to his parents, "steadyness under fire is the great beauty of a soldier[.]"

One is reminded that Robert E. Lee, watching the advance of Burnside's troops at Fredericksburg, said, "It is well that war is so terrible; we should grow too fond of it."[20]

Miller analyzed at length the emotions experienced by the soldier. He admitted the danger inherent in war, but explained "in regard to the danger I have passed through that part is very pleasent[.]" Soldiers amused themselves after battle by sitting around campfires and laughing over stories of "hairbreadth escapes" told in a "gay reckless carless way." An observer "would be very apt to think that we were the happiest set of men" he had ever seen.

"But if you should go with us to the battle field and see those that are so gay thier faces pale and thier nervs tremblings and see an ankziety on every countenance almost bordering on fear," Miller said, "you would be very apt to think we were all a set of cowardly poltrouns[.]" The soldiers should be imagined this way "just before the fight begins and the enemy is in sight and the dul ominous silence that generaly takes place before the battle begins[.]" The soldier does not fear the dangers he has been through already, but he fears those that are to come.

Once skirmishers had been deployed, and the firing of cannons and small arms had begun, Miller observed that the soldiers' expressions changed remarkably. They could now "see the solid columns of the foe advance in plain sight every man seeming to step as proudly and steadily as if on parad and even while the artilery tears large gaps in thier line still on they come hardly faltiring for a moment[.]" This spectacle of war left the men still pale, "but see the firm compressed lips the eye fixed and [persevering?] and blood shot and the muscels rigid and the veins corugated and knoted and looking more like fiends than men[.]" When the order to charge came, "away we in to the very jaws of death and never for one moment faltering but yeling like devils to the mouths of the Canon and then to hear the wild triumphant cheer[.]" Yet in a few hours these men who had resembled devils would be ministering to the wounded left on the field, both friends and enemies, "with the kindness and tenderness of a woman[.]" Miller concluded that, "by the time you have seen this you will begin to think that a soldier has as many carackters as a cat is said to have lives[.]"[21]

Miller's description points to the fact that a soldier could not be well-defined in simple terms – either as patriotic hero or as savage beast. The war demanded a full range of responses from men. Miller understood that "a soldiers life is a sucession of extreems, first a long period of inactivity folowed by a time when all his energies both mental and phsical are taxed to the utmost[.]" The rapid and extreme changes that men underwent increased the anxiety created by the war. No one "character" would serve for a man in such an environment.[22]

This was true in other ways. The Massachusetts college student, Samuel Storrow, wrote home about the various physical tasks in which military life required proficiency. "When I get home I shall be qualified for any position, either that of a boot black, a cleaner of brasses, a washer – (wo)man, cook, chambermaid, hewer of wood & drawer of water, or, failing in all these I can turn beggar & go from door to door asking for 'broken vittles'. In all these I should feel prefectly at home by long practise therein." Storrow was middle class and was perhaps more amused – or chagrined – by his new roles than most soldiers were. But the occupations he lists were all notable for their lack of dignity. Most of them were associated with servants and other dependents; beggars commanded even less respect; and "hewer of wood & drawer of water" was a Biblical phrase that usually denoted a slave. These demeaning roles were unwelcome additions to one's image as a soldier and hero; they were ways in which military life broke down civilian ideas of status and identity.[23]

Another contradiction experienced by the soldier was that between his image of the volunteer as the preeminently virtuous patriot and the reality of the men with whom he shared army life. Where he had expected to find paragons, he found mortal men. Both the Union and Confederate armies had their share of petty thieves, drunkards, slackers, and other lowlife.

The camp was simultaneously immoral and virtuous, full of temptation and full of piety. Christopher Keller of the 124th Illinois was shocked by the temptations to vice open to men when they first went into camp after his regiment was raised in the fall of 1862. Apparently the other men of his company were shocked as well, for they soon voted to have their captain teach a regular Bible class. Shortly after their arrival Keller wrote a description of his camp that caught the two contrary impulses displayed there. "My bunkmate is reading his bible and in the bunk below they are having a prayer meeting on a small scale while others are cutting up, some swearing, some laughing, some writing, and others reading." He concluded that camp was "the place to see human nature in all its different varieties."[24]

Luther C. Furst, who volunteered early in the war, noted that "The history of the four kings" was the most popular book in camp. His discouragement with the immorality of the camp was deepened by his belief that the war was brought on by national wickedness. And a soldier in the 140th New York observed that the only reason many men in camp knew when it was Sunday was that stores were closed that day and they could buy no liquor.[25]

One Confederate pronounced camp "the last place for me or any other sivil man." The noise and misconduct of his fellow volunteers appalled him. And another deplored the absence of religion in camp. "I haven't heard a sermon in I can't tell when. You hear no more talk about religion here than if there was no such thing. The army is more demoralizing than I ever dreamed of. Three-fourths I recon, of the officers and men in this Regiment are profane swearers and card players."[26]

The contradiction between image and reality, the excitement and fear of combat, the psychological exhaustion caused by the extremes in a soldier's life, the dehumanization of the army, even the risk of bestialization – the volunteer had to suffer all these to fight for his cause. It is not surprising that he sometimes felt resentful of those who had remained at home and that he acquired a new identity as a soldier. It is not even surprising that some soldiers did act like the beasts that most soldiers feared they might become.

After the surrender of Confederate Gen. Joseph E. Johnston's army, Union Gen. W. T. Sherman marched his victorious soldiers north from Bennett Place, North Carolina, to Washington, DC Along the way they stopped to visit the battlefields of the east, where the Army of the Potomac had long struggled with Robert E. Lee's forces. Robert Strong's company passed through the Wilderness, where one of the greatest battles of the war had been fought. "Right in the line of breastworks stood a lone house," Strong remembered. "When we passed the house it was occupied only by women, not a single living man. They were surrounded by the bones of thousands of dead men."

The women in the house came to the door to watch the Union soldiers march by. One of Strong's fellow soldiers had picked up a skull from the battlefield. He greeted the women and asked them, "Did you have any friends in this fight?"

One of them replied her brother had been killed in the battle.

"Here is his head," the soldier said, and "tossed the skull in among them."[27]

Notes

1 S. H. Baldy to mother, May 31, 1861. Confederate Miscellany. Emory University Atlanta (hereafter EMORY).

2 David Herhert Donald, ed., *Gone for a Soldier: The Civil War Memoirs of Private Alfred Bellard* (Boston, 1975), 13.

3 John William DeForest's *Miss Ravenel's Conversion from Secession to Loyalty*, a fine novel written by a Union officer, touches upon this phenomenon and reveals particular bitterness about the place of the veteran in postwar America. For an account from another war, see Ford Madox Ford's *Parade's End*. Soldiers serve as a standing moral rebuke to civilians in times of crisis; one suspects that much of the contempt shown them by civilians springs from the need to project outward the emotions produced by one's own failure to participate in the great struggle. See also Charles Royster, " 'The Nature of Treason': Revolutionary Virtue and American Reactions to Benedict Arnold," *The William and Mary Quarterly*, 3rd Series, XXXVI (April 1979), 163–93, for a discussion of civilian attitudes during the American Revolution.

4 Rudolphe Rey to Miss Lizze DeVoe, June 14, 1865. Rey Papers. New-York Historical Society (NYHS). George Starbird to Marianne Starbird, October 21, 1863. Starbird Letters. Schoff Collection, Clements Library, University of Michigan (hereafter SCHOFF).

5 Habun R. Foster to Charles A. Wills, September 11, 1862. Mary J. Wills Papers, WM. Rufus W. Cater to Cousins Laurence and Fannie, June 1, 1863. Douglas J. and Rufus W. Cater Papers. Library of Congress (LC).

6 Benjamin F. Ashenfelter to father, September 26, 1862. Harrisburg Civil War Round Table collection. US Army Military History Institute (hereafter USAMHI).

7 Douglas J. Cater to Laurence, June 24, 1864. Douglas J. and Rufus W. Cater Papers. LC. Clifford Dowdey and Louis H. Manarin, eds., *The Wartime Papers of R. E. Lee* (Boston, 1961), 80.

8 Susan Previant Lee and Peter Passell, in their analysis of Claudia Goldin and Frank Lewis, "The Economic Cost of the American Civil War," *Journal of Economic History* 35 (June 1975), 304–9, reveal some of the limitations of economic history by admitting it cannot explain why the soldiers of both armies fought for so much less money than they should have received in light of "risk premiums" and "loss of future wages." They suggest, in the case of the Union army, "the difference between the actual human capital loss and the required risk premium paid reflected unmeasured non-material benefits the soldiers received in fighting for their cause(s)." *A New Economic View of American History*, (New York, 1979), 224–5. It would be disingenuous of me, however, to pretend that the Confederate and Union soldiers were not very much concerned with money; resentful of better-paid officers, bounty-jumping volunteers, and stay-at-homes who earned enough to buy their way out of the army, the soldiers worried about economic matters frequently. Patriotism does not blind, nor are those who experience it insensible to everything else.

9 John Pierson to daughter, March 26, 1863. John Pierson Letters. SCHOFF.

10 John Pierson to Joanna, July 15, 1863. John Pierson Letters. SCHOFF. See also the letter of a Pennsylvania laborer. "I also feele sorry that I could not send you some Money yet the pay day is past for over a month ago But as long as we are marching and fighting wee wont Draw any money and it wouldent do To draw any money now for wee could not send any home in any safety at at preasant for the is no express from here but I hope wee will soon get into camp and get our money I know you would need it veary Bad But I hope your friends will not lieve you suffer you must do the Best you can I hope everything will come rite after all for all that Abel Herrold wouldent Trust you that flower I ecspect the cause is becase he is a copper head and they cant any Thing Better be exspected of such a man as he is for that is coper head princiapels The time I Boated for him I had to wait 18 months for 40 dollars of my pay and he wont trust 5 dollars for a couple of weeks" John Carvel Arnold to wife, June 5, 1864. John Carvel Amold Papers. LC.

11 Henry H. Seys to Harriet Seys, October 23, 1863. Henry H. Seys Letters. SCHOFF.

12   John Rogers to family, May 15, 1862. Rogers Family Papers. Harrisburg Civil War Round Table Collection. USAMHI.

13   Christopher Howser Keller to George and Esther Keller, October 3, 1862. Christopher Howser Keller Letters. SCHOFF.

14   Harry Lewis to Mrs. John S. Lewis, February 15, 1863. Harry Lewis Papers. Southern Historical Collection, University of North Carolina, Chapel Hill (SHC).

15   Lyman C. Holford Diary, November 4, 1863. LC.

16   S. H. Eells to friends, June 25, 1862. S. H. Eells Papers. LC.

17   Henry I. Greer to mother, July 16, 1864. Henry I. and Robert Greer Papers. LC. R. S. Webb to mother, May 26, 1864. Webb Family Papers. SHC.

18   Harry Lewis to Mrs. John E. Lewis, August 20, 1863. Harry Lewis Papers. SHC. John Fleming, Civil War Recollections, 50, NYHS.

19   Pellona Alexander to Manning P. Alexander, April 14, 1862. Manning P. and Pellona David Alexander Letters. University of Georgia (UG).

20   James T. Miller to Joseph Miller, May 24, 1863. James T. Miller to Robert and Jane Miller, June 6, 1863. Miller Brothers Letters. SCHOFF.

21   James T. Miller to William Miller, June 8, 1863. Miller Brothers Letters, SCHOFF.

22   James T. Miller to Robert and Jane Miller, February 18, 1863. Miller Brothers Letters. SCHOFF.

23   Samuel Storrow to parents, December 4, 1862. Samuel Storrow Papers. Massachusetts Historical Society, Boston.

24   Christopher H. Keller to Caroline M. Hall, September 14, 1862, September 21, 1862; to George and Esther Keller, September 14, 1862. Christopher H. Keller Letters. SCHOFF.

25   Luther C. Furst Diary, May 12, 1861, June 1, 1861, June 2, 1861. Harrisburg Civil War Round Table Collection. USAMHI. Frank Appleton Badger to mother, September 21, 1862. Alfred M. Badger Papers. LC.

26   H. H. Green to J. M. Davis, May 28, 1862. Malcolm Letters. UG. Alexander Smith Webb to sister, February 6, 1862. Webb Family Papers. SHC.

27   Ashley Halsey, ed. *A Yankee Private's Civil War by Robert Hale Strong* (Chicago, 1961), 205.

Questions to consider

- How would you describe the relationship between soldiers and civilians in Civil War armies?

- How do wars change social relationships in societies?

- How was the experience of returning Civil War soldiers similar to, or different from, those of other wars?

Chapter 9

"For the Boys in Blue":
Organizing the US Sanitary Commission

Jeanie Attie

Soldiers weren't the only people transformed by the experience of the Civil War. Like their counterparts who left home, civilians who stayed behind – especially women – found themselves faced with tasks they had never previously undertaken. Sometimes these tasks were relatively simple, like milking a cow. Other times they were more complex, like running a business. Even before the war, some American women distinguished themselves as having the desire and talent to move far beyond their accepted "sphere" of home and family, often by using the imperatives of home and family to justify challenging the status quo.

The Civil War created many more opportunities of this kind than had ever existed before for American women. Of particular importance in this regard was the formation of the United States Sanitary Commission, an organization that gathered supplies, distributed relief, provided nursing services, and in countless other ways served soldiers in the field and in hospitals. The USSC demonstrated the tremendous, even awesome, power of a modern institution in an industrial society – and, to the evident nervousness of some – the tremendous, even awesome, power of American women in that society.

In this excerpt from her 1998 book *Patriotic Toil: Northern Women and the American Civil War*, Jeanie Attie explores the challenges – challenges of logistics as well as challenges to authority – faced by the men who enlisted women's help in launching the USSC.

Jeanie Attie, " 'For the Boys in Blue': Organizing the Home Front," in *Patriotic Toil: Northern Women and the American Civil War* (Ithaca, NY: Cornell University Press, 1998), pp. 87–91; 99–104. Copyright © by Cornell University. Used by permission of the publisher, Cornell University Press.

The men who created the United States Sanitary Commission never anticipated that the greater part of their energies would be occupied by persuading northern women to participate in their project. Having witnessed the explosion of female support for mobilization during the first days and weeks of the war, they assumed that women would embrace a plan that promised to maximize the impact of their benevolence. For Sanitary Commission leaders, the key to success lay in their "wise foresight and perfect comprehension" of the gendered division of social authority in American society, an understanding that would enable them to manipulate the nonpolitical arena of feminized benevolence to serve their own version of nationhood. The "most novel and striking characteristics of our American civilization," wrote commission historian Charles Stillé, was the fact that benevolent organizations "had been for a long time under the control and management almost excusively of women." When the USSC "sought to make the women of the country its agents in the vast work of supplying . . . the Government in its care of the Army," it did so with a unique appreciation of the antebellum compromise on gender or, as Stillé phrased it, the "peculiar position which [women] occupy in a democratic society like ours."[1]

At the outset of USSC operations, the commissioners expected that their most challenging task would involve revamping an outmoded, entrenched War Department bureaucracy and advising the Medical Bureau to adopt modern sanitary and medical procedures. The commission's "great object," recalled Henry Bellows, was to "develop, strengthen and support the regular medical and military authorities and methods." Yet by war's end, people believed the commission's "chief business" had been "the collection and distribution of voluntary supplies." "The vast proportions [relief] assumed, during the progress of the war," remarked Stillé, "were due to circumstances, which it was impossible to have foreseen from the beginning."[2]

What the men of the USSC did not foresee was the extent to which their relief scheme involved an incursion into the social prerogatives middle-class women had acquired in the decades before the war, namely dominance over the welfare needs of their communities and the labor conducted within their households. The commission, of course, was not repudiating female philanthropy; in fact, it called for greater discretionary efforts on the part of the public. But its assertion of control over the destination and uses of women's gifts carried with it the imputation that customary methods of benevolence were inadequate to winning a war, even perilous for a nascent army requiring systematic care. By declaring that a national emergency rendered unpaid female labor a form of military materiel that could legitimately be requisitioned for the war, the commission plan suffused housework and voluntarism with national political purposes. At the same time, however, by defining benevolence as a province of the state requiring the supervision of elite men, it also declared that women's control over domesticity and charity was no longer inviolate.

Making claims in the name of defending the nation for rights to the products of women's household labor was one thing; commanding that labor was another matter. Indeed, as soon as the commission postulated that women's homemade gifts were goods owed the state in a military emergency, it broached a number of potentially disruptive problems that were only dimly glimpsed in the early weeks of the war. What, in fact, was a woman's obligation to the state in wartime? What was more important for the Union cause: women's labor or women's loyalty? Did female benevolence extend past community boundaries to the nation as a whole? How could a plan that was predicated on the antebellum gender ideology – a romanticized construction that asserted women's inherent proclivities for domesticity and charity – expect easy compliance when it erased the allocation of power that gave the gendered separation of economic responsibilities its legitimacy? By placing so much emphasis on the products of women's housework, the Sanitary Commission scheme came close to unmasking the fiction that household labor produced no market value, that it was merely a leisurely or instinctual endeavor.

The confidence with which the commissioners began their enterprise was reinforced by the early successes of the Woman's Central Relief Association. The women's organization appeared to have gained acceptance from local women's groups with relative ease. But the WCRA's structure and mode of operation differed significantly from the organization Bellows and his colleagues created. In contrast to the WCRA's willingness merely to coordinate the workings of existing charitable groups, the Sanitary Commission's nationalist vision was premised on a network of uniformly structured societies dedicated to soldier relief and answerable solely to the central agency. Intent on fostering wholly new benevolent entities, the commission devoted considerable energy to communicating with the loyal female public about the bureaucratic framework and the procedures it considered essential for maintaining competent aid societies.

Among the USSC's first messages to the female homefront was a call to form a soldiers' aid society in every village and city in the North. In order to justify such a sweeping step, it reiterated stories that women's spontaneous benevolence was creating chaos at the front by deluging the army with useless goods. Explaining to women the problems they had caused, the commission carefully couched its criticism within a sentimentalized account of the work they had already initiated: "The churches, the schools, the parlors, the bedchambers, were alive with the patriotic industry of those whose fingers could not rest while a stitch could be set, a bandage torn, for the relief of the brave soldiers." Before long, the "little circles and associations, with patriotic intent . . . were multiplying, like rings in the water, over the face of the whole country."[3] But the cumulative impact of these random efforts was problematic, for although "the stream" was in "full flow," it was guided by zeal rather than discretion. Worse still, the army was "inundated by a flood of public bounty, wasting itself where it was not wanted." Given the "immense mischief" such charitable efforts might create "if allowed to run wild," it was necessary to establish some control over these "national impulses." The commission's "purpose" was "to systematize the impulsive, disorderly, and uninformed sympathies and efforts of the women of the country so as to make effective . . . the generous and restless desires to help the young army."[4]

Although the commission justified its intervention in homefront relief on the grounds that women's early wartime benevolence had been effusive and disorganized, the reality was very different. While many women had taken it upon themselves to aid departing relatives and outfit local regiments, these activities were usually conducted on an ad hoc, personal, and temporary basis. In fact, by the middle of 1861, many towns were still without a soldiers' aid society. "The Spring of 1861 & nearly the whole Summer passed away, without any organized movement in this place," explained the secretary of the Fayetteville, New York, Ladies Soldiers Aid Society. Though "every loyal woman felt constantly self-reproved for her inaction" and "many sent their offerings through distant societies," the remoteness of this "small country village" inhibited a more concerted effort.[5]

Women who did not see fit to establish permanent soldiers' aid societies may not have been apathetic or inexperienced in civic affairs, for no one expected a long or exceedingly destructive war. The first call for volunteers stipulated only a three-month military term, and men rushed to volunteer in part because they shared the belief that the war would be brief. Young men raised with literary images of military heroes welcomed the opportunity to attain their own piece of historical glory.[6] One soldier remembered that, during the early days of the war, "the belief then was almost universal throughout the North that the war would amount to nothing much but a summer frolic, and would be over by the 4th of July."[7] Like the men who volunteered for military service, homefront women too assumed that violence and bloodshed would be kept to a minimum. Mrs. Bordwell from Corinovia, New York, noted that the women in her town "accepted Secretary Seward's prophecy respecting the duration of the struggle, and did not at first deem any organization necessary." (Corinovia women did not organize formally until the middle of 1862).[8] For a brief and doubtlessly triumphant conflict, local regiments could be adequately cared for by the redirected energies of existing philanthropic agencies.

Whether or not it was aware of the fragile state of homefront organizing, the commission moved ahead with its scheme to create a network of local societies that would form a resilient infrastructure for its welfare experiment. In October 1861, it distributed 40,000 copies of a circular, composed by Frederick Law Olmsted, endorsed by President Lincoln, and addressed to the "Loyal Women of America," that spelled out the USSC plan for structuring relief and channeling supplies to the army.[9]

[. . .]

Forming a soldiers' aid society was a far cry from sustaining it. Although few groups were as short-lived as the Patriotic Aid Society of Dickinson Centre, New York, which lasted only five days, many were only intermittent affairs. "The maintaining of an organization of this kind is far more difficult than one would imagine," reported the secretary of the Black Creek Aid Society of New York. Attendance at meetings "grew less and less until there were but two or three who manifested any interest," and the group managed to stay together only for "a season." The women of Bloomsburg, Pennsylvania, credited a Sanitary Commission directive for their decision to organize, but "as time wore and discouragements arose, a great number wearied and fell by the way." A number of societies dispersed and reconstituted themselves over the course of the war. The women of Ashville, New York, organized themselves in October 1861, disbanded after a brief period of work, and then reconstituted a society in the summer of 1862. Even a male correspondent to the WCRA recognized that warwork imposed unusual burdens on busy women; explaining in early 1864 why his wife and other women of Vernon, New Jersey, no longer sent contributions, he noted, "you have no idea what hard work those ladies found it."[10]

Though the USSC enjoyed only limited success in reforming women's charitable behavior, it was remarkably, if inadvertently, effective in stimulating correspondence from women throughout the North. From the moment the organization undertook the coordination of supply work and stretched its probing arm into the hinterland, news from the homefront poured into both national headquarters and branch offices from a female public anxious to explain its successes and failures. Women wrote unsolicited letters as well as answers to personal inquiries and, later, formal questionnaires. Stimulating a unique dialogue among the male commissioners, the female branch leaders, and themselves, northern women created an arena in which they could articulate the enormity of housework, the economic and political complexions of their communities, and the special hardships the war had imposed on their lives. Usually written to explain why they were unable to satisfy specific USSC requests, their correspondence challenged prevailing assumptions about household labor and revealed common difficulties among women in various regions. Repeatedly, women pointed to the lack of economic resources, conflicting personal and family responsibilities, and skepticism about the project's rationale as the most persistent hindrances to regular warwork. The sources of homefront resistance to Sanitary Commission entreaties were varied, but fostering sustained, voluntary labor for national purposes was clearly an unreliable and politically charged undertaking.

In industrial towns and agricultural regions alike, the commission scheme jeopardized delicately balanced economies, now under the added burdens of war. For towns such as Altoona, Pennsylvania, whose inhabitants were "mainly railroad operatives of limited means," there was the problem of enlisting working-class women to assume middle-class functions. As the Altoona Society's secretary, Charlotte Lewis, explained, little was accomplished, "there being a great scarcity of the class of women at all accustomed to act outside the home." Around the country the commission heard numerous complaints of distressed households. "A great many plead poverty," wrote Mrs. Bradfield from Hardin County, Iowa. The women of North

Billerica, Massachusetts, who collected donations at the beginning of the war, reported that "living became so expensive" they accomplished little more.[11]

Poor women in the WCRA region wrote to Louisa Lee Schuyler and her associates intimate, oftentimes moving, descriptions of households and local economies hard hit by the war. The head of the Dorcas Society in Lodi, New York, wrote in April 1862 that they were forwarding their last package to the commission. "And I am very sorry," she added, "but the place is a factory village and the inhabitants are mostly Hollanders and all are a laboring class of people and lately work has been scarce and Money hard to get and consequently have no funds to work with."[12] "I hardly dare now to make another specific and immediate requisition," explained a Cortland Village, New York, woman in November 1861. Though hers was "a charming rural region," farm sizes were small and the soil "only adapted to grasing." In a pointed rebuke to USSC assumptions about appealing for the "boys in blue," she elucidated the economic realities of her town's women. "We have *three* flourishing academies, no thieves or beggars, but there are not a dozen opulent individuals in the county! Nineteen out of every twenty articles I have sent to you have been made by the personal labor of people who employ no servants. . . . With such facts, in view, dear Madam, you can easily conceive why it would not be very gracious in me to cry 'another for Hector' *too* often."[13]

Notwithstanding high transportation costs and war-inflated prices for cotton and wool, it appeared that rural women were disproportionately generous contributors to the Sanitary Commission project. The women of Ellsworth, New York, may have been typical: describing themselves as "merely country people with slender purses," they regularly donated to the army.[14] In the commission's estimation, the reason that provincial areas proved more generous than did major cities such as New York was obvious: urban bourgeois women who had established their own philanthropic organizations stood to lose the most by relinquishing authority to a national organization and, as Louisa Schuyler recognized, were most likely to feel competitive with the commission. "The *love of power*, which so blinds the eyes of the city people, does not extend in the country," she wrote to Olmsted in 1863. "I feel as if I never could say enough about the noble spirit of self sacrifice found in these little villages. They never *see* anything & work from pure faith & principle."[15]

Moved by the sentiments of poorer women from rural locales, Schuyler nevertheless knew that the organization's well-being depended on its ability to tap the assets of wealthy men and the philanthropic capacities of upperclass women. As early as the fall of 1861, the Woman's Central Relief Association boasted of maintaining correspondence with "several hundred names of prominent ladies in different states." Eliza Schuyler routinely called upon her elite peers to sustain flagging supply work and direct their attentions to the commission. "I am engaged in writing to influential ladies," she reported to Alfred Bloor at the end of 1862, "to inform their circles, and influence them against local and partial organisations." Propertied women, after all, were "so much more easily affected by personal influences."[16]

Yet even the advantages of class could not undo the constraints posed by gender inequities in economic power; the reality was that nearly all women were dependent on their male relatives for money. After women's personal household surpluses were exhausted, contributions from individual men and local businesses sometimes constituted the only means for continuing soldier aid work. When commission agent William Hobart Hadley found people in Portsmouth, New Hampshire, expressing the "strong belief that they have done more for their soldiers than any other towns or cities in the Union," the women confided to him that such views held by the men dimmed the prospects for continuing warwork. "Their ladies assured me that they were unable to beg enough of the men to purchase materials to keep themselves in work."[17]

If women lacked influence over men in public forums, they were equally vulnerable to men's decision making power at home. Some correspondents alluded to the inequitable balance of power in nineteenth-century marriages to illuminate why their donations were not as large as they had hoped. Mrs. Delilah Allen confided to the WCRA: "My husband lacks or has not my opinions of doing for those who have fought for our country's freedom. . . . I have with my horse and carriage done much but it has been to the distaste of my husband." "Politics ran high with us," Mrs. Augustus Lippincott admitted to Commissioner Blatchford at the war's end, "and Mothers and daughters were apt to work according to the opinions of Husbands & Fathers." Given the political polarization in her Hills Grove, New York, town, "there was not much harmony in regard to things relating to the war." A Bergen, New York, correspondent complained of women who "were more interested in their husbands' politics than in the suffering of soldiers," adding a special partisan rebuke for Republican women; since their men had caused the war, she reasoned, "their wives might take care of the soldiers."[18]

But the greatest constraints on women's abilities to participate in warwork were the rigors of their domestic labors. Time and again female correspondents cited household chores, childcare responsibilities, and family illnesses as the chief reasons for neglecting requests for their charity. For the majority of women, who employed no household help, housework burdens were onerous. Explaining why her neighbors failed to sustain a soldiers' aid society, Miss Denroche wrote that the few who wanted to work felt they could not do it alone and added that "some have large families of sick or young children." Sarah Bradford of Geneva, New York, informed the WCRA that she had to resign as secretary of her local aid society, "having many other cares & duties claiming my attention."[19]

These letters were extraordinary in their explication of the laborious nature of household tasks. For decades northern women had been surrounded by dictates that cast their domestic work as the antithesis of labor, indeed, as something approaching a leisurely pursuit.[20] Bellows himself had employed the language of leisure to explain how women were able to produce so much for the army during the war. But the escalating demands for the products of housework led some women to glimpse problems in cultural formulations that cast their existence as free of work. Women such as Miss Denroche used the opportunity of corresponding with the commission to delineate the realities of their household labor, possibly to acquire recognition for the otherwise invisible efforts that defined their lives: "I am shut in school from 8 ½ untill 4 PM every day. I have all my own housekeeping to do and we have no baker here. . . . I have an acre and three quarters of land to take care of out of school and in winter all my wood to saw and split at least I had to do it until a week since I found it was injuring my health. . . . you must see I have not much leisure."[21]

Notes

1 Charles J. Stillé, *History of the United States Sanitary Commission* (Philadelphia, 1866), pp. 170–1.

2 Bellows, "U.S. Sanitary Commission," p. 73; Stillé, *History of the United States Sanitary Commission*, p. 166.

3 "The origin, organization, and working of the women's Central Association of Relief", in us Sanitary Commission document no. 32, *Report Concerning the Women's Central Association of Relief* (New York, 1861) I.S (all USSC numbered documents are collected in *Documents of the US Sanitary Commission*, (2 vols.) [New York, 1866] hereafter cited as Documents). *Documents*, 1:5.

4 "Statement of the Object and Method of the Sanitary Commission – with Supplement," December 7, 1863, no. 69, *Documents*, 2:49; Bellows, "U.S. Sanitary Commission," p. 73.

5   Fayetteville Ladies Soldiers Aid Society, 1866, Box 981, USSC Papers.
6   Charles Royster, *The Destructive War: William Tecumseh Sherman, Stonewall Jackson, and the Americans* (New York, 1991), pp. 252–3.
7   Leander Stillwell, *The Story by a Common Soldier of Army Life in the Civil War, 1861–1865* (Erie[?] KSN., 1920), p. 9.
8   Mrs. P. Bordwell to USSC, 1866, Box 981, USSC Papers.
9   The "Letter" was addressed to all "Countrywomen," though the only branch in existence was the Woman's Central Relief Association, which covered women living in New York State and parts of Connecticut, Rhode Island, Massachusetts and New Jersey. See "To the Loyal Women of America," October 1, 1861, no. 32, *Documents*, 1:35–43. Olmsted noted the number of appeals in a letter to his half-sister, Frederick Law Olmsted to Mary Olmsted, November 6, 1861, in *FLO Papers*, 4:219–22.
10 Mrs. L. M. Stowe, April 30, 1866; Mrs. J. E. Caldwell, April 9, 1866; Hannah J. John to Jno. S. Blatchford, April 6, 1866; Mrs. R. Roselle Ticknor to Blatchford, April 16, 1866, Box 981; C. Allen, M.D., to Miss Marshall, January 25, 1864, Box 671, USSC Papers.
11 Charlotte L. Lewis to Jno. S. Blatchford, April 19, 1866, Box 980; Mrs. L. M. Bradfield to Mr. Blatchford, April 19, 1866, Box 986; Eliza A. Rogers to Blatchford, April 28, 1866, Box 983, USSC Papers.
12 A. D. Amerman to Louisa L. Schuyler, April 21, 1861, Box 655, USSC Papers.
13 Mrs. Henry S. Randall to Louisa L. Schuyler, November 24, 1861, Box 654, USSC Papers.
14 Rhoda S. Briggs, 1866, Box 981, USSC Papers.
15 Louisa L. Schuyler to Frederick L. Olmsted, May 20, 1863, Box 955, USSC Papers. See also William Quentin Maxwell, *Lincoln's Fifth Wheel: The Political History of the United States Sanitary Commission* (New York, 1956), p. 91.
16 Eliza H. Schuyler to F. L. Olmsted, November 8, 1861, Box 965; Eliza H. Schuyler to A. J. Bloor, December 3, 1862, Box 954, USSC Papers.
17 See George O. Glavis to Dr. Bellows, February 7, 1863, on reliance on upper-class women to raise money; H. Hadley to H. Bellows, December 2, 1861, Box 640, USSC Papers.
18 Mrs. Delilah Allen, February 11, 1863, Box 669; Mrs. Augustus Lippincott to Blatchford, July 2, 1866, Box 980; Mrs. Michstrussen, 1866, Box 981, USSC Papers.
19 E. S. Denroche to Mrs. Helen W. Marshall, January 25, 1864, Box 671; Sarah H. Bradford to Mrs. Marshall, January 25, 1864, Box 671, USSC Papers.
20 Jeanne Boydston argues that rhetoric about women's leisure constituted a central feature in what she terms the "pastoralization of housework." See *Home and Work: Housework, Wages, and the Ideology of Labor in the Early Republic* (New York, 1990), pp. 147–52.
21 Denroche to Marshall, January 25, 1864, Box 671, USSC Papers.

Questions to consider

- What were some of the challenges facing men who wished to enlist the help of women in relief work?

- How would you describe the relationship between local and national relief efforts led by women?

- How did the kind of work women did at home affect the quality and quantity they did for the USSC?

- What would you say were the strengths and limitations of volunteer labor, military or civilian, in wartime? Is professional paid labor more desirable? In what ways?

Chapter 10

The Home Front: Primary Sources

Diary Entry

Gertrude Clanton Thomas

Soldiers were not the only people to experience the deprivation and despair of war, and not only because the line between home front and battle front collapsed in places like Fredericksburg, VA, or Vicksburg, MS, (not to mention countless farms elsewhere literally caught in the crossfire). The war cast long shadows even on those far from the fighting. Gertrude Clanton Thomas was the mistress of a relatively large plantation in Georgia when she wrote the following diary entry in the summer of 1864. What has the war done to her life – and what has the war done to her thinking?

Diary of Gertrude Clanton Thomas, (September 17, 1864), in "Slavery, War, and Emancipation," from *The Secret Eye: The Journal of Gertrude Clanton Thomas*, ed. Virginia Ingraham Burr (Chapel Hill: University of North Carolina Press, 1990), pp. 276–7.

[. . .]

Saturday, September 17, 1864 . . . How I do wish this war was over. I wish to breathe free. I feel pent up, confined – cramped and shall I confess it am reminded of that Italian story of *The Iron Shroud* where daily – daily hourly and momently the room contracts, the victim meanwhile utterly impotent to avert the impending doom. Never have I so fully realised the feeble hold upon this world's goods as I do now. I don't think I have ever enjoyed that peculiarly charming season the Indian Summer more than I have during the past few weeks. Looking up the three Avenues and at the Goats Cows and Horses so quietly walking about, listening at the cooing of Pigions, the chirping of the different fowls in the yard – I imagine this contrasted with men clad in Yankee uniform rudely violating the privacy of my home. I imagine the booming of Yankee cannon and the clash of Yankee sabres and I ask myself how soon shall this thing be?? Nor does it require an imaginative mind to foretell such an event but the last page of my Journal must bear no such cowardly record.

I have sometimes doubted on the subject of slavery. I have seen so many of its evils chief among which is the terribly demoralising influence upon our men and boys but of late I have become convinced the Negro *as a race* is better off with us as he has been than if he were made free, but I am by no means so sure that we would not gain by his having his freedom given him. I grant that I am not so philanthropic as to be willing voluntarily to give all we own for the sake of the principle, but I do think that if we had the same invested in something else as a means of support I would willingly, nay gladly, have the responsibility of them taken off my shoulders....

[...]

Letter to Norfleet Perry

Fannie Perry

For many loved ones, the essence of the Civil War experience was separation. Fanny Perry was a slave in Texas; her husband, Norfleet, accompanied his master's son, who served in the Texas Cavalry. This letter was probably written by Fanny Perry's mistress. How would you describe the feelings Fanny expresses toward her husband? How does she seek to comfort him and herself?

Fanny Perry, "Letter to Norfleet Perry, Spring Hill, Texas" (December 28, 1862), in *We Are Your Sisters: Black Women in the Nineteenth Century*, ed. Dorothy Sterling (New York: Norton, 1984), p. 240. From *The Journal of Negro History*, vol. 65, no. 4, (Autumn 1980), 363–4. Reprinted by permission of the Association for the Study of African American Life and History.

My Dear Husband: Spring Hill, [Texas,] December 28, 1862.

I would be mighty glad to see you and I wish you would write back here and let me know how you are getting on. I am doing tolerable well and have enjoyed very good health since you left. I haven't forgot you nor I never will forget you as long as the world stands, even if you forget me. My love is just as great as it was the first night I married you, and I hope it will be so with you. If I never see you again, I hope to meet you in Heaven. There is no time night or day but what I am studying about you. I heard once that you were sick but I heard afterwards that you had got well. I hope your health will be good hereafter. Master gave us three days Christmas. I wish you could have been here to enjoy it with me for I did not enjoy myself much because you were not here. Mother, Father, Grandmama, Brothers & Sisters say Howdy and they hope you will do well. Be sure to answer this soon for I am always glad to hear from you. I hope it will not be long before you can come home.

Your Loving Wife
Fannie

Letter to Solomon Steward

Emma Steward

The ultimate form of separation was death, a gulf experienced by millions of Americans in the Civil War. The pain was all the greater when people died far from those who loved them. This moving letter was sent by Emma Steward to her husband Solomon, who served in the First South Carolina Volunteers, the first regiment of former slaves to be inducted into the US Army. How does she depict the death of their child? And what kinds of struggles does she continue to face?

Emma Steward to Solomon Steward, Fernandina, Florida, (February 8, 1864), in *We Are Your Sisters: Black Women in the Nineteenth Century*, ed. Dorothy Sterling (New York: Norton, 1984), p. 241.

My Dear Husband: Fernandina, Florida, February 8, [1864]

   This Hour I Sit Me Down To write you In a Little world of sweet sounds. The Choir In the Chapel near Here are Chanting at The Organ and Thair Morning Hymn are sounding and The Dear Little birds are joining Thair voices In Tones sweet and pure as angels whispers. But My Dear a sweeter song Than That I now Hear and That Is The song of a administering angel Has Come and borne My Dear Little babe To Join with Them. My babe only Live one day. It was a Little Girl. Her name Is alice Gurtrude steward. I am now sick in bed and have Got nothing To Live on. The Rashion That They Give for six days I Can Make It Last but 2 days. They dont send Me any wood. I dont Get any Light at all. You Must see To That as soon as possible for I am In want of some Thing To Eat.

All the family send thair love to you. No more at pressant

Emma Steward

Letter to Lydia Bixby

Abraham Lincoln

One of the most difficult challenges for anyone who wishes to provide comfort to those in grief involves coming up with meaningful words of condolence. The challenge was all the greater during the Civil War, when death was numbingly common, and efforts to solace inevitably sounded clichéd. Abraham Lincoln, who undertook this task frequently as the conflict raged, was understandably daunted when he sat down to write a letter to Lydia Bixby, whom he mistakenly believed had lost five sons (it later turned out that only two died in the service, and a third, who was captured, may have died in a Confederate prison). How would you describe his strategy in expressing sympathy for Mrs. Bixby? How effective is it?

Abraham Lincoln to Lydia Bixby, Washington, DC, in *Abraham Lincoln: Speeches and Writings*, 1859–1865, ed. Don Fehrenbacher (New York: Library of America, 1989), p. 644.

Executive Mansion, Washington

Dear Madam, – I have been shown in the files of the War Department a statement of the Adjutant General of Massachusetts, that you are the mother of five sons who have died gloriously on the field of battle.

I feel how weak and fruitless must be any words of mine which should attempt to beguile you from the grief of a loss so overwhelming. But I cannot refrain from tendering to you the consolation that may be found in the thanks of the Republic they died to save.

I pray that our Heavenly Father may assuage the anguish of your bereavement, and leave you only the cherished memory of the loved and lost, and the solemn pride that must be yours, to have laid so costly a sacrifice upon the altar of Freedom. Yours, very sincerely and respectfully,

Part V

Wartime Economies

Plate 7 Heavy Metal: Washington, DC, Workmen in front of the Trimming Shop, April, 1865. The Civil War both created possibilities and imposed limits on industrial workers seeking to organize for better working conditions. (Selected Civil War photographs, Library of Congress)

Chapter 11

Industrial Workers and the Costs of War

Philip S. Paludan

Wars transform the ways societies work – "work" in the specific sense of the manner in which people perform their occupations, as well as "work" in the more general sense of how effectively a community functions. Wars expand and collapse economies, create and spread new forms of technology, hasten the rise and fall of private fortunes, and subject citizens to economic shocks (like rapidly rising prices) that are beyond anyone's control. The outcome of battles on remote fields often shape the destinies of nations, but the reality of wars for ordinary citizens is often felt in shops and homes not even singed by gunfire.

It is generally agreed that the American Civil War was a major turning point in American economic history. Instead of a nation based on agriculture, whether feudal, capitalistic, or both, the die was cast – to use a fitting metaphor – for a nation built on industrial capitalism. Factories and free labor, not farms and slaves, would represent the future. For the South, this change would mark the end of a way of life; for the North, it would intensify trends (particularly the importance of financial institutions) whose outlines were already clearly established.

Yet the term "free labor," coined to identify the alternative to slave labor, did not seem entirely accurate for the millions of American workers, many of them immigrants, who labored in Union factories during the Civil War. Often paid subsistence wages at best, and regarded with disdain or worse by nativists, these people struggled with multiple kinds of adversity, even as they made crucial contributions (sometimes reluctantly or even with hostility) to the war effort. They also made efforts to organize themselves by occupation, a quest that proved quite difficult during the war and after, and yet one that would persist, with real success, in the coming century.

In this excerpt from his 1988 book *"A People's Contest": The Union and Civil War*, Phillip Shaw Paludan explores the challenges facing industrial workers during the conflict. The war, Paludan argues, was a crucible for a labor movement not yet ready for prime time. Yet the obstacles workers and their leaders faced helped them formulate the strategies that would bear fruit later.

Phillip Shaw Paludan, "Industrial Workers and the Costs of War," in "A People's Contest":
The Union and Civil War, 1861–1865 (New York: Harper & Row, 1988), pp. 170–97.

There were more than 9 million workers in the North. Almost 3,500,000 of them, farmers and farm laborers, directly benefited from the boom in agriculture. Another 5,600,000 workers found employment off the farms or engaged in professional or domestic service, trade, transportation, manufacturing, mining, and mechanical industries. These were domestic servants, laborers, teachers, clerks, railroad workers, middlemen, blacksmiths, boot and shoemakers, carpenters, cotton mill workers, miners, tailors. Those linked to the farm economy experienced good times, too. But a growing proportion of Northern workers lived in the growing industrial world, gathering together in increasing numbers in shops and factories and on work gangs. In this population about a million people were self-employed and/or company officials, but the majority worked for someone else. These were the workers who forecast the future structure of the economy. They were also the workers whose fate had caused so much prewar attention.[1]

Although their work experience forecast a modern industrial society, that society was not yet in place in the war years. Older localistic contexts endured side by side with a burgeoning industrial environment. Workers experienced this new world in that older context. While nationalizing forces moved in the land, local communities were dominant in the lives of almost everyone. Few workers were organized. A reasonable estimate puts the number at approximately 300,000, less than 10 percent of all industrial workers in the 1860s belonging to local or regional organizations. As of 1860 there were only five national unions: the Printers, the Stonecutters, the Hat Finishers, the Iron Molders, and the Machinists. When workers sought protection or progress they formed local mixed trade assemblies – uniting delegates from workingmen's clubs, trade unions, and general reform societies that were interested in workingmen's problems. Such assemblies usually sought political power, but occasionally they supported boycotts and strikes by member organizations or acted as bargainers in settlements.

Most organizations were weak. In a one-industry town, workers could control politics. Shoemakers in Lynn, Massachusetts, created the Workingman's party in 1860 and took over town government. But in larger cities assemblies lacked the numbers for political clout. When workers tried to oust a Republican mayor of Philadelphia in 1865, they failed. Efforts to organize national trade assemblies during the war were equally unsuccessful. When Robert Gilchrist, president of the Louisville assembly, called for a July 1864 meeting of all the trade assemblies in Canada and the United States, the response was so poor that he issued another call, this time for September. "There are 200,000 mechanics now represented in protective unions in the United States and Canada," he proclaimed. Twelve delegates showed up representing eight cities in eight states. After writing a constitution and planning an organization they disbanded, calling for a second conference in 1865. This meeting never took place.[2]

The National Iron Molders – perhaps the strongest of the national unions – suggests the puny power of organized labor. Membership in the eighteen locals was mixed. Some locals consisted of skilled workers only; others mixed skilled and unskilled. Some had only a handful of members; others, like that at Troy, New York, hundreds. Dues ranged from ten cents a month in Philadelphia to fifty dollars a year in Troy and Albany. Some locals could spend hundreds of dollars to carpet meeting halls; others had trouble paying rent. Some of the locals were quite businesslike, focusing on economic issues and discussions; others resembled secret lodges with mysterious initiation ceremonies, secret passwords, and even public silence about being union members.

The driving force of the national organization was William Sylvis, who became secretary of the Philadelphia local in 1859 and helped found the national organization. Defeated for the presidency, he was chosen national secretary and by 1863 took over as president, a post with no treasury and no control over the locals. Sylvis set out to create a national union in fact. Throughout the winter of 1862–3 he begged and borrowed his way from city to city. Some locals paid for his visits, others didn't. Some promised to and never did. At some stops he raised money for the next leg of his journey. At other stops he met local police and employers who put him quickly back on the train. Sylvis created an impressive number of new locals. But the national body remained frail.

There were strong locals that might win strikes at times. The number of locals grew under Sylvis' activity. But even at the end of the war in 1866 Sylvis could still deplore "the selfish and senseless croaking and opposition of some whose vision is so contracted that they cannot see beyond the narrow limits of the little village in which they live."[3]

Sylvis foresaw the shape of a national economy to come. But the immediate situation saw local communities confronting the early inroads of a national economy. Conflict of interest between labor and management was often difficult to visualize, as small communities engendered social and personal relationships between employer and worker. Even in a good-sized place like Lynn, Massachusetts, where the process of industrialization was unmistakable, workers still called for harmony of interest between owners and workers. During their great strike of 1860 workers applauded some of the factory owners even while protesting against others. And the outrage that most disturbed these workers was an effort by some of the larger owners to bring outside police into the community to enforce order. Other communities witnessed alliances between local workers and local merchants and businessmen against the efforts of national companies, usually railroads, to put down worker demands for better pay, shorter hours, and improved working conditions.[4]

The generally small size of the workplace also restrained labor militance. The most outspoken criticism of the industrial system targeted factories where masses of men and women swarmed like machines serving other machines. But the average manufacturing establishment as of 1860 did not look like that. There were about 19 workers per manufacturing establishment in New England, slightly over 10 in the middle states, and a little under 6 in the West. The whole North as of 1860 found an average of 9.34 workers in each of the approximately 140,433 manufactories.

But these figures hid signs of growing industrialization in the United States, and the growth of labor consciousness in certain pockets in the North, especially in textiles, shoes, iron, and machine manufacture. While most factories in the cities were not large by modern standards, every large city had factories of considerable size. By 1870 Cincinnati had about 4,400 manufacturing establishments employing some 61,000 workers – an average of about 14 hands per firm. But 17 of those firms employed over 5,250 of Cincinnati's workers. This small number averaged 310 hands. In New York City the average number of hands employed in the city's leading manufactories was 24.4, but almost 40 percent of the employees worked in the clothing industries where shops averaging over 70 were the rule.[5]

The factory work force reflected the concentration of industry, which had been going on for several years. The work force grew in size, but the number of places people worked diminished. This concentration worried observers. The *New York Times* headlined an 1869 story: "Concentration of Capital in the Hands of Few – Employers Becoming Fewer and

Laborers More Numerous – the Rich Richer, the Poor Poorer." The *Times* suggested that if more workers would decide to live outside the big cities, this trend might be reversed, but the figures kept on going the other way, and the paper caught the analogy that had become common throughout the war era: "The capitalists or masters are becoming fewer and stronger and richer.... the laborers or slaves are becoming more numerous or weaker and poorer."[6]

These forces were at work in the country as it moved into the Civil War. But their effect varied from place to place, and attitudes about how permanent they were, of course, also varied. Practically nowhere was there complete despair. Even in New York, Boston, Philadelphia, where things were worst, stories could be told in workers' neighborhoods of men who had escaped poverty. Newspapers and politicians reiterated endless rags-to-riches tales. Few people could in fact exchange their rags for better clothing in one generation, but even among the poorest classes incremental improvement in conditions could be seen: unskilled laborers whose sons became semiskilled and whose grandsons became skilled workers and then foremen. In industries that recent immigrants dominated, laborers took orders from their countrymen and could visualize moving up. Workers were more likely to be impressed by the personal instances they encountered of success, however modest, than with a statistical pattern showing the odds against them. Statistics on such matters were, in fact, a phenomenon of the postwar world.[7]

Opportunities varied according to industry and job situation. Benefits existed alongside disadvantages. In larger shops where worker influence was limited, wages might be higher than in smaller shops. Industries that were growing offered greater opportunities for advancement than more attractive craft occupations. And within the larger factories, which employed increasingly larger percentages of the work force, a range of jobs existed that produced a labor aristocracy of higher paid, more highly skilled workers laboring alongside lower paid and less skilled counterparts. Common laborers in these conditions might learn skilled jobs by observation, and so move up.[8]

This confused diversity was reflected in the very language with which people spoke of economic occupation and class. Newly emerging manufacturers sometimes said that they were capitalists and called their workers "labor" or "workingmen." But they more frequently called themselves part of the "producing classes" or even "workingmen" and/or "labor." They called the older merchant elite "capitalists." The term "middle class" was just starting to make its appearance and was used in quotation marks when it was used at all. And when people spoke of the economic system as a whole they did not call it capitalism, they called it the "free labor system."

Social communities and traditional work patterns often softened the power of economic forces over workers. Friends helped with food and clothing when times were hard. Churches provided economic assistance and focused attention on spiritual matters. Ethnic-religious communities also provided the basis for effective organization to protest against the power of their bosses. Unions often served social as well as economic roles, especially among the Irish and Germans. Workers in factories often demanded respect for their traditional work habits and styles of living. They offset the forces of industry by taking days off work to celebrate traditional holidays. Owners protested but throughout much of the nineteenth century could do little about it. Workers also shortened their work week. "Blue Monday" was a constant irritant to owners, but the practice of not coming back to work on the first day of the week persisted. "King Friday" also provoked owners. Workers frequently left one job for another, especially in larger cities when jobs were plentiful and times good. And, of course, there could be strikes over specific grievances.[9]

Workers' cultural values thus helped soften the impact of industrialism. They also hindered widespread organizing. The dominant power of religion in their culture divided workers as it did the larger population. In the mid-1850s Irish Catholics, who comprised a large percentage of the unskilled workers in the larger cities, were the targets of nativist attacks by Protestant workers who burned and vandalized Catholic schools and churches. Catholics for their part feared the quasi-religious fraternal orders that attracted many Protestant workers. Priests warned about the potential corruption of the faith in workers who joined such groups. Catholic fears that public schools threatened the religious values of their children led to demands for public assistance to parochial schools. Protestants responded by proclaiming the separation of church and state and expressing fears about public money paid to support "popish" indoctrination. The great Protestant revival that swept the cities in 1858 hardly diffused this religious antagonism.

Workers were also divided by political allegiances, which were interwoven with religious values. Republican leaders such as Henry Wilson and Nathaniel Banks had many supporters among the workers and also had been prominent in the nativist American party. Democratic politicians played on the Catholic allegiances of their working-class supporters by insisting that the meddling Republicans wanted to destroy the rights of others to drink and pray and simply be let alone. Both parties claimed to be the party of the workingman, and gained the allegiance of workers and further divided them. It is no wonder that a leading labor newspaper observed that two iron molders from the same shop might be political enemies, and proclaimed that parties were "the curse of working-men."[10]

The power of labor was further limited because many workers refused to see themselves as imprisoned in an industrial workingclass. Immigrants came to the United States hoping to buy farms in the nation with the largest open frontiers in the world. Native citizens who worked in the cities kept their rural ties. Most of them had been born in the country, even more had relatives living on farms. They retained their rural memories and their self-image as something other than hopeless prisoners of urban toil. They moved from the cities back to the farms for harvests and other jobs. Winter factory workers were often summer farmers. Unemployed mill workers became hired hands and plowboys. Even those forced by circumstances or temporarily attracted to industrial work might keep family farms. Many a worker, both immigrant and native, followed the admonition that Irish-American Mark Sullivan recalled his immigrant father giving him: "Never sell the farm: no matter what happens to you in the cities, this will be a shelter to you."[11]

On the eve of conflict the workers of the North lived in a world of conflicting and contrasting experiences, of local community attachments, with an economy predominantly rural but one where industrialization was a force of growing size and potential danger. Class consciousness was a fact in some places but mitigated in many others by hopes, by strategies, by options kept open, by lack of experience with the evils that called it forth. There was widespread concern about the shape of things to come, but that concern focused inevitably on the controversy over slavery, which symbolized so well the anxieties they felt.[12]

The secession crisis found labor divided in its sympathies, though more inclined to peace. German laborers in the Midwest offered their staunch support to Lincoln as he traveled to Washington. Troy, New York, workers pledged loyalty. Milwaukee workers resolved that if the crisis were not solved peacefully, "revolutionary" means would be justified since the South was responsible for the crisis. In Cincinnati Lincoln was told that

we, the German free working men of Cincinnati, avail ourselves of this opportunity to assure you . . . of our sincere and heartfelt regard. . . . Our vanquished opponents have in recent times made frequent use of the term workingmen and workingmen's meetings in order to create the impression that the mass of workingmen were in favor of compromise between the interests of free labor and slave labor. . . . We firmly adhere to the principle which directed our votes to your favor.[13]

But if some labor organizations supported Lincoln at this time, signs of opposition were more frequent. Just recovering from the impact of the mid-1850s depression, many workers feared that disunion would bring economic disaster. They also knew that they would be the ones on the battlefields of any war. Pro-Southern factory owners had helped foster opposition by closing their factories. Other businessmen had nurtured fears by retracting activity in the face of the crisis. Workers in all parts of the nation thus joined large antiwar rallies. Meetings in the East, in Philadelphia, Newark, and Boston, were balanced with Western gatherings in Reading, St. Louis, and Louisville. Sylvis of the Iron Molders was in Louisville and then in Philadelphia publishing a call that brought five thousand worker representatives to that city to demand compromise. The future founder of the Knights of Labor, Ira Stewart, joined in attacking the extremists who had spawned the crisis. The Louisville meeting damned "disorganizing traitors" and "congressional extremists" and insisted that both were disloyal and enemies to labor.[14]

But wishes for peace could not withstand the Confederate attack on Fort Sumter. Workers throughout the North surged forward to crush an attack on the nation and to punish the slave power. Industrial conflicts were quickly submerged in the rush to arms. The ironworkers of Troy were organizing a strike when the news from Sumter came in. Large numbers of the membership enlisted. The weakened union lost more ground when management used the opportunity to hire nonunion workers, required that these workers not join any union, and brought charges against the union for conspiracy. By early fall 1861 Troy ironworkers were largely disbanded, meeting only three times in five months. One Philadelphia local ended its 1861 meeting in this way: "It having been resolved to enlist with Uncle Sam for the War, this union stands adjourned until either the union is safe or we are whipped." Throughout the North the story was the same. Workers of all sections and all ethnic groups flocked to the army. In proportion to their percentage of the population, more industrial workers served in the Union army than any other group except for professionals. Looking at military service after the war, statistician Benjamin Gould noted that for every 1,000 soldiers there were likely to be 487 farmers or farm workers, 421 mechanics and laborers, 35 workers involved in commerce, 16 professionals, and 41 from a range of other occupations.[15]

But if the workers were willing to fight for their country, the war also gave them the chance to fight for their own interests as well. The ideology of the conflict had a strong impact on them. Lincoln's description of the war as a people's contest, a struggle to remove burdens from the backs of labor and give to everyone an equal chance in the race of life, spoke directly to their feelings. Furthermore, the president made clear on several occasions a sympathy for the workers. As early as his speech at Cooper Union he applauded a system where workers could strike. In the aftermath of the great Lynn strike, when a delegation of machinists and blacksmiths came to see him at the White House, he allegedly told them that "I know in almost every case of strike the men have just cause for complaint." He told another delegation, "I know the trials and woes of workingmen. I have always felt for them." A believer in the labor theory of value, Lincoln commented that labor "deserves much higher consideration" than capital. "I myself was a hired laborer," he reminded several audiences. Such words suggested that the war might directly benefit workers. From being a single group contesting others for support, the cause of labor became linked to the cause of all loyal Northerners.[16]

And yet this same phenomenon also might undercut labor's advancement. Workers' special needs and aspirations might be absorbed into the general, ill-defined free labor cause. With the

North united under this banner all classes could lay claim to the patriotic ideals of the Union, and worker protest might lose its strength. More tellingly, the workers themselves fell prey to this patriotic homogenizing. Many began to identify their cause with that of the Republican party. They thus fell into bed with the very businessmen that they had been challenging. Lynn offers an example of this phenomenon at work in the most striking way. The Workingmen's party had won city elections in 1860 and 1861, but by 1863 the Republican party was in control, and by 1864 no votes at all were cast for anyone but the Republican candidate. Small towns growing into cities, like Springfield, Massachusetts, were often Republican strongholds, and workers in most of the major Northern cities throughout the war voted Republican.[17]

Experienced Republican party politicians with reputations as friends of the workers, such as Henry Wilson, argued that his party was the free labor party. "We have made labor honorable," Wilson declared, "even in the rice swamps of the Carolinas and Georgia; we have taken the brand of dishonor from the brow of labor throughout the country and in so doing that grand work we have done more for labor, for the honor and dignity of laboring men, than was ever achieved by all the parties that arose in this country from the time the Pilgrims put their feet upon Plymouth Rock up to the year 1860." Such appeals were frequently persuasive even to working-class leaders. Samuel Gompers cast the first vote of his life in 1872 for Grant in the belief that the Republican struggle against slavery showed party dedication to the cause of free labor. But Democrats also tried to collect labor votes by a similar appeal to the general and widely popular idea that the end of slavery was a victory for the working classes. In early 1865 the party published a pamphlet, "America for Free Working Men!" collecting material from the *New York Evening Post* to show how Democrats fought slavery for years, thus earning the support of free workers of the North.[18]

[...]

[...] the ideology of the North also served to diffuse the claim of workers for special attention. Since all of society was linked in the free labor struggle, owners, industrialists, capitalists, might equally assert their devotion to free labor goals, thus weakening the special force of labor's claim to the idea. In a society not yet clearly industrialized, a society just beginning to develop the clear divisions between wage earners and independent owners, it was, in fact, easy to deny the permanence of the growing gap. By its emphasis on unity and loyalty the war helped hide this distinction. On the other hand, the war, with the economic costs it exacted from labor and the organization it stimulated, with the contrasts between free labor ideology and wage slavery reality, provoked many labor leaders to greater efforts. These would have their impact in fostering a stronger labor movement after the conflict. One of the reasons for the endurance of the labor movement and its growth after the war was the fact that the war did very little, if anything, to decrease the actual economic inequality in the nation. Possibly Northern labor made minimal gains overall, but the gap between rich and poor and between wage earner, hired laborer, and the owners of shops, factories, and farms narrowed hardly at all. The war taught labor the need and efficacy of organizing to achieve its goals. It did little to bring those goals much closer.[19]

Notes

1   Calculated from the *Ninth Census of the United States* (1870), vol. 3, 808–9. This was the first census to list occupations. National occupational figures have been discussed by David Montgomery, *Beyond Equality: Labor and the Radical Republicans* (New York, 1967) pp. 28–9, 448–50; Daniel

Rodgers, *The Work Ethic in Industrial America* (Chicago, 1978), pp. 36–7; and Carl Siracusa, *Mechanical People: Perceptions of the Industrial Order in Massachusetts, 1815–80* (Middletown, Conn., 1978). Also helpful is Lebergott, *Manpower in Economic Growth*. See Clyde Griffin, "Occupational Mobility in 19th-Century America: Problems and Possibilities," *Journal of Social History* 5 (Spring 1972): 310–30, for the complexities of determining occupational status.

2 Norman J. Ware, *The Labor Movement in the United States, 1860–1890* (New York, 1929), pp. 1–5; Dawley, *Class and Community*, pp. 101–4; Sylvis, *Life of William Sylvis*, pp. 61–3; John R. Commons et al., *History of Labour in the United States* (New York, 1918), vol. 2, pp. 33–9; Stanley Lebergott, "The American Labor Force," in Lance Davis et al., *American Economic Growth* (New York, 1971), p. 220.

3 Grossman, *William Sylvis*, pp. 34, 55–67, 72–80; Montgomery, *Beyond Equality*, pp. 223–5.

4 Dawley, *Class and Community*, pp. 86–8, 102–3, 200–2 (Dawley fails to notice this phenomenon, although his evidence clearly reveals it); Herbert Gutman, "Social and Economic Structure and Depression: American Labor in 1873 and 1874," PhD diss., University of Wisconsin, Madison, 1959, pp. xii–xv; Daniel Walkowitz, *Worker City, Company Town* (Urbana, 1978), pp. 12–13; Michael Frisch, *Town into City: Springfield, Massachusetts, and the Meaning of Community* (Cambridge, MA, 1972) pp. 127–28.

5 Calculated from the *Eighth Census of the United States*, "Manufacturers," pp. 677–701, 705–11, 729–30; Henry Pelling, *American Labor* (Chicago, 1960), pp. 25–26; Gutman, "Social and Economic Structure and Depression," pp. 234–36; Lawrence Costello, "The New York City Labor Movement, 1861–1873," PhD diss., Columbia University, New York, 1967.

6 *New York Times*, February 22, 1869, p. 2.

7 Stephen Thernstrom, *Poverty and Progress* (Cambridge, MA., 1964); Walkowitz, *Worker City, Company Town;* Daniel Walkowitz, "Statistics and the Writing of Working-Class Culture," *Labor History* 15 (Summer 1974): 416–60; Peter Knights, *The Plain People of Boston, 1830–1860: A Study of City Growth* (New York, 1971), pp. 78–102. Knights and Thernstrom, who present the darkest picture of upward mobility, still report upward climbing for even their lowest groups. Two-thirds of the lowest classes in Newburyport who stayed in the town improved their position. See Thernstrom, pp. 149–50. Almost 15 percent of those who stayed in Boston between 1850 and 1860 moved up; 2.8 percent moved down. See Knights, 99. Dawley, *Class and Community*, finds an upward mobility of about 10 percent per decade in Lynn, Massachusetts, between 1860 and 1880. (pp. 161–5)

8 Bruce Laurie, Theodore Hershberg, and George Alter, "Immigrants and Industry: The Philadelphia Experience, 1850–1880," *Journal of Social History* 9 (Winter 1975): 219–48.

9 Daniel T. Rogers, "Tradition, Modernity and the American Industrial Worker," *Journal of Interdisciplinary History* 7 (Spring 1977): 655–81; Herbert Gutman, "Work, Culture, and Society in Industrializing America, 1815–1919," *American Historical Review* 78 (June 1973): 531–89. Montgomery, *Beyond Equality*, pp. 14–15, notes the vagueness of class rhetoric. For surveys of the literature of the "new labor history," which emphasizes working class consciousness and the impact of diverse religious and intellectual perspectives on the condition of workers, see David Brody, "Labor History in the 1970s: Toward a History of the American Worker," in Michael Kammen, ed., *The Past Before Us* (Ithaca, 1980); David Brody, "The Old Labor History and the New: In Search of an American Working Class," *Labor History* 20 (Winter 1979); David Montgomery, "To Study the People: The American Working Class," *Labor History* 21 (Fall 1980); Sean Wilentz, "Against Exceptionalism: Class Consciousness and the American Labor Movement, 1790–1920," paper delivered at Organization of American Historians meeting, Los Angeles, 1984. Wilentz especially has tried to link the intellectual and cultural perspectives of workers with their class consciousness. See his *Chants Democratic: New York City and the Rise of the American Working Class* (New York, 1984).

10 Montgomery, *Beyond Equality*, pp. 42–4; Timothy Smith, *Revivalism and Social Reform: American Protestantism on the Eve of Civil War* (New York, 1957), pp. 45–79; Ray Allen Billington, *The Protestant Crusade, 1800–1860* (New York, 1938), pp. 305–7; Kelley, *The Cultural Pattern in American Politics;* Paul Kleppner, "Lincoln and the Immigrant Vote: A Case of Religious Polarization," *Mid-America* 48

(July 1966): pp. 176–95; Ronald P. Formisano, "Ethnicity and Party in Michigan, 1854–1860," in Frederick Luebke, ed., *Ethnic Voters and the Election of Lincoln* (Lincoln, Neb., 1971), pp. 175–95.

11   Dawley, *Class and Community*, 48–52; Robert Cross, "The Changing Image of the City Among American Catholics," *Catholic Historical Review* 48 (April 1962): 33–52; Montgomery, *Beyond Equality*, pp. 35–38; Mark Sullivan, *The Education of an American* (New York, 1938), 11; Schob, *Hired Hands and Plowboys*.

12   The religious, ethnic, and class differences that divided workers were still generally vague, as were the distinctions between employer and employee. Using cultural analysis to describe the condition of the workers in this period thus "involves a sacrifice of historical complexity for descriptive clarity," in the words of Leonard S. Wallock, "The Limits of Solidarity: Philadelphia's Journeymen Printers in the Mid-Nineteenth Century," paper delivered at OAH meeting, Los Angeles, 1984, 21. See the warning on this point by Bruce Laurie, *Working People of Philadelphia, 1800–1850* (Philadelphia, 1980). Also see Friedrich Lenger, "Class, Culture, and Class Consciousness in Antebellum Lynn: Critique of Alan Dawley and Paul Faler," *Social History* 6 (October 1981): 317–32.

13   *New York Daily Tribune*, January 8, February 16, February 20, 1861. On the complicated issue of German-American support for Lincoln, see Luebke, ed., *Ethnic Voters and the Election of Lincoln*. Most contributors to this volume argue that the German vote was divided, with Lincoln likely to have received the Lutheran votes but very unlikely to have gotten Catholic support. See also David Potter, *The Impending Crisis* (New York, 1976), pp. 435–36.

14   Montgomery, *Beyond Equality*, pp. 92–93; Grossman, *William Sylvis*, pp. 44–46; Terence Powderly, *Thirty Years*, 44; Commons et al., *History of Labour*, vol. 2, pp. 10–12.

15   Gould, *Investigations in Military and Anthropological Statistics*, pp. 5, 10–14, 209–10; Grossman, *William Sylvis*, 46–55; Powderly, *Thirty Years*, p. 57; Dawley, *Class and Community*; Walkowitz, "Working Class Culture," 186ff. McPherson, *Ordeal by Fire*, disputes the argument that industrial workers served in especially high percentages. (pp. 357–9)

16   Borritt, *Lincoln and Economics*, pp. 183–85, 218–21.

17   Montgomery, *Beyond Equality*, pp. 108–10; Dawley, *Class and Community*; Frisch, *Town into City*, 53–5.

18   Samuel Gompers, *Seventy Years of Life and Labour* (New York, 1925), vol. 2, p. 49; Carl Siracusa, *Mechanical People*, pp. 216–18; George McNeill, *The Labor Movement: The Problem of Today* (New York, 1887), pp. 123–4; Charles Nordhoff, "America for Free Working Men!" (New York, 1865).

19   Soltow, *Men and Wealth*, pp. 99–104; Williamson and Lindert, *American Inequality*, pp. 38–9, 46–8.

Questions to consider

- What are some of the obstacles that faced Union industrial workers during the war?

- What role did cultural values – religion and ethnicity, to name two examples – play in shaping workers' identities?

- In what ways did the free labor ideology of the North foster working class consciousness? In what ways did it inhibit that consciousness?

Chapter 12

Wartime Economies: Primary Sources

The Mind of the South

Wilbur J. Cash

One of the great unifying ideas in American national life is the American Dream – the notion that anything is possible if you want it badly enough. The power of the idea is in its elasticity; there can be as many American Dreams as there have been Americans. Yet there are broad classes of dreams – like upward mobility and home ownership – and most American Dreams have a strong economic component.

The American Dream had considerable appeal in the antebellum South, where acquiring a home or a business had as much appeal as anywhere else. Yet the Southern American Dream had distinctive elements, rooted in an economic system where capital was invested in sources of wealth (like human beings) that were both more mythic and less liquid than one could find elsewhere. The Civil War would destroy this particular American Dream, but its memory would inform (and perhaps haunt) others even after the region embraced its own style of capitalism and recaptured its original stature as the leading economic region of the nation.

Journalist W. J. Cash (1900–41) produced only one book in his lifetime, but that book, published months before his premature death, is widely regarded as a classic. With almost poetic intensity, Cash describes the big dreams of the small antebellum planter, and the ways that dream could – and did – become reality.

W. J. Cash, *The Mind of the South* (New York: Knopf, 1941), pp. 15–17. Copyright © 1941 by Alfred A. Knopf, Inc. and renewed 1969 by Mary R. Maury. Used by permission of Alfred A. Knopf, a division of Random House, Inc.

[...]

A stout young Irishman brought his bride into the Carolina upcountry about 1800. He cleared a bit of land, built a log cabin of two rooms, and sat down to the pioneer life. One winter, with several of his neighbors, he loaded a boat with whisky and the coarse woolen cloth woven by the women, and drifted down to Charleston to trade. There, remembering the fondness of his woman for a bit of beauty, he bought a handful of cotton seed, which she planted about the cabin with the wild rose and the honeysuckle – as a flower. Afterward she learned, under the tutelage of a new neighbor, to pick the seed from the fiber with her fingers and to spin it into yarn. Another winter the man drifted down the river, this time to find the half-way station of Columbia in a strange ferment. There was a new wonder in the world – the cotton gin – and the forest which had lined the banks of the stream for a thousand centuries was beginning to go down. Fires flared red and portentous in the night – to set off an answering fire in the breast of the Irishman.

Land in his neighborhood was to be had for fifty cents an acre. With twenty dollars, the savings of his lifetime, he bought forty acres and set himself to clear it. Rising long before day, he toiled deep into the night, with his wife holding a pine torch for him to see by. Aided by his neighbors, he piled the trunks of the trees into great heaps and burned them, grubbed up the stumps, hacked away the tangle of underbrush and vine, stamped out the poison ivy and the snakes. A wandering trader sold him a horse, bony and half-starved, for a knife, a dollar, and a gallon of whisky. Every day now – Sundays not excepted – when the heavens allowed, and every night that the moon came, he drove the plow into the earth, with uptorn roots bruising his shanks at every step. Behind him came his wife with a hoe. In a few years the land was beginning to yield cotton – richly, for the soil was fecund with the accumulated mold of centuries. Another trip down the river, and he brought home a mangy black slave – an old and lazy fellow reckoned of no account in the rice-lands, but with plenty of life in him still if you knew how to get it out. Next year the Irishman bought fifty acres more, and the year after another black. Five years more and he had two hundred acres and ten Negroes. Cotton prices swung up and down sharply, but always, whatever the return, it was almost pure velvet. For the fertility of the soil seemed inexhaustible.

When he was forty-five, he quit work, abandoned the log house, which had grown to six rooms, and built himself a wide-spreading frame cottage. When he was fifty, he became a magistrate, acquired a carriage, and built a cotton gin and a third house – a "big house" this time. It was not, to be truthful, a very grand house really. Built of lumber sawed on the place, it was a little crude and had not cost above a thousand dollars, even when the marble mantel was counted in. Essentially, it was just a box, with four rooms, bisected by a hallway, set on four more rooms bisected by another hallway, and a detached kitchen at the back. Wind-swept in winter, it was difficult to keep clean of vermin in summer. But it was huge, it had great columns in front, and it was eventually painted white, and so, in this land of wide fields and pinewoods it seemed very imposing.

Meantime the country around had been growing up. Other "big houses" had been built. There was a county seat now, a cluster of frame houses, stores, and "doggeries" about a red brick courthouse. A Presbyterian parson had drifted in and started an academy, as Presbyterian parsons had a habit of doing everywhere in the South – and Pompeys and Cæsars and Ciceros and Platos were multiplying both among the pickaninnies in the slave quarters and among the white children of the "big houses." The Irishman had a piano in his house, on which his daughters, taught by a vagabond German, played as well as young ladies could be expected to. One of the Irishman's sons went to the College of South Carolina, came back to grow into the chief lawyer in the county, got to be a judge, and would have been Governor if he had not died at the head of his regiment at Chancellorsville.

As a crown on his career, the old man went to the Legislature, where he was accepted by the Charleston gentlemen tolerantly and with genuine liking. He grew extremely mellow in age and liked to pass his time in company, arguing about predestination and infant damnation, proving conclusively that cotton was king and that the damyankee didn't dare do anything about it, and developing a notable taste in the local liquors. Tall and well-made, he grew whiskers after the Galway fashion – the well-kept whiteness of which contrasted very agreeably with the brick red of his complexion – donned the long-tailed coat, stove-pipe hat, and string tie of the statesmen of his period, waxed innocently pompous, and, in short, became a really striking figure of a man.

Once, going down to Columbia for the inauguration of a new Governor, he took his youngest daughter along. There she met a Charleston gentleman who was pestering her father for a loan. Her manner, formed by the Presbyterian parson, was plain but not bad, and she was very pretty. Moreover, the Charleston gentleman was decidedly in hard lines. So he married her.

When the old man finally died in 1854, he left two thousand acres, a hundred and fourteen slaves, and four cotton gins. The little newspaper which had recently set up in the county seat spoke of him as "a gentleman of the old school" and "a noble specimen of the chivalry at its best"; the Charleston papers each gave him a column; and a lordly Legaré introduced resolutions of respect into the Legislature. His wife outlived him by ten years – by her portrait a beautifully fragile old woman, and, as I have heard it said, with lovely hands, knotted and twisted just enough to give them character, and a finely transparent skin through which the blue veins showed most aristocratically.

Questions to consider

- In what ways is the figure described by Cash similar or different to other legends of upward mobility, like Andrew Carnegie – or Oprah Winfrey?

- The figure Cash describes here corresponds to some of the legendary characters in novels written by his contemporaries, like Gerald O'Hara in Margaret Mitchell's *Gone with the Wind* (1936) and William Faulkner's Thomas Sutpen in *Absalom! Absalom!* (also 1936). Such figures were created in part to contest an older vision of the Southern plantation as solely the domain of the blue-blooded. Why do you think the notion of "finely transparent skin through which the blue veins showed most aristocratically" had special appeal in the antebellum South? What ramifications might there have been in trying to demolish that view?

Letters to Secretary of War Edwin Stanton

Mary Herrick

According to an old saying, the only certain things in life are death and taxes. Both tend to accelerate in wartime, creating economic burdens that the more vulnerable members of society are ill-equipped to handle. In these 1863 letters to Secretary of War Edwin Stanton, an upstate widow protests taxes she does not feel she can afford.

Consider as you read Mrs. Herrick's notion of what she thinks she owes her government, and what she thinks her government owes her. How different is she in her attitudes than women in more recent wars?

Mary Herrick, "Letters to Edwin Stanton, Nunda, NY" (May 30, 1863), in *Root of Bitterness: Documents of the Social History of American Women Second Edition*, eds. Nancy F. Cott, Jeanne Boydston, Ann Braude, Lori D. Ginzberg, and Molly Ladd-Taylor (Boston, MA: Northeastern University Press, 1996), pp. 268–9. Copyright © 1996 by Nancy F. Cott. Reprinted with the permission of Northeastern University Press.

E. M. Stanton   Nunda, [NY] May 30, 1863
Secretary of War.

I am a widow my Son is in the army vollenteered last august to fill up the 33 went as a nine months man was promised to be discharged when the time of the regiment was out my husband has been dead 15 years and George B. Herrick of the 33 was all the child I ever had so I am left all alone I have a small plase and dont want to be taxed to death. that is I don't want the copperhead collecter to take what lidle I have for taxes. he threatened to sell my things for the vollenteer tax because I am poor and did not have the money as soon a he wanted it. My son George B. Herrick is a printer by trade inlisted in Rochestr was well aquainted with Col. Tayler before the war broke out. George B. Herrick my son paid one hundred and fifty dollars of his heard earnings towards *this war* before he inlisted I did not think him well anough to go but he was better when he went south 5 years ago and I consented to let him go and he has done as much as eney in his department being *Agitants cleark*! Mr Stanton and Lincan and co that is what they call you dont you think you and the President could find *some means* to Protect those of us that have given all we had towards this war but a plase to stay. I would like to keep a plase to stay if possible. if I dont have eney thing but bread and water! by good rights you should pass a law to exempt such as I am from heavey taxes as you have money so plenty you could verrey easy make me a donation of one hundred and fiftey dollars and then I can have something to pay the extrey taxes with. it is unjust and cruel to tax a poor woman to death *you* have plentey of simpathy for the slaves and I think slavery is an abomination in the sight of god. that is one reason why I don't want to be a slave to this *war*! eney reffrences you want you can have Mr. Morey of the dayley Union is aquainted with Georg he has worked in there office. Doct Chaffee of Springfield Massachusetts is likewise aquainted and George is a member of the Typographical union.

With Respect, Mary W. Herrick

Nunda, Jun 13, 1863

Sir I received yours of the 8 on the 11 and enclosed was 6 sheets of a sercler [circular] in pamphlet form; and as the letter had bin opened I did not [k]now as I received all that you enclosed: thanks maney thanks for your reply as I did [not] expect eney: I was somewhat surprised to find an answer and more so to find that the envelope had been opened and I think in the office here and I am afraid the Post master done it himself; I think a *woman* has all the rights of a *free* american sitisen and I want the uneion as it was without *slavery*: I dont want one state or stripe less in that dear old flag that has floated over me ever since I was born in this land of the brave and this *contrey of the free*: my son is a firm suporter of the war gave all he had and then went himself: and has done more than some that was in perfect health when they arrived in dixey: hoping *not to live if the uneion* is to be *severed*: hoping this cruel rebellion may soon be *crushed out*. if I was a man I would fight to *crush it*, but my son think it is no plase for me eaven as nurse in the hospitals. but I can pray for peace once more to fold her blessed wings around us and return each son to his dessolate mother.

With Respect, ... Mrs. Mary W. Herrick, Livingston c[ou]n[ty]

Letters Received, 1863, Enlisted Branch, Adjutant General's papers, box 22, RG 94, National Archives. The editors are grateful to Rachel Filene Seidman for locating and providing a copy of this document.

Part VI

Slavery During Wartime

Plate 8 Black Market: Slave brokerage house, Atlanta, 1864. The slave trade continued in earnest during the Civil War, even as the institution began to buckle. This picture was taken after the fall of the city by George N. Barnard, official photographer of the Chief Engineer's Office under General William Tecumseh Sherman. (Selected Civil War photographs, Library of Congress)

Chapter 13

A Loss of Mastery

James L. Roark

While there has long been disagreement on its centrality, most observers agree that the preservation of slavery was an important objective for at least some Southerners in the Civil War. Herein lies a paradox, for waging the war endangered the very thing Confederate forces fought to protect. In part this is because Southern secession became the rationale (or, to some, the pretext) for the Lincoln administration to implement the policy some Southerners feared it would all along: abolition. (The administration claimed the Emancipation Proclamation was justified as a military measure, because the rebels were using slave labor as an instrument of their insurrection.) Yet other forces in play worked to erode slavery's hold in the South even without the external threat of emancipation. The urgent demand for slave labor generated pressures to offer incentives – like the hotly contested proposal, approved just as the war was ending, to offer slaves freedom in return for military service – for those who might otherwise have little reason to fight for the Confederacy. And the absence of masters from their farms and plantations gave slaves responsibilities – and opportunities – that belied the frequent assertion that they were essentially children incapable of managing on their own.

Still, for all the obstacles they faced, it is clear that some slave owners remained deeply, even fiercely, committed to the peculiar institution, and would have acted by any means necessary to restore slavery to its antebellum status in the event of Confederate victory. That victory proved elusive, of course, but there were a number of years where the outcome of the war remained in doubt. What happened to slaves in these years – and, in particular, what happened to those who wished to keep them in slavery – is among the subjects covered in James Roark's highly regarded 1977 study *Masters Without Slaves: Southern Planters in the Civil War and Reconstruction*. In this excerpt, Roark describes the concrete day-to-day realities of slavery under siege – and the attitudes of those who hoped it would survive.

James L. Roark, "A Loss of Mastery," in *Masters Without Slaves: Southern Planters in the Civil War and Reconstruction* (New York: Norton, 1977), pp. 68–91. Copyright © 1977 by W. W. Norton & Company, Inc. Used by permission of W. W. Norton & Company, Inc.

"War is father of all and king of all, and some he shows as gods, others as men; some he makes slaves, others free."

Heraclitus

[...]

The slave-plantation system stood at the center of the antebellum Southern economy, and at the center of the plantation stood the planter. Before the war, the slaveholder presiding over his isolated estate had been largely free, within only a few broad constraints, to organize, operate, and rule or misrule as he pleased. Almost without outside imposition, he could set his own rules and follow or evade statute law as he pleased. And for very practical reasons he was jealous of his prerogatives. In a forced-labor system, it was imperative that authority remain clearly defined and absolute. Competing centers of power could only disrupt. Order and control demanded that mastership be undivided and complete.

The slave master was an object of fascination among contemporary Americans, but descriptions often clashed. On the eve of the war, one Southern observer, Daniel Hundley, described the planter as an impeccable aristocrat, with a blue-blooded lineage, faultless physique, a well-trained mind, gracious manners and openhanded hospitality, a way with horses, guns, and hounds, and a highly honed sense of honor and duty.[1] But a Northern contemporary, Frederick Law Olmsted, questioned the existence of such a being as the Southern gentleman. He found the planter class to be composed of stupid, uneducated, loutish, vulgar men, who crassly and brutally exploited the lower classes of both colors.[2] Actually, the sprawling plantation country was broad enough to encompass planter personalities of a number of types, from the chivalrous and genteel to the illiterate and tobacco-stained – from the Sartoris to the Sutpen. Some plantations resembled patriarchal families, networks of authority and warm affection, subordination and genuine responsibility, while others were organized in the crudest manner, revolving entirely around profit, with men and beasts treated brutally and considered of equal value.

Despite their enormous differences in refinement and humanity, planters had in common the practical task of managing large numbers of black slaves in the production of staple crops. While slaveholders played many roles, practical economic duty provided an important element of uniformity within the planter class. Tradition commonly portrays the planter as a casual manager, uninterested in production and cost figures, careless about routine and organization, generally slipshod and disorderly in his agricultural operations.[3] Planters bull-headedly clung to some inefficient ways, certainly, but they were often practical-minded men who were decidedly not indifferent to the realities of managing plantation finances and plantation labor. As U. B. Phillips has explained, financial loss endangered more than a planter's bank account. His economic pursuit was often more than a means of maintaining his way of life. It was his life. Nor could slaveholders afford to be careless about their labor force. The situation of Alfred Huger was typical. He said before the war, "I am utterly dependent as to property & as to the safety of my family for peace and tranquility among our Negroes."[4] And tranquil slaves were the product of careful supervision and stern discipline. The most famous antebellum plantations, while hardly modern scientific enterprises, were run in a relatively methodical manner, with planters monitoring both the finances and the labor, seeking to maximize both order and control.

The Civil War threatened to destroy planter control and plantation order by shattering the shield of isolation which protected rural estates. War transformed the Southern countryside from a supportive environment to hostile territory. It ate away at the vital relationships between master and slave and between slave and plantation. It disrupted routine and system and diminished mastery. Before the fighting ended, a score of assailants breached the walls of the plantations. Although none but those who wore blue uniforms were lethal, each inflicted a painful wound on the slave regime.

In the early years of the war, planters seemed to see the protection of slavery largely in terms of controlling slave behavior. Since slaves themselves had always been considered the chief threat to the institution, it was natural that the thinking of planters begin there. Masters constructed a strategy of defense based on the prewar precedent – isolation. Their aim was to keep the slaves in and abolitionist ideas out. If dangerous notions could be kept out of the slave quarters and the slaves kept on the plantations, slavery would be secure. The Reverend C. C. Jones and his son agreed that their "entire social system" depended on their ability to "*seal* by the most rigid police all ingress and egress" to the plantation. They realized, however, that "this is most difficult."[5] Had they been medieval barons, planters would likely have filled their moats to the brim and pulled up their drawbridges until the danger passed.

The worry that the slaves themselves might destroy slavery was as old as the institution itself. It rested in large part on the planters' image of the black personality. This was a dual image, as George Fredrickson has explained, including a "hard" portrait and a "soft" one – painting the black on the one hand as a lower order of human, nearly a beast, and on the other as an immature human, a child.[6] Catherine Edmondston, a long-time observer of life in the slave quarters, believed blacks were a rudimentary type. "I do not think negroes possess natural feelings," she said during the war. In the treatment of their young and their old, they showed none of the "natural sentiments," while in their sexual activity, their feelings were unnaturally heightened. In March, 1862, she witnessed a slave marriage which followed an engagement of one day. "So Cupid gave place to Hymen in a shorter time than usual – primitive customs one will say, but Cuffee strips off the elegancies and refinements of civilization with great ease."[7]

Vying with the image of the black as a lower order of human was the image of the undeveloped and childlike black personality. "I see from your letter, as from many others I receive," Henry Watson, Jr., of Alabama said to a Northern friend on the eve of the war, "that you at the North think we live in perpetual dread of our servants. There could not be possibly a greater mistake. As well might you suppose that we lived in terror of our children." Most slaveholders, he explained, felt "an attachment for the servants similar, in some respects, to that we feel for our children. We feed them, clothe them, nurse them when sick and in all things provide for them. How can we do this and not love them?" As for the slaves, "they too feel an affection for their master, his wife and children and they are proud of his and their success." Watson thought there was a "charm" in the name "Master." Slaves "look upon and to their master with the same feeling that a child looks to his father. It is a lovely trait in them. This being the case how can we fear them?"[8]

Both images existed simultaneously, though uneasily, in most white Southern minds. A Georgia woman, for instance, called away from her plantation for a few days, was "perplexed" at having to leave her "people" without "white protection and control."[9] Whites offered blacks both safety and discipline; they were at once guardians and jailers of the black child-beast. Regardless of which image dominated in the mind of any particular planter, all agreed that blacks were inherently inferior. Unequal and thus unfit for freedom, they could only be enslaved. Either as children or as beasts, they required close and continuous supervision. Either foolish or irrational, they could easily be persuaded to flight or worse. Blacks were not an ideal laboring class, but if isolated from all noxious ideas and kept under the firm authority of the master, they were capable of steady, even affectionate, service.

Slavery spawned its own defense, and in addition, continuous abolitionist attack forced Southerners to construct rigorous arguments in support of their peculiar institution. Southern spokesmen turned to the Bible, biology, social theory, history, and law for justification. Theoretically inclined Alfred Huger, for instance, declared that slavery was not merely a "legal interpretation" or a "treaty between men," but "a separate and distinct 'institution' ordained by the Almighty!"[10] More often, however, working planters constructed their defense of slavery around what they knew best – the everyday, practical circumstances of Southern slaves.

Planters' arguments often took the form of a discussion comparing the welfare of their slaves with that of free labor. In reply to those who argued that blacks were savagely treated in the South, plantation dwellers pointed to the blacks' fate in the North. Planters who visited the North were often genuinely shocked by what they saw. In 1854, a Mississippi man wrote home to his sister on the plantation that he was sickened by the way blacks lived in Philadelphia. "As for the negroes," he said, "there is as many as ten or fifteen living in one little hut about ten feet long and twelve feet wide, with nothing to eate one half of the time, and I might add nothing to sleepe on. . . . " Some, he declared, were "actually starving for something to eat."[11]

The defenders of slavery also contrasted the well-being of Southern slaves with the pitiful state of Northern white labor. In 1857, a North Carolina planter – sounding something like a more illustrious Southerner, George Fitzhugh – reported that all of "his people" were "healthy, contented and happy, with plenty to eat" and "well clothed." Each had a house supplied by the owner, "with a pile of wood" and "a nice garden of about half an acre." Negroes had "their supply of meal, pork, molasses and tobacco weekly, with a meeting house to which they resort every Sunday, to sing and pray, and a clergyman to preach . . . and a physician to attend them when sick." When he saw the "comfort" of his slaves, he said, "I sincerely pity the condition of the poor operatives in the northern factories who are turned loose to starve with all the horrors of winter staring them in the face. Without employment, without wages or food, without clothing, without fire, without houses to shelter them, they are turned adrift by their employers. . . . " He could not understand why Northerners, with troubles enough at home, busied themselves "in destroying the peace, confidence, and affection subsisting between the master and his slaves."[12]

Sometimes planters ranged beyond the black and white laboring classes of the North to comparisons on the international level. In 1862 Catherine Edmondston was struck with the bounty and nutritiousness of the slaves' ration, even in the midst of a war. She thought it must be "more than any other laboring class on the globe gets regularly." She made a list: "Think of what the Irish get – 'potatoes & porid [sic],' the French – 'bread & grapes,' Italiens [sic] – Maccaroni & olive oil, the Spanish – Black bread & garlic, the Swedes – but it is useless to go through the catalogue. The object of their misplaced sympathy, the poor negro, fares better than any of them & has as much freedom."[13] Compared with other members of the same race or class, Southern planters concluded, the slaves were fortunate indeed.

Though they argued that Southern slaves fared better than Northern blacks, Northern white workers, and the world's working class, planters knew that Northerners did not accept this view, and feared that the slaves did not realize their good fortune. And the planters' constant references to it may have revealed their own doubts. But certainly after John Brown's attack at Harpers Ferry, Southerners had little doubt about Northern attitudes. In Southern eyes, the Northern response to this atrocity proved that the North was an abolitionist nation. For decades, Southerners had labored to make the South safe for slavery, smothering debate and insisting on an orthodox proslavery position, but with John Brown's raid their efforts became deadly earnest. In December, 1859, David Gavin of South Carolina was thrilled to hear that so many "abolitionist emissaries have been lynched and expelled from the country." He was dissatisfied, however, with the degree of protection that had been achieved. He thought that "there should be sound and efficient laws passed and a good and sufficient police or number of soldiers enlisted to enforce them, and stringent laws about free negroes, persons of Colour and all white persons who have not a visible means of an honest living."[14]

The secession crisis pushed the South to the edge of frenzy. Rumors of "servile insurrection" raced from Virginia to Texas. Antisecessionists in the South did their share to feed the panic by arguing that disunion would trigger a massive uprising among the slaves. Abolitionists in the North also promised that the first shot would serve as a signal for the slave revolution. Docility among slaves, planters knew, was not inherent, but the product of careful discipline. Consequently, as one planter noted in the fall of 1860, "A little offense of a negro may cost him his life."[15]

After secession, one of the first orders of business was to tighten controls over slaves and all those who came into contact with them. David Gavin must have been pleased as Southerners put more bite into their laws against "tampering," buttressed their slave patrols and canceled exemptions from duty, called home slaves on hire in the cities, and voided slaves' passes to visit families on other plantations. Individuals also did what they could to tighten security. William Cooper of Mississippi captured four runaways in 1862, and instead of returning all of them to their owners, he returned three and hanged one as a public lesson.[16] Gentlemen in Henry A. Middleton's neighborhood in South Carolina adopted the same punishment but a different mathematics. When they captured six runaways, they returned three and hanged three. "The blacks were encouraged to be present," Middleton reported. "The effect will not soon be forgotten."[17]

But fears of insurrection would not die. Plantation dwellers kept their ears to the ground, listening for rumbles of black revolution. Waves of dread and fear drifted back and forth across the Confederacy. In late 1861, a Mississippi woman heard a rumor that Natchez officials had recently quashed an attempted "servile insurrection" in their city. She told a friend that the revolutionaries "were supposed to come to this co. next[;] they were to kill every Negro that wouldn't join them."[18] More often, letters between planters contained a line or two confirming the fact that their blacks were still quiet. Six weeks after Sumter, William Kirkland let his anxious sister know that the "Negroes here are as subordinate as ever and if properly managed and well treated will I think continue so. . . . "[19] Two years later Fanny I. Erwin remarked that the "negroes too are as quiet & well-contented as they can be, in spite of the fears of a great many who apprehend trouble this winter."[20] The planters repeated descriptions of the slave's docility doubtlessly revealed their nagging fears of his rebelliousness.

Dread reached a crescendo in September, 1862, with Lincoln's Emancipation Proclamation. Planters saw in it the most unprincipled villainy. John Houston Bills of Tennessee thought Lincoln was trying his mightiest to inaugurate "servile War" and feared "a great loss of property and perhaps of life."[21] The young mayor of Savannah looked upon the act "as a direct bid for insurrection," an "infamous attempt to incite flight, murder, and rapine on the part of our slave population." Is it not an effort "to subvert our entire social system, desolate our homes, and convert the quiet, ignorant dependent black son of toil into a savage incendiary and brutal murderer?" he asked his father. His father agreed that Lincoln's message reeked of the "same heartless, cold-blooded, and murderous fanaticism that first began and has marked the war. . . . "[22] When January 1, the day the Proclamation went into effect, came and went quietly, planters breathed a sigh of relief. But as long as slavery existed they were never released from anxiety.

The abolitionist threat was not restricted to speeches and proclamations from Washington. War meant that the South was filled with Yankee soldiers, each of whom, the planters said, was itching to foment rebellion. In Virginia, Thomas Watson declared his "main dread" to be "that the Yankees will attempt to liberate and arm the slaves."[23] The path of Northern armies was marked by the trail of rumors it left behind. Hugh Torrance of Mississippi reported that raiding Yankees had told slaves that to be free "all they would have to do would be to kill their owners & take possession & live as white people."[24] When Federal troops invaded North Carolina, a rumor marched with them that the slaves were only waiting for the signal "to rise up against their masters & strike a blow for Union."[25] Louis Manigault of South Carolina charged that the South was dealing with "an Enemy of no principle whatsoever, whose only aim is . . . to arm our own Negroes against their very Masters; and entice by every means this misguided Race to assist them in their diabolical programme." With "this species of Warfare none of us can boast of our positions," he said, "for never with more truth can it be said None of us can tell 'what a day may bring forth.' "[26]

Yankees, however, were only one source of abolitionist ideas. Some two dozen planters from Marion District, South Carolina, pointed their fingers at another that was closer to home. In a May, 1862, appeal to their governor, they reported that there was in their neighborhood a family of "nonslaveholders" who traded with blacks, who sent no men to serve in the Confederate forces, and whom they believed to be responsible for the burning of several buildings. This family was "dangerous to the Community, subversive of all discipline among our Slaves and hostile to our Government." Soon, the planters declared, these people might even "incite an insurrection among the slaves in the neighborhood." If the government did not act, "we will be compelled for the protection of our families and our property to take the matter in our own hands."[27] Not all nonslaveholders were suspected of being provocateurs, but as a class, they received special scrutiny.

[. . .]

Disruptions of traditional plantation routine resounded in the slave cabins and were often reflected in slave behavior. The impact may have been muted but it was rarely entirely muffled. Almost any change alarmed Southern planters. "I certainly agree with you that the negroes must have meat," Langdon Cheves II told a worried friend. "They have been so regularly accustomed to it that a sudden change would produce great discontent. . . ."[28] But sudden change became commonplace during the war. Two sources of change which promised to be particularly disruptive were the transformation of the agricultural base of the plantations and the government's policy of slave impressment.

Planters were apprehensive about shifting away from staple crops. Staples–slaves–plantations was the traditional pattern, and they feared that the remaining two elements could not withstand the defection of the first. Without a cash crop, how would they maintain their farms? Loss of income was one fear, but they were also worried about how the change would affect the slaves. One argument planters used against a sharp contraction of the cotton acreage was, What would you do with the slaves? The cultivation of staples kept the slaves in the fields for the entire year, providing constant work, known work schedules, and defined tasks. The ruts were deep and therefore safe, stable, and predictable. Food crops, on the other hand, were seasonal, requiring new routines and untried schedules. They made increased supervision necessary just when supervisors were in short supply. Behind the debate on staples versus provisions, then, lurked the older issue of slave discipline.

Only overseers and managers, apparently, were able to see a bright side to the agricultural revolution. Perhaps they were pleased at being relieved of the pressure to produce so many bales to the hand or pounds to the acre. An Alabaman argued that the switch in crops "will change the face of our country very much & is desirable in every view." He explained that "it will rest the lands . . . beautify the whole canebrake with grasses clover stock & other improvements, & perhaps not materially diminish . . . incomes in the end."[29] In answer to a question from the owner about what to do with the slaves when there was so little cotton, an overseer in Mississippi responded, "O, plenty to do, that ought to have been done before, but we were run down after cotton-cotton! We shall have time to ditch, and the plantation needs it much, and long has needed it. We shall fix our fences and hedges; we shall move the negro cabins, and put them up right, and in order, and with brick chimneys. We shall do a heap, that we have heretofore left undone."[30]

The transformation was successful; the South produced enough food, and did it without a slave insurrection. But the transition from cotton to corn was not smooth. It disrupted routine and often affected slave behavior. When slaves were pressed into work that was unfamiliar or outside the old routine, slaveholders often complained of "demoralization," a generic term that referred to every sort of misbehavior from rudeness to rebellion. One Gulf coast planter surveyed his slaves and concluded that he needed to get them back to the discipline and routine of cotton production before they became as useless as the staple they had once produced.[31]

Confederate impressment of slaves was another intrusion that particularly worried planters. They opposed impressments on principle and on practical grounds. When John Houston Bills faced the loss of four of his bondsmen to the military in the fall of 1861, he argued that impressment was unconscionable. "A most villainous call," he cried, one which the government has "no right to make & [which] is the beginning of a despotism worse than any European Monarchy." He reminded the authorities that the South was "fighting for liberty," but he thought "we had more 'Liberty' & prosperity 12 months ago than we shall ever see again. . . ."[32] Toward the end of the war, the Richmond *Examiner* attempted to explain the stubborn refusal of planters to part with their laborers. Planters have been accused of selfishness, the paper pointed out, but their objections were "not so much to the employment of the Negro in itself, as to the shock to the rights of property which is involved." On this one kind of property, the *Examiner* explained, "the South has concentrated all its proprietary feeling, and the man who would submit without a murmur to the impressment of his horses or his crops may very likely shrink back with a species of superstition . . . from the attempt by his own government to deprive him of these very slaves for whom he had already fought a long and desperate war."[33]

The *Examiner* was correct when it argued that encroachments on slavery called forth especially fierce responses for reasons of principle. But very practical considerations also motivated the objections. Planters were naturally reluctant to give up their valuable labor and expensive property, especially after they learned that slaves in government service were often brutally treated and miserably cared for. Also, planters were supposed to receive compensation for the use of the slaves, but payment was erratic. Terms of service were explicit and short, but once the slaves were enrolled they were difficult to get back. And the government had a way of asking for slaves just at harvest time. Howell Cobb declared that planters had a right to expect "reason and common sense in the officials of Government."[34] An objection that was as important as any of the rest was expressed by a Georgia planter in 1862. "If my negroes are carried to Savannah under this order," he declared, "I will abandon them. I do not want them to return to the plantation to demoralize the balance." Removed from their plantation homes and set down in strange and distant places, slaves could develop "dangerous habits" and acquire "foolish ideas."[35] A single infected individual, planters believed, could contaminate an entire slave population.

What was at stake was not only the planter's pride, his prickly individualism, his property, and his liberties, but more than these, the institution of slavery itself. The right to control one's own slaves was paramount. To weaken the authority of the master, to loosen the fetters of slavery, was to tamper with the vital workings of the institution. No wonder, then, that planters failed to respond satisfactorily to the government's call for slave labor. In a report written to explain the shortage of slaves being made available, an official in South Carolina said, "For the end in view, even for what has been accomplished, how trifling has been the sacrifice." In exasperation he explained that "only one month's labor" was being required, but even "that much has not been furnished." In fact, "the greatest complaints . . . have been from those who have furnished least."[36] In Virginia, while slave labor played a crucial role in the state's war effort, planters were less and less willing to serve up their slaves. By 1864, only about 75 per cent of those legally requisitioned by the government were ever provided.[37]

How well slavery functioned on a particular plantation could have been determined, before the war, by a glance at the production figures – the bales of cotton, hogsheads of sugar, pounds of tobacco or rice – but such indicators were useless in the disrupted economy of the Confederacy. One of the crudest ways of keeping track of the situation was simply to list all of one's slaves and then cross out the names of those who ran away to "Lincoln land." Most planters used more subtle methods, however. They scrutinized the behavior of the slaves to see how slavery was withstanding the assault of war. How well did the blacks work in the fields? A bit of hesitancy in the stroke? How did they speak to the white family? A trace of defiance? Planters kept their fingers on the pulse of the plantation for signs of "Yankee fever."

The reaction of slaves to war spanned the widest possible spectrum – from taking up the rifle of a slain master and firing at the vile Yankee to putting on the blue uniform and firing at the vile master. The behavior of most was concentrated in the middle portion of the spectrum, ranging from faithful service throughout the war to slipping away from the plantation at the first opportunity. While the loyal and devoted servant was by no means a myth, he loomed much larger in postwar fiction than he did in wartime reality. Slaves did not often revolt, but they did not remain "loyal" either. Most planters reported more theft and malingering and less diligence and deference. As discipline loosened and routine crumbled, blacks found more and more freedom in the crevices of plantation life.

On one of the South's most famous plantations, Susan Dabney Smedes later remembered, "life went on as usual." If anything, in fact, the servants "went about their duties more conscientiously than before. They seemed to do better when there was trouble in the white family, and they knew there was trouble enough. . . ."[38] Similarly, a South Carolinian reported on Christmas Day of 1864 that his position was "wretched," but, at least, "Our negroes are as orderly as usual. . . . They are anxious about the future & seem to sympathize with us in our distress."[39] Near the end of the war, John Edwin Fripp, owner of two plantations on Saint Helena Island, off the coast of South Carolina, reported that Federals had burned his house and stripped his plantations. "I am happy to say my negroes have acted orderly and well all the time," he announced, "none going off excepting one or two Boys who accompanied the yanks for plunder but have returned home and appear quite willing to go to work." The others "acted nobly[,] furnishing my family with provisions and return[ing] all they saved by begging the Yankees[.]"[40]

More often, planters were gravely disappointed. In North Carolina, Catherine Edmondston witnessed the "total demoralization" of her bondsmen. When the war began, her slaves were "diligent and respectful," and she responded as their kindly protector. She recorded that when they learned that "the Yankees were trying to steal them," they "entreated me not to leave them & I have promised to remain at home & take what care I can of them." A month later she noted that slaves on neighboring plantations were behaving badly, but she thought they were "the indulged negroes, servants of widows & single ladies who have not been kept in proper subordination." She was thankful that none of hers thought he was "as good as a Yankee." Shortly afterward, however, she began to be troubled by the behavior of her own slaves. She believed the problem stemmed from her husband's absence and her own frequent trips away from the plantation. "These constant absences...are telling on the servants," she declared. "They are getting so awkward, inefficient & even lazy!" By the end of the year, her patience was exhausted. "[A]s to the idea of a *faithful servant, it is all a fiction*," she exclaimed. "I have seen the favorite & most petted negroes the first to leave in every instance." They had changed from dutiful servants to impudent slaves in a few short months, she observed sorrowfully.[41]

When planters spied insubordinate behavior among their slaves, they responded in a variety of ways. James Lusk Alcorn, noticing laziness among his bondsmen, "whipped several in the field" and was pleased with the result.[42] A Georgian promised harsher punishment. After capturing two runaways, he said that if "Jim and Ike tried it again," he would "kill them both."[43] Others sought to maintain control by removing their slaves from proximity to Union troops. The South was filled with masters and slaves searching for a "safe place." The British observer A. J. Fremantle was on hand in 1863 when General Nathaniel Banks marched into Louisiana's Red River valley. "The road today was alive with negroes," he reported. They were "being 'run' into Texas out of Banks' way."[44] Others simply sold their troublemakers. In 1863, a Georgia man reported continual difficulty with a particular slave. At the end of the year he simply noted, "I sold Big Henry for $2400."[45]

Despite the planters' best efforts, however, on some estates power clearly shifted from the "big house" to the slave cabins. Mrs. C. C. Clay, Sr., of Alabama, for instance, was soon forced to rely on "moral suasion" to "get them to do their duty." She noted that her efforts were only occasionally successful. And a year later, her situation had declined to the point where she "begged ... what little is done."[46] Although the shift was rarely this complete, power did tend to gravitate toward the slave quarters.

Responses of planters to their bondsmen during the war depended a great deal, naturally, on the slaves' behavior. And planters often oscillated between optimism and pessimism as the scene out their front windows changed. But their feelings also depended on their basic assumptions about slaves and slavery. Some felt deep responsibility for and devotion to their slaves. Alfred Huger, for instance, once heard that a cholera epidemic was threatening the Cooper River plantations. If it came to his, he declared, "I shall join my Negroes immediately and shall share their fate." He explained that "the system of slavery is perfectly in keeping with my principles as a Politician & as a Christian, but the Master should in my opinion be the last to run away when danger comes."[47] Others showed a total lack of affection or empathy. An Alabama planter wrote home in 1862 that he "was not very sorry to hear of old Will's demise and if he had only held on until the crop was laid by I could have given him up with all my heart." His wife's news that the slaves were idle did not surprise him, he added. "You must have them whiped [sic] when they need it. You must pay particular attention to the hogs...." The following year, in reply to his wife's inquiry about selling a slave to pay some debts, he said that he "didn't care much" one way or the other, but he certainly did not want her sold at less than "the market price."[48]

Planters sometimes maintained their fondness and concern for their slaves even when their "black family" deserted them. The disloyalty of slaves did not so much shock as sadden them, and they directed their anger at the enticer rather than the enticed. After all, how could whites condemn the Negro for following the dictates of his own immature nature? Planters commonly referred to runaways as "poor deluded wretches" and "poor deluded creatures." A Georgian reported that many of his servants had left, "deserting their best friends, to enjoy the poor Negroes['] idea of freedom, that is perfect idleness, not knowing that God meant all his creatures to work."[49] A South Carolinian said, "Poor fools! how deceived & mistaken they are." He was truly disturbed when he heard that the Federal authorities had taken the men "without regard to family separations and sent [them] any & every where under guards, where they are hard worked & miserably fed."[50] In his eyes at least, slavery had never been so brutal and inhumane. Another planter explained the behavior of runaways in understandable human terms. They fled, he explained, because the "temptation of change, the promise of freedom, and of pay for labor, is more than most can stand."[51] Many planters responded to the plight of the blacks with genuine pity, feeling almost as sorry for them as they felt for themselves.

Many others, however, registered shock, hurt, disillusionment, and rage. They shut off empathy for insubordinate blacks just as they closed off concern for disrespectful poor whites. Many saw themselves as having sacrificed considerable time and effort in training and uplifting *their* "people," only to be betrayed. Louis Manigault was cut deeply by the "ingratitude evinced in the African character." "In too many instances," he said, "those we esteemed the most have been the first to desert us."[52] Catherine Edmondston could neither understand nor forgive and wished "that there was not a negro left in this country."[53] The change of heart was reflected clearly in the nomenclature planters used in referring to their slaves. Before the war, those of the least refinement almost never employed the blunt term "slaves" in speaking of their own bondsmen. They resorted to an abundance of euphemisms, ranging from the plain "servants" and "laborers" to the intimate "my black friends," "my black family," and "my people." In the final years of the war, however, planters commonly spoke of their "slaves" and even of their "niggers." From servant to slave was a long journey. It meant that something had died which would be difficult to resurrect. It marked the early stages of a trend that would lead to disdain and hostility toward blacks during Reconstruction.

Instead of being sympathetic, disappointed, or angry, some planters were simply terrified. For years they had heard orators describe the bloody scenes that would occur if slavery were ever disrupted. And now, all around them, the system was breaking down. Early in 1865, six of South Carolina's most illustrious families – among them the Allstons and the Sparkmans – rushed a petition to the Federal Military Command to plead for protection from the Negroes. Freed by invading Union troops, they were "in the most disorderly & lawless condition, if not savage and barbarous." The petitioners begged in the "name of common humanity & Christian civilization" that the Northern commander send soldiers to save the Pee Dee planters from this "insurrectionary force."[54]

Whatever a planter's feeling toward his slaves, he was bound eventually to agree with the Reverend C. C. Jones that "no reliance can be placed *certainly* upon any."[55] Inevitably, if not his own servant, then the trusted servant of an acquaintance would abscond. But, ironically, just at the moment when planters had the least faith in their bondsmen, they relied most heavily on their loyalty. With the normal supervisors away, blacks were largely on their own on many plantations. Drivers were often pressed into service as overseers. Mary Jones of Georgia explained that one of her plantations was "necessarily left to Andrew's fidelity."[56] When a Mississippi man departed for the army he made his carriage driver foreman of his estate. Realizing that he was asking his slave to assume increased responsibility just when the rewards for disloyalty were highest, he offered him a bribe, telling him that "if the south was successful and he was faithful to his trust," he would "give him his freedom."[57] A promise of personal manumission by a planter was far from the enemy's pledge of general emancipation; still, the very fact that a master felt compelled to match the enemy's offer of freedom with a similar offer of his own meant that the war was turning plantations and slavery upside down.

[...]

Perhaps the single most powerful force tempting planters to acquiesce in the destruction of slavery was the weariness produced by the long, vastly destructive war. Days of worry stretched into months and years. Unrelieved strain sapped energy, health, and confidence.

Anxiety – about unpredictable poor whites, untrustworthy blacks, an unreliable government; about where to find food and how to fend off destruction – became the companion of every planter. Other Southerners suffered more, with even fewer cushions, but in the end some planters were brought to their knees, victims of physical and emotional exhaustion. For these, the desire to cease struggling, the need to find a quiet place, became paramount.

War played havoc with the participants' emotions, whipsawing them between grief and rage. Few families escaped the trauma of death. Sometimes it was the loss of a son or husband that touched them first, sometimes the loss of a friend. A Georgia woman who heard of the deaths of several neighbors said, "*Their deaths* have brought the war home to me more forceably than could the deaths of a regiment of soldiers from any other place."[58] While the news of death came suddenly, rage against the enemy built gradually. In 1864, a young planter declared, "Day by day and hour by hour does the deep seated enmity I have always had... for the accursed Yankee nation increase & burn higher.... they have slaughtered our kindred[,]... destroyed our prosperity as a people & filled our whole land with sorrow.... I have vowed that if I should have children – the first ingredient of the first principle of their education shall be uncompromising hatred & contempt of the Yankee."[59]

Planters were exhausted by the rush of emotion that flung them from one pole to the other. A Louisiana man thought that constant "excitement is not quite death but pretty near."[60] Ella Clanton Thomas of Georgia said that a "life of emotion, quick rapid succession of startling events," wore upon "the constitution and weakened the physical nature." Her "nervous organization" was "so completely disorganized" that she needed perfect quiet. "I feel as if I did not have energy to raise my head," she reported. "My mind is sluggish and my will is weak and undecided. I lack energy... spiritually, intellectually, & physically. I have been... dull inert and desponding." The problem was, she said, that "the human mind is so constituted that it cannot stand a constant pressure" and "the war has been going on for a much longer time than we could have thought."[61] David Gavin hardly understood his problem at all. "I have plenty of provisions," he said, "and yet I am sick, dull and low spirited.... sick, sick, heart, soul, mind, body & spirit."[62] Some could not even escape into sleep. In the week the war ended, William Cooper dreamed "of flood & planks to walk on... amid mud [and] water – & of my driving [a] wagon amid rain & high water with 2 mules... in flight from the enemies."[63]

The unrelieved tension pushed the minds of men and women to the edge of sanity, and sometimes beyond. The British observer A. J. Fremantle recounted the tragedy of a Mississippi planter he met in the summer of 1863. "We had a crazy old planter... with us," he recalled. "He insisted upon accompanying the column, mounted on a miserable animal which had been left him by the enemy as not being worth carrying away. The small remains of this poor old man's sense had been shattered by the Yankees a few days ago. They had cleaned him completely out, taking his horses, mules, cows, and pigs, and stealing his clothes and anything they wanted, destroying what they could not carry away." This broken planter, Fremantle said, had "insisted on picking some of the silk of Indian corn, which he requested I would present to Queen Victoria to show her how far advanced the crops were in Mississippi."[64]

By the end of the war anything that promised relief was tempting. In October, 1864, Octavia Otey of Alabama felt "quite desperate... like I could struggle no longer."[65] William J. Minor, owner of three plantations in Louisiana, cried out, "Peace – peace – peace – God grant it – and stop this most unnatural & most bloody war."[66] The fiery Southern patriot Ella Clanton Thomas said that "the time and circumstances somehow appears to create a reckless, careless feeling, an impatience to have it over." She craved freedom from war. "At times," she said in March, 1865, "I feel as if I was drifting on, on, ever onward to be at last dashed against some rock and I shut my eyes and almost wish it was over, the shock encountered and I prepared to know what destiny awaits me." She was "tired, oh so tired" and wanted to "breathe free." "I feel the restraint of the blockade and as port after port becomes blockaded I feel shut up, pent up and am irresistably reminded of the old story of the iron shroud contracting more and more each hour...." She thought that someday she might "be glad that I have lived through this war," but "now the height of my ambition is to be *quiet*...."[67] By 1865, peace and quiet had become for some planters the primary object.

Another powerful force operating to detach planters from slavery was the institution's unprofitability in wartime. By 1865 most Southern plantations had become economic burdens rather than financial blessings. Each year of the war, incomes fell off more sharply. Louis Bringier, a large planter in Louisiana, said in December, 1864, "I do not know what we will do with our darkies. They are a great source of annoyance, and but very little profit at the present." He concluded that "they will have to become more profitable or we shall have to give them up in self-defence."[68] Bringier's urge toward voluntary emancipation was only momentary, for in April, 1865, he was willing to take up guerrilla warfare for the Confederate cause. But the fact remains that most planters could not afford to be indifferent to the financial difficulties accompanying slavery in wartime. A few had indicated all along that a handsome profit was their only objective. Before the war, a Virginian had complained that slavery did not pay in his state. "It may be different in Cotton Country," he said, but "it has been a losing business in Virginia." He had decided, therefore, to "clear out every thing but portraits and go right to a city."[69] Planters whose only interest in slavery was profit were sometimes ready and relieved by 1865 to rid themselves of their nonproducing consumers.

An extensive debate grew up among planters about what was the most secure investment during wartime. Until the last year of the war, they engaged in a brisk trade in slaves. But while slave property had always been admired for its liquidity, during the war that characteristic proved a serious problem. Hundreds of thousands of slaves spilled over into the Union lines. Slaveowners sometimes expressed a willingness to sell all their bondsmen if they could find a safer investment. Robert Newell of Louisiana thought "cows and mares" were his best bet,[70] but most planters who sought an alternative to slaves looked to land or Confederate bonds. Henry L. Graves advised his father that "land is the only safe investment now."[71] Another Georgian declared that he would "rather have land than Negroes."[72] If the Federals invaded his Saint Johns River plantation, a Florida man asserted, "I shall take black and white of the family into Georgia and turn the blacks into Confederate Bonds."[73]

Without the income to provide properly for their slaves, sensitive planters found them a heavy emotional burden. John Jones, a minister-planter from Georgia, brooded over his responsibilities. "I am truly tired of my daily cares," he said in 1863, "they are without number. To clothe and shoe and properly feed our Negroes and pay our taxes requires more than we make by planting, especially when debts have to be paid." In his opinion, "the most pressed people in our Confederacy are the owners of slaves who have no way to support them. Sometimes I think that Providence by this cruel war is intruding to make us willing to relinquish slavery by feeling its burdens and cares."[74] Whether they were more sensitive to their own burdens or to those of their slaves, planters could sometimes see in the emancipation of blacks their own personal liberation.

Another force which wore down some planters' dedication to slavery was the slaves' "demoralized" behavior. Insubordination and defection angered many slaveholders. Planters learned how little they knew of their slaves, even their most trusted and "most petted." Shortly after the end of the war, Ella Clanton Thomas learned that "Susan, Kate's nurse, Ma's most trusty servant, her advisor, right hand woman and best liked house servant has left her."[75] They were pained to find that "those we loved best, and who loved us best – as we thought – were the first to leave us."[76] Piqued by their bad behavior, one Virginia planter was for the moment at least genuinely glad that the invading Yankee army had relieved him of "the plague, vexation & expense of so many idle, worthless & ungrateful house servants."[77] Disloyalty among the slaves tended to deaden those warm feelings of paternal responsibility which were a significant buttress, as well as an important reward, of the institution of slavery.

Some plantation dwellers entered the war with doubts about the morality of slavery, and four years of destruction sometimes transformed their doubt into certainty. "Southern women are I believe all at heart abolisionists [sic]," Ella Clanton Thomas of Georgia had said in 1858. The institution, she thought, "degrades the white man more than the Negro and oh exerts a most deleterious effect upon our children." During the war she read proslavery books to convince herself that slavery was right, but she concluded that it was morally indefensible. "This is a subject upon which I do not like to think," she said in 1864, but "taking my stand upon the moral view of the subject, I can but think that to hold men and women in *perpetual* bondage is wrong."[78] Southerners were accustomed to finding the hand of God in all things, and some wondered if the disastrous war was not divine retribution for the sin of slavery. Dolly Burge of Georgia said that she had "never felt that slavery was altogether right for it is abused by many."[79] The wartime movement to humanize the institution of slavery was probably built in part upon doubt and guilt. Despite their efforts, it is likely that some plantation folk saw in the destruction of slavery the fiery cleansing of sin.

In addition, either an indomitable American patriotism or a vibrant Southern nationalism could operate to undermine a planter's attachment to slavery. Although not all Unionists believed their patriotism automatically linked them with the cause of abolition, many persistent Unionists were committed to supporting the Union whatever the cost, even if it meant emancipation. One such Unionist planter claimed after the war that he was "not opposed to secession merely" but even approved "the acts that established the freedom of the slaves."[80] A real, whole-souled devotion to the cause of Confederate independence also could convince a planter that any independence, even one without slavery, was preferable to subjugation and renewed Yankee domination. An exemplar of this viewpoint was Jefferson Davis, that Mississippi slaveholder who as president of the Confederate States of America was willing to sacrifice slavery to win Southern nationhood. Intense patriotism directed to either the United States or the Confederacy, therefore, could diminish a Southerner's attachment to slavery.

By the end of the war, some planters were receiving few financial, political, social, or psychological rewards from slavery. Financially, they considered slavery more a burden than an asset. Politically, they found their views shouldered aside by men with military and diplomatic perspectives. Socially, they recognized that as military and governmental service grew in prestige, slave ownership was no longer the single avenue to status. And psychologically, they received little benefit from plantations filled with restless and footloose slaves. As bad as things were, moreover, they threatened to get worse. By 1865, blacks were moving through the South at will, and nonslaveholding whites were growing increasingly surly and disrespectful. Planters feared a total breakdown of order. Lawlessness and chaos, they thought, were imminent. In a somewhat similar situation in Brazil some twenty years later, slaveholders accepted abolition in order to check further disintegration.[81] It is probable that some planters acquiesced in the final abolition of slavery in 1865 because slavery's rewards had shriveled and its burdens increased. Peace, in some minds, offered the only hope for rest, relief, order, and security.

Notes

1   Daniel R. Hundley, *Social Relations in Our Southern States*, pp. 49, *passim*.

2   Frederick Law Olmsted, *The Cotton Kingdom, passim*.

3   One perpetuator of the myth of the planter as a disinterested, ineffectual manager was George Bagby. In his description of the "Virginia gentleman," he said that "the whole of the character is fully told only when you come to open his 'secretary.' There you will find his bonds, accounts, receipts, and even his will, jabbed into pigeon-holes or lying about loose in the midst of a museum of powder-horns, shot-gourds, turkey-yelpers, flints, screws, pop-corn, old horseshoes and watermelon seed." George W. Bagby, *The Old Virginia Gentleman and Other Sketches*, p. 57. Several historians have recently attempted to replace one myth with another. Rejecting the notion that planters were primitive businessmen, they argue that planters actually anticipated the Frederick W. Taylor school of scientific management. See R. Keith Aufhauser, "Slavery and Scientific Management," *Journal of Economic History (JEH)*, 33 (Dec., 1973), 811–24; and Robert William Fogel and Stanley L. Engerman, *Time on the Cross: The Economics of American Negro Slavery*, pp. 200–6.

4   Alfred Huger to John Preston, Dec. 11, 1856, Alfred Huger Papers, Duke.

5   Charles C. Jones, Jr., to Rev. C. C. Jones, July 25, 1862; Rev. C. C. Jones to Charles C. Jones, Jr., July 10, 1862, in Robert Manson Myers, ed., *The Children of Pride: A True Story of Georgia and the Civil War*, pp. 940, 929.

6   George M. Fredrickson, *The Black Image in the White Mind: The Debate on Afro-American Character and Destiny, 1817–1914*, pp. 43–70.

7   Mrs. Catherine Ann Edmondston Diaries, June 27, 1863, and March 26, 1862, North Carolina Department of Archives and History, Releigh (hereafter NCAH).

8   Henry Watson, Jr., to Sarah Carrington, Jan. 28, 1861, Henry Watson, Jr., Papers, Duke.

9   Mrs. Mary Jones to Charles C. Jones, Jr., May 28, 1863, in Myers, ed., *Children of Pride*, p. 1063.

10 Alfred Huger to J. Harleston Read, Nov. 9, 1854, Alfred Huger Papers, Duke.

11 H. L. Green to his sister, Oct. 29, 1854, Crabtree Jones Papers, NCAH.

12 Clipping from Sarah J. B. Cain's scrapbook, signed "North Carolina planter," Oct. 12, 1857, John Lancaster Bailey Papers, Southern Historical Collection, University of North Carolina, Chapel Hill (SHC). While in New York in 1859, a Louisianan wrote to his wife, "I have seen more misery since I have been in this city than I have since I have ben in the union [;] it is awful." He had also seen a great many "expensive things," he said, but he thought that if the money had been spent on "the poore of this City it would have been a greate deal better." Robert A. Newell to Sarah Newell, June 1, 1859, Robert A. Newell Papers, Louisiana State Department of Archives, Louisiana State University, Baton Rouge (LSU).

13 Mrs. Catherine Ann Edmondston Diaries, June 1, 1862, NCAH.

14 David Gavin Diary, Dec. 17, 1859, SHC.

15 C. D. Whittle to L. N. Whittle, Oct. 30, 1860, Lewis Neale Whittle Papers, SHC.

16 William Cooper Diaries, April, 1862, SHC.

17 Henry A. Middleton to Harriott Middleton, Nov. 5, 1862, Langdon Cheves Collection, South Carolina Historical Society, Charlesten (SCHS).

18 S. M. Hunt to "Jennie," Oct. 15, 1861, Hughes Family Papers, SCH.

19 William Kirkland to Octavia Otey, May 22, 1861, Wyche and Otey Family Papers, SHC.

20 Fanny I. Erwin to Cadwallader Jones, Jr., Jan. 17, 1863, Cadwallader Jones, Jr., Papers, SHC.

21 John Houston Bills Diary, Dec. 13, 1862, John Houston Bills Papers, SHC.

22 Charles C. Jones, Jr., to Rev. C. C. Jones, Sept. 27, 1862; Rev. C. C. Jones to Charles C. Jones, Jr., Sept. 30, 1862, in Myers, ed., *Children of Pride*, pp. 967, 969. Because planters believed that emancipation was Lincoln's aim from the beginning, some responded to the proclamation calmly, thinking it a mere formality. See, for example, Ella Gertrude (Clanton) Thomas Journal, Oct. 7, 1862, Duke.

23 Diary of Thomas Watson, July 4, 1862, Watson Papers, University of Virginia (UVA).

24 Hugh Torrance to Mrs. T. M. Reid, Feb. 16, 1863, George F. Davidson Papers, Duke.

25 Mrs. Catherine Ann Edmondston Diaries, March 23, 1863, NCAH.

26 Louis Manigault Diary, Sept., 1862, in Albert V. House, ed., "Deterioration of a Georgia Rice Plantation during Four Years of Civil War," *Journal of Southern History*, 9 (Feb., 1943), 106.

27 An appeal to the governor, May 2, 1862, James M. Chestnut, Jr., Letters and Papers, Duke. Even if the Yankees and the Southern nonslaveholders could not convince the slaves to pick up the torch and knife, the planters feared, they could tempt them into running away. C. C. Jones pointed out that runaways destroyed slavery just as effectively as barn burners. And, besides, they might "pilot an enemy into your *bedchamber!*" Rev. C. C. Jones to Charles C. Jones, Jr., July 10, 1862, in Myers, ed., *Children of Pride*, p. 929.

28 Langdon Cheves II to William T. Haskell, March 5, 1862, Langdon Cheves Collection, SCHS. Eugene Genovese brilliantly analyzes the process by which slaves took what masters perceived as privileges and reinterpreted them as rights, which they demanded. Eugene D. Genovese, *Roll, Jordan, Roll: The World the Slaves Made, passim.*

29 J. A. Wemyss to Henry Watson, Jr., Jan. 28, 1862, Henry Watson, Jr., Papers, Duke.

30 Quoted in John K. Bettersworth, ed., *Mississippi in the Confederacy: As They Saw It*, p. 224.

31 James Allen to his wife, Jan., 1864, James Allen and Charles B. Allen Papers, SHC.

32 John Houston Bills Diary, Oct. 8, 1861, John Houston Bills Papers, SHC.

33 Quoted in Harrison A. Trexler, "The Opposition of Planters to the Employment of Slaves as Laborers by the Confederacy," *Mississippi Valley Historical Review (MVHR)*, 27 (1940), 213.

34 Ibid., 217.

35 Quoted in T. Conn Bryan, *Confederate Georgia*, p. 132.

36 Report of William M. Shannon, 1864, Miscellaneous Manuscripts, SCHS.

37 James H. Brewer, *The Confederate Negro: Virgina's Craftsmen and Military Laborers, 1861–1865*, pp. 152–3.

38 Susan Dabney Smedes, *Memorials of a Southern Planter*, pp. 196–7.

39 James B. Heyward to Maria Heyward, Dec. 25, 1864, Heyward and Ferguson Family Papers, SHC.

40 John Edwin Fripp Diary, 1864 or 1865, John Edwin Fripp Papers, SHC.

41 Mrs. Catherine Ann Edmondston Diaries, Feb. 12, 1862, March 31, 1862, May 10, 1862, and Sept. 9, 1862, NCAH.

42 James Lusk Alcorn to Amelia Alcorn, Dec. 18, 1862, James Lusk Alcorn Papers, SHC.

43 M. M. Green to Mary Jones, Dec. 7, 1863, Crabtree Jones Papers, NCAH.

44 A. J. Fremantle, *Three Months in the Southern States: April–June 1863*, p. 45. After Port Royal fell and it appeared that Federal troops would drive up the Savannah River, the Manigaults, simply as a precautionary measure, removed ten slaves from their plantation, "selecting such as we deemed most likely would cause trouble." Charles and Louis Manigault Records, June 12, 1862, Georgia Historical Society (GaHS).

45 Quoted in Bryan, *Confederate Georgia*, p. 125.

46 Quoted in H. E. Sterkx, *Partners in Rebellion: Alabama Women in the Civil War*, p. 132.

47 Alfred Huger to Thomas Bee Huger, Sept. 15, 1854, Alfred Huger Papers, Duke. Agreeing with Huger's sentiment, another South Carolinian argued that a master should never "desert his negroes." In fact, she declared, "where negroes are deserting to the enemy, their master left them first." Mrs. Manning to John Manning, June 17, 1861, Williams-Chesnut-Manning Papers, South Carolina Library (SCL).

48 N. W. E. Long to his wife, June 17, 1862, and Feb. 18, 1863, N. W. E. Long Confederate Soldier's Letters, Emory.

49 William King Diary, Sept. 6, 1864, William King Papers, SHC.

50 "Max" to "Buss," Sept. 19, 1862, Williams-Chesnut-Manning Papers, SCL.

51 Rev. C. C. Jones to Mrs. Eliza G. Robarts, July 5, 1862, in Myers, ed., *Children of Pride*, 925.

52 Louis Manigault Diary, June 12, 1862, in House, ed., "Deterioration of a Georgia Rice Plantation," 102.

53 Mrs. Catherine Ann Edmondston Diaries, Sept. 9, 1862, NCAH.

54   Petition to the Federal Military Command, Georgetown District, March 6, 1865, Sparkman Family Papers, SHC.

55   Rev. C. C. Jones to Mrs. Eliza G. Robarts, July 5, 1862, in Myers, ed., *Children of Pride*, p. 925.

56   Mrs. Mary Jones to Charles C. Jones, Jr., May 28, 1863, in Myers, ed., *Children of Pride*, p. 958.

57   Quoted in James W. Silver, ed., *Mississippi in the Confederacy: As Seen in Retrospect*, p. 286.

58   Ella Gertrude (Clanton) Thomas Journal, July 21, 1861, Duke.

59   Henry Graves to a cousin, Oct. 10, 1864, Graves Family Papers, SHC.

60   A. F. Rightor to Andrew McCollam, Aug. 10, 1864, Andrew McCollam Papers, SHC.

61   Ella Gertrude (Clanton) Thomas Journal, Dec. 31, 1863, June 28, 1864, July 12, 1864, and March 29, 1865, Duke.

62   David Gavin Diary, July 8, 1863, SHC.

63   William Cooper Diaries, April, 1865, SHC.

64   Fremantle, *Three Months in the Southern States*, pp. 19–22.

65   Octavia Otey Diary, Oct. 3, 1864, Wyche and Otey Family Papers, SHC.

66   Quoted in J. Carlyle Sitterson, "The Transition from Slave to Free Economy on the William J. Minor Plantations," *AgH*, 17 (Oct., 1943), p. 219.

67   Ella Gertrude (Clanton) Thomas Journal, Dec. 26, 1864, and March 29, 1865, Duke.

68   Louis Bringier to "Stella," Dec. 31, 1864, Louis Amedee Bringier Papers, LSU.

69   C. D. Whittle to L. N. Whittle, July 24, 1860, and Sept. 29, 1860, Lewis Neale Whittle Papers, SHC.

70   Robert Newell to Sarah Newell, Jan. 24, 1863, Robert A. Newell Papers, LSU.

71   Henry L. Graves to Iverson Graves, Feb. 29, 1864, Graves Family Papers, SHC.

72   Quoted in Bryan, *Confederate Georgia*, p. 125.

73   John L'Engle to Edward L'Engle, March 11, 1863, Edward McCrady L'Engle Papers, SHC.

74   Rev. John Jones to Mrs. Mary Jones, Dec. 7, 1863, in Myers, ed., *Children of Pride*, p. 1121.

75   Ella Gertrude (Clanton) Thomas Journal, May 29, 1865, Duke.

76   Quoted in Bell Irvin Wiley, *The Plain People of the Confederacy*, p. 83.

77   C. Chesnut to Mrs. Manning, Nov. 8, 1863, Williams-Chesnut-Manning Papers, SCL.

78   Ella Gertrude (Clanton) Thomas Journal, Jan. 2, 1858, and May 23, 1864, Duke.

79   Dolly Burge Diary, Nov. 8, 1864, Burge-Gray Papers, Emory.

80   Quoted in Frank W. Klingberg, *The Southern Claims Commission*, p. 108.

81   Robert Brent Toplin, "The Specter of Crisis: Slaveholder Reactions to Abolitionism in the United States and Brazil," *CWH*, 18 (June, 1972), 132; Robert Brent Toplin, *The Abolition of Slavery in Brazil*, pp. 225–46.

Questions to consider

- What were some of the challenges that planters faced in maintaining control over their property before and during the Civil War?

- How did the war change the uses for, and perceptions of, slaves?

- What were some of the reasons some planters were willing to conceive the end of slavery by 1865? (You might also consider what reasons were *not* part of their considerations.)

Chapter 14

"Answering Bells is Played Out": Slavery and the Civil War

Tena W. Hunter

For some, a loss of mastery was a worry; for others it was a hope. The war brought rapid changes to the South, changes that were both independent of, and intertwined with, race relations. Nowhere was this truer than in Atlanta, a new Southern city whose fortunes rose and fell with those of the Confederacy. (Indeed, Atlanta is a virtual character in its own right in Margaret Mitchell's 1936 novel *Gone with the Wind*.) The war created tremendous new complications for white property owners there – and prized new opportunities for an increasingly restive slave population. In this opening chapter from her 1999 book *To 'Joy My Freedom: Southern Black Women's Lives and Labors After the Civil War*, Tera W. Hunter describes the changes the war wrought, and the way slave women dealt with, and made the most of, those changes.

Tera W. Hunter, "Answering Bells is Played Out," in *To 'Joy My Freedom: Southern Black Women's Lives and Labors after the Civil War* (Cambridge, MA: Harvard University Press, 1997), pp. 4–20. Copyright © 1997 by the President and Fellows of Harvard College. Reprinted by permission of the publisher.

Ellen, a house slave in Atlanta, violated a long-established code of racial etiquette by wearing her mistress's toiletries during the early years of the Civil War. Imagine Ellen standing in the master bedroom of the Big House, playfully staring at her likeness reflected in a looking-glass mounted on a Victorian vanity. She primps her hair, rearranges her clothing, and shifts the view of her profile from front to side. Taking her pick among an array of dainty crystal bottles, she sniffs earthy and then floral fragrances and carefully applies one of the perfumes. While reveling in the crisp, cool feel of amber-tinted drops of liquid against her skin, she dreams about a life far away from the drudgery of her circumscribed existence – a life she believes could soon be within her reach.

Ellen audaciously indulged these vicarious pleasures repeatedly, even after being reprimanded by her owner, Samuel P. Richards, and eventually whipped. In pampering and adorning her body with the magical elixir, Ellen transgressed feminine beauty rituals intended to enhance white bodies only. She laid claim to a measure of possession of her own person – and a womanly person at that. The Civil War, as Ellen perceived, could erode the rituals of daily life in the South. Bondwomen like Ellen notified slaveowners that they could neither take servile obedience for granted nor be assured that chattel slaves would cook, clean, wash, mend, or greet arriving visitors as they had before. As another slave woman abruptly replied in response to her owner's command to attend to her duties: "answering bells is played out."[1]

Such incidents expose the increasingly pronounced clash of expectations between masters and slaves during the Civil War. Ellen waged her bets on the destruction of slavery, which strengthened her resolve to take risks in testing the limits of bondage as she awaited its official demise. Samuel P. Richards, by contrast, believed the war was a temporary annoyance and inconvenience; he predicted that "when we come to a successful end to the war" slavery would continue. Despite Richards's disinclination to concede to the winds of change, Ellen's defiance and similar acts by other slaves exasperated him as he struggled to protect his diminishing authority. Richards complained: "I am disgusted with negroes and feel inclined to sell what I have. I wish they were all back in Africa, – or – Yankee Land. To think too that this 'cruel war' should be waged for them."[2] The war of nerves conducted by slaves taxed Richards's patience more severely than any actions on the battlefields and served as a harbinger of future difficulties in Southern labor relations long after the Confederacy's defeat. However small and symbolic this friction may appear, conflicts and renegotiations over the meaning of slavery and freedom increased as the war progressed, with prolonged consequences for all Southerners.

Similar vignettes of contestation between slaves and masters were repeated throughout the region. As the Union and Confederate troops faced off at Fort Sumter, African Americans were poised to intervene in this revolutionary moment to influence the outcome of the war in their favor.[3] A slave mistress in Savannah summed up the changed dispositions of slaves who were testing the limits of the institution: the Negroes "show a very different face from what they have had heretofore."[4] Slave resistance was not unique to the Civil War, but black countenances evinced new meanings not readily discernible to masters under normal conditions in the antebellum era. African Americans articulated objections against the system of human bondage more consciously and openly than ever before.

Slaveholders formerly secure in their privileged positions and confident in the docility and loyalty of their most prized slaves in the Big House showed new faces as well – the faces of disillusion and betrayal. Slaves, the critics most cognizant of the constraints of human bondage, rejected the long-held beliefs of masters. Planters learned of "the perfect impossibility of placing the least confidence in any Negro" very early in the war, as one Savannah patrician noted. "In too many numerous instances those we esteemed the most have been the first to desert us."[5] And those who stayed were no more reliable inasmuch as they ceased to labor on former terms. "I was sorely tried with Fanny, my cook a very dull, obstinate servant," remarked another Georgian. "I make our coffee every morning and then find great difficulty in getting her to get our simple breakfast."[6] Masters had not yet discerned that the worrisome, but seemingly innocuous, concessions they reluctantly made, such as making coffee or cajoling the cook to prepare the morning meal, would hasten the collapse of slavery.

As the certainty of slavery became more tenuous during the War, latent tensions and sharply contrasting world views and ambitions of various groups surfaced. The internecine battles between slaves and masters, North and South, slaveholding and nonslaveholding whites prefigured conflicts that would continue to plague the region for many years. In cities like Atlanta, where urban conditions made slavery precarious long before the war began, the sudden and dramatic population growth and commercial expansion during the war helped to secure slavery's demise.

In the antebellum period, Atlanta was barely a blip on the map. In the 1820s, it served as a railroad depot in the foothills of north Georgia for neighboring farmers. By the 1850s, a fusion of Northern entrepreneurs along with the native-born yeomen inaugurated the business of city building. The expansion of railroad lines enabled swifter commerce west, further south, north, and to the Atlantic coast, enhancing the city's strategic geography by the eve of the Civil War.[7]

Atlanta's growth was fostered by the Civil War and by the railroad. Its dramatic rise countered an emblematic feature of Southern economic development. The South lagged behind the North in urbanization and industrialization, a tribute to the overwhelming predominance of plantation slavery and agriculture. Cities of any significance in the antebellum era, such as Savannah, New Orleans, and Charleston, catered to the needs of the planter elite.[8] The Southern states seceded to conserve plantation slavery and its urban subordinates, but secession produced unexpected consequences: the war destroyed slavery, and it transformed several inauspicious towns into developing metropolises. By the end of the war, New South cities like Atlanta began eclipsing the eminence of Old South cities.

Atlanta was conspicuous within the region from its inception. The predominance of merchants and manufacturers and the absence of planters within the city's economic elite invited early comparisons to the commercial ambitions of cities in the North. Even at this incipient stage of urban development, some Atlantans took pride in an entrepreneurial spirit that attracted young, upwardly mobile white men dedicated to commerce and industry, and this foreshadowed events and accolades to come. Upstarts were welcomed to the city to help build the railroads that stood at the center of the economy, and to develop related industries, like foundries and rolling mills. Other businesses included hotels, a brewery, a saw mill, a flour mill, a shoe factory, wagon builders, furniture shops, cigar factories, leather tanneries, a whiskey distillery, and agricultural implement manufacturers.[9] This diversity of businesses offered opportunities for consumers and workers, slave and free, not typical of the region. But even as Atlanta self-consciously touted itself as a progressive divergence from the South's dependence on one-crop agriculture, it also resisted social and political change.

Atlanta's distinctive economy presented conflicting interests for the city's power brokers as the Civil War approached. Most businessmen initially opposed secession out of fear that alienation from the Union would obstruct interregional trade, though they relented in due course.[10] Their apprehension regarding the adverse consequences of military invasion and Confederate government policies was well-founded. Farmers and traders fearful of impressment refrained from bringing their wares to city markets, which led to a shortage of foodstuffs and dry goods. Acute class conflict among whites surfaced as deprived consumers rioted, looted provision houses, and stole from wealthy residents in protest over spiraling prices, greedy speculation, and government impressment. Poverty led destitute patriots to turn against their allies. In March 1863, starving wives of Confederate soldiers rioted and pilfered provision houses in the central business district on Whitehall Street. The wives of artisans, factory workers, and Confederate soldiers displayed similar disenchantment in boisterous crowds in other towns. An Atlanta newspaper castigated these "women seizures" as a movement of "very wicked and ignorant women, generally instigated thereto and led by rascally individuals."[11]

Though commerce plummeted as predicted, no one could have foreseen the salutary impact of the war on the growth and development of manufacturing and urban expansion. The centrality of cities as distribution centers for the rebel forces boosted the importance of Atlanta as a strategic location, second only to Richmond. The military demand for ordnance and the fabrication of other items for civilian and military use, such as boots, buckles, buttons, saddles, uniforms, revolvers, and railroad cars, encouraged the building of new factories and the retooling of old operations. The influx of slaves, soldiers, runaways, military laborers, military officials, and refugee slaveholders generated a tremendous population expansion. In 1860, Atlanta's population had stood at less than ten thousand; two years later it had nearly doubled.

This sudden expansion of inhabitants presented an immediate problem of social control. In its earlier frontier days, Atlanta had a reputation as a "crossroads village" that attracted rowdies, vagabonds, bootleggers, and prostitutes. These "disreputable" sorts congregated in Snake Nation, along Peter's Street, and Murrell's Row, near Decatur Street, the beginnings of red-light districts and a thriving "underworld." Early city officials had a difficult time enforcing laws against prostitution, cockfighting, discharging firearms in the streets, and rolling live hogs in hogsheads down hills. Murder, larceny, gambling, insobriety, disorderly conduct, and indecent exposure filled the pages of the court dockets in the antebellum period – an inclination only heightened by the chaos of the war.[12]

Ramblers and roughnecks did not present the most formidable challenge to the city unless they also happened to be black. Slavery, as it was known in most of the plantation South, did not take root in Atlanta in the same way, where commerce and a complementary "urban promotive creed" prevailed. In the rural South, slavery ordered labor relations and plantation life; in the urban South, slavery was only one source of labor and was merely incidental to a city's character. In 1860 there were only 1,900 blacks in Atlanta, 20 percent of the population, and all but twenty-five persons were slaves. Individual slaves performed important labor in a wide variety of occupations, including brakemen, blacksmiths, boilermakers, and paper mill workers. Yet most African Americans were concentrated in domestic work, as in other antebellum cities, mainly in hotels and boardinghouses.[13] Even with such a relatively small number of slaves in the city, however, they were difficult to control, since the usual mechanisms were simply not as effective. Slaves were freer to roam about in the larger society among a denser populace, rather than being quarantined on isolated farms. The kind of labor they performed in small workshops or hotel establishments did not lend itself as easily to direct and constant supervision as did gang labor in the fields.

The economic and political priorities of Atlanta as a relatively young city were different from those of more established Southern cities where slaves were more numerous, but they did not deter slavery altogether. Samuel P. Richards, a British-born merchant, bought slaves for his farm in the countryside, hired the slaves of other owners, and purchased servants specifically to work in his Atlanta home. In December 1862, he purchased thirteen-year-old Ellen after two years of hiring her: "I have committed the unpardonable sin of the Abolitionists in buying a negro. I am tired of the trouble of getting a servant every Christmas and we have found Ellen a pretty good girl."[14] A few months later he purchased a family of three slaves: Joe, Caroline, and their three-year-old child. Richards sent the husband to work on the farm in the country and the wife and child to the city residence. Though somewhat skeptical at first about the outcome of his investment, Richards was soon optimistic about high returns. He purchased Ellen for $1,225, several hundred dollars below her former owner's asking price, and within five months he estimated that her value had risen to $2,000. Gloating over the appreciation of his property, despite the exigencies of an economy spun out of control, Richards predicted a Confederate victory and the continuance of slavery. He believed that "negroes will command very high prices as there will be so much demand for labor to raise cotton and a great many will have been taken by the Yankees."[15]

In reality, Ellen's price rose because of wartime inflation as well as the scarcity of household slaves. As one slaveholder wrote to another about the prospects of finding experienced domestics in the city: "Many desirable negroes are daily offered by people who are obliged to sell – but the kind most offered are field hands – men[,] boys and young women."[16] The relatively lower prices for field hands advertised by slave dealers lends credence to this observation.[17] The influx of refugee whites into the city may have contributed to the market for domestic slaves. But the urgent need for able-bodied field workers to sustain the plantation system and to raise crops for the subsistence of civilians and soldiers alike made it more difficult to find slaves hired expressly for domestic labor.[18]

The impressment of slaves by the Confederacy was a further drain on waning supplies. Samuel Stout, the head surgeon for the Army of Tennessee, headquartered in Atlanta, wrote to patrons in Florida for help for one of the Confederacy's largest hospitals. "In nothing can you aid us more than by sending us fruits and vegetables. Labor is also very much in demand. Every negro hired to the hospital, enables us to send an able-bodied soldier to the field."[19] Domestic servants were especially in demand – men as nurses, women as laundresses, and both as cooks.[20]

The hire-out system alleviated some of the inconveniences of scarcity by permitting slaves or owners to make short-term arrangements for daily, monthly, or yearly work. Given the diverse and fluctuating needs of urban economies, whites in cities relied on the hiring system to balance the demands for labor with the legal constraints that slavery imposed on bound workers. Many owners hired out their chattel property to friends as favors. Some sought to lighten their financial hardships by relieving themselves of the daily care of slaves, or to rid themselves of the burdens of managing unruly and willful slaves.[21] Ellen Campbell, an Augusta ex-slave, described the circumstances leading to her working for hire at age fifteen: "My young missus wus fixin' to git married, but she couldn't on account de war, so she brought me to town and rented me out to a lady runnin' a boarding house." But the arrangement was short-lived. Campbell dropped a serving tray, and the boardinghouse keeper stabbed her in the head with a butcher's knife in punishment. Campbell's enraged mistress revoked the contract immediately.[22] Slaveholders, however, were often willing to bear the risks of abuse when the profits reaped from hire contracts provided their sole income.[23]

The hire-out system democratized access to slaves by enabling white wage-earners to benefit from the system, even as some white workers were forced to compete with slaves. If they could not afford to buy a slave outright, some could afford to hire slaves as helpers as their needs demanded them. Thus, the proportion of the white population that owned slaves in the cities was higher than in the rural areas, even though individual holdings were smaller.[24] Jennie Akehurst Lines, the wife of a union printer in Atlanta, wrote letters to her sister detailing a dilemma of white workers' hiring practices. The spiraling costs of living and the insecurity of her husband's trade during a period marked by workplace strife and uncertain wages limited the Lineses' family income. Yet Jennie Lines remained steadfast in her opinion of the necessity of hiring domestic labor. "I presume you think I ought not to keep help," she wrote. "If I did not I should have to pay out the same amount for washing. True we should save the food and clothing but I do not believe we should save one dime more."[25] Aside from the economic rationale, the drudgery and quantity of the work also provided a motivation, which the printer's wife described as her lack of "taste" for certain kinds of work.[26] "Besides I could never look nice myself, keep my baby or my house clean. Sylvanus dont want me to do kitchen drudgery in this country – says he will break up house keeping if I insist on doing without help."[27] Slaves for hire raised the standard of living for a segment of the white working class and gave some nonslaveowners a direct investment in preserving the institution. The effect of such white racial unity and the contradictory relations between blacks and whites of similar economic circumstances would become more apparent in later years – especially in the strained relations between household workers and poor white employers.

Some aspects of urban slavery were similar to those of rural slavery. The sexual exploitation of women was equally onerous whether it occurred on plantations or in urban households.

Black women were subjected to sexual abuse by slaveowners, overseers, and drivers. They were assaulted by individual men and gangs. Though most women were helpless in the face of violations of their persons, some fought their assailants directly at great risk. Others devised strategies to evade molestation without open confrontation. Louisa, a Georgia house slave, avoided the clutches of her master by sleeping in the room with his children or nailing up the windows of her own house. He persisted and found a way into her room, however, and she turned up the light of lamps to distract and dissuade him. Still undaunted, he made efforts to cajole and coerce Louisa by offering "two dollars to feel her titties," which she also refused. Afforded little protection against unwanted sexual advances and exploitation of their reproductive capabilities, many black women who resisted were beaten, mutilated, sold, or killed.[28] During the Civil War, Union and Confederate soldiers took advantage of their positions of power and authority to rape slave women, sometimes in the presence of the women's parents, husbands, children, and grandchildren who were forced to stand by, helpless and horrified.[29]

In other ways, urban slavery had distinct advantages and disadvantages compared to rural slavery. The small slaveholding units in urban areas almost inevitably meant that slave families were torn apart. As we saw, when Samuel P. Richards purchased a family consisting of parents and child, he split the group by sending the father to the country and the mother and child to the city. Urban house slaves often suffered double isolation: they were cut off from their families as well as from other slaves.[30] The small holdings of individual owners also put greater burdens on slaves to perform labor beyond their capability. With few or no other slaves to share the work load, slave exertion could be pushed to the limits, which was especially burdensome for domestic servants expected to perform on constant call.[31] A former slave from Nashville recounted the onerous labor that she endured when she was hired out. "They hired me to nurse, but I had to nurse, cook, chop in the fields, chop wood, bring water, wash, iron and in general just do everything," she recalled as an adult.[32] She awoke before the sun rose, made the fire, and commenced both house and field work, which was remarkable because she was only six years old at that time.

Children were especially vulnerable to exploitation in isolation from their parents or other adult slaves. Jennie Lines summed up the logic of hiring girls: "We have a negro girl sixteen years old. She is large enough and strong enough to do everything, and I mean she shall if I keep her. We pay $4 a month for her besides clothes; that you know is cheap for a grown woman."[33] After some complaints about twelve-year-old Beckie's master raising her rate, despite her poor performance, Lines wrote with increased confidence: "She improves. Perhaps she will in a few months be just the help I need. I can make her do my work just as I want it done, which I can not do with an older one."[34] Lines expected the young ones to perform with the same degree of skill and perseverance as women twice their age – cooking, washing, cleaning, and caring for an infant.

Despite the hardships of urban bondage, the system could not enforce the same degree of coercion as rural bondage did. Slaves living in cities were afforded many opportunities for living a relatively autonomous life. Anonymity within a dense population and customary practices that permitted slaves of absent owners to find their own shelter in sheds, attics, basements, single rooms, or small houses encouraged independence. In addition, urban slavery permitted casual contact between unfree and free people, black and white. Pass systems, curfews, and other laws were designed to limit the mobility of slaves while away from their official workplaces without the permission of owners, but in reality, these mechanisms were usually not strictly enforced. Threadbare municipal infrastructures and minuscule resources did not allow for controlling any segment of the population, slave or free. Though some owners tried to limit interactions among blacks by spreading slave housing all over the city, they did not have the wherewithal to keep close watch over slaves. Slaves took advantage of the lax patrol to move around the city, to participate in a rich, if still limited, communal life almost as if they were free. They gathered to socialize in markets, grocery stores, grogshops, street corners, churches, and the homes of friends – clandestinely during the day and openly at night.[35]

Slaves living independent of their masters' constant supervision posed a persistent threat to the system and tested the capability of the municipal government to act as a surrogate for the owners. The demands of the Civil War and the conditions it created frustrated antebellum mechanisms of control. In 1863, the Atlanta City Council made an extra effort to enforce a pass system to regulate the large influx of slave military laborers. But overlapping civilian and military authority blurred the chain of command, hindering the city from implementing unilateral decisions. The city council made another futile attempt in the same year to limit black mobility by requiring all blacks, except body servants, to "be kept in some negro yard or house, and not [be] permitted to go at large through the city" after work hours.[36]

During the war, a number of factors contributed to the growing number of slaves who were living and working independently. The unanticipated growth of the black population made any attempts to control slaves impractical. The inflated costs and shortages of housing for everyone, regardless of race or status, made it difficult to govern who should live where. The increasing demand for black labor in a broad range of enterprises made it beneficial for slaveowners to defy the laws and allow their slaves to earn their own living. Many whites suffered the psychological effects of the loss of bound labor, but many were still eager to reap its profits. Other slaveowners facing privation abandoned slaves in cities, forcing more blacks into the self-hire system to avoid destitution. The city's futile attempts to control all of these unforeseen forces created a general atmosphere of lax regulation of the conventional constraints of slavery and even greater tolerance of blacks who committed petty crimes.[37]

As city officials and masters in Atlanta lost their grip on bound labor, fear of outright slave rebellion troubled the white residents. In 1863, this anxiety increased when two female slaves were arrested for setting a boardinghouse on fire. In addition, slaves organized "Negro balls" in local hotels, ostensibly to raise money for Confederate soldiers and their body servants. Though the city initially approved these seemingly innocent amusements, people came to see them as public disturbances with the potential to stir up rebellion. But these "Negro balls," no matter how annoying, prompted only occasional cause for concern. The city's bigger problem was the more pervasive and less dramatic daily struggle between slaves and masters that undermined the changing institution as the war lingered on.[38] African Americans seized the moment to pursue their aspirations and in the process revealed latent contending notions of freedom that shook the confidence and ideology of slaveholders. The conspicuous defiance of house slaves shattered illusory assumptions, and their behavior exposed the conflicts that would continue once slaves were free.

The arrival in Atlanta of refugee slaveholders with their slaves who were fleeing embattled areas of the Confederacy multiplied the city's problems of social control. Refugee slaves and oldtimers used the occasion of social disarray to flee. The Lineses' young slave who had been denied extended contact with her mother ran away. Beckie, her replacement, also deserted, though she was caught and beaten before she completed her escape. Undaunted, she left again a few months later on a professed trip to pick blackberries and never returned.[39]

Slaves took greater liberties through the hire system in their quest for freedom during the war. "Old Clarissa" was sent to Savannah with the understanding that she would remit a certain portion of her wages to her master on a regular basis. But upon her arrival she repudiated the agreement by sending a smaller portion of her earnings. Her perplexed master weighed the merits of acquiescence versus punishment, knowing that an alienating gesture could risk forfeiting his property and lone source of income.[40] Once exposed to urban life, slaves were not easily coerced into returning to plantations. Another slave, Rachel, grew accustomed to the independent life afforded by renting a room and working as a washerwoman in Atlanta. No amount of persuasion from her mistress could convince Rachel to avoid the imminent dangers of the approaching Union Army and return to her owner's protective care. As Rachel stated, she "preferred to await the coming of Sherman in her present quarters."[41]

The majority of slaves remained on plantations or in white urban households until the war's end. The heavily armed white civilian populace, the power of the Confederate troops, and the rough terrain of north Georgia made it difficult for slaves to escape. Some, no doubt, conformed to their masters' expectations of ideal servants – in outward appearance if nothing else. But outward compliance could be deceptive as slaves harbored deeper resentments that would resurface after they were free and subjected to conditions reminiscent of slavery. At least a few slaves may have shown genuine concern toward their masters who were in dire straits or faced plundering Yankees. Some slaves bought Confederate bonds, raised money to help Confederate soldiers, buried valuables or sewed silverware into mattresses to escape detection by Union invaders, or even donated their savings to cash-poor slaveowners.[42]

Acts of generosity clearly required slaves to go beyond the call of duty, but they did not dampen the yearning for freedom. Phyllis, a much beloved slave of Grace Elmore, gently tried to articulate this lesson to her owner. Elmore professed regard for Phyllis and spoke of her in this way: "She is very intelligent, reads, writes, [is] half white and was brought up like a white child by her former mistress." But Elmore did not appreciate Phyllis's answer to an important question: "I asked Phyllis if she liked the thought of being free." Phyllis replied that yes, she wanted to be free, "tho' she'd always been treated with perfect kindness, and could complain of nothing in her lot." Despite her good treatment Phyllis insisted that she "wanted the power to do as she liked." Disappointed by the reply from an "intelligent" slave, Elmore mocked Phyllis's and other slaves' views about freedom which in her estimation failed to comprehend the magnitude of the responsibilities.[43]

Masters increasingly, if begrudgingly, recognized that kind gestures and appearances of orderly behavior could be feigned as many slaves demonstrated their contempt for bound labor, overtly or covertly, when opportunities arose. Slaves who helped to hide their owners' heirlooms and valuables one day might lead the Yankees directly to the loot the next day.[44] Some house slaves directly attacked the most visible signs of their oppression by claiming the products of their uncompensated labor, such as cash, clothing, jewelry, household items, or food from the table or pantry. Others defaced the ostentatious mansions that stood in marked contrast to their own sparse shanties.[45] While many refused to work at all, others changed their work pace and the quality of their output, provoking typical complaints like the following: "Fanny as usual cooked miserably: the worst turkey dressing I have seen in my life."[46] As the mistress Lines reported of the infamous Beckie: she "makes me a great trouble ironing days. She is so careless and stupid."[47] In sheer exasperation, another mistress complained: "I think O, if I had a good cook; it would be a pleasure to keep house." This slaveholder's highest aspiration at that moment was to find just "one who would take care or even do what they are told to do."[48]

Some slaves who remained in their masters' households used the mobility and independence afforded by urban bondage to fight against the system. A slave woman in Richmond spent her earnings from washing the clothing of rebel soldiers on baking bread for Union prisoners of war. According to one account: "she got in to the prisoners through a hole under the jail-yard fence; knowing all the while she'd be shot, if caught at it."[49] Aggie Crawford, an Athens cook, defied prohibitions against slave literacy designed to keep blacks ignorant of current affairs. She stole newspapers to keep fellow slaves abreast of the war and sold whiskey, probably to save money for a planned escape.[50] Similarly, Tiny, the "last and *dearest* girl" of Samuel P. Richards's brother Jabez, made preparations for fleeing to freedom. She stole "first, about $150 from him and receiving no punishment she next stole about the same amount from Dr Doyle!" In another case, "Patience (who had been especially petted) managed to steal enough coffee, sugar, and flour to live on for many weeks."[51]

The resilience exhibited by house slaves in their increased shows of defiance during the war meant that work that had been performed by slaves exclusively might not get done at all, which translated into more physical labor for white women. "John, Sarah and Rose have left and I did the washing for six weeks," a Natchez, Mississippi, slaveowner remarked. I "came near ruining myself for life as I was too delicately raised for such hard work," she stated.[52] Others noted the added encumbrances of physical labor imposed on other whites beyond their own households. "For the first time in my life, I saw & had white people to wait on me," noted a mistress during a stopover at a boardinghouse outside Atlanta. "The lady where we boarded waited on the table & cooked sometimes. She was kind hearted & very obliging but I could not bear for her to wait on us."[53] Other white women encountered dire privation that forced them to do what they had always considered unthinkable for women of their race – sell their own labor. "Many who were well supplied for months and some for a year, have been compelled to come to town and perform day work for a living, the man making $30. & $35. per month and the woman 5 cents or 10 cents a piece for washing," observed a Georgia slaveholder.[54] These excursions by whites into paid or unpaid labor dramatize the topsy-turvy world produced by the war, but they were temporary inconveniences. Few white women in the South, no matter how poor, worked as domestics either during or after the war.

White soldiers in the trenches echoed the sentiments of the women they left behind to maintain the home front as the men suddenly discovered the arduousness of housework. An army veteran and planter wrote sympathetically to Jefferson Davis, the President of the Confederacy, with a plan to send domestic help to the soldiers' camps. "The *hardest*, and *most painful duty* of the *young Volunteers*, is to *learn how* to *Cook*, and *wash*." Emphasizing the novelty of this ordeal, he stated: "At *home*, the *young* Soldier, has his *Food Cooked* for *him*, by his *Mother, Sister's or* by *our Slaves* – but not *so* in the *Field* of *Battle*."[55] A Union soldier in Georgia suffered similar agony. "I spend the afternoon in washing, mending and baking. I was very tired at night and wondered how women gets through with as much work as they do. Washing, etc. is the hardest work I have to do."[56]

Not all slaveholders acquiesced to the changing conditions of slavery. Many extolled slave loyalty at the same time that they took extra measures to subjugate their slaves further. The fears and bitterness that slaveowners harbored in the years immediately before the war in anticipation of its arrival induced some to exercise brutal force once the war began. If some slaves became more unruly during the war, they were responding not only to new opportunities for freedom but also to increased violence from their masters. Many owners, even some who were mild-mannered under normal circumstances, became more abusive or more neglectful as they realized they would eventually lose their investment in human chattel.[57]

The much anticipated arrival of the Union Army in northwest Georgia occurred in May 1864. Sherman's march toward the Gate City en route to the sea, more than any other single event heretofore, inspired songs of jubilee among slaves and excited fears of rebellion among whites. Sherman plotted the invasion of Atlanta, a strategic interior city in Dixie, to destroy its key military resources and asphyxiate the network feeding supplies to Robert E. Lee's forces in Virginia. Sherman's arrival shattered the last remnants of slaveholders' authority and control.

White women on the home front were bearing more responsibility for slave management than they were accustomed to doing. In the absence of fathers and husbands they quickly had to learn new skills in negotiation to deal with recalcitrant slaves not apt to respect their authority. After Sherman's arrival, a group of almost one hundred white women from Jonesboro, near Atlanta, submitted a petition to Governor Joseph E. Brown, in haste: "There are no men left here scarcely and the few who are, are almost impotent to afford any protection to us the females and our children." They requested an exemption of military service for the town marshal because the slaves in the vicinity "have been taught by long experience to regard [him] with awe & fear."[58] But despite such efforts to inculcate trepidation, slaveholders had to face another contingent of willful slaves. Runaways trailed the Northern liberators into Atlanta for the chance to participate directly in the destruction of slavery and the Confederacy. African Americans deserted their masters en masse – about nineteen thousand followed the General as he moved through the state. One planter captured the overwhelming feeling of betrayal this scene evinced: "Every servant gone to Sherman in Atlanta . . . We thought there was a strong bond of affection on their side as well as ours!"[59] The sight of blacks and whites looting and destroying fortifications and private property bore out the worst fears of many white Atlantans.[60]

As the Union Army approached Atlanta, slaveholders were reminded once again that outward appearances could mask the true feelings of their slaves. House slaves considered to be the most faithful and diligent were the first to refuse to work or to desert to the rear of Sherman's troops. Slaveowners voiced both surprise and dismay in recalling the characteristics of runaway slaves like Tiny and Patience – the "dearest" and the "most petted" slaves of Jabez Richards, mentioned previously. Other examples were plentiful: Mary, a "faithful girl" was "near free & did as she pleased – but waited on her [mistress] & like a dog – was by her side constantly." But when the Yankees arrived, a different Mary emerged as she helped her mistress's family prepare the carriage for escape and refused to climb aboard herself. "To her [mistress's] surprise, she held back & said I am not going – an officer (Yank) will come to take me; after awhile & he did."[61]

Some slaveholders dismayed by the acts of betrayal as they evacuated the city sought revenge. The Union Army arrived at one Georgia plantation to discover that the owners had chained down a house slave before vacating to avoid the indignity of her defection. When the slaves began running away, "her master swore she should stay and cook for him and his family. He 'would fix her'; so he had heavy iron shackles put on her feet so she could not run off."[62] While some slaves were left behind in dire straits, others were taken away with little regard for the impact on black families. When Emma Prescott departed she took along Patience, a child-nurse, ignoring the needs of Patience, who had recently married Allen Slayton of Columbus. Prescott justified splitting up the black family by emphasizing her own suffering: "I had to be separated from my husband too." By acting in her own best interest, Prescott shattered any illusion of reciprocal relations between slaves and masters.[63]

Sherman besieged the city of Atlanta on September 1, 1864, as the civilian evacuation was well under way. Confederate officers admitted defeat and surrendered the next day. They began to demolish military ordnance and machinery, including the Atlanta Rolling Mill and locomotives filled with ammunition, to deprive enemy invaders of their benefits. In November, the Union Army systematically destroyed all remaining manufacturing plants, torching four to five thousand buildings and the entire business district. Renegade soldiers, without the authority of their commanding officers, added to the damage by pillaging private residences. Few edifices outlasted the demolition.

Black residents in the city were not left unscathed by General Sherman, whose contempt for them was well known. Sherman's troops raped black women and destroyed black-owned property, including a church. En route to Savannah at the end of the year, Sherman's men caused the death of hundreds of blacks trailing in the rear by removing a pontoon bridge before the refugees could cross over a river, leaving them at the mercy of advancing Confederates.[64] But Sherman's abuse of African Americans did not dissipate white anxieties as slaveholders returned to Atlanta during the winter months.[65] As one woman stated: "Several old men are left & they go from one plantation to another with guns in their hands trying to keep [slaves] down." She continued, "we fear the negroes now more than anything else."[66]

As the Battle of Atlanta ended, it was undeniable that Ellen, the recalcitrant slave playing with her mistress's toiletries in front of the vanity, had calculated the bleak prospects for slavery more accurately than her master. The destruction of slavery was accomplished with the participation of slaves themselves, not just by military maneuvers or decisions promulgated in the White House or the halls of Congress. The slaves who ran away to join the Union Army; those who scraped and saved funds to rescue captured Union soldiers; those who cooked, washed, and spied for the federal troops; and those who remained in the custody of plantations and urban households and refused to accept preexisting terms for their uncompensated labor – all in their own way helped to erode human bondage. As African Americans asserted themselves during the heat of the war, they set the stage for the renegotiation of labor and social relations for many years to come.

Notes

1   As quoted in Armstead L. Robinson, " 'Worser dan Jeff Davis': The Coming of Free Labor during the Civil War, 1861–1865," in *Essays on the Postbellum Southern Economy*, ed. Thavolia Glymph and John J. Kushma (College Station, Tex.: Texas A&M University Press, 1985), p. 37.

2   Entries for 5 May 1862, 2 May 1863, and 13 September 1863, Samuel P. Richards Diary, Atlanta History Center (hereafter cited as AHC). Details of the Ellen incident embellished. In an effort to preserve the historical integrity of the documents, I have quoted from sources exactly as they were written, as much as is consistent with clarity. Irregular and erroneous grammar, syntax, spelling, capitalization, and punctuation have been retained. Readers should assume that quotations throughout this book follow the original sources.

3   On this perspective see for example, Ira Berlin et al., *Slaves No More: Three Essays on Emancipation and the Civil War* (Cambridge: Cambridge University Press, 1992); Eric Foner, *Reconstruction: America's Unfinished Business, 1863–1877* (New York: Harper & Row, 1988), pp. 1–76; Leon F. Litwack, *Been in the Storm So Long: The Aftermath of Slavery* (New York: Alfred A. Knopf, 1979).

4   [Louisa F. Gilmer] to my dear father [Adam L. Alexander], 17 November 1861, Alexander-Hillhouse Family Papers, Southern Historical Collection, University of North Carolina, Chapel Hill (hereafter cited as SHC).

5   Louis Manigault, as quoted in Edmund L. Drago, *Black Politicians and Reconstruction in Georgia: A Splendid Failure* (Baton Rouge: Louisiana State University Press, 1982), p. 3.

6   Entry of 14 January 1862, Laura Beecher Comer Diary, SHC. See Robinson, " 'Worser dan Jeff Davis,' " pp. 34–7.

7   On the impact of the war on Atlanta and the urbanization of the South, see James Michael Russell, *Atlanta, 1847–1890: City Building in the Old South and the New* (Baton Rouge: Louisiana State University Press, 1988), pp. 91–116; Clarence L. Mohr, *On the Threshold of Freedom: Masters and Slaves in Civil War Georgia* (Athens: University of Georgia Press, 1986), pp. 190–209; and Don H. Doyle, *New Men, New Cities, New South: Atlanta, Nashville, Charleston, Mobile, 1860–1910* (Chapel Hill: University of North Carolina Press, 1990), pp. 31–6.

8   See Richard C. Wade, *Slavery in the Cities: The South 1820–1860* (New York, 1964), pp. 4–16.

9 See Jonathan W. McLeod, *Workers and Workplace Dynamics in Reconstruction-Era Atlanta* (Los Angeles: Center for Afro-American Studies, University of California, 1989), pp. 5–6.

10 Russell, *Atlanta*, pp. 91–116; Mohr, *Threshold of Freedom*, pp. 190–209; and Doyle, *New Men*, pp. 31–6.

11 Russell, *Atlanta*, pp. 99–100; Atlanta *Southern Confederacy*, 16 April 1863, quoted in Steven Hahn, *The Roots of Southern Populism: Yeoman Farmers and the Transformation of the Georgia Upcountry, 1850–1890* (New York: Oxford University Press, 1983), p. 129; Drew Gilpin Faust, "Altars of Sacrifice: Confederate Women and Narratives of War," *Journal of American History* 76 (March 1990): 1224–7; George C. Rable, *Civil Wars: Women and the Crisis of Southern Nationalism* (Urbana: University of Illinois Press, 1989), pp. 108–10; Victoria E. Bynum, *Unruly Women: The Politics of Social and Sexual Control in the Old South* (Chapel Hill: University of North Carolina Press, 1992), pp. 112, 120–9, 145–6.

12 Russell, *Atlanta*, pp. 72–4, 91–116; Mohr, *Threshold of Freedom*, pp. 190–209; Doyle, *New Men*, pp. 31–6; McLeod, *Workers and Workplace*, p. 6.

13 Russell, *Atlanta*, pp. 70–1; Wade, *Slavery in the Cities*, pp. 20–3.

14 Entry of 27 December 1862, Richards Diary, AHC.

15 Ibid., entry of 2 May 1863.

16 Ro. Cornilius Robson to Colonel David Barrow, 15 October 1863, David Barrow Papers, Hargrett Library, University of Georgia.

17 Atlanta *Daily Intelligencer*, 14 July 1863.

18 See Wade, *Slavery in the Cities*, pp. 32–3.

19 Samuel Stout to Isabel Harmon, 22 September 1863, Samuel H. Stout Papers, Robert W. Woodruff Library, Emory University.

20 Mohr, *On the Threshold of Freedom*, p. 133.

21 Wade, *Slavery in the Cities*, pp. 38–54. For examples of hiring out see entries of 15 July and 4 August 1864, William H. King Diary, SHC; entry of 29 October 1862, Laura Beecher Comer Diary, SHC.

22 George P. Rawick, ed., *The American Slave: A Composite Autobiography* (Westport, C.: Greenwood Press, 1941; 1972); *Georgia Narratives*, vol. 13, pt. 4, p. 222 (hereafter cited as WPA Ga. Narr.). See also testimony of Sallie Blakley, WPA Ga. Narr., suppl., ser. 1, vol. 4, pt. 1.

23 T. C. Howard to [James] Gardener, 15 September 1860, James Gardener Papers, Georgia Department of Archives and History.

24 Wade, *Slavery in the Cities*, p. 43.

25 Jennie to Maria, 2 December 1862, in Amelia Akehurst Lines, *To Raise Myself a Little: The Diaries and Letters of Jennie, a Georgia Teacher 1851–1886*, ed. Thomas Dyer (Athens: University of Georgia Press, 1982), p. 193.

26 Ibid., entry of 24 July 1863, p. 204.

27 Ibid., entry of 2 December 1862, pp. 193–4.

28 As quoted in Herbert G. Gutman, *The Black Family in Slavery and Freedom, 1750–1925* (New York: Pantheon Books, 1977), p. 80. For other examples of sexual abuse of slave women see testimony of Aunt Carrie Mason, WPA Ga. Narr., vol. 13, pt. 3, pp. 112–13; testimony of Mollie Kinsey, WPA Ga. Narr., suppl. ser. 1, vol. 4, pt. 2, p. 373; and testimony of Tunis G. Campbell, 31 October 1871, in 42nd Congress, 2nd Session, House Report no. 22, pt. 6, *Testimony taken by the Joint Select Committee to Inquire into the Condition of Affairs in the Late Insurrectionary States* (Washington, DC: Government Printing Office, 1872), vol. 2, p. 862. Also see Deborah Gray White, *Ar'n't I a Woman? Female Slaves in the Plantation South* (New York: W. W. Norton, 1985), p. 78; Jacqueline Jones, *Labor of Love, Labor of Sorrow: Black Women, Work, and the Family from Slavery to Freedom* (New York: Basic Books, 1985), pp. 20, 27–8, 37–8; Elizabeth Fox-Genovese, *Within the Plantation Household: Black and White Women of the Old South* (Chapel Hill: University of North Carolina Press, 1988), pp. 189, 315, 323–6, 374; Thelma Jennings, " 'Us Colored Women Had to Go Through A Plenty': Sexual Exploitation of African-American Slave Women," *Journal of Women's History* 1 (Winter 1990): 60–3.

29 Gutman, *Black Family*, p. 386.

30 "Sixty-Five Years a 'Washer & Ironer,' " in *God Struck Me Dead: Religious Conversion Experiences and Autobiographies of Negro Ex-Slaves*, ed. A. Watson, Paul Radin, and Charles S. Johnson (Nashville, 1945; reprint ed. Westport, Conn.: Greenwood Press, 1972), p. 186; see also Emma J. S. Prescott, "Reminiscences of the War," typescript, p. 53, AHC.

31 Wade, *Slavery in the Cities*, pp. 30–1.

32 " 'Washer & Ironer,' " pp. 185–6.

33 Entry of 30 April 1862, in Lines, *Diaries and Letters*, p. 188.

34 Ibid., entry of 14 February 1863, p. 198.

35 See Wade, *Slavery in the Cities*, pp. 55–79, 143–79; Mohr, *Threshold of Freedom*, pp. 190–209.

36 As quoted in Mohr, *Threshold of Freedom*, pp. 202, 198–9; Russell, *Atlanta*, pp. 70–1, 110–11.

37 Mohr, *Threshold of Freedom*, pp. 201–9.

38 Russell, *Atlanta*, pp. 110–11.

39 Entries of 8 February and 24 July 1863, in Lines, *Diaries and Letters*, pp. 197, 204.

40 See Mohr, *Threshold of Freedom*, p. 206.

41 Mary A. H. Gay, *Life in Dixie After the War* (Atlanta: C. P. Byrd, 1897), p. 162.

42 Benjamin Quarles, *Negro in the Civil War* (Boston: Little, Brown, 1953; 1969), pp. 49–51; Drago, *Black Politicians*, pp. 4, 8.

43 Entry of 24 May 1865, Grace Elmore Diary, SHC.

44 See Rable, *Civil Wars*, p. 158.

45 For example, see A Richmond Lady [Sally A. Brock Putnam], *Richmond During the War; Four Years of Personal Observation* (Richmond: G. W. Carlton, 1867), pp. 264–266.

46 Entry of 22 January 1862, Comer Diary, SHC. See also entries of 5 May 1862 and 9 September 1864, Richards Diary, AHC.

47 Entry of 1 July 1863, in Lines, *Diaries and Letters*, p. 203. See also ibid., entry of 7 February 1863, p. 197.

48 Entries of 12 and 22 January 1862, Comer Diary, SHC.

49 Quoted in John T. Trowbridge, *The South: A Tour of Its Battle-Fields and Ruined Cities* (Hartford, 1866; reprint ed., New York: Arno, 1969), p. 171.

50 WPA Ga. Narr., vol. 12, pt. 1, p. 257.

51 Entry of 28 February 1863, Richards Diary, AHC; Sidney Root, "Autobiography," typescript, p. 16, AHC. On the general problem of domestic "crime," see, for example, entry of 29 July 1864, King Diary, SHC; Imogene Hoyle to Amaryllis Bomar, 28 November 1864, Bomar-Killian Papers, SHC; entry of 13 September 1863, Richards Diary, AHC; and entry of 29 July 1862, Comer Diary, SHC.

52 As quoted in Robinson, " 'Worser dan Jeff Davis,' " p. 36. See also Rable, *Civil Wars*, pp. 118–19.

53 Prescott, "Reminiscences of the War," p. 43, AHC.

54 Entry of 15 July 1864, King Diary, SHC.

55 A. Hayne to Jefferson Davis, 8 August 1863 [1861], in *Freedom: A Documentary History of Emancipation, 1861–1867*, ser. 1, vol. 1, *The Destruction of Slavery*, ed. Ira Berlin et al. (Cambridge: Cambridge University Press, 1985), p. 695.

56 George C. Lawson, "Reminiscences of the March Through Georgia and the Carolinas: From Letters and Journal Written by George C. Lawson of the 45th Illinois Volunteers," 2 March 1865, pp. 73–4, Lawson Correspondence, AHC.

57 See Bynum *Unruly Women*, pp. 112–14. Mohr. *Threshold of Freedom*, pp. 44–51.

58 "Petition from 95 Females in Jonesboro, Georgia" to Governor Joseph E. Brown, 26 May 1864, Telamon Cuyler Papers, AHC.

59 As quoted in Drago, *Black Politicians*, p. 4.

60 Ibid., pp. 7–12; Franklin M. Garrett, *Yesterday's Atlanta* (Miami: E. A. Seeman, 1974), pp. 23–40; Elise Reid Boylston, *Atlanta: Its Lore, Legends and Laughter* (Doraville, GA: Foote & Davies, 1968), pp. 87–90.

61 Prescott, "Reminiscences of the War," p. 63, AHC. See also entry of 26 December 1864, Grace B. Elmore Diary, SHC; and testimony of Mrs. Ward, 15 November 1883, in US Congress, Senate,

Committee on Education and Labor, *Report Upon the Relations Between Labor and Capital* (Washington, DC: Government Printing Office, 1885), vol. 4, p. 329.

62 Elizabeth H. Botume, *First Days Amongst the Contrabands* (Boston: Lee and Shepard, 1893), p. 140.

63 Prescott, "Reminiscences of the War," pp. 59–60, AHC; Mohr, *Threshold of Freedom*, p. 103.

64 Drago, *Black Politicians*, pp. 10–15; Gutman, *Black Family*, p. 386; Mohr, *Threshold of Freedom*, pp. 90–5; Berlin et al., *Slaves No More*, pp. 68, 175.

65 Russell, *Atlanta*, pp. 113–15; Doyle, *New Men*, pp. 31–3.

66 Imogene Hoyle to Amaryllis Bomar, 28 November 1864, Bomar-Killian Papers, AHC. See also John Richard Dennett, *The South As It Is: 1865–1866*, ed. Henry M. Christman (New York: Viking, 1965), p. 269.

Questions to consider

- How was slavery in a city like Atlanta different from that of a large plantation?

- What role did slaves themselves play in the destruction of slavery? In what ways did they consciously and unconsciously loosen their bonds?

- What kinds of sources does Hunter use to make her case? Which are the most compelling?

Chapter 15

Slavery During Wartime: Primary Sources

Diary Entry

Mary Chesnut

The greatest terror in the heart of every slaveholder was the murderous slave. Though rare – and rarer still were slave insurrections – the coming of the war greatly intensified fears about the vengeful slave, particularly among Southern white women. Few were more powerful in writing about this subject than Mary Chesnut. The wife of a former US Senator from South Carolina, Chesnut enjoyed access to the highest levels of the Confederate government, whose leaders she wrote about with tart insight in her celebrated diary. Chesnut was also an excellent barometer of everyday Southern life for the elite, and charted the fall of the Confederacy with melancholy precision. In this dairy entry from early in the war, she is unexpectedly forced to consider one of her deepest fears. Consider in particular Chesnut's invocation of her cousin Betsey Witherspoon's "own people."

"Diary of Mary Chesnut" (21 September 1861), in *Mary Chesnut's Civil War*, ed. C. Vann Woodward (New Haven: Yale University Press, 1981), p. 198.

September 21, 1861. Last night when the mail came in, I was seated near the lamp. Mr. Chesnut, lying on a sofa at a little distance, called out to me, "Look at my letters and tell me about them."

I began to read one aloud; it was from Mary Witherspoon – and I broke down. Horror and amazement was too much for me. Poor Cousin Betsey Witherspoon was murdered! She did not die peacefully, as we supposed, in her bed. Murdered by her own people. Her negroes.

Letter from Wilson's Landing, Virginia

Sgt. George W. Hatton

Every once in a while, there were moments in the Civil War where, to use the slave expression, one would find the "bottom rail on top." One such moment was witnessed by Sergeant George W. Hatton, a member of the United States Colored Infantry serving in Virginia during Gen. Ulysses S. Grant's Wilderness campaign of 1864. Consider the tone of this account of a captured slave owner, and the moral Hatton draws from the story. Do you share his feelings?

G. W. Hatton, "Letter, Wilson's Landing, Virginia" (May 28, 1864), in *A Grand Army of Black Men: Letters from African-American Soldiers in the Union Army, 1861–1865*, ed. Edwin S. Redkey (New York: Cambridge University Press, 1992), pp. 95–6. Reprinted by permission of Cambridge University Press.

You are aware that Wilson's Landing is on the James River, a few miles above Jamestown, the very spot where the first sons of Africa were landed in the year 1620, if my memory serves me right, and from that day to the breaking out of the rebellion was looked upon as an inferior race by all civilized nations. But behold what has been revealed in the past three or four years; why the colored men have ascended upon a platform of equality, and the slave can now apply the lash to the tender flesh of his master, for this day I am now an eyewitness of the fact. The country being principally inhabited by wealthy farmers, there are a great many men in the regiment who are refugees from this place. While out on a foraging expedition, we captured a Mr. Clayton, a noted reb in this part of the country, and from his appearance, one of the F.F.V.s [First Families of Virginia]; on the day before we captured several colored women that belonged to Mr. C., who had given them a most unmerciful whipping previous to their departure. On the arrival of Mr. C. in camp, the commanding officer determined to let the women have their revenge, and ordered Mr. C. to be tied to a tree in front of head-quarters, and William Harris, a soldier in our regiment, and a member of Co. E, who was acquainted with the gentleman, and who used to belong to him, was called upon to undress him and introduce him to the ladies that I mentioned before. Mr. Harris played his part conspicuously, bringing the blood from his loins at every stroke, and not forgetting to remind the gentleman of the days gone by. After giving him some fifteen or twenty well-directed strokes, the ladies, one after another, came up and gave him a like number, to remind him that they were no longer his, but safely housed in Abraham's bosom, and under the protection of the Star Spangled Banner, and guarded by their own patriotic, though once down-trodden race. Oh, that I had the tongue to express my feelings while standing upon the banks of the James River, on the soil of Virginia, the mother state of slavery, as a witness of such a sudden reverse!

The day is clear, the fields of grain are beautiful, and the birds are singing sweet melodious songs, while poor Mr. C. is crying to his servants for mercy. Let all who sympathize with the South take this narrative for a mirror.

Part VII

Emancipation

Plate 9   Free Movement: Fugitive slaves ford the Rappahannock River around the time of the Second Battle of Bull Run near Manassas, VA, in the summer of 1862. President Lincoln's Emancipation Proclamation, issued in September of 1862, both reflected and intensified the reality that ending slavery would further Union war aims – and realize the implicit promises of the nation's founding. (Photo by Timothy H. O'Sullivan; Selected Civil War photographs, Library of Congress)

Chapter 16

The Meaning of Freedom in the Age of Emancipation

Eric Foner

Perhaps no word in American history is more potent – and more elusive – than "freedom." The Puritans who went to New England in the early seventeenth century, for example, arrived seeking a kind of freedom – the right to worship God as they saw fit – that they lacked at home. Yet they had little interest in allowing others such freedom; for them, "tolerance" was a dirty word (should one tolerate, never mind accept, that which is evil? That's not freedom – that's licentiousness). Similarly, the adventurers who settled Virginia around the same time were also seeking freedom, though this form tended to be more economic in nature: the freedom to get rich. Yet their dreams of wealth often involved getting other people to do most of the actual work; their freedom depended on slavery. Indeed, the very concept of freedom was defined, even depended, upon the highly visible alternative of bondage. This was the great paradox that the distinguished American historian Edmund Morgan had in mind when he wrote his groundbreaking 1975 book *American Slavery, American Freedom*.

Even the end of the most obvious, literal form of slavery in the Civil War was marked by ambiguity. Abraham Lincoln issued his Emancipation Proclamation on September 17, 1862, in which he decreed that slavery would end in all rebel territory as of January 1, 1863. Yet this seemingly bold assertion was, initially at least, meaningless: Lincoln ended slavery precisely where he had no effective authority to do so. In fact, the Emancipation Proclamation did have a significant long-term impact. For one thing, the word got out – like the puncturing of a great container, the Emancipation Proclamation led to a steady drain of slaves away from their masters toward freedom. For another, it changed the terms of the war, in which abolition was now finally official US-government policy. Lincoln justified the Emancipation Proclamation as an emergency wartime measure made in his capacity as commander-in-chief, one designed to strip the rebels of a tool – slave labor – they used to resist federal authority. Yet he also made clear that he would henceforth support ending slavery everywhere on a permanent, constitutional basis. In February 1865, as one of his final acts in office, he signed just such a measure – the Thirteenth Amendment – that stands as his, and the Civil War's, greatest legacy.

And yet, again, freedom was not necessarily what it seemed. As Lincoln himself had observed in his 1858 debates with Stephen Douglas, freedom was not the same thing as equality, and inequality could itself be a form of slavery – which is, in essence, what the twentieth century Civil Rights Movement was all about. The very former slave owners James L. Roark writes about in Part VI of this book realized that the tenant farming system could itself be a de facto form of slavery. Nor were African Americans the only ones to be confused and frustrated by the elusive search for freedom in the century after the Civil War. The pursuit of freedom, like the pursuit of like happiness, seemed to be something that could be pursued endlessly without ever being attained (or guaranteed).

No historian has done more to clarify the ambiguities of freedom than Columbia University historian Eric Foner. In this address to the Organization of American Historians in 1994, a precursor to his 1999 book *The Story of American Freedom*, Foner traces the various shapes and sizes of freedom in American life from the time of the Revolution to the time of the Civil War.

Eric Foner, "The Meaning of Freedom in the Age of Emancipation," *The Journal of American History*, vol. 81, no. 2 (Sept 1994), 435–60. Copyright © 1994 Organization of American Historians. Reprinted with permission.

[. . .]

In the years preceding the Revolution, "slavery" became a central feature of the language of American politics. Already widely used in the eighteenth-century Atlantic world to signify a loss of personal and political rights, the word acquired special force in America because of the proximity of hundreds of thousands of genuine slaves (about 20 percent of the colonial population in 1776). In resisting British policies, many colonists chose to describe their relationship to the mother country as enslavement. Sometimes their language directly invoked the harsh conditions under which African Americans lived, as in warnings that Britain planned to rule the colonists "with a rod of iron" and to reduce them to "beasts of burden." Actual slaves, however, rarely figured in this discourse. Slavery meant denial of the right of self-government or dependence on the will of another, not being reduced to a species of property. "Those who are taxed without their own consent," said John Dickinson, "are slaves." Paine defined hereditary rule as "a species of slavery"; "representative government," he added, "is freedom." In a reversal of previous usage, the contrast between England as "the land of slavery" and America as "*the country of free men*" became a standard part of the idiom of national independence, employed with no sense of irony even in states where the majority of the population consisted of slaves. South Carolina, declared one writer in 1774, was a land of freedom, and it was impossible to believe "that in this sacred land slavery shall soon be permitted to erect her throne."[1]

Even though rarely mentioned explicitly, black slavery was intimately related to the meaning of freedom for the men who made the American Revolution. In his famous speech to the British Parliament warning against attempts to coerce the colonies, Edmund Burke insisted that in the South at least, it was familiarity with actual slavery that made colonial leaders so sensitive to the threat of metaphorical slavery. Where freedom was a privilege, not a common right, he observed, "those who are free are by far the most proud and jealous of their freedom." Burke's insight in some ways anticipated the argument of Edmund S. Morgan's brilliant presidential address on the "American paradox," delivered before this organization over twenty years ago. Slavery for blacks, Morgan maintained, made republican freedom possible for whites, for by eliminating the great bulk of the dependent poor from the political nation, it left the public arena to men of propertied independence, in eighteenth-century political theory the only sure basis of republican government. Indeed, for many Americans owning slaves offered a route to that economic independence widely deemed indispensable to genuine freedom (a point driven home by a 1780 Virginia law that rewarded soldiers in the war for independence with three hundred acres of land and a slave). Whether Morgan's ingenious argument applies equally well to the northern colonies, where slavery was far less imposing a presence, may well be questioned. But his insight reminds us that slavery for blacks did not necessarily contradict white Americans' understanding of freedom. The republican vision of a society of independent men actively pursuing the public good could easily be reconciled with slavery for those outside the circle of citizenship. So, too, the liberal definition of liberty as essentially a private quality and of the political community as a collection of individuals seeking protection for their preexisting natural rights could, if one wished, be invoked to defend bondage. The right of self-government and the protection of property against interference by the state were essential to political freedom; taken together, these principles suggested that it would be an infringement on liberty to deprive a man of his property (including slave property) without his consent. The war, one group of Virginians insisted in the 1780s, had been fought for "the full, free, and absolute enjoyment of every species of our property, whatsoever." To divest owners of their slave property would reduce *them* to slavery.[2]

Some leaders of the Revolution were fully aware that slavery contradicted its professed ideals. James Otis insisted that to be worthy of the name, freedom must be indivisible and, alone among patriot leaders in the 1760s, declared blacks to be British subjects "entitled to all the civil rights of such." Arthur Lee noted in 1767 that if freedom was "the birth-right of all mankind," keeping Africans "in a State of slavery is a constant violation of that right, and therefore of Justice." Most dramatically, slaves themselves appreciated that by contrasting freedom so starkly with slavery and by defining freedom as a universal right rather than the privilege of a particular community or nation, the revolutionists had devised a rhetoric that, despite its palpable limitations, could readily be deployed against chattel bondage. The language of liberty echoed in slave communities, North and South, as slaves appropriated the patriotic ideology for their own purposes. The first concrete steps toward emancipation were "freedom petitions" by enslaved African Americans, who hailed the efforts of colonial leaders "to free themselves from slavery" and suggested, with more than a touch of irony, that legislation regarding blacks aspire toward "that same grand object." "Every principle from which America has acted," declared another petition, demanded emancipation. By 1800, the slave rebel Gabriel could plan to emblazon on a silk flag the colonists' own celebrated words, "Death or Liberty," to demonstrate, as one of his followers noted, that "we had as much right to fight for our liberty as any men."[3]

Two developments set in motion or greatly accelerated by the Revolution transformed the language of freedom and slavery in the nineteenth-century United States. The first was the rise of universal manhood suffrage, which itself reflected the eclipse of the older idea that public virtue and propertied independence were the bases of political freedom. Increasingly, voting came to be viewed – in popular usage if not, strictly speaking, in the law – as a right rather than a privilege, "the grandest right of a freeman," as a Maryland essayist put it in 1776. By the eve of the Civil War, nearly every state in the Union had enfranchised the vast majority of its white male citizens. Beginning with demands for the right to vote by lesser artisans, journeymen, and wage laborers during the Revolution, insistent pressure from below for an expansion of the suffrage did much to democratize American politics. Simultaneously, by severing ownership of productive property from membership in the political nation, these popular movements both exemplified and reinforced an emerging definition of public virtue as available to all citizens, not just the propertied, and of autonomy as resting on self-ownership rather than economic independence. There were "thousands of men without property," wrote Francis Lieber in his influential antebellum disquisition on American political institutions, "who have quite as great a stake in the public welfare as those who may possess a house or enjoy a certain amount of revenue."[4]

In a country that lacked more traditional bases of nationhood – long-established physical boundaries, historic ethnic, religious, and cultural unity – political institutions came to define both nationality and freedom itself. The right to vote, said one advocate of democratic reform, was the first mark of liberty, "the only true badge of the freeman." Those denied this right, said another, were "put in the situation of the slaves of Virginia." By the time Alexis de Tocqueville visited America, the axiom that "the people" ruled was repeated ad infinitum. But who were the people of the United States? As older kinds of exclusion fell away – property and religious qualifications for voting, for example – others were retained, and new ones added. Everywhere, with the quixotic exception of New Jersey between 1776 and 1807, women, whether married or single, propertied or dependent, were denied the suffrage. And, in a society in which slavery was expanding rapidly, both in geographical scope and economic centrality, the rights of free men inevitably took on a racial component. In 1800, no free state limited the suffrage on the basis of race. But every state that entered the Union after that year, except Maine, restricted the right to vote to white males. And in states such as Pennsylvania and New York, the right of free blacks to vote was either narrowed or eliminated entirely. The United States, said a delegate to the convention that disenfranchised Pennsylvania's black population, was "a political community of white persons." In effect, race had replaced class as the boundary defining which American men were to enjoy political freedom.[5]

As the bases for exclusion from this central definition of citizenship shifted, so too did their intellectual justification. These were the years when Americans spoke most insistently of liberty as the unique genius of their institutions, of territorial expansion as, in the oft-repeated words of Andrew Jackson, "extending the area of freedom." This rhetoric of self-congratulation knew no geographical borders; it was, said British visitor Harriet Martineau, a "wearisome cant" found in newspaper editorials, political addresses, and sermons, North and South. But the very pervasiveness of the claim to freedom among whites encouraged the rise of a racialist ideology that located in nature itself reasonable grounds for the unique forms of unfreedom to which blacks were subjected. How could belief in freedom as a universal human right be reconciled with exclusion of blacks from liberty in the South and the rights of free men in the North? Exclusion based on natural incapacity was not really exclusion at all.[6]

Of course, as John Stuart Mill asked rhetorically, "was there ever any domination which did not appear natural to those who possessed it?" Yet even Mill's argument for universal freedom, in his great work *On Liberty*, applied "only to human beings in the maturity of their faculties." The immature included not only children, but entire "races" of less than "civilized" peoples, deficient in the qualities necessary in the democratic citizen – the capacity for self-control, rational forethought, devotion to the nation. These were precisely the characteristics that Jefferson, in his famous comparison of the races in *Notes on the State of Virginia*, claimed blacks lacked, partly due to natural incapacity and partly because the bitter experience of bondage had rendered them (quite understandably, he felt) disloyal to America. Jefferson still believed that black Americans might eventually enjoy the natural rights enumerated in the Declaration of Independence, but he felt they should do so in Africa or the Caribbean. Blacks formed no part of the "imagined community" of Jefferson's republic. The violent slave revolution in Saint-Domingue not only revealed how the existence of slavery distorted white America's understanding of freedom (for the rebellious slaves were viewed not as men and women seeking their freedom in the tradition of 1776, but as a danger to American institutions, who must be quarantined and destroyed) but also reinforced the conviction that blacks were by nature uncivilized. Their incapacity for personal self-government – that is, the ability to subordinate their passions to rational self-discipline – rendered them unqualified for political self-government and, it was increasingly argued by defenders of slavery in the North as well as the South, for freedom itself.[7]

Women, too, ostensibly lacked the capacity for independent judgment and rational action, a conviction that contributed to the emerging ideology of separate spheres, which defined women of all classes and races as by nature fundamentally different from men. Gender and racial differences were widely understood as being part of a single, natural hierarchy of innate endowments. "How did woman first become subject to man, as she now is all over the world?" asked the *New York Herald* in 1852. "By her nature, her sex, just as the negro is and always will be, to the end of time, inferior to the white race, and, therefore, doomed to subjection." The Creator, said a delegate to Virginia's 1829 constitutional convention, had rendered woman "weak and timid, in comparison with man, and had thus placed her under his *control*, as well as under his protection." Since the right of suffrage "necessarily implied *free-agency* and *intelligence*," nature itself had decreed women's "incapacity to exercise political power." Indeed, the political world of the nineteenth century, so crucial an arena for the exercise of masculine freedom, was itself constructed through a contrast with the feminine sphere of the home. If no longer necessarily a property holder, the free man was still defined as the head of a family and master of a household, whose personal independence rested on the enforced dependence of wives and children. Thus, rather than being aberrations in a broader story of the expansion of freedom, the exclusions from political rights were intrinsically related to the ways the idea of freedom was constructed in the nineteenth-century United States.[8]

The second development that reshaped the idea of freedom after 1800 was the rapid expansion of capitalism. Although both North and South experienced the market revolution, its consequences in the two regions were profoundly different, consolidating, in the South, the greatest slave society the modern world has known, while setting the North on a path of economic modernization. Economic change, in other words, powerfully sharpened the dichotomy between slavery and freedom. One indication of this was the rapid decline of the varieties of partial freedom that had coexisted with slave and free labor in colonial America. Indentured servitude, a form of voluntary unfreedom, provided a major part of the nonslave labor force, North and South, before the Revolution. As late as the early 1770s, nearly half the immigrants who arrived in America from England and Scotland had entered into contracts for a fixed period of labor in exchange for passage. Although not slaves, indentured servants could be bought and sold and subjected to corporal punishment, and the obligation to carry out their duties ("specific performance" in the language of the law) was enforced by the courts. They occupied, a Pennsylvania judge remarked in 1793, "a middle rank between slaves and free men." This was not freedom as the nineteenth century would understand it. But in the generation after the Revolution, with the rapid decline of indentured servitude and apprenticeship and the identification of paid domestic service as an occupation for blacks and white females, the halfway houses between slavery and freedom disappeared. At the same time, the abolition of slavery in the North drew a geographical line across the Union, separating free and slave states. These developments would eventually make possible the emergence of an ideology that glorified the North as the home of "free labor."[9]

If the democratization of politics consolidated the right to vote as the political definition of freedom, the market revolution greatly encouraged the spread of liberal individualism, and broad dissemination of a "negative" definition of freedom as the absence of external constraints on autonomous, self-directed individuals. Even as political participation expanded, the power of government waned. Whigs such as John Quincy Adams might insist that government could enhance the realm of freedom by creating the conditions for ordered economic development, thereby maximizing individual choices. More popular, however, was the Democratic view of government as a source of unwarranted privilege, a "danger to liberty," understood as the capacity of citizens to pursue their interests and cultivate their individual talents. "In this country," declared the *New York Journal of Commerce* in 1848, contrasting American definitions of freedom with those of French socialists, "liberty is understood to be the *absence* of government from private affairs."[10]

In a world in which personal freedom increasingly meant the opportunity to compete in the marketplace in the pursuit of economic gain, slavery remained the master metaphor for describing impediments to individual advancement. To temperance advocates, drink, which deprived an individual of the capacity for self-realization, was a form of enslavement; some described the "chains of intoxication" as "heavier than those which the sons of Africa have ever worn." For nativists, Catholicism was a form of slavery at odds with American conceptions of liberty, since Catholics were obligated to follow authority blindly rather than displaying the manly independence of Protestants; their unfamiliarity with the principle of personal liberty allegedly explained why so many Catholic immigrants remained poor. And the discontent of those Americans who believed the material conditions of autonomy were slipping from their grasp just when the rhetoric of freedom was flourishing crystallized in the idea of "wage slavery."[11]

There was nothing uniquely American in the rhetorical mobilization of chattel slavery to criticize labor relations under capitalism. But this vocabulary took on a special power in the United States. Because slavery was an immediate reality, not a distant symbol, and the small producer still a powerful element in the social order, the idea that the wage earner, because of economic dependence, was less than fully free retained considerable power as a criticism of the emerging order. Despite obvious exaggeration, the idea of wage slavery provided American labor and its allies with a critique of emerging capitalism in which workplace exploitation, not control of the government by placemen and nonproducers (as in nineteenth-century Britain), took center stage. The idea of wage slavery also served to deconstruct, as it were, the sharp contrast between slavery and freedom, to expose the forms of coercion and hidden inequalities inherent in ostensibly free economic institutions. Freedom, Noah Webster's *American Dictionary* declared, was both the opposite of slavery, and "a state of exemption from the power or control of another." The Jacksonian labor movement asked how many wage earners truly enjoyed such "exemption." Even as employers celebrated the labor contract as a voluntary agreement between autonomous individuals, the very antithesis of slavery, critics of wage labor demonstrated that the moral authority of the contrast with slavery could be used for very different purposes. Wage labor, insisted Philadelphia labor spokesman Langdon Byllesby, was the "very essence of slavery."[12]

Northern laborers were not alone in criticizing marketplace understandings of freedom. The rapid expansion of slavery and the consolidation of a distinctive southern ruling class promoted the emergence of a proslavery ideology in which the contrast between freedom and slavery became an ideological weapon against the self-proclaimed "free society" of the North. The northern free laborer, insisted defenders of slavery such as John C. Calhoun and George Fitzhugh, was little more than "the slave of the *community*," a situation far more oppressive than to be owned by an individual master, shielded from the exploitation of the competitive marketplace. Repudiating not only Jefferson's rhetoric of universal natural rights but also his conviction that slavery distorted the character of the white population by training it in despotism, southern spokesmen returned to the older idea that freedom was a privilege; Calhoun called it a "reward to be earned, not a blessing to be gratuitously lavished on all alike."

Slavery allowed propertied men the leisure to cultivate their talents and participate actively in government, thus producing economic, social, and political progress. If northerners, broadly speaking, accepted the idea of boundaries excluding nonwhites from political freedom, the white South extended this logic to insist that some people were not suited to freedom of any kind. The white man, was "made for liberty," while blacks, said Gov. George McDuffie of South Carolina, were "utterly unqualified . . . for rational freedom." Far from being the natural condition of mankind, wrote Fitzhugh, "universal liberty" was an aberration, an experiment carried on "for a little while" in "a corner of Europe" and the northern United States, and with disastrous results. Taking the world and its history as a whole, slavery was "the general, ... normal, natural" basis of "civilized society." Freedom meant not simply being uncoerced, but exercising sovereignty over subordinates. In a word, as the *Richmond Enquirer* put it, "Freedom is not possible without slavery."[13]

Even as proslavery ideologues challenged prevailing definitions of freedom in the antebellum North, these ideas were tested and reshaped in entirely different ways by their northern abolitionist adversaries. The contribution of the crusade against slavery to redefining the meanings of freedom was both profound and complex. Abolitionists, quite understandably, resented equations of northern labor with southern bondage, whether emanating from the slave South or the labor movement of the free states. The wage earner's "freedom of contract" discredited the analogy between wage and chattel slavery, insisted Edmund Quincy, since the free laborer had the right to "choose his employer," "contract for wages," and leave his job if he became dissatisfied. In affirming the uniqueness of the evil of slavery, abolitionists helped popularize the sharp dichotomy between slavery's illegitimate coercions and the condition of labor in the North, and the related concept, fortified by the market revolution, that autonomy derived, not from the ownership of productive property, but from property in oneself and the ability to enjoy the fruits of one's labor. "Self-right is the *foundation* right," insisted Theodore Weld, the basis of all other rights in society, a formula that diverted attention from the many ways in which the independence of free men and women was limited. Abolitionists of the Garrisonian stripe extended this definition of freedom as self-direction into a critique of coercive institutions in general, including government, the church, and, on occasion, the family. Others, particularly those who led the antislavery movement into politics in the 1840s, rejected the practice of "confounding" slavery "with other relations and institutions from which it is in reality and essentially distinct." The cause of freedom meant emancipating the slaves. It would only injure the cause to identify abolitionists as enemies of institutions "which the great body of its members cherish as objects of great regard – family authority and our republican government."[14]

"Family authority," however, was inevitably drawn into the debate over slavery. Like wage slavery, the concept of the "slavery of sex" demonstrated the power of the slavery metaphor to shape understandings of freedom. The idiom of freedom and unfreedom empowered early feminists to develop a pervasive critique of male authority. Feminist abolitionists did not invent the analogy between marriage and slavery. Mary Wollstonecraft had invoked in the 1790s, and it had become prominent in the writings and speeches of Robert Owen, Frances Wright, and other early communitarians, who insisted that true equality was impossible until the institution of marriage had been fundamentally transformed. At New Harmony, Owen had promised, women would no longer be "enslaved" to their husbands. (Actual conditions for women there proved to be somewhat less than utopian.) But the analogy between free women and slaves gained prominence as it was swept up in the accelerating debate over chattel slavery. Even Sarah Josepha Hale, editor of *Godey's Lady's Book* and a strong opponent of the movement for women's rights, spoke of how the common law reduced "woman to the condition of a slave." Proslavery ideologues such as Fitzhugh said much the same thing by defending both slavery and marriage as systems of subordination based upon natural differences in the capacity for freedom and by maintaining that, by logical extension, abolition threatened established gender relations.[15]

There were indeed real and disturbing parallels between chattel slavery and marriage. "Woman is a slave, from the cradle to the grave," asserted Ernestine Rose. "Father, guardian, husband – master still. One conveys her, like a piece of property, over to the other." Marriage was "voluntary," but the common law reduced the wife to an appendage of her husband, one who did not enjoy the fruits of her own labor. Until after the Civil War, married women could neither sign independent contracts nor control the wages they might earn, and even then, the husband's proprietary right to his wife's person and domestic labor remained unquestioned. Women's rights advocates turned the abolitionist definition of freedom as self-ownership into a critique of men's property rights in women and of marriage as a system of domination. The analogy with slavery suggested the remedy – emancipation – understood to include not only political enfranchisement but also such demands as liberalization of divorce laws and access to all the educational and economic opportunities of men. Whether married or not, women deserved the autonomy and range of individual choices that constituted the essence of freedom. Feminism, therefore, was an extension of nineteenth-century liberal principles, but it was also much more. For even as it sought to apply liberalism to women, the movement posed a fundamental challenge to some of its central tenets – that the capacity for independence and rationality were quintessentially male traits, that the world was divided into autonomous public and private realms, and that the family's internal relations fell beyond the bounds of scrutiny on the basis of justice and freedom.[16]

For the early movement for women's rights, the slavery of sex became an all-encompassing critique of the subordination of women, and the female slave an emblem for the condition of all women. The emphasis in abolitionist literature on the physical violation of the slave woman's body helped give the idea of self-ownership a concrete reality, a literalness, that encouraged application to free women as well. Women's ensuing demands for the right to regulate their own sexual activity and procreation and to be protected by the state against violence at the hands of their husbands were so explosive that they were rarely raised publicly until after the Civil War. These issues, however, frequently arose in the private correspondence of feminist leaders. (Lucy Stone, who believed a woman must have an "absolute right" to her "body, and its uses," admitted that the movement was not yet ready for this question, since "no two of us think alike about it.")[17]

Like the metaphor of wage slavery, the description of free women as living in "legalized slavery" both obscured and illuminated social realities. Even many feminists understood that the intense individualism of a Lucy Stone or an Elizabeth Cady Stanton was far removed from family life as actually experienced by most women, and that their theories did not take into account the emotional dependencies, the sacrifice of "freedom," that marriage and parenthood inevitably entail. Just as most abolitionists repudiated the wage slavery metaphor, black feminist abolitionists such as Sarah Parker Remond rejected the analogy between free women and slaves because they understood that a stable family life had special meaning to those who experienced slavery. Even though free women deserved more rights, Remond declared, slave women, as the "worst victims" of slavery, stood in dire need of "the protection . . . enjoyed by the white." Yet even if the "slavery of sex" remained of little relevance to actual slaves, the inclusion of slave women in the category of woman enabled feminists to redefine social difference as sexual inequality, and that inclusion proved liberating for free women.[18]

If, in popularizing the identification of autonomy with personal self-ownership rather than propertied independence, abolitionists narrowed the definition of freedom, the idiom of the "slavery of sex" demonstrates the capacity of this definition to reinvigorate the idea of freedom as a truly universal entitlement. When applied to African Americans, this principle challenged both southern slavery and the racial boundaries that confined free blacks to second-class status throughout the nation. Drawing on eighteenth-century traditions of natural rights, the Declaration of Independence, and the perfectionist creed of evangelical religion, abolitionists insisted that personal liberty took precedence over such forms of freedom as the right of citizens to accumulate and hold property or the enjoyment of self-government by political communities. Stripping away many of the metaphorical usages of slavery, they helped focus the debate over freedom on actually existing chattel slavery. Moreover, despite their alienation from a succession of presidential administrations that seemed firmly in the grasp of the Slave Power, abolitionists glimpsed the possibility that the national state might become the guarantor of freedom, rather than its enemy. At a time when the authority to define the rights of citizens lay almost entirely with the states, abolitionists maintained that emancipation would imply not simply an end to the legal status of bondage, but a national guarantee of the equal civil rights of all Americans, black as well as white. In seeking to define the core rights to which all Americans were entitled – the meaning of freedom in concrete legal terms – abolitionists pioneered the concept of equality before the law regardless of race, one all but unknown in American jurisprudence before the Civil War.[19]

Most adamant in contending that the struggle against slavery required a redefinition of freedom were black members of the abolitionist crusade. "He who has endured the cruel pangs of slavery," wrote Frederick Douglass in 1847 in the inaugural issue of his newspaper, the *North Star*, "is the man to advocate liberty," and black abolitionists developed an understanding of freedom that went well beyond the usage of most of their white contemporaries. Those who had known slavery firsthand were among the most penetrating critics of the proslavery argument. "Flimsy nonsense," Douglass called it, that men would be "ashamed to remember" once slavery had been abolished. Equally nonsensical were the nation's pretensions as a land of liberty, which slaves ridiculed when they had the chance and black abolitionists repudiated at every opportunity. Indeed, free blacks dramatically reversed the common association of the United States with the progress of freedom. In choosing to celebrate the anniversary of West Indian emancipation, rather than July 4, and holding up Britain as a model of devotion to liberty, black communities in the North offered a stinging rebuke to white Americans' claims to live in a land of freedom.[20]

Even more persistently than their white counterparts, black abolitionists articulated the ideals of egalitarian constitutionalism and color-blind citizenship. "The real battleground between liberty and slavery," wrote Samuel Cornish, "is prejudice against color." African Americans, slave and free, understood that the sharp dichotomy between freedom and slavery failed to encompass the actual experience of free blacks, who, in the South, lived, worked, and worshipped alongside slaves and, in the North, were relegated to a quasi freedom of inequality. True freedom, the free black experience suggested, meant more than the absence of coercion. "No people can be free," wrote Martin Delany, "who themselves do not constitute an essential part of the *ruling element* of the country in which they live," a sentiment shared by the many black abolitionists who did not hold Delany's emigrationist views. Abolishing slavery implied empowering African Americans with all the rights – civil, social, political – enjoyed by whites, a wholesale transformation of the institutions and culture of the society that had supported and legitimated slavery in the first place. More than white abolitionists, black abolitionists identified the widespread poverty of the free black population as a consequence of slavery and insisted that freedom had an economic as well as a personal dimension. It must be part of the "great work" of the antislavery crusade, insisted Charles L. Reason, "to abolish not only chattel slavery, but that other kind of slavery, which, for generation after generation, dooms an oppressed people to a condition of dependence and pauperism." In the black abolitionists' expansive definition of freedom and in their understanding of the limits slavery placed on freedom even in the northern states lay roots of future struggles over the consequences of emancipation.[21]

Thus, by the eve of the Civil War, the debate over freedom and slavery had at last come to focus on actual, rather than metaphorical, slavery. In the hands of the Republican party, the antithesis between freedom and slavery or, as Republicans put it, "free society" and "slave society," coalesced into a comprehensive ideology glorifying the North as the home of true freedom. In the Republican ideology, "free labor" – labor not subject to the coercions of slavery and enjoying the opportunity for physical mobility and social advancement – was not only the foundation of freedom but a universal entitlement, not confined to any particular set of persons, a point Abraham Lincoln drove home in his debates with Stephen A. Douglas by choosing as his example a black woman. In the Republicans' rallying cry "Freedom National," the intentions of the founding fathers and the text of the Constitution were reinterpreted to demonstrate that freedom was, in the words of William H. Seward, the "perpetual, organic, universal" principle of the American republic and slavery an aberration, which would soon be done away with. And the scale of the Union's triumph in the Civil War, along with the sheer drama of emancipation, fused nationalism, morality, and the language of freedom into an entirely new combination. "Liberty and Union have become identical," wrote Douglass; for Lincoln, the war's deepest meaning lay in the "new birth of freedom" for all Americans occasioned by the destruction of slavery for blacks. A new nation had emerged from the war, declared Lincoln's Illinois friend Congressman Isaac N. Arnold. "This new nation is to be wholly free."[22]

The varied understandings of freedom shaped by the struggle over slavery profoundly affected how Americans, North and South alike, responded to the social revolution wrought by emancipation. "What is freedom?" asked Congressman James A. Garfield in 1865. "Is it the bare privilege of not being chained? If this is all, then freedom is a bitter mockery, a cruel delusion."[23] Did freedom mean simply the absence of slavery, or did it imply other rights for the emancipated blacks, and if so, which: Civil equality, the suffrage, ownership of property? The bitter debates of the Reconstruction era revolved in large measure around the definition of freedom in the aftermath of emancipation. The concrete historical reality of emancipation posed freedom as a historical and substantive issue, rather than a philosophical or metaphorical one. The destruction of slavery raised in the most direct form the relationship between property rights and personal rights, between personal, political, and economic freedom.

In the postemancipation South, most whites, especially those who assumed that the survival of the plantation system was essential to maintaining economic stability and racial supremacy, defined black freedom in the narrowest conceivable manner. Before the Civil War, the white South had condemned free labor as a disguised form of general slavery. After the war, it responded to emancipation by trying to subject blacks to precisely the generalized slavery it had previously condemned. As the northern journalist Sidney Andrews discovered late in 1865.

> The whites seem wholly unable to comprehend that freedom for the negro means the same thing as freedom for them. They readily enough admit that the Government has made him free, but appear to believe that they still have the right to exercise over him the old control. . . . They acknowledge the overthrow of the special servitude of man to man, but seek to establish the general servitude of man to the commonwealth.

Rejecting the idea that emancipation implied civil or political equality for the freedmen or even those opportunities to acquire property and advance in the marketplace that northerners took for granted as indispensable to any free society, southern leaders insisted that blacks remain as a dependent plantation labor force, in a work situation not very different from slavery. The emancipated slave, a southern newspaper insisted, needed to be taught that "he is *free*, but free only to labor." To enforce this definition of the meaning of black freedom, state governments during Presidential Reconstruction enacted the notorious Black Codes, denying blacks equality before the law and political rights and, through vagrancy laws and statutes making breach of contract a criminal offense, attempting to circumscribe their economic opportunities so that plantation agriculture could survive the end of slavery.[24]

"Will the United States give them freedom or its shadow?" a northern educator had written from North Carolina shortly after the end of the Civil War. Northern Republicans, imbued with a free-labor ideology sanctified by the triumph in the Civil War, refused to accept a definition of black freedom that seemed to make a mockery of the struggle for emancipation. As the war drew to a close, the Republican-dominated Congress, in debates over the Thirteenth Amendment, struggled to define precisely the repercussions of the destruction of slavery. Even Congressman William Holman, an Indiana Democrat hardly known as an emancipationist, noted that "mere exemption from servitude is a miserable idea of freedom." All agreed that property rights in man must be abrogated, contractual relations substituted for the discipline of the lash, and the master's patriarchal authority over the lives of the former slaves abolished. The phrase most often repeated in the debates – the "right to the fruits of his labor" – was thought to embody the distinction between slavery and freedom. These debates also made clear what emancipation did not encompass. Several congressmen expressed concern that the amendment's abolition of "involuntary servitude" might be construed to apply to relations within the family. "A husband has a right of property in the service of his wife," said one congressman, which the abolition of slavery was not intended to touch. Indeed, slavery's destruction of family life (including the husband's role as patriarch and breadwinner) had been one of abolitionism's most devastating criticisms of the peculiar institution. Republicans assumed emancipation would restore to blacks the right to family life, with women assuming their natural roles as daughters, wives, and mothers within the domestic sphere. Along with the right to "personal liberty," the male-headed family, embodying the "right of a husband to his wife" and of a "father to his child," declared Congressman John Kasson of Iowa, constituted the "three great fundamental natural rights of human society." Thus, even as they rejected the racialized definition of freedom that had emerged in the first half of the nineteenth century, Republicans left the conventions of gender relations largely intact. Women would remain, as Stanton put it, "in a transition period from slavery to freedom."[25]

The Thirteenth Amendment, said one Democratic senator in December 1865, had abolished the right of one person to own another, "and that I think ought to be sufficient for the lovers of freedom in this country." But it was not. "We must see to it," announced Sen. William Stewart at the opening of Congress in December 1865, "that the man made free by the Constitution of the United States ... is a freeman indeed." By 1866 a consensus had emerged within the Republican party that civil equality was an essential attribute of freedom, and in a remarkable, if temporary, reversal of political traditions, the newly empowered national state emerged, not as a threat to individual liberty, but as the "custodian of freedom," obligated to identify and protect the rights of all American citizens. The Fourteenth Amendment enshrined the notion of equality before the law in the Constitution, and many Republicans believed that the Thirteenth Amendment, which irrevocably abolished slavery, also empowered Congress to overturn such "badges of slavery" as state legislation discriminating among citizens on the basis of race. Soon afterward, blacks were accorded political rights equal to those of whites.[26]

The Republican party thus proved a potent instrument in breaking down the civil and political barriers to equal citizenship for the freedmen. The importance of this accomplishment ought not to be underestimated: repudiating the racialized definition of democracy that had emerged in the first half of the nineteenth century was a major step toward reinvigorating the idea of freedom as a universal entitlement. When it came to defining the economic conditions of freedom in the postbellum South, however, Republicans found themselves divided. All believed that the Civil War had demonstrated the superiority of the northern system of labor; all believed that emancipation implied the construction of a "free labor society" in the former slave states. What the victorious North found difficult to define was the new economic status of the former slaves. Republican policy makers were perfectly willing to exert the power of the federal government in an attempt to guarantee the marketplace freedoms of blacks – the rights to choose a livelihood, acquire property, sign contracts, and enjoy access to the courts, on the same terms, formally, as whites. Further than this, they were unwilling to go. Only a minority, most notably Thaddeus Stevens, sought to resurrect the older view that without ownership of productive property, genuine freedom was impossible. "Small independent landholders," Stevens told the House, "are the support and guardians of republican liberty." By the time of Reconstruction, however, few Republicans seem to have believed that wage labor and republican freedom were incompatible, so long as the unfettered market offered the laborer the opportunity to achieve, through diligence and hard work, economic independence. Thus, the pleas of Stevens, George W. Julian, and a few others that Congress redistribute southern land fell on deaf ears.[27]

There was, of course, one further protagonist in the story, whose voice we have, thus far, not heard. "The Negroes are to be pitied," wrote a South Carolina educator and minister. "They do not understand the liberty which has been conferred upon them." In fact, blacks carried out of bondage an understanding of their new condition shaped both by their experience as slaves and by observation of the free society around them. Slavery negates both individual rights and community self-determination, and as free people, blacks sought both the personal liberties of whites and collective empowerment. Along with an end to the myriad injustices associated with slavery – separation of families, punishment by the lash, denial of access to education – freedom meant, as Henry McNeal Turner put it, the "enjoyment of our rights with other men" and independence from white control. One element of this independence was the right to vote; in the words of Douglass, "Slavery is not abolished until the black man has the ballot." In a democracy where universal manhood suffrage was the political norm, Douglass explained, to deny blacks the vote was "to brand us with the stigma of inferiority," to accept as valid the false ascription of personal deficiencies to blacks in order to exclude them from the American political community. Anything less than full citizenship rights would doom former slaves to the quasi freedom to which free blacks had been subjected before the Civil War.[28]

Also central to their definition of freedom was economic autonomy. In January 1865 Gen. William T. Sherman and Secretary of War Edwin M. Stanton met with a group of black leaders in Savannah, Georgia, recently occupied by the Union army. Asked what he understood by slavery, the group's spokesman, Garrison Frazier, responded that it meant one man's "receiving . . . the work of another man, and not by his consent." Freedom he defined as "placing us where we could reap the fruit of our own labor." The way to accomplish this was for the former slaves to own land; without land, their labor would continue to be subject to exploitation by the former owners. Only land, said former Mississippi slave Merrimon Howard, would enable "the poor class to enjoy the sweet boon of freedom."[29]

In its individual elements and in much of its language, the attempt by former slaves to breathe substantive meaning into emancipation coincided with definitions of freedom widely shared among white Americans – self-ownership, family stability, marketplace equality, political participation, and economic autonomy. But these elements coalesced into a vision very much their own. Freedom meant something quite different to those who had long enjoyed it than to those to whom it had always been denied. For whites, freedom, no matter how defined, was a given, a heritage to be defended. For American blacks, steeped in a Christian eschatology in which the story of Exodus played a central role, emancipation was a critical moment in the history of a people, while freedom was a broad, multifaceted concept, a millennial transformation of every facet of their lives. Rather than a metaphor, slavery was a historical experience, which would remain central to their conception of themselves and their place in history. Long after white America had forgotten or retrospectively sugarcoated the actual history of slavery, its brutal reality would remain alive in blacks' collective memory. Whenever blacks discussed slavery, historian Walter L. Fleming complained at the turn of the century, "we hear the clank of chains and the cutting swish of the lash." The antithesis of slavery was not "simple" freedom, but a share of the political and economic power previously enjoyed by the planter class. To put it another way, the emancipated slaves raised the time-honored question of the conditions of freedom: whether to be socially stigmatized, deprived of political power, and lacking in economic resources is, in some essential sense, to be less than truly free.[30]

In 1865 a young Bostonian, A. Warren Kelsey, was dispatched to the South by a group of cotton manufacturers to investigate economic and political conditions. From Orangeburg, South Carolina, Kelsey penned a revealing account of how blacks understood the meaning of freedom.

> The sole ambition of the freedman at the present time appears to be to become the owner of a little piece of land, there to erect a humble home, and to dwell in peace and security at his own free will and pleasure. If he wishes, to cultivate the ground in cotton on his own account, to be able to do so without anyone to dictate to him hours or system of labor, if he wishes instead to plant corn or sorghum or sweet potatoes – to be able to do *that* free from any outside control, in one word to be *free*, to control his own time and efforts without anything that can remind him of past sufferings in bondage. This is their idea, their desire and their hope.[31]

Thomas Jefferson would have well understood this desire – to be master of one's own time, free from the coercions of either an arbitrary master or the impersonal marketplace. Here was an ideal of freedom commensurate with the vision of a polity resting on the consent of truly autonomous individuals. But in Reconstruction America, how many whites enjoyed freedom thus defined? And in a society where most whites no longer enjoyed economic autonomy, could blacks reasonably expect the nation to guarantee it for them? In being forced to deal with freedom as a matter of concrete policy, Americans were compelled to recognize how thoroughly their own society had changed. The debates unleashed by the end of slavery, in other words, may well have forced Americans to appreciate how far they had traveled from the world in which freedom rested on ownership of productive property. In retrospect, Reconstruction emerges as a decisive moment in fixing the dominant understanding of freedom as self-ownership and the right to compete in the labor market, rather than propertied independence. Even as the overthrow of slavery reinforced the definition of the contract as the very opposite of the master–slave relationship, the policy of according black men a place in the political nation while denying them the benefits of land reform fortified the idea that the free citizen could be a dependent laborer. Reconstruction helped to solidify the separation of political and economic spheres, the juxtaposition of political equality and economic inequality, as the American way. Henceforth, it would be left to dissenters – populists, labor radicals, socialists, and the like – to resurrect the older idea of economic equality as the essence of freedom.

In the end, the black political leader John Mercer Langston declared shortly after the end of Reconstruction, emancipation proved to be severely limited, for the former slaves had not acquired that "practical independence" so indispensable to real liberty. History, unfortunately, does not move in a whiggish progress from unfreedom to freedom, a straight line toward ever greater liberty and human dignity. The death of slavery did not automatically mean the birth of freedom. Instead, it thrust the former slave into a kind of no-man's-land, a partial freedom that made a mockery of the American ideal of the independent citizen. Once Reconstruction had been overthrown, as Douglass put it in 1883, African Americans remained "only half free," standing in "the twilight of American liberty." Indeed, viewing the nineteenth century as a whole, the transition from slavery to freedom appears not simply as a narrative of liberation, but as a far more complex story in which the descendants of Africa came to enjoy greater freedom than they had known, but by no means freedom as they had come to understand it, while many small white farmers and craftsmen descended into the dependency of tenancy and wage labor, still experienced by many Americans as the antithesis of freedom.[32] Emancipation, therefore, settled for all time Professor Morgan's American paradox, the simultaneous existence of slavery and freedom, while reopening another: the coexistence of political democracy and economic dependence. And that American paradox – the meaning of freedom in a land pervaded by inequality – still bedevils our society today.

Notes

1   On the percentage of slaves in the colonial population in the 1770s, see US Bureau of the Census, *Historical Statistics of the United States, Colonial Times to 1970* (2 pts., Washington, 1975), pt. I, p. 168; and cf. Duncan J. MacLeod, *Slavery, Race, and the American Revolution* (New York, 1974), p. 62. Bernard Bailyn, *Ideological Origins of the American Revolution* (Cambridge, MA., 1967), pp. 119, 232–33; Jack P. Greene, " 'Slavery or Independence?': Some Reflections on the Relationship among Liberty, Black Bondage, and Equality in Revolutionary South Carolina," *South Carolina Historical Magazine*, 80 (July 1979), 197–203, esp. 201; Reid, *Concept of Liberty in the Age of the American Revolution*, pp. 38–45. For John Dickinson's remark, see Bailyn, *Ideological Origins of the American Revolution*, pp. 232–3. Philip S. Foner, ed., *The Complete Writings of Thomas Paine* (2 vols., New York, 1945), I, p. 390; Wood, *Creation of the American Republic*, p. 32; Peter Force, ed., *American Archives* (6 vols., Washington, 1837), I, p. 512. Cf. F. Nwabueze Okoyo, "Chattel Slavery as the Nightmare of the American Revolutionaries," *William and Mary Quarterly*, 37 (Jan. 1980), pp. 3–28.
2   Edmund Burke, *The Works of the Right Honourable Edmund Burke* (16 vols., London, 1803), III, p. 54; Edmund S. Morgan, "Slavery and Freedom: The American Paradox," *Journal of American History*, 59 (June 1972), 5–29; Edmund S. Morgan, *American Slavery, American Freedom: The Ordeal of Colonial Virginia* (New York, 1975), p. 385; Davis, *Problem of Slavery in Western Culture*, pp. 412–13; Davis, *Problem of Slavery in the Age of Revolution*, pp. 259–60. For the argument by the group of Virginians, see Sylvia R. Frey, "Liberty, Equality, and Slavery: The Paradox of the American Revolution," in *The American Revolution: Its Character and Limits*, ed. Jack P. Greene (New York, 1987), pp. 241–2.
3   Judith N. Shklar, *American Citizenship: The Quest for Inclusion* (Cambridge, MA, 1991), p. 41; Roger Bruns, ed., *Am I Not a Man and a Brother: The Antislavery Crusade of Revolutionary America, 1688–1788* (New York, 1977), p. 108; Peter H. Wood, " 'Liberty is Sweet': African-American Freedom Struggles in the Years before White Independence," in *Beyond the American Revolution*, ed., Young, pp. 152–9; Thomas J. Davis, "Emancipation Rhetoric, Natural Rights, and Revolutionary New England: A Note on Four Black Petitions in Massachusetts, 1773–1777," *New England Quarterly*, 62 (June 1989), 255; Winthrop D. Jordan, *White over Black: American Attitudes toward the Negro, 1550–1812* (Chapel Hill, 1968), p. 291; *Calendar of the Virginia State Papers and Other Manuscripts, 1652–1869* (11 vols., Richmond, 1875–93), IX, pp. 160, 164.
4   *Annapolis Maryland Gazette*, Aug. 15, 1776; Robert J. Steinfeld, "Property and Suffrage in the Early American Republic," *Stanford Law Review*, 41 (Jan. 1989), 335–76; Sean Wilentz, "Property and Power: Suffrage Reform in the United States, 1787–1860," in *Voting and the Spirit of American Democracy: Essays on the History of Voting and Voting Rights*, ed. Donald W. Rogers and Christine Scriabine (Urbana, 1992), pp. 31–41; James A. Henretta, "The Rise and Decline of 'Democratic-Republicanism': Political Rights in New York and the Several States, 1800–1915," in *Toward a Usable Past: Liberty under State Constitutions*, ed. Paul Finkelman and Stephen E. Gottlieb (Athens, GA, 1991), p. 58; Lieber, *On Civil Liberty and Self-Government*, pp. 176–7.
5   William B. Scott, *In Pursuit of Happiness: American Conceptions of Property from the Seventeenth to the Twentieth Century* (Bloomington, 1977), pp. 76–8, esp. p. 77; Merrill D. Peterson, ed., *Democracy, Liberty, and Property: The State Constitutional Conventions of the 1820's* (Indianapolis, 1966), esp.

pp. 60–1; Daniel T. Rodgers and Sean Wilentz, "Languages of Power in the United States," in *Language, History, and Class*, ed. Penelope J. Corfield (Cambridge, MA, 1991), p. 254; Marc W. Kruman, "The Second American Party System and the Transformation of Revolutionary Republicanism," *Journal of the Early Republic*, 12 (Winter 1992), 517–18; Robert J. Cottrol and Raymond T. Diamond, "The Second Amendment: Toward an Afro-Americanist Reconsideration," *Georgetown Law Journal*, 80 (Dec. 1991), 334. For the remark by the Pennsylvania delegate, see Leon F. Litwack, *North of Slavery: The Negro in the Free States, 1790–1860* (Chicago, 1961), p. 77.

6   Rush Welter, *The Mind of America, 1820–1860* (New York, 1975), p. 253. For Andrew Jackson's words, see Major L. Wilson, *Space, Time, and Freedom: The Quest for Nationality and the Irrepressible Conflict, 1815–1861* (West-port, 1974), p. 33. For Harriet Martineau's comment, see Potter, *Freedom and Its Limitations in American Life*, pp. 1–2. Reginald Horsman, *Race and Manifest Destiny: The Origins of Racial Anglo-Saxonism* (Cambridge, MA, 1981), 1–4, 146–53.

7   Susan Moller Okin, *Women in Western Political Thought* (Princeton, 1979), p. 215; Richard Bellamy, *Liberalism and Modern Society: A Historical Argument* (University Park, 1992), p. 25; Thomas Jefferson, *Notes on the State of Virginia* (New York, 1964), pp. 132–4; Benedict Anderson, *Imagined Communities: Reflections on the Origin and Spread of Nationalism* (New York, 1991); Michael Zuckerman, "The Color of Counterrevolution: Thomas Jefferson and the Rebellion in San Domingo," in *The Languages of Revolution*, ed. Loretta Valtz Mannucci (Milan, 1988), pp. 83–109; Joyce Appleby, "The Radical *Double-Entendre* in the Right to Self-Government," in *The Origins of Anglo-American Radicalism*, ed. Margaret Jacob and James Jacob (Boston, 1984), pp. 275–9.

8   Elizabeth Cady Stanton, Susan B. Anthony, and Matilda Joslyn Gage, eds., *History of Woman Suffrage* (6 vols., Rochester, 1881–1922), I, p. 854; Peterson, ed., *Democracy, Liberty, and Property*, pp. 293–4. See also Paula Baker, "The Domestication of Politics: Women and American Political Society, 1780–1920," *American Historical Review*, 89 (June 1984), 628–31; and Joan R. Gunderson, "Independence, Citizenship, and the American Revolution," *Signs*, 13 (Autumn 1987), 71–6.

9   Robert J. Steinfeld, *The Invention of Free Labor: The Employment Relation in English and American Law and Culture, 1350–1870* (Chapel Hill, 1991), 3–5, 46, 101–2, esp. 101, 122–33; Bernard Bailyn, *Voyagers to the West: A Passage in the Peopling of America on the Eve of the Revolution* (New York, 1986), p. 166; Sharon V. Salinger, *"To Serve Well and Faithfully": Labour and Indentured Servants in Pennsylvania, 1682–1800* (New York, 1987), pp. 142–53; Bernard Elbaum, "Why Apprenticeship Persisted in Britain but Not in the United States," *Journal of Economic History*, 49 (June 1989), 346; Albert Matthews, "Hired Man and Help," *Publications of the Colonial Society of Massachusetts*, 5 (March 1898), pp. 225–56.

10 L. Ray Gunn, *The Decline of Authority: Public Economic Policy and Political Development in New York, 1800–1860* (Ithaca, 1988), pp. 1–3, 155, 184–8; Adrienne Koch and William Peden, eds., *The Selected Writings of John and John Quincy Adams* (New York, 1946), p. 342; "Introduction," *United States Magazine and Democratic Review*, 1 (Oct. 1837), 1–15; Welter, *Mind of America, 1820–1860*, p. 416. For the *New York Journal of Commerce* quotation, see ibid., 127.

11 W. J. Rorabaugh, *The Alcoholic Republic: An American Tradition* (New York, 1979), pp. 200–1, 214–15; Heman Humphrey, *Parallel Between Intemperance and the Slave Trade: An Address Delivered at Amherst College, July 4, 1828* (Amherst, 1828); Amy Bridges, *A City in the Republic: Antebellum New York and the Origins of Machine Politics* (New York, 1984), p. 31.

12 Gareth Stedman Jones, *Languages of Class: Studies in English Working Class History, 1832–1982* (New York, 1983), pp. 90–178; Noah Webster, *An American Dictionary of the English Language* (2 vols., New York, 1828), s. v. "freedom"; Sean Wilentz, *Chants Democratic: New York City and the Rise of the American Working Class, 1788–1850* (New York, 1984), pp. 271–84; Christopher Lasch, *The True and Only Heaven: Progress and Its Critics* (New York, 1991), p. 203.

13 Marcus Cunliffe, *Chattel Slavery and Wage Slavery: The Anglo-American Context, 1830–1860* (Athens, GA, 1979), pp. 4–7, esp. p. 4–7; Eugene D. Genovese, *The Slaveholders' Dilemma: Freedom and Progress in Southern Conservative Thought, 1820–1860* (Columbia, SC, 1992), pp. 33–4, 48; Richard K. Crallé, ed., *The Works of John C. Calhoun* (6 vols., New York, 1851–1856), I, p. 55. For Gov. George McDuffie's remark, see "Diversity of the Races; Its Bearing upon Negro Slavery," *Southern Quarterly Review*, 3 (April 1851), 406. William M. Wiecek, *The Sources of Antislavery Constitutionalism in America, 1760–1848* (Ithaca, 1977), p. 180; George Fitzhugh, *Sociology for the*

South; or, The Failure of Free Society (Richmond, 1854), pp. 238–9; Drew Gilpin Faust, ed., *The Ideology of Slavery: Proslavery Thought in the Antebellum South, 1830–1860* (Baton Rouge, 1981), p. 285. For the *Richmond Enquirer* quotation, see James Oakes, *Slavery and Freedom: An Interpretation of the Old South* (New York, 1990), p. 80.

14   Jonathan A. Glickstein, "'Poverty is Not Slavery': American Abolitionists and the Competitive Labor Market," in *Antislavery Reconsidered: New Perspectives on the Abolitionists*, ed. Lewis Perry and Michael Fellman (Baton Rouge, 1979), pp. 207–11. For Edmund Quincy's argument, see the *Liberator*, Oct. 1, 1847. Ronald G. Walters, "The Boundaries of Abolitionism," in *Antislavery Reconsidered*, ed. Perry and Fellman, p. 9; Lewis Perry, *Radical Abolitionism: Anarchy and the Government of God in Antislavery Thought* (Ithaca, 1973), pp. 24, 51–9; *Emancipator*, March 26, 1840.

15   Clare Midgley, *Women against Slavery: The British Campaigns, 1780–1870* (New York, 1992), p. 27; Carol A. Kolmerten, *Women in Utopia: The Ideology of Gender in American Owenite Communities* (Bloomington, 1990), pp. 8–11, esp. pp. 8, 79–94; Norma Basch, *In the Eyes of the Law: Women, Marriage, and Property in Nineteenth-Century New York* (Ithaca, 1982), p. 120; Stephanie McCurry, "The Two Faces of Republicanism: Gender and Proslavery Politics in Antebellum South Carolina," *Journal of American History*, 78 (March 1992), 1251–5.

16   Basch, *In the Eyes of the Law*, p. 162; Amy Dru Stanley, "Conjugal Bonds and Wage Labor: Rights of Contract in the Age of Emancipation," *Journal of American History*, 75 (Sept. 1988), 477–82; Elizabeth B. Clark, "Matrionial Bonds: Slavery and Divorce in Nineteenth-Century America," *Law and History Review*, 8 (Spring 1990), 34–5, 48–9; Jean Matthews, "Race, Sex, and the Dimensions of Liberty in Antebellum America," *Journal of the Early Republic*, 6 (Fall 1986), 276–80; Wendy Brown, "Finding the Man in the State," *Feminist Studies*, 18 (Spring 1992), 17–20.

17   Blanche Glassman Hersh, *The Slavery of Sex: Feminist-Abolitionists in America* (Urbana, 1978), pp. 9, 196–98; Ellen Carol DuBois, "Outgrowing the Compact of the Fathers: Equal Rights, Woman Suffrage, and the United States Constitution, 1820–1878," *Journal of American History*, 74 (Dec. 1987), 837–40, 856; William Leach, *True Love and Perfect Union: The Feminist Reform of Sex and Society* (New York, 1980), pp. 81–2; Elizabeth Pleck, "Feminist Responses to 'Crimes Against Women,' 1868–1896," *Signs*, 8 (Spring 1983), 453–7; Karen Sánchez-Eppler, *Touching Liberty: Abolitionism, Feminism, and the Politics of the Body* (Berkeley, 1993), pp. 1–5, 19–21. For Lucy Stone's comment, see Hersh, *Slavery of Sex*, p. 66.

18   Myra C. Glenn, *Campaigns against Corporal Punishment: Prisoners, Sailors, Women, and Children in Antebellum America* (Albany, NY, 1984), pp. 70–1; Clark, "Matrimonial Bonds," pp. 40–1; Shirley J. Yee, *Black Women Abolitionists: A Study in Activism, 1828–1860* (Knoxville, 1992), pp. 4–5. For Sarah Parker Remond's comments, see Clare Midgley, "Anti-Slavery and Feminism in Nineteenth-Century Britain," *Gender and History*, 5 (Autumn 1993), 352; and C. Peter Ripley et al., eds., *The Black Abolitionist Papers* (5 vols., Chapel Hill, 1985–1992), I, p. 445. See also ibid., p. 23.

19   Stanley N. Katz, "The Strange Birth and Unlikely History of Constitutional Equality," *Journal of American History*, 75 (Dec. 1988), 753; Harold M. Hyman, *A More Perfect Union: The Impact of the Civil War and Reconstruction on the Constitution* (New York, 1973), pp. 452–62; William E. Nelson, *The Roots of American Bureaucracy, 1830–1900* (Cambridge, MA, 1982), pp. 42–56.

20   Philip S. Foner, ed., *The Life and Writings of Frederick Douglass* (4 vols., New York, 1950–1955), I, pp. 191, 281; Ripley et al., eds., *Black Abolitionist Papers*, IV, pp. 74, 256–57; John R. McKivigan and Jason H. Silverman, "Monarchial Liberty and Republican Slavery: West Indian Emancipation Celebrations in Upstate New York and Canada," *Afro-Americans in New York Life and History*, 10 (Jan. 1986), pp. 10–12.

21   Jane H. Pease and William H. Pease, *They Who Would Be Free: Blacks' Search for Freedom, 1830–1861* (New York, 1974), pp. 3–9; Donald G. Nieman, "The Language of Liberation: African Americans and Equalitarian Constitutionalism, 1830–1850," in *The Constitution, Law, and American Life: Critical Aspects of the Nineteenth-Century Experience*, ed. Donald G. Nieman (Athens, GA, 1992), pp. 68–70. For Samuel Cornish's comment, see Ripley et al., eds., *Black Abolitionist Papers*, III, pp. 3, 365–6. Ira Berlin, *Slaves without Masters: The Free Negro in the Antebellum South* (New York, 1974), pp. 269–71; Vincent Harding, *There Is a River: The Black Struggle for Freedom in America* (New York, 1981), pp. 186; Julia Griffiths, ed., *Autographs for Freedom* (Aubum, NY, 1854), pp. 15.

22   Yehoshua Arieli, *Individualism and Nationalism in American Ideology* (Cambridge, MA., 1964), pp. 308–9, 315–17; Eric Foner, *Free Soil, Free Labor, Free Men: The Ideology of the Republican Party before the Civil War* (New York, 1970), pp. 11–39, 73–102; Roy P. Basler, Marion Dolores Pratt, and Lloyd A. Dunlap, eds., *The Collected Works of Abraham Lincoln* (9 vols., New Brunswick, 1953–1955), II, pp. 405; George E. Baker, ed., *The Works of William H. Seward* (5 vols., Boston, 1853–1884), I, pp. 74, 86–87; Foner, ed., *Life and Writings of Frederick Douglass*, III, pp. 214; V. Jacque Voegeli, *Free but Not Equal: The Midwest and the Negro during the Civil War* (Chicago, 1967), pp. 162.

23   Burke A. Hinsdale, ed., *The Works of James Abram Garfield* (2 vols., Boston, 1882–1883), I, p. 86.

24   Sidney Andrews, "Three Months Among the Reconstructionists," *Atlantic Monthly*, 16 (Feb. 1866), 243–4; Eric Fonet, *Reconstruction: America's Unfinished Revolution, 1863–1877* (New York, 1988), pp. 132–4, esp. p. 134, pp. 198–201.

25   H. S. Beals to Samuel Hunt, Dec. 30, 1865, American Missionary Association Archives (Amistad Research Center, Tulane University, New Orleans, LA); Lea S. Vander Velde, "The Labor Vision of the Thirteenth Amendment," *University of Pennsylvania Law Review*, 138 (Dec. 1989), 437–504, esp. 443n; *Congressional Globe*, 38 Cong., 2 sess., Jan. 10, 1865, p. 193; ibid., Jan. 11, 1865, p. 215; Peggy C. Davis, "Neglected Stories and the Lawfulness of *Roe v. Wade*," *Harvard Civil Rights-Civil Liberties Law Review*, 28 (Summer 1993), 309, 318–20; Clark, "Matrimonial Bonds," p. 34.

26   *Congressional Globe*, 39 Cong., 1 sess., Dec. 13, 1865, p. 42; ibid., Dec. 21, 1865, p. 111; Foner, *Reconstruction*, pp. 23–30, esp. p. 24, pp. 228–80.

27   Eric Foner, *Politics and Ideology in the Age of the Civil War* (New York, 1980), pp. 128–49, esp. p. 135.

28   Foner, *Reconstruction*, pp. 75–123, esp. pp. 77, 67; Ripley et al., eds., *Black Abolitionist Papers*, III. p. 66.

29   "Documents: Colloquy with Colored Ministers," *Journal of Negro History*, 16 (Jan. 1931), 88–94, esp. 91; Merrimon Howard to Adelbert Ames, Nov. 28, 1873, Ames Family Papers (Sophia Smith Collection, Smith College, Northampton, MA.).

30   Derek Q. Reeves, "Beyond the River Jordan: An Essay on the Continuity of the Black Prophetic Tradition," *Journal of Religious Thought*, 47 (Winter–Spring 1990–1991), 43; James Oliver Robertson, *American Myth, American Reality* (New York, 1980), pp. 98–9; Harding, *There is a River*, p. 260; King, *Civil Rights*, pp. 29–31; John David Smith, *An Old Creed for the New South: Proslavery Ideology and Historiography, 1865–1918* (Westport, 1985), p. 9. See also, David Brion Davis, *Revolutions: Reflections on American Equality and Foreign Liberations* (Cambridge, MA, 1990), p. 29.

31   A. Warren Kelsey to Edward Atkinson, Sept. 9, 1865, Edward Atkinson Papers (Massachusetts Historical Society, Boston, MA).

32   John Mercer Langston, *Freedom and Citizenship* (Washington, 1883), pp. 233–4; Robert Miles, *Capitalism and Unfree Labor: Anomaly or Necessity?* (New York, 1987), p. 5; Foner, ed., *Life and Writings of Frederick Douglass*, IV, p. 430.

Questions to consider

- What were the legacies of freedom for Americans in the aftermath of the American Revolution?

- How has the meaning of freedom been understood and contested for American women (black as well as white)?

- In his classic 1988 book *Battle Cry of Freedom*, a book which takes its title from a popular song in both the North and South, Civil War historian James McPherson notes that the Confederacy, no less than the Union, understood the war to be a struggle for freedom. What did freedom mean for white men of the South? Insofar as you recognize the limits of their vision, in what ways do you imagine there to be limits to yours? Can freedom be – should it be – absolute?

Chapter 17

Emancipation: Primary Sources

Letter to Abraham Lincoln

Lydia Maria Child

Writer and activist Lydia Maria Child had enjoyed a long and varied career (including authorship of the much-loved poem "Over the River and Through the Woods") even before she joined the abolitionist cause in the 1830s. Before and during the war, Child was among the most militant of those calling for an end to slavery, repeatedly expressing impatience with the Lincoln administration's cautious approach. In this letter, published in at least two abolitionist newspapers, she urges Lincoln to do the right thing – for slaves, for God, and for the Union.

L. Maria Child, "Mrs L. Maria Child to the President of the United States", in *A Lydia Maria Child Reader*, ed. Carolyn L. Karcher (Durham, NC: Duke University Press, 1997), pp. 254–61. Copyright © 1997 Duke University Press. All rights reserved. Used by permission of the publisher.

It may seem a violation of propriety for a woman to address the Chief Magistrate of the nation at a crisis so momentous as this.[1] But if the Romans, ages ago, accorded to Hortensia[2] the right of addressing the Senate on the subject of a tax unjustly levied on the wealthy ladies of Rome, surely an American woman of the nineteenth century need not apologize for pleading with the rulers of her country in behalf of the poor, the wronged, the cruelly oppressed. Surely the women of America have a right to inquire, nay, demand, whether their husbands, sons, and brothers are to be buried by thousands in Southern swamps, without obtaining thereby "indemnity for the past and security for the future."

In your Appeal to the Border States, you have declared slavery to be "that without which the war could never have been," and you speak of emancipation as "the step which at once shortens the war."[3] I would respectfully ask how much longer the nation is to wait for the decision of the Border States, paying, meanwhile $2,000,000 a day, and sending thousands of its best and bravest to be stabbed, shot, and hung by the rebels, whose property they are employed to guard. How much longer will pro-slavery officers be permitted to refuse obedience to the laws of Congress, saying, "We shall continue to send back fugitives to their masters until we receive orders from the *President* to the contrary."[4] What fatal spell is cast over your honest mind, that you hesitate so long to give such orders? Be not deceived; God is not mocked. Neither nations nor individuals sin against His laws with impunity. Hear the old Hebrew Prophet, whose words seem as if spoken for *us*: "Thou should'st not have stood in the crossway to cut off those that did escape; neither should'st thou have delivered up those that did remain in the day of distress. For thy violence against thy brother, shame shall cover thee, and thou shalt be cut off forever. The pride of thine heart hath deceived thee, saying, who shall bring *me* down to the ground? Though thou exalt thyself as the *eagle*, and though thou set thy nest among the *stars*, thence will I bring thee down, saith the Lord."[5]

The American people have manifested almost miraculous patience, forbearance, and confidence in their rulers. They have given incontrovertible proof that their intelligence, their love of country, may be trusted to any extent. They are willing to sacrifice their fortunes and their lives, but they very reasonably wish to know what they are sacrificing them for. Men, even the bravest, do not go resolutely and cheerfully to death in the name of diplomacy and strategy. The human soul, under such circumstances, needs to be lifted up and sustained by great ideas of Justice and Freedom.

President Lincoln, it is an awful responsibility before God to quench the moral enthusiasm of a generous people. It wastes thousands of precious lives, causes an unutterable amount of slow, consuming agony, and tarnishes our record on the pages of history. Again I respectfully ask, how much longer we are to wait for the Border States, at such tremendous cost and with such a fearful risk? When a criminal is on trial, it is not deemed prudent to try by a jury who are interested in the crime. Slavery is on trial, and the verdict is left to slaveholders in the Border States. The report of their majority shows them to be slaveholders in heart and spirit. The process of reasoning and entreaty has been very properly tried with them, and the people of the free States have waited long and patiently for some obvious good result. They are getting restive; very restive. Everywhere I hear men saying: "Our President is an honest, able man, but he appears to have no firmness of purpose. He is letting the country drift to ruin for want of earnest action and a consistent policy." This is not the utterance of any one class or party. It may be heard everywhere; by the wayside, in the cars, and at the depots. Nor can I deny that some speak with less moderation. Shall I tell you what I said when cold water was thrown on the spark of enthusiasm kindled by the brave, large-hearted Gen. Hunter?[6] I exclaimed, with a groan, "Oh, what a misfortune it is to have an extinguisher instead of a Drummond[7] Light in our watchtower, when the Ship of State is reeling under such a violent storm, in the midst of sunken rocks, with swarms of unprincipled wreckers everywhere calculating on the profit they may derive from her destruction." The crew are working at the pumps with manly vigor and almost superhuman endurance. They look out upon a prospect veiled by dense fog, and their cry is, "Oh! God, let us know whither we are driving. Give us a clear, steady light to guide us through the darkness of the storm."

I trust you will not deem me wanting in respect for yourself or your high position, if I say frankly that you seem to trust too much to diplomatic and selfish politicians, and far too little to the heart of the people. You do them wrong, irreparable wrong, by stifling their generous instincts, and putting an extinguisher on every scintillation of moral enthusiasm. Are you not aware that moral enthusiasm is the mightiest of all forces? It is the fire which produces the steam of energy and courage, and the motion of all the long train of crowded cars depends on its expansive power. In the name of our suffering country, for the sake of a world that needs enfranchisement, I beseech you not to check the popular enthusiasm for freedom!

[. . .]

Oh, President Lincoln, God has placed you as a father over these poor oppressed millions. Remember their forlorn condition! Think how they have been for generations deprived of the light of knowledge and the hope of freedom! Think of the cruel lashes inflicted on them for trying to learn to read the Word of God! Think of their wives polluted, and their children sold, without any means of redress for such foul and cruel wrongs! Imagine them stealing through midnight swamps, infested with snakes and alligators, guided toward freedom by the North Star, and then hurled back into bondage by Northern bloodhounds in the employ of the United States[!] Think how long their groans and prayers for deliverance have gone up before God, from the hidden recesses of Southern forests! Listen to the refrain of their plaintive hymn, "Let my people go!" Above all, think of their present woeful uncertainty, scourged and driven from one to another, not knowing whom to trust! We are told that uncounted prayers go up from their bruised hearts, in the secrecy of their rude little cabins, that "God would bress Massa Lincoln." Is there nothing that touches your heart in the simple trust of these poor, benighted suffering souls? In view of it, can you still allow the officers of the United States to lash them at their pleasure and send them back to their masters, on the plea that the *President* has given no orders on the subject? Shall *such* officers go unrebuked, while Gen. Hunter is checked in his wise and humane policy, and when the great, honest soul of Gen. Phelps[8] is driven to the alternative of disobeying the convictions of his own conscience, or quitting the service of his country? If you *can* thus stifle the moral enthusiasm of noble souls; if you *can* thus disappoint the hopes of poor, helpless wretches, who trust in you as the appointed agent of their deliverance, may God forgive you! It will require *infinite* mercy to do it.

I can imagine, in some degree, the embarrassments of your position, and I compassionate you for the heavy weight of responsibility that rests upon your shoulders. I know that you are surrounded by devils that have squeezed themselves into the disguise of toads. I pray you to lose no more time in counting these toads and calculating how big a devil each may contain. Look upward instead of downward. Place your reliance on *principles* rather than on men. God has placed you at the head of a great nation at a crisis when its free institutions are in extreme peril from enemies within and without. Lay your right arm on the buckler of the Almighty, and march fearlessly forward to universal freedom in the name of the Lord!

Pardon me if, in my earnestness, I have said aught that seems disrespectful. I have not so intended. I have been impelled to write this because night and day the plaintive song of the bondmen resounds in my ears:

"Go down, Moses, go down to Egypt's land,
And say to Pharaoh: 'Let my people go.' "[9]

That you may be guided by Him who has said: "First righteousness; and then peace," is the earnest prayer of

Yours, respectfully,
L. Maria Child

Notes

1   This letter was prominently featured on p. 1 of the *National Republican* of 22 August 1862, and reprinted in the *Liberator* of 29 August and the *National Anti-Slavery Standard* of 6 September. It was one of many urging Lincoln to issue an emancipation proclamation. See also *New York Tribune* editor Horace Greeley's "The Prayer of Twenty Millions" (20 Aug. 1862) and Harriet Beecher Stowe's "Prayer" (*Independent* 28 Aug. 1862).

2   Hortensia, daughter of the Roman orator Quintus Hortensius, protested to the Roman Senate in 43 BC when Mark Anthony, Octavian, and Lepidus sought to raise money for a civil war against the assassins of Julius Caesar by taxing the property of 1,400 wealthy women. Arguing that women should not be taxed to support a war they had not voted to approve, she succeeded in reducing the number of women taxed to 400 and in having a similar tax levied on men.

3   Child is referring to a presidential message of 6 March 1862 in which Lincoln asked Congress to pass a joint resolution offering financial aid to "any state which may adopt a gradual abolishment of slavery" – a proposition he urged slaveholders in the border states to consider. Child had greeted this message with jubilation and had been disappointed when nothing came of it.

4   At the beginning of the war, anxious not to alienate slaveholders loyal to the Union, Lincoln instructed military officers to send all fugitive slaves who fled to Union army camps back to their masters – a policy that outraged Child and other abolitionists. On 10 March 1862, Congress enacted an article of war forbidding officers to return fugitive slaves to their masters, on the grounds that it would shorten the war to deprive Confederates of their labor force and to employ those laborers on the Union side.

5   Child quotes, in order, from Obadiah 1.14, 1.10, 1.3, and 1.4.

6   On 9 May 1862 General David Hunter (1802–86), acting as head of the Department of the South, declared all the slaves in his jurisdiction free. Lincoln promptly revoked the proclamation on the grounds that Hunter had no authority to issue it.

7   The Drummond light, named after its 1825 inventor, was a limelight.

8   General John Wolcott Phelps (1813–85), an abolitionist from Vermont, resigned his commission on 21 August 1862 when his superior, General Benjamin Butler, refused to allow him to recruit "contrabands" as soldiers and ordered him to set them at chopping wood instead.

9   The spiritual "Go Down, Moses" was first transcribed and published in 1861 by the Reverend Lewis C. Lockwood, a missionary organizing relief work among the "contrabands" of Fort Monroe. He sent Child a copy of it, which she refers to as "The Song of the Contrabands"; see LMC to Mary Stearns, 15 Dec. 1861, *SL* 400. In the next sentence Child paraphrases Isaiah 32.17 ("The work of righteousness shall be peace") and James 3.18 ("And the fruit of righteousness is sown in peace of them that make peace").

Questions to consider

- How would you describe the tone of this letter? What words do you think Child would use to describe Lincoln to other abolitionists?

- What does Child understand the role of the Presidency to be? How does she reinforce that?

- How convincing is this letter? What do you think Lincoln might have said in response?

Letter to Horace Greeley

Abraham Lincoln

"We think you are strangely and disastrously amiss," *New York Tribune* editor (and future presidential candidate) Horace Greeley wrote in an open letter to Lincoln in August

1862. Greeley was dismayed by both Lincoln's caution in dealing with slavery, and what some regarded as his pandering to the sensibilities of border states that had not left the Union ("I'd like to have God on my side," Lincoln had reputedly joked at one point during the secession crisis, "but I must have Kentucky.") In private, Lincoln strongly encouraged slaveholders from Border States to consider a negotiated end to slavery, just as he remonstrated with antislavery activists whom he believed were pushing too far too fast. Lincoln's response to Greeley, which was widely reprinted in newspapers across the nation, has long been regarded as his definitive statement about his priorities in the Civil War. What do you think about those priorities?

Abraham Lincoln to H. Greeley (August 22, 1862), Washington, DC, in *Abraham Lincoln: Slavery and the Civil War: Selected Writings and Speeches*, ed. Michael Johnson (New York: Bedford/St. Martins, 2001), pp. 204–5.

Executive Mansion,
Washington

Hon. Horace Greely:

Dear Sir

I have just read yours of the 19th. addressed to myself through the New-York Tribune.[1] If there be in it any statements, or assumptions of fact, which I may know to be erroneous, I do not, now and here, controvert them. If there be in it any inferences which I may believe to be falsely drawn, I do not now and here, argue against them. If there be perceptable in it an impatient and dictatorial tone, I waive it in deference to an old friend, whose heart I have always supposed to be right.

As to the policy I "seem to be pursuing" as you say, I have not meant to leave any one in doubt.

I would save the Union. I would save it the shortest way under the Constitution. The sooner the national authority can be restored; the nearer the Union will be "the Union as it was." If there be those who would not save the Union, unless they could at the same time *save* slavery, I do not agree with them. If there be those who would not save the Union unless they could at the same time *destroy* slavery, I do not agree with them. My paramount object in this struggle *is* to save the Union, and is *not* either to save or to destroy slavery. If I could save the Union without freeing *any* slave I would do it, and if I could save it by freeing *all* the slaves I would do it; and if I could save it by freeing some and leaving others alone I would also do that. What I do about slavery, and the colored race, I do because I believe it helps to save the Union; and what I forbear, I forbear because I do *not* believe it would help to save the Union. I shall do *less* whenever I shall believe what I am doing hurts the cause, and I shall do *more* whenever I shall believe doing more will help the cause. I shall try to correct errors when shown to be errors; and I shall adopt new views so fast as they shall appear to be true views.

I have here stated my purpose according to my view of *official* duty; and I intend no modification of my oft-expressed *personal* wish that all men every where could be free.

Yours,
A. LINCOLN

Notes

1   *CW*, V, 389.

Emancipation Proclamation

Abraham Lincoln

In an important sense, Lincoln's conversations with various parties in the slavery controversy obscured the fact that he had come to a resolution on the subject months before he announced it. At the advice of Secretary of State Seward, however, he waited to reveal his position until the Union had won a decisive victory, lest that statement be seen as an act of desperation. Robert E. Lee's withdrawal from Maryland following the battle of Antietam on September 17, 1862 was not necessarily the best occasion for such a move (Lincoln himself was frustrated by Gen. George McClellan's failure to crush Lee, whose battle plans had fallen into Union hands), but the President decided it was the best one he was likely to get.

As noted earlier, the Emancipation Proclamation had little immediate practical effect, since it addressed slavery in rebel-held territory. Yet over time its impact was great not only in the South, but in working to keep Great Britain, which did not want to take a decisively proslavery position, out of the conflict. And while Lincoln paid a steep political price in the short term – Democrats made major gains in the mid-term elections of 1862, explicitly invoking the Emancipation as a foolish, if not outrageous, recasting of military objectives – it put the war on a durably moral footing.

Since Lincoln has long been recognized as a highly deliberative writer and thinker, it is deeply striking that the Emancipation Proclamation is written in notably legalistic, even off-putting, language. Why do you think he did so? And what do you make of the (military) logic by which he justifies his actions?

Abraham Lincoln, "Emancipation Proclamation" (September 22, 1862).

BY THE PRESIDENT OF THE UNITED STATES OF AMERICA:
A PROCLAMATION.
Whereas, on the twentysecond day of September, in the year of our Lord one thousand eight hundred and sixty two, a proclamation was issued by the President of the United States, containing, among other things, the following, towit:

"That on the first day of January, in the year of our Lord one thousand eight hundred and sixty-three, all persons held as slaves within any State or designated part of a State, the people whereof shall then be in rebellion against the United States, shall be then, thenceforward, and forever free; and the Executive Government of the United States, including the military and naval authority thereof, will recognize and maintain the freedom of such persons, and will do no act or acts to repress such persons, or any of them, in any efforts they may make for their actual freedom.

"That the Executive will, on the first day of January aforesaid, by proclamation, designate the States and parts of States, if any, in which the people thereof, respectively, shall then be in rebellion against the United States; and the fact that any State, or the people thereof, shall on that day be, in good faith, represented in the Congress of the United States by members chosen thereto at elections wherein a majority of the qualified voters of such State shall have participated, shall, in the absence of strong countervailing testimony, be deemed conclusive evidence that such State, and the people thereof, are not then in rebellion against the United States."

Now, therefore I, Abraham Lincoln, President of the United States, by virtue of the power in me vested as Commander-in-Chief, of the Army and Navy of the United States in time of actual armed rebellion against authority and government of the United States, and as a fit and necessary war measure for suppressing said rebellion, do, on this first day of January, in the year of our Lord one thousand eight hundred and sixty three, and in accordance with my purpose so to do publicly proclaimed for the full period of one hundred days, from the day first above mentioned, order and designate as the States and parts of States wherein the people thereof respectively, are this day in rebellion against the United States, the following, towit:

Arkansas, Texas, Louisiana, (except the Parishes of St. Bernard, Plaquemines, Jefferson, St. Johns, St. Charles, St. James[,] Ascension, Assumption, Terrebonne, Lafourche, St. Mary, St. Martin, and Orleans, including the City of New-Orleans) Mississippi, Alabama, Florida, Georgia, South-Carolina, North-Carolina, and Virginia, (except the fortyeight counties designated as West Virginia, and also the counties of Berkley, Accomac, Northampton, Elizabeth-City, York, Princess Ann, and Norfolk, including the cities of Norfolk & Portsmouth[)]; and which excepted parts are, for the present, left precisely as if this proclamation were not issued.

And by virtue of the power, and for the purpose aforesaid, I do order and declare that all persons held as slaves within said designated States, and parts of States, are, and henceforward shall be free; and that the Executive government of the United States, including the military and naval authorities thereof, will recognize and maintain the freedom of said persons.

And I hereby enjoin upon the people so declared to be free to abstain from all violence, unless in necessary self-defence; and I recommend to them that, in all cases when allowed, they labor faithfully for reasonable wages.

And I further declare and make known, that such persons of suitable condition, will be received into the armed service of the United States to garrison forts, positions, stations, and other places, and to man vessels of all sorts in said service.

And upon this act, sincerely believed to be an act of justice, warranted by the Constitution, upon military necessity, I invoke the considerate judgment of mankind, and the gracious favor of Almighty God. . . .

ABRAHAM LINCOLN

Emancipation Proclaimed

Frederick Douglass

Born in slavery near the eastern shore of Maryland, Frederick Douglass (ca. 1817–95) escaped to freedom in 1838 and began a legendary career as a writer, speaker and activist in the abolitionist cause. Douglass was every bit as impatient as other abolitionists with the Lincoln administration about Emancipation. Ambivalent about Lincoln himself, Douglass alternated between seeing him as not up to the task of governing and being impressed by his inner poise and relative lack of racial superiority. For Douglass the cause itself (in which two of his sons enlisted) was paramount, and the litmus test by which he measured the administration. When it delayed, he lambasted it; when it acted, he congratulated it. The following editorial was published in Douglass's newspaper in the weeks following the Emancipation Proclamation.

Frederick Douglass, "Emancipation Proclaimed", in *Douglass' Monthly* (October 1862), in *Frederick Douglass: Selected Writings and Speeches*, ed. Philip S. Foner, abridged and adapted by Yuval Taylor (1950; Chicago: Lawrence Hill Books, 1999), pp. 517–20. Reprinted by permission of the publisher.

Common sense, the necessities of the war, to say nothing of the dictation of justice and humanity have at last prevailed. We shout for joy that we live to record this righteous decree. *Abraham Lincoln*, President of the United States, Commander-in-Chief of the army and navy, in his own peculiar, cautious, forbearing and hesitating way, slow, but we hope sure, has, while the loyal heart was near breaking with despair, proclaimed and declared: "*That on the First of January, in the Year of Our Lord One Thousand, Eight Hundred and Sixty-three, All Persons Held as Slaves Within Any State or Any Designated Part of a State, The People Whereof Shall Then be in Rebellion Against the United States, Shall be Thenceforward and Forever Free.*" "Free forever" oh! long enslaved millions, whose cries have so vexed the air and sky, suffer on a few more days in sorrow, the hour of your deliverance draws nigh! Oh! Ye millions of free and loyal men who have earnestly sought to free your bleeding country from the dreadful ravages of revolution and anarchy, lift up now your voices with joy and thanksgiving for with freedom to the slave will come peace and safety to your country. President Lincoln has embraced in this proclamation the law of Congress passed more than six months ago, prohibiting the employment of any part of the army and naval forces of the United States, to return fugitive slaves to their masters, commanded all officers of the army and navy to respect and obey its provisions. He has still further declared his intention to urge upon the Legislature of all the slave States not in rebellion the immediate or gradual abolishment of slavery. But read the proclamation for it is the most important of any to which the President of the United States has ever signed his name.

Opinions will widely differ as to the practical effect of this measure upon the war. All that class at the North who have not lost their affection for slavery will regard the measure as the very worst that could be devised, and as likely to lead to endless mischief. All their plans for the future have been projected with a view to a reconstruction of the American Government upon the basis of compromise between slaveholding and non-slaveholding States. The thought of a country unified in sentiments, objects and ideas, has not entered into their political calculations, and hence this newly declared policy of the Government, which contemplates one glorious homogeneous people, doing away at a blow with the whole class of compromisers and corrupters, will meet their stern opposition. Will that opposition prevail? Will it lead the President to reconsider and retract? Not a word of it. Abraham Lincoln may be slow, Abraham Lincoln may desire peace even at the price of leaving our terrible national sore untouched, to fester on for generations, but Abraham Lincoln is not the man to reconsider, retract and contradict words and purposes solemnly proclaimed over his official signature.

The careful, and we think, the slothful deliberation which he has observed in reaching this obvious policy, is a guarantee against retraction. But even if the temper and spirit of the President himself were other than what they are, events greater than the President, events which have slowly wrung this proclamation from him may be relied on to carry him forward in the same direction.[1] To look back now would only load him with heavier evils, while diminishing his ability, for overcoming those with which he now has to contend. To recall his proclamation would only increase rebel pride, rebel sense of power and would be hailed as a direct admission of weakness on the part of the Federal Government, while it would cause heaviness of heart and depression of national enthusiasm all over the loyal North and West. No, Abraham Lincoln will take no step backward. His word has gone out over the country and the world, giving joy and gladness to the friends of freedom and progress wherever those words are read, and he will stand by them, and carry them out to the letter. If he has taught us to confide in nothing else, he has taught us to confide in his word. The want of Constitutional power, the want of military power, the tendency of the measure to intensify Southern hate, and to exasperate the rebels, the tendency to drive from him all that class of Democrats at the North, whose loyalty has been conditioned on his restoring the union as it was, slavery and all, have all been considered, and he has taken his ground notwithstanding. The President doubtless saw, as we see, that it is not more absurd to talk about restoring the union, without hurting slavery, than restoring the union without hurting the rebels. As to exasperating the South, there can be no more in the cup than the cup will hold, and that was full already. The whole situation having been carefully scanned, before Mr. Lincoln could be made to budge an inch, he will now stand his ground. Border State influence, and the influence of half-loyal men, have been exerted and have done their worst. The end of these two influences is implied in this proclamation. Hereafter, the inspiration as well as the men and the money for carrying on the war will come from the North, and not from half-loyal border States.

The effect of this paper upon the disposition of Europe will be great and increasing. It changes the character of the war in European eyes and gives it an important principle as an object, instead of national pride and interest. It recognizes and declares the real nature of the contest, and places the North on the side of justice and civilization, and the rebels on the side of robbery and barbarism. It will disarm all purpose on the part of European Government to intervene in favor of the rebels and thus cast off at a blow one source of rebel power. All through the war thus far, the rebel ambassadors in foreign countries have been able to silence all expression of sympathy with the North as to slavery. With much more than a show of truth, they said that the Federal Government, no more than the Confederate Government, contemplated the abolition of slavery.

But will not this measure be frowned upon by our officers and men in the field? We have heard of many thousands who have resolved that they will throw up their commissions and lay down their arms, just so soon as they are required to carry on a war against slavery. Making all allowances for exaggeration there are doubtless far too many of this sort in the loyal army. Putting this kind of loyalty and patriotism to the test, will be one of the best collateral effects of the measure. Any man who leaves the field on such a ground will be an argument in favor of the proclamation, and will prove that his heart has been more with slavery than with his country. Let the army be cleansed from all such pro-slavery vermin, and its health and strength will be greatly improved. But there can be no reason to fear the loss of many officers or men by resignation or desertion. We have no doubt that the measure was brought to the attention of most of our leading Generals, and blind as some of them have seemed to be in the earlier part of the war, most of them have seen enough to convince them that there can be no end to this war that does not end slavery. At any rate, we may hope that for every pro-slavery man[2] that shall start from the ranks of our loyal army, there will be two anti-slavery men to fill up the vacancy, and in this war one truly devoted to the cause of Emancipation is worth two of the opposite sort.

Whether slavery will be abolished in the manner now proposed by President Lincoln, depends of course upon two conditions, the first specified and the second implied. The first is that the slave States shall be in rebellion on and after the first day of January 1863 and the second is we must have the ability to put down that rebellion. About the first there can be very little doubt. The South is thoroughly in earnest and confident. It has staked everything upon the rebellion. Its experience thus far in the field has rather increased its hopes of final success than diminished them. Its armies now hold us at bay at all points, and the war is confined to the border States slave and free. If Richmond were in our hands and Virginia at our mercy, the vast regions beyond would still remain to be subdued. But the rebels confront us on the Potomac, the Ohio, and the Mississippi. Kentucky, Maryland, Missouri, and Virginia are in debate on the battlefields and their people are divided by the line which separates treason from loyalty. In short we are yet, after eighteen months of war, confined to the outer margin of the rebellion. We have scarcely more than touched the surface of the terrible evil. It has been raising large quantities of food during the past summer. While the masters have been fighting abroad, the slaves have been busy working at home to supply them with the means of continuing the struggle. They will not down at the bidding of this Proclamation, but may be safely relied upon till January and long after January. A month or two will put an end to general fighting for the winter. When the leaves fall we shall hear again of bad roads, winter quarters and spring campaigns. The South which has thus far withstood our arms will not fall at once before our pens. All fears for the abolition of slavery arising from this apprehension may be dismissed. Whoever, therefore, lives to see the first day of next January, should Abraham Lincoln be then alive and President of the United States, may confidently look in the morning papers for the final proclamation, granting freedom, and freedom forever, to all slaves within the rebel States. On the next point nothing need be said. We have full power to put down the rebellion. Unless one man is more than a match for four, unless the South breeds braver and better men than the North, unless slavery is more precious than liberty, unless a just cause kindles a feebler enthusiasm than a wicked and villainous one, the men of the loyal States will put down this rebellion and slavery, and all the sooner will they put down that rebellion by coupling slavery with that object. Tenderness towards slavery has been the loyal weakness during the war. Fighting the slaveholders with one hand and holding the slaves with the other, has been fairly tried and has failed. We have now inaugurated a wiser and better policy, a policy which is better for the loyal cause than an hundred thousand armed men. The Star Spangled Banner is now the harbinger of Liberty and the millions in bondage, inured to hardships, accustomed to toil, ready to suffer, ready to fight, to dare and to die, will rally under that banner wherever they see it gloriously unfolded to the breeze. Now let the Government go forward in its mission of Liberty as the only condition of peace and union, by weeding out the army and navy of all such officers as the late Col. Miles, whose sympathies are now known to have been with the rebels. Let only the men who assent heartily to the wisdom and the justice of the anti-slavery policy of the Government be lifted into command; let the black man have an arm as well as a heart in this war, and the tide of battle which has thus far only waved backward and forward, will steadily set in our favor. The rebellion suppressed, slavery abolished, and America will, higher than ever, sit as a queen among the nations of the earth.

Now for the work. During the interval between now and next January, let every friend of the long enslaved bondman do his utmost in swelling the tide of anti-slavery sentiment, by writing, speaking, money and example. Let our aim be to make the North a unit in favor of the President's policy, and see to it that our voices and votes, shall forever extinguish that latent and malignant sentiment at the North, which has from the first cheered on the rebels in their atrocious crimes against the union, and has systematically sought to paralyze the national arm in striking down the slaveholding rebellion. We are ready for this service or any other, in this, we trust the last struggle with the monster slavery.

Douglass' Monthly, October 1862

Notes

1 Lincoln himself observed in 1864: "I claim not to have controlled events, but confess plainly that events have controlled me." (Philip S. Foner, ed., *Abraham Lincoln: Selections from His Writings*, p. 22.)

2 General McClellan, however, denounced the Proclamation, warned Lincoln that the Administration must under no circumstances abandon its conservative policies, and issued a counter-proclamation to the army denouncing any and all proposals to free the slaves. (See George B. McClellan, *McClellan's Own Story*, New York, 1887, pp. 487–8.)

Questions to consider

• How would you describe the tone of the editorial? Compare its content and style with that of Lydia Maria Child's letter.

• What does Douglass understand the role of the Presidency – and the government – to be? What is the particular responsibility of the American people?

• In retrospect, how accurate would you say Douglass was in describing the fate of slavery as its situation developed in the months and years following the Emancipation Proclamation?

Address at Gettysburg

Abraham Lincoln

The Emancipation Proclamation officially took effect on January 1, 1863. Eleven months later, Lincoln journeyed to Gettysburg, Pennsylvania to deliver what has become what is widely considered the most famous speech in American history. Lincoln used the occasion to honor the Union dead – and, as some historians (notably Garry Wills) have argued, to rewrite the purpose of the Civil War. How do you view this document in light of the Emancipation Proclamation?

Abraham Lincoln, "The Gettysburg Address" (November 19, 1863).

Four score and seven years ago our fathers brought forth on this continent, a new nation, conceived in Liberty, and dedicated to the proposition that all men are created equal.

Now we are engaged in a great civil war, testing whether that nation, or any nation so conceived and so dedicated, can long endure. We are met on a great battle-field of that war. We have come to dedicate a portion of that field, as a final resting place for those who here gave their lives that that nation might live. It is altogether fitting and proper that we should do this.

But, in a larger sense, we can not dedicate – we can not consecrate – we can not hallow – this ground. The brave men, living and dead, who struggled here, have consecrated it, far above our poor power to add or detract. The world will little note, nor long remember what we say here, but it can never forget what they did here. It is for us the living, rather, to be dedicated here to the unfinished work which they who fought here have thus far so nobly advanced. It is rather for us to be here dedicated to the great task remaining before us – that from these honored dead we take increased devotion to that cause for which they gave the last full measure of devotion – that we here highly resolve that these dead shall not have died in vain – that this nation, under God, shall have a new birth of freedom – and that government of the people, by the people, for the people, shall not perish from the earth.

ABRAHAM LINCOLN.

Second Inaugural Address

Abraham Lincoln

Here's a thought experiment. Imagine, for a moment, Franklin Delano Roosevelt or Harry Truman going before the American people in 1945 and telling them that World War II is almost over – and that rather than celebrate, Americans should feel shame for failing to act sooner to stop the Holocaust. Or imagine Lyndon Johnson or Richard Nixon announcing troop withdrawal from Vietnam, because like Great Britain in the American Revolution, the United States was wrong to prevent Vietnam's independence. Such implausible scenarios can allow one to imagine what a striking speech Abraham Lincoln's Second Inaugural was. At the very moment of triumph – his own as well as that of his country – Lincoln speaks a language of guilt and unrealized redemption.

Consider, as you read this speech, its relationship to Lincoln's letter to Horace Greeley from two years earlier. What has changed both in the world he is addressing, and in Abraham Lincoln's mind?

Abraham Lincoln, "Second Inaugural Address" (March 4, 1865).

[Fellow Countrymen:]

At this second appearing to take the oath of the presidential office, there is less occasion for an extended address than there was at the first. Then a statement, somewhat in detail, of a course to be pursued, seemed fitting and proper. Now, at the expiration of four years, during which public declarations have been constantly called forth on every point and phase of the great contest which still absorbs the attention, and engrosses the enerergies [sic] of the nation, little that is new could be presented. The progress of our arms, upon which all else chiefly depends, is as well known to the public as to myself; and it is, I trust, reasonably satisfactory and encouraging to all. With high hope for the future, no prediction in regard to it is ventured.

On the occasion corresponding to this four years ago, all thoughts were anxiously directed to an impending civil-war. All dreaded it – all sought to avert it. While the inaugeral address was being delivered from this place, devoted altogether to *saving* the Union without war, insurgent agents were in the city seeking to *destroy* it without war – seeking to dissol[v]e the Union, and divide effects, by negotiation. Both parties deprecated war; but one of them[1] would *make* war rather than let the nation survive; and the other would *accept* war rather than let it perish. And the war came.

One eighth of the whole population were colored slaves, not distributed generally over the Union, but localized in the Southern part of it. These slaves constituted a peculiar and powerful interest. All knew that this interest was, somehow, the cause of the war. To strengthen, perpetuate, and extend this interest was the object for which the insurgents would rend the Union, even by war; while the government claimed no right to do more than to restrict the territorial enlargement of it. Neither party expected for the war, the magnitude, or the duration, which it has already attained. Neither anticipated that the *cause*[2] of the conflict might cease with, or even before, the conflict itself should cease. Each looked for an easier triumph, and a result less fundamental and astounding. Both read the same Bible, and pray to the same God; and each invokes His aid against the other. It may seem strange that any men should dare to ask a just God's assistance in wringing their bread from the sweat of other men's faces; but let us judge not that we be not judged. The prayers of both could not be answered; that of neither has been answered fully. The Almighty has His own purposes. "Woe unto the world because of offences! for it must needs be that offences come; but woe to that man by whom the offence cometh!"[3] If we shall suppose that American Slavery is one of those offences which, in the providence of God must needs come, but which, having continued through His appointed time, He now wills to remove, and that He gives to both North and South, this terrible war, as the woe due to those by whom the offence came, shall we discern therein any departure from those divine attributes which the believers in a Living God always ascribe to Him? Fondly do we hope – fervently do we pray – that this mighty scourge of war may speedily pass away. Yet, if God wills that it continue, until all the wealth piled by the bond-man's two hundred and fifty years of unrequited toil shall be sunk, and until every drop of blood drawn with the lash, shall be paid by another drawn with the sword, as was said three thousand years ago, so still it must be said "the judgments of the Lord, are true and righteous altogether."[4]

With malice toward none; with charity for all; with firmness in the right, as God gives us to see the right, let us strive on to finish the work we are in; to bind up the nation's wounds; to care for him who shall have borne the battle, and for his widow, and his orphan – to do all which may achieve and cherish a just, and a lasting peace, among ourselves, and with all nations.

Notes

1   That is, the Confederacy.
2   That is, slavery.
3   Matthew 18: 17.
4   Psalms 19: 9.

Part VIII

Resistance

TO THE

LABORING MEN

OF NEW YORK.

COMRADES :---Do you want to pay heavy taxes ? Do you want to suffer loss and ruin ? Do you want to be trampled under foot by ambitious demagogues ? Do you want to have your homes filled with sorrow, and your eyes run over with tears ? If not, then

STOP AND THINK!

The property destroyed by a riot must be paid for by the city, and in this way every act of disorder, violence and house-burning, is only laying heavier taxes on your own shoulders. Every disorderly act that is done only calls for greater expenses on the part of the city government. The United States does not pay the damages, but the City of New York alone. Of course, all the disturbances, losses and damages, only

FALL UPON OUR OWN HEADS.
COMRADES,

STAND BY THE LAW !

Stand by good order and good sense, and you will find it good policy. If any law is bad, let it be settled by the courts in a proper form. Do not listen to bad men who are only leading you to your ruin.

The politicians and business men of New York must stand by the law and the Constitution.

It is cheaper and better to Stand by the Law!

For when the law is broken and property destroyed, and lives lost, we all suffer more or less by the injury. Comrades! In the name of God---in the name of our wives and children---in the name of every thing that is dear to us---

STOP and THINK!

Stand up as Democratic Workingmen should stand up before the world, and show the traitors of the South, and the friends of tyranny all over the world, that

The Workingmen of New York are able to govern themselves!

Stand by the Union, the Constitution and the Laws ! Then peace, freedom and prosperity will be secure to you and to your children after you.

KEEP HONESTLY AT YOUR WORK!
GIVE NO HEED TO BAD ADVICE!

Any man that advises you to break the law is your enemy, and the enemy of your wives and children. These troubles will make the times only the worse for us all. High prices, heavy rents, and heavier taxes. Comrades! Keep the peace and all will be well.

Saturday, July 18, 1863.   **A Democratic Workingman.**

Plate 10   Reading the Riot Act: This broadside, printed during the New York Draft Riots of 1863, warns residents that they will be the ones to pay the price for ongoing unrest. How do you imagine the person (or people) who crafted this message? How persuasive do you think such reasoning would be? (Printed Ephemera Collection, Library of Congress)

Chapter 18

A Multiplicity of Grievances

Iver Bernstein

As long as there have been wars fought on the North American continent, there have been those who refused to fight in them. Perhaps the best-known examples are the Tories of the American Revolution and the antiwar protesters of the Vietnam War. Yet even the so-called "Good War," World War II, had its (often overlooked) opponents, whether they were Isolationists, pro-Fascists, or conscientious objectors. Sometimes such people have quietly opposed conflicts; at other times their opposition has been vocal, even spectacular.

The Civil War was notable for the variety of internal dissent that was present on both sides throughout the war. Very generally speaking, it is possible to map enthusiasm for the war along a spectrum if you visualize a map of the United States in which New England is deep red, the lower South is deep blue, and the shades edge toward purple as you get toward the center. Strong pro-Confederate sentiment in the Union's so-called "butternut" region (so named for the color of the homespun clothing residents wore) included southern Ohio and Indiana. Conversely, Unionist sentiment was strong in parts of Confederate states like east Tennessee. In western Virginia, Unionism was so strong, in fact, that the region seceded from the seceded Virginia to form the new state of West Virginia in 1863.

Yet opposition to the war was not strictly a matter of geography. Both Jefferson Davis and Abraham Lincoln were strongly criticized by their respective allies for suspending the writ of Habeas Corpus, in which a prisoner is promptly informed of the charges against him. Davis was hounded on this and other counts by Georgia governor Joseph Brown; Lincoln, for his part, had to endure the attacks of Ohio Representative Clement L. Vallandigham, who advocated a negotiated settlement to the war. Arrested by Union General Ambrose Burnside for an allegedly treasonous speech in 1863, Lincoln changed Vallandigham's sentence from imprisonment to banishment, and had him deposited – no doubt with some glee – behind Confederate lines. (Vallandigham returned in 1864, but his expected arrest never materialized; the administration apparently concluded it could afford to tolerate his opposition.)

Some forms of war resistance were not legal or political, but economic. From Mobile, AL, to Boston, MA, seemingly spontaneous demonstrations against the war protested the absence, or prohibitive expense, of daily necessities. Some of the most dramatic events were led by women, notably the so-called Richmond Bread Riots of 1863, in which civilians, many of them armed wives of soldiers, took to the streets and demanded that "speculators" turn over hoarded supplies like bacon and flour. Jefferson Davis personally confronted the mob, and it finally dispersed.

Yet by far the most powerful demonstrations against the war were the New York City Draft Riots of July, 1863. The immediate cause of this conflagration was the conscription law passed by Congress that March, which required all male citizens and immigrant applicants for citizenship to register for a draft whose numbers would be determined by geographic quotas. Draftees could obtain an exemption from the draft by finding a substitute or paying $300 – a huge sum for the time, and one that generated widespread complaints that the Union was practicing warfare against the working class as well as the planter class, all for the benefit of slaves.

Interest in the New York Draft Riots has intensified in recent years, thanks to Martin Scorsese's *Gangs of New York* (2002) and Kevin Baker's comparably compelling novel *Paradise Alley* (also 2003). But the standard account remains Iver Bernstein's 1990 book *The New York City Draft Riots: Their Significance for American Society and Politics in the Age of the Civil War*. In this opening chapter, Bernstein provides a narrative account of an event which – coming on the heels of Union victories at Gettysburg and Vicksburg – served as a sharp reminder that the Civil War could be lost at home before it was ever won on the battlefield.

Iver Bernstein, "A Multiplicity of Grievances," in *The New York City Draft Riots: Their Significance for American Society and Politics in the Age of the Civil War* (New York: Oxford University Press, 1990), pp. 17–42. Copyright © 1990 by Iver Bernstein. Used by permission of Oxford University Press, Inc.

On Friday, July 17, 1863, the last day of the [New York] draft riots, Peace Democrat Congressman and newspaper editor James Brooks published a brief article entitled "The Riot – Its History." By the 17th, New Yorkers had developed their own versions of the riot-week events and interpretations of the rioters' motives.[1] But Brooks, a popular uptown figure intimately familiar with the attitudes of his constituents, was one of the few observers to draw up a calendar of the rioters' activities:

Sunday – A day of leisure, thousands of Workingmen pondering upon the draft of Saturday.
Monday – The Conscription Riot, developed in attacks upon the Provost Marshals and their places, etc.
Tuesday – The Riot of Thieves, not only from New York – but from Philadelphia, Boston, and all quarters, who rushed here to steal.
Wednesday – Not a Conscription Riot nor a Thief Riot – but the consequences of the collisions of the military and the mob.[2]

Brooks's calendar discriminated among the rioters' targets and chronicled the day-to-day progression of the violence. He did not figure the riot's various forms of racial violence into his account and his notion that rioters who looted were marauders from other cities seems farfetched – he doubtless wished to rehabilitate the event as a pure revolt against Republican Party centralization. But his observation that the insurrection went through phases and that each phase reflected the prominence of different rioters and targets is supported by much of the available evidence. The draft riots involved diverse groups of workers and a multiplicity of grievances against Republican rule. Each group had its own understanding of what the strike against conscription meant.

Monday, July 13

The draft riots began Monday morning not at the hour of the draft but at the hour of work. Between six and seven o'clock, four hours before the Ninth District draft selection was scheduled to begin, employees of the city's railroads, machine shops, and shipyards, iron foundry workers, laborers for an uptown street contractor, and "hundreds of others employed in buildings and street improvements" failed to appear at their jobs.[3] By eight o'clock, many of these workers were streaming up Eighth and Ninth avenues, closing shops, factories, and construction sites along the way and urging workmen to join the procession. After a brief meeting at Central Park, the crowd broke into two columns and, with "No Draft" placards held aloft, marched downtown to the Ninth District Provost Marshal's Office, at Third Avenue and Forty-seventh Street, scene of the draft lottery to be held later that morning.[4] On the way, some rioters cut telegraph poles and committed the first acts of theft, breaking into a hardware store to steal broadaxes.[5] On Third Avenue, a crowd had begun to hack down telegraph poles and lines. Not long afterwards, Irish women used crowbars to pull up the tracks of the Fourth Avenue railway, and soon crowds had stopped the Second and Third Avenue cars.[6] Rioters also attacked several police officers. Superintendent of Police John A. Kennedy, out of uniform, was spotted by a crowd, dragged through the mud and beaten on the head until "unrecognizable."[7] Kennedy was later rescued by John Eagan, a Tammany politician in the Nineteenth Ward.[8] During the course of the morning, rioters who attended the Central Park meeting may have encountered others who had assembled further downtown to close Allaire's Works, the Novelty Works, and other factories along the East Side waterfront. The convergence of rioters from different parts of the city was more likely a result of rumor and circumstance than explicit and coordinated design.[9]

At ten-thirty, draft selection began in the Ninth District Office while the now sizable crowd milled outside. After fifty or so names had been drawn, the Black Joke Engine Company Number Thirty-three arrived dressed in full fire company regalia. One of their men had been selected in Saturday's lottery. Many firemen thought their traditional exemption from militia service should extend to the federal draft, and over the weekend the Black Joke Company had resolved to halt Monday's Ninth District proceedings.[10] A pistol shot rang out, and the Black Joke men burst into the office, smashed the selection wheel, and set the building on fire. A deputy provost marshal who tried to persuade the Black Joke men to fight the flames was beaten to the ground.[11] The throng outside listened to a Virginia lawyer and Confederate sympathizer named John U. Andrews deliver an anti-draft speech; some mistook Andrews for the Peace journalist Benjamin Wood.[12] As the blaze spread to tenements next door, Chief Engineer John Decker of the Fire Department urged the crowd to let his men through and spare the belongings of poor workingmen. He was seconded by Black Joke foreman, uptown building contractor, and Democratic alderman Peter Masterson, who approved the destruction of the draft office but hoped the rioters would now let Decker and his company do their job. The crowd applauded Masterson and cleared a path, but a mob returning to the scene after a battle with police drove

Decker and his men away. By eleven-thirty that morning, orders were given to suspend the draft and transfer government papers to Governor's Island for safekeeping.[13]

By this time, the rioters had virtually halted the business of the city, particularly in the uptown wards. In one reporter's account, "men left their various pursuits; owners of inconsiderable stores put up their shutters; factories were emptied, conductors or drivers left their cars, employees at railroad depots all added formidable accessions to the depots. . . . " The crowds on the Upper East Side avenues had now swelled into a "concourse of over twelve thousand" that included men, women, and children of every social grade who had put down their work to discuss the Conscription Act or merely to watch the disturbance and ponder what direction it would take. As most of the city turned its attention toward the rioters and their activities, the draft became Monday's "all-absorbing subject."[14]

Rioters now began to gather at sites emblematic of the political choices of the day to voice their approval or objection. One cohort paid a friendly visit to Democratic General George B. McClellan's house on East Thirty-first Street.[15] Shortly after noon, rioters appeared at Printing House Square, the journalistic thoroughfare, where one could always find the makings of a crowd awaiting the latest war news. They huzzahed McClellan and the buildings of the Peace Democrat *Daily News* and *Weekly Caucasian* and groaned at the offices of the Republican *Times* and *Daily Tribune*. To many New Yorkers, the round, bespectacled face, drooping figure, and telltale white overcoat of Horace Greeley, editor of the *Tribune*, embodied the Republican Party and the anti-slavery cause. James H. Whitten, a neighborhood barber known for his extreme Confederate views, challenged Greeley to show himself and threatened to kill the abolitionist and gut the office. The crowd resisted Whitten's urgings and left the building alone when Greeley failed to appear. After chasing a policeman across City Hall Park, the rioters dispersed and Whitten returned to his barber's chair.[16]

During the morning, divisions among the rioters began to emerge. One committee that closed factories on the East Side explicitly limited its aims to halting the draft. James Jackson, owner of an iron works, reported a conversation with a delegation from an assemblage of one hundred men and boys outside his factory between nine and ten o'clock: "The leaders said they wanted the shop to close and [I] asked how long it must close. They said I might go to work the next day. They stated that their only object was to make a big show to resist the draft. They said they had no other motive than to have the men join them to put down the draft."[17] Employee Charles Clinch heard the leader of the deputation, cartman Thomas Fitzsimmons, say "he did not wish to injure Mr. Jackson, but wished the mob to go away."[18] Jackson closed his shop and his property was left unharmed, while the crowd marched off to nearby Franklin's Forge.[19] For Fitzsimmons and his committee, the "strike" against conscription was a one-day affair. They sought to interrupt the draft but wanted no wholesale onslaught against private property. Their notion of a peaceable "demonstration" may have been shared by the rioters who counseled restraint at the Provost Marshal's Office and the *Tribune* building. Fitzsimmons's action was already different in style and scope from that of the rioters who committed the early morning thefts, interfered with transportation and communication lines or encouraged the spread of flames from the Ninth District office to adjacent buildings.

After Monday noon the revolt against conscription began to expand beyond the limited protest of rioters like Fitzsimmons and his associates. By midday enrollment officers around the city had received orders to suspend the draft; soon there was a popular awareness that the draft had been interrupted and "all its machinery [put] speedily beyond reach of any such undertaking as that of the Black Joke."[20] The deserted Eighth District Provost Marshal's Office at Broadway and Twenty-ninth Street was burned at five o'clock by Patrick Merry, an Irish cellar digger who lived in the neighborhood, and two or three hundred men and boys. Before firing the draft office, Merry ordered a gang of marble cutters at a Broadway construction site to stop work and join his "band" and then attempted to close down John W. Onderdonk's hardware shop next door to the draft office.[21] Meeting resistance at Onderdonk's, Merry and his comrades then sacked the Provost Marshal's Office and set it and the hardware shop ablaze. While the fire spread down the block, the crowd went on a looting spree. Gold bracelets and brooches were taken from a jewelry store and valuables grabbed from upstairs apartments. Finally, the crowd attacked a black fruit vendor and stole his produce.[22]

Here was the closing of work sites and shops, the assault on federal property – the same sort of strike against the Republican draft – that Thomas Fitzsimmons and most Monday morning rioters would have found familiar. But the Merry episode had a new twist. The strike was aimed more at purging the neighborhood of the draft apparatus, since the Eighth District lottery had been interrupted hours earlier. Now, too, the rioters' anti-draft action was joined with looting, destruction of property, and an assault on a black man, activities soon to be repudiated by some of the participants in the revolt.

By five o'clock Monday, the list of the rioters' targets had lengthened considerably. Beginning Monday, homes suspected of harboring policemen were burned by the crowd. Policemen caught by the rioters were often stripped of their clothing and literally defaced – beaten on the face and head until unrecognizable.[23] Bitter assaults against the police would continue through the week. By mid-afternoon Monday, hostility toward the police was combined with an animus against well-dressed gentlemen and the houses of wealthy Republicans.[24] Rioters tore through expensive Republican homes on Lexington Avenue and took – or more often, destroyed – "pictures with gilt frames, elegant pier glasses, sofas, chairs, clocks, furniture of every kind, wearing apparel, bed clothes. . . ."[25] At three o'clock, a nine-year-old black boy was attacked by a downtown mob at the corner of Broadway and Chambers Street.[26] Later in the afternoon, a crowd threatened the Eighteenth Ward Police Station, raided an armory in search of weapons, and drove off the police sent to protect government property. When police reinforcements arrived, the crowd torched the building.[27] Another crowd left the charred site of the Ninth District draft building to burn Allerton's Bull's Head Hotel, which housed an office of the American Telegraph Company. The gathering at Bull's Head "divided into two or three gangs, with leaders bearing pieces of boards for banners on which were written . . . 'No draft,' etc., and it was unsafe to express a single word in dissent from the proceeding." One of these gangs held up a tantalizing sign that read "Independent."[28] By supper time, one group had set fire to the splendid Colored Orphan Asylum on Fifth Avenue and another began attacking black men and boys in the tenement district along the downtown waterfront. But anti-Republicanism remained the refrain of the violence as crowds returned to Greeley's *Tribune* office in the early evening, stormed the building, and set it afire before police drove them away.[29]

Late Monday we also find the earliest evidence of some rioters abandoning the violence and in many cases joining forces with city authorities to protect property and suppress the uprising. Thomas Fitzsimmons, leader of the committee which closed Jackson's Foundry during the morning hours, had by nightfall organized a patrol to guard property on his block.[30] The other leader of the Twenty-eighth Street patrol was Richard Hennessey, a local soap manufacturer and acquaintance of the Fitzsimmons family.[31] Fitzsimmons and his vigilante police force maintained a twenty-four-hour watch through the week and successfully protected a black man from a lynch mob on Wednesday.[32] Meanwhile Fitzsimmons's assurance that Jackson could reopen his shop Tuesday morning proved false. The iron works was kept closed through the riot week and well into the next by threats of arson from a new committee with intentions far different from those of Fitzsimmons's Monday delegation.[33]

The most obvious repudiation of the violence [of] Monday evening was that of the volunteer fire companies. Firemen were prominent in the anti-draft demonstration of Monday morning but solidly arrayed against the rioters by Tuesday. Engine Company Number Thirty-three, leader of the Monday assault on the Ninth District draft office, was by Tuesday defending its Upper West Side neighborhood against riot and arson.[34] Local residents furnished the Black Joke men with refreshments through the week, and railroad directors and property owners published a letter of gratitude to the fire laddies in the city press.[35] On Tuesday evening, Hook and Ladder Company Number Twelve fought its way through a barricade to douse the flames at the Twenty-second Street Police Station, and then, clearing another set of barricades, rushed to a Fourteenth Street lumberyard where the firemen battled rioters until dawn.[36] Engineer Henry Lewis and his vigilance committee arrested eight "thieves" nearby and recovered $1,200 worth of stolen property in the course of their patrol.[37] Still, many fire companies feared their efforts to uphold public order would obscure their ongoing hostility toward the draft. The Forrest Engine Company Number Three printed a notice affirming their opposition to the draft, which it declared to be "unnecessary and illegal." "But in the present exciting times," the resolution continued, "we deem it our duty . . . to protect the property of the citizens of the Eleventh Ward to the best of our abilities."[38] Some rioters, then, continued to denounce the policies of the Republican administration even when they disavowed or campaigned against the unfolding insurrection against property and the social order.

The tensions among Monday's crowds and the abandonment of the revolt by some rioters suggest that from the outset the uprising had different sorts of participants with diverse grievances. At least through early Monday afternoon, the course of violence was much influenced by rioters concerned primarily with the administration of the draft. These workingmen and their families, whose actions call to mind Brooks's "Conscription Riot," denounced Republicans Lincoln and Greeley, carried placards against the draft, and cheered as the Ninth District draft office burned.[39] Like the committee at Jackson's Foundry they used the technique of marching from shop to shop and corraling men into the crowd to increase their numbers and inform the city's workers about their action. This style of protest was familiar to all New York City workers in the 1850s and 1860s as a method of enforcing strikes.[40] These rioters displayed great hostility toward government representatives and property and even condoned the burning of federal buildings and the attacks on Metropolitan Police and United States Army Invalid Corps arriving to investigate the disturbance on Third Avenue. It was even conceivable that a rioter of this sort might have joined in the savage beating of Police Superintendent Kennedy on Monday morning.[41] But these rioters seem to have shunned the looting, the hanging and mutilation of black men, and the attacks on war industries that began Monday and continued through the week; this was the crowd William O. Stoddard (private secretary to President Lincoln and a member of the "volunteer special" police during the bloody week) described as "honest laboring men, of all political parties, thousands of them . . . willing to parade the streets in an 'anti-Draft demonstration,' and to do any required amount of shouting and all that sort of thing, who were at the same time not at all inclined to commit either burglary or arson or murder."[42] Their enemies were the Republican administration and the draft law with its offensive substitution and three-hundred-dollar commutation clauses. Some of these rioters may have regarded a conscription law without the invidious provisions as a legitimate and equitable way to hasten a Northern victory.[43]

Alongside Monday's rioters of limited aims were others with larger designs. These men, women, and children helped to destroy the Provost Marshal's Office, attacked city police and federal officials, and closed factories. But this cohort also severed telegraph lines, tore up railroad tracks and committed the first acts of theft Monday morning. It was probably rioters of this sort who later in the week destroyed the track of the Hudson River Railroad, attacked the Weehawken and Fulton ferries, and attempted to burn the Harlem and McComb's Dam bridges and the Manhattan and Metropolitan gas works.[44] Early Monday, one crowd within earshot of a reporter cut down telegraph poles after discussing the possibility of the authorities summoning troops from Albany.[45] The assaults on telegraph lines, ferry slips, railroad tracks, and gas factories went beyond mere machine breaking to disclose a grander anticipation of – or even plan for – protracted confrontation with the authorities.[46] We do not know how elaborate this plan was or whether such attacks were coordinated, but the appearance of deliberate scheming was compelling enough to convince Republicans and Democrats alike that the destruction of transportation and communication lines and efforts to darken the city were the *coup de main* in a Confederate conspiracy to coordinate Southern military victories with a mob takeover of New York.[47] Contrary to such perceptions, the rioters' attacks seem to have been independent in motive and free from outside manipulation. If anything, the attacks revealed these crowds' keen sense of the dynamics and structure of the city.

Only as the violence entered its second day – the rioters of limited aims now retired and the more ambitious crowds in full force – did it become possible to identify each of the riot's constituencies. Monday's rioters were by no means all Irish and Catholic. Some were German-speaking (one observer thought the early morning procession looked like "some German festival") and some were native-born and Protestant.[48] Artisans in the building trades, who formed the backbone of the uptown fire companies, figured prominently in reports of the Monday morning factory closings and anti-draft procession.[49] These were the painters, carpenters, bricklayers, stonecutters, and small building contractors who pushed the city's line of settlement north toward Central Park in the 1850s and 1860s.[50] By the middle of the week, the social complexion of the crowds had changed. Midweek rioters were more predictably Irish and Catholic, and they were more likely to be members of trades restricted to sons of Erin.[51] German-Americans had by Tuesday organized against the insurrection and were commended by the Republican press for their loyal and orderly comportment.[52] Tuesday's and Wednesday's rioters tended to be industrial workers and common laborers employed in the city's iron foundries, railroad shops, and dock and street construction gangs, especially in the upper wards. The laborer rioters, it should be said, generally did not toil alongside or under the supervision of skilled craftsmen; instead, these quarrymen, street pavers, cartmen, and longshoremen independently organized and managed their own work. Observers frequently commented on the role of "half-grown boys" in the midweek crowds.[53] Of the two dozen identifiable wounded rioters brought into Bellevue Hospital on Thursday of riot week, seven were listed as "minors," six as "laborers," two as "boilermakers," and one as a "cartman." Only one, sixteen-year-old plumber John Ennis, was associated with the building trades. By midweek, artisans in building had largely disappeared from the newspaper accounts and presumably had abandoned the streets.[54]

The lines between constituencies were sometimes blurred. Some Germans appeared among Tuesday's and Wednesday's rioters, some Irish left the streets Monday afternoon. Occasionally artisans rioted through the week, and sometimes industrial workers and laborers dropped out of the crowds early on. But the most clear and abrupt social division was that between journeymen in the older artisan trades, who limited their participation to Monday's demonstrations, and workers in newer industrial occupations and common laboring, who persisted in the midweek revolt. By Tuesday the riot had entered a new phase in which the animus came primarily from Monday's most violent rioters.

As the uprising began its second day, it also became clear that the rioters had altogether failed to lure one important segment of the work force onto the streets. Observers noted that neighborhoods which had witnessed the most violent antebellum strikes and riots were relatively quiet in July 1863. Street violence had time and again punctuated the political life of the "Bloody Sixth" Ward: an anti-abolitionist riot in 1834, a bread riot in 1837, a tailors' strike in 1850 and finally the sanguinary police riot of July 1857.[55] The "Irish Fourteenth" Ward had been home to Michael Walsh and his boisterous "Unterrified Democracy" of the forties and early fifties. During the draft riots, the *Tribune* remarked, "the people of the Sixth and Fourteenth Wards . . . refrained from participating in the outrageous conduct of the mob. . . . "[56] This was meager consolation for resident black families, who found themselves abandoned by white neighbors and easy prey for marauding bands.[57] Notwithstanding such racial violence, the demonstration against the draft in either of its phases never took root in the heartland of antebellum labor protest. Instead Tammany officials including Alderman John Fox, Judge Joseph Dowling, and Comptroller Matthew Brennan presided over an early return to work on July 15.[58] Though this area had long been Democratic, midweek events confirmed it as Tammany territory. Tammany editor John Clancy told his readers on July 18, "Let us hear no more the libellous epithet 'Bloody Sixth.' "[59]

The Bloody Sixth and its northern neighbor the Fourteenth were the heart of the seaport's downtown manufacturing district. The hundreds of sweatshops clustered in the Sixth and Fourteenth turned out clothing and shoes for the trade in consumer-finishing goods and employed the city's most proletarianized poor.[60] These workers toiled in occupations where craft skills had largely been eroded by industrialization. That the employees of the sweatshop district were uninterested in draft rioting – though they were generally faithful Democrats likely to be critical of Republican policies – did not augur well for the laborers and industrial workers who resumed the revolt Tuesday morning.

Tuesday, July 14, to Friday, July 17

The line dividing the riot-week movements of common laborers and industrial workers was more finely drawn than the broad stroke that separated their activities from those of the artisans. The artisan penchant for discipline and rationalism, which may have helped to bring the limited demonstrations to a halt Monday afternoon, was foreign to the thinking of both laborers and industrial workers. These more destructive rioters were ardent foes of the Republican government and all its works, emancipation and federal taxation no less than the draft. They regarded the strike as their most potent weapon against Republican rule and continued to tour the city closing factories and laboring sites. The account of the riot's second and last phase thus begins with Tuesday's vandalism of Republican homes and hostile displays against patriotic symbols, episodes that may well have involved all types of midweek rioters. But increasingly the rift between laborers and industrial workers appeared in vivid relief. The account ends with a discussion of differences in the relations of these two groups with the black community, the "better classes," and the official representatives of Republican authority.

A rage against well-known Republicans and their property remained a dominant theme of the violence. Rumors of an attack planned against the home of abolitionists James Sloane Gibbons and Abby Hopper Gibbons and that of their neighbor James Sinclair (a relative of Greeley's) circulated through the uptown shops Tuesday afternoon.[61] Indeed the Gibbonses' problems with "the Irish mob" had begun the previous winter when they celebrated the Emancipation Proclamation by illuminating their house and draping the windows with red, white, and blue bunting; later that evening they found their front door, steps, and pavement smeared with pitch.[62] The draft rioters' raid on the Gibbonses' house seems to have been one of the more concerted and systematic attacks of the riot week. Late in the afternoon of July 14, two men on horseback waving swords and shouting "Greeley! Gibbons! Greeley! Gibbons!" (the journalist had boarded at the Gibbonses' and was rumored among the rioters to live there) galloped up to the house; a crowd of men and women followed close behind. The horsemen stopped one at each side of the courtyard and allowed about a dozen men with pick-axes into the house while they kept the rest of the mob back. Inside the men "destroyed what they could and threw things out the windows."[63] Finally the advance team was joined by the throng without. The rioters were driven away by a company of soldiers on two occasions but each time returned to the house. Fires were lit and the house was saved only by the intervention of neighbors afraid of spreading flames.

The rioters vented their greatest anger against the Gibbonses' domestic effects:

> The witnesses all agree that a great deal of the furniture was thrown out of the windows, most of it having been previously injured. . . . Many of the books and papers in the library were used to kindle the fires, placed under the furniture collected for that purpose; others were scattered about and trampled upon. . . . The pictures and works of art were mostly defaced or injured in the house. . . . The crockery, etc., was demolished in the house. The carpets and oil cloths were greatly injured, and after having been nearly destroyed, were mostly carried away.[64]

The official who would later examine the Gibbonses' claim for riot damages estimated that only "20 per cent of the articles lost were stolen."[65] James Gibbons recalled that "the piano was actually fired and broken up, and carried off in fragments."[66] The "riot of thieves" à la Brooks was in this instance bent primarily on defacing and destroying property. It was as if demolishing cultural possessions – what one friend of the Gibbonses reverently referred to as the "household gods" – was the rioters' way of destroying the essential attribute of the Republican elite and guaranteeing their departure from the neighborhood.[67]

During the vandalism of the Gibbons home, two drunken Irishmen, Michael O'Brien and John Fitzherbert, led a nearby crowd in the tearing of an American flag to Fitzherbert's chants of "Damn the Flag!"; in a later incident Fitzherbert cheered "Jeff Davis."[68] Midweek rioters saluted a long list of Peace Democrat and Confederate heroes, from Horatio Seymour and General McClellan to the Wood Brothers to Jefferson Davis.[69] By contrast, the Wednesday rioters who marched through Pitt and Broome streets closing factories and machine shops held an American flag aloft.[70] Such diverse and often conflicting demonstrations of allegiance suggest that pro-Confederate statements were a convenient way for some rioters to denounce the Republican Party. More likely than not, these displays and salutes did not represent deep-seated Confederate sympathy. The most striking historical analog to this use of pro-Confederate cheering as a rallying point for anti-Republican Party sentiment was pro-French sloganeering during the violent popular resistance to the Militia Act in Ireland in the summer of 1793. Militia rioters in the late eighteenth-century Irish uprising spoke of their expectations of aid from France.[71] As the draft rioters began to lose hope late in the week, they seized upon any negative point of reference to the Republican authorities. If they only held out a little longer, some whispered, "Baltimore" would come to their assistance. The rioters may have remembered Baltimore as the city in which crowds attacked the Massachusetts Sixth Regiment on its way to the front in April 1861.[72] This heightened and often desperate feeling against the government was characteristic of much of the midweek violence.

After Monday the crowds increasingly turned their attention toward the local black community. Threats of violence, and the occasional attacks on black workingmen which gave such threats their bite, were a regular feature of race relations in the city during this era. But racial tension was high during late spring 1863 because of the shipping companies' decision to employ black labor to break a longshoremen's strike. The week before the riots, Police Superintendent Kennedy reported a growing incidence of physical assaults on black people. Fearing an outbreak, he urged Secretary of War Stanton not to parade the black Fifty-fifth

Massachusetts Regiment through the city as planned.[73] On Sunday, July 12, there were a number of arson attempts against houses on Carmine Street, the heart of one of the city's several black enclaves.[74] In a sense, the racial violence of the draft riots was the quickening of an already accelerated tempo of intimidation and assault.

What made the July riots' brand of racial attack new was its sweeping character. Intimations that white working people were going to approach the matter of racial domination with new intensity and thoroughness could be found in the Monday afternoon razing of the Colored Orphan Asylum, followed by the smashing of its furniture and the uprooting of surrounding trees, shrubbery, and fences.[75] The crowds' desire not merely to destroy but to wipe clean the tangible evidence of a black presence surfaced a few hours later when a waterfront lynch mob hanged William Jones, then burned his body.[76]

The riots were an occasion for gangs of white workingmen in certain trades to introduce into the community the "white-only" rule of their work settings. Bands of Irish longshoremen, many of whom lived within blocks of the piers they worked, began the first racial attacks Monday afternoon. Committees of the "Longshoremen's Association" patrolled the piers in the daylight hours insisting that "the colored people must and shall be driven to other parts of industry, and that the work upon the docks, the stevedoring, and the various jobwork therewith connected, shall be attended to solely and absolutely by members of the 'Longshoremen's Association,' and such white laborers as they see fit to permit upon the premises."[77] Irish street pavers, cartmen, and hack drivers followed suit in other parts of the city, though not with the longshoremen's visible organization and proclamations.[78] Any talk of associations ceased at sunset when parties of men and boys abandoned watch over the piers, factories, and laboring sites for a tour of the surrounding tenements. "Dock laborers" were responsible for the Wednesday night beating and near drowning of black workingman Charles Jackson.[79] They were probably also involved in the Monday, Tuesday, and Wednesday evening attacks on waterfront dance houses, brothels, and boarding houses that catered to black laborers and sailors or, as one city official put it, "negroes . . . of the lowest class."[80] Regardless of their own race, boardinghouse keepers and runners known for black clienteles were stripped of their clothes and threatened with the hangman's rope or driven from the area.[81] On Roosevelt Street, tenements that housed black families were torched and the victims' furniture demolished and burned in sidewalk bonfires. The crowds directed their greatest fury against black men, though black women who protected their husbands and sons could become targets through association. Waterfront rioters seized Jeremiah Robinson, a black man trying to escape to Brooklyn wearing his wife's clothing, beat him senseless and threw his body into the East River.[82] By midweek, the rioters had virtually emptied the harbor front of people of color.[83]

The most violent racial purges of tenement districts were the special province of the men and boys of laborer families. Black sailor William Williams was assaulted by longshoreman Edward Canfield and two other laborers at dawn Tuesday when he walked ashore at an Upper West Side pier to ask directions.[84] Like many of the racial murders, this attack developed into an impromptu neighborhood theater with its own horrific routines. Each member of the white gang came up to the prostrate sailor to perform an atrocity – to jump on him, smash his body with a cobblestone, plant a knife in his chest – while the white audience of local proprietors, workmen, women, and boys watched the tragedy with a mixture of shock, fascination, and, in most instances, a measure of approval. A couple of onlookers did slip away to notify the police, but, as was so often the case, no member of the white audience tried to intervene. To the contrary, milkman Daniel Greenleif reported, "after the occurrence there were several cheers given and something said . . . about vengeance on every nigger in New York." The performance over, the assemblage retired to a nearby liquor store. Some minutes later and down the block, a cartman opening his stable to begin the workday was warned by a man, possibly Canfield, "not to put any niggers to work." When the police arrived, they found the street quiet and Williams in a bleeding and insensible condition from which he died soon after.[85]

Elaborate dramas of a similar kind were reenacted during the course of three Upper West Side lynchings. At dawn Wednesday, nineteen-year-old William Mealy spotted black shoemaker James Costello on West Thirty-second Street and gave chase; Costello fired a shot in self-defense.[86] The shot drew the attention of five or six white men, laborer Matthew Zweick maybe among them.[87] The party pulled Costello from the house where he sought refuge, alternately beat, kicked, and stoned him, trampled on his body, and finally hanged him. Before the episode was complete, two of the party dragged him half-dead to a mudhole where, in a variation on the theme of tar and feather, one immersed him in water while the other emptied a barrel of ashes over his head. Finally the rioters plundered and burned down the house where Costello had attempted to hide.[88] Some hours later laborer George Glass yanked crippled black coachman Abraham Franklin and his sister Henrietta from their rooms a few blocks away, roughed up the girl and dragged Franklin through the streets. A lamppost was found and Franklin was hanged. The military arrived, scattered the crowd and cut down Franklin's body, but when the soldiers departed, the corpse was hoisted up again with cheers for Jefferson Davis.[89] Then the crowd pulled down Franklin's body for the final time. In a grisly denouement, sixteen-year-old Irishman Patrick Butler dragged the body through the streets by the genitals as the crowd applauded.[90] After yet another hanging in this neighborhood, rioters cut off their black victim's fingers and toes.[91] The houses of these black residents were often identified, if they needed to be, by bands of small boys who "marked" them by stoning the windows. The boys later returned with their male elders to pull out the black tenants and complete the bloody mission.[92] Through such elaborate routines, these white workingmen and boys cultivated a dehumanized view of their black neighbors.

Sexual mutilation, burning, and drowning of victims call to mind a traditional and highly symbolic strain of popular violence dating at least as far back as the early modern era.[93] Patrick Butler's public display and appropriation of Abraham Franklin's body and one crowd's amputation of a victim's fingers and toes pointed to a need among rioters of this stripe to prove sexual conquest of the black male community through symbolic acts. Startling even to New Yorkers accustomed to the bloody street melee, these acts no doubt served to dehumanize and objectify black men further in the minds of their white attackers.[94] After the manhood of black workingmen had been publicly reified and debased, white laborers seem to have imagined, an objective black male presence could be cleansed from the neighborhoods. We must be careful here not to ascribe too much structure and rationality to such emotional behavior. But it is certainly worth wondering whether bonfire lynch murders and drownings of black victims were the final acts in much improvised dramas of conquest and purification. Fire and water would symbolically render harmless what these rioters perceived as the post-emancipation social power of their black neighbors. In the view of many white Northerners, the political ascendancy of the Republican Party was causing a revolution in race relations in their communities. The demise of slavery as an institution and a national question, almost inevitable by summer 1863, seemed to signal the end of an era in the North as well as the South. But no one set of rules emerged to replace an older *modus vivendi* between the races in Northern cities. Through sexual conquest and purification, many white workingmen may have hoped to erase the threat of a new black dignity at a time when the social and political status of black people was especially unsettled.[95]

The behavior of Patrick Butler requires additional comment. The image of the Irish youth dragging Franklin's corpse through the streets burns itself into the mind even as our sensibilities become dulled from many descriptions of bloody scenes. Butler himself, it should be noted, was listed in the court records as a "butcher": practitioner of an old and violent craft as renowned for knife-flourishing on the streets as within the market stalls. Nonetheless it is hardly sufficient to associate this rioter's brutality with the behavior of an occupational group. The sexual intensity, exaggerated gestures and bravado of Butler's act call to mind, more than anything, the mentality of a sixteen-year-old boy.[96]

Boys often led the most violent and sexually charged attacks on black men. Young and unmarried males were, of course, especially liable to be drafted. But, as Mayor George Opdyke noted in his account of the riots, so many of the rioters were younger than the minimum draft age of twenty that the simple motive of self-protection against the Conscription Act does not explain their actions.[97] If not always vulnerable to the draft law, New York's young immigrant workers were vulnerable in a larger economic and social sense. They were easily the most underemployed members of the white male labor force. The marginality of young male workers was especially acute at a moment when, in many trades, older traditions of apprenticeship were breaking down or altogether gone and a factory work force based in part on youth labor was only beginning to emerge. During this especially bleak interregnum, many poor boys, regardless of their chosen trade, may have wondered whether they would ever become full-fledged participants in the family and job networks that defined social maturity for the mid-nineteenth-century adult workingman. Attacks on both Republican draft offices and the bodies of black workingmen make sense if we imagine white working-class youths to be seeking to restore to the community not just political order but also social and sexual order. If a sense of insecurity helped to inspire the racial attacks of white laborers who competed with black workers, it played an even larger role in the white youth riot that figured as a leitmotif in the mid-week violence.[98]

Fear of racial amalgamation, the theme of so many earlier anti-black riots in New York City, was also an element of the violence.[99] Crowds visited and often attacked the homes of racially mixed couples and white women who kept company with black men. Tuesday night, downtown saloonkeeper and small-time Democratic politician William Cruise tried unsuccessfully to instigate a crowd of men and boys to burn the house of Mary Burke, a white prostitute who included black men among her clientele.[100] Cruise had better luck when he gave straw and matches to a gang of boys and led them around the corner to the rooms of William Derrickson, a black laborer at a local loading depot. William escaped but his son Alfred was pulled out on the street, stripped, and beaten. A fire was started under a lamppost, and Alfred would have been lynched and burned to death were it not for the eleventh-hour intercession of grocer Frederick Merrick and a group of local German residents who chased the rioters away.[101] That same evening, laborer Thomas Cumiskie joined physician Thomas Fitzgerald and a crowd in an unsuccessful effort to burn the house of Harlem abolitionist and Internal Revenue Collector Edgar Ketchum.[102] The next night Cumiskie led rioters around East Harlem to solicit money for a round of drinks. The rowdies' destination was the shanty of Ann Martin, where they interviewed Mrs. Martin and debated whether her dwelling should be burned.[103] In these incidents, the women involved – Ann Derrickson and Ann Martin – were white wives of men of color. The sexual policing of black men may have been a motive here much as it was in the murder of Abraham Franklin.

For many crowds in which laborers were prominent, it became important to confirm the loyalty of friends and identify enemies among the neighborhood "chamber of commerce." On Wednesday, Martin Hart, a gaspipe layer recently arrived from Ireland, Adam Schlosshauer, a German gardener, and John Halligan, another laborer, led a band of "at least eight" revellers around Harlem asking storekeepers and employers for liquor money. One man made the request for fifty cents or a dollar while two others serenaded with flute and tin kettles. The group marked the names of stinters on a card and left them with the warning "We'll settle with you tonight."[104] John Piper, a teamster whose name had come up in the lottery, asked Upper West Side slaughterhouse owner Thomas White for "money to treat the boys" and, receiving a few shillings, invited some bystanders into White's office for a drink. Piper announced that he hoped to rally "all the G. D. drafted men to resist the draft" but had come "to inform his friends" what the mob was going to do and "see that his friends would be protected." Promising White immunity, the teamster boasted that a neighboring abbatoir owner would be burned out because "he was a mean G.D.S. of a B.," he had prevented the burning of a black residence, he was German, and "he had informed on the rioters."[105]

In these and other incidents, treating was serious business. The crowds often brandished clubs and revolvers; the threat of arson was carried out against proprietors who refused to pay up.[106] Under such duress, the offer to stand drinks cannot be said to have been freely given. But even then treating carried connotations of friendship and sympathy between donor and recipient, connotations magnified by the black and white moral universe of mid-week in which capitulation to the mob furnished grounds for suspicion of treason. While the motives of Hart and company were more purely bacchanalian than those of Piper, the issue of support for the ongoing draft riot never wholly disappeared from these interchanges.

Some rioters were easily appeased: a suspicious party who performed an act of generosity, produced the proper "friendly" sponsorship, or proclaimed anti-draft sentiments could readily undermine the damning evidence of dress, occupation, or political views. In the Piper episode Policeman William McTaggart was among the bystanders ushered into White's establishment after White had offered to stand drinks. Piper asked White if McTaggart was "reliable," and when reassured, proceeded to reveal the rioters' plans of destruction on the Upper West Side.[107] A speech could be as effective as an offer to treat in quelling the rioters' suspicions. Director of the Sixth Avenue Railroad Alfred G. Jones was pulled from his depot on Tuesday by a gang seeking to force those men still working to join their ranks. "I promenaded arm in arm with a drunken Irishman," Jones confided to his diary, "and was let go upon making 'a speech against the draft.'... They said I was all right and left me after shaking hands generally."[108] For these rioters – and they were frequently laborers – the project of sweeping the city clean of individuals and institutions responsible for the draft was as much one of social inclusion as it was one of exclusion. A rage against elite offenders went hand-in-hand with chivalry toward elite friends.

As the week progressed, the attention of such crowds began to drift from the Republican government and its works to other community institutions they suspected of hostility to the insurrection, exploitative behavior, or moral reform. On Monday evening, fifty or more boys set fire in the parlor of Republican Postmaster Abram Wakeman's abandoned Yorkville townhouse. Next the crowd burned a police station across the street. Then the rioters moved to the Magdalen Asylum, a home for aging prostitutes on Eighty-eighth Street. The moral reform of prostitution had been a favorite project among the evangelical Protestant middle class since the 1830s, but the Magdalen Asylum hardly qualified as a Republican Party outpost.[109] With laborers Richard Lynch and Nicholas Duffy at the fore (Duffy was a well-known local character), the crowd interviewed the asylum superintendent, departed, and then returned for a follow-up discussion; finally they announced "they were going 'to burn the building the same as they had [the Republican] Wakeman's house.'... " They took a desk, fired the building, and released the prostitutes.[110]

In this speculative fashion some rioters explored the political and social allegiances of the Protestant middle and upper classes. Such attacks often surprised the victims themselves who, like the Magdalen superintendent, were not sure why they had become targets. Late Monday, rioters approached Professor John Torrey's house near the grounds of Columbia College "wishing to know if a republican lived there, and what the College building was used for."[111] "They were going to burn Pres. King's house," Torrey wrote, "as he was rich, and a decided republican. They barely desisted when addressed by the Catholic priests. The furious bareheaded and coatless men assembled under our windows and shouted aloud for Jefferson Davis!"[112] The Catholic priests calmed the rioters' suspicions, as did the family of a Doctor Ward later that evening. The Ward family saved their nearby Fifth Avenue mansion by assuring the crowd that "they were all Brackenridge [sic] democrats and opposed to the draft."[113] The entreaties of the superintendent of the Magdalen Asylum were less persuasive. Some rioters lengthened their list of enemies to include an array of middle- and upper-class Protestant individuals and institutions. For these crowds, the midweek revolt had moved beyond an attack on the agencies of the wartime state.

As the Magdalen and Columbia episodes suggest, Catholic loyalties mattered and Catholic antipathies could broaden the swath of the midweek riot. At Tuesday dawn a Harlem temperance and music room was burned, and later in the week two Protestant missions were wrecked.[114] On Wednesday we find the first evidence of rioters proclaiming Irish and Catholic identity as an explanation or legitimation for their attacks. In one incident a Central Park laborer named Doherty incited a gang of Irishmen to warn away and burn the house of Republican lawyer Josiah Porter, whom they called a "black orangeman [and]...a black republican at that"; Porter had refused Doherty permission to build a shanty on Porter's land.[115] Earlier that morning Michael McCabe announced his membership in the "Hibernian Society" in the course of extorting forty dollars from a Harlem grocer (whose connection to the Republican Party, if any, remains unknown).[116] Wednesday night, uptown rioters' query to well-dressed gentlemen, "Are you for the Union?" was safely if evasively answered, "I am a Democratic Catholic."[117] While Catholic resentment of Protestant authority smoldered through both phases of the riot, it glowed brightest in the midweek violence.

Another "illegitimate" personality rioters sought to drive away was the waterfront brothelkeeper. The brothel district along the downtown West Side docks was the scene of attacks beginning Tuesday night. Unlike the firing of Roosevelt Street dance houses Monday night and William Cruise's threats to prostitute Mary Burke's rooms on Tuesday, the destruction of the West Side brothels was not necessarily linked to racial animosities. "Bands of rioters" toured the waterfront stores and wharves during the day on Tuesday and rallied laborers for the "procession" that evening.[118] A little after eight o'clock the assemblage divided into two parties and the march began.

Consisting "almost entirely" of boys and led by a man sporting a white hat with a feather, one group headed up Washington Street while another column turned up West Street along the wharves.[119] The first group, now joined by a party of women and men, entered and destroyed the saloon and brothel of Heinrich Strückhausen on Greenwich Street. Wash basins and water pitchers were broken, furniture smashed, liquor and cigars carried off.[120] The crowd continued on to John Smith's brothel at 157 Greenwich, where boys began throwing bricks at the door. Young longshoreman Martin Haley was about to usher his comrades inside when the proprietor Smith suddenly appeared in the doorway and shot him dead; the marchers scattered.[121]

Prostitutes were never injured in these attacks – the rioters sought only to tear down the offending structure and drive the owner out of business. Musical instruments were thus the first objects to meet with the rioters' axes.[122] German proprietors were frequent victims, but these were not anti-German attacks per se. Though there is no direct evidence on this point, rioters may have regarded brothelkeepers, especially those who catered to German or black workingmen, as petty exploiters who attracted large numbers of migrant laborers to their districts and undermined their ability to control the labor market.[123] The raids on houses of ill-fame Tuesday night and through the week reflected the special social situation and needs of the waterfront laborer families.[124]

Such attacks were at best loosely linked to concurrent goals of repudiating the Republicans and their draft and destroying telegraph lines, ferries, and bridges.[125] Irish rioters now began to attack German and Jewish store owners.[126] Some of these shopkeepers were known Republicans, and occasionally attacks began with a formal discussion (a *Kleindeutschland* bartender managed to save his employer's premises by treating rioters to a round of drinks).[127] More often, though, mobs dispensed with interviews and tests of allegiance and attacked the German shops on sight.[128] One of the earlier reasons for destroying property – to prevent those parties "connected to the draft" from returning to the neighborhood – now disappeared in favor of outright theft.[129]

The most troublesome obstacle Irish rioters faced as they struggled to keep uptown factories and work sites closed through the week was the attitude of their German neighbors and fellow workers. Though many German workers had turned out for Monday's uprising, by Tuesday their enthusiasm for the strike against the draft had flagged. A report came into the *Tribune* office Tuesday night that a gang had approached the German residents of Third Avenue between Fortieth and Forty-first streets "and threatened that if they did not join the rioters, they [the gang] would set the whole block on fire."[130] But what began as an attack on local scab elements had now become an indiscriminate race riot. On Wednesday, downtown rioters included on their list of targets a few defenseless Chinese peddlers suspected of liaisons with white women.[131] As the revolt drew to a close, some crowds seem to have assaulted all groups which on sight could be labeled exploitative, responsible for the presence of a strike-breaking element (real or imagined) in their districts, or merely unsympathetic. Here systematic and concerted attacks or exploratory interviews gave way to impulse.[132]

As these crowds grew less fastidious in their choice of targets, they also became more open to suasion by Democratic Party leaders. What may have been the last collective act of laborer rioters Thursday evening began as a challenge to Republican authority and ended as a dialogue in which Democratic elites convinced workers not to riot. The Seventh Avenue Armory was the great symbol of government military presence in the uptown wards. Rioters had threatened the building all week, and consequently it was heavily guarded. Rumor of a planned attack on the Armory reached Governor Seymour at the Saint Nicholas Hotel dinner time Thursday. Seymour dispatched N. Hill Fowler – Corporation Attorney, Peace Democrat, and longtime resident of the Upper West Side – to address the hundreds of working people who by nightfall were crowding the streets around the Armory. Fowler read a letter from Seymour suspending the draft in New York City and Brooklyn and received loud applause. After some further remarks advising opposition to the draft in the courts and not on the streets, Fowler left and the throng quietly dispersed.[133] By Thursday, laborers seemed to have imprinted their characteristic outlook on the class dialogue of the Upper West Side.[134] If the Democratic upper classes could protect them from the draft, these workers may have speculated, there would be no immediate need to contest the Republicans for power.

As laborers lengthened their list of social enemies and grew more tentative in their challenges to the federal government, industrial workers focused their choice of targets. Eighteen-year-old blacksmith Peter Dolan led a gang in a Tuesday attempt to destroy Republican Mayor Opdyke's house.[135] On Thursday, boilermaker Edward Clary assaulted and may have tried to shoot point-blank policeman William H. Carman (Clary denied only the final pulling of the trigger).[136] Such direct confrontation with the authorities became the special cachet of industrial worker riot activity by the middle of the week. While laborers and industrial workers agreed that their common political enemy was "Black Republicanism," laborers were more likely to emphasize "black," while industrial workers put their stress upon "Republicanism." Industrial workers wished less to coax upper-class loyalty and good will than to separate their world from that of the Republican elite and its authority.

The racial attacks of industrial workers, while often quite violent, were different in style from those of laborers. Blacksmith John Leavy and his son led a Tuesday night assault on West Indian broker Jeremiah Hamilton's Upper East Side residence. The Leavys worked together at a coach factory a few doors away.[137] Though one of the boys in the raiding party announced with some bravado, "There is a nigger living here with two white women, and we are going to bring him out and hang him on the lamppost," little violence occurred after it was obvious Hamilton was not home. "Sentinels" were posted at the corner of each nearby avenue. The elder Leavy and his gang asked Mrs. Hamilton for liquor and cigars, the boy Leavy requested a suit of old clothes, and the band departed. No attempt was made to burn the house.[138] In fact, few firings of black residences or bonfire murders of black men occurred in districts with large numbers of industrial worker families.[139] The uptown Eleventh Ward, known for its massive machine shops and its bitter hostility toward blacks, Republican politicians, and the draft, witnessed no bonfire lynchings and no arson against black homes, though there were more than a few black dwellings in the area from which to choose.[140] Of course racist sentiment in this neighborhood was intense. But industrial workers connected their racism to their primary targets, the Republicans and the draft. "It would have been far from safe for a negro to have made his appearance in that locality," wrote one reporter of the Eleventh Ward, "for the laboring classes there appear to be of the opinion that the negroes are the sole cause of all their trouble, and many even say that were it not for the negroes there would be no war and no necessity for a draft."[141] Like laborers, industrial workers hoped to drive black families from their districts. But sexually charged purges of black men did not occur in industrial worker neighborhoods.

In those Upper East Side neighborhoods, crowds continued to assault Republican homes and factories through the week (as late as Thursday morning, mobs were threatening the stately Republican residences along Gramercy Park). However, the Republicans who suffered the largest share of violence on the Upper East Side were draft officers, soldiers, and policemen. Women led the rioters' week-long crusade to drive from the factory districts all armed representatives of the Republican government. Women of the industrial Eleventh Ward, an observer noted, "vow vengeance on all enrolling officers and provost marshals and regret that they did not annihilate the officers when they first called to procure the names for the draft."[142] Most draft officials wisely stayed off the streets during the uprising (though in one instance rioters broke into the home of enrollment officer Joseph Hecht, called him "Mr. Lincoln," and beat him in his own parlor).[143] Government troops and police were left to bear the full brunt of popular wrath. On Tuesday an Upper East Side mob attacked, beat, and killed Colonel Henry O'Brien of the Eleventh New York Volunteers. The day before, O'Brien had used a howitzer to clear Second Avenue of rioters and killed a woman bystander and her child. On Monday night, O'Brien's house was gutted.[144] The next morning, neighborhood people spotted O'Brien returning to inspect his property. One man approached O'Brien from behind and clubbed him to the ground. The murder of Colonel O'Brien that afternoon lasted six hours.[145] Women dominated the crowds that first beat his face to a pulp, later pulled him through the streets and into his own backyard, stripped him of his uniform, and finally "committed the most atrocious violence on the body" before he died.[146] The crowds turned on a local druggist who offered the half-dead soldier a drink of water and wrecked the druggist's store. A girl who protested the violence was beaten and the house where she boarded destroyed. Only Father Clowry of nearby Saint Gabriel's managed to calm the crowd sufficiently to administer O'Brien the extreme unction.[147]

The assault on O'Brien was not special treatment reserved for Irish supporters of the government or the murderers of women and children, though O'Brien's deeds no doubt distinguished him as a target. A similar pattern of violence characterized the dozens of assaults on policemen and soldiers through the week.[148] Fierce beatings were administered to these officials, but the women and men in the O'Brien crowd and others like it were not concerned with purification as were the racist lynch mobs. There were no burnings or drownings of police or soldiers. The participation of working-class wives suggests these events were not merely the outgrowth of the male workplace experience and may have relied as well on the neighborhood networks of poor Irish women. No rioter announced that his or her attacks on policemen and soldiers were inspired by hostility to the Republican Party. Yet there is reason to suspect that the city's immigrant poor did associate such armed authority with Republicanism. It was not that all soldiers and policemen were Republicans (many were not). Rather, the Union Army and Metropolitan Police were institutions that had emerged under the auspices of the Republican Party. The Army's relation to the Republican national government was self-evident; the Metropolitan Police was a creation of the local Republican elite, which had wrested control of city law enforcement from the Democratic Party in July 1857 only after suppressing a riot opposing the change.[149] Under the zealous leadership of Superintendent John A. Kennedy, whom the rioters singled out for vengeance early on, the Metropolitan Police practically became an arm of the Republican government in Washington. Secretary of War Stanton appointed Kennedy a special provost marshal and the police a provost marshal's guard in August 1862, as the city prepared for the state draft. Kennedy's police now had the power to apprehend any who interfered with the war effort, and they exercised that power to the utmost. They arrested four thousand deserters in little over a year, defined disloyalty broadly enough to include harmless statements against the Republican Party, detained suspects on meager evidence, and on Election Day 1862 used information procured during state draft enrollment to challenge the legal status of immigrant (and presumably Democratic) voters.[150] This was the context in which Kennedy's police were popularly identified with Republican authority.

The O'Brien incident and others like it set the tone for the titanic struggles between the crowds and the police and military in the Upper East Side factory district. Monday's and Tuesday's battles for control of the Union Steam Works on East Twenty-second Street presaged the entrenched style of conflict soon to characterize the fighting in this neighborhood. Working-class families from the blocks surrounding the firearms factory hoped to seize the hundreds of carbines rumored to be inside. A wire factory converted to wartime arms production, the Steam Works was owned by Mayor Opdyke's son-in-law George Farlee. "Mr. Opdyke's Armory" had become a popular symbol of Republican control of the uptown industrial landscape.[151]

Rioters broke into the factory on Monday afternoon. In some of the most bitter hand-to-hand encounters of the week, Inspector George W. Dilks and two hundred policemen drove off with clubs the crowds of men and women streaming into the factory. Through the day neighborhood working people stormed the armory and several times seized the building. Police wrested the factory back only after a stair-by-stair struggle.[152] Tuesday afternoon, crowds captured the factory again and repulsed an attempt of the Eighteenth Ward police to dislodge them.[153] Inspector Dilks and Captain John C. Helme then returned to the scene with a company of the Twelfth United States Infantry.[154] In this next encounter, the women were "very desperate," barring the policemen's path and assaulting them with stones and clubs.[155] Only repeated volleys of gunfire into the dense mass of working people enabled the combined forces of police and military to rescue the remaining boxes of weapons from the building.[156] Tuesday night, the rioters finally did assert their claim to the Union Steam Works, burning the building to the ground. The Eighteenth Ward Police Station on the same block was also burned that evening.[157]

What Brooks called the "collisions of the military and the mob" were now centered on the streets surrounding the large uptown factories, as the crowds battled to seize and hold the industrial terrain. On Tuesday barricades went up east of First Avenue in the Seventeenth and Eleventh wards, east of Third Avenue in the Eighteenth Ward, and along Ninth Avenue in the Twentieth Ward.[158] These boundaries cordoned off the waterfront residential and work world of the heavily Irish Catholic industrial working class from the center island that was the domain of a more native-born and Protestant middle and upper class.[159] Eighth and Third avenues, thoroughfares of retail stores and artisan shops, were both decidedly on the far side of the barricades from this working-class perspective. By Wednesday, Second Avenue had become the critical boulevard for workers to control: "Crowds of excited men occupied the corners of the streets and no one was allowed to cross the Second Avenue without first being placed under a rigid and scrutinizing examination."[160] East of that avenue, as one reporter so examined put it, any "stranger" was suspected of being an agent of the Republican authorities, either a "special officer or a spy."[161] It was here, under the shadow of the massive factories of the Upper East Side riverfront, more than on the West Side, that industrial workers were concentrated and their involvement in the riot was most evident.[162] Through the middle of the week laborers remained highly mobile: touring the city, closing factories, and demanding obeisance from proprietors in the uptown neighborhoods. By contrast industrial workers and their families now became intensely local in their thinking. They hoped to establish zones of the city free from a Republican presence. Irish Catholicism was an important part of the identity of many East Side rioters, and by excluding Republicans, they may have believed that their territory of justice would also be free from the usurpations of a nativistic and homogenizing Protestant rule.[163] When the wives of Upper East Side workingmen enjoined their husbands to "die at home" on Wednesday and Thursday, "home" meant the dozen or so square blocks in which these families lived and worked.[164]

One of the large factories behind this working class *cordon sanitaire* was Jackson's Foundry, scene of Thomas Fitzsimmons' peaceable Monday demonstration against the draft. By Wednesday morning, the mob outside the Twenty-eighth Street factory grew so dense that two companies of the Sixty-fifth New York National Guard and a detachment from the Eighth Regiment, along with some police reinforcements, were sent in to occupy and protect the factory.[165] A committee of rioters demanded that the soldiers give up the policemen to the crowd. The committee promised to disperse the gathering outside the foundry if the policemen were "delivered up."[166] Otherwise the rioters threatened to storm the factory at all hazards. The police officers donned workmen's garments and escaped the building in disguise. Hitchcock and Jackson, owners of the iron works, begged Brigadier General Harvey Brown to withdraw the troops from the building "as their presence only exasperated the people."[167] State Senator John Bradley and Judge Michael Connolly repeated the request on Friday, informing Commissioner of Police Thomas Acton that "the presence of the military . . . incited the mob to acts of violence."[168] Brown and Acton both refused to remove any troops, while Acton wrote back, "The Eighteenth Ward is a plague spot and must be wiped out."[169] Meanwhile the committee besieged the foundry and nearly flushed out the starving soldiers before military reinforcements arrived.

The rioters' committees had better success keeping the tenements free of military and police. Committees moved block-by-block through the Upper East Side riverfront district, posting sentinels at street corners and searching each house for soldiers wounded in the fighting and secreted away by sympathetic neighbors. Exacting tests of loyalty were administered by the rioters to those suspected of aiding military men, and the officials were treated ruthlessly when caught. On Wednesday night, a crowd beat and nearly hanged an army surgeon found hiding in an East Nineteenth Street cellar.[170]

By Thursday, regiments returning to the city from Gettysburg seized and occupied the streets and key factories of the uptown wards. An Eighth Regiment artillery troop and a mountain howitzer surveyed the streets around Gramercy Park.[171] One company of the Seventh Regiment occupied Day's India Rubber Factory on East Thirty-fifth Street and took control of that block.[172] Other troops from the Seventh were stationed as pickets from Third Avenue and Thirty-second Street east to the river and north to Fortieth Street. "Not more than one citizen at a time is allowed to enter the picket line, by permission of the officer of the guard," observed one reporter, "and even then he is not permitted to stand still or look around, but must briskly walk to his destination, under penalty of being shot by the sentries. . . ."[173] By Friday, many of the six thousand active troops now in the city were stationed in the uptown districts.[174] Industrial workers' hopes of liberating their neighborhoods from the policies and personnel of the Republican government had to be deferred.

Now the battle on the Upper East Side moved indoors. Late afternoon Thursday, Colonel Thaddeus Mott led a company of volunteers down East Twenty-second Street between Second and Third avenues when a crowd attempted to blockade the street and prevent the soldiers' passage.[176] The residents of the block fired bricks down on the military from the rooftops, and a sniper shot killed Mott's company sergeant. The company beat a quick retreat but returned with police and citizen deputy reinforcements and orders from General Brown to recover the officer's body. General Putnam, commanding the returning troops, retrieved the body and ordered his soldiers to clear the houses of rioters, first on Twenty-second Street and then on Thirty-first Street. The neighborhood barricaded its doors against the soldiers but finally the troops prevailed. Breaking down doors, bayoneting all who interfered, the soldiers drove the crowds to the tenement roofs. "A large number of the crowd" jumped to certain death below.[176] Colonel Mott marched sixteen male prisoners from the two blocks back to General Brown's headquarters. Two of the five traceable Twenty-second Street prisoners were metal workers, one an iron molder and one a blacksmith.[177] On the Upper East Side, the homes of industrial workers became the final redoubts of the draft riots.[178]

A true calendar of the events of July 13–17 reveals that the draft riots unfolded in two phases, each with its own characteristic participants, motives, and dynamics. Through early afternoon Monday, much of the violence bore the stamp of rioters who were conducting a one-day demonstration against the administration and inequitable provisions of the Conscription Act. This "big show against the draft" was hostile to Republican leaders and officials and conceived the draft as one of several obnoxious Republican wartime policies. Such rioters left the streets by late Monday and in many instances joined the organized effort to restore order. Alongside these rioters were others who from the outset were willing to employ far more violent means to put down the draft and were opposed to conscription on any terms. By Tuesday they dominated the action, and the riot entered a new, more murderous and destructive phase. The midweek rioters proceeded to connect the draft to many of its social bases in the community. Only the offensive behavior of an entire cast of characters, these rioters felt, could account for the subversion of just authority and the unprecedented power and arrogations of the Republican Party. A problem of this magnitude called for major surgery. Midweek crowds aimed to cut out the tumor whole, to isolate and remove all manifestations of the Republican social presence. As they watched a centralizing national government become increasingly identified with the prerogatives of a local elite they associated with exploitative and interventionist authority, rioters of all persuasions sought to reclaim the polity in the name of the community.

Would the draft rioters realize their ambition of establishing the political authority of the community in New York? By the end, the riots had revealed a popular opposition to Republican rule broad enough to astonish even the most optimistic Copperhead. The rioters were in most cases not the economically marginal or criminal poor, though vagrants and thieves, ubiquitous in the unruly port city, certainly did join the mob. Nor were the rioters the most proletarianized and degraded workers. The revolt was primarily the doing of wage earners accustomed to considerable control over the conduct of their jobs. Judging from the aggressive tone and wide-ranging scope of the riots, these workers also had a sense of their own political importance. Yet this popular opposition was fragmented, drew upon diverse constituencies, and deployed many, often conflicting, ethnic, religious, racial, class, and political strategies. The theme of varied strategies was clear both in the different ways artisans, laborers, and industrial workers rioted as well as in the decision of workers in the sweatshop district not to participate. The fate of the draft rioters' assertiveness would depend upon what social and political leaders could make of these disparate materials.

One of the questions left open to speculation in mid-July was the political future of those workers who had expressed their grievances independently of Democratic Party leaders. While the employees of the sweatshop district allowed Democratic politicians to speak for them, the artisans, industrial workers, and laborers who rioted did not. These wage earners were doubtless interested in what Democratic orators of all persuasions had to say, but had a capacity for self-directed and sustained collective activity that would make their participation in any future political movement something to be watched closely, not taken for granted. Laborers, who deferred to Democratic leaders at the end of the riot, were hardly less independent-minded than their artisan and industrial worker associates. From the perspective of a Democratic boss, these rioting workers were potentially a fractious lot.

Two other groups opposed to the draft – organized workers in the building trades and German-Americans – expressed their views apart from the party machinery. The strikes and riots of 1863 began a decade of unprecedented organization among New York City workers, but during the war most local trade unions were still new and fragile.[179] Few unions were strong enough to influence the behavior of many wage earners during the July riots. Even when sympathetic to the strike against conscription, most unions preferred not to associate themselves with treasonous and violent acts (the exception here, of course, was the Longshoremen's Association). The one journeymen's society to condemn the riots publicly and warn its members against treason was Patrick Keady's Practical House Painters' Association, which included some uptown Irishmen. Known for his criticism of Republican measures and his insistence that unions be kept free of party politics, Keady sent his membership a letter that began, "I do not for a moment suppose that any of you took part in the late riots. You are too well aware of your own interest to do that; but you can in many ways exercise your influence to prevent recurrence of such disgraceful scenes as were then enacted. . . ."[180] Keady and the organized few for whom he spoke hoped to establish the trade union movement as an independent arena of opposition to both treasonous violence and Republican policies.

Similarly, German-Americans sought to restore peace to their home districts at arm's length from the personnel of the major political parties. When most Germans left the crowds late Monday and organized to protect property and battle rioters, they necessarily placed themselves in league with Republican authorities. But like some of the fire companies, Germans made clear that they acted independently of Republican allies. "We believe," one *Kleindeutschland* group announced on the 16th, "that the draft is unconstitutional and uncalled for, [and] said draft now being stopped we organize ourselves as a body to protect the lives and the property of the people in this district. . . ."[181] While such a stance chilled German relations with the Republican Party, it was by no means a declaration of allegiance to Tammany Hall. Germans tended to take to the streets not as self-proclaimed "Democrats" but as "Germans" (as in the "Germans of Division Street" who patrolled the woodworking district on the 16th) or as squads of *Turnverein* or *Schützenverein*.[182] When the Democrats of *Kleindeutschland* did organize a citizens' brigade to suppress the violence, it was an anti-Tammany or Peace Democrat outfit.[183] The prospects of popular anti-Republicanism also depended on the political identities that the building trades unions and German-American associations would choose for themselves.

Finally, the draft rioters' success or failure rested on the responses of the many groups which comprised the local middle and upper classes. An internally polarized and embattled elite confronted the political challenge of the rioters. The eventual outcome of the Civil War and the fate of the Republican experiment in nation-building were highly uncertain during the second week of July 1863. Unresolved, too, was the outcome of a dramatic contest for authority among New York City's "better classes."

Notes

1   See Bernstein, *The New York City Draft Riots*, Chapter 2 for a discussion of each of these "readings" of the riots.

2   *Evening Express*, July 17, 1863. Though Brooks's calendar ends on Wednesday, it was not until sometime Friday that all areas of the city were pacified and work was generally resumed.

3   *Tribune*, July 14, 1863; *Irish American*, July 18, 1863; *Fincher's Trades Review*, July 18, 1863; Stoddard, *Volcano*, 30–1 (Croton Reservoir laborers); Barnes, *Draft Riots*, 10 (street contractors' men).

4   McCague, *Second Rebellion*, p. 61; *Bloody Week!*, 2. To my knowledge, no record of the proceedings in Central Park survives.

5   McCague, *Second Rebellion*, p. 61.

6   Ibid., 62.

7   Barnes, *Draft Riots*, pp. 10–12; Case of Francis Cusick, Grand Jury Dismissals, Aug. 1863, Supreme Court Cases, Location 9571, New York Municipal Archives and Records Center (MARC); Cook, *Armies of the Streets*, pp. 58–9.

8   Barnes, *Draft Riots*, pp. 11–12; Cook, *Armies of the Streets*, p. 57.

9   Case of Thomas Fitzsimmons, Grand Jury Dismissals, Aug. 1863, and Case of Thomas Sutherland, Indictments, Aug. 1863, MARC. These cases involve the only two groups of East Side rioters from the morning of July 13 that are described in the court records in any detail. We do not know for certain that Fitzsimmons's crowd ever made it to the Ninth District lottery, though the timing of their confrontation with James Jackson (9:00 to 10:00 a.m.), the location (East Twenty-eight Street), and their claim that they were demonstrating against the draft suggest they were headed toward the 10:30 lottery on East Forty-seventh Street. We do know that the Sutherland party, which closed Allaire's, Novelty, and several other shops in the Eleventh Ward, was headed uptown and that they arrived in time to participate in the attack on the Bull's Head (or Allerton's) Hotel, Forty-third Street between Fourth and Fifth avenues. There they joined crowds that had come to Allerton's from the Ninth District Provost Marshal's Office. See *Bloody Week!*, p. 7.

10 Stoddard, *Volcano*, p. 38.

11 Cook, *Armies of the Streets*, p. 60; *Leader*, July 18, 1863.

12 Stoddard, *Volcano*, p. 50; *Bloody Week!*, p. 4; for a biography of "Andrews the Mob Leader," see *Bloody Week!* pp. 30–1.

13 *Bloody Week!* p. 3; *Tribune*, July 14, 1863; Stoddard, *Volcano*, p. 50; for Decker's speech to the Third Avenue crowd, see Cook, *Armies of the Streets*, p. 61.

14 *Herald*, July 14, 1863; for the Monday morning observations of one elite bystander, see *Strong Diary*, III: pp. 335–6.

15 *Herald*, July 14, 1863.

16 Jeter Allen Isely, *Horace Greeley and the Republican Party, 1853–1861: A Study of the New York Tribune* (Princeton, 1847), pp. 10–11; Case of James H. Whitten, Indictments, Aug. 1863, MARC (see official court reporter's account of Whitten's trial for the *Tribune*); Cook, *Armies of the Streets*, pp. 88–9.

17   Case of Thomas Fitzsimmons, Grand Jury Dismissals, Aug. 1863, MARC.

18   Ibid. (deposition of Charles Clinch).

19   Ibid.

20   Stoddard, *Volcano*, p. 50.

21   Case of Patrick Merry, Indictments, July 1863, MARC; Cook, *Armies of the Streets*, p. 247.

22   Headley, *The Great Riots of New York*, p. 169; Claim of James Vincent, Draft Riot Claims, Comptroller's Office, New York County, "Bundles Civil War Related," MARC.

23   *Tribune*, July 14, 1863; Barnes, *Draft Riots*, p. 46 (Eighth Precinct Policemen attacked), pp. 58–9 (Fifteenth Precinct Policemen attacked).

24   *Tribune*, July 14, 1863; *Evening Express*, July 14, 1863.

25   *Irish American*, July 14, 1863. Accounts vary as to whether these houses were attacked because they were owned by Republicans or because their owners sheltered policemen fleeing the mob. Most likely, the rioters had both reasons in mind. See John Rogers, Jr., to Sarah Ellen Derby Rogers, July 18, 1863, Misc. Mss. Rogers, New-York Historical Society (NYHS). Rogers saw the rioters searching for sheltered policemen in the Lexington Avenue homes that were burned down; he also overheard some rioters, possibly the same group, "inquiring where the republicans lived."

26   *Tribune*, July 14, 1863.

27   Ibid. (Eighteenth Ward Police Station House); Cook, *Armies of the Streets*, pp. 68–70 (Twenty-first Street Armory).

28   *Tribune*, July 14, 1863.

29   Case of James H. Whitten, Indictments, Aug. 1863, MARC; for another indictment related to the attack on the *Tribune* office, see Case of George Burrows, Indictments, Oct. 1863, MARC; Cook, *Armies of the Streets*, pp. 89–90.

30   Case of Thomas Fitzsimmons, Grand Jury Dismissals, Aug. 1863, MARC (depositions of Charles Irving, James W. Trimble).

31   Ibid. (deposition of Richard Hennessey).

32   Ibid. (deposition of Charles Irving).

33   See below, note 39.

34   *Daily News*, July 23, 1863.

35   *Tribune*, July 24, 1863.

36   *Daily News*, July 23, 1863.

37   *Leader*, July 18, 1863.

38   *Evening Express*, July 15, 1863.

39   See Cook, *Armies of the Streets*, p. 57, for denunciations of Lincoln and Greeley at the attack on the Ninth District Provost Marshal's Office Monday morning.

40   See David Montgomery, "Strikes in Nineteenth Century America," *Social Science History* 4 (Feb. 1980), 81–104; Carl Degler, "Labor in the Economy and Politics of New York City, 1850–1860: A Study in the Impact of Early Industrialism" (Unpubl. PhD diss., Columbia Univ., 1952).

41   See Case of Daniel Conroy and Thomas Kiernan, Grand Jury Dismissals, Aug. 1863, MARC; Case of Charles Dennin, Indictments, Aug. 1863, MARC (deposition of Peter Fowler). Dennin may have been printer Charles O. Denning.

42   Stoddard, *Volcano*, pp. 30–1.

43   This last observation is based in part on discussion of the commutation and substitution clauses of the March 3rd Act in trade union circles. See *Fincher's Trades Review*, July 18, July 25, 1863. The offensive three-hundred-dollar clause was condemned by all Monday rioters, wrote one reporter, regardless of "whether one liked or disliked the Conscription Act." *Evening Express*, July 14, 1863.

44   *Tribune*, July 14, 1863 (Third Avenue, and Harlem and New Haven Railroads); *Evening Express*, July 15, 1863 (Weehawken Ferry, Hudson River Railroad); *Tribune*, July 15, 1863 (uptown bridges); for an arrest related to such attacks, see Case of Joseph Canary, Grand Jury Dismissals, Aug. 1863, MARC.

45   *Herald*, July 14, 1863.

46   Here the comment of the rioters who were trying to keep the authorities from summoning troops from Albany is relevant (see note 45), as is the report that rioters who attacked the gas house in the

Eleventh Ward later in the week "were heard to say that they would put the city in darkness." *Herald*, July 16, 1863.

The one instance of Luddite-style machine-breaking during the riots occurred Tuesday in *Kleindeutschland*. Rioters burned some patent street-cleaning carts, "which undoubtedly were regarded as depriving rioting people of their profession." *Tribune*, July 15, 1863; on the Luddites, see Malcolm I. Thomis, *The Luddites: Machine-Breaking in Regency England* (New York, 1972).

47 Gideon Welles, *Diary of Gideon Welles* (Boston, 1911), I, entry of July 14, 1863, for one of many Republican claims that the riots were fomented by rebel agents; August Belmont to William H. Seward, Newport, RI, July 20, 1863, in August Belmont, *Letters, Speeches, and Addresses* (New York, 1890), for evidence that some Democrats reached the same conclusion as Welles.

48 German involvement in the Monday processions is mentioned in Maria L. Daly, "Diary of Maria L. Daly," I, July 23, 1863, Charles Patrick Daly Papers, New York Public Library (NYPL). On German rioters in *Kleindeutschland* on Tuesday, see *Tribune*, July 15, 1863. Also see Maria Daly's comment that "the principal actors in the mob were boys and I think many were Americans," in Maria L. Daly, "Diary," I, July 23, 1863, Daly Papers, NYPL.

49 On the building trades' participation in the Monday morning anti-draft procession, see *Irish American*, July 18, 1863; *Fincher's Trades Review*, July 18, 1863; *Tribune*, July 14, 1863.

Two points must be made with regard to the observation that artisans in the building trades formed the backbone of the uptown fire companies in 1863. First, each fire company had three leadership positions (foreman, assistant, secretary). In 26 of the 44 uptown fire companies (59.1 percent), at least one of the three officers was in the building trades. In 9 of those 44 companies (20 percent), at least two of the three officers were in the building trades. Second, among the membership of these companies, 343 of the 1430 uptown firemen (23.9 percent) were in the building trades. All told the building trades were represented heavily among the leadership and substantially among the membership of the uptown fire companies (uptown is defined here as north of Fourteenth Street). For the lists of the officers and members of the New York fire companies, with occupations and addresses noted, that were used to compute these figures, see Office of the Chief Engineer, *Annual Report of the Chief Engineer of the Fire Department, of the City of New York, Document 14* (New York, 1863), pp. 33–4, 36–7, 40–1, 52–7, 62–4, 66–9, 71–2, 79–81, 83–8, 90–1, 103, 112, 120–1, 123, 125, 127, 129, 132–4, 136, 139–40, 143, 145, 147, 152–5, 160–1, Municipal Reference and Research Center, New York.

50 See Bernstein, *The New York City Draft Riots*, chs 3 and 6.

51 Dock work and quarry work were almost exclusively Irish occupations.

52 *Times*, July 14, 1863.

53 *Herald*, July 16, 1863 ("half-grown boys").

54 *Tribune*, July 17, 1863.

55 See Bernstein, *The New York City Draft Riots*, Chapter 3 (1850 tailors' strike) and Chapter 4 (anti-abolitionist riot of 1834, police riot of 1857).

56 *Tribune*, July 18, 1863; *Leader*, July 18, 1863.

57 In this neighborhood, see claims of black women Eugenia Brown, Electra Cox, Elizabeth Dixon, Hannah Spencer, "Draft Riot Claims," Comptroller's Office, New York County, MARC; also Case of William Cruise, James Best, Moses Breen, Indictments, Dec. 1863, MARC.

58 *Herald*, July 16, 18, 1863.

59 *Leader*, July 18, 1863.

60 See Christine Stansell, "The Origins of the Sweatshop: Women and Early Industrialization in New York City," in Michael H. Frisch and Daniel J. Walkowitz, eds., *Working Class America: Essays on Labor, Community and American Society* (Urbana, 1983), pp. 78–103; Wilentz, *Chants Democratic*, pp. 107–42.

61 Lucy Gibbons Morse, "Personal Recollections of the Draft Riot of 1863," 2, Knapp/Powell, Trunk 1, NYHS.

62 Ibid., 1.

63 Ibid., 6; Case of John Corrigan, Grand Jury Dismissals, 1863, MARC (Corrigan was one of the men on horseback).

64   Claim of Abby H. Gibbons, in Board of Supervisors, *Communication*, II; 874.

65   Ibid.

66   Ibid. (affidavit of James S. Gibbons).

67   Mrs. E. B. Sedgwick to Julia Gibbons, July 18, 1863, in Sarah Hopper Emerson, ed., *The Life of Abby Hopper Gibbons Told Chiefly Through Her Correspondence* (New York, 1896), II; pp. 52–3; for a theft claim related to the Gibbons attack, see Case of Mary Kennedy, Indictments, Aug. 1863, MARC.

68   Case of Michael O'Brien and John Fitzherbert, Indictments, Oct. 1863, MARC; Cook, *Armies of the Streets*, pp. 125–6.

69   On cheering for Seymour and Fernando Wood on the afternoon of July 14th, see *Tribune*, July 18, 1863.

70   *Daily News*, July 16, 1863.

71   Thomas Bartlett, "An End to Moral Economy: The Irish Militia Disturbances of 1793," *Past and Present* 99 (May 1983), 41–64, and esp. 57.

72   On the significance of Baltimore as a Southern-sympathizing Northern city, see Barbara Jeanne Fields, *Slavery and Freedom on the Middle Ground: Maryland during the Nineteenth Century* (New Haven, 1985), pp. 40–62. See Joel Tyler Headley, *The Great Rebellion: A History of the Civil War in the United States* (Hartford, 1865), I; pp. 70–82, on Baltimore crowds' attacks on the Massachusetts Sixth Regiment on its way to the front in April 1861. Governor Horatio Seymour's anti-draft agitation in New York State in 1863 was in some ways reminiscent of the attempts of Maryland's Governor Thomas Hicks to prevent federal troops from passing through Baltimore in the early days of the war.

73   John A. Kennedy to E. M. Stanton, July 8, 1863, in US War Department, *The war of the Rebellion: A Compilation of the official Records of the Union and Confederate Armies* (Washington, DC, 1899) (*WOR*), ser. III, vol. III:473.

74   McCague, *Second Rebellion*, p. 56.

75   Committee of Merchants for the Relief of Colored People, Suffering from the Late Riots in the City of New York, *Report*, in James M. McPherson, ed., *AntiNegro Riots in the North, 1863*, p. 25; Cook, *Armies of the Streets*, p. 78.

76   Committee of Merchants, *Report*, p. 16; *Tribune*, July 14, 1863; Case of John Nicholson, Indictments, Oct. 1863, MARC; Cook, *Armies of the Streets*, p. 82.

77   *Daily News*, July 17, 1863; Albon P. Man, Jr., "Labor Competition and the New York Draft Riots of 1863," *Journal of Negro History* 36 (Oct. 1951), 375–405.

78   Case of Frank Shandley, Ann Shandley, James Shandley, James Cassidy, Indictments, Aug. 1863, MARC (street paver); Case of William Rigby, Indictments, July 1863, MARC (hack driver); Case of Edward Canfield, James Lamb, William Butney, Indictments, Aug. 1863, MARC; attacks on Charles Jackson, William Johnson and son, Committee of Merchants, *Report*, 21, *Evening Express*, July 17, 1863, "A Negro's Throat Cut in the First Ward," (longshoremen); Case of Dennis Carey, *Tribune*, July 24, 1863 (cartman).

79   *Evening Express*, July 17, 1863 ("A Negro's Throat Cut in the First Ward").

80   Claims of Mary Johnston, Henry Beverly, William Taylor, in Board of Supervisors of the County of New York, *Communication from the Comptroller . . . Relative to Damage by Riots of 1863*, II, Doc. No. 13 (New York, 1868), 163–64, 797–800, 926–9; Cook, *Armies of the Streets*, pp. 79–80.

81   Cook, *Armies of the Streets*, pp. 79–80; *Evening Express*, July 14, 15, 1863.

82   Committee of Merchants, *Report*, p. 15; Cook, *Armies of the Streets*, pp. 82–3. Women of color were more often stoned or chased away than beaten or killed. For an instance of a white woman attacked because of her association with a targeted black man, see the rioters' beating murder of Ann Derrickson when she tried to shield her son Alfred from attack, Case of William Cruise, James Best, Moses Breen, Indictments, Dec. 1863, MARC.

83   *Evening Express*, July 14, 1863 ("the negroes have completely disappeared from the streets"); and see below, on Wednesday's attacks on Chinese men in the Fourth Ward. Such a change in the racial targets of downtown rioters suggests that by midweek most black people who were able to leave the downtown district had done so.

84 Case of Edward Canfield, James Lamb, William Butney, Indictments, Aug. 1863, MARC; Coroner's Inquest at the Body of William Williams, Indictments, Aug. 1863, MARC.

85 Case of Canfield, Lamb, Butney, Indictments, Aug. 1863, MARC. The reactions of the white witnesses of the murder are recorded in the testimony for the case. Also, see Committee of Merchants, *Report*, p. 20, Cook, *Armies of the Streets* pp. 97–8.

86 Case of Matthew Zweick, Indictments, Oct. 1863, MARC; *Tribune*, July 27, 1863.

87 Case of Matthew Zweick, Indictments, Oct. 1863, MARC. Zweick was indicted for riot, offending public decency, and first-degree murder. The district attorney refused to prosecute on the ground of inconclusive evidence.

88 Ibid. Note that of the 23 rioters killed in a confrontation with Colonel Mott's troops after the lynching murder of James Costello on the 15th, 19 had waterfront addresses, listed in the newspaper as "Eleventh Avenue." Of the 16 men killed, 8 were traceable, with some allowance for error, in the city directory. This group was composed of 3 laborers, 3 grocers, an "agent," and either an employee or proprietor of a stoneyard (listed merely as "stone"). See New York *Times*, July 16, 1863 ("Partial List of the Killed and Wounded on 32nd Street").

89 *Tribune*, July 24, 25, 28, 1863; Cook, *Armies of the Streets*, p. 143.

90 Case of Patrick Butler, Indictments, July 1863, MARC. In his answer to an initial charge of murder, Butler responded, "I am not guilty, all I done was to take hold of his private parts." He later pleaded guilty to the charge of offending public decency. Cook, *Armies of the Streets*, p. 235.

91 *Bloody Week!*, p. 25; *Tribune*, July 16, 1863.

92 See especially the Claim of Maria Prince, County of New York, *Communication from the Comptroller*, 274–6 (Testimony of Enoch W. Jacques).

93 Note the importance of similarly violent rituals of purification in the Catholic religious riots of early modern France. See Natalie Zemon Davis, "The Rites of Violence: Religious Riot in Sixteenth-Century France," *Past and Present* 59 (1973), 51–91.

94 On the nature of street violence in antebellum cities, see Bernstein, *The New York City Draft Riots*, Introduction, above.

95 The rise of the Republican Party and the demise of slavery did provide the context for a new black social and political assertiveness in Northern cities. See discussion below, Ibid. Chapter 6.

96 On butchers, street violence, and gang activity in antebellum New York, see Wilentz *Chants Democratic* pp. 269–70.

97 George Opdyke, *Official Documents, Addresses, Etc., of George Opdyke, Mayor of the City of New York, During the Years 1862 and 1863* (New York, 1866), p. 289.

98 See Susan G. Davis, " 'Making Night Hideous': Christmas Revelry and Public Order in Nineteenth Century Philadelphia," *American Quarterly* 34 (Summer 1982), 185–99, for another argument associating youth rioting with the extreme casual employment and vagrancy of working-class youth at this stage of the industrial revolution. Also, see Michael B. Katz, Michael J. Doucet, and Mark J. Stern, *The Social Organization of Early Industrial Capitalism* (Cambridge and London, 1982), pp. 255–6, on this point.

99 On anti-amalgamationist riots in antebellum New York, see Kerber, "Abolitionists and Amalgamators," pp. 28–39; Richards, "*Gentlemen of Property and Standing*," pp. 150–5; Wilentz, *Chants Democratic*, pp. 264–66. On the social and political issues of miscegenation, see Joel Williamson, *New People: Miscegenation and Mulattoes in the United States* (New York, 1980), pp. 61–110.

100 Case of William Cruise, James Best, Moses Breen, Indictments, Dec. 1863, MARC; Cook, *Armies of the Streets*, pp. 134–6.

101 Case of William Cruise, James Best, Moses Breen, Indictments, Dec. 1863, MARC.

102 Case of Thomas Fitzgerald, Indictments, Aug. 1863, MARC.

103 Case of Patrick Henrady, Daniel McGovern, Thomas Cumiskie, Indictments, Aug. 1863, MARC.

104 Case of John Halligan, Martin Hart and Adam Schlosshauer, Indictments, Aug. 1863, MARC. See especially the affidavit of storekeeper Marcellus E. Randall. Randall saw Martin Hart and his party solicit "Sherwood and Conners," Mrs. Brown's dry goods store, a larger beer saloon, Sheridan's tinsmith shop, Mitchell's grocery store, Mrs. Colman's dry goods store, and Levi Adams's factory.

105 Case of John Piper, Indictments, Nov. 1863, MARC; Cook, *Armies of the Streets*, p. 95.

106 Hart's gang was arrested before it had a chance to carry out its threats, but stores and dwellings were burned for the offense of refusing to treat (this was usually not the only offense). See Case of Henry Saulsman, James Galvin and Thomas Kelly, Indictments, Aug. 1863, MARC, for the burning of a liquor store that was closed up during the early morning of July 27, 1863, and the sparing of a saloon next door that opened up to treat this Yorkville gang.

107 Case of John Piper, Indictments, Nov. 1863, MARC.

108 Alfred Goldsborough Jones, "Diary," XIV, July 14, 1863, Alfred Goldsborough Jones Papers, NYPL.

109 On the evangelical reform of prostitution in New York City, see John Barkley Jentz, "Artisans, Evangelicals, and the City: A Social History of Abolition and Labor Reform in Jacksonian New York" (Unpubl. Ph.D. diss., City Univ. of New York, 1977), pp. 96–97.

110 Case of Richard Lynch and Nicholas Duffy, Indictments, Aug. 1863, MARC.

111 A. H. Dupree and L. H. Fishel, Jr., eds., "Eyewitness Account of the New York Draft Riots, July, 1863," *Mississippi Valley Historical Review (MVHR)* 47 (Dec. 1966), 576.

112 Ibid.

113 Ibid.

114 *Evening Express*, July 14, 1863; Cook, *Armies of the Streets*, p. 145.

115 Case of Matthew Powers, Patrick Kiernan, Bernard Clark, Frederick Hammer, Bernard Fagan, Indictments, Aug. 1863, MARC; Cook, *Armies of the Streets*, p. 145.

116 Case of Michael McCabe, Indictments, Aug. 1863, MARC. McCabe listed his occupation as "workman" in his court affidavit.

117 *Tribune*, July 17, 1863.

118 *Daily News*, July 15, 1863.

119 Claim of Heinrich Strückhausen, Draft Riot Claims, Comptroller's Office, New York County, MARC.

120 Ibid.

121 Case of John Smith, Coroner's Inquisition, July 1863, Supreme Court Collection, Location 7915, MARC.

122 Claim of Franz Rubel, in Board of Supervisors, *Communication*, II:800 (rioters destroy bass viol), and Claim of Moses Lowenstein, II:370–72 (rioters destroy piano).

123 On working-class perceptions of the brothel as an institution of bondage, in the Parisian setting, see Judith Coffin, "Artisans of the Sidewalk," *Radical History Review* 26 (1982), 89–101.

124 See Bernstein, *The New York City Draft Riots* Map 1, "Map of the Attacks on Brothels, July 13–17, 1863," for evidence that attacks on brothels centered on the waterfront districts. There were brothels in other areas of the city; see Timothy J. Gilfoyle, "The Urban Geography of Commercial Sex: Prostitution in New York City, 1790–1860," *Journal of Urban History*, 13 (Aug. 1987), 371–93, and esp. 385, 387–8.

125 Some newspapers remarked that a number of the downtown brothelkeepers were Democrats. See the Monday night attack on a Vandewater Street boarding house of a black man named Lyons. Lyons was reportedly "a well-known Democrat." *Evening Express*, July 14, 1863.

126 *Herald*, July 16, 1863 (Tuesday evening attacks on Jewish clothing stores in the East Thirties); *Tribune*, July 16, 1863 (attacks on Jewish clothing stores of Grand Street).

127 *Tribune*, July 15, 1863; *Evening Express*, July 15, 1863; Claim of Jacob Brush, Draft Riots Claims, Comptroller's Office, New York County, MARC; Cook, *Armies of the Streets*, p. 131 (bartender at 474 Grand Street). Among the targets in *Kleindeutschland* were Lincoln House; the German Republican headquarters, on Allen Street; Mr. Hoechster's hardware store, Avenue B (Hoechster was a known Republican). Prospective targets mentioned in the newspapers included Held's Hotel, owned by the "well-known German Republican" Andreas Willman, and Steuben House, belonging to Sixtus L. Rapp.

128 Cook, *Armies of the Streets*, p. 131 (attack on Elias Silberstein).

129 Weapons and clothing were the most commonly stolen items. See the Tuesday attack on Brooks Brothers's Catherine Street store. The firm had a reputation as a government war contractor, but in

this attack any anti-government animus quickly evaporated in the ensuing free-for-all in which rioters helped themselves to stacks of clothing before police arrived on the scene. Claim of Brooks Brothers, in Board of Supervisors, *Communication*, II:963–1044. Also see Headley, *Great Riots*, p. 215–18; Barnes, *Draft Riots*, pp. 55–6.

130　*Tribune*, July 15 (gang threatens Germans), July 18, 1863 (repudiation of the riots by the Germans of the Democratic Seventeenth Ward).

131　*Herald*, July 16, 1863; *Evening Express*, July 15, 1863.

132　It may be that crowds in the waterfront Fourth Ward turned against these few Chinese after the black residents of that district had been driven away.

133　Indeed the draft in New York City and Brooklyn had been suspended by Provost Marshal General Fry two days earlier, on July 14. On the Fowler episode, *Evening Express*, July 17, 1863; on crowds' earlier threats to the Armory, see *Evening Express*, July 14, 1863.

134　In part, this conjecture is based on evidence that the Upper West Side waterfront and adjacent blocks were home to many longshoremen in the mid- and late-nineteenth century, many of them involved in the coastwise trade in lumber and local traffic in brick and coal. See Joseph Jennings, *The Frauds of New York and the Aristocrats Who Sustain Them* (New York, 1874), p. 38; Charles B. Barnes, *The Longshoremen* (New York, 1915), pp. 48–51, 60–2; and US Commission on Industrial Relations, *Final Report and Testimony*, Sen. Doc. No. 415, Vol. III (Wash., DC, 1916), pp. 2053–67 (on Chelsea piers in the early 20th century). Longshoremen were undoubtedly frequent participants in Upper West Side riot incidents through the week. See esp. Case of Edward Canfield, Indictments, Aug. 1863, and Case of William Patten, Indictments, Aug. 1863, MARC. The Upper East Side had no comparable longshoring population.

135　Barnes, *Draft Riots*, p. 87; McCague, *Second Rebellion*, pp. 73–4. Though we have no supporting affidavits here, Dolan's guilty plea (Cook, *Armies of the Streets*, p. 238) allows one to argue with confidence that he was indeed a leader of the attack on Opdyke's residence.

136　Case of Edward Clary, Grand Jury Dismissals, 1863, MARC.

137　Case of John Leavy and John Leavy, Jr., Indictments, Oct. 1863, MARC.

138　Ibid.

139　See Bernstein, *The New York City Draft Riots*, Map 2, "The Geography of Racial Murders, July 13–July 17."

140　Ibid. Bernstein, *The New York City Draft Riots* Map 3, "Distribution of Black Population in New York City, by Ward, 1860." Note that in the Fourth Ward, listed as having only 67 black residents in 1860, there were violent attacks on black people and black property through the riot week. By comparison, the factory-district Eleventh Ward, with 225 black residents, and Eighteenth Ward, with 404 black residents, had many more black targets from which to choose, but little racial violence.

141　*Herald*, July 18, 1863.

142　Headley, *Great Riots*, p. 357 (Report of Captain Richard L. Shelley on operations near Gramercy Park on Thursday morning); *Strong Diary*, III:338; *Herald*, July 18, 1863.

143　Cook, *Armies of the Streets*, p. 145.

144　Ibid., 118; *Tribune*, July 15, 1863.

145　*Bloody Week!*, p. 32.

146　Headley, *Great Riots*, p. 199.

147　Cook, *Armies of the Streets*, p. 119.

148　David Montgomery, *Beyond Equality*, p. 105, suggests that policemen were targets for the rioters more frequently than soldiers. Soldiers received a share of the violence, but policemen were the most common targets. See Case of Daniel Conroy and Thomas Kiernan, Grand Jury Dismissals, 1863, MARC, for an arrest related to the beatings of members of the U.S. Invalid Corps.

149　See Weinbaum, "Temperance, Politics, and the New York City Riots of 1857," pp. 246–70, on immigrant views of the Metropolitan Police.

150　That the rioters knew who Kennedy was, singled him out for attack, and made much of his near-fatal beating afterward is made clear in Barnes, *Draft Riots*, pp. 10–12, 22; on Kennedy's use of the authority of the provost marshal as a means of consolidating Republican political power, see James

F. Richardson, *The New York Police: Colonial Times to 1901* (New York, 1970), pp. 124–9. In November 1862, Kennedy stationed police at every polling place with a list of those who had sworn themselves to be aliens in order to escape the draft. Those who had so sworn themselves were subject to arrest if they tried to vote. Indeed, some Republican leaders thought that in this and other forms of harassment Kennedy had gone too far. He was criticized by the *Times* and, after one suit for false arrest, censured by the Police Commissioners at a departmental trial. So close was the relation between Kennedy and the Lincoln administration that Kennedy and his detectives were used by Republicans in Washington to investigate a rumored assassination plot against Lincoln in Baltimore in January 1861, on the eve of the inauguration.

151   *Tribune*, July 15, 1863; Opdyke, *Official Documents*, p. 271. The Mayor had a financial interest in the armory, a fact that was widely known.

152   Cook, *Armies of the Streets*, p. 101.

153   Barnes, *Draft Riots*, p. 65.

154   Ibid., pp. 87–8.

155   Ibid., pp. 88; *Tribune*, July 15, 1863.

156   Cook, *Armies of the Streets*, p. 102.

157   *Times*, Oct. 21, 1863 ("Fires during the Riots").

158   *Bloody Week!*, p. 28; *Tribune*, July 31, 1863; Cook, *Armies of the Streets*, pp. 126–7; Walling, *Recollections of a New York Chief of Police*, pp. 81–2, on the "Battle of the Barricades."

159   See Appendix A, "Uptown Social Geography, 1863." See Friedrich Engels, "The June Revolution," in Karl Marx and Friedrich Engels, *The Revolution of 1848–49: Articles from the Neue Rheinische Zeitung* (New York, 1972), pp. 50–9, for a discussion of where Parisian workers drew their class boundaries when the barricades went up in June 1848.

160   *Herald*, July 16, 1863.

161   Ibid., July 17, 1863.

162   While many industrial workers in the metal trades lived and worked on the Upper West Side, the Upper East Side could more properly be called an industrial factory district. See note 134, above, on the Upper West Side. According to one student of the nineteenth-century West Side, "only one large factory, the Higgins Carpet Factory, was in operation down to war time." Otho G. Cartwright, *The Middle West Side: A Historical Sketch* (New York, 1914), pp. 33. There were, in fact, a fair number of metalworking and machine-building factories on the West Side above Twenty-sixth Street during the Civil War years. By contrast, the Eighteenth, Twenty-first, and particularly the Eleventh wards on the Upper East Side were better characterized as industrial worker wards, where large factories devoted to metallurgy were concentrated. Quarrymen, street pavers, and other common laborers did live and work alongside the factory workers of the East Side (though, notably, few longshoremen). But more than the West Side, the Upper East Side featured clusters of large metallurgical establishments along its waterfront. The congregation of huge factories at the northeastern end of the Eleventh Ward, drawing on a vast labor pool of metalworkers residing in the low-income districts along the Upper East Side waterfront, had no counterpart on the West Side.

  Metal-trades workers were frequent participants in Upper East Side riot incidents through the week. See esp. Case of John Leavy and John Leavy, Jr., Indictments, Oct. 1863, Case of Thomas Sutherland, Indictments, Aug. 1863, MARC, and discussion of Twenty-second Street prisoners, below.

163   Evidence that some East Side rioters regarded Catholic identity as grounds for acquitting individuals of whose political loyalties they were uncertain can be found in Leonard, *Three Days' Reign of Terror*, 19.

164   Upper East Side rioters tended to live within a few blocks of their targets. Soldiers later found stolen arms from the Union Steam Works in surrounding tenements on Twenty-second Street and belongings from Colonel Henry O'Brien's gutted Thirty-fourth Street home in the adjacent tenements on that block. See Alan N. Burstein, "Immigrants and Residential Mobility: The Irish and Germans in Philadelphia, 1850–1880," and other essays emphasizing the importance of the

"journey to work" to the experience of nineteenth-century urban workers, in Theodore Hershberg, ed., *Philadelphia: Work, Space, Family and Group Experience in the Nineteenth Century* (New York, 1981). Burstein notes the high residential concentration of Irish and German industrial workers around the factories where they worked. See discussion of New York's factory districts, Bernstein, *The New York City Draft Riots*. 3.

On women's use of the phrase "die at home" on the Upper East Side as "a favorite watch-word," see Leonard, *Three Days' Reign of Terror*, p. 7.

165 *Daily News*, July 17, 1863.
166 Barnes, *Draft Riots*, p. 56.
167 *Weekly Caucasian*, July 25, 1863; *Daily News*, July 17, 1863.
168 *Tribune*, July 17, 1863.
169 Cook, *Armies of the Streets*, pp. 160–2; *Evening Express*, July 17, 1863.
170 Leonard, *Three Days' Reign of Terror*, pp. 16–20.
171 Cook, *Armies of the Streets*, p. 162.
172 Letter of Henry M. Congdon to his Father (Charles Congdon, Esq.?), July 17, 1863, Misc. Mss., NYHS.
173 *Herald*, July 18, 1863.
174 *Daily News*, July 18, 1863.
175 Ibid., July 17, 1863.
176 Ibid.
177 These were Thomas Lube, molder, residing at 131 E. 22nd St., and James Smith blacksmith, 128 E. 22nd St. See *Times*, July 18, 1863 ("Rioters Arrested").
178 Employees on the Upper West Side had returned to work by 2 p.m. Thursday, East Side shipyards and factories remained closed at least until Friday morning. *Daily News*, July 17, 1863.
179 See Bernstein, *The New York City Draft Riots*, Chapter 3, for a discussion of the labor movement of 1863.
180 *Tribune*, July 23, 1863; *Fincher's Trades Review*, July 25, 1863 (Keady's letter).
181 *Times*, July 14, 1863 (Germans organizing to protect property late Monday); *Tribune*, July 15, 1863 (some Germans rioting on Tuesday); *Herald*, July 17, 1863 ("Meeting in the Seventeenth Ward").
182 *Herald*, July 17, 1863 ("Germans of Division Street"); *Strong Diary*, III:343 (Germans of the Seventh Ward); *Tribune*, July 30, 1863 (*Schützen-verein*); Montgomery, *Beyond Equality*, p. 106 (*Turnverein*).
183 *Daily News*, July 17, 1863 ("Peace Democrats of the Thirteenth Ward").

Questions to consider

- What were some of the underlying causes that seem to have sparked the riots? How legitimate do you think the various grievances were?

- How important a factor was racism?

- Describe the role of immigrants in this event. Can one generalize among, or within, particular ethnic groups?

- Toward the end of this piece, Bernstein notes that "the revolt was mainly the doing of wage earners accustomed to considerable control over the conduct of their jobs." What might such an observation suggest about the impact of the Civil War in American life generally? (In answering this question, you might also consider Philip Paludan's essay in Part V of this book.)

Chapter 19

Resistance: Primary Sources

Opinion on the Draft

Abraham Lincoln

When the Civil War began, Lincoln asked for volunteers to serve for three months in what he assumed would be a short war, and the response was enthusiastic. After that, volunteer recruitment was done on a statewide level with a generally satisfactory yield. But by mid-war, the supply of enthusiastic enlistees had dried up, and while Lincoln had authorized the recruitment of African-Americans, whose presence would have a real impact on Union military strength, this asset alone was not sufficient. That's why he signed the Conscription Act of 1863. Lincoln knew that the measure was unpopular, and in response drew up this document. He discussed it with his cabinet, but it was never made public.

Abraham Lincoln, "Opinion on the Draft" (September 14, 1863).

It is at all times proper that misunderstanding between the public and the public servant should be avoided; and this is far more important now, than in times of peace and tranquility. I therefore address you without searching for a precedent upon which to do so. Some of you are sincerely devoted to the republican institutions, and territorial integrity of our country, and yet are opposed to what is called the draft, or conscription.

At the beginning of the war, and ever since, a variety of motives pressing, some in one direction and some in the other, would be presented to the mind of each man physically fit for a soldier, upon the combined effect of which motives, he would, or would not, voluntarily enter the service. Among these motives would be patriotism, political bias, ambition, personal courage, love of adventure, want of employment, and convenience, or the opposites of some of these. We already have, and have had in the service, as appears, substantially all that can be obtained upon this voluntary weighing of motives. And yet we must somehow obtain more, or relinquish the original object of the contest, together with all the blood and treasure already expended in the effort to secure it. To meet this necessity the law for the draft has been enacted. You who do not wish to be soldiers, do not like this law. This is natural; nor does it imply want of patriotism. Nothing can be so just, and necessary, as to make us like it, if it is disagreeable to us. We are prone, too, to find false arguments with which to excuse ourselves for opposing such disagreeable things. In this case those who desire the rebellion to succeed, and others who seek reward in a different way, are very active in accomodating us with this class of arguments. They tell us the law is unconstitutional. It is the first instance, I believe, in which the power of congress to do a thing has ever been questioned, in a case when the power is given by the constitution in express terms. Whether a power can be implied, when it is not expressed, has often been the subject of controversy; but this is the first case in which the degree of effrontery has been ventured upon, of denying a power which is plainly and distinctly written down in the constitution. The constitution declares that "The congress shall have power . . . To raise and support armies; but no appropriation of money to that use shall be for a longer term than two years." The whole scope of the conscription act is "to raise and support armies." There is nothing else in it. It makes no appropriation of money; and hence the money clause just quoted, is not touched by it. The case simply is the constitution provides that the congress shall have power to raise and support armies; and, by this act, the congress has exercised the power to raise and support armies. This is the whole of it. It is a law made in litteral pursuance of this part of the United States Constitution; and another part of the same constitution declares that "This constitution, and the laws made in pursuance thereof . . . shall be the supreme law of the land, and the judges in every state shall be bound thereby, anything in the constitution or laws of any state to the contrary notwithstanding."

Do you admit that the power is given to raise and support armies, and yet insist that by this act congress has not exercised the power in a constitutional mode? – has not done the thing, in the right way? Who is to judge of this? The constitution gives congress the power, but it does not prescribe the mode, or expressly declare who shall prescribe it. In such case congress must prescribe the mode, or relinquish the power. There is no alternative. Congress could not exercise the power to do the thing, if it had not the power of providing a way to do it, when no way is provided by the constitution for doing it. In fact congress would not have the power to raise and support armies, if even by the constitution, it were left to the option of any other, or others, to give or withhold the only mode of doing it. If the constitution had prescribed a mode, congress could and must follow that mode; but as it is, the mode necessarily goes to congress, with the power expressly given. The power is given fully, completely, unconditionally. It is not a power to raise armies *if* State authorities consent; nor *if* the men to compose the armies are entirely willing; but it is a power to raise and support armies given to congress by the constitution, without an if.

It is clear that a constitutional law may not be expedient or proper. Such would be a law to raise armies when no armies were needed. But this is not such. The republican institutions, and territorial integrity of our country can not be maintained without the further raising and supporting of armies. There can be no army without men. Men can be had only voluntarily, or involuntarily. We have ceased to obtain them voluntarily; and to obtain them involuntarily, is the draft – the conscription. If you dispute the fact, and declare that men can still be had voluntarily in sufficient numbers prove the assertion by yourselves volunteering in such numbers, and I shall gladly give up the draft. Or if not a sufficient number, but any one of you will volunteer, he for his single self, will escape all the horrors of the draft; and will thereby do only what each one of at least a million of his manly brethren have already done. Their toil and blood have been given as much for you as for themselves. Shall it all be lost rather than you too, will bear your part?

I do not say that all who would avoid serving in the war, are unpatriotic; but I do think every patriot should willingly take his chance under a law made with great care in order to secure entire fairness. This law was considered, discussed, modified, and amended, by congress, at great length, and with much labor; and was finally passed, by both branches, with a near approach to unanimity. At last, it may not be exactly such as any one man out of congress, or even in congress, would have made it. It has been said, and I believe truly, that the constitution itself is not altogether such as any one of it's framers would have preferred. It was the joint work of all; and certainly the better that it was so.

Much complaint is made of that provision of the conscription law which allows a drafted man to substitute three hundred dollars for himself; while, as I believe, none is made of that provision which allows him to substitute another man for himself. Nor is the three hundred dollar provision objected to for unconstitutionality; but for inequality – for favoring the rich against the poor. The substitution of men is the provision if any, which favors the rich to the exclusion of the poor. But this being a provision in accordance with an old and well known practice, in the raising of armies, is not objected to. There would have been great objection if that provision had been omitted. And yet being in, the money provision really modifies the inequality which the other introduces. It allows men to escape the service, who are too poor to escape but for it. Without the money provision, competition among the more wealthy might, and probably would, raise the price of substitutes above three hundred dollars, thus leaving the man who could raise only three hundred dollars, no escape from personal service. True, by the law as it is, the man who can not raise so much as three hundred dollars, nor obtain a personal substitute for less, can not escape; but he can come quite as near escaping as he could if the money provision were not in the law. To put it another way, is an unobjectionable law which allows only the man to escape who can pay a thousand dollars, made objectionable by adding a provision that any one may escape who can pay the smaller sum of three hundred dollars? This is the exact difference at this point between the present law and all former draft laws. It is true that by this law a some what larger number will escape than could under a law allowing personal substitutes only; but each additional man thus escaping will be a poorer man than could have escaped by the law in the other form. The money provision enlarges the class of exempts from actual service simply by admitting poorer men into it. How, then can this money provision be a wrong to the poor man? The inequality complained of pertains in greater degree to the substitution of men, and is really modified and lessened by the money provision. The inequality could only be perfectly cured by sweeping both provisions away. This being a great innovation, would probably leave the law more distasteful than it now is.

The principle of the draft, which simply is involuntary, or enforced service, is not new. It has been practiced in all ages of the world. It was well known to the framers of our constitution as one of the modes of raising armies, at the time they placed in that instrument the provision that "the congress shall have power to raise and support armies." It has been used, just before, in establishing our independence; and it was also used under the constitution in 1812. Wherein is the peculiar hardship now? Shall we shrink from the necessary means to maintain our free government, which our grand-fathers employed to establish it, and our own fathers have already employed once to maintain it? Are we degenerate? Has the manhood of our race run out?

Again, a law may be both constitutional and expedient, and yet may be administered in an unjust and unfair way. This law belongs to a class, which class is composed of those laws whose object is to distribute burthens or benefits on the principle of equality. No one of these laws can ever be practically administered with that exactness which can be conceived of in the mind. A tax law, the principle of which is that each owner shall pay in proportion to the value of his property, will be a dead letter, if no one can be compelled to pay until it can be shown that every other one will pay in precisely the same proportion according to value; nay even, it will be a dead letter, if no one can be compelled to pay until it is certain that every other one will pay at all – even in unequal proportion. Again the United States House of representatives is constituted on the principle that each member is sent by the same number of people that each other one is sent by; and yet in practice no two of the whole number, much less the whole number, are ever sent by precisely the same number of constituents. The Districts can not be made precisely equal in population at first, and if they could, they would become unequal in a single day, and much more so in the ten years, which the Districts, once made, are to continue. They can not be re-modelled every day; nor, without too much expence and labor, even every year.

This sort of difficulty applies in full force, to the practical administration of the draft law. In fact the difficulty is greater in the case of the draft law. First, it starts with all the inequality of the congressional Districts; but these are based on entire population, while the draft is based upon those only who are fit for soldiers, and such may not bear the same proportion to the whole in one District, that they do in another. Again, the facts must be ascertained, and credit given, for the unequal numbers of soldiers which have already gone from the several Districts. In all these points errors will occur in spite of the utmost fidelity. The government is bound to administer the law with such an approach to exactness as is usual in analogous cases, and as entire good faith and fidelity will reach. If so great departures as to be inconsistent with such good faith and fidelity, or great departures occurring in any way, be pointed out, they shall be corrected; and any agent shown to have caused such departures intentionally, shall be dismissed.

With these views, and on these principles, I feel bound to tell you it is my purpose to see the draft law faithfully executed.

Questions to consider

- How would you describe the tone of this document? Do you consider it persuasive?

- Evaluate the logic Lincoln uses in addressing those who oppose the draft for reasons relating to class, and those who oppose it for reasons relating to race (i.e. emancipation).

- Can you speculate on why this document was never released to the public? Do you think it should have been?

- The United States military suspended its peacetime draft in 1973, and the military has been comprised solely of volunteers ever since. What are the strengths and weaknesses of such an arrangement?

Letter to Henry Fowler

Adelaide Fowler

In this letter to her brother Henry, Adelaide Fowler of Daversport, MA, describes her feelings about draft (there were also riots over it in nearby Boston at this time). How would you summarize her position? Do you agree with it?

Adelaide Fowler, "Letter to Henry Fowler" (July 1863, Daversport, MA), in *Yankee Correspondence; Civil War Letters Between New England Soldiers and the Home Front*, eds. Nina Silber and Mary Beth Sievens (Charlottesville: University of Virginia Press, 1996), p. 120. Reprinted by permission of The Phillips Library at the Peabody Essex Museum.

I am glad that the draft has taken place only it had ought to before now for one man ought to go as well as another. Now it is high time for people to show their patriotism if they have any; of course there are some cases when there has been two or three drafted from one family that are hard but the majority are wise dispensations of Providence. Every man ought to feel willing to do something for this war and I wish it was so. A great many persons think that spending their breath in useless word is all that *they* ought to do and leave the work for others to do you ask them who and they say negroes. The draft has brought a few of such persons out, they must send their sons or sacrifice three hundred dollars (not half enough) and this is the reason why I think the draft is doing good. . . .

Part IX

War on the Frontier

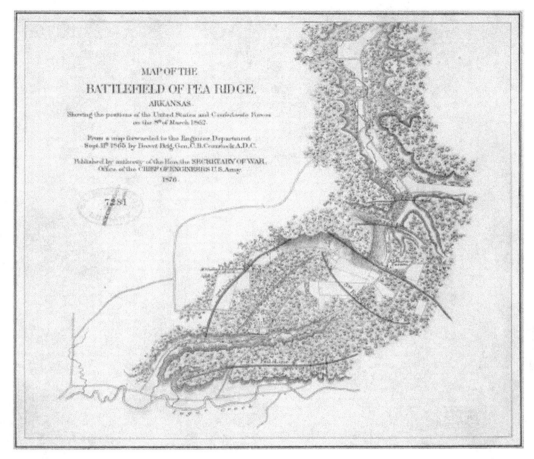

Plate 11 Red Record: An 1876 map of the battlefield of Pea Ridge, Arkansas, showing the positions of the United States and Confederate forces on March 8, 1862. Pea Ridge, a failed Confederate offensive that involved Native American troops, showed that the Civil War was not simply a black-and-white affair. (Geography and Map Division, Library of Congress)

Chapter 20

The Way to Pea Ridge

Alvin M. Josephy, Jr.

When most people think of the Civil War, they think of famous places that were either strategic objectives or sites of famous battles: Gettysburg, Richmond, Appomattox, Atlanta. It is not insignificant that all four of these places are east of the Mississippi River. At the time and ever since, some observers have been chagrined at how obsessed Americans have been with the war in the East, when, they believe, it was actually won and lost in the West. There is a great deal of truth to this view.

There is also a great deal of truth in the assertion, noted earlier, that the American war started well before 1861, and did so on the frontier of "Bleeding Kansas," where partisan fighting between pro-slavery "Bushwackers" and anti-slavery "Jayhawkers" dates back to the mid-1850s. Nor did the war actually end at Appomattox; fighting continued sporadically elsewhere around the country; the last recorded combat death took place in Palmito, Texas, in May 1865. The engagement was a Confederate victory.

There is one other misleading perception worth addressing here: that the Civil War – that American race relations generally – has been a black-and-white affair. In fact, at the very moment the nation was torn from within, both sides were navigating relations with Native Americans in ways that ranged from alliances to open warfare. And Native Americans themselves debated – and sometimes fought – among themselves about which side, if any, to take.

Nowhere does this intersection between the strategic significance of the frontier and the strategic significance of red–white relations come into sharper focus than at the Battle of Pea Ridge, in March 1862. A 16,000-man force under the leadership of Confederate general Earl Van Dorn, based in northwestern Arkansas, hoped to invade Missouri, a slave state under (somewhat tenuous) Union control. To do so, however, the rebels had to overcome a smaller Federal army of 11,000 under the command of Samuel R. Curtis, which was situated near the Arkansas–Missouri border. Some of Van Dorn's numerical advantage came from three regiments of the Five Nations, mostly Cherokee, in modern-day Oklahoma. The Five Nations hoped that a Confederate victory would give them more autonomy than they enjoyed under the Federal government.

The hopes of both sides in this alliance proved unfounded (the resulting battle was a resounding Union victory that sealed Missouri, and thus much of the Midwest, from Confederate offensives). But as Alvin Josephy, Jr. shows in this chapter excerpt from his highly regarded 1991 book *The Civil War in the American West*, the road to Pea Ridge was, literally and figuratively, a fascinating Confederate detour through Indian territory.

Alvin M. Josephy, Jr., "The Way to Pea Ridge," in *The Civil War in the American West* (New York: Alfred A. Knopf, 1991), pp. 319–30. Copyright © 1991 by Alvin M. Josephy, Jr. Used by permission of Alfred A. Knopf, a division of Random House, Inc.

On the cold, wintry morning of March 7, 1862, in the northwestern corner of the border state of Arkansas, blue-coated troops of Iowa and Missouri cavalry, in advance of a large Union force, emerged from a patch of scrubby woods and three hundred yards away, across an open prairie, sighted a mass of Confederate horsemen. In the clear air, the distant thunder and crashing of cannon fire and musketry rolled toward them across the hills and hollows from the opposite side of the heights of Pea Ridge, where the battle was already joined. Now it would open on this second front.

The officer in command of the Federal column, Prussian-born Colonel Peter J. Osterhaus from St. Louis, moved quickly, ordering three guns of Captain G. M. Elbert's 1st Missouri Flying Battery to move out of the woods and disperse the rebels. As the gunners' shells exploded across the clearing, Osterhaus maneuvered his cavalry into position for a charge against the Southerners.

The Confederates beat him to it. With a sudden wild yell, intermingled with war whoops, they headed across the open ground, most of them on ponies, but some dismounted and running, straight toward the artillery battery. In an instant of impressions – of painted faces and long, glistening black hair, of owl and chicken-hawk feathers stuck in floppy-brimmed wool hats and colored-cloth turbans, of moccasined feet, bows and arrows, tomahawks, and flashing knives, and, above all, of the howling, screaming war cries – the Federals realized that most of the fierce mob coming at them were Indians.

Osterhaus tried to get the 5th Missouri Cavalry to countercharge and break up the attack, but the members of that unit were too panic-stricken to move. The next moment, the Indians and a squadron of Texas horsemen who had charged with them swarmed over Elbert's battery and drove the Union gunners and cavalry into headlong retreat. The Confederate charge halted at the guns. Ignoring the rebels' commanding officer, Brigadier General Albert Pike, a puffing, unmilitary-looking man of almost 300 pounds with long, flowing locks and the beard of a prophet, who roared at them in vain to keep after the enemy, the Indians pranced in triumph around the captured battery, whooping excitedly, and mounting the cannons as if they were horses. Some piled up straw from a nearby wheat field and set the gun carriages on fire. In the confusion of smoke and flames, shells in the ammunition chests exploded, killing and maiming some of the Indians.

In twenty minutes, the tables had turned. Osterhaus regrouped and, opening fire from the woods with another of his batteries, drove Pike and the Indians back across the field and into some trees near where they had begun their charge. Some of the Indians managed to retrieve and hold on to the captured artillery pieces, though they were unable to use them.

The Indians did little more to help the Confederate cause during the two days of intense fighting at Pea Ridge. But the charge against Elbert's battery on the first morning led to a scandal that brought condemnation of the Indians and besmirched the name and reputation of their commander, Albert Pike, for the rest of his life. The Arkansas battle, perhaps the most decisive of the Civil War in the Trans-Mississippi West, was a Federal victory, hurling back the Confederacy's last serious threat to Missouri and saving that state for the Union. It came at a time when the North, frustrated by General McClellan's inaction in Virginia, had little else to cheer about. But the good feelings were mixed with rage and horror. Not only had the Confederates used Indians – Cherokees from the Indian Territory – against the Northern troops, but the tribesmen, according to the Union commander, Brigadier General Samuel R. Curtis, had scalped, tomahawked, and mutilated the bodies of Federal wounded and dead during and after the fighting around Elbert's battery. "The warfare," Curtis would later say, "was conducted by said savages with all the barbarity their merciless and cowardly natures are capable of."[1]

The charges of scalping and mutilation were true. "From personal inspection," officers of the 3d Iowa Cavalry, one of the Northern units near the guns, reported finding the bodies of eight members of their regiment that had been scalped and others that had been riddled with musket balls or mutilated with knives.[2] Pike himself was horrified on the second day of the battle to discover that some of the Indians in his command had taken scalps as trophies. "Angry and disgusted," he had at once issued a general order, stating that he had seen an Indian killing a wounded man and knew that scalping had been done, and prohibiting both practices – which he knew were common and accepted in Indian warfare – as "inhuman and barbarous." A copy of the order, he said, was sent "by flag of truce to General Curtis, who acknowledged its receipt."[3]

Far from helping Pike, his attempt at forthrightness, corroborating Curtis's charges, fed the hue and cry that the North raised against him, particularly in the press and by sensationalist pamphleteers. Claiming that the Indians had scalped 100 Union soldiers at Pea Ridge, the Chicago *Tribune* told its readers that, as their commanding officer, Pike "deserves and will undoubtedly receive eternal infamy." The Boston *Evening Transcript*, not content with listing Pike among "the meanest, the most rascally, the most malevolent of the rebels who are at war with the United States Government," added that it was "not to be presumed that a more venemous [sic] reptile than Albert Pike ever crawled on the face of the earth." Referring to him as the leader of "the Aboriginal Corps of Tomahawkers and Scalpers at the battle of Pea Ridge," the New York *Tribune* played on Pike's name to call him "a ferocious fish" and guessed that "upon the recent occasion, he got himself up in good style, war-paint, nose-ring, and all." Less restrained was a pamphlet whose writer reported luridly that before the battle Pike had "maddened" the Indians with liquor "to fire their savage natures, and, with gaudy dress and a large plume on his head, disregarding all the usages of civilized warfare, led them in a carnage of savagery, scalping wounded and helpless soldiers, and committing other atrocities too horrible to mention."[4]

The fifty-two-year-old Pike, in truth, was a great friend of the Indians, knowledgeable about them, and, as a prewar frontier lawyer who had represented them in legal matters, experienced in dealing with their chiefs and councils. Moreover, he was not above wearing Indian dress, appearing from time to time in leggings, moccasins, and even feathered headdresses of the plains Indians. Born in Boston, he had come West as a youth, and after an adventurous tour among Indians in the Southwest, had settled in Arkansas. Although he had been a captain in the Mexican War, he was anything but military-minded. In addition to having had a flamboyant career in the law, he was a poet, a journalist, a successful planter, and a scholar versed in many languages, including Latin, Greek, Sanskrit, and a number of Indian tongues. Eccentric, physically mountainous, and with a conceit to match his size, he had become a legendary figure in Arkansas, the protagonist of tales that dealt with his gluttony and with such idiosyncrasies as his hiring a brass band to follow him about on his backwoods legal circuits to soothe his nerves after busy court sessions. A romantic, also, who found inspiration in the works of Shelley and Keats and tried to emulate them with his own compositions on love and nature, he had little regard for the regulations and protocols of others. When he thought he was right, which was generally always, he could be maddeningly contentious and independent. But he knew Indians, and after the start of the war, the Richmond government had made him its contact with the tribes of the Indian Territory, which lay just west of Arkansas like a buffer between Confederate Texas and Union Kansas.

Even before the outbreak of hostilities, the seceded states had recognized the geographic importance of the Indian Territory to the Confederacy's western flank. A month before the attack on Fort Sumter, Robert Toombs, Jefferson Davis's Secretary of State, had proposed sending a special agent to the Territory to secure for the Southern government the friendship of its Indian inhabitants, particularly of the powerful Five Civilized Tribes, the Cherokees, Creeks, Chickasaws, Choctaws, and Seminoles, who had been forced to remove there in the 1830s from the Southeast.

As the attorney for several of the tribes, Pike had had somewhat the same idea as Toombs, and shortly afterward, with the help of one of Arkansas's Confederate Senators, he had won appointment by Richmond as a special commissioner to deal with the tribes of the Indian Territory. Late in May 1861, he had hoisted his massive frame into a buggy and, at the head of a long line of wagons laden with potted foods, cases of wine, and assorted goods for the Indians, had set off for the Territory, authorized by the Confederacy to spend $100,000 for treaties of alliance with the tribes.

[. . .]

Pike found the Five Civilized Tribes torn with unrest and internal dissension. Ever since they had moved West, each had been divided by bitter feuds between those who had agreed to their removal from their ancient southeastern homelands and those who had opposed and resisted it. Each, also, had experienced angry divisions between their full-bloods, who maintained many of their traditional customs, and the more "progressive" mixed-bloods, who, after long exposure to missionaries, schools, and white society in the Southeast, had become culturally more like Southern whites than Indians.

In the years since the tribes' arrival in the Territory, the feuds had begun to subside, and the Indians had created efficient, white-styled governments, thriving economies, and their own school systems and public institutions. With their five domains spread across 70,000 square miles of woodland and prairie, their combined population of fewer than 100,000 had benefited from an abundance of rich agricultural and grazing land, protected against white intrusion and guaranteed to them by the United States government. Able to develop their fertile, well-watered resources in peace, many of the mixed-bloods had become affluent plantation owners and raisers of livestock, possessing black slaves and living like prosperous whites elsewhere in the South.

The Civil War, Pike discovered, had revived their old internal strife. Joined by Ben McCulloch, he called first on John Ross, the seventy-year-old Principal Chief of the Cherokees, whose porticoed mansion, named Rose Cottage – though it could house forty guests – stood in stately dignity at the end of a half-mile-long driveway at Park Hill, near the Cherokee capital at Tahlequah. Ross had already received soundings concerning the Cherokees' sympathies from Arkansas's secessionist governor, Henry Rector, as well as from McCulloch. The Indians' country was "looked to by the incoming Administration of Mr. Lincoln, as fruitful fields ripe for the harvest of abolitionism, freesoilers, and Northern mountebanks,"

Rector had warned Ross, urging that the Cherokees ally themselves with "the common brotherhood of the slaveholding states."[5] McCulloch had made similar overtures, informing Ross of his appointment to guard the Indian Territory from invasion by the North and proposing the formation of Home Guard units by pro-Confederate Cherokees. To both men, Ross had replied that his tribe would continue to observe the treaties it had made with the Federal government, but would take no part in the white men's quarrel.

Fearing that an occupation of the Indians' lands against their will would drive the tribes into the Union's arms, McCulloch had backed away and established his headquarters at Fort Smith, Arkansas, on the eastern border of the Territory. There, he had busied himself with preparations for the defense of northwestern Arkansas, waiting for the Louisiana, Arkansas, and Texas regiments that had been promised him, and at the same time keeping a watchful eye on the Indians' country. The arrival of Pike in May had given him a new opportunity to put pressure on the Cherokees.

Standing only five and a half feet tall, Ross repeated to McCulloch and Pike the tribe's determination to remain neutral. But the wealthy and dignified chief also faced a dilemma. Despite a political craftiness that had kept him in the leadership of the 21,000 Cherokees since 1828, he was caught uncomfortably between two factions of the tribe that had already chosen sides in the Civil War. Although Ross was only one-eighth Cherokee himself and worked his fields with 100 slaves, he headed the tribe's majority element that was composed mostly of non-slave-owning full-bloods, who years before had resisted removal from the Southeast. Many of them were known as Pin Cherokees – for crossed pins that they wore on their coats or shirts as a sign of their membership in a secret full-blood traditionalist society sponsored by missionaries. Because of the missionaries' influence, the Pins were zealously abolitionist and sympathetic to the North.

Opposed to them was a group of pro-Confederate Cherokees, principally slave-owning mixed-bloods. Composed largely of members of families who had favored removal to the West in the 1830s, they were led by fifty-five-year-old Stand Watie, a longtime rival and enemy of Ross and the lone Indian survivor of those who had signed the treaty with the government agreeing to give up the Cherokee homeland in the East. Ross's angry followers had assassinated the other three signers, one of whom was Watie's famous brother, Elias Boudinot. Well educated at Moravian mission schools in Tennessee, and successful as a planter in the new lands in the Indian Territory, Watie was short and stocky, with legs bowed from years on horseback. Visiting whites described him as "looking Indian," which may have referred to his wide, flat face, broad nose, and swarthy complexion or to his "deep and thoughtful" manner. He spoke little, and when he did, it was usually brief, explosive, and to the point. Three-quarters Cherokee, he had already thrown in with the South and, on his own, was raising and drilling a force of mixed-blood Cherokee horsemen to assist the Confederacy.

Fearful of Watie, Ross was concerned that the Confederates might oust him from office and put Watie in his place as Principal Chief. At the same time, he was afraid of the consequences of supporting Watie and breaking the Cherokees' treaties with the United States government. It would mean forfeiting millions of dollars that Washington held in trust for the tribe, as well as alienating his full-blood Pin supporters who kept him in office. Under the circumstances, the best he could do was to continue to insist on the tribe's neutrality and watch developments.

Angered by Ross's rebuff, McCulloch returned to Fort Smith, warning the chief that if a Northern invasion of the Indian Territory seemed imminent, "I will at once advance into your country, if I deem it advisable."[6] At the same time, both McCulloch and Pike were aware of the pro-Confederate force that Watie was raising, and, pleased at least by knowledge of that support, Pike accepted Ross's decision for the time being and left Tahlequah on June 6.

Traveling south across the Arkansas River, he met next with the Creek Indians, discovering again that the feuds of removal days had been revived and that the Creeks were even more bitterly divided than the Cherokees.

The faction of the tribe that had resisted removal from the East followed wealthy Chief Opothleyahola, a fierce traditionalist full-blood now about eighty years old, who was strongly anti-South and loyal to the Washington government. An opposing element of acculturated mixed-bloods, who had formally agreed to removal from their Georgia and Alabama homes and now favored the slave states, was led by Principal Chief Motey Kennard and Daniel N. and Chilly McIntosh, half brothers and the sons of a pro-removal leader whom Opothleyahola's followers had slain as a traitor. Tension, bordering on an open break and violence, existed between the two factions, but Pike found the McIntosh brothers eager to raise a pro-Southern Creek regiment. On July 10, he signed a treaty with them, providing that the McIntoshes' Creek unit would have to fight only within the borders of the Indian Territory and promising that the Confederacy would help defend them with white troops if they were attacked.

Two days later, Pike had a more successful meeting with representatives of the Chickasaws and Choctaws, who lived in the southern part of the Territory, close to the Red River border with Texas. Under the influence of their pro-Confederate Indian agent, Colonel Douglas H. Cooper, an ambitious, strong-willed Mississippian and a friend of Jefferson Davis, the two tribes had already announced their support of the seceding states and had agreed to form a mounted rifle regiment to be led by Cooper. The spokesmen for both tribes quickly signed a treaty with Pike, making their regiment available for service on behalf of the Confederacy in the Indian Territory.

Going on to the Seminoles' country, Pike again found dissension. Those Indians, who had been exiled forcibly to the Territory from the Florida swamps, were as divided among themselves as their Creek neighbors. Maintaining a disinterest in the North-South conflict, Billy Bowlegs, Alligator, and other traditionalist town chiefs stayed aloof from Pike. An influential headman and ordained minister named John Jumper, however, was pro-South and agreed to enlist Seminoles to join the McIntoshes' Creek regiment.

In high spirits, Pike then set off for the western part of the Territory to try to gain the friendship of the "wild" tribes of the plains. Escorted by his new allies, Motey Kennard, Chilly McIntosh, and John Jumper, and a mounted bodyguard of 60 Creek and Seminole Indians flying a Confederate flag and an array of colored pennants, he met at the Wichita Agency near Fort Cobb with Tonkawas, Caddos, Wacos, and other Indians who had recently been removed from Texas to the Indian Territory, as well as with Wichitas and a large number of chiefs and headmen of bands of buffalo-hunting Comanches. The Indians came willingly to his feasts and, in return for lavish presents of guns, ammunition, saddles, hats, coffee, and tobacco and promises of annual disbursements of rations, livestock, tools, sugar, and other goods, agreed to put themselves "in peace and war forever" under the laws and protection of the Confederate States of America, the Comanches, in addition, promising to end their raids in Texas.[7] Although the Indians "touched the pen" to the treaties, they were largely indifferent to the white men's war, and their agreements did not commit them to overt action in support of the Confederacy. Nevertheless, Pike was pleased by the Comanches' promise to end their hostilities against the Texas frontier settlements, and for a year the signatory chiefs more or less observed that agreement.

At Tahlequah, meanwhile, John Ross had had second thoughts. For one thing, Stand Watie's force of pro-Southern Cherokees had become a menacing reality. Impatient with Ross, Ben McCulloch had commissioned Watie a colonel in the Confederate Provisional Army, and Watie was formally organizing his regiment of mixed-blood followers to stand watch over the northeastern part of the Indian Territory against Union forces from Kansas and destroy anything that might be of service to the enemy. At the same time, Pike's treaties with Indian leaders were isolating Ross from the other tribes. Finally, to the worried Cherokee Principal Chief, the Confederates now appeared to be winning the war. In the East, they had beaten the Federals at Bull Run and were even threatening to take Washington, DC. On August 10, closer to the Cherokees' country, McCulloch, now leading the Arkansas, Louisiana, and Texas regiments that had been promised him, and General Sterling Price, the commander of Missouri's pro-Southern State Guard, had combined their forces at Wilson's Creek in Missouri and defeated the Union Army in that state. The Federal general, Nathaniel Lyon, had been killed, and his shattered troops had retreated north. To Ross, flanked on the east by Confederates in control of Arkansas and southern Missouri, the prospect of being able to reestablish relations with Washington – which had shown little interest or ability in maintaining contact with the tribes of the Indian Territory – seemed dashed forever.

Aware that events were strengthening the hand of Watie and the pro-Confederate mixed-bloods within his tribe, Ross decided to act. At a mass meeting on August 21 at Tahlequah, the canny chief undercut Watie by persuading the tribe to authorize negotiations for a treaty of alliance with the Confederacy. "The State on our border [Arkansas] and the Indian Nations about us," he told the Cherokees, "have severed their connection with the United States and joined the Confederate States. Our general interest is inseparable from theirs and it is not desirable that we should stand alone."[8] Reluctantly, the full-bloods agreed to his proposal to ask Pike to return to Tahlequah and to offer him the service of a Cherokee regiment of Home Guards, to be led by Colonel John Drew, a loyal Ross follower.

Elated by Ross's change of heart, Pike hurried back to Tahlequah. On October 7, with Drew's mounted recruits, mostly full-blood Pin Cherokees, and some of Watie's mixed-blood horsemen lined up uneasily together, Pike signed a treaty of alliance with the Cherokee Nation. The agreement provided that the Confederates would assume the Federal government's financial obligations to the tribe and would seat a Cherokee delegate in the Confederate Congress in Richmond. As in the other treaties, Pike promised that the Cherokees would not be called upon to fight unless their lands in the Indian Territory were invaded, in which event they could count on protection by white troops of the Confederate Army. At Tahlequah, Pike also signed treaties with groups of Osage, Quapaw, Seneca, and Shawnee Indians, whose leaders, at Pike's request, Ross had summoned to the Cherokee capital from the northeast section of the Indian Territory, where the Federal government had previously resettled them after dispossessing them of their original homelands.

Grateful for the success of his mission, the Confederates appointed Pike a brigadier general and in November put him in charge of the Indian troops as commander of the Department of Indian Territory. Although worn out by his labors, he prepared to go to Richmond to oversee the ratification of his treaties and to secure funds for the treaty obligations and for the equipping of the Indian regiments. On the eve of his departure from Fort Smith, he received distressing messages that fighting had broken out in the Indian Territory between the Confederate and Union factions of the Creek Indians.

Notes

1   Robert Lipscomb Duncan, *Reluctant General: The Life and Times of Albert Pike*, E. P. Dutton, New York, 1961, p. 227.
2   Ibid., pp. 227–8.

3   Robert Lipscomb Duncan, *Reluctant General: The Life and Times of Albert Pike*, E. P. Dutton, New York, 1961, p. 225.
4   Ibid., pp. 228–9; Annie Heloise Abel, *The American Indian as Participant in the Civil War*, Arthur H. Clark Co., Cleveland, 1919, n. 65, p. 31.
5   *The War of the Rebellion: Official Records* . . . (hereafter cited as *O.R.*), Series I, vol. 1, pp. 683–4; see also Gary E. Moulton, ed., *The Papers of Chief John Ross*, vol. 2, University of Oklahoma Press, Norman, 1985, p. 465.
6   Wilfred Knight, *Red Fox: Stand Watie's Civil War Years in Indian Territory*, Arthur II. Clark Co., Glendale, Calif., 1988, p. 62.
7   A. M. Gibson, "Confederates on the Plains: The Pike Mission to Wichita Agency," *Great Plains Journal*, Vol. 4, No. 1 (Fall 1964), p. 10.
8   *O.R.*, I, 3, pp. 673–5; see also Moulton, *Papers of John Ross*, vol. 2, p. 481.

Questions to consider

- What words would you use to describe the process by which the Confederate government sought Native American support in the Civil War?

- How, by contrast, would you describe the struggle among Native Americans themselves to decide upon their stand in the conflict?

- Some observers at the time and since have noted an irony in a Cherokee–Confederate alliance, given that 30 years before, it had been Southerners who had driven them out of their homelands in Georgia. How plausible do you consider their choice – in particular that of Stand Watie, perhaps the most famous Native American to emerge from the conflict?

Chapter 21

War on the Frontier: Primary Sources

Account of Sioux Executions

St. Paul Pioneer Press

In August 1862, Sioux Indians in Minnesota revolted against the US government for its failure to make promised payments in exchange for Indian lands. The brief but intense struggle culminated in the suppression of the rebellion and the conviction of over 300 Sioux, who were condemned to death in trials presided over by the state's governor, who had also led Federal forces. White Minnesotans were pleased with this outcome, but President Lincoln was not – in November he asked for the court records and the following month commuted almost 90 percent of the sentences. These decisions were controversial, with settlers feeling the president was far too lenient and the Natives feeling he was still far too severe. On December 26, 1862, the government performed 38 hangings, one of the highest mass executions in American history. The following account comes from the *St. Paul Pioneer Press*. What glimpses of cultural attitudes does it reveal?

St. Paul Pioneer Press (December 26, 1862), "Hangings End Sioux Uprising" in *The Civil War Chronicle*, ed. J. M. Gallman (New York: Crown Publishers, 2000), pp. 259–60.

At precisely ten o'clock the condemned were marshaled in a procession and, headed by Captain Redfield, marched out into the street, and directly across through files of soldiers to the scaffold, which had been erected in front, and were delivered to the officer of the day, Captain Burt. They went eagerly and cheerfully, even crowding and jostling each other to be ahead, just like a lot of hungry boarders rushing to dinner in a hotel. The soldiers who were on guard in their quarters stacked arms and followed them, and they in turn, were followed by the clergy, reporters, etc.

As they commenced the ascent of the scaffold the death song was again started, and when they had all got up, the noise they made was truly hideous. It seemed as if Pandemonium had broken loose. It had a wonderful effect in keeping up their courage. . . .

The scene at this juncture was one of awful interest. A painful and breathless suspense held the vast crowd, which had assembled from all quarters to witness the execution.

Three slow, measured, and distinct beats on the drum by Major Brown, who had been announced as signal officer, and the rope was cut by Mr Duly (the same who killed Lean Bear, and whose family were attacked) – the scaffold fell, and thirty-seven lifeless bodies were left dangling between heaven and earth. One of the ropes was broken, and the body of Rattling Runner fell to the ground. The neck had probably been broken, as but little signs of life were observed; but he was immediately hung up again. While the signal-beat was being given, numbers were seen to clasp the hands of their neighbors, which in several instances continued to be clasped till the bodies were cut down.

As the platform fell, there was one, not loud, but prolonged cheer from the soldiery and citizens who were spectators, and then all were quiet and earnest witnesses of the scene.

Patriotic Iowa!

Mary A. Livermore

The outbreak of the Civil War found the Boston-born Mary Livermore in Chicago, where she co-directed the Northwestern branch of the United States Sanitary Commission. Three years later, her organizing efforts brought her to Iowa, where she helped prepare a fund-raising event. In this passage from her 1888 memoir *My Story of the War*, Livermore describes what she saw on the frontier. How would you describe this decidedly Eastern perspective on the West?

Mary A. Livermore, *My Story of the War: A Woman's Narrative* (Hartford, CT: A. D. Worthington & Co., 1888), pp. 610–12.

[. . .]

From the beginning of the war Iowa had nobly responded to the call of the country. From her sparse population she had sent forth her sons to assist in the defence of freedom and the subduing of the rebellion, until she was then twenty thousand ahead of her quota. On every battle-field Iowa men had won an imperishable name for the lofty courage with which they had contemned death. From almost every home in Iowa, wives and mothers, sisters and lovers, had surrendered to the exigencies of war those dear to them as their heart's blood. Under the call for men for the "hundred days' service," the colleges and institutions of learning had sent forth their entire senior classes, so that there was not a college Commencement that year in Iowa. And for the same reason the courts had adjourned, and all legal and United States business had been postponed for the present.

But while Iowa had contributed so nobly of her sons to the country, she had not kept pace with the other Northwestern states in the sanitary work for the relief of the sick and wounded. There had been reasons for this. A diversity of opinion as to the best methods of doing this work was probably the most potent. The sanitary supplies had largely been sent through unreliable channels, and so had failed to reach those for whom they were intended. This had brought discouragement throughout the state. But this evening meeting in the Congregational church quickened the whole state into intense activity; and in the furor which followed, she outdid her sister states, which had been longer at work.

After making arrangements at home for my absence, I spent some months in Iowa, riding in "mud-spankers," in stages, "prairie schooners," on railroads, and in every conceivable way. I held meetings, and did whatever was necessary, in connection with the men and women who had organized for this purpose, to make their sanitary fair a great success.

It opened in the last week of June, 1864. I had been kept informed of its steady growth, and was prepared for something creditable, but was surprised by its beauty and magnitude. It was a wonderful fair, when all that pertained to it was fully comprehended. It was held west of the Mississippi, where the refinements and luxuries of civilization were not supposed to exist in large measure. It was held in a new state, where railroads were not numerous, and where prairie stage-coaches were still the principal conveniences for travelling.

At that time more than half the territory of the state was in the hands of Eastern speculators, who refused to open it to immigration. The male population had been so drained by the repeated calls of the country, that women were aiding in the outdoor work of the farms, all through the state, ploughing, reaping, mowing, and threshing. The fair was held in a state not rich, save in the great hearts of its loyal men and women, and its broad acres of virgin prairie, holding uncounted wealth in its bosom. There were no ladies and gentlemen of elegant leisure among her people. Few idlers or listless hangers-on were there, all being, engaged in the earnest work of subduing nature, – in building highways and railroads, bridges and steam-boats, school-houses and warehouses, and in bringing the soil under cultivation.

As I entered the spacious City Hall building, three stories high, completely occupied by the fair, and went from one department to another, each filled with articles tasteful, beautiful, and useful, I was astonished at the great variety of wares displayed. This latest born of the great sisterhood of fairs seemed, at a *coup d'œuil*, equal in beauty and general effect to any of its predecessors.

It was intended to hold the fair for one week only. But, finding it impossible to carry out the purpose of the executive committee, it was decided to continue it a week longer. The gross receipts of the first week were sixty thousand dollars. It was a splendid result, and an unparalleled success, when all the circumstances were considered. At the end of the second week the managers of the fair were able to announce their net profits as nearly sixty thousand dollars. In estimating all the disadvantages under which this far-away state labored from the outset, and recalling her patriotism, loyalty, and generosity, one is forced to say, "Many states did excellently; but Iowa excelled them all!"

Part X

Wartime Politics

Plate 12 Still Standing: Abraham Lincoln in a portrait from Matthew Brady's studio, taken January 8, 1864. For most of that year, Lincoln's political situation was tenuous and his reelection in doubt. (Selected Civil War photographs, Library of Congress)

Chapter 22

The Confederate South at High Tide

Emory M. Thomas

"Politics are almost as exciting as war, and quite as dangerous," Winston Churchill once remarked. "In war you can only be killed once, but in politics many times." Yet as Churchill knew first hand, politics also affords the possibilities of resurrections, and in the Civil War there were a number of politicians – notably the men at the top – who counted on more than one.

Governing both the Union and the Confederacy were daunting challenges, not only because of the pressure to deal effectively with an armed foe, but also because any policy could be opposed from within the political system (as well as outside it, as many riots attest). On the surface, the Lincoln administration had a more daunting challenge because there was an organized opposition – the Democratic Party – as well as internal challengers within Republican party ranks (and, for that matter, within Lincoln's own cabinet). Yet the absence of a party system in the Confederacy meant that disagreements could – and did – become personal and thus often unproductive. Moreover, while the struggle for survival helped foster solidarity within the Confederacy in the aftermath of secession, it could also serve to intensify conflicts and foster dissension.

The Confederate States of America existed for only four years – assuming, of course, its identity was recognized as such – and the sense of crisis in its government was perpetual. And yet for a season it functioned as a bona fide republic with elected representatives, a constitution, and all the challenges of administration that come with it. In his 1979 book *The Confederate Nation, 1861–1865*, Emory M. Thomas offers a vivid snapshot of a moment – early 1863 – when it was possible to imagine a lasting future.

Emory M. Thomas, *The Confederate Nation, 1861–1865* (New York: Harper & Row, 1979), pp. 190–9. Copyright © 1979 by Emory M. Thomas. All rights reserved. Reprinted by arrangement with HarperCollins Publishers, Inc.

During the early months of 1863 as the Confederacy marked the second anniversary of its founding and the first year of its permanent government, the new nation appeared to be normal. The Southern nation had endured, indeed prevailed, for two campaigning seasons without the loss of truly critical land or battles. And even though the war went on, Confederate prospects in 1863 looked far more hopeful than they had in 1862. At Richmond a distinguished foreign visitor, Arthur James Lyon Fremantle, found an orderly government and "at least as much difficulty in gaining access to the great men as there would be in European countries." On the surface at least the South seemed to have achieved wartime stability.[1]

Yet beneath this superficial stasis the Confederacy was far from normal. The continued strain of wartime exposed new flaws in the fabric of Confederate nationality. On January 6, 1863, for example, Dodson Ramseur's division of Lee's army marched through Richmond with many of its members barefoot. No wonder that in 1863 the Confederate Patent Office issued four separate patents for wooden shoe soles; shoes were a small matter until men had to march without them.[2]

The new challenges which beset the Confederacy in 1863 were, more accurately, new versions of old challenges. They called for novel responses which transformed the Confederate South still more from its ante-bellum origins. Jefferson Davis faced a new political crisis with a Congress whose members faced their own political crises in upcoming fall elections. Southern soldiers and civilians encountered increasing shortages of supplies and provisions, and the Confederate government confronted a shortage of specie and a declining faith in inflated treasury notes. And Southern armies again faced Northern invasions during another campaigning season. These circumstances, whether interpreted as chronic problems or crises, clamored for resolution as the year 1863 began.

President Davis' new political difficulties had begun back in the fall of 1862 with his cabinet. George W. Randolph had been a capable secretary of war. By October 1862, Randolph had impressed upon Davis and Richmond officialdom the significance of the west as a theater of military operations and had argued successfully for some relaxation in the departmental command structure.[3] Beyond the Appalachians, Randolph perceived, the war demanded a fluidity too often unappreciated in Richmond. But when he attempted to act on his enthusiasm by shifting some troops in the western command without consulting the President, Davis responded by reminding Randolph of the relative powers of commander-in-chief and secretary of war. Randolph resigned in haste on November 15, and Davis accepted the resignation in greater haste. When Randolph described the war secretary's job as that of a "chief clerk," the quarrel became public and the antiadministration press elaborated upon the theme.[4]

To cope with the situation, Davis installed General Gustavus W. Smith in the War Office ad interim and cast about for Randolph's replacement. On November 22 he gave the war portfolio to James A. Seddon and thus forestalled political crisis. Seddon was a Virginian, a disciple of Calhoun, and a staunch secessionist. He was, however, more scholar than warrior, and his sickly appearance raised questions about his capacity to sustain the work load of the War Office. But he proved to be a practical and clear-eyed administrator, bowing to the President's expertise in military matters but contributing a large measure of common sense and efficiency in the day-to-day conduct of the war. Press and public reaction to Seddon's appointment was generally favorable. The Richmond *Examiner* and Charleston *Mercury*, two of the administration's most consistent critics, endorsed the new secretary, and Virginians were satisfied that one of their own was again in the cabinet.[5]

Although Seddon was the President's first choice to replace Randolph, Davis had seriously considered Joseph E. Johnston. The Virginian general had spent most of the campaigning season of 1862 recovering from wounds sustained at Seven Pines, and just about the time that the Randolph-Davis squabble came to crisis, he reported himself fit for duty. What Johnston wanted most was command of the Army of Northern Virginia, which he still considered his own. That army was now Lee's, but Johnston did merit an important command, and even though the General and the President had had their differences, Davis held Johnston's generalship in high esteem. Seddon had much to do with the solution to the problem of finding a use for Johnston, and in so doing built upon Randolph's legacy of concern for coordination of the western command. In late November, Seddon and Davis decided to make a superdepartment, a theater actually, of the Confederate heartland between the Appalachian Mountains and the Mississippi River, and command of this new military structure went to Johnston. The command included three field armies: Edmund Kirby Smith's in east Tennessee, Braxton Bragg's in middle Tennessee, and John C. Pemberton's covering Vicksburg. Johnston's mission was coordination. Beyond this fact, however, his duties and authority were somewhat ambiguous.[6]

Aware at last of problems in the western theater, Davis resolved to view the situation at first hand. He wished to confer with Bragg, inspect the armies, visit political leaders, and show himself to the people – all in the hope, as he wrote to Lee, that "something may be done to bring out men not heretofore in service, and to arouse all classes to united and desperate resistance."[7]

Traveling first to Murfreesboro, where Bragg stood between two Federal armies at Nashville and Chattanooga, Davis made a speech to the troops, then, with commanding General Johnston in tow, hurried on to visit Pemberton at Vicksburg. On December 26 he addressed the Mississippi legislature and a few days later returned to Richmond, stopping on his way to consult with local leaders and test the climate of public opinion.[8]

Returning to the capital on the night of January 5, Davis found to his surprise a band and a modest crowd at the station. The occasion demanded a speech, and Davis rose to the occasion with accounts of Southern heroism, tales of Yankee atrocities, and exhortations to greater patriotism which stirred his audience. Yet through the speech ran a current of estrangement between President and people; Davis spoke as a visitor to the city in which he had lived for nearly two years. He protested that "constant labor in the duties of office, borne down by care, and with an anxiety which has left me scarcely a moment for repose, I have had but little opportunity for social intercourse among you," and concluded with the hope "that at some future time we shall be better acquainted."[9] As President, Jefferson Davis led the Southern revolution as capably, perhaps, as any man could have led it, but his political personality had severe limitations, and Confederate Southerners had to look beyond him to find inspiration for the cause.[10]

While the President was traveling to Richmond, Bragg's army fought a major battle at Murfreesboro on December 31, 1863.[11] Bragg described the battle as a victory, and Davis accepted the word but not the fact. How was he to explain Bragg's subsequent retreat to Tullahoma? Acting decisively Davis ordered Johnston to investigate the matter, then to take command of Bragg's army and send the "victorious" general to Richmond to make a personal accounting. A series of circumstances having little relation to the military situation frustrated these plans, however, and Johnston's role in the structure of command remained unclear in all but outline. Davis and Seddon probably thought of Johnston as a sort of trouble-shooter; Johnston himself believed and wrote to his friends in Congress that he had been exiled and elevated to a position of inconsequence.[12]

Having dealt with the politics of administration in the Randolph crisis, the politics of command in Johnson's theater assignment, and the politics of personality in his western tour, President Davis girded himself to face the politics of politicians when Congress came back into session on January 12, 1863.

The session lasted until May, and for the first two months the Southern solons distinguished themselves more by what they did not do than by what they did. Congress debated but did not enact bills to establish a Supreme Court, seat cabinet members in Congress, create a general staff for the army, and renew the President's authority to suspend habeas corpus. The Supreme Court and habeas corpus bills had the support of Davis and the administration, which in part explained their failure; for in an election year, congressmen were reluctant to expand the power of the central government and were sensitive to the abuses of martial law by some commanders. Even though the Confederate Constitution made provision for a Supreme Court, Congress never passed the requisite enabling legislation. Consequently ultimate judicial authority remained in the state courts instead of the central government. Still, to an amazing degree state courts in the Confederacy upheld the prerogative of the Davis government. Hence the Confederate judicial system remained fragmented in structure but centralized in substance.[13]

Author of the general staff and the cabinet member seating bills was Senator Louis T. Wigfall of Texas. The idea of permitting commanders to appoint their own staffs had considerable merit, but the merits of the bill got lost in what became a conflict of prerogative and personality between president and senator. The President had already vetoed Wigfall's general staff proposal once, on the ground that it infringed upon presidential power, and from that moment Wigfall became an open political enemy of Davis. Wigfall reintroduced his general staff bill and offered the cabinet member seating bill as opposition measures, and as such the Senate rejected them. Thus, although the Confederate Constitution made provision for the seating of cabinet members in Congress, no member of Davis' cabinet ever got the opportunity to explain his program to Congress in person. That was not all to the bad; cabinet members were able to escape the invective of antiadministration men like Wigfall in the Senate or Henry S. Foote in the House. But it was unfortunate that Wigfall's general staff scheme, which could only have improved the normally poor quality of staff work in Southern armies, lost to personal rancor and Davis' inflexibility.[14]

The fate of these four pieces of legislation dramatized the erosion of administration influence, erosion which increased during the remaining two years of the Confederacy's life. That the opposition never coalesced into a party structure gave some index of its fragmentation. Ultimately antiadministration sentiment in Congress, like the attempted obstruction of national policies in some of the states, was a measure of the political metamorphosis within the Confederate South. With some allowance for individual quirks and for the limitations of Jefferson Davis' political personality, the fundamental issue which divided the Davis government from its foes was state rights versus nationalism. In the name of wartime emergency, the Davis administration had all but destroyed the political philosophy which underlay the founding of the Southern republic. Interestingly, the Confederate Congress sometimes led the way.[15]

During the final month and a half of the session, Congress debated and enacted three crucial bills which expanded still further the authority of the Richmond government. In March, Congress authorized quartermaster and commissary officers to seize private property for the use of field armies.[16] In reality the law merely legitimized the existing practice by which armies lived off the land when necessary. The army paid for the impressed items in accord with a War Department schedule of standard prices. Unfortunately for producers, the schedule consistently fixed prices below the open market value, and the government paid in depreciated currency. Unfortunately for civilian consumers, army agents often seized supplies en route to local markets and thus produced a scarcity of food and forage in Southern cities and towns. The impressment process, with its ills and inequities, was doubtless necessary as a supplement to the efforts of the Commissary and Quartermaster Bureaus, and though Southern civilians complained, they generally submitted to this infringement of property rights for the sake of the cause. Ironically that cause had originally included concern for the sanctity of private property in slaves, yet the act of March 26 gave sanction to the impressment of slaves as military laborers.[17]

Congress began debating ways and means of financing the Southern nation and its war early in the 1863 session. Secretary of the Treasury Memminger reported on January 10 what Congressmen already knew too well: the policy of financing the war by issuing treasury notes had produced rampant inflation.[18] In January 1863, a gold dollar in Richmond brought three dollars in treasury notes.[19] And the trend worsened every day. Yet clearly the government needed enormous amounts of money to sustain its existence. Memminger's solution was simple and logical – for a peacetime economy. He proposed to remove as much as two-thirds of the paper money from circulation by offering to exchange non-interest-bearing notes for interest-bearing bonds.[20] On March 23, Congress enacted the policy and authorized Memminger to issue each month up to $50 million in treasury notes which could be exchanged for thirty-year bonds bearing 6 percent interest.[21] Under the provisions of this act the government printed more than $500 million worth of notes, the largest issue of notes ever made in the Confederacy, but the inflation rate discouraged investment in bonds, and only $21-million worth of notes were withdrawn from circulation. By January 1, 1864, a gold dollar in Richmond was worth eighteen to twenty dollars in Confederate notes, reflecting an inflation rate of over 600 percent. The wonder was that the government survived for another fifteen months thereafter.[22]

In January 1863, Memminger renewed his consistent plea for taxation as a necessary method of producing revenue and of restraining inflation. The treasury note authorization of March 23 was only half of the government's financial policy in 1863. The other half was a collection of measures designed to generate revenue to support government paper. On April 24 Congress passed a tax law which was stern to the point of being confiscatory. The act levied an 8-percent ad valorem tax on agricultural products grown in 1862 and taxed bank deposits and commercial paper at the same rate. The act levied a 10-percent tax on profits from buying and selling foodstuffs, clothing, and iron, thus requiring speculators in these commodites to share their profits with the government. It levied a license tax on just about every form of occupation or business, a graduated income tax whose scale varied from 1 percent of incomes less than $500 to 15 percent of incomes over $10,000, and a tax-in-kind tithe on agricultural produce and livestock: 10 percent of everything grown or slaughtered in 1863.[23]

The tax law was bitter medicine. The unchallenged income tax, for example, anticipated the United States federal income tax by fifty years. Nevertheless at first Congress received praise for its courage and wisdom. Before long, however, the difficulties of equitable enforcement became apparent. The tax in kind, especially, proved onerous, and the "TIK men," agents appointed to collect the tithe, too often acted like licensed thieves. Some dissenters declared the tax unconstitutional, and it probably was, but the President countered with the plain truth that the nation's survival depended upon collection of the tax.[24] The tax bill and other significant legislation of 1863 dealt with the problem of distributing wealth, food, and supplies among armies and people. The year before, the main thrust of government activity had been the organization of manpower when Confederates faced the challenge of reconciling state rights and individual liberties with the demands of a multifront war fought by the largest bodies of armed men ever assembled in North America. Actually these two efforts, material distribution and manpower organization, were opposite sides of the same coin. The Confederates were learning the hard lessons of modern warfare: to survive, a combatant nation must be able to mobilize its military population, its economy, and its social institutions in support of the war. The Confederates had submitted to conscription and martial law; now they faced impressment, confiscatory taxation, and fiat currency.

Notes

1   Walter Lord (ed.), *The Fremantle Diary: Being the Journal of Lieutenant Colonel Arthur James Lyon Fremantle, Coldstream Guards, on his Three Months in the Southern States* (New York, 1954), p. 164. Jefferson Davis went so far as to state in his first message to Congress in 1863, "we have every reason to expect that this will be the closing year of the War." Davis to Congress, January 12, 1863, James D. Richardson (ed.), *Messages and Papers of the Confederacy*, 2 vols. (Nashville, TN. 1906), I, p. 277.

2   Kate Mason Rowland, Ms. Diary, Confederate Museum, Richmond, VA, *Report of the Commissioner of Patents* (Richmond, VA, 1864).

3   For Randolph's accomplishments see Archer Jones, "Some Aspects of George W. Randolph's Service as Confederate Secretary of War," *Journal of Southern History*, XXVI (1960), 299–314.

4   The Randolph–Davis correspondence is in Dunbar Rowland (ed.), *Jefferson Davis, Constitutionalist: His Letters, Papers and Speeches*, 10 vols. (Jackson, MS., 1923), V, pp. 371–2, 374–5. On the status of cabinet secretaries and clerks, the Richmond *Examiner* (November 17, 1862) commented, "Indeed, if cabinet ministers are to continue mere automations, it matters little by what names those machines are called." Among historians, Jones ("Randolph's Service") blames Davis for the incident; Rembert W. Patrick (*Jefferson Davis and His Cabinet* [Baton Rouge, LA, 1944], pp. 127–31) blames Randolph.

5   Patrick, *Davis and His Cabinet*, pp. 131–49; Roy W. Curry, "James A. Seddon, a Southern Prototype," *Virginia Magazine of History and Biography*, LXIII (1955), 123–50.

6   Patrick, *Davis and His Cabinet*, pp. 132–35; For assessments of Davis, Johnston and theater command, see Frank E. Vandiver, *Rebel Brass: The Confederate Command System* (Baton Rouge, LA, 1956), pp. 34–7; Archer Jones, *Confederate Strategy from Shiloh to Vicksburg* (Baton Rouge, LA, 1961), pp. 96–110; and Thomas L. Connelly, *Autumn of Glory: The Army of Tennessee, 1862–1868 (Baton Rouge, LA, 1971)*, pp. 30–8.

7   Davis to Lee, December 8, 1862, Rowland (ed.), *Jefferson Davis*, IV, 384.

8   For Davis' travels see Hudson Strode, *Jefferson Davis*, 3 vols. (New York, 1955–1959, 1964), II, pp. 343–56; and Jones, *Confederate Strategy*, pp. 111–22.

9   Richmond *Enquirer*, January 7, 1863, cited in Rowland (ed.), *Jefferson Davis*, V, pp. 390–5.

10 On Davis and public morale see Bell I. Wiley *Road to Appomattox*, (New York, 1968), pp. 28–31, 105–8.

11 Connelly, *Autumn of Glory*, pp. 44–68; Grady McWhiney *Braxton Bragg and Confederate Defeat: Field Command* (New York, 1969), pp. 349–73.

12 Davis, on the night he returned to Richmond, referred to the "victory" at Murfreesboro (Rowland [ed.], *Jefferson Davis*, V, 392). The President's instructions to Johnston are contained in letters of January 22 and February 19 (Rowland [ed.], *Jefferson Davis*, V, 420–1, 433–5). Johnston's account is in his *Narrative of Military Operations*, ed. by Frank E. Vandiver (Bloomington, IN., 1959), pp. 161–2. To Texas Senator Louis T. Wigfall, Johnston wrote on March 8, 1863: "I am told that the President and Secretary of War think that they have given me the highest military position in the Confederacy, that I have full military power in all this western country. . . . If they so regard it, ought not our highest military officer to occupy it? It seems so to me that principle would bring Lee here. I might then, with great propriety be replaced in my old Command." (Louis T. Wigfall Papers, University of Texas Archives, Austin) See also Gilbert E. Govan and James W. Livingood, *A Different Valor: The Story of General Joseph E. Johnston, C.S.A.* (New York, 1956), pp. 166–74.

13 Wilfred Buck Yearns, *The Confederate Congress* (Athens, GA, 1960), pp. 155, 37–8, 228; "Proceedings of the Confederate Congress," I Congress, II Session, *Southern Historical Society Papers*, XLVI, 9, 110; William M. Robinson, Jr., *Justice in Grey: A History of the Judicial System of the Confederate States of America* (Cambridge, MA, 1941).

14 See Alvy L. King, *Louis T. Wigfall: Southern Fire-Eater* (Baton Rouge, LA, 1970), pp. 157–60, 166–8.

15 See Emory M. Thomas, *The Confederacy as a Revolutionary Experience* (Englewood Cliffs, NJ, 1971), pp. 73–8. The Congress too often led in the degree of rancor as well. The Supreme Court bill sparked a brawl in which Georgia Senator Benjamin H. Hill hurled an inkwell at Alabama Senator William Loundes Yancey (King, *Wigfall*, p. 150).

16 James M. Matthews (ed.), *The Statutes at Large of the Confederate States of America... Third Session... First Congress* (Richmond, VA, 1863), pp. 102–4, 127–8.

17 Thomas B. Alexander and Richard E. Beringer, *The Anatomy of the Confederate Congress: A Study of the Influences of Member Characteristics on Legislative Voting Behavior, 1861–1865* (Nashville, TN., 1972), pp. 139–44; Yearns, *Confederate Congress*, pp. 116–120. See also Harrison A. Trexler, "The Opposition of Planters to the Employment of Slaves as Laborers by the Confederacy," *Mississippi Valley Historical Review* XXVII (1940), 211–24.

18 Memminger to Thomas S. Bocock, January 10, 1863, in Raphael P. Thian (comp.), *Reports of the Secretary of the Treasury of the Confederate States of America, 1861–1865*, Appendix III (Washington, DC, 1878), 99–115.

19 Richard Cecil Todd, *Confederate Finance* (Athens, GA, 1954), p. 198.

20 See ibid, pp. 110–11

21 Matthews (ed.), *Statutes at Large... Third Session... First Congress*, pp. 97–98, 99–102.

22 Todd, *Confederate Finance*, pp. 111, 119–20, 198. From hindsight Charles W. Ramsdell once stated, "If I were asked what was the greatest single weakness of the Confederacy, I should say, without much hesitation, that it was in this matter of finances. The resort to irredeemable paper money and to excessive issues of such currency was fatal, for it weakened not only the purchasing power of the government but also destroyed economic security among the people." (*Behind the Lines in the Southern Confederacy* [Baton Rouge, LA, 1944], p. 85).

23 Matthews (ed.), *Statutes at Large... Third Session... First Congress*, pp. 115–26. Todd, *Confederate Finance*, pp. 136–41.

24 Todd, *Confederate Finance*, pp. 141–8. Todd estimates the value of taxes in kind collected from 1863 to 1865 at $62 million (p. 148). See also James L. Nichols, "The Tax-in-Kind in the Department of the Trans-Mississippi," *Civil War History*, V (1959), pp. 382–9. On the larger issues of Confederate fiscal policy see three articles by Eugene M. Lerner, "Monetary and Fiscal Programs of the Confederate Government," *Journal of Political Economy*, LXII (1954), 506–22; "Money, Prices, and Wages in the Confederacy," *Journal of Political Economy*, LXIII (1955), 20–40; and "Inflation in the Confederacy, 1861–1865," in Milton Friedman (ed.), *Studies in the Quantity Theory of Money* (Chicago, 1956), pp. 163–78.

Questions to consider

- What were some of the challenges the Confederacy confronted at mid-war? How well do you think it met them?

- Thomas concludes this piece by noting a contradiction: that a nation founded on states' rights was relying on ever-greater central authority by the national government. Was this a fatal contradiction?

- Note that the book from which this excerpt is taken is called *The Confederate Nation*. Do you agree the Confederacy *was* a nation? What criteria are you using to make this determination?

Chapter 23

To Finish the Task: The Election of 1864

William E. Gienapp

The essence of representative democracy lies in giving citizens – a term whose definition is almost always limited in one form or another – the right to choose their leaders. Yet wartime makes such practices difficult, if not impossible, and even of questionable value (as in the common Confederate practice of allowing men to choose their officers, something that was often as much a function of popularity as merit). Wars are often times when the public will suspend normal rules, and when leaders emerge through extralegal means. So it is all the more notable that, amid all the hatred and hypocrisy that has coursed through the American body politic from the very beginning, regular elections were held in the wartime Union as scheduled, including the presidential election of 1864. Perhaps no fact testifies so clearly to the intensity of Americans' faith in the democratic process.

Their faith in their president was another matter. Given his virtual deification in decades following his death, it may sometimes be easy to forget that Abraham Lincoln was not especially well regarded by many of his fellow citizens. Indeed, his election in 1860 was at least to some degree a function of his anonymity: he had not made enemies the way the outspoken front-runner, William Seward, had. Once in office, Lincoln annoyed abolitionists with his caution, and angered much of the rest of the electorate with the Emancipation Proclamation, which was widely cited as the explanation for major Democratic gains in the mid-term elections of 1862. While he did have some passionate supporters, he had at least as many skeptics, and more than a few people who loathed him.

In the end, it would be the course of war itself that would determine Lincoln's future. In the first half of 1864, after three years of inconclusive fighting and growing resistance at home, it was far from clear to many Republicans – far from clear to Lincoln himself – that he would have the privilege of a second term, something that had not happened since the presidency of Andrew Jackson almost 25 years earlier. In his masterful short biography *Abraham Lincoln and Civil War America* (2002), the late Harvard historian William Gienapp recreates the sense of uncertainty, even desperation, that surrounded the Lincoln administration at the crucial turning point of the war

[. . .]

In the summer of 1864 Lincoln found himself under attack from all sides. Radicals were unhappy with his policies on slavery and Reconstruction, conservatives doubted his leadership abilities, and everyone blamed him for failing to end the war. In this dark and discouraging period, he manifested his steadfastness in the face of criticism, his determination to do what he believed right, and his refusal to seek mere partisan advantage.

When the new government in Louisiana, established under Lincoln's guidelines, failed to grant additional rights to African Americans, opposition in Congress to Lincoln's program increased. Two leading radicals, Benjamin F. Wade in the Senate and Henry Winter Davis in the House, introduced a bill that established a more stringent program of Reconstruction. The Wade–Davis bill placed the Confederate states temporarily under a military governor. Rather than Lincoln's nucleus of 10 percent, it required a majority of a state's 1860 voters to take the loyalty oath before forming a new state government. Large categories of southern whites were disqualified from participating in the restoration process by mandating they take a so-called iron-clad oath that they had never voluntarily supported the Confederacy. In addition, slavery was abolished in the state, and Confederate officials barred from holding office. With strong radical support, the bill passed Congress on July 2, shortly before adjournment.

Radical leaders rushed to the White House to press Lincoln to sign the bill, but he laid it aside. When Senator Zachariah Chandler stressed the importance of its provision abolishing slavery in the reconstructed states, Lincoln replied, "That is the point on which I doubt the authority of Congress to act." Reminded that he had issued the Emancipation Proclamation, Lincoln answered, "I conceive that I may in an emergency do things on military grounds which cannot be done constitutionally by Congress." While Lincoln had issued the Emancipation Proclamation as a military act based on the executive's war powers, he never believed Congress had the constitutional power to abolish slavery in a state. In the end, he pocket-vetoed the bill (if a president does not sign a bill after Congress has adjourned, it has the effect of a veto).

Lincoln then issued a proclamation explaining his action. Declaring that he was unwilling "to be inflexibly committed to any single plan of restoration," he objected to abandoning the new governments already in place in Louisiana and Arkansas. He further roused the radicals' ire by noting that the Wade–Davis bill provided one plan, which the people of the South were free to accept if they wished (an unlikely occurrence, as he well knew).

Wade and Davis responded by publishing a manifesto that harshly assailed Lincoln as a political usurper, bent on creating "shadows of Governments" in the South to aid his reelection. Insisting that "the authority of Congress is paramount" on the matter of reconstruction, they characterized Lincoln's proclamation as a "studied outrage on the legislative authority of the people." Wade and Davis's vehemence sorely tried Lincoln's well-known patience. "To be wounded in the house of one's friends," he lamented, "is perhaps the most grievous affliction that can befall a man."

The division between Lincoln and the radicals over Reconstruction involved more than whether Congress or the president would play the major role in formulating a program of Reconstruction. Also involved were different perceptions of how best to restore loyal governments in the South. Radicals had little faith in white southern Unionists and believed that blacks were the only loyal group of any size in the South. Therefore, they demanded immediate emancipation and saw black suffrage as the best way to establish loyal governments. Lincoln, in contrast, shrank from inaugurating a fundamental upheaval in southern society and mores, and by stressing future over past loyalty, he was willing to allow recanting Rebels to dominate the new southern governments. Moreover, Lincoln believed that the best strategy was to introduce black suffrage in the South by degrees in order to accustom southern whites to blacks voting. How far he was willing to go in extending rights to former slaves remained unclear, but his gradualist approach to social change remained intact, just as when he had tried to get the border states in 1862 to adopt gradual emancipation. Finally, the radicals and Lincoln held quite different views of the relationship of Reconstruction to the war effort. By erecting impossibly high standards that no southern state could meet, the Wade–Davis bill sought to postpone Reconstruction until the war was over. For Lincoln, in contrast, a lenient program of Reconstruction would encourage southern whites to abandon the Confederacy and thus was integral to his strategy for winning the war.

At the same time, Lincoln was harshly denounced by antiwar Democrats. Northern war weariness, which peaked in the summer of 1864, fostered a powerful peace movement on the home front. The extreme Copperheads claimed that a negotiated settlement was possible if Lincoln would only drop his insistence on emancipation. Lincoln correctly understood that Jefferson Davis would never agree to a restoration of the Union, but many Northerners, sickened by the bloodshed, clutched almost in desperation at any hope for peace.

Already under attack from the peace wing of the Democratic party, Lincoln came under heavy pressure from Horace Greeley to open peace negotiations with the Confederacy. "Our bleeding, bankrupt, almost dying country also longs for peace – shudders at the prospect of fresh conscriptions, of further wholesale devastations, and of new rivers of human blood," Greeley plaintively wrote in early July. Informed that Confederate diplomats with authority to negotiate a peace settlement were in Niagara Falls, Greeley urged the president to confer with them. The belief that the administration did not favor peace, he added, was doing great political damage and was certain to do even more as the election approached.

Tired of Greeley's censorious attitude and his flip-flops on public policy, Lincoln hit upon the brilliant strategy of sending the New York editor to Niagara Falls to meet these purported commissioners. He drafted a letter, addressed "To Whom It May Concern," laying out his peace terms, which he gave to his secretary, John Hay, to take to Niagara Falls. "Any proposition" from the Confederate government, the letter read, "which embraces the restoration of peace, the integrity of the whole Union, and the abandonment of slavery ... will be received and considered by the Executive government of the United States, and will be met by liberal terms on other substantial and collateral points."

Lincoln no doubt smiled as he sent Greeley on what he knew was a wild goose chase. When Greeley reported (as Lincoln suspected all along) that the Confederates had no power to conduct peace negotiations, the editor of the *Tribune* found himself the target of northern ridicule. His eyes twinkling, Lincoln chuckled to Charles A. Dana, one of Greeley's former associates who was now working in the War Department, "I sent Brother Greeley a commission. I guess I am about even with him now."

Realizing that a negotiated peace was impossible, Lincoln adopted the strategy of appearing to be willing to open peace talks, while setting the preconditions high enough that Davis would reject them out of hand. His demand for the abandonment of slavery in his letter outlining his peace terms was more sweeping than the terms of his Emancipation Proclamation and the ambiguous language of his Reconstruction program.

Lincoln's strategy backfired. All through the summer, Democrats made effective use of his "To Whom It May Concern" letter to argue that Lincoln was prolonging the war because of a fanatical desire to end slavery. That demand out of the way, Democrats insisted, a settlement with the Confederacy could quickly be reached. The unfriendly *New York Herald* proclaimed that the letter "sealed Lincoln's fate in the coming Presidential campaign."

In this battle for northern public opinion, Lincoln was ironically aided by Jefferson Davis, who blundered by not proposing an armistice and peace talks without conditions. He also benefited when two unofficial emissaries, following an interview with Davis in Richmond, quoted the Confederate president as having delivered an ultimatum that "the war...must go on...*unless you acknowledge our right to self-government.* We are not fighting for slavery. We are fighting for Independence, – and that, or extermination, we *will* have."

Even so, Lincoln remained on the defensive. His peace terms failed to mollify the radicals, still smarting over his veto of the Wade–Davis bill, while they constituted a sharp blow to the prowar Democrats, who were opposed to emancipation as a Union war aim. Conservative and moderate Republicans were also discontented, believing that Lincoln's letter would strengthen Confederate resistance; they also feared that it would usher in wild scenes of revolutionary upheaval in the postwar South. With the president under attack whichever way he turned, his old friend Orville Browning flatly pronounced him a "failure" as president.

Nevertheless, Lincoln decided to stick to his position. He could not give up the nearly 130,000 black men now serving in the Union ranks, he explained, nor would he consent that slaves once freed be reenslaved. "I should be damned in time and in eternity for so doing." In an interview with several Wisconsin Republicans, Lincoln insisted that the war was being waged solely to save the Union, but that "no human power can subdue this rebellion without using the Emancipation lever as I have done."

By the beginning of August, despair was evident among Republicans, who believed that they were staring defeat in the face. Military victory appeared as far away as ever, party divisions were deepening, and Lincoln seemed unable to rally public opinion to his side. There had been griping all summer among disaffected Republicans about Lincoln's candidacy, but the movement to convene a new convention and dump Lincoln now came to a head. At a meeting in New York City, a number of prominent Republicans canvassed the possibility and a call soon appeared, urging that a convention be held in Cincinnati on September 28. "Mr. Lincoln is already beaten," Greeley contended in endorsing the call. "He cannot be elected. And we must have another ticket to save us from utter overthrow."

Disheartened reports from party leaders in a number of key states poured in to Henry J. Raymond, chairman of the Republican National Committee and editor of the *New York Times*. Raymond attributed Lincoln's problems to the military situation and the prevailing opinion that the administration was prolonging the war solely to end slavery. "The suspicion is widely diffused that we *can* have peace with Union if we would," he wrote the president on August 22. "It is idle to reason with this belief – still more idle to denounce it. It can only be expelled by some authoritative act, at once bold enough to fix attention and distinct enough to defy incredulity and challenge respect." He urged that a commissioner be appointed to negotiate with Davis, specifying only reunion as a condition for peace. Davis would certainly reject such terms, Raymond added, but the offer would dampen the cry in the North for peace negotiations. At a subsequent meeting at the White House with the leaders of the National Committee, Lincoln rejected this proposal, insisting that it "would be worse than losing the Presidential contest – it would be ignominiously surrendering it in advance."

Gloom pervaded the White House. "Everything is darkness and doubt and discouragement," Nicolay reported in late August. Lincoln remained outwardly determined, but in reality he was deeply discouraged. On August 23, after reading Raymond's bleak letter, he took out a sheet of paper and wrote the following: "This morning, as for some days past, it seems exceedingly probable that this Administration will not be re-elected. Then it will be my duty to so co-operate with the President elect, as to save the Union between the election and the inauguration; as he will have secured his election on such ground that he can not possibly save it afterwards." Lincoln was certain that party pressure would force any Democratic president, no matter how committed to the war, to agree to an armistice, which he knew would be fatal to the Union cause. After sealing this statement in an envelope, he had each of his cabinet members sign the back without revealing the contents to them. Only after the election was over did he open the envelope and read to his advisers the statement they had blindly endorsed.

The Democrats had postponed their convention until the end of August in order to see what the military situation was before selecting a ticket. Among the delegates who assembled in Chicago was Clement Vallandigham, the Copperhead leader who had been banished the year before, and who now returned from Canada breathing fire and daring the administration to arrest him. Lincoln instructed his generals to leave Vallandigham alone, convinced that he was doing more harm to the Democrats than the Republicans.

The Democrats nominated former general George McClellan for president. McClellan was the choice of the regular Democrats, who favored a war to save the Union but balked at emancipation. The platform, however, reflected the views of the peace wing of the party. Largely written by Vallandigham, the 1864 Democratic platform pronounced the war a failure and called for an armistice and peace negotiations with the Confederacy. "After four years of failure to restore the Union by the experiment of war," the controversial plank read, "... justice, humanity, liberty, and the public welfare demand that immediate efforts be made for a cessation of hostilities, with a view of an ultimate convention of the States, or other peaceable means, to the end that, at the earliest practicable moment, peace may be restored on the basis of the Federal Union...." In his acceptance letter, McClellan repudiated the assertion that the war was a failure and, after much indecision, rejected the idea of an armistice.

Privately, Confederate leaders considered McClellan their last hope of victory. His triumph would signal the North's unwillingness to continue the war; certainly it would revive southern morale and determination. McClellan's election would lead to southern independence, the *Charleston Mercury* assured its readers following the Democratic convention, and thus it was "essential" that "for the next two months *we hold our own and prevent military success by our foes.*"

Democrats' – and Confederates' – optimism was short lived. Word soon arrived from Sherman that "Atlanta is ours, and fairly won," which completely transformed the existing political situation. Sherman's capture of the city on September 2 came on the heels of Admiral David Farragut's stirring success at Mobile Bay. Shortly thereafter, Philip Sheridan smashed Jubal Early's army and began to devastate the Shenandoah Valley so that Lee could no longer draw supplies from that fertile agricultural region. It was apparent that the Union was much closer to victory than Northerners had previously realized. Republican spirits revived, and Democratic ones correspondingly declined. Almost overnight, Abraham Lincoln became the favorite to win the 1864 presidential election.

The prospect of a Republican victory in November did wonders to close the party's internal breach. The movement to hold a new national convention promptly collapsed, and even "sorehead republicans," in the words of the *New York Herald*, scrambled aboard the Lincoln bandwagon. At this point Zachariah Chandler, who considered McClellan a traitor, apparently worked out an arrangement whereby Frémont would withdraw from the race and Montgomery

Blair, the radicals' chief nemesis, would leave the cabinet. Lincoln disliked giving up Blair, who had been a loyal supporter, but he realized that Blair's endless personal quarrels and slashing attacks on his critics negated his political usefulness. In late September Frémont withdrew as a candidate, and Lincoln accepted Blair's long-standing offer to resign and named William Dennison of Ohio the new Postmaster General. Radicals took to the campaign trail, though sometimes stumping with less than good grace for the national ticket.

Three key northern states – Pennsylvania, Ohio, and Indiana – held their state elections in October. Unlike the other two states, Indiana failed to adopt a procedure that would allow Union soldiers to vote in the field. With an eye on the contest, Lincoln asked Sherman to furlough as many Indiana troops as possible to go home and vote in the state election. Sherman complied, and two of his generals, John Logan and Frank Blair, Jr., both notable politicians and former Democrats, campaigned for Lincoln in the state and elsewhere. When the Republicans, aided by the soldier vote, carried all three states, Lincoln's success in November seemed likely, but the result in Pennsylvania was uncomfortably close. Two days later, Lincoln estimated that he would narrowly squeak through in the November balloting.

As was the custom for presidential candidates in the nineteenth century, Lincoln refrained from actively campaigning, but he kept a close eye on developments in various states. Indeed, Fessenden reported that "the President is too busy looking after the elections to think of anything else." He especially used his enormous tact and great powers of persuasion to paper over personal feuds and party divisions in several states, including Pennsylvania. "I confess that I desire to be re-elected," Lincoln remarked. "God knows I do not want the labor and responsibility of the office for another four years. But I have the common pride of humanity to wish my past four years Administration endorsed."

Following such a heated campaign, the balloting on November 8 was surprisingly peaceful. Election day was "dull, gloomy and rainy" in Washington. Calling around noon, Noah Brooks found the White House virtually deserted. In talking to Hay during the day, Lincoln reflected, "It is a little singular that I who am not a vindictive man, should have always been before the people for election in canvasses marked for their bitterness." Except for the 1846 congressional race, "the contests in which I have been prominent have been marked with great rancor." That evening Hay accompanied the president as he went over to the War Department to receive the returns by telegraph, just as Lincoln had done four years earlier at the office of the *Illinois State Journal* in Springfield. The early returns were generally favorable, and the Republican trend grew more pronounced as the evening wore on. Lincoln was in a genial mood, and it was not until around three that he at last went home.

The final returns gave Lincoln a popular majority of more than 400,000 votes. Lincoln carried all but three states (New Jersey, Delaware, and Kentucky) and won an overwhelming victory in the electoral college, 212 to 21. The election was closer than these numbers suggest, however, for Lincoln's margin was very small in several key states, including New York. His vote in 1864 followed the same lines as in 1860, except in the border states, where the Republican party now was much stronger.

One of the most striking features of the balloting was Lincoln's support among Union soldiers. Nineteen states made provisions for troops to vote in their camps. Lincoln won almost 80 percent of the their votes, evidence of the great affection ordinary soldiers had for him, as well as the deep resentment they bore toward the Copperheads and the Democratic platform. One Democratic soldier who voted for Lincoln explained, "I had rather stay out here a lifetime (much as I dislike it), than consent to a division of our country. . . . We all want peace, but none *any* but an *honorable* one." The vote of soldiers provided Lincoln's margin of victory in New York and Connecticut, and probably Indiana and Maryland as well.

During the course of the war, Lincoln had developed a very special relationship with Union troops, who affectionately called him "Uncle Abe" and "Father Abraham." His unpretentious manner, common looks, and homespun ways appealed to ordinary soldiers, who felt a kinship with him. When he reviewed the troops, he did not cut a dashing figure on horseback (one of Grant's aides said he reminded him of "a country farmer riding into town wearing his Sunday clothes"), but the men spontaneously broke into cheers as he rode by. A New York soldier wrote home after Lincoln visited the army in 1862, "The boys liked him. In fact, his popularity with the army is and has been universal." On another occasion, when Lincoln reviewed the Army of the Potomac, Noah Brooks observed, "It was noticeable that the President merely touched his hat in return salute to the officers, but uncovered to the men in the ranks." The troops appreciated the interest he took in their condition and treatment, and when he told them to bring their personal problems to his attention, many did. This relationship grew stronger as the war continued, and the 1864 election confirmed that Union soldiers were the strongest supporters Abraham Lincoln had.

Two nights later Lincoln made a brief speech to a crowd of well-wishers who came to the White House. "The election was a necessity," he affirmed. "We can not have free government without elections; and if the rebellion could force us to forego, or postpone a national election, it might fairly claim to have already conquered and ruined us." The election caused strife, but it also did good. "It has demonstrated that a people's government can sustain a national election, in the midst of a great civil war."

The election of 1864 marked the final turning point of the Civil War. Its outcome constituted a great personal triumph for Lincoln after four years of vicious and unrelenting criticism. It also evinced the renewed commitment of the northern people, after the Union's recent military victories, to continue the struggle until the war was won. Finally, it represented an endorsement of the policy of emancipation, against which Democrats had directed their fire in the recent campaign, and ended any doubt that slavery would be abolished as a result of the war. "The crisis has been past," George Templeton Strong wrote in his diary, "and the most momentous popular election ever held since ballots were invented has decided against treason and disunion."

To be sure, Jefferson Davis remained defiant and announced that the Confederacy would fight on until independence was achieved, but in the wake of Lincoln's victory southern morale rapidly deteriorated. With the defeat of the Confederacy now only a matter of time, Lincoln turned his thoughts to peace.

Questions to consider

- Gienapp notes that Lincoln had poor relations with the radical wing of his party in 1864 because of his relatively cautious approach to Reconstruction. How would you compare Lincoln's handling of this matter with Emancipation (you may wish to look at documents in Part VII)? Do you think he was right to go slow?

- Had Lincoln lost or never been elected, can you imagine a negotiated settlement for the Civil War? What might it have looked like?

- How much political danger do you think Lincoln faced in 1864?

Chapter 24

Wartime Politics: Primary Sources

Chiefly About War Matters

Nathaniel Hawthorne

Nathaniel Hawthorne was a major (if not exactly best-selling) novelist during the Civil War – and an avowed Democrat who had held an important diplomatic post during the administration of his friend Franklin Pierce, who held the presidency from 1857 to 1861. In 1862, on assignment for *Atlantic Monthly*, Hawthorne went to the White House and met a man who he was inclined to regard with some suspicion. The brief sketch that resulted, part of a much larger look at the wartime situation, was complex, suggesting both admiration as well as condescension (and, perhaps, Hawthorne's customary skepticism about those who think they can change the world for the better, a skepticism that grew directly out of his ambiguous attempts to explore his Puritan heritage).

Nathaniel Hawthorne, "Chiefly About War Matters. By a Peaceable Man," *Atlantic Monthly*, vol. 10, no. 57 (July 1862), 43–61.

[...]

Of course, there was one other personage, in the class of statesmen, whom I should have been truly mortified to leave Washington without seeing; since (temporarily, at least, and by force of circumstances) he was the man of men. But a private grief had built up a barrier about him, impeding the customary free intercourse of Americans with their chief magistrate; so that I might have come away without a glimpse of his very remarkable physiognomy, save for a semi-official opportunity of which I was glad to take advantage. The fact is, we were invited to annex ourselves, as supernumeraries, to a deputation that was about to wait upon the President, from a Massachusetts whip-factory, with a present of a splendid whip.

Our immediate party consisted only of four or five (including Major Ben Perley Poore, with his notebook and pencil), but we were joined by several other persons, who seemed to have been lounging about the precincts of the White House, under the spacious porch, or within the hall, and who swarmed in with us to take the chances of a presentation. Nine o'clock had been appointed as the time for receiving the deputation, and we were punctual to the moment; but not so the President, who sent us word that he was eating his breakfast, and would come as soon as he could. His appetite, we were glad to think, must have been a pretty fair one; for we waited about half an hour in one of the antechambers, and then were ushered into a reception-room, in one corner of which sat the Secretaries of War and of the Treasury, expecting, like ourselves, the termination of the Presidential breakfast. During this interval there were several new additions to our group, one or two of whom were in a working-garb, so that we formed a very miscellaneous collection of people, mostly unknown to each other, and without any common sponsor, but all with an equal right to look our head-servant in the face.

By and by there was a little stir on the staircase and in the passage-way, and in lounged a tall, loose-jointed figure, of an exaggerated Yankee port and demeanor, whom (as being about the homeliest man I ever saw, yet by no means repulsive or disagreeable) it was impossible not to recognize as Uncle Abe.

Unquestionably, Western man though he be, and Kentuckian by birth, President Lincoln is the essential representative of all Yankees, and the veritable specimen, physically, of what the world seems determined to regard as our characteristic qualities. It is the strangest and yet the fittest thing in the jumble of human vicissitudes, that he, out of so many millions, unlooked for, unselected by any intelligible process that could be based upon his genuine qualities, unknown to those who chose him, and unsuspected of what endowments may adapt him for his tremendous responsibility, should have found the way open for him to fling his lank personality into the chair of state, – where, I presume, it was his first impulse to throw his legs on the council-table, and tell the Cabinet Ministers a story. There is no describing his lengthy awkwardness, nor the uncouthness of his movement; and yet it seemed as if I had been in the habit of seeing him daily, and had shaken hands with him a thousand times in some village street; so true was he to the aspect of the pattern American, though with a certain extravagance which, possibly, I exaggerated still further by the delighted eagerness with which I took it in. If put to guess his calling and livelihood, I should have taken him for a country schoolmaster as soon as anything else. He was dressed in a rusty black frock-coat and pantaloons, unbrushed, and worn so faithfully that the suit had adapted itself to the curves and angularities of his figure, and had grown to be an outer skin of the man. He had shabby slippers on his feet. His hair was black, still unmixed with gray, stiff, somewhat bushy, and had apparently been acquainted with neither brush nor comb that morning, after the disarrangement of the pillow; and as to a night-cap, Uncle Abe probably knows nothing of such effeminacies. His complexion is dark and sallow, betokening, I fear, an insalubrious atmosphere around the White House; he has thick black eyebrows and an impending brow; his nose is large, and the lines about his mouth are very strongly defined.

The whole physiognomy is as coarse a one as you would meet anywhere in the length and breadth of the States; but, withal, it is redeemed, illuminated, softened, and brightened by a kindly though serious look out of his eyes, and an expression of homely sagacity, that seems weighted with rich results of village experience. A great deal of native sense; no bookish cultivation, no refinement; honest at heart, and thoroughly so, and yet, in some sort, sly, – at least, endowed with a sort of tact and wisdom that are akin to craft, and would impel him, I think, to take an antagonist in flank, rather than to make a bull-run at him right in front. But, on the whole, I like this sallow, queer, sagacious visage, with the homely human sympathies that warmed it; and, for my small share in the matter, would as lief have Uncle Abe for a ruler as any man whom it would have been practicable to put in his place.

Immediately on his entrance the President accosted our member of Congress, who had us in charge, and, with a comical twist of his face, made some jocular remark about the length of his breakfast. He then greeted us all round, not waiting for an introduction, but shaking and squeezing everybody's hand with the utmost cordiality, whether the individual's name was announced to him or not. His manner towards us was wholly without pretence, but yet had a kind of natural dignity, quite sufficient to keep the forwardest of us from clapping him on the shoulder and asking him for a story. A mutual acquaintance being established, our leader took the whip out of its case, and began to read the address of presentation. The whip was an exceedingly long one, its handle wrought in ivory (by some artist in the Massachusetts State Prison, I believe), and ornamented with a medallion of the President, and other equally beautiful devices; and along its whole length there was a succession of golden bands and ferrules. The address was shorter than the whip, but equally well made, consisting chiefly of an explanatory description of these artistic designs, and closing with a hint that the gift was a suggestive and emblematic one, and that the President would recognize the use to which such an instrument should be put.

This suggestion gave Uncle Abe rather a delicate task in his reply, because, slight as the matter seemed, it apparently called for some declaration, or intimation, or faint foreshadowing of policy in reference to the conduct of the war, and the final treatment of the Rebels. But the President's Yankee aptness and not-to-be-caughtness stood him in good stead, and he jerked or wiggled himself out of the dilemma with an uncouth dexterity that was entirely in character; although, without his gesticulation of eye and mouth, – and especially the flourish of the whip, with which he imagined himself touching up a pair of fat horses, – I doubt whether his words would be worth recording, even if I could remember them. The gist of the reply was, that he accepted the whip as an emblem of peace, not punishment; and, this great affair over, we retired out of the presence in high good-humor, only regretting that we could not have seen the President sit down and fold up his legs (which is said to be a most extraordinary spectacle), or have heard him tell one of those delectable stories for which he is so celebrated. A good many of them are afloat upon the common talk of Washington, and are certainly the aptest, pithiest, and funniest little things imaginable; though, to be sure, they smack of the frontier freedom, and would not always bear repetition in a drawing-room, or on the immaculate page of the Atlantic.[1]

Good Heavens! what liberties have I been taking with one of the potentates of the earth, and the man on whose conduct more important consequences depend than on that of any other historical personage of the century! But with whom is an American citizen entitled to take a liberty, if not with his own chief magistrate? However, lest the above allusions to President Lincoln's little peculiarities (already well known to the country and to the world) should be misinterpreted, I deem it proper to say a word or two in regard to him, of unfeigned respect and measurable confidence. He is evidently a man of keen faculties, and, what is still more to the purpose, of powerful character. As to his integrity, the people have that intuition of it which is never deceived. Before he actually entered upon his great office, and for a considerable time afterwards, there is no reason to suppose that he adequately estimated the gigantic task about to be imposed on him, or, at least, had any distinct idea how it was to be managed; and I presume there may have been more than one veteran politician who proposed to himself to take the power out of President Lincoln's hands into his own, leaving our honest friend only the public responsibility for the good or ill success of the career. The extremely imperfect development of his statesmanly qualities, at that period, may have justified such designs. But the President is teachable by events, and has now spent a year in a very arduous course of education; he has a flexible mind, capable of much expansion, and convertible towards far loftier studies and activities than those of his early life; and if he came to Washington a backwoods humorist, he has already transformed himself into as good a statesman (to speak moderately) as his prime-minister.

Note

1   The above passage relating to President Lincoln was one of those omitted from the article as originally published, and the following note was appended to explain the omission, which had been indicated by a line of points:

We are compelled to omit two or three pages, in which the author describes the interview, and gives his idea of the personal appearance and deportment of the President. The sketch appears to have been written in a benign spirit, and perhaps conveys a not inaccurate impression of its august subject; but it lacks *reverence*, and it pains us to see a gentleman of ripe age, and who has spent years under the corrective influence of foreign institutions, falling into the characteristic and most ominous fault of Young America.

Questions to consider

- How would you describe the style Hawthorne employs here? Are you amused, annoyed or both? Why?

- Some of this portrait was trimmed from *Atlantic Monthly* when it was published in 1862, because Hawthorne's editors deemed it insufficiently respectful of the President. Do you agree?

Work

Boston Evening Transcript

Politics is about people, but it is also about principles and interests. In this article from the *Boston Evening Transcript* about three weeks before the election of 1864, one senses an impatience with personalities and a desire to clarify what the contest – political and military – was really about. How persuasive is this writer's point of view?

Boston Evening Transcript (October 15, 1864), "Work", in *The Civil War: Ironweed American Newspapers and Periodicals Project*, ed. Brayton Harris (Forest Hills, NY: Ironweed Press, 1999), pp. 540–1.

It may be considered settled that of the two candidates for the presidency, Abraham Lincoln is to be elected by a very large majority of the electoral vote. In ordinary times this would be enough. But more than this is wanted now. In one sense, the men in this political contest are of little account. Their respective merits or demerits have entered into the canvass, merely as one side or the other has endeavored to win votes by showing its fitness or unfitness to stand as the head of the administration of a great republic. The real issue is an issue of principles, and in view of this fact, an overwhelming expression of public sentiment on the right side is to be labored for with unremitted diligence and unwearied earnestness.

Grant that the Chicago party means to insist upon a Union of some sort as a condition of peace; grant that it means to stand upon its own solemnly resolved platform, or upon whatever of definite purpose can be inferred from the adroit and ambiguous letter of McClellan; great this, and it is still easy to see what policy must come of giving the whole power in the management of public affairs, or even of any considerable influence as a strong minority, to the political plotters who have disguised their antirepublican designs by assuming to represent the democracy. That policy, to make the best of it, means to try negotiations first with the leaders of the rebellion, not with the people of the South, and in these negotiations the Chicago party would stand ready to concede as those leaders their old relations to the Federal government.

This is what they intend by making "Union" the only condition of peace. They do not start with the fact that Jefferson Davis and his fellow conspirators are traitors and guilty of armed treason – the authors by the admission of Alexander H. Stephens, of a civil war with all in horrors, for which they had, at the time of its assaults upon the national flag, no justification.[1] They do not start with this fact. They have an entirely different theory as to the past doings and the present attitude of the Richmond leaders. At most, they are misguided political adversaries, who are to be conciliated, and won back to the allegiance they have spurned, by compromise. This is the policy: Armistice, conference concession, and such a Union as the secessionists may be pleased to agree to. If this encouragement fails, then, say a portion of the Chicago party, we will fight on for a Union. But amid the contradictions in that party, the fighting, even in the last resort, will be a very mild kind of skirmishing.

On the other side, the ground taken is that the nation is engaged in overcoming rebellion, in compelling treason to submit unconditionally, and in restoring the authority of the Federal government all over the land, so that it shall not be again periled by sectional treason and an ambitious aristocracy that holds free institutions and popular rights in supreme contempt.

Here is the issue of principles and of policy presented to the voters of the North on the 8th of November. The result of the election is not to be merely the expression of a choice as between the two nominees, but a pronunciamento by the people as to the view they take of the war and the sort of nation they mean to be. This being the case, how clear is the duty of working in season and out of season to secure an overwhelming expression of the popular will in favor of Union and free institutions – a democratic nationality.

Note

1   Alexander H. Stephens served as Davis's vice president (1861–65) and, after the war, as congressman and governor of Georgia.

Part XI

Gender Battles

Plate 13 Family Values: Alfred Waud's "Mustered Out" (see photo of him in the Introduction of this book) captures the exuberance of the Little Rock, Arkansas, African American community as US Colored Troops return home on April 20, 1865. This drawing was published in *Harper's Weekly* on May 19, 1866 amid struggles over Reconstruction and the rights of freedmen and women. (Prints and Photographs Division, Library of Congress)

Chapter 25

What Shall We Do?:
Confederate Women Confront the Crisis

Drew Gilpin Faust

In the mid-nineteenth century the concept of separate spheres for men and women was common sense, even with regional variations. In theory, it was all very simple: the good Lord made man and woman (actually, woman was made from man) and set them on the Earth to love and serve each other and their children. This involved the understanding that each sex had distinct tasks particular to them: men to hunt, gather, and protect the family from external threats; women to feed, nurture, and protect it from internal ones. Men were to cultivate diligence, independence, and self-restraint; women, as the moral centers of the home, were understood to be instinctively pious, gentle, and submissive. In the modern world of the nineteenth century, hunting and gathering was more of a metaphor than a fact (at least in cities and towns), and nurturance could involve the cultivation of domestic arts and even sciences. But the prescribed roles were reasonably clear. Biological sex differences were directly correlated with gender roles.

Or so it seemed. In fact, the lines between spheres could get blurred when half of the equation was out of the picture for one reason or another. And there were times when some women – like abolitionists – felt that the only way to preserve their private domestic sphere was to venture out into the public one to correct what they saw to be egregious moral failures. Naturally, such people were viewed with suspicion.

The complexities intensified still further in wartime. During the Civil War era men and women lived apart from each other for long stretches of time, and the press of events could force them to perform tasks (from cooking to plowing) that they never would have imagined performing (or being able to perform) under other circumstances. Even when the tasks didn't change, ideas did, ideas that could lead to conflicts or new realities in the war's aftermath.

Few Civil War historians have explored these questions with as much depth as Harvard University historian Drew Gilpin Faust. A direct descendant of Confederates, Faust has devoted much of her career to plumbing the complexities of Southerners' lives. In a controversial 1994 article in the *Journal of American History*, Faust turned her focus exclusively to women, going so far as to suggest that one reason that the South lost the Civil War may have been because elite Southern white women had had enough, and that their desertion from the cause had crippling effects. In this opening chapter from her 1999 book *Mothers of Invention: Women of the Slaveholding South in the Civil War,* Faust illustrates how the war's outbreak unsettled gender relations even for women who were not particularly interested in challenging the status quo.

Drew Gilpin Faust, "What Shall We Do?," in *Mothers of Invention: Women of the Slaveholding South in the American Civil War* (Chapel Hill: University of North Carolina Press, 1996), pp. 9–18. Copyright © 1996 by the University of North Carolina Press. Used by permission of the publisher.

As the nation passed anxiously through the long and uncertain months of the "secession winter" of 1861–2, Lucy Wood wrote from her home in Charlottesville, Virginia, to her fiancé, Waddy Butler. His native South Carolina had seceded just before Christmas, declaring itself sovereign and independent, but Virginia had not yet acted. Just a week before Lucy Wood's letter of January 21, her state's legislature had voted to call a secession convention, and Wood thought disunion was "fast becoming the order of the day." Yet these momentous events had already changed Lucy's life. Waddy Butler, preoccupied with new military obligations in service of what Wood pointedly called "*your* country," had been neglecting his intended bride, failing to write as frequently as she had come to expect. Affianced they still might be, but, Wood noted, they had become citizens of different nations, officially "foreigners to each other now."[1]

In January 1861 Lucy Wood was more bemused than genuinely troubled by this intrusion of grave public matters into her personal affairs, and she fully expected Virginia's prompt secession to reunite her with Butler in "common cause." But beneath the playful language of her letter lay an incisive perception. Waddy Butler's new life as a soldier would ultimately not just deprive his future wife of "hearing from you as often as I otherwise should," but would divide the young couple as he marched off to war and she remained home in a world of women. By removing men to the battlefield, the war that followed secession threatened to make the men and women of the South foreigners to one another, separating them into quite different wartime lives. As the sense of crisis mounted through the early months of 1861 and as political conflict turned into full-scale war, southern ladies struggled to make the Confederacy a common cause with their men, to find a place for themselves in a culture increasingly preoccupied with the quintessentially male concerns of politics and of battle. Confederate women were determined that the South's crisis must be "certainly ours as well as that of the men."[2]

Public Affairs Absorb Our Interest

Like most southern women of her class, Lucy Wood was knowledgeable about political affairs, and her letter revealed that she had thought carefully about the implications of secession. Her objections to disunion, she explained to Waddy Butler, arose from her fears that an independent southern nation would reopen the African slave trade, a policy she found "extremely revolting." Yet as she elaborated her position, detailing her disagreements with the man she intended to wed, Wood abruptly and revealingly interrupted the flow of her argument. "But I have no political opinion and have a peculiar dislike to all females who discuss such matters."[3]

However compelling the unfolding drama in which they found themselves, southern ladies knew well that in nineteenth-century America, politics was regarded as the privilege and responsibility of men. As one South Carolina lady decisively remarked, "woman has not business with such matters." Men voted; men spoke in public; ladies appropriately remained within the sphere of home and family. Yet the secession crisis would see these prescriptions honored in the breach as much as the observance. In this moment of national upheaval, the lure of politics seemed all but irresistible. "Politics engrosses my every thought," Amanda Sims confided to her friend Harriet Palmer. "Public affairs absorb all our interest," confirmed Catherine Edmondston of North Carolina. In Richmond, Lucy Bagby crowded into the ladies' gallery to hear the Virginia Convention's electrifying secession debates, and women began customarily to arrive an hour before the proceedings opened each morning in order to procure good seats. Aging South Carolina widow Keziah Brevard confessed that she was so caught up in the stirring events that when she awoke in the night, "My first thought is 'my state is out of the union.' "[4]

Like Lucy Wood, however, many women thought this preoccupation not entirely fitting, even if irresistible. Few were as adamant in their opposition to women's growing political interest and assertiveness as Louisianian Sarah Morgan, who longed "for a place where I would never hear a woman talk politics" and baldly declared, "I hate to hear women on political subjects." But most ladies were troubled by feeling so strongly about matters they could only defensively claim as their rightful concern. "I wonder sometimes," wrote Ada Bacot, a young widow, "if people think it strange I should be so warm a secessionist, but," she continued more confidently, "why should they, has not every woman a right to express her opinions upon such subjects, in private if not in public?" The "Ladies of Browards Neck" Florida demonstrated a similar mixture of engagement and self-doubt when they united to address the "politicians" of their state in a letter to the *Jacksonville Standard*. Their positive views on secession, they assured their readers, were not frivolous or ill-founded but were supported in fact and argument. "And if any person is desirous to know how we come by the information to which we allude, we tell them in advance, by reading the newspapers and public journals for the ten years past and when we read we do so with inquiring minds peculiar to our sex." Rather than accepting their womanhood as prohibiting political activism or undermining the legitimacy of their political views, these Florida ladies insisted on the special advantages of their female identity, boldly and innovatively claiming politics as peculiarly appropriate to the woman's sphere.[5]

Catherine Edmondston worried about the vehemence of her secessionist views because of the divisions they were causing in her own family. Before Lincoln's call for troops in April 1861, Edmondston's parents and sister remained staunch Unionists, although Catherine and her husband of fifteen years strongly supported the new southern nation. Edmondston found the resulting conflict very "painful" and was particularly distressed at having to disagree with her father. "It is the first time in my life that my judgment & feelings did not yeild to him." It was a "pity," she observed, that politics had become so heated as to "intrude into private life." Boundaries between what she had regarded as public and private domains were being undermined, as were previously unquestioned definitions of women's place within them. As war consumed the South, Edmondston would find that little space was left to what she called "private life." The private, the domestic, would become part of the homefront, another battlefield in what was by 1865 to become total war.[6]

In 1861, however, southern women still largely accepted the legitimacy of divisions between the private and the public, the domestic and the political, the sphere of women and the sphere of men. Yet they nevertheless resisted being excluded from the ever more heated and ever more engrossing political conflict that surrounded them. Women's politics in the secession crisis was necessarily a politics of ambivalence. Often women, like men, were torn about their decision to support or oppose secession. Few white southerners of either sex left the Union without a pang of regret for the great American experiment, and just as few rejected the newly independent South without a parallel sense of loss. "It is like uprooting some of our holiest sentiments to feel that to love [the Union] longer is to be treacherous to ourselves and our country," remarked Susan Cornwall of Georgia. As Catherine Edmondston explained, it seemed to her perfectly acceptable for a Confederate to "mourn over" the United States "as for a lost friend."[7]

But women's political ambivalence in the secession crisis arose from a deeper source as well: their uncertainty about their relationship to politics altogether. Admitting that they as women had no place in the public sphere, they nevertheless asserted their claims within it. Yet they acted with considerable doubt, with reluctance and apology, longing to behave as ladies but declining to stand aside while history unfolded around them. War had not yet begun, but southern women had already inaugurated their effort to claim a place and an interest in the national crisis.

Your Country Calls

What one Alabama lady called the "unexpected proportions" of the Civil War would take most Americans North and South by surprise. Many southerners anticipated that the Union would not contest southern secession, and James Chesnut, former United States senator from South Carolina, confidently promised that he would drink all the blood spilled in the movement for independence. Yet as soon as their states seceded, southern men began to arm and drill, and expectations of military conflict at once thrilled and frightened the region's women. Looking back on those early days, one Virginia lady remarked that war had at first seemed like "a pageant and a tournament," but others wrote of "foreboding for the future" or of a "trembling fear" of what might be in store. Disunion troubled Julia Davidson for reasons entirely apart from divisions of politics. "I study about it sometimes," she wrote her husband, John, "and get The blues so bad I do not know what to do. God grant That all things may yet be settled without *bloodshed*." As an elderly widow living alone on a large plantation, Keziah Brevard feared not just military bloodshed but worried too about what she called the "enemies in our midst," the vulnerability of the South to slave uprisings.[8]

White southern women felt far freer than their men to admit – and even no doubt to feel – fears that, however unmanly, were entirely justified by the perilous circumstances facing the South. Women voiced apprehensions about war and anxieties about loss of particular loved ones, fears that masculine conventions of honor and courage would not permit men to express. From the outset this touch of realism tempered women's politics and women's patriotism; the culturally accepted legitimacy of women's private feelings and everyday obligations posed a counterweight to the romantic masculine ideology of war. Soon after the passage of the Ordinance of Secession, a South Carolina lady offered her womanly resolution of the inconsistency between these imperatives, explicitly privileging the personal over the political, loyalty to family over obligation to the state. "I do not approve of this thing," she declared. "What do I care for patriotism? My husband is my country. What is country to me if he be killed?" Kate Rowland of Georgia admitted that her "patriotism is at a very low ebb when Charlie comes in competition." When her husband joined the army, she had no ambition for him to garner fame and glory; instead she wished him to secure a post as far as possible from all fighting. "Charlie is dearer to me than my country, & I cannot willingly give him up," she confessed.[9]

The conflict between women's emergent patriotism and their devotion to the lives and welfare of their families became clear as southern men prepared for war. Very precise expectations of men's appropriate behavior in wartime enhanced many women's enthusiasm for the Confederacy. The romance of the military and the close association of manhood with honor, courage, and glory outweighed the reluctance many women felt to give up their loved ones, for they had come to believe that the very value of these men was inseparable from their willingness to sacrifice their lives in battle. A "man did not deserve the name of man if he did not fight for his country," Kate Cumming concluded. One lady of the Shenandoah Valley sent her son off to camp with a triumphant proclamation in the columns of the *Winchester Virginian*: "Your country calls. . . . I am ready to offer you up in defense of your country's rights and honor; and I now offer you, a beardless boy of 17 summers, – not with grief, but thanking God that I have a son to offer." Sarah Lawton of Georgia celebrated the opportunities she thought war would provide to make men more manly and to arrest what she regarded as men's failure to fulfill her expectations of them. "I think something was needed to wake them from their effeminate habits and [I] welcome war for that." Mary Vaught ceased speaking to those of her gentleman friends who had not enlisted, and a group of young women in Texas presented hoopskirts and bonnets to all the men in the neighborhood who did not volunteer.[10]

But the call for soldiers deeply troubled many women, who anticipated that their husbands and sons might well meet death rather than glory on the battlefield. Alabama widow Sarah Espy was distressed by her son's determination to enlist. "I do not like it much," she wrote, "but will have to submit." Lizzie Ozburn of Georgia endured just a few weeks of army service by her husband, Jimmie, before herself arranging for a substitute to complete his term of enlistment. "Then if you don't come," she warned him, "you wont have any lady to come to when you do come."[11]

The conflicting imperatives of patriotism and protectiveness played themselves out dramatically in the ritualized moment of troop departures. Communities gathered en masse to wish the soldiers farewell and often to present them with uniforms or flags sewn by local ladies. Patriotic addresses were the order of the day, and the soldiers marched off, as one young member of the elite Washington Artillery described it, "pelted with fruit, flowers, cards & notes" from throngs of ladies. Ceremonies of colorful uniforms, waving banners, patriotic speeches, and martial music displayed all the romance of war as well as unbounded expectations of personal courage and glorious victory.[12]

The ebullience of the crowd, however, often came at the expense of considerable repression of feeling. Gertrude Thomas spoke of the "speechless agony" with which she bade her husband good-bye, and Emily Harris seemed almost resentful that "It has always been my lot to be obliged to shut up my griefs in my own breast." When one woman burst into tears before two young soldiers, their mother chastised her, "How could you, let them see you crying? It will unman them." Men could evidently be men only with considerable female assistance.[13]

But often enough, women, especially younger ones, did break down. Sixteen-year-old Louisiana Burge described the reactions of her boarding school friends to the departure of a regiment from their Georgia town. Almost all the girls were weeping. "Em Bellamy spent nearly the whole evening in my room crying about the war and John T. Burr who leaves tonight. . . . Between her and cousin Emma Ward crying about Ed Gwinn I have had a time of it. . . . Ginnie Gothey's feelings have overcome her; she has gone to bed, sick with crying about Bush Lumsden who don't care a snap for her. Ridiculous! I can hear Susie Clayton screaming way down in her room."[14]

A seventeen-year-old bride loudly voiced her rejection of the masculine ethos of war for the feminine ideal of domestic love. "Oh Dan! Dan!" she sobbed, "I don't want to be proud of you. I just don't want you to get hurt! . . . I don't want fame or glory! I want you!" Catherine Edmondston, more mature as well as considerably invested in her new claims to a political identity and new sense of public responsibility, contrasted her behavior with the likes of this young bride. As her husband, Patrick, departed with his men, "The women, many of them wept, sobbed, nay even shreiked aloud, but I had no tears to shed then. With a calm, stern, determined feeling I saw them depart. The sentiment of exalted Patriotism which filled my heart found no echo in Lamentations, no vent in tears. He is gone, gone in the highest exercise of man's highest & holiest duty! . . . I would not have him here, would not have him fail in one duty, falter in one step."[15]

Catherine Edmondston's posture embodied the prescriptions of an emergent ideology of wartime womanhood. Confederate females could not privilege their personal needs above the demands of the nation. In the moment of crisis, country had to come before husband or son. If the South was to survive, women had to become patriotic, had to assume some of the political interests of men, and had to repress certain womanly feelings and expectations for the good of the Cause. Woman should cultivate a spirit of "self reliance," should practice "self denial," wrote Leila W. in a piece for the *Southern Monthly* that she entitled "Woman A Patriot." But, the essayist was careful to add, "we do not mean to say that she should become masculine."[16]

By the summer of 1861 the effort to create a new Confederate woman was well under way in the South's public press. Military manpower needs required a rationalization of female sacrifice and a silencing of women's direct interest in protecting husbands and sons. The nineteenth-century creed of domesticity had long urged self-denial and service to others as central to woman's mission, but war necessitated significant alterations – even perversions – of this ideology of behavior and identity. Women's self-sacrifice for personally significant others – husbands, brothers, sons, or family – was transformed into sacrifice *of* those individuals to an abstract and intangible cause.[17]

Redefining women's sacrifice in this manner created both logical and emotional difficulties for southerners, who endeavored to address and resolve these contradictions in extensive public discussion. Gender thus became an explicit subject of widespread debate. Songs, plays, poems, even official presidential pronouncements sought to enlist women of all classes in the work of filling the ranks. One popular theme urged young women to bestow their favors only on men in uniform. In a much reprinted song, a male songwriter assumed a female voice to proclaim, "I Would Like to Change My Name." This fictionalized heroine was searching for a husband,

> But he must be a soldier
> A veteran from the wars,
> One who has fought for "Southern Rights"
> Beneath the Bars and Stars.

A letter from "Many Ladies" to the *Charleston Daily Courier* in August 1861 warned cowards and slackers, "None but the brave deserve the fair." Even Jefferson Davis addressed the question of women's appropriate marital choice, declaring the empty sleeve of the mutilated veteran preferable to the "muscular arm" of "him who staid at home and grew fat."[18]

One song published early in the war acknowledged the clash between woman's traditional role and the conflict's new demands. From "stately hall" to "cottage fair," every woman rich or poor was confronted by her own "stormy battle" raging within her breast.

> There Love, the true, the brave,
>   The beautiful, the strong,
> Wrestles with Duty, gaunt and stern–
>   Wrestles and struggles long.[19]

Like male songwriters who addressed that theme, the "Soldiers Wife" who had penned the lyrics was certain that, like soldiers, women themselves would win "heart victories" over their emotions and in their "proudest triumphs" send their menfolk off to war. Stirring marches commemorated the scene of parting, with men striding nobly into the horizon while women such as Catherine Edmondston just as nobly waved handkerchiefs and cheered their departure. "Go fight for us, we'll pray for you. Our mothers did so before us." Popular songs and poems deplored the very behavior Edmondston had found so upsetting, urging women to repress their grief, lest they weaken soldiers' resolve. "The maid who binds her warrior's sash/And smiling all her pain dissembles" or "The mother who conceals her grief" accomplished woman's highest duty, a poem in the *Richmond Record* affirmed. Women, one newspaper proclaimed, had been offered a "glorious privilege" in the opportunity to contribute to the Cause by offering up their men. Yet popular expression acknowledged that women often harbored lingering doubt. A newspaper poem, "I've Kissed Him and Let Him Go," was among the frankest of such treatments.[20]

> There is some, I know, who feel a strange pride
>   In giving their country their all,
> Who count it a glory that boys from their side
>   In the strife are ready to fall,
> But I sitting here have no pride in my heart
>   (God forgive that this should be so!)
> For the boy that I love the tears will still start.
>   Yet I've kissed him and let him go.

Best was to feel right, so dedicated to the Cause that personal interest all but disappeared. Next best was to stifle lingering personal feeling. But the minimal requirement was to silence doubt and behave properly, even if right feeling proved unattainable. Catherine Edmondston and Gertrude Thomas both knew how they were expected to act, as did the Louisiana woman who confided to her diary, "How I do hate to give him up, but I suppose I have to be a martyr during this war."[21]

Notes

1   Title from *New Orleans Daily Picayune*, June 9, 1861; Lucy Wood to Waddy Butler, January 21, 1861, Lucy Wood Butler Papers, UVA. Because the subject of this book is elite, white, southern women, I will not endlessly repeat the adjectives *elite, white,* and *southern* when discussing this group. I will assume that, like a pronoun with a clear referent, my meaning will usually be evident. I will repeat the adjectives in order to make distinctions clear when I am also discussing other groups of women and from time to time to emphasize an awareness of the dangerous tendency in some early women's history to conflate women of all classes and races and to ignore their differences. The construction and reconstruction of class and racial difference is central to my project in this book, as it was to the identity work that characterized the wartime experience of women of the South's master class. See Elizabeth Spelman, *Inessential Woman: Problems of Exclusion in Feminist Thought* (Boston: Beacon, 1988); Bonnie Thornton Dill, "Race, Class, and Gender: Prospects for an All-Inclusive Sisterhood," *Feminist Studies* 9 (Spring 1983); 131–50; and Nancy A. Hewitt, "Beyond the Search for Sisterhood: American Women's History in the 1980s," in *Unequal Sisters: A Multicultural Reader in U.S. Women's History*, ed. Vicki L. Ruiz and Ellen Carol DuBois, 2nd edn (New York: Routledge, 1994), pp. 1–19.

2 Lucy Wood to Waddy Butler, January 21, 1861, Butler Papers, Manscripts Department, Alderman Library, University of Virginia (UVA); Kate Cumming, *Kate: The Journal of a Confederate Nurse*, ed. Richard Barksdale Harwell (Baton Rouge: Louisiana State University Press, 1959), p. 39.

3 Lucy Wood to Waddy Butler, January 21, 1861, Butler Papers, UVA. Wood's opposition to the African slave trade was shared by many Virginians, and the Confederate constitution prohibited the trade partly as a gesture to win over the wavering border states, especially Virginia.

4 Ada Bacot Diary, December 12, 1860, South Carolina Library, University of South Carolina, Columbia (SCL); Amanda Sims to Harriet Palmer, December 9, 1861, Palmer Family Papers, SCL; Catherine Ann Devereux Edmondston, April 16, 1861, in *Journal of a Secesh Lady: The Diary of Catherine Ann Devereux Edmondston, 1860–1866*, ed. Beth G. Crabtree and James W. Patton (Raleigh: Division of Archives and History, 1979), p. 50; "Reminiscences of Lucy Bagby," Bagby Family Papers, Virginia Historical Society Richmond VA (VHS); Keziah Brevard Diary, January 6, 1861, SCL. See also Amy E. Murrell, "Two Armies: Women's Activism in Civil War Richmond" (senior honors thesis, Duke University, 1993). Elizabeth Varon's recent dissertation argues that these prescriptions were often honored in the breach rather than the observance in the prewar South as well. She documents much wider political activism by Virginia women than scholars have hitherto recognized, but she also shows the persistence of a conflicting ideology. See Varon, " 'We Mean to Be Counted': White Women and Politics in Antebellum Virginia" (PhD dissertation, Yale University, 1993). On women and politics generally, see Paula Baker, "The Domestication of Politics: Women and American Political Society, 1780–1920," *American Historical Review* 89 (June 1984), 620–47, and Michael McGerr, "Political Style and Women's Power, 1830–1930," *Journal of American History* 77 (December 1990), 864–85.

5 Sarah Morgan, *The Civil War Diary of Sarah Morgan*, ed. Charles East (Athens: University of Georgia Press, 1991), pp. 121, 73–4; Bacot Diary, January 19, 1861, SCL; Samuel Proctor, ed., "The Call to Arms: Secession from a Feminine Point of View," *Florida Historical Quarterly* 35 (January 1957), 267.

6 Edmondston, *Journal of a Secesh Lady*, pp. 54, 34.

7 Susan Cornwall Diary, February 4, 1861, Southern Historical Collection University of North Carolina, Chapel Hill (SHC); Edmondston, *Journal of a Secesh Lady*, p. 35. Slaveowing women of the Confederate South adopted the language of separate male and female spheres, of distinct public and private realms, to express their uneasiness with war's transformations and to understand and negotiate the changes in their lives. We must be careful to recognize that these are their analytic or conceptual characterizations and to distinguish their rendering of their experience from our own assessments of the shape of their world. In the course of the war, Confederate women used the language of "spheres" to legitimate resistance to change, to ease the shock of change by denying it altogether, and, on occasion, to make change more palatable by describing it in familiar terms. Their characterizations often represent ideals or prescriptions that seem to the historian strikingly at odds with their own behavior or circumstances. Their contradictory comments and actions in regard to secession politics make this clear at the outset. I have been more interested in the ideological and social strategies that their use of this language reveals than I have been in the accuracy of these terms as descriptions of their behavior and lives. Although I state in the Preface that private lives essentially ended in the South with the outbreak of war, Confederate women came to this realization slowly, haltingly, painfully, and incompletely. It is this evolution that is at the heart of their war story. For a discussion of how women's historians have often failed to separate their own analytic uses of "separate spheres" from those of their nineteenth-century subjects, see Linda K. Kerber, "Separate Spheres, Female Worlds, Woman's Place: The Rhetoric of Women's History," *Journal of American History* 75 (June 1988), 39.

8 N. Van Beel to Jefferson Davis, August 14, 1861, LRCSW, RG 109, reel 10, p. 5521, NA; Mary Early Scrapbook, p. 17, VHS; Edmondston, *Journal of a Secesh Lady*, p. 44; Fannie Page Hume Diary, April 17, 1861, UVA; Julia Davidson to John Davidson, January 8, 1861, Davidson Family Papers, AHC; Brevard Diary, April 13, 1861, SCL.

9 Margaret Crawford Adams, "Tales of a Grandmother," in *South Carolina Women in the Confederacy*, ed. Mrs. Thomas Taylor, Mrs. A. T. Smythe, Mrs. August Kohn, Miss M. B. Poppenheim, and Miss Martha Washington, 2 vols. (Columbia, SC.: State Co., 1903), 1;210; Kate Rowland Diary, December 12, 29, 1863, EU.

10 Cumming, *Kate*, p. 49; letter from Ann Catron, *Winchester Virginian*, May 8, 1861; Sarah Lawton to General Henry Rootes Jackson, September 9, 1861, Sarah Lawton Papers, GDAH; Mother to William Vaught, March 18, 1862, William Vaught Papers, RU; J. M. Fain to Huldah Fain Briant, May 19, 1862, Huldah Annie Briant Papers, DU.

11 Sarah Espy Diary, April 19, 1861, ADAH; Lizzie Ozburn to Jimmie Ozburn, October 14, 1861, Katherine Elizabeth Ozburn Papers, GDAH.

12 William Vaught to Mary Vaught, August 9, 1862, Vaught Papers, RU.

13 Ella Gertrude Clanton Thomas, *The Secret Eye: The Journal of Ella Gertrude Clanton Thomas, 1848– 1889*, ed. Virginia Ingraham Burr (Chapel Hill: University of North Carolina Press, 1990), p. 192; *The Journals of David Golightly Harris*, ed. Philip N. Racine (Knoxville: University of Tennessee Press, 1990), p. 268; Betty Herndon Maury, *The Confederate Diary of Betty Herndon Maury, 1861– 1863*, ed. Alice Maury Parmalee (Washington, DC: privately printed, 1938), pp. 3–4.

14 Richard B. Harwell, "Louisiana Burge: The Diary of a Confederate College Girl," *Georgia Historical Quarterly* 36 (June 1952), 153.

15 Myrta Lockett Avary, ed., *A Virginia Girl in the Civil War, 1861–1865* (New York: Appleton, 1903), p. 27; Edmondston, *Journal of a Secesh Lady*, p. 69.

16 Leila W., "Woman A Patriot," *Southern Monthly* 1 (October 1861), 115.

17 Public discourse and popular culture in the Confederacy might appropriately be considered what Michel Foucault has called "technologies of power," designed to rework human identities in accordance with shifting cultural and social needs. See Foucault, *The Discourse on Language* (New York: Random House, 1971) and *Power/Knowledge: Selected Interviews and Other Writings, 1972– 1977*, ed. Colin Gordon (New York: Pantheon, 1980).

18 Theodore von La Hache, *I Would Like to Change My Name: A Favorite Encore Song* (Augusta: Blackmar & Bro., 1863); *Charleston Daily Courier*, August 15, 1861; Davis quoted in unidentified newspaper clipping in George Bagby Scrapbook, 2:128, George Bagby Papers, VHS.

19 "Heart Victories," in *Songs of the South* (Richmond: J. W. Randolph, 1862), pp. 68–69.

20 "Our Mothers Did So before Us," in ibid., pp. 70–1; *Richmond Record of News, History and Literature*, September 3, 1863, p. 105; *Charleston Daily Courier*, August 19, 1861; "I've Kissed Him and Let Him Go," clipping in Bagby Scrapbook, 5:99, George Bagby Papers, VHS.

21 Priscilla Munnikhuysen Bond Diary, June 29, 1862, Louisiana State University, Baton Rouge, LA.

Questions to consider

- What are some of the ways the Civil War divided men from women?

- What did it mean for a Southern woman to be patriotic? Do you think the Southern answer to this question was different from the Northern one? (Consider, for example, the United States Sanitary Commission described in Part IV and the lack of a Southern counterpart.)

- What role did popular culture play in articulating gender roles?

Chapter 26

When God Made Me I Wasn't Much, But I's a Man Now

Jim Cullen

What happens when a group of people suddenly gets engendered in a dramatically new way? Slaves were always identified by sex – it was an important classification tool for masters, to be exploited. But many of the distinctions white people made in the roles of men and women were deemed irrelevant for slaves, who did not have the option of living their family or work lives in ways that allowed much in the way of differentiation. A slave "lady," for example, was a virtual contradiction in terms. But for African American men in particular, the war, emancipation, and the eventual use of black troops on a large scale transformed their identity in profound ways, allowing them to claim, and explore, a term whose meaning is still sometimes elusive: manhood. In this 1992 essay, Jim Cullen describes this crucial turning point in the history of African American men.

Jim Cullen, "I's a Man Now: Gender and African American Men," in *Divided Houses: Gender and the Civil War*, eds. Catherine Clinton and Nina Silber (New York: Oxford University Press, 1992), pp. 76–91. Copyright © 1992 by Catherine Clinton and Nina Silber. Used by permission of Oxford University Press, Inc.

At one point in the 1989 film *Glory*, a former slave named Rawlins who has enlisted in the Union army gets angry at a fellow soldier. A runaway South Carolinian private named Trip has just insulted Searles, an educated Bostonian, by telling him he acts like "the white man's dog." Offended by this remark, Rawlins gives Trip a piece of his mind, criticizing him for his insolent attitude toward whites, his fellow soldiers, and the war effort in general. "The time's comin' when we're goin' to have to ante up and kick in like men," Rawlins tells Trip. "Like men!" Trip is not instantly transformed by these remarks, and he will take some of his rebellious skepticism to a sandy grave off the coast of Charleston. But while he later tells his commanding officer that he does not wish to carry the regimental colors, he echoes Rawlins by saying he plans to "ante up and kick in." And on the eve of the battle, he tells his fellow black soldiers that whatever may happen, "we men, ain't we." (They affirm him in unison.)

Like so much popular culture, these fictionalized characters reveal – and conceal – a good deal about American history and culture. Cast in an unabashedly heroic light where even rebels like Trip ultimately carry the flag, *Glory* obscures the ambivalence, ambiguity, and disillusionment that military experience held for many African American men and women during the Civil War. Indeed, the absence of black women in the film belies their presence in many military encampments as civilians, nurses, or, in the case of Harriet Tubman, crucial strategic combatants. On the other hand, *Glory* does suggest the diversity of black life in the United States in its cast of characters, and does, like many recent popular and academic histories, recognize the role African Americans played in securing their own emancipation.

Glory is also illuminating in the way it deals with gender. As the above example suggests, a concern with becoming and behaving like a man is an important theme of the movie, as indeed it was for many actual black soldiers. In newspaper articles, government affidavits, and letters to officials, families, and each other, manhood surfaces again and again as an aspiration, a concern, or a fact of life. But while it's one thing to note the recurring reference to manhood in such documents, it's another to know exactly what these people meant by it. Is one born (slave or free) with manhood, or must one earn it? Is it derived by virtue of one's sex, or is it the result of acting in a particular way? Did manhood mean the same thing to black people as it did to white people? Since many of these men were semi-literate – or had to depend on others to write for them – they were not inclined to elaborate on their terminology. Even those who were quite literate did not bother to explain what they assumed their readers would understand.

However varied their understanding of the term, what's striking in looking over the records these men left behind is a widely shared sense that the Civil War did indeed mark a watershed for black manhood. As the *material* conditions of their lives changed – as they joined the armed forces, were freed from slavery, or both – so too did their *ideological* conceptions of themselves as men. In some cases these new ideas were expressed explicitly; other times implicitly. As historian Joan Scott has noted, an awareness of sexual difference as fact or metaphor has always been important, though the concept of gender as a separate analytic category is very much a late-twentieth-century invention.[1] This means any exploration of gender in historical contexts should proceed with some caution. But proceed it should, because the attempt, however imperfect, to understand how other people understood themselves can perhaps still teach us something about them – and ourselves.

The outbreak of war in 1861 led men all over the country to volunteer for military service, and African Americans were no exception. In Washington, Pittsburgh, Cleveland, Boston, and many other cities and towns, black men offered their services singly or in groups to recruiting officers. Almost without exception, they were turned down. Ironically, black men had some of their best success in the Confederacy, though they were generally put to work building fortifications or other kinds of tasks requiring heavy labor. In one sense, this is hardly surprising: southern society had been organized for blacks to perform these roles, which were probably accepted during wartime in the hope of being looked upon with favor in the event of Confederate victory. Except in emergencies, southern blacks were not permitted to fight, and organizations like New Orleans's Native Guards (a part of the state militia composed of free African Americans) found offers of their services declined. Rejections varied in tone, but their content often echoed that of a Cincinnati man who said, "We want you damn niggers to keep out of this; this is a white man's war."[2]

Officially, he was right – at first it was a white man's war. The efforts of abolitionists to the contrary, secession, not slavery, was the pretext for the outbreak of hostilities, and the Lincoln administration assiduously courted slaveholding states still in the Union by avoiding any appearance of restructuring existing race relations. President Lincoln personally countermanded the orders of generals like John Fremont and David Hunter who attempted to free slaves in occupied Confederate territory, and resisted Congressional efforts to punish rebellious slaveholders by confiscating their "property."

Under such circumstances, one might wonder why African Americans wanted to fight at all. And in fact some did question getting involved. "We have nothing to gain, and everything to lose, by entering the lists as combatants," wrote one man from Troy, New York. Wrote another from Colorado: "I have observed with much indignation and shame, their [African Americans'] willingness to take up arms in defence of this unholy, illbegotten would-be Republican government." Many of those opposed to African American involvement were appalled by the prospect of fighting for a country that made no promise of redressing centuries of injustice. "I, as the Captain, in behalf of the company, am resolved never to offer or give service, except be it on equality with all other men," stated a prospective volunteer from Philadelphia.[3]

At the same time, however, many African Americans were eager to join the struggle even before the Emancipation Proclamation was issued, and cast their advocacy in gendered terms. On May 1, 1861, a group of freemen in New York City met and voted down a resolution offering to fight they knew would be rejected. Nevertheless, the *Anglo-African*, a weekly newspaper that circulated in the metropolitan area, urged its readers to remain in a state of readiness. Acknowledging the argument that the conflict was "a white man's war," the paper nevertheless asserted that the northern way of life offered privileges of free labor, education, and freedom from divided families that should be guarded, if not expanded. "Are these rights worth the having?" the *Anglo-African* asked. "If they are then they are worth defending with all our might and at any cost. It is illogical, unpatriotic, nay mean and unmanly in us to shrink from the defence of these rights and privileges." While some men challenged the *Anglo-African*'s position in letters to the editor, still others wrote to support it. "The issue is here; let us prepare to meet it with manly spirit," wrote one Philadelphia man in rebuke to another who had argued for a more neutral approach to the war.[4]

In mid-nineteenth-century America, the word "manly" was rich with connotations of an acquired sense of civilization and duty.[5] For participants in the *Anglo-African* debate, the manly thing to do was defend, and perhaps expand, a way of life by fighting, a behavior considered the unique province of males. It also meant having the will to act on one's own behalf. "God will help no one that refuses to help himself," the Philadelphia writer said in his letter. "The prejudiced white man North or South never will respect us until they are forced to by deeds of our own."[6]

Yet a willingness to fight, and thus achieve manhood by waging a war for freedom, seemed moot if African Americans were barred from fighting. "Why does the Government reject the negro?" asked a frustrated Frederick Douglass in August of 1861. "Is he not a man? Can he not wield a sword, fire a gun, march and countermarch, and obey orders like any other?"[7] For Douglass, of course, the questions were rhetorical. All black men needed was the chance to demonstrate the important truth that they were the white man's equal in war as well as peace.

Actually, some men had been quietly getting the chance from the very beginning. Despite the official federal ban on black recruitment, unofficial African American units were organized in Kansas, South Carolina, and Louisiana, and saw action in the early years of the war (indeed, blacks had been participants in the guerrilla warfare over "Bloody Kansas" for years). Moreover, as readers of Herman Melville's fiction know, the American navy had long been a multiracial institution.[8] Some men also worked as spies. Many others weakened the

Confederate war effort with acts of insubordination on plantations or by escaping from them, often finding refuge behind Union lines and working as cooks or laborers.

All these actions made official policy increasingly irrelevant. Meanwhile, intractable rebel resistance, military defeat, and growing difficulties in meeting manpower needs from white volunteers impelled the Lincoln administration to widen its war aims and turn the political screws on the Confederacy. It is in this context that the President issued the preliminary Emancipation Proclamation in September of 1862, which placed the war on new footing and placed the status of African Americans at the very center of national life.

Even as the political tide on slavery was turning in the summer of 1862, so was the US position on arming African Americans. In July, Congress passed a confiscation act enabling the President "to employ as many persons of African descent as he may deem necessary and proper for the suppression of this rebellion." It also repealed a 1792 law that barred blacks from the military. Lincoln himself also made the case for black enlistments that month when discussing emancipation with the Cabinet, and gave the go-ahead even before the proclamation was issued in September or took effect in January of 1863.

Simultaneously, military considerations became even more urgent than political ones. In the spring of 1862, the Confederate-spurned Native Guards of New Orleans offered to join the Union effort after General Benjamin Butler occupied the city. Butler at first refused, but when threatened by a Confederate attack in August, he changed his mind and recruited three black regiments. At the same time, the need to withdraw cavalry forces from captured territory in the South Sea Islands off the coast of South Carolina led to the formation of the "Department of the South," under which freed slaves were permitted to become soldiers.

It was the Emancipation Proclamation, however, that opened the floodgates for black enlistment. Now possessing the means – and promised a worthy end – leaders of the black community enthusiastically joined the recruitment effort. John S. Rock, William Wells Brown, Sojourner Truth, and many other luminaries from the northern abolitionist community worked as recruitment agents. The first two northern regiments were formed in Massachusetts, though in fact they were comprised of men from all over the North and even Canada. Meanwhile, over 20,000 volunteers were raised in the Mississippi valley between April and December of 1863 alone. By the end of the war, approximately 180,000 African Americans served in the United States Armed Forces. Constituting less than 1 percent of the North's population, African American soldiers comprised roughly 10 percent of the army.[9]

One of the most tireless proponents of black enlistment was Frederick Douglass, whose own sons joined the fabled Massachusetts 54th Volunteer Infantry. "Let the black man get upon his person the brass letters 'U.S.'; let him get an eagle on his button, and a musket on his shoulder and bullets in his pocket, and there is no power on earth which can deny that he has earned the right to citizenship in the United States," he wrote in one widely quoted article.[10]

The editor of *Douglass's Monthly* was also fond of drawing on the manly rhetoric of action. In another piece, he asserted that African Americans were fighting "for principle, and not from passion," and that the black soldier secures "manhood and freedom" via civilized warfare. Douglass went on to make an unfortunate comparison between blacks and Native Americans, "who go forth as a savage with a tomahawk and scalping knife," but in doing so he revealed a definition of manhood as less the amoral use of brute force than the controlled application of power to achieve a just objective.[11]

It wasn't only Douglass – or the black leadership – who drew on the language of manhood. Enlisted soldiers often appeared as featured speakers during recruitment drives and made such appeals to their audience. The remarks of one soldier in Nashville in 1863 are highly revealing in this regard:

Come boys, let's get some guns from Uncle Sam, and go coon hunting; shooting those gray back coons that go poking about the country nowadays (Laughter)...Don't ask your wife, for if she is worth having she will call you a coward for asking her. (Applause and waving of hankerchiefs by the ladies.)[12]

This passage is striking in two ways. First, it draws on the southern white habit of describing slaves as animals. Here, the blacks are the men and the rebels are the animals, rendered in a mode of male bravado that is still common in our own day. Second, these comments also suggest a definition of manhood derived from gender conventions understood – and endorsed – by women, of man as fighter who leaves the home in order to protect it.

Unfortunately, the story of the struggle for black enlistment is not an altogether happy one, and not only because these men fought for the right to kill and be killed. A variety of factors marred the effort. First among these was racism, which impeded the project in the North and checked it in the Confederacy until the very end of the war. "If you make [the African American] the instrument by which your victories are won," an Ohio congressman warned, "you must treat him as a victor is entitled to be treated, with all decent and becoming respect." Others supported black enlistment because they would rather have blacks die than whites. "But as for me, upon my soul!/So liberal are we here / I'll let Sambo be murthered instead of myself / On every day of the year" went a popular song attributed to Irish-Americans. Nor were such attitudes limited to the working classes. "When this war is over & we have summed up the entire loss of life it has imposed on the country I shall not have any regrets if it is found that a part of the dead are *niggers* and that *all* are not white men," wrote the Governor of Iowa to the general-in-chief of the army in 1862.[13]

Indeed, white eagerness to have blacks serve in the army reached vicious proportions. Civilians and government officials soon realized that enlisted blacks could be credited toward conscription quotas, and coercion and terror were often the result, as some black men were literally abducted from their homes and forced into the army. Northern states would send agents to enlist "underemployed" men of the occupied South for a fee, and they wandered the countryside in search of recruits, often impeding military operations and demanding food, forage, and transportation from their "hosts." In many cases, these men also bilked enlistees of their bounties.[14]

Even those who entered the army freely and enthusiastically quickly encountered situations making it clear that even if the Union was committed to freedom, it had no intention of offering equality. Once black enlistment became official policy, the government ordered that all black units should have only white commissioned officers, barring advancement to enlisted African Americans. Many blacks who were already officers, especially in New Orleans, were systematically hounded into resigning their commissions. The army did permit the commissioning of chaplains and surgeons, and there were some exceptions made to the rule, most notably Martin Delany, who was promoted to major at the very end of the war. Noncommissioned officers were also allowed, but these had much less prestige.[15]

Another source of frustration was pay. Despite the promise of receiving the same amount of money as whites, black soldiers were paid only about half of what their white counterparts were. Some black units refused their pay in protest, at great personal cost to themselves and their families, and still others threatened to lay down their arms. Some were shot or jailed for their protests. Some 80 percent of US soldiers shot for mutiny were black.[16]

A letter to the Governor of Massachusetts by a commander of black troops suggests how central a place manhood – more specifically, a sense of manhood that insisted upon an equality previously limited to whites – occupied in such disputes:

They enlisted because *men* were called for, and because the Government signified its willingness to accept them as such not because of the money offered them. They would rather work and fight until they are mustered out of the Service, without any pay than accept from the Government less than it gives to other soldiers from Massachusetts, and by so accepting acknowledge that because they have African blood in their veins, they are less men, than those who have saxon.[17]

When, after much delay, Congress finally acted to correct the situation in June of 1864, it did so by making an invidious distinction between those who had been slaves before the war and those who were free. Such a policy impaired morale within these regiments, and exacerbated tensions between northern and southern blacks, and the previously slave and previously free.[18]

Finally, African Americans were often given a disproportionate amount of fatigue duty. Ordered to dig ditches, build fortifications, clean latrines, or other dirty work, they were often denied the opportunity to drill or perform the more esteemed tasks of soldiering. Such practices not only bred resentment but also contributed to the higher disease rate among blacks, many of whom shouldn't have been in the army in the first place or who were overworked by their officers. Whereas two white soldiers died of disease for every one who died in battle, for blacks the ratio was about ten to one. One in twelve whites in the Union army died of disease in the war; one in five blacks did.[19]

The flagrant abuses suffered by these men led many recruiters, including Douglass, to suspend their efforts, while those oppressed by these injustices sought the aid of sympathetic officers or government officials. Here, too, the language of manhood was used, not so much as an assertion that African Americans were entitled to the same challenges whites were, but as a request for decency for those whose identities could not be reduced to that of a mere worker, as was the case under slavery. "The black men has wives and Sweet harts Jest like the white men," stated an anonymous New Orleans black man in 1863:

> it is rettin that a man can not Serve two master But it Seems that the Collored population has got two a rebel master and a union master the both want our Servises one wants us to make Cotton and Sugar and the Sell it and keep the money the union masters wants us to fight the battles under white officers and the injoy both the money and the union.[20]

"Today the Anglo Saxon Mother, Wife, or Sister are not alone, in tears for departed Sons, Husbands, and Brothers," wrote another man to President Lincoln, describing the apathy and contempt with which blacks were treated, and the deprivations endured by the "needy Wives, and little ones" at home. "We have done a Soldiers Duty," he said. "Why cant we have a soldier's pay?"[21] Implicit in such writings was a belief that manhood meant responsibility not only to the nation or even one's race but to the "Sweet harts" and families whose pride – and, more pointedly, whose livelihoods – depended on those in the service. Indeed, it seems there were times when men affirmed their manhood by preferring family over the army. "I poor man, wid large famerly – my wife Rinah she can't work," said one husband, who had already served in the army, to a recruiter. "Dey took me an' kep me tree mont' an' nebber pay me, not one cent. My wife hav notting to eat – mus' starve."[22]

Despite the multiple setbacks these African American soldiers endured, some did find entrance into the armed forces to be an affirming experience. "Now we sogers are men – for the first time in our lives," a sergeant based in South Carolina told a meeting in Philadelphia. "Now we can look our old masters in de face. They used to sell and whip us, and we did not dare say one word. Now we ain't afraid, if they meet us, to run the bayonet through them." A former slave agreed with this assessment. "This was the biggest thing that ever happened in my life," he said. "I feel like a man with a uniform on and a gun in my hand." Even whites who worked with these men were struck by the transformation. "Put a United States uniform on his back and the *chattel* is a *man*," observed one white soldier. "You can see it in his look. Between the toiling slave and the soldier is nothing but a god could lift him over. He feels it, his looks show it."[23]

Becoming a "man" killed two racist conceptions of African Americans with one stone. In the years before the war, southern whites had defended their peculiar institution by describing blacks as children or animals, depending on which description made their "stewardship" more rhetorically defensible.[24] As armed soldiers, these people were neither. War has always been seen as a place where "boys" become men, but for African American men in the Civil War, this was particularly true, even poignant. Soldiering also endowed these men with a new power to prevent the capricious abuse of those who could no longer be considered property. "The fact is, when colored Soldiers are about they are afraid to kick colored people on the streets as they usually do," black minister Henry Turner told the secretary of war in February of 1866.[25]

Becoming a man also had sexual dimensions. Turner described an experience eight months before, when the men in his regiment stripped their clothes to cross a stream:

> I was much amused to see the secesh women watching with the utmost intensity, thousands of our soldiers, in a state of nudity. I suppose they desired to see whether these audacious Yankees were really men, made like other men, or if they were a set of varmints. So they thronged the windows, porticos, and yards, in the finest attire imaginable. Our brave boys would disrobe themselves, hang their garments upon their bayonets and through the water they would come, walk up on the street, and seem to say to the feminine gazers, "Yes, though naked, we are your masters."[26]

In this striking passage – and, one imagines, widely elsewhere – manhood becomes sexual power. In the antebellum South, intercourse (sexual and otherwise) was either taboo or cast African American men in a subordinate position. Now, however, these men have attained mastery over their bodies which they use for their own purposes, a mastery that compels white southerners to observe it in action. No force is used, no words are exchanged, but the effect of a new sexual order is unmistakable, symbolized by bayonets supporting (Yankee) uniforms.

For many men, black and white, the ultimate test of manhood was combat. As noted, African Americans participated in a number of land and sea battles in the first two years of the war, but three engagements in 1863 went far to validate – and valorize – the contributions of African Americans. The first of these was at Port Hudson in Louisiana, a key Confederate stronghold for the control of the Mississippi River. Black troops participated on an assault on the fort, which failed. But their performance impressed many observers. "It is no longer possible to doubt the bravery and steadiness of the colored race, when rightly led," the New York *Times* reported.[27] There is more than a little paternalism in this statement, as in Thomas Wentworth Higginson's remark that the men under his charge were "growing more like white men – less naive and less grotesque."[28] Yet just as much as the black soldiers it was white observers who were re-evaluating their perceptions in light of new developments.

This is true even of Confederates. Barely ten days after Port Hudson, at the battle of Milliken's Bend, African Americans played a crucial role in resisting a rebel attack designed to weaken the Federal grip around Port Hudson and Vicksburg. Perhaps the best explanation of what followed was offered by a southern general: "The charge was resisted by the negro portion of the enemy's force with considerable obstinacy, while the white or true Yankee portion ran like whipped curs almost as soon as the charge was ordered."[29] Even though "true" Yankees are white, this man allows that it was black soldiers who defeated the Confederates.

The most celebrated battle involving black troops was the struggle for Fort Wagner off the coast of Charleston in July of 1863. (This event forms the backdrop for *Glory*.) In part this stems from the participation of the Massachusetts 54th led by Robert Gould Shaw, the son of prominent abolitionists, who would die in the assault and be lionized for the next century. As in the case of Port Hudson, the assault on Wagner was a failure in military terms, but a resounding political and cultural victory for blacks. "It is not too much to say that if this Massachusetts 54th had faltered when its trial had come, two hundred thousand colored troops for whom it was a pioneer would never have been put into the field," according to the New York *Tribune*.[30] Black troops would later play an important role in the Virginia theater in 1864, and were the first to march into Charleston when the city finally fell in 1865.

As in so many other aspects of black life, these victories came at a price. First among these costs was death. At Milliken's Bend, one Louisiana regiment lost almost 45 percent of its men to death or casualties, one of the highest proportions of any battle in the whole war.[31] There is a cruel irony that black men did so much dying on the battlefield – considered the very zenith of manhood – even as they were still dismissed as less than men.

There was also a persistent concern that African Americans were used as cannon fodder. Seven months after the Fort Wagner attack, an attack all knew would be a bloodbath for the unit that led it, a correspondent from the New York *Tribune* testified before the American Freedmen's Inquiry Commission that a battle planner had said, "Well, I guess we will let [abolitionist general George] Strong lead and put those d—d niggers from Massachusetts in the advance; we may as well get rid of them, one time or another."[32] Ironically, even when white commanders had relatively good intentions, they could backfire. At the last minute, black units trained to lead the attack at the Battle of the Crater in 1864 were held back in favor of white units to avoid charges of treating black life casually. But when white units foundered in the assault, the blacks were sent to assist, got trapped, and the result was disaster for all.

Another problem was the enemy. The Confederacy refused to treat black soldiers as prisoners of war in exchange negotiations, which led the Union to stop exchanges altogether, with particularly tragic results for those in dangerously unhealthy prison camps. Threats to execute all black soldiers were never officially enacted, perhaps in fear of reprisals President Lincoln promised would follow. But rebel hatred for black troops led to widespread reports of brutal massacres, most notably at Fort Pillow, Tennessee, where future Ku Klux Klan founder Nathan Bedford Forrest allegedly allowed black soldiers who had surrendered to be executed and allegedly condoned the burning of a hospital. "Remember Fort Pillow!" became a rallying cry for black soldiers who subsequently fought with even greater ferocity, often flying a black flag that signified that they would not expect – or give – any mercy.

The most sincere form of flattery is imitation, and the Union's success in mobilizing black manpower led to proposals from leading Confederates to arm African Americans. To do so, however, would create difficult ideological contradictions for a would-be nation predicated on white supremacy and slavery, and such proposals were rejected. Still, as one proslavery theorist told Jefferson Davis in 1865, blacks could fight and be granted their freedom, but that's all – no voting, legal protection, or any form of equality. Indeed, such a suggestion seems prescient in suggesting the fate of African Americans before and after Reconstruction.[33] Even more persuasive than the force of such logic was the deteriorating military situation, and the support of General Robert E. Lee in enlisting blacks led the Confederate government to change its mind in the spring. By then, however, it was too late; within weeks, black Union troops would be among the first to march into Richmond. They would also be among the last to leave the army; the black proportion of the armed forces went from about one-tenth to over one-third by the fall of 1865, as earlier enlistees were mustered out first and some blacks were sent to remote outposts.[34]

The passage of the Thirteenth Amendment and Union victory in 1865 represented a watershed in African American history, one in which the actions of many blacks, North and

South, slave and free, man and woman, had participated. The sense of pride of – and in – army veterans was especially strong, and many went on to become leaders in their communities. Some, like naval hero Robert Smalls and army officer Martin Delany, became important political leaders in state and national politics. For the rest of their lives, black men would relish their contributions. "If we hadn't become sojers, all might have gone back as it was before," former slave and army veteran Thomas Long wrote after the war. "But now tings can neber go back, because we have showed our energy and our courage and our naturally manhood."[35]

Perhaps the most important, and lasting, change freedom and fighting wrought was in African American families. For Long, demonstrating manhood was important not only for what it taught the outside world but also for the authority it would give him at home. "Suppose you had kept your freedom witout enlisting in dis army; your chilen might have grown up free and been well cultivated as to be equal to any business," he speculated. "But it would always have been flung in dere faces – 'Your fader never fought for he own freedom' – and what could dey answer? Neber can say that to dis African Race any more."[36]

For some men, military experience provided a sense of empowerment even while they were away during the war. "Don't be uneasy my children I expect to have you," wrote a Missouri soldier to his two enslaved daughters in September of 1864. To their master, he wrote, "I want you to understand that mary is my Child and she is a God given rite of my own and you may hold on to hear as long as you can but I want you to remember that the longor you keep my Child from me the longor you will have to burn in hell."[37] (The man was hospitalized on this day with chronic rheumatism and it's not known what happened; one can only hope the girls were recovered – and that father and daughters took solace from a sense of assertiveness that well might have been unimaginable three years before.)

Before the war, the white gender conventions of separate spheres and the cult of true womanhood were at best irrelevant and at worst oppressive to African Americans. Unlike elite white women, for example, black women were expected to work outside the home. Like some whites, black men performed physical labor, but as historian James Horton argues, "slavery demanded that black men forego the intellectual, emotional and temperamental traits of manhood. The ideal slave recognized his inability to control his life." The coming of emancipation then offered black women the possibility of returning to the home, and gave black men a powerful sense of agency over their own lives and responsibility for their families.[38]

In this regard, the war realigned gender conventions in the black community; as a result, they more closely resembled those of whites.[39] Indeed, at this point in their history, many African Americans rejected any attempt to suggest racial difference. Much to his frustration, Martin Delany, often considered a father of black nationalism, found it "dangerous to go into the country and speak of color in any manner whatever, without the angry rejoiner 'we don't want to hear that; we are all one color now.' "[40] This rejection of racial difference would not remain in place for all people and all times; by the end of the century, for example, some black women were finding that white conceptions of womanhood were still irrelevant or oppressive, and some white men were arguing that true manhood was predicated on whiteness.[41]

"How extraordinary, and what a tribute to ignorance and religious hypocrisy, is the fact that in the minds of most people, even those of liberals, only murder makes men," W. E. B. Du Bois would later write. "The slave pleaded, he was humble; he protected the women of the South, and the world ignored him. The slave killed white men; and behold, he was a man."[42] Yet if manhood was often conflated with the power to kill and destroy, the documents explored here suggest that at least some black men also saw it as a source of power to preserve and create. The key to that power was a personal transformation, a fusion of biological fact and social aspiration that allowed a man to help change his world. "What are you, anyhow," a white man insultingly asked a South Carolina soldier in the middle of the war. "When God made me I wasn't much," came the answer, "but I's a man now."[43]

Notes

1   Joan Scott, *Gender and the Politics of History* (New York, 1988), p. 41.
2   James McPherson, *The Negro's Civil War: How Americans Felt and Acted During the War for the Union* (Urbana, 1965), p. 22.
3   Ibid., pp. 33–4, 29.
4   Ibid., p. 31.
5   This definition of manly – in contrast to masculine, which has more innate connotations – is developed in Gail Bederman, "Manly Civilization/Primitive Masculinity: Race, Gender, and Evolutions of Middle-Class American Manhood" (PhD dissertation, Brown University, 1992).
6   *The Negro's Civil War*, pp. 32–3.
7   Ibid., p. 162.
8   On p. 230 of *The Negro in the Civil War* (Boston, 1969), Benjamin Quarles estimated one-quarter of naval enlistments were black. More recent calculations show the figure to be around 9 percent.
9   Ibid., p. 198; Ira Berlin, Joseph P. Reidy, and Leslie S. Rowland, eds., *Freedom: A Documentary History of Emancipation 1861–1867*, Series II: *The Black Military Experience* (New York, 1982), p. 14.
10 Leon F. Litwack, *Been in the Storm So Long: The Aftermath of Slavery* (New York, 1980), p. 72.
11 Douglass quoted in *Black Writers and the Civil War*, ed. Richard A. Long (Secaucus, 1988), p. 313.
12 *Been in the Storm So Long*, p. 74.
13 Ibid., pp. 66, 71; *Freedom*, p. 85.
14 Ibid., p. 77.
15 Joseph Glatthaar, *Forged in Battle: The Civil War Alliance Between Black Soldiers and White Officers* (New York, 1991), pp. 9, 36. For the specific ways black officers were harassed, see documents in *Freedom*, pp. 303–47.
16 *Forged in Battle*, p. 115.
17 *Freedom*, p. 387.
18 The inequality of the Union pay structure is well documented, and is discussed in much of the literature on African American soldiers in the Civil War. For one particularly good discussion, see McPherson's *The Negro's Civil War*, pp. 193–204.
19 For documents pertaining to fatigue duty, see *Freedom*, pp. 483–516; for figures on disease and explanations for the disparity between blacks and whites, see pp. 633–37.
20 Ibid., p. 153.
21 Ibid., pp. 385–6.
22 Willie Lee Rose, *Rehearsal for Reconstruction: The Port Royal Experiment* (New York, 1964), p. 267.
23 *Been in the Storm So Long*, pp. 64, 101; *Forged in Battle*, p. 79.
24 For a discussion of such strategies, see William Taylor, *Cavalier and Yankee: The Old South and the American National Character* (New York, 1961).
25 *Freedom*, p. 757.
26 Ibid., p. 97.
27 *Forged in Battle*, p. 130.
28 Thomas Wentworth Higginson, *Black Life in an Army Regiment* (1869; New York, 1984), p. 224.
29 *The Negro's Civil War*, pp. 186–87; *Forged in Battle*, p. 133.
30 *The Negro's Civil War*, p. 191.
31 *Forged in Battle*, p. 134.
32 Ibid., p. 137.

33 *Freedom*, pp. 291–95.
34 Ibid., p. 733.
35 *Been in the Storm So Long*, p. 102.
36 Ibid.
37 *Freedom*, pp. 689–90. The owner of the girls wrote a letter to the commander of the Department of the Missouri asking that the soldier be forced to leave the state. "To be insulted by such a black scoundrel is more than I can stand," he said, claiming he had always been a Unionist, and, as such, his property should be protected (p. 691).
38 James Oliver Horton, "Freedom's Yoke: Gender Conventions Among Antebellum Free Blacks," *Feminist Studies* 12, no. 1 (Spring 1986): 53. For the work strategies of African American women, see Jacqueline Jones, *Labor of Love, Labor of Sorrow: Black Women, Work and the Family from Slavery to Freedom* (New York, 1985).
39 See the discussion of gender roles in *Freedom*, pp. 30–2.
40 Eric Foner, *Reconstruction: America's Unfinished Revolution* (New York, 1988), p. 288.
41 Hazel Carby, *Reconstructing Womanhood: The Emergence of the Afro-American Novelist* (New York, 1987); Gail Bederman, "Civilization, the Decline of Middle-Class Manliness, and Ida B. Wells's Anti-Lynching Campaign (1892–1894)," *Radical History Review* (Winter 1992).
42 W. E. B. Du Bois, *Black Reconstruction* (New York, 1935), p. 110.
43 *The Negro in the Civil War*, p. 199.

Questions to consider

- What are some of the meanings of "manhood" for African American men in the Civil War? Have these definitions changed?

- "I's a man *now*," a South Carolina soldier announces at the end of this piece. What does the word "now" imply about the definition of manhood? Do men make themselves?

- How do these soldiers understand the changing role of womanhood for their mothers, wives, and daughters?

Chapter 27

Gender Battles: Primary Sources

General Order No. 28

Benjamin Butler

Union naval power allowed Federal forces to invade the city of New Orleans with relative ease in 1862, but the occupying army did not find a warm welcome. Commanding General Benjamin Butler was particularly dismayed about widespread reports of women residents emptying their chamber pots onto the heads of Union soldiers who walked under their windows. In response to these and other such outrages, Butler issued General Order No. 28, which did not endear him to the locals. What assumptions did Butler make here? Did those assumptions cross sectional lines?

Benjamin Butler, "General Order No. 28," in *The Civil War Chronicle*, ed. J. M. Gallman (New York: Crown Publishers, 2000), p. 177.

As the officers and soldiers of the United States have been subject to repeated insults from the women (calling themselves ladies) of New Orleans in return for the most scrupulous non-interference and courtesy on our part, it is ordered that hereafter when any female shall by word, gesture, or movement insult or show contempt for any officer or soldier of the United States she shall be regarded and held liable to be treated as a woman of the town plying her avocation.

Letter from Beaufort, South Carolina

Harriet Tubman

In an ironic way, Harriet Tubman (1821–1913) benefited from white racist assumptions about gender and race: since she wasn't "really" a woman, she could do things no "respectable" female would ever contemplate, and she would consistently be underestimated by white Southerners. Nicknamed "General Tubman" by the radical abolitionist John Brown, Tubman, who escaped from bondage in 1849, was legendary for her daring exploits with the Underground Railroad, in which she helped hundreds of slaves escape to freedom. When the Civil War broke out, Tubman went to South Carolina to work as a spy. In this (dictated) letter, Tubman seeks bloomers – widely regarded as scandalous alternatives to long dresses – as a practical solution to the problems she faces on her operations. How would you characterize her tone here? What does she assume about gender conventions?

Harriet Tubman, (June 30, 1863), in *We Are Your Sisters: Black Women in the Nineteenth Century*, ed. Dorothy Sterling (New York: Norton, 1984), p. 260.

Beaufort, South Carolina, June 30, 1863

Last fall, when the people here became very much alarmed for fear of an invasion from the rebels, all my clothes were packed and sent to Hilton Head and lost; and I have never been able to get any trace of them since. I want, among the rest, a *bloomer* dress, made of some coarse, strong material, to wear on *expeditions*. In our late expedition up the river, in coming on board the boat, I was carrying *two pigs* for a poor sick woman, who had a child to carry, and the order "double quick" was given, and I started to run, stepped on my dress, it being rather long, and fell and tore it almost off, so that when I got on board the boat there was hardly anything left of it but shreds. I made up my mind then that I would never wear a long dress on another expedition of the kind, but would have a *bloomer* as soon as I could get it. So please make this known to the ladies, for I expect to have use for it very soon.

You have without doubt seen a full account of the Combahee expedition. We weakened the rebels by bringing away seven hundred fifty-six heads of their most valuable livestock. Of these seven hundred and fifty-six contrabands, nearly or quite all the able-bodied men have joined the colored regiments here.

I have now been absent two years almost, and have just got letters from my friends in Auburn, urging me to come home. My father and mother are old and in feeble health, and need my care and attention. I do not see how I am to leave at present. Among other duties which I have, is that of looking after the hospital here for contrabands. Most of those coming from the mainland are very destitute, almost naked. I am trying to find places for those able to work, so as to lighten the burden on the Government as much as possible, while at the same time they learn to respect themselves by earning their own living.

Faithfully and sincerely your friend,

Harriet Tubman

Obtaining Supplies

Louisa May Alcott

Literally and figuratively a child of the Transcendentalists, Louisa May Alcott (1832–88) had about as rarefied a childhood as any American has ever had (Henry David Thoreau was one of her teachers, and Ralph Waldo Emerson was a frequent family guest). Despite – or perhaps because of – such an upbringing, the outbreak of the Civil War led Alcott to crave authentically intense experience, and so she went off to Washington to serve as a nurse (still a generally male profession, though the Civil War would change that). Her first book, the 1863 novella *Hospital Sketches*, offered readers a thinly veiled, and sometimes self-mocking, autobiography. Alcott, who never married, went on to a highly successful career as a writer and breadwinner for her family. In subsequent books like *Little Women* (1868) – which was also thinly veiled autobiography set during the Civil War – Alcott both confirmed and challenged the conventional wisdom of her time.

Louisa May Alcott, "Obtaining Supplies," in *Hospital Sketches* (Boston, MA: Applewood Books, 1986), pp. 3–8.

"I want something to do."

This remark being addressed to the world in general, no one in particular felt it their duty to reply; so I repeated it to the smaller world about me, received the following suggestions, and settled the matter by answering my own inquiry, as people are apt to do when very much in earnest.

"Write a book," quoth the author of my being.

"Don't know enough, sir. First live, then write."

"Try teaching again," suggested my mother.

"No thank you, ma'am, ten years of that is enough."

"Take a husband like my Darby, and fulfill your mission," said sister Joan, home on a visit.

"Can't afford expensive luxuries, Mrs. Coobiddy."

"Turn actress, and immortalize your name," said sister Vashti, striking an attitude.

"I won't."

"Go nurse the soldiers," said my young neighbor, Tom, panting for "the tented field."

"I will!"

So far, very good. Here was the will, and plenty of it; now for the way. At first sight not a foot of it appeared; but that didn't matter, for the Periwinkles are a hopeful race. Their crest is an anchor, with three cock-a-doodles crowing atop. They all wear rose-colored spectacles, and are lineal descendants of the inventor of aerial architecture. An hour's conversation on the subject set the whole family in a blaze of enthusiasm. A model hospital was erected, and each member had accepted an honorable post therein. The paternal P. was chaplain, the maternal P. was matron, and all the youthful P.'s filled the pod of futurity with achievements whose brilliancy eclipsed the glories of the present and the past. Arriving at this satisfactory conclusion, the meeting adjourned; and the fact that Miss Tribulation was available as army nurse went abroad on the wings of the wind.

In a few days a townswoman heard of my desire, approved of it, and brought about an interview with one of the sisterhood which I wished to join, who was at home on a furlough, and able and willing to satisfy all inquiries. A morning chat with Miss General S. – we hear no end of Mrs. Generals, why not a Miss? – produced three results: I felt that I could do the work, was offered a place, and accepted it, promising not to desert, but stand ready to march on Washington at an hour's notice.

A few days were necessary for the letter containing my request and recommendation to reach headquarters, and another, containing my commission, to return; therefore no time was to be lost; and heartily thanking my pair of friends, I tore home through the December slush as if the rebels were after me, and like many another recruit, burst in upon my family with the announcement –

"I've enlisted!"

An impressive silence followed. Tom, the irrepressible, broke it with a slap on the shoulder and the graceful compliment –

"Old Trib, you're a trump!"

"Thank you; then I'll *take* something:" which I did, in the shape of dinner, reeling off my news at the rate of three dozen words to a mouthful; and as every one else talked equally fast, and all together, the scene was most inspiring.

As boys going to sea immediately become nautical in speech, walk as if they already had their "sea legs" on, and shiver their timbers on all possible occasions, so I turned military at once, called my dinner my rations, saluted all new comers, and ordered a dress parade that very afternoon. Having reviewed every rag I possessed, I detailed some for picket duty while airing over the fence; some to the sanitary influences of the wash-tub; others to mount guard in the trunk; while the weak and wounded went to the Work-basket Hospital, to be made ready for active service again. To this squad I devoted myself for a week; but all was done, and I had time to get powerfully impatient before the letter came. It did arrive however, and brought a disappointment along with its good will and friendliness, for it told me that the place in the Armory Hospital that I supposed I was to take, was already filled, and a much less desirable one at Hurly-burly House was offered instead.

"That's just your luck, Trib. I'll take your trunk up garret for you again; for of course you won't go," Tom remarked, with the disdainful pity which small boys affect when they get into their teens. I was wavering in my secret soul, but that settled the matter, and I crushed him on the spot with martial brevity –

"It is now one; I shall march at six"

I have a confused recollection of spending the afternoon in pervading the house like an executive whirlwind, with my family swarming after me, all working, talking, prophesying and lamenting, while I packed my "go-abroady" possessions, tumbled the rest into two big boxes, danced on the lids till they shut, and gave them in charge, with the direction, –

"If I never come back, make a bonfire of them."

Then I choked down a cup of tea, generously salted instead of sugared, by some agitated relative, shouldered my knapsack – it was only a traveling bag, but do let me preserve the unities – hugged my family three times all round without a vestige of unmanly emotion, till a certain dear old lady broke down upon my neck, with a despairing sort of wail –

"Oh, my dear, my dear, how can I let you go?"

"I'll stay if you say so, mother."

"But I don't; go, and the Lord will take care of you."

Much of the Roman matron's courage had gone into the Yankee matron's composition, and, in spite of her tears, she would have sent ten sons to the war, had she possessed them, as freely as she sent one daughter, smiling and flapping on the door-step till I vanished, though the eyes that followed me were very dim, and the handkerchief she waved was very wet.

My transit from The Gables to the village depot was a funny mixture of good wishes and good byes, mud-puddles and shopping. A December twilight is not the most cheering time to enter upon a somewhat perilous enterprise, and, but for the presence of Vashti and neighbor Tom, I fear that I might have added a drop of the briny to the native moisture of –

"The town I left behind me;"

though I'd no thought of giving out: oh, bless you, no! When the engine screeched "Here we are," I clutched my escort in a fervent embrace, and skipped into the car with as blithe a farewell as if going on a bridal tour – though I believe brides don't usually wear cavernous black bonnets and fuzzy brown coats, with a hair-brush, a pair of rubbers, two books, and a bag of ginger-bread distorting the pockets of the same. If I thought that any one would believe it, I'd boldly state that I slept from C. to B., which would simplify matters immensely; but as I know they wouldn't, I'll confess that the head under the funereal coal-hod fermented with all manner of high thoughts and heroic purposes "to do or die," – perhaps both; and the heart under the fuzzy brown coat felt very tender with the memory of the dear old lady, probably sobbing over her army socks and the loss of her topsy-turvy Trib. At this juncture I took the veil, and what I did behind it is nobody's business; but I maintain that the soldier who cries when his mother says "Good bye," is the boy to fight best, and die bravest, when the time comes, or go back to her better than he went.

Till nine o'clock I trotted about the city streets, doing those last errands which no woman would even go to heaven without attempting, if she could. Then I went to my usual refuge, and, fully intending to keep awake, as a sort of vigil appropriate to the occasion, fell fast asleep and dreamed propitious dreams till my rosy-faced cousin waked me with a kiss.

A bright day smiled upon my enterprise, and at ten I reported myself to my General, received last instructions and no end of the sympathetic encouragement which women give, in look, touch, and tone more effectually than in words. The next step was to get a free pass to Washington, for I'd no desire to waste my substance on railroad companies when "the boys" needed even a spinster's mite. A friend of mine had procured such a pass, and I was bent on doing likewise, though I had to face the president of the railroad to accomplish it. I'm a bashful individual, though I can't get any one to believe it; so it cost me a great effort to poke about the Worcester depot till the right door appeared, then walk into a room containing several gentlemen, and blunder out my request in a high state of stammer and blush. Nothing could have been more courteous than this dreaded President, but it was evident that I had made as absurd a demand as if I had asked for the nose off his respectable face. He referred me to the Governor at the State House, and I backed out, leaving him no doubt to regret that such mild maniacs were left at large. Here was a Scylla and Charybdis business: as if a President wasn't trying enough, without the Governor of Massachusetts and the Hub of the Hub on top of that.

"I never can do it," thought I. "Tom will hoot at you if you don't," whispered the inconvenient little voice that is always goading people to the performance of disagreeable duties, and always appeals to the most effective agent to produce the proper result. The idea of allowing any boy that ever wore a felt basin and a shoddy jacket with a microscopic tail, to crow over me, was preposterous, so giving myself a mental slap for such faint-heartedness, I streamed away across the Common, wondering if I ought to say "your Honor," or simply "Sir," and decided upon the latter.

Questions to consider

- What are some of the underlying assumptions in the replies Tribulation Periwinkle gets when she says, "I want something to do?" How are such assumptions internalized, and what stratagems does Periwinkle employ to get beyond them?

- Explore the humor here: does Periwinkle's self-deprecating style work as cultural critique?

- What role does Tom play in motivating Periwinkle? How does his gender status as a boy shape that role?

Part XII

The Written War

Plate 14 Front Lines: A newspaper vendor hawks his wares in Virginia in late 1863. More than any war before or after, the Civil War was a war of print in a highly literate society. (Selected Civil War photographs, Library of Congress)

Chapter 28

Popular Literary Culture in Wartime

Alice Fahs

"The real war will never get in the books," Walt Whitman famously asserted in 1882. That didn't stop writers – including Whitman himself – from trying, during the war and long after. (We still haven't given up, as this book attests.) More than in any war before or after, the United States in the Civil War was a culture of print in a society of literacy. Letters, newspapers, dime novels, sermons, political tracts, histories and more created a blizzard of paper that blanketed soldiers at the front as well as the folks back home.

But what did this literature say – or, perhaps more importantly – what did this literature do? It is impossible to answer this question completely, or even to prove that it did anything at all. And yet there is a palpable sense that it made an enormous difference in helping people come to terms with the conflict, of confirming, challenging, or maybe even changing their beliefs. At the very least, wartime literature provides a compelling, durable record of the way people were (and were not) thinking while the war raged around them.

Alice Fahs, a historian at the University of California, Davis, waded through this flood of writing in her 2001 book *The Imagined Civil War: Popular Literature of the North & South, 1861–1865*. In this opening chapter she provides an overview of the wartime literary landscape.

Alice Fahs, "Popular Literary Culture in Wartime," in *The Imagined Civil War: Popular Literature of the North & South, 1861–1865* (Chapel Hill: University of North Carolina, 2001), pp. 17–41. Copyright © 2001 by the University of North Carolina Press. Used by permission of the publisher.

Beat! beat! drums! – Blow! bugles! blow!
Through the windows – through doors – burst like a
    force of ruthless men,
Into the solemn church, and scatter the congregation;
Into the school where the scholar is studying:

> Leave not the bridegroom quiet – no happiness must
>   he have now with his bride;
> Nor the peaceful farmer any peace, plowing his field or
>   gathering in his grain;
> So fierce you whirr and pound, you drums – so shrill
>   you bugles blow.
>   (Walt Whitman, "Beat! Beat! Drums!,"
>   Harper's Weekly, September 28, 1861)

"Men cannot think, or write, or attend to their ordinary business," Oliver Wendell Holmes reported from Boston in the fall of 1861. "They stroll up and down the streets, they saunter out upon the public places." War fever had produced a "nervous restlessness of a very peculiar character." An "illustrious author" confessed that he "had laid down his pen," unable to "write about the sixteenth century," while the nineteenth "was in the very agony and bloody sweat of its great sacrifice." An eminent scholar "read the same telegraphic dispatches over and over again in different papers, as if they were new, until he felt as if he were an idiot." In South Carolina, Mary Chesnut confided to her diary that she had "tried to rise above the agonies of everyday life" by reading Emerson. "Too restless," she concluded of her failed attempt in June 1861. "Manassas on the brain."[1]

In both the North and the South, war permeated the wide-ranging set of practices and beliefs that constituted popular literary culture. War changed what people read, what was available to read, and how, where, and with what expectations they read it. It altered the plans and prospects of publishers, pushing some to the brink of failure while giving new energy to a few well-positioned firms. It reshaped literary careers, forcing established authors to reconsider their writing plans, inspiring new authors to enter the literary marketplace, and deeply affecting what both found possible to imagine. Most profoundly, war catalyzed a rethinking of prevailing beliefs about the connecting links between literature and society and between individual and nation. In the South, war produced an urgent discussion of the place of literature within the larger project of nation building and of the role of the patriotic reader within a larger literary culture. In the North, an explosion of war-related popular literature and patriotic print goods, part of an expansive commercial culture of war, tightly bound the individual to the nation and yet, ironically, complicated attempts to fix the meanings of the war. Both north and south, war became not just an obsessive, all-consuming subject but also a mode of perception and way of life that disrupted and reorganized authors' and readers' conceptions of identity, nationhood, and even time itself. "How long it is since Sumter!" Jane Woolsey wrote to a friend from New York only three weeks after war began. "I suppose it is because so much intense emotion has been crowded into the last two or three weeks that the 'time before Sumter' seems to belong to some dim antiquity. It seems as if we never were alive till now; never had a country till now."[2]

The all-consuming nature of war was a subject frequently remarked on early in the war, both north and south. "Tonight," Kate Stone of Augusta, Georgia, recorded in her diary in May 1861, "we all gathered around" the fire to hear a friend "read the papers. Nothing but 'War, War' from the first to the last column. Throughout the length and breadth of the land the trumpet of war is sounding." "Town talk has but one topic these days," George William Curtis commented in the columns of *Harper's Monthly* during July and August. "The beat of the drum, the bugle-call, the shrill, passionate shock of martial music fill the air by night and day." Not only did "the bookshops have only placards of books of tactics and the drill," but "the windows glow[ed] with portraits of the heroes." The "photograph galleries are crowded with living soldiers looking at pictured soldiers upon the walls," while "the theatres revive old battle melodramas and invent new." Even "the piles of brick and rubbish in the streets are covered with posters bearing a charging Zouave for illustration, and with General Orders, and calls for recruits and notices of warlike meetings."[3]

Reading habits changed dramatically with the onset of war, a fact that numerous observers noted both north and south. Newspapers suddenly became an urgent necessity of life, with readers eagerly gathering at bulletin boards outside newspaper offices in order to read the news as soon as it was printed. In Boston, Oliver Wendell Holmes reported that one person he knew always went through the "side streets on his way for the noon *extra*, – he is so afraid somebody will meet him and *tell* the news he wishes to *read*, first on the bulletin-board, and then in the great capitals and leaded type of the newspaper." The newspaper was "imperious," according to Holmes. "It will be had, and it will be read. To this all else must give place. If we must go out at unusual hours to get it, we shall go, in spite of after-dinner nap or evening somnolence." "We haunt the bulletin board," Mary Chesnut concurred from Columbia, South Carolina, in 1862, while in New York, George William Curtis reported that "the crowds assemble daily before the bulletins of the newspaper offices, and the excitement of important news flutters along Broadway or Nassau Street like the widening ripples in water. You feel something in men's motions; you see something in the general manner of the throng in the street before you read it recorded upon the board or in the paper. There is but one thought and one question. The people are soldiers. The country is a camp. It is war."[4]

The ability of newspapers to satisfy the public's feverish desire for news on an hourly, not just daily, basis struck many contemporary observers as remarkable, signifying a fundamental shift not only in the nature of warfare but also in the very "manner of existence" itself. Already in the fall of 1861, Holmes mused that "new conditions of existence," including the railroad and telegraph, made this war "very different from war as it [had] been." From Memphis the *Southern Monthly* agreed, asserting in early 1862 that this war had no parallel in history, as "the railroad, the steamer, and the telegraph are a trinity which has killed all parallel. Mechanical ingenuity, in a thousand ways, has completely revolutionized war." One revolutionary aspect of war, said Holmes, was "perpetual intercommunication, joined to the power of instantaneous action," which keeps us "alive with excitement." No longer was the news delivered by a "single bulletin" or courier, as in the past; instead, "almost hourly paragraphs" made readers "restless always for the last fact or rumor they are telling."[5]

Such restlessness meant that initially during the war, reading the newspaper displaced other forms of literary culture. In November the *Southern Literary Messenger* commented, "In times like the present, very little interest is felt in literature. Nothing that does not relate to the war itself is read." The *Southern Monthly* concurred: "[The time is not] propitious to reading, or reflection, or study, as people's minds are filled with anxiety and expectation; and until this excitement shall subside, it cannot be expected that a different feeling will prevail." In the North, the trade journal of the book publishing industry noted a radically changed literary landscape, commenting, "The entire absorption of public interest by current events has caused a nearly complete cessation in the demand for new books, and publishers have in consequence discontinued their usual issues." There was abundant evidence of the truth of this remark: while in July 1860 the prestigious Boston publisher Ticknor and Fields, for instance, had had some thirty volumes in press, in July 1861 the firm had only four in production. Longfellow remarked on visiting Ticknor and Fields's "Old Corner" bookstore, "Nothing alive but the military. Bookselling dead." After a second visit he noted, "The 'Corner' looks gloomy enough. Ticknor looks grim and Fields is fierce. Business is at a standstill. So much for war and books."[6]

Books published during the spring of 1861, like George William Curtis's society novel, *Trumps*, tended to fizzle in the marketplace, and many projected books had to be put off. James T. Fields, editor of Ticknor and Fields, wrote to several of his authors to delay publication of their works: "The Times are so shaky," he wrote to Bayard Taylor, "we postpone 'The Poets' Journal' till autumn." To Thomas Wentworth Higginson he wrote that Higginson's *Outdoor Papers* must wait "till we see how McClellan is doing." The outlook for books was "hazy," he said; "the Trade is in a state of apathy I never saw approached." Metaphors of paralysis were common: the secession winter had "paralysed business for a time, utterly," James Perkins Walker of Boston's Walker, Wise and Company commented; the "national troubles" had "paralyzed all but military and periodical literature," *Harper's Monthly* agreed. In the South, William Gilmore Simms noted, "People here breathe nothing but war, & read none but military books now."[7]

Under the exigencies of war, literary careers were delayed or took unexpected turns, as the crisis affected what could be imagined as well as what could be published. In Charleston, the poet Henry Timrod wrote to a friend in September that he had "planned several poems of length during the present summer" but that "all of them, I am afraid, will remain the skeletons which they are as yet, until more peaceable times. The lyre of Tyrtaeus is the only one to which the Public will listen now; and over that martial instrument I have but small command." In Concord a worried Louisa May Alcott, who wished to submit a story to the *Atlantic Monthly*, reported in November that editor James T. Fields had told her "he has Mss. enough on hand for a dozen numbers & has to choose war stories if he can, to suit the times. I will write 'great guns' Hail Columbia & Concord fight, if he'll only take it for money is the staff of life & without one falls flat no matter how much genius he may carry."[8]

Alcott's comment suggested a developing reality of wartime popular literary culture. Just as Northerners and Southerners experienced the early disruptions of war in remarkably similar ways, so too authors and publishers in both sections rapidly responded to readers' all-absorbing interest in the conflict by producing popular war literature. But these efforts exposed deep economic and cultural divisions between the two sections, divisions that would only deepen over the course of the war. First and foremost was the fact that most major publishing firms and presses were in the North, not in the South. The 1860 census made the disparity dramatically clear: it counted 986 printing offices in New England and the middle states, with only 151 printing establishments in the South. Of these, the 21 presses in Tennessee produced the most work – yet Tennessee, with the only stereotype foundry in the South, fell under Union control early in the war. There were 190 bookbinders in New England and the middle states – but only 17 in the South. No printing presses were manufactured in the South, meaning that it would be difficult, if not impossible, to replace broken presses. The Richmond Type Foundry did advertise "Southern Type, Manufactured on Southern Soil," but it also acknowledged that it was "the only establishment of the kind in the South." At the same time there were only 15 paper mills in the South in 1861, which "could barely meet half the requirements Southern publishers placed upon them every day." There were no facilities in the South for making wood-pulp paper, which in the North became an important substitute for paper made from cotton rags during the war. The *Daily Richmond Enquirer*'s January 1862 advertisement for "Paper and Ink: – Wanted immediately" was a plaintive motif reiterated in many journals during the war. "Attention Everybody! Rags! Rags! Rags! I want to buy ten thousand pounds of well cleaned Cotton and Linen Rags" was an advertisement placed by one printer in the *Southern Literary Companion* in June 1864. The Georgia firm of Burke, Boykin and Company advertised in verse for rags:

Save your rags, and save your tags,
Save your good-for-nothing bags –
Bring them to this office, soon,
Bring them morning, eve, or noon.

Bring us scraps and cotton thread,
Bring the night cap from your head,
Bring the shirt upon your back,
Bring us pieces white or black.[9]

On the eve of the war there were only a few established Southern book publishers, including West and Johnston and J. W. Randolph of Richmond; S. H. Goetzel of Mobile; Evans and Cogswell of Charleston; and Burke, Boykin and Company in Macon. Few other firms, except for religious publishers, were of any considerable size. Among the few established periodicals were the Richmond literary monthly the *Southern Literary Messenger*, established in 1834; the critical monthly *De Bow's Review*, first published in New Orleans in 1845; the weekly *Southern Field and Fireside*, first published in 1859 in Augusta, Georgia; and the *Southern Literary Companion*, begun in 1859 in Newnan, Georgia. Yet relatively few Southerners read these periodicals, instead depending on Northern books and periodicals for their reading matter.[10]

By the end of 1861, both the blockade of Southern ports and the end of federal mail service meant that Southerners no longer had access to the Northern literature on which they had long depended. Henry Timrod, for one, bemoaned the disappearance of literary culture as he had known it: "No new books, no reviews, no appetizing critiques, no literary correspondence, no intellectual intelligence of any kind! Ah! It is a weary time! To volunteer is now the only resource against *ennui*. The Camp is *life*. Thither flow exclusively all the currents of thought and action, and thither, I suppose, I must betake myself if I would not die of social and intellectual atrophy." Confronting cultural separation from the North, many Southern readers privately worried over the loss of Northern literature even as they proclaimed their sectional loyalty. "We take quite a number of papers," Kate Stone said in May 1861, listing among them the Northern journals *Harper's Weekly* and *Monthly*, the *New York Tribune*, and the *Journal of Commerce*. "What shall we do when Mr. Lincoln stops our mails?" Near Augusta, Georgia, Ella Thomas wrote in her diary in July, "The Blockade has prevented the importation of new Books and loyal as I am and wish to be I think that for a time this will prove a serious inconvenience."[11]

While privately readers worried about the impact of war on valued reading habits, publicly numerous Southern periodicals celebrated cultural separation from the North. "Now that Northern journals have become, as long ago they should have been, contraband articles at the South, it is hoped that the subscriptions for Southern literary journals will be rapidly increased," the *Southern Literary Messenger* said. "Literary journals of a high order must be sustained at the South, if we would have an actual and not a merely nominal independence of the North." "We must have a periodical literature," the *Charleston Courier* agreed. "The need is great and it is felt. Forced from our dependence on the North, we must see to it, that we meet this pressing demand with cheerfulness, earnestness, and liberality." The *Southern Monthly* stressed the importance of increasing the number of Southern book publishers, "by the sustainment of which alone are we to have a flourishing and healthy literature. It will be found that they go hand in hand, and when the one languishes, the other etiolates and withers."[12]

Many commentators stressed the connections between literary and political nationhood, arguing that nation building was a vital cultural as well as political project. "A nation cannot live upon bread alone," the *New Orleans Delta* commented in the fall of 1861. Although "the development of the South, up to this time, has been almost purely economical and political," the "destiny of the South will be but a crude and unfinished attempt" unless "along with her political independence she achieves her independence in thought and education, and in all those forms of mental improvement and entertainment which by a liberal construction of the word, are included in literature." Commentators celebrated the literary opportunities opened by secession and war: "We have risen to the dignity and importance of a nation," the *Charleston Courier* proclaimed in an article entitled "Literature in the South." "We are now treading the path to independence; we have begun a new career; unbounded prosperity and glory, such as our fathers never dreamed of in the wildest flights of their imagination, invite and stimulate our efforts and energies."[13]

Such comments envisioned war as an exhilarating opportunity finally to create an independent Southern literature. Calls for an independent Southern literature and the end of dependence on Northern print culture had been a familiar part of antebellum Southern literary culture, but many critics now agreed that the antebellum project had been a failure. One reason often cited was the disproportionate power of Northern cultural institutions. The literature that the South had been "able to claim for her own," the *New Orleans Delta* wrote, though "intrinsically rich and vigorous as much of it may have been, was wofully inadequate to cope with the literature arrayed against her. The pens and the presses, the books, the periodicals and the journals, the pulpits, the lecture desks, and the school rooms" of the North and of Europe were "openly or insidiously hostile to her institutions, her rights, her interests, her aspirations," and "placed her at a fearful disadvantage in the controversy she was compelled to maintain before the tribunal of public opinion."[14]

Yet few critics solely blamed Northern institutions for a perceived lack of Southern literary independence. What the *Southern Monthly* termed Southern "literary laziness" was also a culprit. Musing over the question of why the South was "dependent upon the north," Ella Thomas wrote in her journal, "We have plenty of talent lying latent in the South to make for us a glorious name. We have one great drawback – indolence – to contend against. Say what we may it is more this than indifference or anything else which prevents so many from improving their God given talent."[15]

If the "laziness" of would-be writers was partially at fault for the failure of Southern literary independence, the habits of readers were even more to blame. From the pages of newspapers and periodicals, Southerners reprimanded their compatriots for reading Northern literature and urged them to support Southern literature as a patriotic duty. "I trust though the present crisis has lost you Northern patronage," a "lady of Jackson, Mississippi" wrote to the *Southern Literary Messenger*, "it will not be long before Southerners, who have wasted their money to pay for the demoralizing trash, sent forth by the Northern press, will awake to a full sense of the duty they owe themselves and to Southern Literature." The South had for too long been tied to the "wheels of Northern publishers"; but now she trusted that "the Literary bonds will fall with the political ones, and that henceforth we may have the patriotism to sustain our own literature." Writing in the *Southern Field and Fireside*, Ella Swan scolded Southern women, accusing them of having "united with the entire North in supporting a literature at war with your dearest interests. Uncle Tom's Cabin, Dred Scott and other works as poisonous as the deadly Upas tree, have been freely circulated in your midst, while Southern authors have met with little encouragement at your hands. Are not Southern papers, periodicals and books as worthy of your patronage?" The *Southern Illustrated News* asserted that it did not "believe that the people of the South will ever again welcome a Northern periodical into their households – we cannot for a moment believe that they are so devoid of interest for the welfare of the rising generation – so lost to all reason and honor"; the *Charleston Courier* said simply, "Our patronage of magazines published at the North has heretofore been both a folly and a shame."[16]

As such comments made clear, the act of reading itself now took on a strongly ideological cast. Suffused with nationalistic aims, reading was less a private act than a vital part of a larger, public, patriotic culture. Furthermore, such patriotic reading involved not only what one did read but also what one did not; it demanded not just the embrace of Southern literature but also the repudiation of Northern literature – the two were intimately intertwined. Early in the war it was a commonplace to begin discussions of Southern literature with denunciations of Northern literature; Northern works pandered to popular taste; they were "trashy," "poisonous," "contemptible." Never one to shrink from hyperbole, the *Southern Illustrated News* in the fall of 1862 called "Yankee literature," with "a very few exceptions, the opprobrium of the Universe." Yankee books were "of the worst possible description," merely a "very bad imitation of the most indifferent class of English literature." Southern literature would come "in due time," and when it did, it would "in no way resemble the Yankee abortion."[17]

Despite these nearly universal public denunciations of "Yankee trash," however, many commentators expressed uneasiness over whether Southerners would ever give up their love of Northern literature, even under the conditions of civil war. While the *Magnolia Weekly* asserted, "We must build up a popular literature of our own, and it must be as far removed in style from that of our invaders as it is possible for it to be," it also acknowledged, "We have a most powerful *habit* to contend against." After all, perennial antebellum calls for an independent Southern literature largely had fallen on deaf ears. "Not one Southern book" had lain on the antebellum Southern parlor table, the *Southern Monthly* claimed in a scathing editorial in its inaugural September 1861 issue; instead the *Atlantic Monthly*, with "Harriet Beecher Stowe's last novel *continued*" and "Holmes' ingenious diatribes against our country," lay next to "the arrant *Harper*, with its Editor's Table, an essay on the value of the Union," while "on chair and sofa" lay "*Ledger* and *Mercury*, filled with the infectious and mephitic exhalations of Sylvanus Cobb, and others as innocent of ability as of decency." The *Southern Literary Messenger* agreed: "If the angel Gabriel had gone into very heart of the South, if he had even taken his seat on the top of the office of the Charleston Mercury and there proclaimed the immediate approach of the Day of Judgment, that would not have hindered the hottest secessionist from buying the New York Herald and subscribing for Harper's Magazine." The *Messenger* concluded, "Southern patriotism is, and has always been, a funny thing – indeed the funniest of things. It enables a man to abuse the Yankees, to curse the Yankees, to fight the Yankees, to do everything but quit taking the Yankee papers. Nothing less than a battery of 10-inch Columbiads can keep Southern patriotism away from Yankee papers. Even that is doubtful. We suspect that the animating impulse which will ere long carry the Army of the Potomac into Washington City, will, when it is analyzed, be found to be, merely the inappeasable desire of Southern patriotism to obtain a copy of Bonner's Ledger."[18]

Given this "just conception of Southern patriotism," the editor of the *Messenger* promised – tongue in cheek – that the magazine would attempt to appeal to its readers by combining "all of the most trashy, contemptible and popular features of *Harper, Godey, Frank Leslie*, the *Herald, Home Journal, Ledger, Yankee Notions, Nick Nax, Budget of Fun*, and the *Phunny Phellow*."

We shall have nothing but pictures. We shall have nothing but the latest news and the fashions. Diagrams of baby clothes, worked slippers, edgings, frills, cuffs, capes, furbelows, faraboves, and indeed all of the most interior and intricate feminine fixings, shall be supplied in much profusion.... We shall furnish each month not less than 1800 different photographic views of the proper way to do up the back hair. We shall devote eleven-ninths of each number to crochet work and fancy pincushions. Meantime we shall devote our entire space to riddles, charades, acrostics and questions in arithmetic. But the greater part of the magazine shall be given to little dabs of light literature *a la* Fanny Fern. Our exclusive exertions, however, shall be strained for the procurement of tales, stories, narratives, novels, novellettes, serials and serialettes.[19]

This was parody clearly meant to establish the grounds of Southern literary difference from Northern "trash." Yet it also suggested some of the complexities inherent in Southern attempts to establish a new national literature. Even as Southerners denounced Northern literature, it remained a powerful standard against which they defined their literature. According to the *Magnolia Weekly*, for instance, the "Northern weeklies abounded in stuff calculated to appease the cravings of the uncultured appetites" of the "vulgar rabble." The *Magnolia Weekly* sought instead to create "a style of literature which is at once useful and pure." "This is the true popular literature," it claimed. Yet such an attack on Northern literature did not so much dislodge its power within Southern cultural life as shift the terms on which that power was organized.[20]

One aspect of Southern literature that several commentators agreed might make it "useful and pure" was its depiction of slavery. Before the war, the *Southern Monthly* asserted, Southern poets and Southern novelists had failed to paint "in beauty" and idealize "into still higher fascination the domestic ties that breed elevating affections in our negroes" or to paint "the negro nurse, and the negro playmate, remembered by all of us with thrills of affection." "Had a Southern novelist" in the antebellum period "truly painted in as engaging a style" as *Uncle Tom's Cabin* "the real workings of our Biblical system of labor, and its truly Christianizing and elevating effects on the slave, the power of the misrepresentation" offered by Stowe "to mislead would have been checkmated," and the "baneful effect" of Northern literature would have been counteracted.[21]

The *Southern Monthly* argued for the importance of the institution of slavery not just within Southern life but within Southern literary culture as well. It thus made explicit linkages between Southern literary nationalism and slavery that in effect racialized and politicized the very definition of Southern literature at the outset of war. Southern literature, in this and many other accounts, carried a deeply political charge: seen by many observers as a critical component in the building of a new nation, it also had the task of defending the Southern "way of life" – always shorthand for the life of white Southern slaveholders. As many commentators in the early months of war continued to look back with bitterness on the powerful impact of *Uncle Tom's Cabin*, they assumed that a new Southern literature must continue to counteract what were perceived and represented as uniform Northern views. Thus it is not surprising that a number of journals continued to publish defenses of slavery, even after Confederate nationhood was established: in December 1861, for instance, the strongly proslavery *Southern Literary Messenger* began a series of articles by William H. Holcombe entitled "Characteristics and Capabilities of the Negro Race." These articles, like many proslavery manifestos of antebellum years, supported a modified version of polygenesis: "The negro is not a white man with a black skin," the series began, "but, if not a distinct species, at least a permanent variety of the human race." Attempting to find a biological justification for slavery in supposed Negro difference "from all other races of men," this series suggested that Southern wartime literature would continue to be preoccupied with justifications of slavery.[22]

Many commentators agreed on an agenda for Southern literature, but war quickly undercut their plans. Southern periodicals operated under a number of severe constraints during the war. Already in November 1861 the *Southern Literary Messenger* offered extended commentary on the difficulties of publishing in wartime. "In common with other Southern interests, and especially with publications, *The Messenger* has felt, and still feels, severely, the pressure of the war," it said. "While newspaper after newspaper has been suspended, and even the staunchest journals have been compelled to retrench and economise; while De Bow's *Review* is published but once in two months, *The Messenger* has steadily held its own, despite of bad ink, a scarcity of paper and of printers, a great falling off in contributions, and almost a suspension of payments." But "this cannot last," it concluded.[23]

Most dispiriting, the *Messenger* found, was the lack of wartime support from Southern subscribers. Before the war, the editors had "derived comfort from the assurance that the neglect of the Magazine" was "due not so much to Southern indifference to them, and to native literature, as to that habit of dependence on the North, from which nothing less than the horrors of war could ever have delivered us." But now "the war has come, Northern newspapers and magazines have been totally cut off, yet *The Messenger* is in no better plight than before." The publishers had "no more appeals to Southern patriotism to make. All they want is the money that is due them."[24]

The *Messenger*, like many other Southern publications, struggled for its existence during 1861 and early 1862. In April 1862 the editor confessed, "Never were we so 'put to it' for suitable contents for our Table. The Yankees have penetrated so far into the Confederacy – have menaced so many interior points, that our correspondents have had neither leisure nor inclination to furnish contributions." So "driven to the wall" was the magazine that the editor chose to print "some selections from old English writers." In the fall of 1862 it faced new problems, as "the government seized the paper mills in this city, and we failed to get paper" elsewhere. It published a double issue in the fall of 1862, a solution to publishing difficulties to which *De Bow's Review* also resorted. However, after publishing a quadruple number for May through August 1862, *De Bow's* suspended publication entirely except for one single issue in July 1864. As the editor, J. D. B. De Bow, explained in August 1862, "More than half of our subscribers are in Texas, Louisiana, Arkansas, and in parts of the other states held by the enemy, and to them, for some time to come, it may be our fate to be voiceless."[25]

Yet if the war undermined established periodicals such as the *Messenger* and *De Bow's Review*, it acted as inspiration for a new literature of war that appeared in daily newspapers throughout the South. Inspired by the war, for instance, numbers of ordinary citizens, both male and female, contributed a profusion of patriotic poetry to newspapers, a fact that many observers at the time found striking. In September 1861 the *Southern Monthly* noticed that "the daily journals of the South" had become the "depositories of much of that finished poetry generally reserved for the more careful monthly." The *Monthly* reprinted several of these, approvingly commenting that "as specimens of what our patriotism has called forth," the poems compared "favorably with the majority of fugitive pieces found in Northern periodicals." The *Messenger* also remarked on "the many excellent little poems which the war has called forth," and to rescue them from "newspaper oblivion," it offered its readers "a few specimens clipped from our exchanges." Two Richmond literati, Professor Chase and John R. Thompson, were making a collection of these poems, the *Messenger* informed its readers. In mid-1862, some of this collection became the basis for William G. Shepperson's *War Songs of the South*, intended to celebrate a new flowering of Southern literature.[26]

Shepperson, the correspondent "Bohemian" for the *Richmond Daily Dispatch*, argued that newspaper poems were compelling evidence of popular nationalism in the South – a nationalism arising from the people rather than from the government. They revealed a "spontaneous outburst of popular feeling" that gave "the lie to the assertion of our enemy that this revolution is the work of politicians and party leaders alone." Not only had many of the poems been written by women, whose "instinct" had "anticipated the logic of our statesmen," but many had also been composed by "soldiers in camp," and they possessed "all the vitality and force of the testimony of eye-witnesses to a glorious combat, or even of actors in it." Through "the Poet's Corner in the newspaper," these poems had "sped their flight from and to the heart and mind of the people." Such comments assumed that popular patriotic poetry was both an important indication and a creator of popular nationalism.[27]

Many Southerners highly valued this war poetry as an integral part of the war experience, copying favorite poems into their journals or pasting them into scrapbooks along with news clippings of important battles. Mary Chesnut, for instance, copied lines from James R. Randall's stirring and enormously popular "My Maryland" in a January 1862 diary entry. Kate D. Foster, living near Natchez, Mississippi, pasted two newspaper copies of the famous "All Quiet along the Potomac Tonight" on the inside of the front cover of her diary. William Galt, a cadet at the Virginia Military Institute, copied "Maryland My Maryland" and "The Bonnie Blue Flag" in a wartime notebook. M. J. Solomons of Savannah, Georgia, created a scrapbook from a used account book – a sign of how severe the paper shortage was even early in the war – and into it pasted numerous poems from a variety of newspapers.[28]

Drawn from the "Poet's Corner" of a variety of newspapers, these poems revealed how the well-established newspaper "exchange" system worked to link Southerners at wide distances from one another. Under the exchange system, newspapers sent one another copies of their papers as a courtesy, with the understanding that reprints were allowable as long as they were credited. Thus one newspaper might draw poems and articles from a variety of sources, providing a window into a broader culture beyond the local arena. Certainly in the pages of Solomons's scrapbook, poems and news accounts are credited as being drawn from an astonishing array of sources, including the *Richmond Dispatch*; *Southern Advocate*; *Southern Field and Fireside*; *Richmond Daily Examiner*; *Natchez Courier*; *Charleston Mercury*; *Bowling Green (Kentucky) Daily Courier*; *Atlanta Intelligencer*; *New Orleans Picayune*; *Petersburg (Virginia) Daily Express*; *Savannah Republican*; *Atlanta Confederacy*; *Memphis Appeal*; *Montgomery Advertiser*; *Norfolk Day Book*; *Richmond Whig*; and *Southern Illustrated News*, among many others. Although Solomons probably did not have access to all of these newspapers herself, she nevertheless could, through the limited number of newspapers available to her, participate in a wider literary culture of war.[29]

The many scrapbooks kept by Southerners are an important indication of how precious the print culture of war was to a widespread Southern reading public, who were deeply involved in the project of creating a print memory of the war. It is important to note, too, that the newspaper, typically associated with politics rather than the arts, was at the center of this Southern literary culture of war. But many Southerners were also proud that, inspired by the war, and despite the many hardships associated with it, publishers were printing new books and even creating new periodicals. The *Southern Literary Messenger* commented with surprise and pleasure on new Confederate books in December 1861. "Yankee publishers having ceased to subsidize us with presentation copies of their trashy publications, we had closed the 'Book Notice' department for the war, as we supposed. In this, we are glad to find ourselves mistaken," the *Messenger* said, before reviewing new military publications printed by the Richmond firm of West and Johnston. The *Messenger* was especially pleased that, "at a time when paper and printing ink are so scarce and costly," these books were printed and bound "in a superior style."[30]

Several new periodicals were also founded during the first years of war. The first number of the Memphis-based *Southern Monthly*, published by Hutton and Freligh, appeared in September 1861. The spring of 1862 saw the founding of Joseph Addison Turner's idiosyncratic the *Countryman*, unique for being published on a plantation in Putnam County,

Georgia, as well as for employing the fourteen-year-old Joel Chandler Harris as printer's assistant. Modeled after both the *Spectator* and the *Rambler*, the *Countryman* had a small readership, at one time reaching "a circulation of nearly two thousand copies," according to Harris.[31]

In the fall of 1862, as the military fortunes of the Confederacy ran high, so too did Southern literary ambition. In September Charles Bailie founded the Richmond-based *Magnolia: A Southern Home Journal*, which became the *Magnolia Weekly* the next year. In September, too, the Richmond publishers Ayres and Wade founded the most ambitious of the new Southern periodicals, the *Southern Illustrated News*, an illustrated weekly meant as an answer to such popular Northern weeklies as *Frank Leslie's Illustrated Newspaper* and *Harper's Weekly*. The most popular of the new Confederate periodicals, it reportedly sometimes printed some twenty thousand copies. A number of Southern readers and authors alike registered the founding of this new Southern publication as a significant event: nineteen-year-old Lucy Breckinridge, for instance, an avid reader who lived in Grove Hill, Virginia, noted in her diary on September 10, 1862, that she had just received "the first copy of *The Southern Illustrated News*" from Richmond. Twice more during the war would she note that she had been sent a copy of the *News*.[32]

Though war created severe difficulties for an established literary monthly such as the *Southern Literary Messenger*, it created opportunities for an upstart such as the *Southern Illustrated News*. As the *Southern Literary Messenger* ruefully noted, "a pictorial paper, started in this city not much more than a month ago, has already a circulation quadruple that obtained by THE MESSENGER after twenty seven years." The difference between the two publications was not so much an economic one – the *Southern Illustrated News* had great difficulties obtaining paper, too, for instance – as a cultural one: the *Southern Illustrated News* offered a fresh viewpoint for the South, with a fresh combination of voices and features. Moreover, it was deliberately popular in a way that the more gentlemanly *Southern Literary Messenger* not only avoided but sometimes actively scorned. "We wish to pay our weekly visits to thousands of homes in our sunny Southern land," the *News* stated in its first issue, "homes that are lonely in the absence of loved ones in the army – and impart something of cheer to their loneliness. We shall send, far and wide, throughout our borders, carefully executed portraits of our distinguished leaders, that the people may know what manner of men they are, in bodily likeness, in the council and in the field. And we shall count, with something of confidence, upon furnishing our brave soldiers, in their summer bivouac and their winter cantonment, with a pleasant and not unprofitable companion."[33]

Imagining a Confederacy linked through its own readership, the *News* sketched a form of literary nationalism rooted most deeply in the war itself. Indeed, from the first the *Southern Illustrated News* concentrated primarily on the war, providing an eclectic group of war-related features including stories, profiles of generals, editorials on the war, humorous sketches of life in camp, reflections on women's home-front role, and war poems. The *News* commented with amazement on the number of poetic submissions it received: "We have lyrics enough, were they worthy of print," it said after being in print only eight weeks, "to supply the poet's corner for as many years. At a time when writing paper is preposterously high, and so constantly advances in price that it cannot, with any propriety, be called *stationery*, and when postage is a burden which might deter any one from needlessly cumbering the mails, we receive daily piles of poetical contributions." Unfortunately these "innumerous song-offerings" were "not remarkable for celestial fire," the *News* added, commenting, "The 'rebel' muse, we grieve to say, is so disobedient and wayward a child, so slip-shod a Sibyl, that she rebels against all the laws of rhyme, and cares less than nothing about her *feet*."[34]

As these comments revealed, the early reverence with which commentators treated the appearance of amateur war poems had dissipated by the fall of 1862: in January 1863, the *News* even predicted that in the "flour barrel full" of war poems it had received, "not one poetic expression or thought, coming from the heart would be found." The *Southern Literary Messenger* concurred, saying in July 1863, "We are receiving too much trash in rhyme." In September 1863 the *Magnolia Weekly* even ran a brief, pointed story in which a newspaper poet was exposed as nothing more than a "dandy clerk" and shirker. Newspaper war poetry was "all a humbug and imposture from beginning to end," according to this story. "Every man of us, thank God, is ready, heart and hand, to strike for his country's cause, without the necessity of newspaper poets calling upon them to arise," it concluded. Nevertheless, the *Magnolia Weekly*, like other Southern periodicals, continued to print a substantial collection of war poems, including dirges, narrative poems, ballads, and "national hymns," among others.[35]

Given the *News*'s avowedly popular purpose, it is perhaps surprising that two of the most revered antebellum literary names in the South – the poets William Gilmore Simms and Paul Hamilton Hayne – soon not only published poems in the *News* but also appeared on its masthead as regular contributors. But there were compelling reasons for their willingness to appear in the pages of a weekly "story paper." First, cultural separation from the North meant that Simms and Hayne could no longer publish in Northern journals. Only two months before war had broken out, *Frank Leslie's Illustrated Newspaper*, sympathetic to the South throughout the secession crisis, had published a flattering profile of Paul Hayne. But with the onset of war Hayne not only lost his Northern audience for the duration but also, like his Southern compatriots, angrily denounced the "Northmen" as "ruffians," "robbers," and "invaders."[36]

Second, there were very few literary publications in which Southern poets and other writers could publish during the war, and even fewer still that promised to pay much to their authors, if anything at all. The *Southern Monthly*, for instance, simply told its readers that "when Southern readers enough pay for reading" the magazine, "the publishers will pay Southern writers enough for writing it." The *Southern Literary Messenger* bluntly told one would-be contributor in July 1862, "The pressure of the times is such as to forbid any engagements with contributors. None receive compensation at this time." In contrast, the *Southern Illustrated News* did make promises of payment – although it did not always fulfill them, apparently. A plaintive letter from Hayne to a friend in May 1864 complained, "Since Jan. last the 'Illus. News' has paid me *not one* cent for the Poems of mine which have appeared in its columns"; he had expected to receive between fifteen and thirty dollars each for seven poems, most of them war poems. Still, Hayne admitted that he published with the *News* "almost entirely," as he was "constrained to work for *money*." Even the uncertain prospect of payment was a significant inducement for writers who had seen their literary livelihood cut off by war.[37]

Finally, the world of Southern literary publishing was small and inbred. Southern wartime literary publications tended to be edited by a small group of literary men who moved from publication to publication, often knew one another well, and published one another's work. John R. Thompson, for instance, had been the editor of the *Southern Literary Messenger* before the war, joined the staff of the *Southern Field and Fireside* for a brief period in 1860, and then later in the war worked as editor of the *Southern Illustrated News*, among other editorial duties. James D. McCabe was editor of the *Magnolia Weekly* in 1863, but after giving that position up in 1864, he was listed as a contributor to the *Southern Illustrated News* and the *Mercury*. George William Bagby of the *Southern Literary Messenger* also contributed to the *Southern Illustrated News*. And Paul Hamilton Hayne and William Gilmore Simms were listed as contributors to the *Southern Field and Fireside*, the *Southern Illustrated News*, the *Magnolia Weekly*, and the *Mercury*. In short, the exigencies of war encouraged a blending of voices within the pages of a story paper such as the *News*, as revered authors who had published in avowedly literary journals were joined by self-consciously popular authors and by first-time authors newly inspired by the war.[38]

By far the most important aspect of the *News* in its own reckoning was its claim to be "Illustrated." But here its ambitions far outreached its capabilities, emphasizing the extreme difficulties under which Confederate publications labored. The *News* promised to provide illustrations "honestly and faithfully drawn and engraved by competent and experienced artists." The first issue of the weekly, however, contained only one illustration, a small, crude engraving of Stonewall Jackson in the center of the first page. With a certain amount of defensive bluster, the *News* said, "We expect each week to increase the number of engravings, yet our aim shall be, not *number*, but *quality*."[39]

A central problem for the *News* was finding experienced artists and engravers in the South. The *News* may have promised illustrations, but it simply did not have the personnel to produce them: within only a few weeks of its first issue it advertised "Wanted Immediately – Two competent Wood Engravers." Admitting that "the Illustrated department of our paper is not yet complete," it nevertheless reassured its readers, "We hope in a few weeks to have a corps of competent Artists engaged solely in illustrating the pages of this journal with accurate and neatly executed wood cuts."[40]

Some months earlier, the *Southern Monthly* had had to admit defeat in its own quest to be illustrated. "With no small feeling of chagrin, and some of shame, we are forced to confess that a well-illustrated magazine *cannot* yet be produced in the South," it said in March 1862. "Good artists we can procure, but good engravers on wood are scarce among us, and even if they were more numerous, the wood itself is not to be had." A letter from a reader named Lucy complained, "The pleasant anticipations with which I opened the February number of your monthly were checked and my nerves experienced a violent shock when the things called *pictures* met my eyes." Calling them a "burlesque on the fine arts," Lucy assured the magazine that if these illustrations were indeed " 'increased in number as the circulation of the Magazine increases,' " she would "exert what influence I may have to *diminish* its circulation as fast as possible." Under such circumstances, and meeting with "general condemnation," the *Monthly* decided it was "best to discontinue giving 'more of the same sort.' " Illustrating the magazine " 'must wait upon opportunity' to do better," it concluded.[41]

Unlike the *Southern Monthly*, the *Southern Illustrated News* eventually did manage to "do better" by hiring several competent artists, including one who had been "actively and prominently engaged on Frank Leslie's Pictorial." Yet the illustrations in the *News* remained sparse and remarkably crude by Northern standards, their subjects usually portraits rather than scenes of action or battle, which were more difficult to engrave. Other illustrated periodicals faced similar problems. The *Mercury* of Raleigh, which advertised itself as "Beautifully Illustrated," published its first issue in April 1864 without any illustrations whatsoever, explaining that the ink it had purchased was of "such a very inferior quality" that it was impossible to work with. Such difficulties underscored a distinct and important difference between the popular literary culture of war in the North and in the South: whereas in the North the war was imagined visually in *Harper's Weekly, Frank Leslie's Illustrated Newspaper*, in dozens of other publications and forms of print ephemera, as well as in photographs exhibited in galleries such as Matthew Brady's New York gallery, in the South the literary war remained primarily a war of words, not pictures; of poetic images and oratorical flourishes, rather than painted or engraved representations.[42]

This was not for Southern lack of interest in a visual war: within a large city such as Richmond, newspapers advertised theatrical attractions such as Lee Mallory's "Pantechnoptomon," consisting of "War Illustrations Exhibiting the Soldier's Life in Camp, March, Bivouac, Battle." Mallory himself advertised that he needed "Sketches of Scenes and Incidents connected with our army, such as Views of Camps, Battle-Fields, Maps, etc.," and that "any drawings that will be interesting to the public, will be promptly acknowledged and paid for." In mid-1862 a "Confederate Reading Room" advertised "YANKEE PICTORIALS OF THE WAR giving all the scenes and illustrations of the recent great battles and portraits of the most promising actors." These had been "just received, by special order, through a party just arrived from the North." Monthly subscribers paid fifty cents, while a single admission – "good for all day" – cost ten cents.[43]

As this last advertisement revealed, war hardly annihilated interest in Northern periodicals, despite the expressed hopes of numerous Southern publications. Indeed, war may have intensified interest in Northern "pictorials." Not only were they virtually the only visual representations of the war available in the South, but they were so scarce as to be especially valuable commodities. Certainly numerous Southerners recorded the receipt of a Northern "pictorial" as a signal, noteworthy event.[44]

In a myriad ways Northern literature continued to hold power for Southern readers, writers, and publishers. The *Richmond Whig* advertised for "Northern Journals" in December 1862, saying that "any person arriving from the states north of the Potomac, and bringing Northern or European newspapers," would "confer a favor upon the Editors of the Whig by leaving or sending the same" to the *Whig* office. In the *Magnolia Weekly* in 1863, the columnist "Refugitta" (Constance Cary) confessed to missing "that charming Atlantic." Despite the blockade, and despite Southern calls for a boycott of Northern literature, at least one Richmond firm advertised both *Harper's Monthly* and the *Atlantic Monthly* for sale during the summer of 1863. The *Southern Illustrated News* was scandalized that "loyal citizens of the State and the Confederacy should encourage the sale of this pernicious trash." Yet the *News* itself secretly borrowed liberally from Northern periodicals for its own contents, republishing at least four *Harper's Weekly* war romances during 1863 and 1864.[45]

At the same time, though the *News* excoriated the "Yankees" at every opportunity, it nonetheless also sometimes measured its worth in a Northern mirror, professing to be jubilant, for instance, when *Frank Leslie's Illustrated Newspaper* gave it a negative notice. *Leslie's* had reprinted one of the *News*'s diatribes against the North, sarcastically commenting that "the South is going to have an art as well as a literature of its own" and noting that the *Southern Illustrated News* was "called illustrated, because it has one picture – an archaic portrait of 'Stonewall Jackson.' "[46]

Yet the *Southern Illustrated News* claimed to be delighted at this notice. "We ask no greater triumph," the *News* said, "than that of knowing we have excited the ire of these immaculate Yankees, the Harpers and Leslie, for with the advent of the 'Southern Illustrated Newspaper' they clearly perceive that the prospect for the circulation of their miserable sheets ever again in the South, is poor indeed. Hence, we welcome their criticism and abuse of us as a bright harbinger." The *News* even claimed, falsely, that "in New England and New York, the exigencies of the war, and the closing up of the Southern market, have well nigh extinguished authorship and its lights, from the little farthing candle of Mr. James Russell Lowell to the bright gas burner of Dr. Oliver Wendell Holmes." In contrast, "the publishing house of West & Johnston" had "issued more new books from original mss. during the past year, than any firm in Yankee land, not excepting our friends Sharper & Brothers of New York." The *News* concluded with satisfaction that "there has been a healthy stimulus given to literary production among us."[47]

It was true that war stimulated Southern literary production. By late 1862 the *Southern Illustrated News* reflected with some satisfaction (and a good deal of boosterism) on a changed literary world: "A Southern book, at one time, was a dreg in the market," the *News* said, but "now it immediately springs into popularity and is eagerly sought after." Southern authors had once "looked to the Harpers, the Appletons, and others of a like character, to publish their books for them," but now they relied on

> those enterprising merchants, Messrs. West and Johnston, who are extensively engaged in the publishing business. We have now upon our table a variety of military and other works gotten up in a very superior manner by these gentlemen. The typography will compare favorably with the Harpers, while the binding and general getting up is not inferior, and in many respects superior, to any work ever issued from the press of any Northern publishing house. Thus we will no longer be compelled to read the trashy productions of itinerant Yankees, worthless as their hearts are black; but will, in future, have Southern books, written by Southern gentlemen, printed on Southern type, and sold by Southern publishing houses.[48]

This was promotional rhetoric, of course. Not only was the West and Johnston list, consisting of mostly military books, minuscule by Northern standards, but there were other publishers operating in Richmond as well. Still, such a statement was an important indication of the considerable ambitions of many Southern authors, publishers, and periodicals.

In 1863 in particular, during an extended period of confidence in Confederate war fortunes, several new publications were established. The first issue of the humorous weekly the *Southern Punch* appeared in Richmond on August 15, and two other humorous periodicals, the Griffin, Georgia, *Bugle Horn of Liberty* and the Mobile, Alabama, *Confederate Spirit and Knapsack of Fun*, were announced during the summer and fall. At Christmastime the first issue of a new Richmond periodical, the *Bohemian*, appeared. In April 1864 William B. Smith began to publish the *Raleigh Mercury* after a hiatus of three years. In May the publishers of the *Magnolia Weekly* began a monthly periodical called *Smith and Barrow's Monthly*. The editors of such journals often talked of unrealistically ambitious plans for the future: the *Southern Punch*, for instance, planned to issue "a monthly supplement, consisting of a series of Historical Engravings, Equestrian Portraits of Generals, etc., printed on fine proof sheet paper, in the highest style of the art."[49]

By 1864, however, several commentators provided a more realistic assessment of the state of Southern popular literature. "It is useless to attempt to disguise the fact," the *Magnolia Weekly* stated, that "*in spite of our boasted desire to make our literary enterprises succeed, the combined circulation of all the literary journals in the South does not equal the circulation in the South of the New York Ledger, before the War.*" Not only had Southern periodicals not gained the audience they desired, but throughout the conflict war threatened their very existence. The *Southern Monthly*, located in Memphis, Tennessee, had alerted its readers in April 1862 that it had moved to Grenada, Mississippi, as the "occupation of Memphis by the Abolitionists" was "within the bounds of possibility." It promised, nevertheless, that the *Monthly* "will cease but with the Confederacy that gave it birth." Instead it ceased publication, forever, the next month. "But for the capture of Nashville by the Yankees, whereby the large stereotype foundry of that city was lost to us for the war," the *Southern Illustrated News* informed its readers in November 1862, "many valuable fresh books and new editions of old ones would have been brought out in a style highly creditable to the taste and enterprise of the South." Fear of invasion underlay a move by Charleston publisher Evans and Cogswell in 1864, but there was high irony in its choice of Columbia, South Carolina, as a safe haven.[50]

The war stymied the projects of numerous authors, as well. John R. Thompson collected poems for a volume of war poetry that he hoped would be published by a British publisher, but this project never came to pass. In January 1862 William Gilmore Simms wrote to several correspondents suggesting an elaborate plan for the publication of a "Library of the Confederate States," including "new works to be interspersed as prepared, and a wholesome variety to be sought in History, Biography, Statesmanship, Poetry & Fiction." But this plan remained only an idea. In mid-1863 the *Southern Illustrated News* announced that George William Bagby, the editor of the *Southern Literary Messenger*, was "collecting materials for two books, to be entitled respectively, 'Southern Heroes and Heroic Incidents,' and 'Humorous Anecdotes of the War.' " Neither book was published. In early 1865 the poet John Henry Boner wrote that he had been solicited to contribute to a volume compiled "from the writings of different authors of the confederacy – something, as I understand it, in the style of Griswold's 'Poets of America' " (a popular Northern anthology). But this project, too, never came to fruition.[51]

Several authors commented on the havoc war wrought with their literary careers. "My occupation utterly gone, in this wretched state of war & confusion, I have no refuge in my wonted employments," William Gilmore Simms lamented, adding, "Nobody reads nowadays, and no one prints. My desks are already filled with MS.S. Why add to the number?" Paul Hamilton Hayne remarked in 1864 that "all social, intellectual pleasures [had] been ruthlessly destroyed" by the war. "One cannot *think* calmly; the sympathies, fears, passions of the heart being abnormally excited, there is hardly any chance left for that cool, consistent mental action, essential to Artistic success." The poet James Wood Davidson, who fought with the Thirteenth Regiment SC Volunteers, simply said, "War is a very unliterary thing," telling a correspondent, "My lyric harp I rarely touch – One cannot easily carry a harp in addition to the usual outfit of a camp dweller!"[52]

In January 1863, four months after beginning publication, the *Southern Illustrated News* congratulated itself on having survived the difficulties it faced. At the time of its first issue, it commented, "Such was the scarcity of materials that the oldest, ablest, most widely circulated journals in the Confederacy were printed on dingy sheets, which in time of peace would hardly have passed muster as wrapping paper." At the same time "the printing ink then in use was of a quality which we doubt not so soiled the hands of every reader as to have left an indelible impression on every mind." Paper was "so scarce that many deemed it impossible to obtain enough to print a decent edition of a new paper." Moreover, "we had to ransack every State for artists and the materials which artists use – box-wood being then, as now, exceedingly scarce; so much so, indeed, that we had to *discover* some other wood to supply the deficiency." While the *News* had found the best supplies and artists that it could in the South, it had also "sent agent after agent into the lines of the enemy to purchase what could not be obtained at home" and in "more than one instance" had been "twiddled out of large sums by blockade runners."[53]

Still, even the enterprising *News* could not overcome the difficulties of war entirely. As problems with paper and ink supplies, machinery, and personnel became increasingly desperate during the war, it, like many other periodicals, sometimes suspended publication. Although the *Southern Literary Messenger* early in the war had boasted that it had not been forced to resort to double issues, in contrast to *De Bow's Review*, in fact it began to publish on a bimonthly basis in 1862. In October 1862 it informed its readers, "The present double number would have contained as much matter as the last, had not the government seized the paper mills in this city and we failed to get paper in North Carolina." In August 1864 the *Magnolia Weekly* explained to subscribers who complained of missing issues that in fact the *Weekly* had only been published three times during the last three months "owing to the calls made upon the employees of this office for military duty." Under the exigencies of war the *Southern Literary Messenger* was sold in January 1864 and published its last issue in June that same year. Most popular publications quietly folded with the defeat of the Confederacy.[54]

In April 1863 the *Southern Field and Fireside*, commenting that "the condition of the country [was] not favorable to literature," warned, "However violent may be our animosity against the North now, the possibility of our again becoming subservient to Northern pens, and Northern publications is not so unlikely as one might at first imagine." In August the *Southern Illustrated News*, indignantly noting the sale of "Yankee" magazines in Richmond, expressed a fear that "such was the slavishness of the South," that "the old patrons of the Yankee weeklies and monthlies would buy them at any price." In February 1864 the *Southern Punch* mentioned a letter from a correspondent who feared that " 'when this cruel war is over,' the Southern people will again patronise Yankee flash weeklies and monthlies" such as the *New York Ledger*, *Harper's Weekly*, and *Harper's Magazine*. The *Southern Punch* used this letter as the occasion for another spirited call for "literary independence" from the North. But in the event the letter writer was prescient. With the end of the conflict both Southern readers and authors returned, however ironically, to their dependence on Northern literature.[55]

Notes

1   Oliver Wendell Holmes, "Bread and the Newspaper," *Atlantic Monthly* 8 (September 1861), 347; Chesnut, *Mary Chesnut's Civil War*, p. 72.

2   Dannett, *Noble Women of the North*, pp. 45–6.

3   Stone, *Brokenburn*, p. 14. George William Curtis, "Editor's Easy Chair," *Harper's New Monthly Magazine* 23 (July 1861), 266; (August 1861), 411.

4   Holmes, "Bread and the Newspaper," 347, 348. Chesnut, *Mary Chesnut's Civil War*, p. 354. Curtis, "Editor's Easy Chair," *Harper's New Monthly Magazine* 23 (August 1861), 411.

5   Holmes, "Bread and the Newspaper," 346, 348; *Southern Monthly* 1 (April 1862): 632. Holmes, "Bread and the Newspaper," 348.

6   *Southern Literary Messenger* 33 (November 1861), 395; *Southern Monthly* 1 (November 1861), 231–32; *American Publishers' Circular and Literary Gazette*, July 20, 1861, 229; Ticknor and Fields, Rough Cost Book, 1860 and 1861, Ticknor and Fields Archives, Houghton Library; Henry Wadsworth Longfellow as quoted in Tryon, *Parnassus Corner*, 252, 253.

7   Tryon, *Parnassus Corner*, 253–4; James Perkins Walker to "Friends," 1866, James Perkins Walker Papers, Firestone Library, Princeton University; *Harper's New Monthly Magazine* 23 (August 1861), 414; Simms, *Letters of William Gilmore Simms*, 4, 326.

8   Henry Timrod to Rachel Lyons, September 6, 1861, as quoted in Timrod, *Last Years of Henry Timrod*, 9–10; Alcott, *Selected Letters*, p. 72.

9   *Manufactures of the United States in 1860*, pp. cxxxii–cxlv; *Richmond Whig*, April 19, 1861. See also the Southern Literary Messenger 32 (June 1861), 481, which announced, "We take pleasure in informing our Southern friends that Messrs. Henry L. Pelouze & Co., have established a Type Foundry in Richmond, and are prepared to supply those in want, with printing material generally. Should the Southern printers give them proper encouragement, we have no doubt that they will, in time, establish a foundry here equal to any in the Northern cities." Parrish and Willingham, *Confederate Imprints*, 12. On printing in wartime, see Detlefson, "Printing in the Confederacy." *Daily Richmond Enquirer*, January 9, 1862; *Southern Literary Companion*, June 15, 1864; advertisement of Burke, Boykin & Co., Macon, GA, in *Confederate States Almanac* (Macon, 1864), 24, as reprinted in Harwell, *Confederate Belles-Lettres*, 26.

10   At the same time, a smaller reading audience existed in the South than in the North. Approximately 70 percent of the free male population in the South was literate, in contrast to some 90 percent in the more populous North. See Kaser, *Books and Libraries in Camp and Battle*, 3–4.

11   Henry Timrod to Rachel Lyons, December 10, 1861, in Timrod, *Last Years of Henry Timrod*, p. 10; Stone, *Brokenburn*, p. 14; Thomas, *Secret Eye*, 188–9.

12 "Editor's Table," *Southern Literary Messenger* 33 (August 1861), 160; *Charleston Courier* as quoted in the *Southern Field and Fireside*, May 18, 1861, 2; *Southern Monthly* 1 (November 1861), 231–2.

13 *New Orleans Delta* as quoted in the *Southern Literary Messenger* 33 (October 1861): 317; *Charleston Courier* as quoted in *Southern Field and Fireside*, May 18, 1861, 2. For more calls for a new Southern literature, see "To the Literati," *Mercury*, April 30, 1864, 4, and "Literature of the South," *Mercury*, June 11, 1864, 6.

14 On antebellum calls for a Southern literature, see Hubbell, *South in American Literature*, pp. 363–6. *New Orleans Delta* as quoted in "Editor's Table," *Southern Literary Messenger 33* (October 1861), 317–18. Paul Hamilton Hayne reflected on the market realities of Southern popular literary culture in 1864, commenting, "The curse of the South has been that we have had *no* organized Literary fraternity, – no persons constituting a class, whose labors were worth as much *in the Market*, as those of the Lawyer, Doctor, Merchant, or any other *practical* workmen! Our Periodicals, have all failed, chiefly because they started with no *capital*." See Paul Hamilton Hayne to Clara Dargan, March 27, 1864, Clara Victoria Dargan Maclean Papers, Special Collections Library, Duke University, Durham, N.C.

15 *Southern Monthly* 1 (September 1861), 3; Thomas, *Secret Eye*, 188–89.

16 *Southern Literary Messenger* 33 (August 1861), 160; *Southern Field and Fireside*, May 18, 1861, 2; *Southern Illustrated News*, October 4, 1862, 5; *Charleston Courier* as quoted in *Southern Field and Fireside*, May 18, 1861, 2.

17 *Southern Illustrated News*, September 13, 1862, 5.

18 *Magnolia Weekly*, April 11, 1863, 129; *Southern Monthly* 1 (September 1861), 2; "Editor's Table," *Southern Literary Messenger* 33 (September 1861), 237.

19 Ibid.

20 "The Magnolia Stories," *Magnolia Weekly*, April 11, 1863, 129; "Popular Literature," *Magnolia Weekly*, May 30, 1863, 184.

21 *Southern Monthly* 1 (September 1861), 4.

22 For another example of commentary on Northern depictions of slavery, see *Southern Field and Fireside*, December 15, 1860, 236. In such accounts Southerners rarely acknowledged Northern diversity of opinion concerning slavery or the stridently antiblack party culture of Northern Democrats. On that party culture, see especially Baker, *Affairs of Party*. William H. Holcombe, "Characteristics and Capabilities of the Negro Race," *Southern Literary Messenger* 33 (December 1861), 401. On polygenesis and antebellum justifications of slavery, see especially Gould, *Mismeasure of Man*, and Faust, *Sacred Circle*.

23 *Southern Literary Messenger* 33 (November 1861), 395.

24 Ibid.

25 *Southern Literary Messenger* 34 (April 1862), 266; "Editor's Table," *Southern Literary Messenger* 34 (September–October 1862), 581; *De Bow's Review 33* (May–August 1862), 96.

26 *Southern Monthly* 1 (September 1861), 6; *Southern Literary Messenger* 34 (January 1862), 70. For the publication date of *War Songs of the South*, see the *Richmond Daily Dispatch* of July 5, 1862, which commented, "This book of patriotic lyrics, although issued but a few days since, has met with general favor with the public."

27 Shepperson, *War Songs of the South*, 3–4.

28 Chesnut, *Mary Chesnut's Civil War*, 282. Interestingly enough, C. Vann Woodward chose throughout Mary Chesnut's diary to excise the poetry she copied into her text – one of his few excisions of the text. Kate D. Foster Diary, Manuscript Department, Special Collections Library, Duke University. William Galt Notebook, Ms. 0362, Virginia Military Institute Archives, available online at www.vmi.edu. M. J. Solomons Scrapbook, Manuscript Department, Special Collections Library, Duke University. See additional examples of scrapbooks kept by Southern women during the war in the collection of the Eleanor S. Brockenbrough Library, the Museum of the Confederacy, Richmond, VA.

29 "The Poet's Corner" was a term used by many writers to describe the spot where poems were published in the newspaper. Indeed, they were often published in the corner of a page, though not

always. For the use of the term, see, for instance, Edmondston, "*Journal of a Secesh Lady,*" p. 282, and John Henry Boner to Clara Dargan, April 14, 1864 Clara Victoria Dargan Maclean Papers, Manuscript Department, Special Collections Library, Duke University.

30 *Southern Literary Messenger* 33 (December 1861), 468. The publications mentioned were *Chisholm's Manual of Military Surgery; Gilham's Manual for Volunteers and Militia; Ordnance Manual, 1861; Confederate States Army Regulations; Handbook of Artillery*; and *The Volunteer's Hand Book.*

31 Harris, *On the Plantation*, pp. 21–2. On the *Countryman*, see also Turner, *Autobiography of "The Countryman."*

32 Coulter, *Confederate States of America*, 509. A good comparison to the *Southern Illustrated News* is the *Southern Field and Fireside*, which advertised in 1864 that it had "some 13,000 subscribers." *Southern Field and Fireside*, March 6, 1864, 5. Breckinridge, *Lucy Breckinridge of Grove Hill*, 50, 130, 133.

33 "Editor's Table," *Southern Literary Messenger* 34 (September–October 1862), 581; *Southern Illustrated News*, September 13, 1862, 4.

34 *Southern Illustrated News*, November 1, 1862, 3.

35 *Southern Illustrated News*, January 3, 1863, 8; *Southern Literary Messenger* 37 (July 1863), 447; "Uncle John on Poetry," *Magnolia Weekly*, September 19, 1863, 316. In 1864 Paul Hamilton Hayne expressed a similar weariness with war poetry. Pronouncing himself "thoroughly disgusted" with "contemporary themes," he said, "I shall not, probably, compose *another* line upon battles, sieges, or Generals, however distinguished." See Paul Hamilton Hayne to Clara Dargan, March 27, 1864, Clara Victoria Dargan Maclean Papers, Manuscript Department, Special Collections Library, Duke University.

36 "We take pleasure in enrolling this morning among our list of regular contributors the name of Paul H. Hayne, Esq., one of the sweetest poets of our own sunny land," the *Southern Illustrated News* announced in its December 6, 1862, issue. *Frank Leslie's Illustrated Newspaper*, February 2, 1861, 168, 170. Moore, *Paul Hamilton Hayne*, 53.

37 *Southern Monthly* 1 (September 1861): 5; *Southern Literary Messenger* to Clara Dargan, July 24, 1862, Clara Victoria Dargan Maclean Papers, Manuscript Department, Special Collections Library, Duke University; Paul Hamilton Hayne to John R. Thompson, May 1, 1864, Paul Hamilton Hayne Papers, Special Collections Library, Duke University; Paul Hamilton Hayne to Clara Dargan, February 26, 1864, Clara Victoria Dargan Maclean Papers, Special Collections Library, Duke University.

38 On John Reuben Thompson's career, see especially Garmon, *John Reuben Thompson*, and Moss, *Confederate Broadside Poems*, 1–49. For McCabe, see *Southern Illustrated News*, March 19, 1864, 84; *Mercury*, May 21, 1864, 4. For Bagby, see *Southern Illustrated News*, February 14, 1863, 2. For Simms and Hayne, see *Southern Field and Fireside*, November 5, 1863, 4; *Southern Illustrated News*, February 14, 1863, 2; *Magnolia Weekly*, June 13, 1863, 200, and *Mercury*, June 18, 1864, 4.

39 *Southern Illustrated News*, September 13, 1862, 4.

40 Ibid., 5. For another ad for engravers, see *Mercury*, June 11, 1864, 1.

41 *Southern Monthly* 1 (March 1862): 557–58. On attempts to obtain boxwood for engraving, sometimes from blockade runners, see *Southern Illustrated News*, May 9, 1863, 2, 8; *Southern Monthly* 1 (March 1862): 580.

42 *Southern Illustrated News*, October 4, 1862, 8; "Our Illustrations," *Mercury*, April 30, 1864, 4.

43 *Southern Illustrated News*, October 4, 1862, 8; *Daily Richmond Examiner*, July 26, 1862.

44 See, for instance, "Christmas in Camp," *Richmond Whig*, January 1, 1863: "A large file of papers from Nashville was handed us this morning. New York Pictorials, Cincinnati and Louisville papers were among them."

45 *Richmond Whig*, December 10, 1862; Refugitta, "A Confederate Christmas," *Magnolia Weekly*, October 3, 1863, 6. For the advertisement of "Yankee literature" and the reaction of the *Southern Illustrated News*, see *Southern Illustrated News*, August 8, 1863, 36–37. For republished stories, see the October 17, 1863, "The Blue Flowers"; a reprinting of *Harper's Weekly*'s September 5, 1863, "The Blue Flowers"; the November 7, 1863, "Sybil Miller, or the Wounded Soldier," first published in *Harper's Weekly* as "A Gift by the Wayside; the July 30, 1864, "The Heart of Miriam Clyde," published under that same title in the February 27, 1864, *Harper's Weekly*; and the

November 5, 1864, "Worth a Leg," published under that title in *Harper's Weekly* on October 22, 1864.

46 *Frank Leslie's Illustrated Newspaper*, September 27, 1862, 3.

47 *Southern Illustrated News*, October 11, 1862, 5; November 8, 1862, 2.

48 *Southern Illustrated News*, September 27, 1862, 4.

49 For announcements of *The Bugle Horn of Liberty* and the *Confederate Spirit and Knapsack of Fun*, see *Magnolia Weekly*, August 8, 1863, 264, and *Magnolia Weekly*, October 31, 1863, 36. On the *Mercury*'s hiatus, see "A Card," *Mercury*, April 30, 1864, 4. *Southern Punch*, August 15, 1863, 2.

50 "Southern Literature," *Magnolia Weekly*, January 23, 1864, 132; *Southern Monthly* 1 (April 1862): 626; *Southern Illustrated News*, November 8, 1862, 2; London, "Confederate Literature and Its Publishers," 84.

51 On Thompson's attempts to publish a volume of war poetry, see Moss, *Confederate Broadside Poems*, 12, and Garmon, *John Reuben Thompson*, 111. William Gilmore Simms to John Reuben Thompson, January 16, 1862, in Simms, *Letters of William Gilmore Simms*, 6:223. See also Simms to William Porcher Miles, January 31, 1862, in *Letters of William Gilmore Simms*, 4:396–8. John Henry Boner to Clara Dargan, February 5, 1865, Clara Victoria Dargan Maclean Papers, Manuscript Department, Special Collections Library, Duke University.

52 Moss, *Confederate Broadside Poems*, 10; Paul Hamilton Hayne to Clara Dargan, March 27, 1864, James Wood Davidson to Clara Dargan, April 4, 1862, Clara Victoria Dargan Maclean Papers, Manuscript Department, Special Collections Library, Duke University.

53 "Our Paper," *Southern Illustrated News*, January 3, 1863, 2.

54 "Editor's Table," *Southern Literary Messenger* 34 (September–October 1862): 581. *Magnolia Weekly*, August 6, 1864, 292. Likewise, in January 1863 the *Southern Field and Fireside* commented on the "suspension of this paper, during a part of November and all of December." *Southern Field and Fireside*, January 10, 1863, 12.

55 "Southern Literature," *Southern Field and Fireside*, April 4, 1863, 110. *Southern Illustrated News*, August 8, 1863, 37. "Literary Convention," *Southern Punch*, February 6, 1864, 6.

Questions to consider

- What were some of the things Northern and Southern readers had in common during the Civil War? In what ways was the North different from the South?

- Does the failure of the South to sustain a separate literary culture suggest anything about the failure of the Confederate cause generally? Conversely, would you say that the South has managed to create a distinct literary (and general popular) culture generally? Is there a paradox here?

- "The act of reading itself now took on a strongly ideological cast," Fahs writes at one point. What does she mean by this? Is there any sense in which reading today is an "ideological" act? What does your reading lately say about *you*?

Chapter 29

The Written War: Primary Sources

The Great Army of the Sick

Walt Whitman

During the Civil War, Walt Whitman (1819–92) was not quite the "Good Gray Poet" he would later become to a small, but rapidly growing, group of devotees in the closing decades of the nineteenth century. Though he had admirers (among them Ralph Waldo Emerson, at least until Whitman annoyed Emerson by publishing the latter's praise of *Leaves of Grass* in the second edition of that book in 1856), Whitman scandalized at least as many people as he impressed with his often explicitly erotic poetry. Though he had been a Democrat before the war, Whitman, who lived in Washington for much of the struggle, became deeply engaged in the Union effort and a particular fan of Abraham Lincoln, who he observed coming and going from the White House and who he would later memorialize in a series of poems included in *Leaves of Grass*.

For much of his life, Whitman made his living as a journalist. In this 1863 piece for the *New York Times*, he tries to convey life and death in army hospitals, where he spent a great deal of time volunteering to help the sick. How would you describe the strategies he uses to bring this piece of reporting to life? Is there anything poetic here?

Walt Whitman, "The Great Army of the Sick", in *New York Times* (February 26, 1863), in *The Real War Will Never Get in the Books: Selections from Civil War Writers*, ed. Louis Masur (New York: Oxford University Press, 1995). Pp. 258–9.

The military hospitals, convalescent camps, &c. in Washington and its neighborhood sometimes contain over fifty thousand sick and wounded men. Every form of wound, (the mere sight of some of them having been known to make a tolerably hardy visitor faint away,) every kind of malady, like a long procession, with typhoid fever and diarrhoea at the head as leaders, are here in steady motion. The soldier's hospital! how many sleepless nights, how many woman's tears, how many long and aching hours and days of suspense, from every one of the Middle, Eastern and Western States, have concentrated here! Our own New-York, in the form of hundreds and thousands of her young men, may consider herself here – Pennsylvania, Ohio, Indiana and all the West and North-west the same – and all the New-England States the same.

Upon a few of these hospitals I have been almost daily calling as a missionary, on my own account, for the sustenance and consolation of some of the most needy cases of sick and dying men, for the last two months. One has much to learn in order to do good in these places. Great tact is required. These are not like other hospitals. By far the greatest proportion (I should say five-sixths) of the patients are American young men, intelligent, of independent spirit, tender feelings, used to a hardy and healthy life; largely the farmers are represented by their sons – largely the mechanics and workingmen of the cities. Then they are *soldiers*. All these points must be borne in mind.

People through our Northern cities have little or no idea of the great and prominent feature which these military hospitals and convalescent camps make in and around Washington. There are not merely two or three or a dozen, but some fifty of them, of different degrees of capacity. Some have a thousand or more patients. The newspapers here find it necessary to print every day a directory of the hospitals; a long list, something like what a directory of the churches would be in New-York, Philadelphia or Boston. . . .

A Sight in Camp in the Daybreak Gray and Dim

Walt Whitman

In December 1862, Whitman left New York for Virginia in a successful quest to find his brother George, who had been wounded near Fredericksburg (largely as a result of this trip he would spend the next eleven years in the nation's capital). His experiences at the front made a deep impression on him, which he incorporated into his work. This poem was included in his 1865 book *Drum Taps*, which was later incorporated into *Leaves of Grass*. How would you describe his depiction of death?

Walt Whitman, "A Sight in Camp in the Daybreak Gray and Dim," in *Drum Taps* (New York: Bunce & Huntington, 1865), p. 48.

A sight in camp in the daybreak gray and dim,
As from my tent I emerge so early sleepless,
As slow I walk in the cool fresh air the path near by the hospital tent,
Three forms I see on stretchers lying, brought out there untended lying,
Over each the blanket spread, ample brownish woolen blanket,
Gray and heavy blanket, folding, covering all.

Curious I halt and silent stand,
Then with light fingers I from the face of the nearest the first just lift
  the blanket;

Who are you elderly man so gaunt and grim, with well-gray'd hair,
  and flesh all sunken about the eyes?
Who are you my dear comrade?

Then to the second I step – and who are you my child and darling?
Who are you sweet boy with cheeks yet blooming?

Then to the third – a face nor child nor old, very calm, as of beautiful
  yellow-white ivory;
Young man I think I know you – I think this face is the face of the
  Christ himself,
Dead and divine and brother of all, and here again he lies.

Battle Hymn of the Republic

Julia Ward Howe

The epitome of Yankee abolitionism, Julia Ward Howe (1819–1910) embraced the Civil War as a crusade for justice (her husband, Samuel Gridley Howe, had been one of the "Secret Six" who funded John Brown's freedom fighter/terrorist operations of the 1850s). One night in 1861, while visiting an army camp near Washington, DC with the party of Governor Andrew of Massachusetts, Howe found herself unable to sleep. In a flurry of creative activity, she wrote the following poem in the dark of her tent, setting its cadences to the rhythm of "John Brown's Body," a popular abolitionist song. "The Battle Hymn of the Republic" was published – on the cover – of the February, 1862 edition of The Atlantic Monthly. What is its vision of the war? If you knew this song before, do you see it differently now?

Julia Ward Howe, "Battle Hymn of the Republic," in *The Atlantic Monthly* vol. 9, no. 52 (February 1862).

Mine eyes have seen the glory of the coming of the Lord:
He is trampling out the vintage where the grapes of wrath are stored;
He hath loosed the fateful lightning of His terrible swift sword:
        His truth is marching on.

I have seen Him in the watch-fires of a hundred circling camps,
They have builded Him an altar in the evening dews and damps;
I can read His righteous sentence by the dim and flaring lamps;
        His day is marching on.

I have read a fiery gospel writ in burnished rows of steel:
"As ye deal with my contemners, so with you my grace shall deal;
Let the Hero, born of woman, crush the serpent with his heel,
        Since God is marching on."

He has sounded forth the trumpet that shall never call retreat;
He is sifting out the hearts of men before His judgment seat;
Oh, be swift, my soul, to answer Him! be jubilant my feet!
                    Our God is marching on.

In the beauty of the lillies Christ was born across the sea,
With a glory in his bosom that transfigures you and me;
As He died to make men holy, let us die to make men free,
                    While God is marching on.

John Lamar

Rebecca Harding Davis

In many ways, Rebecca Harding Davis (1831–1910) lived her life in an ambivalent neutral zone between North and South. Born in Pennsylvania, Harding spent her early childhood in Alabama before her family moved to Wheeling, Virginia, an Ohio River border town poised between the agricultural South and the rapidly industrializing North. (This strongly Unionist section of Virginia would become part of the new state of West Virginia in 1863.) Harding's first novella, *Life in the Iron Mills* (1861) was published in *The Atlantic Monthly* and is now recognized as one of the founding texts of the movement literary historians know as realism. One year later, *The Atlantic Monthly* published another of what would be a string of Davis stories, "John Lamar," a tale of an escaped slave that suggests that the Civil War was far from a simple struggle of good against evil.

Rebecca Harding Davis, "John Lamar," in *The Atlantic Monthly*, April 1862, 411–23.

The guard-house was, in fact, nothing but a shed in the middle of a stubble-field. It had been built for a cider-press last summer; but since Captain Dorr had gone into the army, his regiment had camped over half his plantation, and the shed was boarded up, with heavy wickets at either end, to hold whatever prisoners might fall into their hands from Floyd's forces. It was a strong point for the Federal troops, his farm, – a sort of wedge in the Rebel Cheat counties of Western Virginia. Only one prisoner was in the guard-house now. The sentry, a raw boat-hand from Illinois, gaped incessantly at him through the bars, not sure if the "Secesh" were limbed and headed like other men; but the November fog was so thick that he could discern nothing but a short, squat man, in brown clothes and white hat, heavily striding to and fro. A negro was crouching outside, his knees cuddled in his arms to keep warm: a field-hand, you could be sure from the face, a grisly patch of flabby black, with a dull eluding word of something, you could not tell what, in the points of eyes, – treachery or gloom. The prisoner stopped, cursing him about something: the only answer was a lazy rub of the heels.

"Got any 'baccy, Mars' John?" he whined, in the middle of the hottest oath.

The man stopped abruptly, turning his pockets inside out.

"That's all, Ben," he said, kindly enough. "Now begone, you black devil!"

"Dem's um, Mars'! Goin' 'mediate," – catching the tobacco, and lolling down full length as his master turned off again.

Dave Hall, the sentry, stared reflectively, and sat down.

"Ben? Who air you next?" – nursing his musket across his knees, baby-fashion.

Ben measured him with one eye, polished the quid in his greasy hand, and looked at it.

"Pris'ner o' war," he mumbled, finally, – contemptuously; for Dave's trousers were in rags like his own, and his chilblained toes stuck through the shoe-tops. Cheap white trash, clearly.

"Yer master's some at swearin'. Heow many, neow, hes he like you, down to Georgy?"

The boatman's bony face was gathering a woful pity. He had enlisted to free the Uncle Toms, and carry God's vengeance to the Legrees. Here they were, a pair of them.

Ben squinted another critical survey of the "miss'able Linkinite."

"How many wells hev *yer* poisoned since yer set out?" he muttered.

The sentry stopped.

"How many 'longin' to de Lamars? 'Bout as many as der's dam' Yankees in Richmond 'baccy-houses!"

Something in Dave's shrewd, whitish eye warned him off.

"Ki yi! yer white nigger, yer!" he chuckled, shuffling down the stubble.

Dave clicked his musket, – then, choking down an oath into a grim Methodist psalm, resumed his walk, looking askance at the coarse-moulded face of the prisoner peering through the bars, and the diamond studs in his shirt, – bought with human blood, doubtless. The man was the black curse of slavery itself in the flesh, in his thought somehow, and he hated him accordingly. Our men of the Northwest have enough brawny Covenanter muscle in their religion to make them good haters for opinion's sake.

Lamar, the prisoner, watched him with a lazy drollery in his sluggish black eyes. It died out into sternness, as he looked beyond the sentry. He had seen this Cheat country before; this very plantation was his grandfather's a year ago, when he had come up from Georgia here, and loitered out the summer months with his Virginia cousins, hunting. That was a pleasant summer! Something in the remembrance of it flashed into his eyes, dewy, genial; the man's leather-covered face reddened like a child's. Only a year ago, – and now –. The plantation was Charley Dorr's now, who had married Ruth. This very shed he and Dorr had planned last spring, and now Charley held him a prisoner in it. The very thought of Charley Dorr warmed his heart. Why, he could thank God there were such men, True grit, every inch of his little body! There, last summer, how he had avoided Ruth until the day when he (Lamar) was going away! – then he told him he meant to try and win her. "She cared most for you always," Lamar had said, bitterly; "why have you waited so long?" "You loved her first, John, you know." That was like a man! He remembered that even that day, when his pain was breathless and sharp, the words made him know that Dorr was fit to be her husband.

Dorr was his friend. The word meant much to John Lamar. He thought less meanly of himself, when he remembered it. Charley's prisoner! An odd chance! Better that than to have met in battle. He thrust back the thought, the sweat oozing out on his face, – something within him muttering, "For Liberty! I would have killed him, so help me God!"

He had brought despatches to General Lee, that he might see Charley, and the old place, and – Ruth again; there was a gnawing hunger in his heart to see them. Fool! what was he to them? The man's face grew slowly pale, as that of a savage or an animal does, when the wound is deep and inward.

The November day was dead, sunless: since morning the sky had had only enough life in it to sweat out a few muddy drops, that froze as they fell: the cold numbed his mouth as he breathed it. This stubbly slope was where he and his grandfather had headed the deer: it was covered with hundreds of dirty, yellow tents now. Around there were hills like uncouth monsters, swathed in ice, holding up the soggy sky; shivering pine-forests; unmeaning, dreary flats; and the Cheat, coiled about the frozen sinews of the hills, limp and cold, like a cord lying a dead man's jaws. Whatever outlook of joy or worship this region had borne on its face in time gone, it turned to him to-day nothing but stagnation, a great death. He wondered idly, looking at it, (for the old Huguenot brain of the man was full of morbid fancies,) if it were winter alone that had deadened color and pulse out of these full-blooded hills, or if they could know the colder horror crossing their threshold, and forgot to praise God as it came.

Over that farthest ridge the house had stood. The guard (he had been taken by a band of Snake-hunters, back in the hills) had brought him past it. It was a heap of charred rafters. "Burned in the night," they said, "when the old Colonel was alone." They were very willing to show him this, as it was done by his own party, the Secession "Bush-whackers"; took him to the wood-pile to show him where his grandfather had been murdered, (there was a red mark) and buried, his old hands above the ground. "Colonel said 't was a job fur us to pay up; so we went to the village an' hed a scrimmage," – pointing to gaps in the hedges where the dead Bush-whackers yet lay unburied. He looked at them, and at the besotted faces about him, coolly. Snake-hunters and Bush-whackers, he knew, both armies used in Virginia as tools for rapine and murder: the sooner the Devil called home his own, the better. And yet, it was not God's fault, surely, that there were such tools in the North, any more than that in the South Ben was – Ben. Something was rotten in freer States than Denmark, he thought.

One of the men went into the hedge, and brought out a child's golden ringlet as a trophy. Lamar glanced in, and saw the small face in its woollen hood, dimpled yet, though dead for days. He remembered it. Jessy Birt, the ferryman's little girl. She used to come up to the house every day for milk. He wondered for which flag *she* died. Ruth was teaching her to write. *Ruth!* Some old pain hurt him just then, nearer than even the blood of the old man or the girl crying to God from the ground. The sergeant mistook the look. "They'll be buried," he said, gruffly. "Ye brought it on yerselves." And so led him to the Federal camp.

The afternoon grew colder, as he stood looking out of the guard-house. Snow began to whiten through the gray. He thrust out his arm through the wicket, his face kindling with childish pleasure, as he looked closer at the fairy stars and crowns on his shaggy sleeve. If Floy were here! She never had seen snow. When the flakes had melted off, he took a case out of his pocket to look at Floy. His sister, – a little girl who had no mother, nor father, nor lover, but Lamar. The man among his brother officers in Richmond was coarse, arrogant, of dogged courage, keen palate at the table, as keen eye on the turf. Sickly little Floy, down at home, knew the way to something below all this: just as they of the Rommany blood see below the muddy boulders of the streets the enchanted land of Boabdil bare beneath. Lamar polished the ivory painting with his breath, remembering that he had drunk nothing for days. A child's face, of about twelve, delicate, – a breath of fever or cold would shatter such weak beauty; big, dark eyes, (her mother was pure Castilian,) out of which her little life looked irresolute into the world, uncertain what to do there. The painter, with an unapt fancy, had clustered about the Southern face the Southern emblem, buds of the magnolia, unstained, as yet, as pearl. It angered Lamar, remembering how the creamy whiteness of the full-blown flower exhaled passion of which the crimsonest rose knew nothing, – a content, ecstasy, in animal life. Would Floy – Well, God help them both! they needed help. Three hundred souls was a heavy weight for those thin little hands to hold sway over, – to lead to hell or heaven. Up North they could have worked for her, and gained only her money. So Lamar reasoned, like a Georgian: scribbling a letter to "My Baby" on the wrapper of a newspaper, – drawing the shapes of the snowflakes, – telling her he had reached their grandfather's plantation, but "have not seen our Cousin Ruth yet, of whom you may remember I have told you, Floy.

When you grow up, I should like you to be just such a woman; so remember, my darling, if I" –. He scratched the last words out: why should he hint to her that he could die? Holding his life loose in his hand, though, had brought things closer to him lately, – God and death, this war, the meaning of it all. But he would keep his brawny body between these terrible realities and Floy, yet awhile. "I want you," he wrote, "to leave the plantation, and go with your old maumer to the village. It will be safer there." He was sure the letter would reach her. He had a plan to escape to-night, and he could put it into a post inside the lines. Ben was to get a small hand-saw that would open the wicket; the guards were not hard to elude. Glancing up, he saw the negro stretched by a camp-fire, listening to the gaunt boatman, who was off duty. Preaching Abolitionism, doubtless: he could hear Ben's derisive shouts of laughter. "And so, good bye, Baby Florence!" he scrawled. "I wish I could send you some of this snow, to show you what the floor of heaven is like."

While the snow fell faster without, he stopped writing, and began idly drawing a map of Georgia on the tan-bark with a stick. Here the Federal troops could effect a landing: he knew the defences at that point. If they did? He thought of these Snake-hunters who had found in the war a peculiar road for themselves downward with no gallows to stumble over, fancied he saw them skulking through the fields at Cedar Creek, closing around the house, and behind them a mass of black faces and bloody bayonets. Floy alone, and he here, – like a rat in a trap! "God keep my little girl!" he wrote, unsteadily. "God bless you, Floy!" He gasped for breath, as if he had been writing with his heart's blood. Folding up the paper, he hid it inside his shirt and began his dogged walk, calculating the chances of escape. Once out of this shed, he could baffle a blood-hound, he knew the hills so well.

His head bent down, he did not see a man who stood looking at him over the wicket. Captain Dorr. A puny little man, with thin yellow bair, and womanish face: but not the less the hero of his men, – they having found out, somehow, that muscle was not the solidest thing to travel on in war-times. Our regiments of "roughs" were not altogether crowned with laurel at Manassas! So the men built more on the old Greatheart soul in the man's blue eyes: one of those souls born and bred pure, sent to teach, that can find breath only in the free North. His hearty "Hillo!" startled Lamar.

"How are you, old fellow?" he said, unlocking the gate and coming in.

Lamar threw off his wretched thoughts, glad to do it. What need to borrow trouble? He liked a laugh, – had a lazy, jolly humor of his own. Dorr had finished drill, and come up, as he did every day, to freshen himself with an hour's talk to this warm, blundering fellow. In this dismal war-work, (though his whole soul was in that, too,) it was like putting your hands to a big blaze. Dorr had no near relations; Lamar – they had played marbles together – stood to him where a younger brother might have stood. Yet, as they talked, he could not help his keen eye seeing him just as he was.

Poor John! he thought: the same uncouth-looking effort of humanity that he had been at Yale. No wonder the Northern boys jeered him, with his slothways, his mouthed English, torpid eyes, and brain shut up in that worst of mudmoulds, – belief in caste. Even now, going up and down the tan-bark, his step was dead, godden, like that of a man in whose life God had not yet wakened the full live soul. It was wakening, though, Dorr thought. Some pain or passion was bringing the man in him out of the flesh, vigilant, alert, aspirant. A different man from Dorr.

In fact, Lamar was just beginning to think for himself, and of course his thoughts were defiant, intolerant. He did not comprehend how his companion could give his heresies such quiet welcome, and pronounce sentence of death on them so coolly. Because Dorr had gone farther up the mountain, had he the right to make him follow in the same steps? The right, – that was it. By brute force, too? Human freedom, eh? Consequently, their talks were stormy enough. To-day, however, they were on trivial matters.

"I've brought the General's order for your release at last, John. It confines you to this district, however."

Lamar shook his head.

"No parole for me! My stake outside is too heavy for me to remain a prisoner on anything but compulsion. I mean to escape, if I can. Floy has nobody but me, you know, Charley."

There was a moment's silence.

"I wish," said Dorr, half to himself, "the child was with her cousin Ruth. If she could make her a woman like herself!"

"You are kind," Lamar forced out, thinking of what might have been a year ago.

Dorr had forgotten. He had just kissed little Ruth at the door-step, coming away: thinking, as he walked up to camp, how her clear thought, narrow as it was, was making his own higher, more just; wondering if the tears on her face last night, when she got up from her knees after prayer, might not help as much in the great cause of truth as the life he was ready to give. He was so used to his little wife now, that he could look to no hour of his past life, nor of the future coming ages of event and work, where she was not present, – very flesh of his flesh, heart of his heart. A gulf lay between them and the rest of the world. It was hardly probable he could see her as a woman towards whom another man looked across the gulf, dumb, hopeless, defrauded of his right.

"She sent you some flowers, by the way, John, – the last in the yard, – and bade me be sure and bring you down with me. Your own colors, you see? – to put you in mind of home," – pointing to the crimson asters flaked with snow.

The man smiled faintly: the smell of the flowers choked him: he laid them aside. God knows he was trying to wring out this bitter old thought: he could not look in Dorr's frank eyes while it was there. He must escape to-night: he never would come near them again, in this world, or beyond death, – never! He thought of that like a man going to drag through eternity with half his soul gone. Very well: there was man enough left in him to work honestly and bravely, and to thank God for that good pure love he yet had. He turned to Dorr with a flushed face, and began talking of Floy in hearty earnest, – glancing at Ben coming up the hill, thinking that escape depended on him.

"I ordered your man up," said Captain Dorr. "Some canting Abolitionist had him open-mouthed down there."

The negro came in, and stood in the corner, listening while they talked. A gigantic fellow, with a gladiator's muscles. Stronger than that Yankee captain, he thought, – than either of them: better breathed, – drawing the air into his brawny chest. "A man and a brother." Did the fool think he didn't know that before? He had a contempt for Dave and his like. Lamar would have told you Dave's words were true, but despised the man as a crude, unlicked bigot. Ben did the same, with no words for the idea. The negro instinct in him recognized gentle blood by any of its signs, – the transparent animal life, the reticent eye, the mastered voice: he had better men than Lamar at home to learn it from. It is a trait of serfdom, the keen eye to measure the inherent rights of a man to be master. A negro or a Catholic Irishman does not need "Sartor Resartus" to help him to see through any clothes. Ben leaned, half-asleep, against the wall, some old thoughts creeping out of their hiding-places through the torpor, like rats to the sunshine: the boatman's slang had been hot and true enough to rouse them in his brain.

"So, Ben," said his master, as he passed once, "your friend has been persuading you to exchange the cotton-fields at Cedar Creek for New-York alleys, eh?"

"Ki!" laughed Ben, "white darkey. Mind ole dad, Mars' John, as took off in der swamp? Um asked dat Linkinite ef him saw dad up Norf. Guess him's free now. Ki! ole dad!"

"The swamp was the place for him," said Lamar. "I remember."

"Dunno," said the negro, surlily: "him's dad, af'er all: tink him's free now," – and mumbled down into a monotonous drone about

"Oh yo, bredern, is yer gwine ober Jordern?"

Half-asleep, they thought, – but with dull questionings at work in his brain, some queer notions about freedom, of that unknown North, mostly mixed with his remembrance of his father, a vicious old negro, that in Pennsylvania would have worked out his salvation in the under cell of the penitentiary, but in Georgia, whipped into heroism, had betaken himself into the swamp, and never returned. Tradition among the Lamar slaves said he had got off to Ohio, of which they had as clear an idea as most of us have of heaven. At any rate, old Kite became a mystery, to be mentioned with awe at fish-bakes and barbecues. He was this uncouth wretch's father, – do you understand? The flabby-faced boy, flogged in the cotton-field for whining after his dad, or hiding away part of his flitch and molasses for months in hopes the old man would come back, was rather a comical object, you would have thought. Very different his, from the feeling with which you left your mother's grave, – though as yet we have not invented names for the emotions of those people. We'll grant that it hurt Ben a little, however. Even the young polypus, when it is torn from the old one, bleeds a drop or two, they say. As he grew up, the great North glimmered through his thought, a sort of big field, – a paradise of no work, no flogging, and white bread every day, where the old man sat and ate his fill.

The second point in Ben's history was that he fell in love. Just as you did, – with the difference, of course: though the hot sun, or the perpetual foot upon his breast, does not make our black Prometheus less fierce in his agony of hope or jealousy than you, I am afraid. It was Nan, a pale mulatto house-servant, that the field-hand took into his dull, lonesome heart to make life of, with true-love defiance of caste. I think Nan liked him very truly. She was lame and sickly, and if Ben was black and a picker, and stayed in the quarters, he was strong, like a master to her in some ways: the only thing she could call hers in the world was the love the clumsy boy gave her. White women feel in that way sometimes, and it makes them very tender to men not their equals. However, old Mrs. Lamar, before she died, gave her house-servants their free papers, and Nan was among them. So she set off, with all the finery little Floy could give her: went up into that great, dim North. She never came again.

The North swallowed up all Ben knew or felt outside of his hot, hated work, his dread of a lashing on Saturday night. All the pleasure left him was, possum and hominy for Sunday's dinner. It did not content him. The spasmodic religion of the field-negro does not teach endurance. So it came, that the slow tide of discontent ebbing in everybody's heart towards some unreached sea set in his ignorant brooding towards that vague country which the only two who cared for him had found. If he forgot it through the dogged, sultry days, he remembered it when the overseer scourged the dull tiger-look into his eyes, or when, husking corn with the others at night, the smothered negro-soul, into which their masters dared not look, broke out in their wild, melancholy songs. Aimless, unappealing, yet no prayer goes up to God more keen in its pathos. You find, perhaps, in Beethoven's seventh symphony the secrets of your heart made manifest, and suddenly think of a Somewhere to come, where your hope waits for you with late fulfilment. Do not laugh at Ben, then, if he dully told in his song the story of all he had lost, or gave to his heaven a local habitation and a name.

From the place where he stood now, as his master and Dorr walked up and down, he could see the purplish haze beyond which the sentry had told him lay the North. The North/Just beyond the ridge. There was a pain in his head, looking at it; his nerves grew cold and rigid, as yours do when something wrings your heart sharply: for there are nerves in these black carcasses, thicker, more quickly stung to madness than yours. Yet if any savage longing, smouldering for years, was heating to madness now in his brain, there was no sign of it in his face. Vapid, with sordid content, the huge jaws munching tobacco slowly, only now and then the beady eye shot a sharp glance after Dorr. The sentry had told him the Northern army had come to set the slaves free; he watched the Federal officer keenly.

"What ails you, Ben?" said his master. "Thinking over your friend's sermon?"

Ben's stolid laugh was ready.

"Done forgot dat, Mars'. Wouldn't go, nohow. Since Mars' sold dat cussed Joe, gorry good times't home. Dam' Abolitioner say we ums all goin' Norf," – with a stealthy glance at Dorr.

"That's more than your philanthropy bargains for, Charley," laughed Lamar.

The men stopped; the negro skulked nearer, his whole senses sharpened into hearing. Dorr's clear face was clouded.

"This slave question must be kept out of the war. It puts a false face on it."

"I thought one face was what it needed," said Lamar. "You have too many slogans. Strong government, tariff, Sumter, a bit of bunting, eleven dollars a month. It ought to be a vital truth that would give soul and *vim* to a body with the differing members of your army. You, with your ideal theory, and Billy Wilson with his 'Blood and Baltimore!' Try human freedom. That's high and sharp and broad."

Ben drew a step closer.

"You are shrewd, Lamar. I am to go below all constitutions or expediency or existing rights, and tell Ben here that he is free? When once the Government accepts that doctrine, you, as a Rebel, must be let alone."

The slave was hid back in the shade.

"Dorr," said Lamar, "you know I'm a groping, ignorant fellow, but it seems to me that prating of constitutions and existing rights is surface talk; there is a broad common-sense underneath, by whose laws the world is governed, which your statesmen don't touch often. You in the North, in your dream of what shall be, shut your eyes to what is. You want a republic where every man's voice shall be heard in the council, and the majority shall rule. Granting that the free population are educated to a fitness for this, – (God forbid I should grant it with the Snake-hunters before my eyes!) – look here!"

He turned round, and drew the slave out into the light: he crouched down, gaping vacantly at them.

"There is Ben. What, in God's name, will you do with him? Keep him a slave, and chatter about self-government? Pah! The country is paying in blood for the lie, to-day. Educate him for freedom, by putting a musket in his hands? We have this mass of heathendom drifted on our shores by your will as well as mine. Try to bring them to a level with the whites by a wrench, and you'll waken out of your dream to a sharp reality. Your Northern philosophy ought to be old enough to teach you that spasms in the body-politic shake off no atom of disease, – that reform, to be enduring, must be patient, gradual, inflexible as the Great Reformer. 'The mills of God,' the old proverb says, 'grind surely.' But, Dorr, they grind exceeding slow!"

Dorr watched Lamar with an amused smile. It pleased him to see his brain waking up, eager, vehement. As for Ben, crouching there, if they talked of him like a clod, heedless that his face deepened in stupor, that his eyes had caught a strange, gloomy treachery, – we all do the same, you know.

"What is your remedy, Lamar? You have no belief in the right of Secession, I know," said Dorr.

"It's a bad instrument for a good end. Let the white Georgian come out of his sloth, and the black will rise with him. Jefferson Davis may not intend it, but God does. When we have our

Lowell, our New York, when we are a self-sustaining people instead of lazy landprinces, Ben here will have climbed the second of the great steps of Humanity. Do you laugh at us?" said Lamar, with a quiet self-reliance. "Charley, it needs only work and ambition to cut the brute away from my face, and it will leave traits very like your own. Ben's father was a Guinea fetich-worshipper; when we stand where New England does, Ben's son will be ready for his freedom."

"And while you theorize," laughed Dorr, "I hold you a prisoner, John, and Ben knows it is his right to be free. He will not wait for the grinding of the mill, I fancy."

Lamar did not smile. It was womanish in the man, when the life of great nations hung in doubt before them, to go back so constantly to little Floy sitting in the lap of her old black maumer. But he did it, – with the quick thought that to-night he must escape, that death lay in delay.

While Dorr talked, Lamar glanced significantly at Ben. The negro was not slow to understand, – with a broad grin, touching his pocket, from which projected the dull end of a hand-saw. I wonder what sudden pain made the negro rise just then, and come close to his master, touching him with a strange affection and remorse in his tired face, as though he had done him some deadly wrong.

"What is it, old fellow?" said Lamar, in his boyish way. "Homesick, eh? There's a little girl in Georgia that will be glad to see you and your master, and take precious good care of us when she gets us safe again. That's true, Ben!" laying his hand kindly on the man's shoulder, while his eyes went wandering off to the hills lying South.

"Yes, Mars'," said Ben, in a low voice, suddenly bringing a blacking-brush, and beginning to polish his master's shoes, – thinking, while he did it, of how often Mars' John had interfered with the overseers to save him from a flogging, – (Lamar, in his lazy way, was kind to his slaves,) – thinking of little Mist' Floy with an odd tenderness and awe, as a gorilla might of a white dove: trying to think thus, – the simple, kindly nature of the negro struggling madly with something beneath, new and horrible. He understood enough of the talk of the white men to know that there was no help for him, – none. Always a slave. Neither you nor I can ever know what those words meant to him. The pale purple mist where the North lay was never to be passed. His dull eyes turned to it constantly, – with a strange look, such as the lost women might have turned to the door, when Jesus shut it: they forever outside. There was a way to help himself? The stubby black fingers holding the brush grew cold and clammy, – noting withal, the poor wretch in his slavish way, that his master's clothes were finer than the Northern captain's, his hands whiter, and proud that it was so, – holding Lamar's foot daintily, trying to see himself in the shoe, smoothing down the trousers with a boorish, affectionate touch, – with the same fierce whisper in his ear, Would the shoes ever be cleaned again? Would the foot move to-morrow?

It grew late. Lamar's supper was brought up from Captain Dorr's, and placed on the bench. He poured out a goblet of water.

"Come, Charley, let's drink. To Liberty! It is a war-cry for Satan or Michael."

They drank, laughing, while Ben stood watching. Dorr turned to go, but Lamar called him back, – stood resting his hand on his shoulder: he never thought to see him again, you know.

"Look at Ruth, yonder," said Dorr, his face lighting. "She is coming to meet us. She thought you would be with me."

Lamar looked gravely down at the low field-house and the figure at the gate. He thought he could see the small face and earnest eyes, though it was far off, and night was closing.

"She is waiting for you, Charley. Go down. Good night, old chum!"

If it cost any effort to say it, Dorr saw nothing of it.

"Good night, Lamar! I'll see you in the morning."

He lingered. His old comrade looked strangely alone and desolate.

"John!"

"What is it, Dorr?"

"If I could tell the Colonel you would take the oath? For Floy's sake."

The man's rough face reddened.

"You should know me better. Good bye."

"Well, well, you are mad. Have you no message for Ruth?"

There was a moment's silence.

"Tell her I say, God bless her!"

Dorr stopped and looked keenly in his face, – then, coming back, shook hands again, in a different way from before, speaking in a lower voice, –

"God help us all, John! Good night!" – and went slowly down the hill.

It was nearly night, and bitter cold. Lamar stood where the snow drifted in on him, looking out through the horizonless gray.

"Come out o'dem cold, Mars' John," whined Ben, pulling at his coat.

As the night gathered, the negro was haunted with a terrified wish to be kind to his master. Something told him that the time was short. Here and there through the far night some tent-fire glowed in a cone of ruddy haze, through which the thick-falling snow shivered like flakes of light. Lamar watched only the square block of shadow where Dorr's house stood. The door opened at last, and a broad, cheerful gleam shot out red darts across the white waste without; then he saw two figures go in together. They paused a moment; he put his head against the bars, straining his eyes, and saw that the woman turned, shading her eyes with her hand, and looked up to the side of the mountain where the guard-house lay, – with a kindly look, perhaps, for the prisoner out in the cold. A kind look: that was all. The door shut on them. Forever: so, good night, Ruth!

He stood there for an hour or two, leaning his head against the muddy planks, smoking. Perhaps, in his coarse fashion, he took the trouble of his manhood back to the same God he used to pray to long ago. When he turned at last, and spoke, it was with a quiet, strong voice, like one who would fight through life in a manly way. There was a grating sound at the back of the shed: it was Ben, sawing through the wicket, the guard having lounged off to supper. Lamar watched him, noticing that the negro was unusually silent. The plank splintered, and hung loose.

"Done gone, Mars' John, now," – leaving it, and beginning to replenish the fire.

"That's right, Ben. We'll start in the morning. That sentry at two o'clock sleeps regularly."

Ben chuckled, heaping up the sticks.

"Go on down to the camp, as usual. At two, Ben, remember! We will be free to-night, old boy!"

The black face looked up from the clogging smoke with a curious stare.

"Ki! we'll be free to-night, Mars'!" – gulping his breath.

Soon after, the sentry unlocked the gate, and he shambled off out into the night. Lamar, left alone, went closer to the fire, and worked busily at some papers he drew from his pocket: maps and schedules. He intended to write until two o'clock; but the blaze dying down, he wrapped his blanket about him, and lay down on the heaped straw, going on sleepily, in his brain, with his calculations.

The negro, in the shadow of the shed, watched him. A vague fear beset him, – of the vast, white cold, – the glowering mountains, – of himself; he clung to the familiar face, like a man drifting out into an unknown sea, clutching some relic of the shore. When Lamar fell asleep, he wandered uncertainly towards the tents. The world had grown new, strange; was he Ben, picking cotton in the swamp edge? – plunging his fingers with a shudder in the icy drifts. Down in the glowing torpor of the Santilla flats, where the Lamar plantations lay, Ben had slept off as maddening hunger for life and freedom as this of to-day; but here, with the winter air stinging every nerve to life, with the perpetual mystery of the mountains terrifying his bestial nature down, the strength of the man stood up: groping, blind, malignant, it may be; but whose fault was that? He was half-frozen: the physical pain sharpened the keen doubt conquering his thought. He sat down in the crusted snow, looking vacantly about him, a man, at last, – but wakening, like a new-born soul, into a world of unutterable solitude. Wakened dully, slowly; sitting there far into the night, pondering stupidly on his old life; crushing down and out the old parasite affection for his master, the old fears, the old weight threatening to press out his thin life; the muddy blood heating, firing with the same heroic dream that bade Tell and Garibaldi lift up their hands to God, and cry aloud that they were men and free: the same, – God-given burning in the imbruted veins of a Guinea slave. To what end? May God be merciful to America while she answers the question! He sat, rubbing his cracked, bleeding feet, glancing stealthily at the southern hills. Beyond them lay all that was past; in an hour he would follow Lamar back to – what? He lifted his hands up to the sky, in his silly way sobbing hot tears. "Gor-a'mighty, Mars' Lord, I'se tired," was all the prayer he made. The pale purple mist was gone from the North; the ridge behind which love, freedom waited, struck black across the sky, a wall of iron. He looked at it drearily. Utterly alone: he had always been alone. He got up at last, with a sigh.

"It's a big world," – with a bitter chuckle, – "but der's no room in it fur poor Ben."

He dragged himself through the snow to a light in a tent where a voice in a wild drone, like that he had heard at negro camp-meetings, attracted him. He did not go in: stood at the tent-door, listening. Two or three of the guard stood around, leaning on their muskets; in the vivid fire-light rose the gaunt figure of the Illinois boatman, swaying to and fro as he preached. For the men were honest, God-fearing souls, members of the same church, and Dave, in all integrity of purpose, read aloud to them, – the cry of Jeremiah against the foul splendors of the doomed city, – waving, as he spoke, his bony arm to the South. The shrill voice was that of a man wrestling with his Maker. The negro's fired brain caught the terrible meaning of the words, – found speech in it: the wide, dark night, the solemn silence of the men, were only fitting audience.

The man caught sight of the slave, and, laying down his book, began one of those strange exhortations in the manner of his sect. Slow at first, full of unutterable pity. There was room for pity. Pointing to the human brute crouching there, made once in the image of God, – the saddest wreck on His green footstool: to the great stealthy body, the revengeful jaws, the foreboding eyes. Soul, brains, – a man, wifeless, homeless, nationless, hawked, flung from trader to trader for a handful of dirty shinplasters. "Lord God of hosts," cried the man, lifting up his trembling hands, "lay not this sin to our charge!" There was a scar on Ben's back where the lash had buried itself: it stung now in the cold. He pulled his clothes tighter, that they should not see it; the scar and the words burned into his heart: the childish nature of the man was gone; the vague darkness in it took a shape and name. The boatman had been praying for him; the low words seemed to shake the night:

"Hear the prayer of Thy servant, and his supplications! Is not this what Thou hast chosen: to loose the bands, to undo the heavy burdens, and let the oppressed go free? O Lord, hear! O Lord, hearken and do! Defer not for Thine own sake, O my God!"

"What shall I do?" said the slave, standing up.

The boatman paced slowly to and fro, his voice chording in its dull monotone with the smothered savage muttering in the negro's brain.

"The day of the Lord cometh; it is nigh at hand. Who can abide it? What saith the prophet Jeremiah? 'Take up a burden against the South. Cry aloud, spare not. Woe unto Babylon, for the day of her vengeance is come, the day of her visitation. Call together the archers against Babylon; camp against it round about; let none thereof escape. Recompense her: as she hath done unto my people, be it done unto her. A sword is upon Babylon: it shall break in pieces the shepherd and his flock, the man and the woman, the young man and the maid. I will render unto her the evil she hath done in my sight, saith the Lord.' "

It was the voice of God: the scar burned fiercer; the slave came forward boldly, –

"Mars'er, what shall I do?"

"Give the poor devil a musket," said one of the men. "Let him come with us, and strike a blow for freedom."

He took a knife from his belt, and threw it to him, then sauntered off to his tent.

"A blow for freedom?" mumbled Ben, taking it up.

"Let us sing to the praise of God," said the boatman, "the sixty-eighth psalm," lining it out while they sang, – the scattered men joining, partly to keep themselves awake. In old times David's harp charmed away the demon from a human heart. It roused one now, never to be laid again. A dull, droning chant, telling how the God of Vengeance rode upon the wind, swift to loose the fetters of the chained, to make desert the rebellious land; with a chorus, or refrain, in which Ben's wild, melancholy cry sounded like the wail of an avenging spirit:

"That in the blood of enemies
    Thy foot imbrued may be:
And of thy dogs dipped in the same
    The tongues thou mayest see."

The meaning of that was plain; he sang it lower and more steadily each time, his body swaying in cadence, the glitter in his eye more steely.

Lamar, asleep in his prison, was wakened by the far-off plaintive song: he roused himself, leaning on one elbow, listening with a half-smile. It was Naomi they sang, he thought, – an old-fashioned Methodist air that Floy had caught from the negroes, and used to sing to him sometimes. Every night, down at home, she would come to his parlor-door to say good-night: he thought he could see the little figure now in its white night-gown, and hear the bare feet pattering on the matting. When he was alone, she would come in, and sit on his lap awhile, and kneel down before she went away, her head on his knee, to say her prayers, as she called it. Only God knew how many times he had remained alone after hearing those prayers, saved from nights of drunken debauch. He thought he felt Floy's pure little hand on his forehead now, as if she were saying her usual "Good night, Bud." He lay down to sleep again, with a genial smile on his face, listening to the hymn.

"It's the same God," he said, – "Floy's and theirs."

Outside, as he slept, a dark figure watched him. The song of the men ceased. Midnight, white and silent, covered the earth. He could hear only the slow breathing of the sleeper. Ben's black face grew ashy pale, but he did not tremble, as he crept, cat-like, up to the wicket, his blubber lips apart, the white teeth clenched.

"It's for Freedom, Mars' Lord!" he gasped, looking up to the sky, as if he expected an answer. "Gor-a'mighty, it's for Freedom!" And went in.

A belated bird swooped through the cold moonlight into the valley, and vanished in the far mountain-cliffs with a low, fearing cry, as though it had passed through Hades.

They had broken down the wicket: he saw them lay the heavy body on the lumber outside, the black figures hurrying over the snow. He laughed low, savagely, watching them. Free now! The best of them despised him; the years past of cruelty and oppression turned back, fused in a slow, deadly current of revenge and hate, against the race that had trodden him down. He felt the iron muscles of his fingers, looked close at the glittering knife he held, chuckling at the strange smell it bore. Would the Illinois boatman blame him, if it maddened him? And if Ben took the fancy to put it to his throat, what right has he to complain? Has not he also been a dweller in Babylon? He hesitated a moment in the cleft of the hill, choosing his way, exultantly. He did not watch the North now; the quiet old dream of content was gone; his thick blood throbbed and surged with passions of which you and I know nothing: he had a lost life to avenge. His native air, torrid, heavy with latent impurity, drew him back: a fitter breath than this cold snow for the animal in his body, the demon in his soul, to triumph and wallow in. He panted, thinking of the saffron hues of the Santilla flats, of the white, stately dwellings, the men that went in and out from them, quiet, dominant, – feeling the edge of his knife. It was his turn to be master now! He ploughed his way doggedly through the snow, – panting, as he went, – a hotter glow in his gloomy eyes. It was his turn for pleasure now: he would have his fill. Their wine and their gardens and – He did not need to choose a wife from his own color now. He stopped, thinking of little Floy, with her curls and great listening eyes, watching at the door for her brother. He had watched her climb up into his arms and kiss his check. She never would do that again! He laughed aloud, shrilly. By God! she should keep the kiss for other lips! Why should he not say it?

Up on the hill the night-air throbbed colder and holier. The guards stood about in the snow, silent, troubled. This was not like a death in battle: it put them in mind of home, somehow. All that the dying man said was, "Water," now and then. He had been sleeping, when struck, and never had thoroughly wakened from his dream. Captain Poole, of the Snake-hunters, had wrapped him in his own blanket, finding nothing more could be done. He went off to have the Colonel summoned now, muttering that it was "a damned shame." They put snow to Lamar's lips constantly, being hot and parched; a woman, Dorr's wife, was crouching on the ground beside him, chafing his hands, keeping down her sobs for fear they would disturb him. He opened his eyes at last, and knew Dorr, who held his head.

"Unfasten my coat, Charley. What makes it so close here?"

Dorr could not speak.

"Shall I lift you up, Captain Lamar?" asked Dave Hall, who stood leaning on his rifle.

He spoke in a subdued tone, Babylon being far off for the moment. Lamar dozed again before he could answer.

"Don't try to move him – it is too late," said Dorr, sharply.

The moonlight steeped the mountain and sky in a fresh whiteness. Lamar's face, paling every moment, hardening, looked in it like some solemn work of an untaught sculptor. There was a breathless silence. Ruth, kneeling beside him, felt his hand grow slowly colder than the snow. He moaned, his voice going fast, –

"At two, Ben, old fellow! We'll be free to-night!"

Dave, stooping to wrap the blanket, felt his hand wet: he wiped it with a shudder.

"As he hath done unto My people, be it done unto him!" he muttered, but the words did not comfort him.

Lamar moved, half-smiling.

"That's right, Floy. What is it she says? 'Now I lay me down' – I forget. Good night. Kiss me, Floy."

He waited, – looked up uneasily. Dorr looked at his wife: she stooped, and kissed his lips. Charley smoothed back the hair from the damp face with as tender a touch as a woman's. Was he dead? The white moonlight was not more still than the calm face.

Suddenly the night-air was shattered by a wild, revengeful laugh from the hill. The departing soul rushed back, at the sound, to life, full consciousness. Lamar started from their hold, – sat up.

"It was Ben," he said, slowly.

In that dying flash of comprehension, it may be, the wrongs of the white man and the black stood clearer to his eyes than ours: the two lives trampled down. The stern face of the boatman bent over him: he was trying to stanch the flowing blood. Lamar looked at him: Hall saw no bitterness in the look, – a quiet, sad question rather, before which his soul lay bare. He felt the cold hand touch his shoulder, saw the pale lips move.

"Was this well done?" they said.

Before Lamar's eyes the rounded arch of gray receded, faded into dark; the negro's fierce laugh filled his ear: some woful thought at the sound wrung his soul, as it halted at the gate. It caught at the simple faith his mother taught him.

"Yea," he said aloud, "though I walk through the valley of the shadow of death, I will fear no evil: for Thou art with me."

Dorr gently drew down the uplifted hand. He was dead.

"It was a manly soul," said the Northern captain, his voice choking, as he straightened the limp hair.

"He trusted in God? A strange delusion!" muttered the boatman.

Yet he did not like that they should leave him alone with Lamar, as they did, going down for help. He paced to and fro, his rifle on his shoulder, arming his heart with strength to accomplish the vengeance of the Lord against Babylon. Yet he could not forget the murdered man sitting there in the calm moonlight, the dead face turned towards the North, – the dead face, whereon little Floy's tears should never fall. The grave, unmoving eyes seemed to the boatman to turn to him with the same awful question. "Was this well done?" they said. He thought in eternity they would rise before him, sad, unanswered. The earth, he fancied, lay whiter, colder, – the heaven farther off; the war, which had become a daily business, stood suddenly before him in all its terrible meaning. God, he thought, had met in judgment with His people. Yet he uttered no cry of vengeance against the doomed city. With the dead face before him, he bent his eyes to the ground, humble, uncertain, – speaking out of the ignorance of his own weak, human soul.

"The day of the Lord is nigh," he said; "it is at hand; and who can abide it?"

Questions to consider

- How does Davis's geographic background inform the setting and logic of this story?

- "John Lamar" complicates *and* reinforces racial and gender stereotypes: how is it like the work of Harriet Beecher Stowe (Part I) and Louisa May Alcott (Part XI) in that way?

- Who, here, is to blame for John Lamar's death? What does this story suggest about the relationship between blacks and whites, and the legacy and meaning of slavery?

Part XIII

Victory and Defeat

Plate 15 No Place Like (This) Home: Appomattox Court House, Appomattox, VA, circa 1865. The house was owned by Wilbur McLean, who moved here after the First Battle of Bull Run in 1861 to get away from the fighting. Four years later, Lee surrendered to Grant in his parlor. (Photo by Timothy H. O'Sullivan; Selected Civil War photographs, Library of Congress)

Chapter 30

The Same Holy Cause

James M. McPherson

It's one thing to justify going to war, the topic of Part II. It's another to actually fight it, as discussed in Part III. It's still another to feel satisfied in having done so, particularly amid shifting objectives and emotional and physical trauma. Indeed, there is a long tradition of hostility toward wars on the part of those who have fought in them, a tradition that was extended, and even intensified, by the Vietnam War, which cast a long shadow over those that followed. And yet it is also true that many veterans, including those who suffered defeat, nevertheless believed in the cause they fought for.

In terms of the cost of human life – for survivors as well as the dead – no war was more costly to Americans than the Civil War. To those who lived through it, the results were astounding, not only in terms of the devastation, but also in terms of the war's outcome: a Union preserved and slavery destroyed. Though the latter was not a stated goal, its accomplishment was the most important to come out of any American war. Amid these results, and the struggle to prevent them, lay another powerful, yet more elusive justification for fighting: honor. It's a word that sounds archaic to modern ears, and yet has a durable history that long preceded, and will no doubt long follow, the birth and death of this republic.

In this excerpt from his 1997 book *For Cause and Comrades*, Princeton University's James McPherson, widely regarded as the dean of Civil War historians, limns the surprising, even moving, idealism of the Civil War soldier.

James McPherson, "The Same Holy Cause," in *For Cause and Comrades: Why Men Fought in the Civil War* (New York: Oxford University Press, 1997), pp. 167–78. Copyright © 1997 by Oxford University Press, Inc. Used by permission of Oxford University Press, Inc.

[. . .]

On July 1, 1864, a captain in the 103rd Illinois, which had suffered grievous casualties in the assault at Kennesaw Mountain four days earlier, told his sister that "this campaign is coming down to a question of muscle and nerve. It is the 62d day for us, over 50 of which we have passed under fire. I don't know anything more exhausting. One consolation is that the Rebels are a good deal worse off than we are.... We'll wear them out yet."[1]

Perhaps he was right. At least one Rebel, a private in the 40th Alabama, was worse off if one can judge from a poem he wrote in his diary in April 1864, *before* the fighting that year began for him:

> I am weary of war, of powder [and] ball
> I am weary & sick of the glory & all....
>
> Too much blood has already flowed like a river
> Too many fond hearts have been parted forever
> Too many farewells with tears have been spoken
> Too many fond circles already been broken
> Footsore and weary over paths steep and rough
> We have fought, we have bled, we have suffered enough.[2]

Yet this bard fought on through another and more terrible year of war. What kept him going? What made the Illinois captain so confident that his side would wear out the enemy in the end? For many of the volunteers of 1861 and 1862, who did most of the fighting and suffered most of the casualties, the answer was pride and conviction. These words summed up the values of duty, honor, courage, and belief in the Cause that had initially propelled them into the army. The interpretation advanced here that these values persisted to the end is not universally accepted. Gerald Linderman's study of Civil War soldiers argued precisely the opposite: their harrowing adventures turned them into hardened skeptics who experienced a "harsh disillusionment" that caused them "to abandon many of the war's initial tenets." Another student influenced by Linderman maintained that "whatever idealism the soldiers brought with them into the army faded" in the latter part of the war. By then they fought not for a cause or for honor, but to stay alive and get the job done so they could go home – or even to go home without getting the job done.[3]

This conclusion seems consistent with common sense. How could soldiers sustain a high level of ideological commitment or belief in noble ideals through the grim experiences of disease, exhaustion, frustration, and death as the war ground on through its fourth year? The weary cynicism of Bill Mauldin's Willie and Joe in World War II, the bitter alienation of the "grunt" in Vietnam, must have had their counterparts in the Civil War. They did. Desertion rates rose in the latter part of the war. Many of the conscripts, substitutes, and bounty men who made up an increasing proportion of both armies were motivated marginally if at all by duty, honor, or ideology. The tone of some soldiers' letters as well as their behavior did take on a more negative, cynical, callous, even brutal quality as time went on. Without question there was a decline in the romantic flag-waving rhetoric of the war's first two years.

But this is not the whole story. Indeed, it is not the most important part of the story. For the fighting soldiers who enlisted in 1861 and 1862 the values of duty and honor remained a crucial component of their sustaining motivation to the end. Their rhetoric about these values was the same in the war's last year as in its first. In a letter of January 12, 1865, summarizing his three and a half years in the army, a young Illinois cavalryman used the word "duty" five times in a single sentence. A Maine veteran who reenlisted for a second three-year term explained why: "*Do your duty* is my motto even though it may clash with my own personal life."[4] The mother of a soldier in the 89th Illinois urged him to get a medical discharge after he was wounded at Pickett's Mills in May 1864. She had already lost one son killed in action and did not want to lose another. But he insisted on returning to the ranks in August. "Because I have done my Duty for the last 23 months," he wrote, "that is no reason why I should not return to the regiment and do my Duty again." After more than two years of fighting, a captain in the 28th Mississippi Cavalry was convinced that war was "an unmixed evil [of]...blood, butchery, death, desolation, robbery, rapine, selfishness, violence, wrong...palliated only when waged in self defence." He was "heartily sick" of it – *and* "sustained alone by a strong sense of duty."[5]

The belief in honor also remained alive and well for many soldiers to the end. To give up the Cause because of reverses, wrote a Tennessee cavalry officer in 1864, would mean "disgrace, dishonor, and slavery forever." When both the mother and wife of an officer in the 40th Tennessee urged him in 1864 to resign because he had done enough for the Confederacy, he rebuked them: "You know me too well to ever mention that to me to desert my country at this time would be awful. I had better die, by that I would not disgrace myself nor the woman I have sworn to love, cherish, & honor....I want to be among the list who can return free from disgrace."[6]

These sentiments were not confined to officers. A private in the 27th North Carolina scorned the "dishonor" of desertion in February 1865 even as the Army of Northern Virginia melted around him. Likewise a private in the 11th Georgia told his mother proudly that for the past four years he had done his "Deuty while in the Noble Army of Northern Va and if I were to desert and lie out of this Strugle as many are doing I could not go any where but that the Eys of man and Woman would look at me....I would feel worse than a Sheep killing Dog."[7]

The language of honor also persisted in the letters of married Union officers whose wives insisted that they had given enough to their country. "Darling you should not have done that," responded a captain in the 2nd Minnesota to his wife in January 1865. "I have risked my life too often for my own & Country's honor to throw both recklessly away." The major of the 10th New York said that in the future his children would look back on the war "either with pride or shame" in their father. This knowledge "has nerved me on & I would rather my children would mourn a Fathers death than his disgrace." When one of the Army of the Potomac's most celebrated soldiers, Joshua Lawrence Chamberlain, proposed to return to the army after partial recovery from a wound once thought to be fatal, his mother pleaded with him to reconsider: "Surely you have done & suffered & won laurels enough in this war." He replied in February 1865 that "I am not scared or hurt enough yet to be willing to face the rear, when other men are marching to the front." To return was the only course "which honor and manliness prompt." Surviving another life-threatening wound at White Oak Road on March 31, he fought through the campaign to Appomattox where Grant designated him to receive the formal surrender of the Army of Northern Virginia.[8]

For many Confederate soldiers in 1864–5 the motive of upholding honor blended with the persistence of their ideological commitment to liberty, independence, and self-government as the only alternatives to the "degradation" of "vassalage" to the Yankees. "The old Troops are not as near whiped as the citizens at home," wrote a veteran in the 32nd Mississippi in early 1864. "Let [the war] be long or short meat or no meat shoes or no shoes [we are] Resolved to fight it out...for the sake of liberty...if we give it up now we will certainly be the most degraded people on earth." A sergeant in the 27th North Carolina admitted in September 1864 that "the soldiers are all tired of the war & would be glad for it to end," but "they are for it ending on honorable terms or none....The south has lost too many of its noble sons to ever submit to A black republican form of government & be striped of its property & rights." If we give up, wrote a planter serving as an officer in the 28th Mississippi, "we lose everything of property – sacrifice our pride of character – of family – everything: – and descend to a depth of degradation unmeasurably below that of the Helots of Greece."[9]

The theme of fighting for liberty remained seemingly as uncomplicated by the existence of slavery in 1864–5 as it had been in 1861. "I went in for the ware," wrote a private in the 47th Alabama in March 1864, "and I do expect to fite till the last for fredom." The last for him came two months later; he was killed at the Wilderness. Another Alabamian, an artillery captain, continued through the final months of the war to fill his diary with references to "the dear rights of freemen" and "the gigantic struggle for liberty," while a private in the 23rd Tennessee remained confident that he would see the "flag of liberty and peace floating to [the] breeze of a united and happy Confederate people."[10] At the end of 1864 a Mississippi officer declared that he was still determined to "battle for freedom a little longer," including the freedom to keep his slaves, for "without slavery little of our territory is worth a cent."[11]

By the winter of 1864–5, however, some Confederate soldiers had come to a new view of the relationship between slavery and liberty. "I can never bear to see the stars and stripes float over this country again," wrote an officer in the 23rd Mississippi. "We would simply be in a deplorable condition of slavery. . . . Almost anything else I am willing to accept, [even to] let the negro go."[12]

This soldier alluded to a great debate then occurring in the Confederacy: whether to arm slaves to fight for the South. The origins of this drastic proposal went back to the previous winter when General Patrick Cleburne had suggested that the Confederate army should remedy its manpower shortage by freeing and arming slaves. This heretical suggestion was squelched because, as one of Cleburne's fellow officers said, "its propositions contravene the principles on which we fight." But it did not stay squelched. By the following winter, discussions of the matter became widespread. In February 1865 Jefferson Davis and Robert E. Lee threw their weight behind a measure to enroll a limited number of slaves in the army – with the assumption, though not the explicit provision, that those enrolled would be freed. This was a desperate move, but these were desperate times. As a Mississippi newspaper put it: "Although slavery is one of the principles that we started to fight for . . . if it proves an insurmountable obstacle to the achievement of our liberty and nationality, away with it!"[13]

After contentious debate, the Confederate Congress finally passed the Negro soldier bill on March 13, 1865. The margin was three votes in the House and one in the Senate. Confederate soldiers who commented on the issue in their letters and diaries mirrored this split: about half reluctantly supported the measure and half angrily opposed it.

The latter condemned the proposal to arm slaves as one of "dishonor and humiliation," in the words of a Louisiana lieutenant. A South Carolina planter's son wrote from the Petersburg trenches that it "throw[s] away what we have toiled so hard to maintain."[14] A Missouri Confederate captain likewise reported that his men believed it contrary to "what they have fought for the last four years." A sergeant in the 17th North Carolina who had served through the whole war said in February 1865 that many men in his company were deserting because of the Negro soldier bill. He was thinking of deserting also if it passed. "Mother," he wrote, "I did not volunteer my services to fight for a free negroes country but to fight for a free white mans country & I do not think I love my country well enough to fight with black soldiers."[15]

Soldiers who favored the arming of slaves saw it as the only alternative to defeat. "Fight negro with negro," wrote an officer on Longstreet's staff, for it would be better even to free them "to gain our independence than be subjugated and lose slaves, liberty, and all that makes life dear." "If we continue to lose ground as we have for the last 12 months," reflected a Louisiana sergeant in January 1865, "we will soon be defeated, and then slavery will be gone any way, and I think we should give up slavery to gain our independence." The son of a wealthy Georgia planter still believed that "the negro's happiest condition is in slavery" but between abolition by the Yankees and emancipation by Confederates he was willing to take "the lesser of two evils."[16] A Tennessee officer agreed in January 1865 that "slavery is lost or will be, & we had better as well emancipate if we can make anything by it now. . . . We can certainly live without negroes better than with yankees and without negroes both." Perhaps reflecting the views of his chief, Robert E. Lee's adjutant Walter Taylor was willing to try the "experiment" of black Confederate soldiers. "It makes me sad however," he told his fiancée, "that the time honored institution will be no more, that the whole social organization of the South will be revolutionized."[17]

The letters and diaries of many Union veterans in the later years of the war also reveal little if any of the disillusionment with their "initial tenets" of patriotism and ideological commitment that some historians have posited. "The cause [is] the same," wrote a lieutenant in the 7th Indiana to his fiancée who had urged him to secure a medical discharge because of his wound so they could get married. "My country [is] as dear. . . . Why should I lay down my arms? I love peace but I love my country more. I am now wedded to war . . . until the issue comes." An eighteen-year-old Illinois private conceded in 1863 that "i dont like [the army] very Well, and they hant many Does," but "Mother, i feal like fighting for My Country as mutch as i ever did. i don't play off Sick like som do to git their Discharge." The next year he was killed at Jonesboro. After more than three years in the army, a lieutenant who commanded his company of the 57th New York from the Wilderness to Petersburg, losing two-thirds of his men, felt "as determined as the first time I took one of the U. S.'s Enfield Rifle Muskets, Ca. .577 into my hands, for the purpose of helping put down the Slave-holder's Rebellion" because "I still love my country."[18]

A key test of this determination came during the winter of 1863–4. Because the three-year terms of 1861 volunteers would soon expire, the Union army faced the dire prospect that many of its best regiments would melt away before the war ended. To meet this exigency the War Department offered several incentives for three-year veterans to reenlist: a $400 bounty (plus state and local bounties in many cases), a thirty-five-day furlough, a "veteran volunteer" chevron to wear on their sleeves, and an appeal to unit pride by allowing a regiment to retain its identity if three-quarters of its veterans reenlisted. This last provision put great pressure on holdouts when a given regiment neared the three-quarters mark. The bounty also helped, though many veterans hesitated to put a price on their lives. For some the furlough was the greatest inducement; they told themselves in January 1864 that since their terms still had five or more months to run, they stood a good chance of being killed anyway so why not seize the opportunity to spend a month with family and friends?

But all of these incentives together do not explain why 136,000 veterans reenlisted – more than half of those whose terms expired in 1864. The persistence of ideological convictions and a determination to finish the job were crucial factors for many soldiers. A reenlisted veteran in the 64th Ohio mentioned in his diary the bounty and furlough and a desire "to remain with my old companions" as reasons for his decision, but "more weighty than any of these [is] love of country and its institutions, and a determination to put down the rebellion." At the end of his reenlistment furlough, this soldier said goodbye to family and friends "to go forth with my life in my hands to fight the battle of freedom for another term of years." The parents of a reenlisted veteran in the 90th New York had opposed his decision, but he explained that although "it is hard to be separated from you so long . . . while duty calls me here and my country demands my services I should be willing to make the sacrifice. . . . Our country needs every man [now] in the service and as many more as possible." A forty-four-year-old father of three tried to assuage his wife's anger when he reenlisted as a captain in the 91st New York, but his choice of words may have made things worse: "I feel as keenly as any other the sacrifice made of home and those I love" as well as the dangers of a soldier's life, but these were "but dust in the balance for my Country's in the scale. . . . My children will remember me [proudly] for having been found among those who challenge treason and battle for the right."[19]

On New Year's Day in 1864, a reenlisted lieutenant in the 57th New York lamented the 50 percent of his comrades who had succumbed to bullets or disease during the past two and a half years. "Amongst the survivors," he wrote, "the excitement and enthusiasm of the early days has long since passed away, but the resolve still remains." They would need every ounce of this grim resolve during the coming campaigns. Writing from the trenches before Petersburg and Atlanta and from active fronts elsewhere in 1864, enlisted men echoed the themes of weariness coupled with determination to see it through. "There is nothing pleasant" about soldiering, wrote a corporal in the 105th Ohio, but "I can endure its privations . . . for there is a *big idea* which is at stake . . . the principles of Liberty, Justice, and of the Righteousness which exalteth a Nation."[20] A few months before he was killed at Fort Fisher, a sergeant in the 9th New York reproved his brother that "this is no time to carp at things which, compared with the success and reestablishment of the Republic, are insignificant." And in letters to his mother, an Irish-born sergeant in the 2nd New Jersey declared that neither the "horrors of the battlefield [nor] the blind acts of unqualified generals" had "chilled my patriotism in the least." "We are still engaged in the same holy cause," he wrote on the third anniversary of his enlistment, "we have yet the same Country to fight for."[21]

Not all Union soldiers felt this way, of course. The beats, the skulkers, the bounty men, substitutes, and draftees, the short-timers who had not reenlisted, the psychiatric casualties who could not take any more – these soldiers wanted nothing so much as to go home or at least to stay as far away from combat as possible. But there were enough who believed in the Cause and were willing to keep risking their lives for it to turn the war decisively in favor of the North in the fall of 1864. Their iron resolve underlay the message conveyed by a dispatch from the American correspondent of the London *Daily News* to his paper in September. "I am astonished," he wrote, by "the extent and depth of the [Northern] determination to fight to the last. . . . They are in earnest in a way the like of which the world never saw before, silently, calmly, but desperately in earnest; they will fight on, in my opinion, as long as they have men, muskets, powder . . . and would fight on, though the grass were growing in Wall Street."[22]

This was chilling news to Southerners who had counted on a waning of the Northern will to fight. Those Southerners might have experienced an even colder chill could they have read the letters of Northern soldiers confirming the observations of the *Daily News* correspondent. "*We must succeed*," wrote an intensely Unionist Missouri officer to his wife in August 1864. "If not this year, why then the next, or the next. And if it takes ten years, why then ten years it must be, for we never can give up, and have a Country and Government left." A lieutenant in the 147th New York wrote from the Petersburg trenches that "I would rather stay out here a lifetime (much as I dislike it) than consent to a division of our country." When the wife of a captain in 28th Wisconsin wrote that she would prefer having him home to winning the war, he replied angrily: "Carrie, don't *ever again* say you don't care *how* they settle this war with the southern traitors – at least *not to me*. . . . I would see the war last twenty years – yes, a lifetime, & while my poor life lasted I would serve my country rather than see her dishonored by yielding to the demands of the wicked crew."[23]

The conviction of Northern soldiers that they fought to preserve the Union as a beacon of republican liberty throughout the world burned as brightly in the last year of the war as in the first. After marching up and down the Shenandoah Valley a couple of hundred miles in Sheridan's 1864 campaign, the last twenty-five miles bare-footed, a private in the 54th Pennsylvania wrote to his wife from the hospital that he was ready to do it again if necessary, for "I cannot believe Providence intends to destroy this Nation, this great asylum for the oppressed of all other nations and build a slave oligarchy on the ruins thereof." A Kansas lieutenant who had spent more than a year in prison after his capture at Chickamauga longed for release but, he wrote his fiancée, he did not want the war to end short of unconditional victory, for if it did "the hope of the freedom of Nations and Millions in Europe and elsewhere [will be] driven back and obscured for ages." An Iowa officer who had risen from the ranks during three years of service while his father and younger sister had died at home and his brother was missing in action after the battle of Atlanta wrote to his distraught mother in September 1864 that he could not resign his commission and come home while the war's outcome remained in doubt. "Thank God," he counseled her, "that you have children that will support the Government that *your* Father supported in the Revolution."[24]

The 1864 presidential election shaped up as a decisive test of these convictions. The Democrats nominated McClellan, who professed to stand for restoration of the Union by military victory. But the Peace Democrats wrote the platform, whose crucial plank, drafted by none other than Clement Vallandigham, branded the war a failure and called for an armistice and peace negotiations. The vice presidential nominee George Pendleton was also a Peace Democrat. Most Northern voters viewed the election as a referendum on the war. So did many Confederates. If Lincoln won, the North would fight on to unconditional victory; if McClellan won, most observers expected a peace short of Union victory.

The overwhelming majority of Northern soldiers saw it this way. Unless they came from Illinois, Indiana, or New Jersey (states with Democratic legislatures) they could vote in camp by absentee ballot. As the election approached, sometimes heated arguments dominated soldiers' campfire bull sessions. The diary entries of a sergeant in the 8th Ohio Cavalry offer a typical chronicle:

Sept. 12, 1864: "Politics the principal topic of the day."
Sept. 13: "Spend a good portion of my time reading the news and argueing politics."
Sept. 21: "Politics keep up quite an excitement in our company."

The regiment then went on a raid (after all, there was a war on), but when they returned to camp the arguments continued.

Oct. 15: "Some considerable excitement on politics in camp."
Nov. 8: The regiment voted 367 for Lincoln, 16 for McClellan.[25]

Peer pressure in this regiment no doubt coerced some of the minority to mark their tickets for Lincoln. But a striking majority of all Union soldiers – 78 percent, compared with 53 percent of the civilian vote – went for Lincoln. This was all the more remarkable because some 40 to 45 percent of soldiers had been Democrats (or came from Democratic families) in 1860, and McClellan retained some residual popularity among old soldiers in the Army of the Potomac. More than one of these veterans said, however, that while they still admired McClellan, they did not like the company he kept. So half of the former Democrats voted for Lincoln. As one of them explained it: "I can not vote for one thing and fight for another."[26]

McClellan's letter accepting the nomination had pledged to proceed with peace negotiations *only* on the condition of reunion. But most soldiers refused to take this seriously. It was the platform that counted, and in the words of a New York lieutenant that platform proclaimed the war "a miserable failure and ask[ed] for peace at the sacrifice of every sense of honor and right. . . . I do not see how any soldier can vote for such a man, nominated on a platform which acknowledges that we are whipped." A corporal in the 19th Michigan explained to his mother that "to ellect McClellan would be to undo all that we have don in the past four years. . . . Old abe is slow but sure, he will accept nothing but an unconditional surrender."[27] The noted cavalry commander Charles Russell Lowell feared that "McClellan's election would [leave] this country . . . in the condition of the South American republics, or worse. . . . Either half a dozen little republics, or *one despotism*, must follow." Lowell did not live to vote for Lincoln; he was killed at Cedar Creek on October 19. But a private in the 122nd New York did live to "give the rebelion another thump this fall by voting for old Abe. I cannot afford to give three years of my life to maintaining this nation and then giving them Rebles all they want."[28]

While service in the army converted many Northern Democrats into Lincoln voters, some of their families back home remained in the McClellan camp. This led to epistolary quarrels.

A Connecticut artillery private could scarcely believe that his brother intended to vote Democratic. How could he "countenance such disloyalty? such infamy and such open insult to the patriots and soldiers of our land and to the martyred dead who have fallen – *they* say for nothing – but we say to save our country's freedom and liberty and . . . the universal cause of liberty and right throughout the world." An Ohio artilleryman sent word to his brother that if he voted for McClellan, "I will never speak to him. . . . He had better go and join the rebel army and have done with it at once." Another Ohioan, an infantry private who was too young to vote, told his father point blank that "when you vote for Mc & Pendleton you put yourself down and go to the ballot box hand in hand *with the vilest trators that America ever knew.*"[29]

When he learned the news of Lincoln's reelection, a naval officer wryly expressed his gratification that "McClellan meets with no better success as a politician than as a general." A private in the 17th Connecticut rejoiced that "our nation has been given new life and vigor and our glorious institutions [are] to be perpetuated."[30] When Lincoln reaffirmed at the Hampton Roads conference in February 1865 that his conditions for peace were unconditional surrender and the end of slavery, a private in the 1st New York Artillery was convinced that the sacrifice of his friends who "died fighting against cruelty and oppression" had been worth it, for "we shall come forth from the fire of trial and have proven to the world that the American people can and will govern themselves and that our country is indeed the land of the free and the home of the' brave." After Lee surrendered at Appomattox, a fifty-one-year-old New Jersey colonel wrote to his wife that he could now come home proud that "it has been our privilege to live and take part in the struggle that has decided for all time to come that Republics are not a failure."[31]

On the third anniversary of his enlistment, which also happened to be his thirty-first birthday, a carpenter who had risen to a captaincy in the 47th Ohio wrote to his ten-year-old son congratulating him on a neatly written birthday letter to the daddy he had scarcely seen during the past three years: "It tells me that while I am absent from home, fighting the battels of our country, trying to restore law and order, to our once peaceful & prosperous nation, and endeavoring to secure for each and every American citizen of every race, the rights garenteed to us in the Declaration of Independence . . . I have children growing up that will be worthy of the rights that I trust will be left for them."[32]

Americans at the end of the twentieth century are also children of that heritage. Whether we are worthy of it will remain a matter of constant reexamination. Civil War soldiers willingly made extraordinary sacrifices, even of life itself, for the principles they perceived to be at stake in the war. Whether Americans today would be willing to make similar wartime sacrifices is unanswerable. One hopes that it will remain unanswered.

Notes

1   Charles Wills to sister, July 1, 1864, in *Army Life of an Illinois Soldier, Letters and Diary of the Late Charles Wills* (Washington, 1906), p. 272.
2   Hiram Smith Williams, diary entry of April 4, 1864, in *This War So Horrible: The Civil War Diary of Hiram Smith Williams*, ed. Lewis N. Wynne and Robert A. Taylor (Tuscaloosa, 1993), pp. 43–4.
3   Gerald F. Linderman, *Embattled Courage: The Experience of Combat in the American Civil War* (New York, 1987), pp. 2, 240; Leif Torkelsen, "Forged in Battle: The Evolution of Small Unit Cohesion in the Union Voluntary Infantry Regiments, 1861–1865" (Senior thesis, Princeton University, 1991), p. 5.
4   Stephen A. Forbes to Frances Snow, Jan. 12, 1865, Forbes Papers, Illinois State Historical Library (ISHL); Abial Edwards to Anna Conant, Dec. 16, 1863, in *"Dear Friend Anna": The Civil War*

Letters of a Common Soldier from Maine, ed. Beverly Hayes Kallgren and James L. Crothamel (Orono, ME, 1992), p. 71.

5 William J. Tomlinson to Emily Tomlinson, July 16, 1864, Tomlinson Papers, in private possession; William L. Nugent to Eleanor Nugent, Nov. 22, 1863, in *My Dear Nellie: The Civil War Letters of William L. Nugent*, ed. William M. Cash and Lucy Somerville Howarth (Jackson, MS., 1977), p. 148.

6 William W. Ward to James B. Hale, Oct. 15, 1864, in *"For the Sake of my Country": The Diary of Col. W. W. Ward, 9th Tennessee Cavalry*, ed. R. B. Rosenburg (Murfreesboro, 1992), p. 145; Urban G. Owen to Laura Owen, March 1, April 8, 1864, in "Letters of a Confederate Surgeon in the Army of Tennessee to His Wife," *THQ Iowa Journal of History*, 4 (1945), 154, 161.

7 David Thompson to mother, Feb. 25, 1865, Samuel Thompson Papers, Southern Historical Collection University of North Grolina at Chapel Hill (SHC UNC); John A. Everett to mother, Feb. 7, March 16, 1865, Everett Papers, Woodruff Library, Emery University, Atlanta (WLEU).

8 John Beatty to Elizabeth Beatty, Jan. 12, 1865, Beatty Papers, Minnesota Historical Society, St. Paul. (MNHS); George Hopper to brother and sister, Dec. 16, 1864, Hopper Papers, US Army Military Institute Carlisle, PA (MHI); Sarah D. B. Chamberlain to Joshua L. Chamberlain, Jan. 1, 1865, Joshua L. Chamberlain to Joshua Chamberlain (father), Feb. 20, 1865, Joshua L. Chamberlain to Sarah Bristow Chamberlain, March 9, 1865, in Alice Rains Trulock, *In the Hands of Providence: Joshua L. Chamberlain and the American Civil War* (Chapel Hill, 1992), pp. 225–7.

9 Neal F. Heendy to Bryant Wright, Feb. 14, 1864, Wright Papers, Perteins Library Duke University (PLDU); Joseph F. Maides to mother, Sept. 23, 1864, Maides Papers, PLDU; Sydney S. Champion to wife, June 1, 1864, Champion Papers, PLDU.

10 James Crowder to brother, March 13, 1864, in *In the Land of the Living: Wartime Letters by Confederates from the Chattahoochee Valley of Alabama and Georgia*, ed. Ray Mathis (Troy, AL, 1981), p. 85; Thomas J. Key, diary entries of Aug. 8, 1864, Feb. 5, 1865, *Two Soldiers: The Campaign Diaries of Thomas J. Key, C.S.A., and Robert J. Campbell, U.S.A.* (Chapel Hill, 1938), pp. 111, 187; T. B. Kelly to L. A. Honnoll, April 25, 1864, Honnoll Papers, WLEU.

11 William L. Nugent to Eleanor Nugent, Aug. 8, Dec. 26, 1864, in *My Dear Nellie*, pp. 197, 229.

12 Joseph Thompson to mother, Feb. 15, 1865, Samuel Thompson Papers, SHC UNC.

13 William B. Bate to William H. T. Walker, Jan. 19, 1864, Civil War Collection, Henry E. Huntington Library, San Marino CA (HEH), *Jackson Mississippian*, reprinted in *Montgomery Weekly Mail*, Sept. 9, 1863, in Robert F. Durden, *The Gray and the Black: The Confederate Debate on Emancipation* (Baton Rouge, 1972), pp. 31–2.

14 R. Howard Browne to wife, undated (Nov. 1864), Browne Papers, SHC UNC; James Wingard to Simon Wingard, Jan. 4, 1865, Wingard Papers, PLDU.

15 Ethan Pennell, Diary, entry of April 8, 1865, Missouri Historical Society, St. Louis (MO HS); Joseph F. Maides to mother, Feb. 18, 1865, Maides Papers, PLDU.

16 Thomas J. Goree to Mary Frances Goree Kittrell, Oct. 21, 1864, in *Longstreet's Aide: The Civil War Letters of Major Thomas J. Goree*, ed. Thomas W. Cutrer (Charlottesville, 1995), p. 137; Robert Patrick, diary entry of Jan. 18, 1865, in *Reluctant Rebel: The Secret Diary of Robert Patrick, 1861–1865*, ed. Jay F. Taylor (Baton Rouge, 1959), p. 250; Richard W. Corbin to father, Dec. 29, 1864, in *Letters of a Confederate Officer to His Family in Europe* (Paris, n.d.), p. 89.

17 James Branch O'Bryan to sister, Jan. 20, 1865, O'Bryan Papers, TSL; Walter Taylor to Bettie Saunders, Feb. 16, 1865, in *Lee's Adjutant: The Wartime Letters of Colonel Walter Herron Taylor, 1861–1865*, ed. R. Rockwood Tower (Columbia, SC, 1995), pp. 223–4.

18 John V. Hadley to Mary J. Hill, Feb. 24, 1863, in. "An Indiana Soldier in Love and War: The Civil War Letters of John V. Hadley," ed. James I. Robertson, Jr., *Indiana Magazine of History* 59 (1963), 230; John D. Shank to family, March 12, April 13, 1863, in *One Flag One Country and Thirteen Greenbacks a Month: Letters from a Civil War Private*, ed. Edna J. Shank Hunter (San Diego, 1980), pp. 61, 68; Cornelius Moore to Adeline Moore, July 7, 1864, in *Cornie: The Civil War Letters of Lt. Cornelius L. Moore*, ed. Gilbert C. Moore (n.p., 1989), p. 192.

19 John A. Gillis, Diary, entries of Jan. 1, March 17, 1864, MN HS; Henry Crydenwise to parents, Jan. 31, June 7, 1864, Crydenwise Papers, WLEU; John G. McDermott to Isabella McDermott, March 10, 1864, McDermott Papers, Wisconsin Historical Society, Madison (WHS).

20   Josiah M. Favill, diary entry of Jan. 1, 1864, in *The Diary of a Young Officer* (Chicago, 1909), p. 273; Bliss Morse to mother, Aug. 29, 1864, and diary entry of Nov. 8, 1864, in *War Diaries and Letters of Bliss Morse*, ed. Loren J. Morse (Tahlequah, OK, 1985), pp. 150, 165.

21   Edward Wightman to Fred Wightman, Aug. 28, 1864, in *From Antietam to Fort Fisher: The Civil War Letters of Edward King Wightman, 1862–1865* (Rutherford, NJ, 1983), p. 206; Edmund English to mother, undated (1864) and April 22, 1864, English Papers, HEH.

22   *London Daily News*, Sept. 27, 1864, quoted in Allan Nevins, *The Organized War to Victory* (New York, 1971), pp. 141–2.

23   Delos Van Deusen to Henrietta Van Deusen, Aug. 21, 1864, Van Deusen Papers, HEH; John Berry to Samuel L. M. Barlow, Aug. 27, 1864, Barlow Papers, HEH; Thomas N. Stevens to Carrie Stevens, Sept. 19, 1864, in *"Dear Carrie"... The Civil War Letters of Thomas N. Stevens*, ed. Georg M. Blackburn (Mt. Pleasant, MI, 1984), p. 250.

24   John Hamer to Eveline Hamer, Aug. 5, 1864, Hamer Papers, MHI; James Love to Molly Wilson, Sept. 24, 1864, Feb. 14, 1865, Love Papers, MO HS; Benjamin Stevens to mother, Sept. 8, 1864, in "The Civil War Letters of an Iowa Family," ed. Richard N. Ellis, *Annals of Iowa*, 3rd Series, 39 (1969), 585.

25   Samuel J. Harrison Diary, Ohio Historical Society, Columbus (OHS).

26   Henry Kauffman to Katherine Kreitzer, Oct. 15, 1864, in *The Civil War Letters (1862–1865) of Private Henry Kauffman*, ed. David McCordick (Lewiston, NY, 1991), 89. For studies of the soldier vote in 1864, see Oscar O. Winther, "The Soldier Vote in the Election of 1864," *New York History* 25 (1944), 440–58, and Josiah Henry Benton, *Voting in the Field: A Forgotten Chapter of the Civil War* (Boston, 1915).

27   Henry Crydenwise to parents, Oct. 25, 1864, Crydenwise Papers, WLEU; Delos Lake to mother, July 12, Nov. 1, 1864, Lake Papers, HEH.

28   Lowell to Josephine Shaw Lowell, Sept. 1, 1864, Lowell to Charles E. Perkins, Oct. 17, 1864, in *Life and Letters of Charles Russell Lowell*, ed. Edward W. Emerson (Boston, 1907), pp. 333, 362; Nathan Buck to sister, July 9, 1864, Saxton Family Collection, HEH.

29   William B. Sniffen to mother, Oct. 18, 1864, Sniffen Papers, MHI; John H. Morse to Belle Morse, Oct. 25, 1864, in *The Letters of Morse*, p. 155; Chauncey B. Welton to father, Oct. 1, 1864, Welton Papers, SHC UNC.

30   William F. Keeler to Anna Keeler, Nov. 9, 1864, in *Aboard the USS Florida, 1863–1865: The Letters of Paymaster William F. Keeler*, ed. Robert W. Daly (Annapolis, 1968), p. 200; Justus Silliman to mother, Nov. 9, 1864, in *A New Canaan Private in the Civil War: Letters of Justus M. Silliman, 17th Connecticut Volunteers*, ed. Edward Marcus (New Canaan, 1984), p. 83.

31   John N. Sherman to parents, Feb. 10, 1865, Sherman Papers, MHI; Robert McAllister to Ellen McAllister, April 9, 1865, in *The Civil War Letters of General Robert McAllister*, ed. James I. Robertson, Jr. (New Brunswick, NJ, 1965), p. 608.

32   Ephraim S. Holloway to John W. Holloway, Aug. 7, 1864, Holloway Papers, OHS.

Questions to consider

- How did Confederate soldiers square their quest for independence for themselves and bondage for slaves?

- How would you describe McPherson's attitude toward the veterans he describes? Would you say his stance toward Confederates is essentially the same as toward Union soldiers? (Do historians have an obligation to have similar stances toward their opposing subjects when analyzing war?)

- Do you think Americans today are willing to make sacrifices comparable to those of Civil War soldiers? Are you? Under what circumstances, if any?

Chapter 31

Victory and Defeat: Primary Sources

Diary Entry

Sarah Morgan Dawson

Sarah Morgan (later Dawson), 1842–1909, a native of Louisiana, was truly from a house divided: her oldest brother was a Unionist, and three others fought for the Confederacy (two died of disease during the War). In this diary entry, which covers the surrender of Lee to Grant and the assassination of Abraham Lincoln, Morgan captures the widespread despair of many Southerners at the dawn of their defeat. How would you describe her attitude toward Lincoln's death? Do you believe she's right in her speculation about the hypothetical response to the murder of Jefferson Davis?

Sarah Morgan Dawson, "Diary Entry for April 19, 1865", in *A Confederate Girl's Diary*, ed. J. I. Robertson, Jr. (Bloomington: Indiana University Press, 1960), pp. 435–7.

No. 211 CAMP ST.,
April 19th, 1865.

"All things are taken from us, and become portions and parcels of the dreadful pasts." . . . Thursday the 13th came the dreadful tidings of the surrender of Lee and his army on the 9th. Everybody cried, but I would not, satisfied that God will still save us, even though all should apparently be lost. Followed at intervals of two or three hours by the announcement of the capture of Richmond, Selma, Mobile, and Johnston's army, even the stanchest Southerners were hopeless. Every one proclaimed Peace, and the only matter under consideration was whether Jeff Davis, all politicians, every man above the rank of Captain in the army and above that of Lieutenant in the navy, should be hanged immediately, or *some* graciously pardoned. Henry Ward Beecher humanely pleaded mercy for us, supported by a small minority. Davis and all leading men *must* be executed; the blood of the others would serve to irrigate the country. Under this lively prospect, Peace, blessed Peace! was the cry. I whispered, "Never! Let a great earthquake swallow us up first! Let us leave our land and emigrate to any desert spot of the earth, rather than return to the Union, even as it Was!"

Six days this has lasted. Blessed with the silently obstinate disposition, I would not dispute, but felt my heart swell, repeating, "God is our refuge and our strength, a very present help in time of trouble," and could not for an instant believe this could end in an overthrow.

This morning, when I went down to breakfast at seven, Brother read the announcement of the assassination of Lincoln and Secretary Seward.

"Vengeance is mine; I will repay, saith the Lord." This is murder! God have mercy on those who did it!

Charlotte Corday killed Marat in his bath, and is held up in history as one of Liberty's martyrs, and one of the heroines of her country. To me, it is all murder. Let historians extol blood-shedding; it is woman's place to abhor it. And because I know that they would have apotheosized any man who had crucified Jeff Davis, I abhor this, and call it foul murder, unworthy of our cause – and God grant it was only the temporary insanity of a desperate man that committed this crime! Let not his blood be visited on our nation, Lord!

Across the way, a large building, undoubtedly inhabited by officers, is being draped in black. Immense streamers of black and white hang from the balcony. Downtown, I understand, all shops are closed, and all wrapped in mourning. And I hardly dare pray God to bless us, with the crape hanging over the way. It would have been banners, if our President had been killed, though!

Letter from Richmond

Chaplain Garland H. White

In early April 1865, the Confederate capital of Richmond – for four years the unrealized goal of Federal armies – finally fell into Union hands. This was perhaps the most exciting event in the Union since the war began; Abraham Lincoln himself visited the city, and savored the experience of sitting in Jefferson Davis's chair at the Confederate White House. But perhaps not even Lincoln, who makes a cameo appearance in the letter that follows, experienced the happiness of Chaplain Garland H. White, who accompanied the first troops – which happened to be African American – into the city. His remarkable story suggests the way in which the public and private dramas of the Civil War could resolve themselves in deeply personal, and deeply moving, ways. What meaning does this moment have for White, given all that has preceded it?

Garland H. White, (April 12, 1865), in *A Grand Army of Black Men: Letters from African-American Soldiers in the Union Army, 1861–1865*, ed. Edwin S. Redkey (New York: Cambridge University Press, 1992), pp. 175–8. Reprinted by permission of Cambridge University Press.

I have just returned from the city of Richmond; my regiment was among the first that entered that city. I marched at the head of the column, and soon I found myself called upon by the officers and men of my regiment to make a speech, with which, of course, I readily complied.

A vast multitude assembled on Broad Street, and I was aroused amid the shouts of ten thousand voices, and proclaimed for the first time in that city freedom to all mankind. After which the doors of all the slave pens were thrown open, and thousands came out shouting and praising God, and Father, or Master Abe, as they termed him. In this mighty consternation I became so overcome with tears that I could not stand up under the pressure of such fullness of joy in my own heart. I retired to gain strength, so I lost many important topics worthy of note.

Among the densely crowded concourse there were parents looking for children who had been sold south of this state in tribes, and husbands came for the same purpose; here and there one was singled out in the ranks, and an effort was made to approach the gallant and marching soldiers, who were too obedient to orders to break ranks.

We continued our march as far as Camp Lee, at the extreme end of Broad Street, running westwards. In camp the multitude followed, and everybody could participate in shaking the friendly but hard hands of the poor slaves. Among the many broken-hearted mothers looking for their children who had been sold to Georgia and elsewhere, was an aged woman, passing through the vast crowd of colored, inquiring for [one] by the name of Garland H. White, who had been sold from her when a small boy, and was bought by a lawyer named Robert Toombs, who lived in Georgia.[1] Since the war has been going on she has seen Mr. Toombs in Richmond with troops from his state, and upon her asking him where his body-servant Garland was, he replied: "He ran off from me at Washington, and went to Canada. I have since learned that he is living somewhere in the State of Ohio." Some of the boys knowing that I lived in Ohio, soon found me and said, "Chaplain, here is a lady that wishes to see you." I quickly turned, following the soldier until coming to a group of colored ladies. I was questioned as follows:

"What is your name, sir?"

"My name is Garland H. White."

"What was your mother's name?"

"Nancy."

"Where was you born?"

"In Hanover County, in this State."

"Where was you sold from?"

"From this city."

"What was the name of the man who bought you?"

"Robert Toombs."

"Where did he live?"

"In the State of Georgia."

"Where did you leave him?"

"At Washington."

"Where did you go then?"

"To Canada."

"Where do you live now?"

"In Ohio."

"This is your mother, Garland, whom you are now talking to, who has spent twenty years of grief about her son."

I cannot express the joy I felt at this happy meeting of my mother and other friends. But suffice it to say that God is on the side of the righteous, and will in due time reward them. I have witnessed several such scenes among the other colored regiments.

Late in the afternoon, we were honored with his Excellency, the President of the United States, Lieutenant-General Grant, and other gentlemen of distinction.[2] We made a grand parade through most of the principal streets of the city, beginning at Jeff Davis's mansion, and it appeared to me that all the colored people in the world had collected in that city for that purpose. I never saw so many colored people in all my life, women and children of all sizes running after Father, or Master Abraham, as they called him. To see the colored people, one would think they had all gone crazy. The excitement at this period was unabated, the tumbling of walls, the bursting of shells, could be heard in all directions, dead bodies being found, rebel prisoners being brought in, starving women and children begging for greenbacks and hard tack, constituted the order of the day. The Fifth [Massachusetts] Cavalry, colored, were still dashing through the streets to protect and preserve the peace, and see that no one suffered violence, they having fought so often over the walls of Richmond, driving the enemy at every point.

Among the first to enter Richmond was the 28th USCT – better known as the First Indiana Colored Volunteers. . . .

Some people do not seem to believe that the colored troops were the first that entered Richmond. Why, you need not feel at all timid in giving the truthfulness of my assertion to the four winds of the heavens, and let the angels re-echo it back to the earth, that the *colored soldiers of the Army of the James were the first to enter the city of Richmond.* I was with them, and am still with them, and am willing to stay with them until freedom is proclaimed throughout the world. Yes, we will follow this race of men in search of liberty through the whole Island of Cuba. All the boys are well, and send their love to all the kind ones at home.

Notes

1   Toombs was a US senator and a Confederate secretary of state and general.
2   Lincoln visited Richmond on April 4, 1865.

Part XIV

Reconstruction

Plate 16 Working Solutions: The Freedmen's Union Industrial School, Richmond, Virginia, from a sketch by James E. Taylor, published in *Frank Leslie's Illustrated Newspaper*, 1866. Northern reformers – particularly women – placed great faith in occupational training as a means for economic, social, and political advancement for former slaves. Were such views naïve or far-sighted?

Chapter 32

"Privilege" and "Protection": Civil and Political Rights During Reconstruction

Laura F. Edwards

Most people would agree that the North won the Civil War. Not quite as many people would agree that it won the peace. To be sure, the conflict destroyed slavery and left the old Southern economy in ruins in ways from which it would take decades to recover. And it is a truism that winners write history. Yet the South showed tremendous resilience in the aftermath of the Civil War – as noted earlier it is now arguably the leading economic region in the United States – and has repeatedly been able to represent its point of view compellingly through channels that range from academic histories to some of the most beloved works of popular culture of all time.

The Southern way of life has proven durable in other ways as well. As a legal matter, slavery ended in 1865, but the tenant farming system that replaced it was for many African Americans virtually bondage in another form. Ironically, the relative racial integration that slavery required was replaced by the separatism of the Jim Crow laws that became common by the 1890s, which allowed different means to the same end: racial supremacy for whites. Leading Southerners used tremendous ingenuity to perpetrate this system, which lasted through the first half of the twentieth century. Of course, as Southern lawyers observed, the South couldn't do it alone: many postwar Jim Crow statutes borrowed their language and intent from prewar Northern ones. In fact, the Southern way of life was in many ways essentially the same as the Northern way of life. The only real difference, you might say, was the accent.

Historians generally describe the dozen years that followed the end of the war in 1865 as "Reconstruction." Reconstruction was a complex process, whose features and outcomes continue to be hotly debated. Yet there is general agreement that it proceeded in three distinct phases. The first of these, "Presidential Reconstruction," actually began before the war was over and ended by 1868. Presidential Reconstruction was begun by Abraham Lincoln around 1863 in Federal-controlled Union territory in Arkansas and Louisiana. Lincoln took a relatively lenient stance with former Confederates, an approach that reflected his temperament as well as his reading of the political situation. Upon his death, Andrew Johnson tried to continue Lincoln's policies. But changed circumstances led long-chafing abolitionist Republicans, now known as Radicals, to challenge Johnson's control over the process. (Johnson was impeached over the firing of his Secretary of War; though not convicted of what was a questionable offense, he was nevertheless rendered politically impotent until replaced by Ulysses S. Grant in 1869.) Radical Reconstruction, which lasted into the mid-1870s, was marked by a military occupation and a tougher stance toward Southern intransigence (embodied most vividly by the rise of the Ku Klux Klan), as well as active party-building collaboration with African American politicians that was alternatively enlightened and corrupt. Radical Reconstruction weakened over the course of the decade as waning Northern will and rising Southern energy led to the third phase of Reconstruction, "Redemption." This phase, in which white supremacists regained control over state governments, began as early as 1869 in Virginia and was completed after the contested presidential election of 1876, in which Southern Democrats acquiesced in the victory of Rutherford B. Hayes, who did not win the popular vote, in return from a withdrawal of all Union forces in the South.

The various overlapping phases of Reconstruction should not obscure the broader patterns that can be traced through the period – and long after. Among these are the sustained efforts by African Americans to gain autonomy over their lives, and the determined efforts of some to prevent this. Crucial to this struggle were the definitions of words like "freedom" and distinctions made within it (As Lincoln himself observed before the war, freedom is by no means the same as equality.) In this selection from her influential 1997 book *Gendered Strife and Confusion: The Political Culture of Reconstruction*, Laura F. Edwards explores the various strategies of North Carolinians, white and black, male and female, to make sense of what was theoretically a new social order.

Laura Edwards, " 'Privilege' and 'Protection': Civil and Political Rights during Reconstruction," in *Gendered Strife and Confusion: The Political Culture of Reconstruction* (Urbana: University of Illinois Press, 1997), pp. 184–98.

As Bella Newton's daughter and son, Susan and William, were walking home one afternoon in 1869, Alexander Noblin, a white neighbor, attempted to assault Susan sexually. Although frustrated in his attempt by William, who pitched a rock at his head, Noblin fired a parting volley. In William's words, he "shook his penis at us and called me a dam little nigger." With this gesture, Noblin symbolically reasserted his power over both children. After learning of the incident, Bella Newton's first response was in keeping with community traditions. She publicized her complaint in the neighborhood and then made an informal bargain with Noblin agreeing not to prosecute in exchange for one dollar and ten pounds of bacon. Noblin delivered the goods, but Newton did not fulfill her end of the deal. Instead of remaining quiet, she filed charges with the local justice of the peace, an extremely bold move for this poor black woman. In so doing, she challenged the privilege of a white man of some prominence. She also chose a course of action that had been closed to her during slavery, when both formal and informal practices sanctioned violence against African-American and, to a lesser extent, poor white women. Much to his chagrin, Alexander Noblin learned that his recent actions carried much different consequences than they had before the war.[1]

Only a small fraction of women launched legal proceedings like this one. But Bella Newton and her daughter did resemble the vast majority of southern women in that they did not measure up to elite white standards of womanhood. And like Bella Newton, these women believed that they deserved the same social respect and legal protection as elite white women, even if they did not live in a domestic setting that would pass muster with Sarah A. Elliott. Newton also insisted on the right to air her grievances in court, demanding that state institutions recognize her legal rights as a woman. Newton challenged not only antebellum conservative political principles that positioned people in relation to public power along racial and class lines but also the postwar reincarnations that articulated the same hierarchies in the language of individual character. In the process she gave substance to the Republican party's lofty principles. Republicans stretched traditional notions of universality to argue that full citizenship rights "naturally" belonged to all men simply because they were men. Thus empowered, men could secure to their women the privileges of maintenance and protection. Of course, party leaders at the state and national levels left their words in places where historians could find them easily. People like Bella Newton did not. Yet, she and other women of both races joined the front lines of political struggle, even though they were excluded from ballot boxes, political podiums, legislative floors, and even party rhetoric.

Poor African Americans and common whites altered the content of public debate, infusing it with their own ideas about men's and women's rights and social roles. But they could not completely reframe these issues, even if they wanted to. By emphasizing gender differences deeply rooted within a patriarchal family structure, they left key components of the antebellum power structure in place. Ultimately, conservatives would use this same scaffolding to rebuild racial and class hierarchies and to constrict the public arena.

Households and Public Power

At the time of southern surrender, it was clear to North Carolina's conservative leaders that all men were not equal. In their minds, men fell out in hierarchical order based on the gradations of independence and dependence created in the private sphere. Among white men, property measured both private and public competence. Property "purchased" a stake in society, the size of which varied directly with the value of the estate. "The acquisition of property," in the words of Jonathan Worth, "proved that [men] had intelligence and interest in the well-being of society." Propertylessness, by contrast, signaled both private and public irresponsibility. "That class," planter John Stafford sniffed in 1860, "possess but little else than moral polution having no property to destroy, no conscience to overcome, no God to fear." Ruled by their passions and improvident of the future, such men were not only poor, they were poor providers. Ineptitude at family governance disqualified them from public power. Even the most honest and well-intentioned of this class would succumb to lures of wily demagogues, or so conservatives believed.[2]

When racial ideology combined with class hierarchy, the result was even more virulent. Conservative whites considered African Americans a permanently dependent race even less politically fit than propertyless whites. The inadequacies of African Americans, unlike those of poor whites, adhered in their very nature. As long as blacks remained under the supervision of their white masters, they were happy, ineffectual minors who needed the guidance of their white masters to survive. Once Sambo and Mammy ventured out on their own, however, their characters changed dramatically. They became the menacing, oversexed black male rapist and black female seductress, images that conveyed the extent to which whites believed African Americans to be incapable of self-governance.[3]

Emancipation only confirmed conservatives' suspicions that the nation was poised too precariously on the slippery slope of universal rights and strengthened their resistance to democratic change. The first state constitution bore the mark of their intransigence, not only excluding blacks from the political process but also restricting the political power of common whites. Even then, many conservatives still saw ominous signs in the few privileges allowed to common whites, particularly those without property. Fighting to keep power out of the hands of those they considered unqualified to exercise it, conservatives opposed the direct election of judges, the abolition of property requirements for office, and the repudiation of Confederate debts. They even reopened the question of free white manhood suffrage. The new apportionment system was also too democratic for the most dogmatic among them. Where the antebellum constitution had counted slaves as three-fifths of a white person, thus favoring slaveholders, the new one based legislative representation on the number of whites only. Thomas Ruffin, the eminent antebellum jurist, scoffed at the new scheme precisely because it implied that political rights were universal. Everyone, according to Ruffin, knew otherwise. Civil rights, which ensured "security in person and property by the Constitution and the laws made under it," were "natural." But political rights, which "consist, not in the rights...as held *under* the law, but of the powers *over* the Constitution and laws," were not. Rights to change and amend the laws, Ruffin argued, should be distributed "according to the sense of the Community of the fitness of particular classes." Political rights, then, were particular, derived from a person's position within the community. Given Ruffin's emphasis on protecting the property of the "intelligent, virtuous, and valuable portion of the population," only those men with wealth and white skin possessed the "fitness" to rule. Other conservatives shared Ruffin's fears of the democratic tendencies in the new constitution. As Jonathan Worth maintained, the "tendency" of democratic government "is to ignore virtue and property and intelligence – and to put the powers of government into the hands of mere *numbers*." When the constitution came to a vote in August 1866, conservatives were instrumental in its defeat.[4]

If rule by "mere *numbers*" rankled the sensibilities of white conservatives, then rule by African Americans was completely inconceivable. Jonathan Worth voiced widely held convictions with his assertion that "the Caucasian race always has been and always will be superior to the negro race." "I know from observation of history," he elaborated, "that the African left to its own self-control, is so indolent and improvident, that he will not – indeed I think he cannot be made a good citizen." His characterization of Henderson Cooper and William Cooper, the two black men accused of raping Susan Daniel, relied on these assumptions. To him they were brutal "monsters," incapable of either understanding or controlling their actions. In fact, it was so difficult for him to imagine African Americans as independent political actors that he remained completely blind to the black community's role in stopping Henderson Cooper's execution and removing him from local jurisdiction. Instead, he lay the blame at the feet of northern military officials, claiming that it was they who created the commotion by "allow[ing]" Henderson Cooper "to go unpunished." In his mind, only wealthy white men could initiate and sustain such weighty political conflicts. The actions of a dependent people, by contrast, carried no public import.[5]

Thomas Ruffin made the association between race and dependency explicit, likening all African Americans to other household dependents. For the same reasons it was "impolitic and unsafe" to grant white women and children political power, the state should bar black men from suffrage "for all time to come, if not forever." B. F. Moore, the principal architect of the state's Black Code, fused class and race in one image of dependency and forecasted doom if African-American men could vote: "The race, long degraded by servitude, ignorant of the politics of government, very low in its grade of morals, and wholly dependent for a living on the ability of the wealthier class of society, would, if allowed to vote, consult their material aid, and speadily engender among the whites, hosts of vile and reckless demagogues." To men of like mind, the state's Black Code granted a dependent race far too many privileges already. These conservatives absolutely refused to consider the possibility of political rights.[6]

When propertyless whites provided the reference point, however, the sharp racial contrasts softened considerably. For conservatives, race never functioned in isolation from other relations of power. Instead, race combined with class and gender to anchor a hierarchical worldview in which the primary line of demarcation separated those who could sustain households from those who could not. Despite all their other differences, neither poor white nor black men were fit for public power. Indeed, this political categorization often caused conservatives to exaggerate the unity of interest and the potential for political cooperation between the two groups. The specter of biracial revolt haunted Jonathan Worth, who described the "majority in all times and in all countries" as "improvident and without property." Without the guidance of the "better class," they would soon degenerate into "a great mob ruled by the will of the hour."[7] He even used racial imagery to describe poor white men, referring to "the black and white negro" and "negroes and albinoes." With these labels, Worth distinguished between the races, while simultaneously destabilizing the racial identity of poor whites to highlight the similarities among all those he considered politically incompetent. "Albinoes" and "white negroes" were only nominally white. In their relation to public power, they occupied a place closer to African Americans than to propertied white men like himself. But the least reliable of all poor white men were those who refused to toe the conservative line and quietly accept their subordinate place in the political order. It was actually politically active poor whites who were the "albinoes" and "white negroes" Worth so scorned – and so feared.[8]

Whereas the likes of Thomas Ruffin and Jonathan Worth dug in their heels, moderate white North Carolinians accepted the inevitability of change and counseled prudent compromise. Some hoped to avoid more radical measures brewing in the North.[9] Others took their cue from unrest within their counties, where angry whites demonstrated their unwillingness to resurrect a social and political order that had so recently betrayed them. As propertyholders and household heads many common white men could identify with some pieces of conservative ideology, but they had never been enthusiastic about some of its more hierarchical elements. The Civil War only solidified their opposition. The burden of the Confederacy's war policies fell heavily on yeoman and poor white families, some of whom had opposed the war in the first place. As their fortunes declined, so did their enthusiasm for the war effort. Locating the problems in a political system that appeared to respond only to the interests of the wealthy, they resorted to extralegal activity. Even those from solid yeoman families often collaborated with propertyless whites, free blacks, and slaves, finding common ground in their opposition to the Confederacy's leaders and their policies.[10]

The bitterness dissipated slowly. At war's end, unionists trumpeted the dawn of a new political regime. According to the *Wilmington Herald*, a unionist newspaper that began publication during the war, the South had not gone down in defeat, only the "aristocrats who desired a government that would give them exclusive privileges and the benefits of *caste*" had. But now "their political and social influence has departed and they will be left high and dry in the future management of the state and general government, while the 'poor whites,' those whom they have looked down on and despised, will assume the reins, and henceforth led by such men as Andrew Johnson and Wm. W. Holden, moral courage and intellectual capacity and brain will govern the country, and the pure democratic principle will prevail." Agreeing with these sentiments, many moderate white leaders openly opposed conservatives' fiscal and political policies. Clearly, the same white people who suffered so much during the war now formed a formidable political force that conservatives ignored at their own peril.[11]

Yet, even as moderates sharply criticized conservatives' stubborn refusal to concede any new ground, they still accepted some of the same conservative ideas about independence and dependence. All men, they admitted, deserved full civil rights, which conferred the means to protect person and property and thus ensured "life, liberty, and the pursuit of happiness." However oppressive the state's Black Code was, it would have been that much worse if not for moderates committed to the idea that certain natural rights extended even to African Americans. While not completely victorious, they did manage to secure key concessions, most notably the right of freedpeople to testify in court, if only in cases where they were directly involved. A few moderates took the next step, including political rights under the rubric of universal rights. But many found the intellectual leap difficult. Unable to see African Americans as anything but helpless dependents requiring constant supervision, white moderates felt far more comfortable advocating the political interests of common white men. As the editor of the *Wilmington Herald* wrote in 1865: "The freed negro is not a citizen in the full sense of the term." Instead, he is "a denizen ... having only the right to hold property, do business, and being at the same time subject to criminal taxation, and other laws, and without the privilege of voting or eligibility to office." Even William W. Holden, who would become one of the state's most fiery Republican leaders, initially opposed granting suffrage to black men.[12]

Like the *Wilmington Herald* editor, most moderates placed suffrage in a different category from civil rights, defining it as a privilege that men earned by meeting certain standards of responsible citizenship, generally property ownership and education. Although drawing heavily on the hierarchical particularism of Jonathan Worth and Thomas Ruffin, they did part ways from conservatives in the emphasis on individual merit, which implied that African-American men might eventually meet the criteria for suffrage, if they applied themselves. The same *Wilmington Herald* editorial that opposed universal suffrage, for instance, also urged the state legislators "to do every thing that they can to elevate this race, and the time *may* come, when, by giving indications of improvement and advancement, their claims for the right of suffrage will be granted by our State." Even then, those who admitted this possibility often pushed it so far in the distant future that they effectively limited the vote to white men or, as some quietly added, to propertied white men. "In our opinion" the editor of the *Herald* assured his readers, black male suffrage "cannot occur during the present, or perhaps the next generation, and consequently we need not give ourselves any uneasiness about it." Moderates, in other words, arrived at the same destination as conservatives, but by a different path. Many did not find the conservatives distasteful enough to jump ship and join the Republican party, but those who did ultimately consigned themselves to the reality of universal manhood suffrage, whether they agreed with it in principle or not.[13]

Within the North Carolina Republican party, other whites, both natives and emigrés, challenged the political significance attached to the categories of independence and dependence. Turning conservative logic on its head, they argued that the denial of full civil and political rights to freedpeople would make a mockery of the nation's founding principles. One of the most forceful proponents was Albion Tourgée, a northern abolitionist who moved to North Carolina after the war and worked actively for the Republican party there. Tourgée believed that the future of the newly reformed Union hung in the balance. But, unlike conservatives who believed that disaster could be averted only through the strict control of freedpeople, Tourgée maintained that the nation's survival depended on granting "equal civil and political rights upon all men, without regard to previous rank or station." William W. Coleman, a substantial North Carolina planter and antebellum legislator, underscored the point with a tragic allusion. "It can easily be shown," he thundered, "that if [freedpeople] are not to be allowed equality before the law, then the principles laid down in the Declaration of Independence upon which our government is based are words 'full of sound and fury signifying nothing.' "[14]

Implicitly linking the interests of African Americans to those of whites, these Republicans charted a new political course in which all men, regardless of race and class, stood as equals in the public sphere. Yet even the most idealistic among them could not completely transcend the influence of class and, more particularly, race. The dangers of which they spoke always seemed to threaten the nation in the abstract, leaving unacknowledged the hazards that freed people alone faced. Furthermore, the focus on the nation's well-being allowed white Republicans to avoid confronting their thoughts about freedpeople's fitness for public governance. Behind their color-blind rhetoric, many white Republicans clearly held reservations about African Americans in general. Even those whites most ardently committed to universal manhood suffrage and biracial political cooperation often depicted blacks as children in need of guidance and as passive recipients of rights they did not yet fully understand or deserve.[15]

The politics of North Carolinian Benjamin Hedrick capture the internal contradictions of Republicans who preached racial equality in theory, but found it difficult to accept in practice. Before the war, Hedrick had opposed the extension of slavery into the territories, a position so unpopular that he resigned his professorship at the University of North Carolina and left the state. With reasoning similar to that of Thomas Jefferson, whom he claimed as an intellectual mentor, Hedrick maintained that slavery corrupted the nation, jeopardizing its republican institutions and damaging the prospects of white freeholders. He did not concern himself with the plight of slaves, who, if anything, only contributed to society's degeneration through their presence. After emancipation, however, Hedrick advocated the extension of full civil and political rights to African Americans as free people. Given " 'Republican Theory,' " he wrote to Jonathan Worth in 1867, "it is a political fallacy to deprive any class of full franchise." Yet he still questioned the actual practicality of granting the vote to a people he considered socially irresponsible and politically ignorant, admitting that it may well be "inexpedient and injurious." In fact, Hedrick ultimately found it impossible to reconcile his deep distrust of African Americans with his theoretical principles. Some of the time theory prevailed, for "as soon as you take the ground of political expediency almost anything may be defended, for instance monarchy, despotism, aristocracy, or any other system that has its admirers and supporters." Having taken this uncompromising stand, Hedrick then fell back on expediency himself: "If it shall be found on fair trial that universal suffrage is not conductive to the public weal, it can then be changed." With the doctrine of racial inferiority and dependency firmly ingrained in the minds of so many white Republicans, it was difficult for even the most progressive among them to include African Americans unconditionally within the rubric of universal rights, let alone accept them as equals.[16]

Most African Americans harbored no such doubts.[17] They believed freedom guaranteed their independence, the establishment and maintenance of which required full civil and political rights. As a group of black men from Goldsboro, North Carolina, wrote: "From a live-long experience as slaves of the men who now administer the laws, we cannot convince ourselves that equal justice will be meted out to us by them; but, on the contrary, we have in a year's experience of freedom, every reason to believe that without the freedmen's bureau, or some similar protection, we shall not be permitted to live even in peace, and our condition thus becomes really worse than when we were slaves and did not expect justice." Although cautiously phrased, theirs was no small claim. These freedmen challenged the idea that their interests coincided with the men who employed them. Since their employers could not represent them and the Freedmen's Bureau was a temporary measure, only one logical solution remained: they should be granted the public power necessary to defend themselves. Others were even more direct. At a mass meeting in New Bern, freedpeople denounced "the many atrocities committed upon our people in almost every section of our country" and "the enforcement of the old code of slave laws" that denied them equal protection under the law. Without public power, their lives would be impossible: Although "our condition has been changed from slavery to that of freedom, we are not insensible as to how unprotected and insecure we are left in the perpetuation of that freedom, without the elective franchise to sustain it."[18]

Black leaders and freedpeople themselves often framed such demands explicitly in the language of universal rights. In so doing, they consciously invoked a long tradition of protest that reached back to the Revolutionary period, when slaves and free blacks appropriated the rhetoric of the time to support their own struggle for freedom. Afterwards, black abolitionists continued to insist that the principles animating the nation's revolt knew no racial bounds, but justified the destruction of slavery and ultimately the extension of full civil and political rights to all free blacks as well. "We see no recognition of color or race in the organic law of the land," a black delegation headed by Frederick Douglass informed President Andrew Johnson in 1866: "It knows no privileged class, and therefore we cherish the hope that we may be fully enfranchised."[19]

In the postemancipation South, freedpeople as well as free blacks wielded these ideas in their efforts to counter efforts to limit or completely deny freedpeople's access to public power. Defining the public interest narrowly, conservatives and even some white Republicans feared that the inclusion of freedpeople within the body politic would introduce conflict into the public arena and endanger social order. For them, "universal" rights extended only to a particular group, delimited by race, gender, and often class as well. In response, African Americans used the political symbols of the nation's founding to pull at the boundaries of universality and, more boldly, to argue that attention to their well-being served the public interest. Quoting directly from the Declaration of Independence, the delegates to an 1866 North Carolina freedmen's convention rebuked the state's conservative leaders for ignoring freedpeople's rights and thus subverting the nation's founding principles. After all, they asked, was it not a white man who said that "all men are born free and equal" and "are endowed by their Creator with inalienable rights"? In the first few years of freedom, the words of the Declaration reverberated across the South, gaining authority with each repetition. Politicians, preachers, and publishers saw no need to rephrase what had already been stated so well and regularly worked pieces of the document into their speeches, sermons, and articles.[20] Like the delegates to the freedmen's convention, they held up a mirror to the nation. The reflection, they argued, told as much about the future of the country as it did about the rights of freedpeople, for the two were one and the same.

African Americans also reworked national icons. Their reading of history openly challenged conservative views by celebrating the role African Americans had played in realizing the promise of the Revolution. Where those like Jonathan Worth and Thomas Ruffin denied African Americans any place in the public arena, black speakers insisted that they had always been there. Henry McNeal Turner, a prominent leader in Georgia, included freedpeople's forefathers among the white founding fathers in a widely republished speech: "The first blood spilt in the revolution for the nation's freedom, was that of Crispus Attucks, a full blooded negro. A negro, then, was the pioneer of that liberty which the American people hold so dear." Attucks was only the first of many who had given their lives for the same principles. The delegates to an 1866 freedmen's convention in Raleigh completed the story, placing African Americans at the center of the Revolution, the War of 1812, and, finally, "in the bloody struggle through which we have just passed." If black people were now free, the delegates insisted, it was because they had fought so hard to free themselves.[21]

Within Granville County, African Americans made the Fourth of July one of their major holidays, thus connecting their own freedom to the nation's founding principles. July Fourth, the *Oxford Torchlight* moaned in 1879, "has well nigh 'played out' with the whites, and has been taken up by the colored people." According to the newspaper, the festivities lasted all day. Early in the morning, people from the surrounding countryside poured into Oxford, where they took over the downtown, decorating the streets, listening to speeches, parading, and picnicking. The Methodists served a meal in the Granville Tobacco Warehouse, while the Baptists dined in Taylor's Warehouse. According to the *Torchlight*, there was quite a "rivalry between the two factions, and each side labored hard" to attract the largest crowd. Pushed aside by African Americans who claimed this "time-honored national holiday" as their own, white Democrats stayed home.[22]

They did not do so willingly. Five years earlier, the county's black militia paraded through the streets of Oxford to celebrate emancipation day. The officers, mounted on horses and with sabers at their sides, led the rest of the uniformed company to the call of fife and drums and the admiration of an enthusiastic crowd. At the request of several white businessmen, the Democratic mayor ordered the procession to stop. The leaders of the march, however, promptly initiated a suit to test the legality of the mayor's order. They emerged victorious. One year later, the North Carolina Supreme Court upheld their right to peaceable assembly and delivered a pointed lesson in postemancipation civics to Oxford officials. "In a popular government like ours," the court declared, "the laws allow great latitude to public demonstrations, whether political, social or moral." To condemn this assembly would set a dangerous precedent that might end "all public celebrations, however innocent or commendable the purpose." It seems only fitting that a parade honoring emancipation provided the vehicle through which African Americans in Granville County demanded recognition of their rights.[23]

As this case suggests, the idea that rights adhered in the individual swept aside racial and class distinctions that were so central to the ideology of those who sought to define freedpeople as something less than full citizens. "If the abstract right to vote inheres in every citizen," asked Benjamin Wood, a prominent white abolitionist quoted in the *Wilmington Herald*, "why not in the native black man?" Echoing these sentiments, an assembly of freedpeople in Alabama announced: "We claim exactly *the same rights, privileges and immunities as are enjoyed by white men*," for "the law no longer knows white nor black, but simply men." Or, as Henry McNeal Turner asked in the same speech that celebrated African-American contributions to the task of nation building, "Was it then because we were not really human that we have not been recognized as a member of the nation's family?" If so, then the proposition was easily refuted, since at the level of "bones, muscles, nerves, veins, organs and functions" all men were clearly the same.[24] This idea of equality actually assumed the presence of racial and class difference: all people should have the same rights even though they did not occupy the same social position or share the same cultural heritage. According to the final stanza of a poem that also appeared in the *Augusta Colored American*:

Fair Afric's *free* and valiant sons
Shall join with Europe's band
To celebrate in varied tongues
Our *free* and happy land.[25]

As the polity expanded to embrace the "varied tongues" of those from different racial and class positions, the "valiant sons" of Africa would stand shoulder to shoulder with their brothers from Europe.

The emphasis on "valiant sons," however, suggests that other differences retained their importance. If all men resembled each other and all women resembled each other, men and women still remained different at the level of "bones, muscles, nerves, veins, organs and functions." Depicting men as courageous defenders of their families' interests, Henry McNeal Turner underscored the importance of this role by portraying "our ladies" as the sexual prey of white slaveholders. The rights of freedom gave black men new power that enabled them to remove the women and children in their families from the exploitative grasp of whites. Black women, by implication, would also experience a new measure of control over their bodies and their lives, but through the protective efforts of their menfolk. Indeed, many African-American leaders referred to political rights in terms of their manhood. Demanding the vote for black men, James T. Rapier, a Republican congressman from Alabama, insisted that "nothing short of a complete acknowledgement of my manhood will satisfy me." As we have seen, African Americans and poor whites did not define the roles of men and women in the same way as more affluent whites. But even those who went so far as to advocate equal civil and political rights for women rarely challenged the basic importance attached to gender difference.[26]

In a struggle that reached back across the nineteenth century, first class and then race, although far less completely, ceased to define which men could legitimately exercise public power. In neutralizing the importance of these differences, reformers advanced a literal definition of manhood rights, emphasizing the commonalities among men. Nonetheless, assuming the mantle of manhood was no easy task, particularly for African-American men, whose proximity to slavery made them appear as perpetual minors in the eyes of many whites. To counter these perceptions, black leaders and their white supporters offered up their military service, their possession of taxable property, and their labor in building the South as proof of their masculinity. Whether in the battlefields or the tobacco fields, black men had worked as courageously and as diligently as white men to support their country.[27]

The presence of families, however, provided the most inclusive defense of manhood and the most compelling justification for full civil and political rights. Regardless of race or class, men could acquire responsibility for dependents as heads of households. All men thus shed the vestiges of dependency and assumed independent status through their essential difference from women, who relied on men for support and protection. Indeed, all men deserved access to public power simply because they were men. Summoning existing laws governing domestic relations that linked familial obligations to public rights, this logic carried great power. After all, the same body of law that required heads of households to support their families also granted them the civil rights and political power necessary to do so. Similarly, women could make claims on the state as dependent wives and daughters. African Americans thus harnessed a traditional definition of the household to serve radical ends. They placed the institution that had once buttressed slavery and defined African Americans as dependents at the center of their efforts to create a very different social order.

African-American men often began their demands for political rights with the same refrain used by the delegates to the 1865 freedmen's convention: "Our first and engrossing concern . . . is how we may provide shelter and an honorable subsistence for ourselves and families." With it, they asserted their position as independent men and affirmed their status as full citizens in a way that they had never been able to use before. "We wish to work and take care of our selfs and familys and benefit the Contary all we can and live upright just and honorable," wrote a group of men from Gates County. "How can we," they asked, when "we hav . . . no protection and no privilege?"[28] In other words, how could they without the civil rights and the political power necessary to enforce recognition of their rights?

In 1865, civil rights and the vote seemed sufficient. "What we want," demanded the editor of the *Raleigh Journal of Freedom* in the fall of that year, "is law to protect our homes, our families and all that is dear to us. When brutal ruffians stalk into our peaceful dwelling[s], insulting our wives and daughters, we want law to bring those ruffians to justice, and the right to call black men to the witness stand to testify against them.... When we have these rights, and not till then, will justice have been vindicated."[29]

Not coincidentally, the extension of civil and political rights prompted another round of violent actions against African Americans. The hooded vigilantes struck at the structural foundations of black power: their households. Bursting in on families in the dead of night, the Klan destroyed their belongings, burned their houses, and then beat, raped, tortured, and murdered their members. During the 1868 elections, the Klan raged with particular intensity in Granville County. "The kukulks klan," Moses M. Hester, Joseph Coley, and Jacob Winston wrote in desperation to Governor Holden, "is shooting out famlys and beeting them notoriously we do not know what to do." Elaborating on the situation, another group claimed that the violence "is geting to be a General thing": "on thursdy night last they went to a Colored mans house and Got him out and Beet him [illegible word] and beet his wife and cut her Dress open and tied her to a tree then told Them if ever they told it or told who it was They would kill them. They then went to another ones house and comence tarring [tearing] the top of his house off... [they] Got hold of his wife... and she Got Loose and ran and they shot her In the back and by [the] side of the face and she now lies in a low state of helth and a Few nights ago they went to a nother colored Mans house and treeted him the same." In this way, vigilantes dealt a double blow. The terror might keep African-American men from voting. If not, the Klan still scored a victory, because the vote meant little as long as black men lacked power to protect their families.[30]

Some African Americans began to doubt that the vote or civil rights would ever amount to anything. A group from Halifax County, for instance, decided to throw in the towel and make a new home for themselves in Liberia. Writing Congressman Elihu Washburne for financial assistance, the men who represented the group explained that they had endured material deprivation and physical violence only to conclude that their hopes for a bare subsistence were illusory: "Some of us have not been paid for our work for two year back & they will not pay us for our work.... The blackman haves his family and feed himself & ... [he] must Starve next winter he cannot live." At this point, they no longer wanted the land "because it is poluted with our blood." In a place where compensation for their labor came in the form of starving families and the likelihood of being "shot like mad dogs," they could never be men. Instead, these black men of Halifax County wished "to get home to our forefathers land." As the proliferation of emigration societies across the South suggests, many other African Americans arrived at a similar decision.[31]

The vast majority, however, determined to stay and fight. By the 1870s, the struggle had acquired a distinctly militant cast. In 1876, for instance, John W. Johnson wrote to Republican governor Curtis Brogden requesting arms for his volunteer militia of sixty African-American men. "Those that have Guns," he explained, "had to take their hard earned dimes and dollars to buy them with owing to the hardness of times there are but few that have purchased guns. We are very anxious for Guns and would like to have improved guns if there is any possible chance for us to get them." African Americans in Granville County organized a similar company. The reports of brutal racial violence that filled every Reconstruction governor's correspondence leave little question as to why these men felt the need to arm themselves.[32] To the extent that justice actually was vindicated, the daily struggles of African Americans contributed as much as Johnson's guns. These people not only worked to realize the principles set down in law but also aimed to revise their content. In this arena, it was women like Bella Newton who often took the lead.

Notes

1   Quote from *State v. Noblin*, 1870, Criminal Action Papers, Granville County. Edwards, "Sexual Violence, Gender, Reconstruction, and the Extension of Patriarchy." See also Clinton, "Reconstructing Freedwomen" and "Bloody Terrain"; and Rosen, "Interracial Rape and the Politics of Reconstruction."

2   Hamilton, *The Correspondence of Jonathan Worth*, 2: 1082; Stafford quoted in Escott, *Many Excellent People*, p. 22. For references to the "better class," see, for instance, Hamilton, *The Correspondence of Jonathan Worth*, 2:1257. The attitude was widespread among conservatives; see, for instance, Escott, *Many Excellent People*, pp. 85–112; McCurry, *Masters of Small Worlds*, pp. 247–51; and Olsen, "An Incongruous Presence," p. 167.

3   For these racialized images, see Jordan, *White over Black*. See also Fields, *Slavery and Freedom on the Middle Ground*; and T. Holt, " 'An Empire over the Mind' " and *The Problem of Freedom*.

4   Quotes from Hamilton, *The Papers of Thomas Ruffin*, 4:63; and Hamilton, *The Correspondence of Jonathan Worth*, 2:1156. Ruffin also argued that the Constitutional Convention had no power because it had been called by military authority in violation of the existing state constitution and the powers vested in the people, since many voters had been disqualified under the president's provisions; see Hamilton, *The Papers of Thomas Ruffin*, 4:62–71. Edward Conigland was so taken with Ruffin's arguments against the constitution that he wrote immediately asking Ruffin for permission to submit the letter for duplication in the *Wilmington Journal* and later sent it to the *Raleigh Sentinel* as well; see Hamilton, *The Papers of Thomas Ruffin*, 4:72–3, 77–8. For opposition to the apportionment system, see Hamilton, *The Papers of Thomas Ruffin*, 4:61–2. For arguments critical of the conservative position, see *North Carolina Standard*, 30 May 1866, 8 Aug. 1866, and 22 Aug. 1866. For an overview of the debate in North Carolina, see Escott, *Many Excellent People*, 105–12. See also Perman, *Reunion without Compromise*.

5   Quotes on Worth's racial views from Hamilton, *The Correspondence of Jonathan Worth*, 2:875, 1095; and on the Cooper-Daniel case from Gov. Jonathan Worth to Pres. Andrew Johnson, 31 Dec. 1867, 9, Worth, Governor's Letter Book, 1867–68. See the introduction for an extended analysis of the Cooper-Daniel case. For the intransigence of North Carolina conservatives under Johnson's Reconstruction plan, see, for instance, Escott, *Many Excellent People*, pp. 85–135; Evans, *Ballots and Fence Rails*, 61–102; and H. Raper, *William W. Holden*, 59–85.

6   Quotes from Hamilton, *The Papers of Thomas Ruffin*, 4:63; and *Raleigh Sentinel*, 29 Aug. 1865. See also Hamilton, *The Papers of Thomas Ruffin*, 4:76–7, 132–4; and Escott, *Many Excellent People*, pp. 106–9, 113–35. In fact, Ruffin was completely incapable of grasping the idea that freedpeople were separate from their masters' households. He argued against apportionment on a white basis, maintaining that all blacks should be included for the same reason that white women, and children were. Although permanently disfranchised, African Americans, white women, and white children "are as much bound by the laws that may be made and therefore, as much interested in them as the white men." Yet, while white women had delegates "who are their neighbors, know their wants and condition and sympathise with them both in their wants and wishes" to represent their interests, African Americans did not. Including them in the apportionment would give former slaveholders, who knew the interests of their black neighbors best, the ability to represent freedpeople in the same way that men represented women. Hamilton, *The Papers of Thomas Ruffin*, 4:64.

7   Quotes from Hamilton, *The Correspondence of Jonathan Worth*, 2:1156, 860. Others echoed these fears; see, for instance, Hamilton, *The Correspondence of Jonathan Worth*, 2:1045. Escott, in *Many Excellent People*, underscores elite white distrust of both poor whites and blacks as well as their enduring fear of biracial alliances in his analysis of nineteenth-century North Carolina politics. See also Goodwyn, *The Democratic Promise*; Kousser, *The Shaping of Southern Politics*; Robinson, "Beyond the Realm of Social Consensus"; and Woodward, *Origins of the New South*.

8   Hamilton, *The Correspondence of Jonathan Worth*, 2:1004, 1048; see also 2:1215. One of Worth's correspondents called a Republican leader one of the "*blackest* radicals" in the state, referring not to his skin color, but to his politics (2:953).

9   For warnings that conservatives would provoke the North's wrath, see *North Carolina Standard*, 26 Sept. 1866 and 3 Oct. 1866. Conservatives refused to heed the advice of even longtime friends. Writing from Washington, DC, Benjamin F. Hedrick, a confidant of Governor Worth, advised him of the rising antagonism toward conservative policies; see, for instance, Hamilton, *The Correspondence of Jonathan Worth*, 2:903, See also Escott, *Many Excellent People*, pp. 104–5.

10   For evidence of biracial collaboration during and immediately after the war, see Edwards, *Gendered Strife and Confusion: The Political Culture Of Reconstruction*, chapter 4, note 60.

11   *Wilmington Herald*, 10 June 1865, reprinted from the *Raleigh Progress*. For the persistence of tensions among whites in postwar North Carolina politics, see Escott, *Many Excellent People*, pp. 136–70; and Olsen, "An Incongruous Presence." See also Hyman, *The Anti-Redeemers*. William W. Holden was particularly critical of elite white conservative rule and published numerous articles on the subject as editor of the *North Carolina Standard*.

12   Quotes from *Wilmington Herald*, 9 June 1865. The *Raleigh Sentinel*'s reports of the legislative debates over the Black Code give the moderates' position. See also R. Alexander, *North Carolina Faces the Freedman*, pp. 39–51; and T. B. Wilson, *The Black Codes of the South*, pp. 96–115. For moderate support for the notion of equal civil rights and an expanded social role for African Americans, see, for instance, *Raleigh Sentinel*, 8 Aug. 1865; *North Carolina Standard*, 14 Feb. 1866, 10 Oct. 1866; and *Wilmington Herald*, 17 July 1865, 30 Jan. 1866, 6 Mar. 1866. The *Wilmington Herald*, however, remained opposed to enfranchising blacks; see, for instance, 8 July 1865 and 27 July 1865. For Holden's initial opposition to universal manhood suffrage, see his address to the 1866 freedmen's convention in the *North Carolina Standard*, 17 Oct. 1866; see also 3 Oct. 1866 and 10 Oct. 1866. In the 1880s, he renounced his support of civil and political rights for African Americans.

13   Quotes from *Wilmington Herald*, 9 June 1865. This distinction between civil and political rights, common to both the North and the South, came up regularly in debates over the status of freedpeople; see, for instance, *North Carolina Standard*, 14 Feb. 1866; and *Wilmington Herald*, 17 July 1865. Moderates assumed that suffrage should be "earned" through intelligence or possession of property; see *Raleigh Sentinel*, 8 Aug. 1865; *Wilmington Herald*, 14 July 1865; *Raleigh Journal of Freedom*, 30 Sept. 1865. For similar debates within the national Republican party, see Foner, *Reconstruction*, pp. 239–61. For white North Carolina Republicans' tenuous commitment to racial equality, see Olsen, "An Incongruous Presence," p. 165.

14   Quotes from Tourgée, *A Fool's Errand*, p. 166; and *Raleigh Journal of Freedom*, 7 Oct. 1865. See also Olsen, *A Carpethagger's Crusade;* and Tourgée, *The Invisible Empire*, pp. 15–20. For "radical" Republicans generally, see Evans, *Ballots and Fence Rails*, pp. 105–27; and Foner, *Reconstruction*, pp. 228–39.

15   These points are most fully elaborated in T. Holt, " 'An Empire over the Mind' " and *The Problem of Freedom*.

16   Hamilton, *The Correspondence of Jonathan Worth*, 2:902, 903. For Hedrick's position on slavery, see Hamilton, "Benjamin Sherwood Hedrick." Hamilton, a conservative apologist and racial reactionary, approves of Hedrick's opposition to slavery precisely because it was "not based upon moral grounds nor did the solicitude for the negro have anything to do with it." Rather, Hedrick and others like him thought "the wrong of slavery was not to the slave, but to the non-slaveholder" (5–6). See also Powell, *Dictionary of North Carolina Biography*, 3:95.

17   There were, however, important differences in strategy among African Americans. Conservatives, for instance, advocated hard work and cooperation with southern whites, while shunning political rights, property redistribution, and other more militant claims that radical leaders supported. Many black leaders fell out somewhere between the two poles, with moderates emphasizing civil and political rights, but not the economic issues supported by poorer blacks in rural areas. For discussions of these issues, see R. Alexander, *North Carolina Faces the Freedmen*, pp. 15–20; Foner, *Reconstruction*, pp. 110–19; T. Holt, *Black over White*; and Reidy, *From Slavery to Agrarian Capitalism*, pp. 179–80, 192–9, 208–9.

18   Quotes from *North Carolina Faces the Freedmen*, p. 80; and *Raleigh Semi-Weekly Record*, 2 Sept. 1865. The editor of the *Nashville Colored Tennessean* echoed these sentiments, arguing that true freedom was impossible without the public power to protect it; reprinted in the *Raleigh Journal of Freedom*, 30 Sept. 1865.

19 *North Carolina Standard*, 14 Feb. 1866. For black abolitionists, see Horton, "Double Consciousness" in *Free People of Color;* Litwack and Meier, *Black Leaders of the Nineteenth Century;* Martin, *The Mind of Frederick Douglass;* and Nash, *Race and Revolution*, pp. 57–87, 167–201. Frederick Douglass, who believed that the emphasis on racial differences obscured the inclusive brotherhood of man implied in the spirit of natural rights, worked fully within the ideology of universal humanism, as Waldo Martin has termed it. Other black leaders placed more importance on the distinctive ways race had shaped the history and identity of African Americans. But the basic principles of universal rights still influenced their arguments, even those who advocated emigration. However much race mattered in their social, economic, and political agendas, they still maintained that all people deserved not just freedom from slavery but also the right to determine the course of their own destiny and the shape of the society in which they lived. Few white abolitionists envisioned the kind of racial equality proposed by black leaders, but they too grounded their opposition to slavery in the ideology of universal rights. Yet white abolitionists tended to see grateful, younger siblings who would then follow the lead of their white patrons, rather than claim their own voice and participate on equal footing in the nation's social and political institutions. See C. Hall, "Missionary Stories" and "Competing Masculinities" in *White, Male, and Middle Class*. Nonetheless, the image of brothers and sisters carried very different implications than the dominant southern one of parent and child.

20 Quoted in R. Alexander, *North Carolina Faces the Freedmen*, 91. In North Carolina and across the South, freedpeople used phrases from the Declaration of Independence and imagery from the Revolution to carry their demands for racial equity. The delegates to the 1865 freedmen's convention hailed emancipation as the culmination of the nation's purpose, describing it as "a triumph of just principles, a practical assertion of the fundamental truths laid down in the great charter of Republican liberty, the Declaration of Independence." See *Raleigh Journal of Freedom*, 7 Oct. 1865. In its previous issue, 30 Sept. 1865, the newspaper invoked the Declaration to justify full political rights: "If the Declaration of Independence was not based on a lie," then "one man or class *can't* legislate for another." Often, a copy of the Declaration even graced Union League meetings; see Foner, *Reconstruction*, p. 283. See also Foner, *Freedom's Lawmakers*, pp. 38, 84, 128, 137.

21 Quotes from the *Augusta Colored American*, 13 Jan. 1866; and R. Alexander, *North Carolina Faces the Freedmen*, p. 91. For similar renderings of African Americans' place in history, see Foner, *Freedom's Lawmakers*, pp. 36, 39, 40, 60, 106, 108, 110, 156, 201. See also Foner, *Reconstruction*, p. 288.

22 *Oxford Torchlight*, 8 July 1879. For Fourth of July celebrations in black communities elsewhere in the South, see Reidy, *From Slavery to Agrarian Capitalism*, p. 179.

23 *State* v. *Hughes* et al., 1874, Criminal Action Papers, Granville County.

24 Quotes from *Wilmington Herald*, 8 July 1865; Foner, *Reconstruction*, p. 288; Turner quoted in *Augusta Colored American*, 13 Jan. 1866. Black legislators' opposition to measures disfranchising former Confederates demonstrates their commitment to an inclusive definition of universal rights; see Balanoff, "Negro Legislators in North Carolina," pp. 32–3; Foner, *Reconstruction*, p. 324; Hume, "Negro Delegates," 141–2; and Perman, *The Road to Redemption*, pp. 36–7. See also Foner, *Freedom's Lawmakers*, pp. 80, 131, 138, 176, 208, 231.

25 Poem quoted in a. Alexander, *Ambiguous Lives*, p. 140.

26 Quotes from Hodes, "The Sexualization of Reconstruction Politics," p. 404; and *Augusta Colored American*, 13 Jan. 1866. For similar statements linking manhood and political rights, see Foner, *Freedom's Lawmakers*, pp. 18, 22, 91, 137, 191, 215. First in the abolitionist movement and later during Reconstruction, many black women, in particular, did work to include themselves in the universal brotherhood of man, arguing for greater public rights. They were joined by a few of their male counterparts, most prominently Frederick Douglass. A few southern African American leaders, including Abraham H. Galloway and James E. O'Hara from North Carolina, supported women's rights. Even for those who supported women's rights, however, the issue remained tied to the movement for racial equality. In both the North and the South, the security of racial privilege allowed middle-class white women to see gender as something distinct from race and led them to separate from the men of their communities to agitate for their own rights. Such a strategy made less sense to African-American women because their own well-being so clearly rose and fell with that of the race as a whole.

This did not mean, however, that black women remained silent on these issues. As Gilmore shows in *Gender and Jim Crow*, black women actually began mobilizing for equal rights and the vote in North Carolina before white women. But in doing so, they were careful not to jeopardize the political and economic goals of their menfolk. See also Carby, *Reconstructing Womanhood*; Higginbotham, *Righteous Discontent*; Horton, "Freedom's Yoke"; and Martin, *The Mind of Frederick Douglass*. For James E. O'Hara and Abraham H. Galloway, see Foner, *Freedom's Lawmakers*, pp. 81–2, 164.

27 For references to taxes and military service, see *Raleigh Journal of Freedom*, 30 Sept. 1865, 7 Oct. 1865; and *Raleigh Semi-Weekly Record*, 2 Sept. 1865. See also Foner, *Freedom's Lawmakers*, pp. 60, 106, 110, 156 for military service; 36, 40, 201 for labor; and 18 for taxes.

28 Quotes from *Raleigh Journal of Freedom*, 7 Oct. 1865; and R. Alexander, *North Carolina Faces the Freedmen*, 102. See also Foner, *Freedom's Lawmakers*, 88; Petition of the Freedmen in the Trent Settlement to Thaddeus Stevens, in Padgett, "Reconstruction Letters from North Carolina: Part 1," 185–7.

29 Quote from *Raleigh Journal of Freedom*, 14 Oct. 1865.

30 Quotes from Moses M. Hester et al. to William W. Holden, 9 Oct. 1868, and Silas L. Curtis et al. to William W. Holden, 11 Oct. 1868, both in Holden Papers. Hodes, in "The Sexualization of Reconstruction Politics," also argues that the Klan targeted households, raped women, and sexually mutilated black men specifically to "unman" black men and thus push them out of the political arena. Contemporary and secondary accounts not only testify to the role of the Klan and other vigilante actions against African Americans in destroying the Republican party but also emphasize that it sought to do so by targeting and destroying black households; see Evans, *Ballots and Fence Rails*, pp. 69–73; Olsen, "The Ku Klux Klan"; *Testimony Taken by the Joint Select Committee to Inquire into the Condition of Affairs in the Late Insurrectionary States*; Tourgée, *The Invisible Empire*; and Trelease, *White Terror*.

31 Petition by thirty-four Halifax County freedmen to Elihu Benjamin Washburne, in Padgett, "Reconstruction Letters from North Carolina: Part 4," 395–6. For African-American emigration from the South, see Cohen, *At Freedom's Edge*; Painter, *Exodusters*; and Reidy, *From Slavery to Agrarian Capitalism*, pp. 181–84, 230–32.

32 John W. Johnson to Curtis H. Brogden, 1876, Curtis H. Brogden, Governor's Papers, North Carolina Department of Archives and History, Raleigh NCDAH. For Granville County's black military company, see *State v. Hughes et al.*, 1874, Criminal Action Papers, Granville County; and *Oxford Torchlight*, 1 Apr. 1879. For black militias elsewhere, see Evans, *Ballots and Fence Rails*, pp. 101–2, 138–9; Foner, *Freedom's Lawmakers*, pp. 119, 131, 223; and Reidy, *From Slavery to Agrarian Capitalism*, pp. 205, 219.

Questions to consider

- How were the terms "privilege" and "protection" used by North Carolina conservatives? What did the distinction between them imply?

- What does Edwards's work suggest about the complicated intersection of blacks and poor whites during Reconstruction?

- Thinking back to Part XI, how did ideas about gender shape the political language and policy of Reconstruction in North Carolina?

- Additionally, how did conceptions of families shape conceptions of politics after the Civil War? In what ways do "family values" continue to affect the electoral discourse?

Chapter 33

Reconstruction: Primary Sources

Letter to Sarah Shaw

Lydia Maria Child

The ending of slavery in 1865 represented the realization of a lifelong dream for abolitionist activist Lydia Maria Child. Yet Child could not help but be disturbed by what she saw happening in the South in the year following Appomattox. In this letter to Sarah Blake Sturgis Shaw, the militant abolitionist and mother of the slain Robert Gould Shaw (who figures prominently in the 1989 film *Glory*), Child surveys the political situation and presents her views. How compelling do you regard her assertion that President Johnson is mistaken to continue the course of Abraham Lincoln?

Lydia Maria Child, "To Sarah Shaw," in *Lydia Maria Child: Selected Letters, 1817–1880*, eds., Milton Meltzer, Patricia G. Holland, and Francine Krasno (Amherst: University of Massachusetts Press, 1982), p. 463

Wayland, Sep. 7'th, 1866.

Darling Sarah,

[. . .]

You ask me what I would have Congress do. In the first place, I think they ought to have done something to diminish the inflated currency of the country, which is having such an unsettling and demoralizing influence. In the next place, I was vexed and grieved, beyond measure, that they voted *themselves* such a large additional salary. They couldn't have put a worse weapon into the hands of Johnson's party; besides, I hold it to be wrong in itself, and dangerous as a precedent, for men to vote how much they themselves shall take out of the public treasury. Thirdly, they ought to have *repealed* the power to grant amnesty, with which they endowed Abraham Lincoln.[1] *Lincoln* had a *good* motive for offering amnesty; for he wanted to use it as a means of *winning over* rebels. But when the war was ended, by their defeat, there was no longer any *good* use to be made of amnesty. Andy Johnson has made use of it, not to lure rebels back to loyalty, but to encourage traitors in persistent treason; and Congress have done nothing to stop his doing it. They ought to have confiscated the lands of rich rebels and opened the way for freedmen to procure portions of the land on easy terms.[2] Under Johnson policy, the old slave holding nabobs hold their thousands of acres, and will not let the freedmen have an acre. If the lands had been confiscated, and sold at low prices, it would also have done more than anything else to gain over the poor whites to the side of the US; and the sale would have helped considerably toward paying the national debt, while it would at the same time have done justice to two much wronged classes. However, I stand by Congress, because they have done a great deal that is good, and because there is nothing else to stand by.

Was there ever such a braying Ass as Johnson? I think that wily fox, Seward encourages him to bray, on purpose to disgust the people, and so give himself a chance to saddle and ride the new party. To think of a man like H. W. Beecher lending himself to the unprincipled schemes of that tippling traitor, that boozy boaster, that devilish demagogue![3] What *can* be his motive? I don't think he is "one of the *devils* unaccountables," but he is certainly one of the *Lord's* unaccountables.

Notes

1 Both Lincoln and Johnson had offered full pardon to all but a few Confederates. Early in 1866 Congress adopted a Reconstruction program that took away Johnson's emergency powers and made Congress supreme in this matter.

2 The abolitionists urged a land confiscation policy, but Congress, the president, and the army would all fail to develop a sound land policy for the blacks. By the end of 1867 the chance to put through land reform in the South had faded.

3 Radical abolitionists by now were squarely opposed to Johnson's Reconstruction policies, but some moderate Republicans who feared risking a split in their party still tagged along with the president.

The Freedmen's Bureau

Margaret Mitchell

Margaret Mitchell (1900–49) was literally and figuratively a child of the South. Her 1936 novel *Gone with the Wind* – a book that is at least as much about Reconstruction as it is the Civil War – remains the most famous book written by an American in the twentieth century, and the film version is arguably the most beloved of all time. Significantly, the only story that could challenge its appeal – the one it supplanted, in fact – was Harriet Beecher Stowe's *Uncle Tom's Cabin*. Mitchell accomplished what Stowe's Southern contemporaries could not provide: a compelling alternative view of the region that made Southern whites the victims, not the perpetrators, of injustice. And despite the efforts of some very determined people in the academy and elsewhere, Mitchell's view continues to inform – perhaps even dominate – the national understanding of the war and its aftermath. Consider, as you read, what Mitchell's strategies are here and in what ways they are effective.

Margaret Mitchell, *Gone with the Wind* (New York: Macmillan, 1936), pp. 655–6.

[. . .] freedom became a never-ending picnic, a barbecue every day of the week, a carnival of idleness and theft and insolence. Country negroes flocked into the cities, leaving the rural districts without labor to make the crops. Atlanta was crowded with them and still they came by the hundreds, lazy and dangerous as a result of the new doctrines being taught them. Packed into squalid cabins, smallpox, typhoid and tuberculosis broke out among them. Accustomed to the care of their mistresses when they were ill in slave days, they did not know how to nurse themselves or their sick. Relying upon their masters in the old days to care for their aged and their babies, they now had no sense of responsibility for their helpless. And the Bureau was far too interested in political matters to provide the care the plantation owners had once given.

Abandoned negro children ran like frightened animals about the town until kind-hearted white people took them into their kitchens to raise. Aged country darkies, deserted by their children, bewildered and panic stricken in the bustling town, sat on the curbs and cried to the ladies who passed: "Mistis, please Ma'm, write mah old Marster down in Fayette County dat Ah's up hyah. He'll come tek dis ole nigger home agin. 'Fo Gawd, Ah done got nuff of dis freedom!"

The Freedmen's Bureau, overwhelmed by the numbers who poured in upon them, realized too late a part of the mistake and tried to send them back to their former owners. They told the negroes that if they would go back, they would go as free workers, protected by written contracts specifying wages by the day. The old darkies went back to the plantations gladly, making a heavier burden than ever on the poverty-stricken planters who had not the heart to turn them out, but the young ones remained in Atlanta. They did not want to be workers of any kind, anywhere. Why work when the belly is full?

For the first time in their lives the negroes were able to get all the whisky they might want. In slave days, it was something they never tasted except at Christmas, when each one received a "drap" along with his gift. Now they had not only the Bureau agitators and the Carpetbaggers urging them on, but the incitement of whisky as well, and outrages were inevitable. Neither life nor property was safe from them and the white people, unprotected by law, were terrorized. Men were insulted on the streets by drunken blacks, houses and barns were burned at night, horses and cattle and chickens stolen in broad daylight, crimes of all varieties were committed and few of the perpetrators were brought to justice.

But these ignominies and dangers were as nothing compared with the peril of white women, many bereft by the war of male protection, who lived alone in the outlying districts and on lonely roads. It was the large number of outrages on women and the ever-present fear for the safety of their wives and daughters that drove Southern men to cold and trembling fury and caused the Ku Klux Klan to spring up overnight. And it was against this nocturnal organization that the newspapers of the North cried out most loudly, never realizing the tragic necessity that brought it into being. The North wanted every member of the Ku Klux hunted down and hanged, because they had dared take the punishment of crime into their own hands at a time when the ordinary processes of law and order had been overthrown by the invaders.

Here was the astonishing spectacle of half a nation attempting, at the point of bayonet, to force upon the other half the rule of negroes, many of them scarcely one generation out of the African jungles. The vote must be given to them but it must be denied to most of their former owners. The South must be kept down and disfranchisement of the whites was one way to keep the South down. Most of those who had fought for the Confederacy, held office under it or given aid and comfort to it were not allowed to vote, had no choice in the selection of their public officials and were wholly under the power of an alien rule. Many men, thinking soberly of General Lee's words and example, wished to take the oath, become citizens again and forget the past. But they were not permitted to take it. Others who were permitted to take the oath, hotly refused to do so, scorning to swear allegiance to a government which was deliberately subjecting them to cruelty and humiliation.

Scarlett heard over and over until she could have screamed at the repetition: "I'd have taken their damned oath right after the surrender if they'd acted decent. I can be restored to the Union, but by God, I can't be reconstructed into it!"

To the Reader

Thomas Dixon

Gone with the Wind continues to be a landmark reading experience of American girls. But when Margaret Mitchell was a girl, the book she cherished was Thomas Dixon's 1905 novel The Clansman (sequel to his equally popular The Leopard's Spots published in 1902 – the title referred to a belief that African Americans, no less than other predators, were incapable of changing their essential natures). The two books were the inspiration for D. W. Griffith's Birth of a Nation (1915), a film hailed as a landmark in the history of cinema and denounced as the most racist film ever made. In this introductory note to The Clansman, Dixon explains that the Ku Klux Klan emerged amid the chaos that followed Lincoln's assassination and the aggressive designs of people like Thaddeus Stevens, the Radical Republican US Senator from Pennsylvania. How would you describe his perspective?

The Ku Klux Klan was first organized in 1866 by former Confederate General Nathan Bedford Forrest as an organization to protect the rights of white Southerners. Forrest denounced the Klan's evolution into a terrorist organization, and dissolved it (an act referred to here), but it carried on, in a secret and decentralized fashion. In the early twentieth century, the Klan revived – some attribute its resurgence to Birth of a Nation – and widened its scope to include hatred of Catholics, Jews, and immigrants, and made major incursions into Midwestern states like Indiana. How would you compare the portrayal here to the one you typically hear about?

Thomas Dixon, "To the Reader," in The Clansman (1905) n.p.

"The Clansman" is the second book of a series of historical novels planned on the Race Conflict. "The Leopard's Spots" was the statement in historical outline of the conditions from the enfranchisement of the Negro to his disfranchisement.

"The Clansman" develops the true story of the "Ku Klux Klan Conspiracy," which overturned the Reconstruction régime.

The organisation was governed by the Grand Wizard Commander-in-Chief, who lived at Memphis, Tennessee. The Grand Dragon commanded a State, the Grand Titan a Congressional District, the Grand Giant a County, and the Grand Cyclops a Township Den. The twelve volumes of Government reports on the famous Klan refer chiefly to events which occurred after 1870, the date of its dissolution.

The chaos of blind passion that followed Lincoln's assassination is inconceivable to-day. The Revolution it produced in our Government, and the bold attempt of Thaddeus Stevens to

Africanise ten great states of the American Union, read now like tales from "The Arabian Nights."

I have sought to preserve in this romance both the letter and the spirit of this remarkable period. The men who enact the drama of fierce revenge into which I have woven a double love-story are historical figures. I have merely changed their names without taking a liberty with any essential historic fact.

In the darkest hour of the life of the South, when her wounded people lay helpless amid rags and ashes under the beak and talon of the Vulture, suddenly from the mists of the mountains appeared a white cloud the size of a man's hand. It grew until its mantle of mystery enfolded the stricken earth and sky. An "Invisible Empire" had risen from the field of Death and challenged the Visible to mortal combat.

How the young South, led by the reincarnated souls of the Clansmen of Old Scotland, went forth under this cover and against overwhelming odds, daring exile, imprisonment, and a felon's death, and saved the life of a people, forms one of the most dramatic chapters in the history of the Aryan race.

THOMAS DIXON, jr.

DIXONDALE, Va., December 14, 1904.

Account of a Ku Klux Klan Visit

Emeline Brumfield

Emeline Brumfield was caring for her rheumatoid 64-year-old husband, Abraham, when the Ku Klux Klan came knocking. Naturally, she and her husband were terrified. But as this undated account suggests, some recipients of racial hatred were willing to stand their ground. In this story, at least, the would-be victim gets the last word.

Emeline Brumfeld, *We Are Your Sisters: Black Women in the Nineteenth Century*, ed. Dorothy Sterling (New York: W. W. Norton & Co., 1984), p. 349.

[...]

They came to my house some time in March. Mr. Brumfield had been lying out for four weeks; he came in all swelled up, and told me to make poultices and poultice his arms and shoulders, and I did, and he laid down, and I laid on two chairs before the fire until midnight, and then his poultice got cold, and he told me to warm it, and when I did, he says, "Now, you go and lay down." I went to bed and was woke up by the alarm of the dog. I seed persons coming up through the woods, running and I says "Ku-Klux! Ku-Klux!" and he just throwed the house 'twixt him and them and run back for the fence. They called for Brumfield, and I says, "Brumfield ain't here," and a man that had come up says, "You're a God-damned liar." I threwed open the door and says, "If I am a God-damned liar, you may come in and get him." He said "Now, you have got to tell me where he is; if you don't I will blow your God-damned brains out." I says, "Then you will have me to shoot tonight."

Part XV

Memory

Plate 17 Early Memory: (Union) flag-raising at Fort Sumter, South Carolina, April 14, 1865 — the fourth anniversary of the fall of the fort to Confederates. Civil War commemoration began even before the war ended, and has shown no sign of ebbing. (Prints and Photographs Division, Library of Congress)

Chapter 34

Quarrel Forgotten or Revolution Remembered? Reunion and Race in the Memory of the Civil War, 1875–1913

David W. Blight

One of the most prominent features on the landscape of the historical profession in the closing decades of the twentieth century was the scholarly subdiscipline that has come to be known as Memory. Scholars of Memory are less interested in describing events of the past per se than in exploring *accounts* of those events – how they were made, contested, and revised over time. As such, Memory is part of a broader current in American culture generally known as Postmodernism – a movement which, among other things, places a new emphasis on the old, in ways that range from classical accents in public architecture to the sampling of old hits in hip-hop songs.

For American historians, there has been no more fertile field for Memory than the Civil War. Indeed, you might say it has become a battleground in its own right. Yet to Yale historian David Blight, a man who has devoted his career to the collective memory of African Americans, that battle began long before the twentieth century. In fact, it began before the war even ended. In this essay, forerunner to his magisterial 2001 book *Race and Reunion: The Civil War in American Memory*, Blight traces some of the sharp – and twisted – stretches in the long road from Appomattox.

David Blight, "Quarrel Forgotten or Revolution Remembered? Reunion and Race in the Memory of the Civil War, 1875–1913," in *Union and Emancipation: Essay on Politics and Race in the Civil War Era* (Kent, OH: Kent State University Press, 1997), pp. 151–79. With permission of The Kent State University Press.

It's gonna hurt now, anything dead coming back to life hurts.
> Amy Denver to Sethe, while helping deliver Sethe's baby, somewhere along the Ohio River during the 1850s, in Toni Morrison's *Beloved*, 1987

I believe that the struggle for life is the order of the world . . . if it is our business to fight, the book
for the army is a war-song, not a hospital sketch.

Oliver Wendell Holmes, Jr., "A Soldier's Faith," 1895

Americans . . . have the most remarkable ability to alchemize all bitter truths into an innocuous but
piquant confection and to transform their moral contradictions, or public discussion of such
contradictions into a proud decoration, such as are given for heroism on the field of battle.

James Baldwin, "Many Thousands Gone," 1951

The historical memory of a people, a nation, or any aggregate evolves over time in relation to
present needs and ever-changing contexts. Societies and the groups within them remember and
use history as a source of coherence and identity, as a means of contending for power or place,
and as a means of controlling access to whatever becomes normative in society. For better and
worse, social memories – ceaselessly constructed versions of a group past – are the roots of
identity formation. In spite of all we would like to think we have learned about how *culture* is
invented, and how *heritage* is a social construct that ultimately defies fixed definition, people
jealously seek to own their pasts. The post-1989 world has demonstrated this dilemma with
tragic consequences. As historian John Gillis has aptly put it, "identities and memories are not
things we think *about*, but things we think *with*."[1] As such, the historical, in the form of social
memory, becomes political.

The study of historical memory might be defined, therefore, as the study of cultural
struggle, of contested truths, interpretations, moments, events, epochs, rituals, or even texts in
history that thresh out rival versions of the past which are in turn put to the service of the
present. As recent events in world politics, curriculum debates, national and international
commemorations and anniversaries have shown, historical memories can be severely
controlled, can undergo explosive liberation or redefinition from one generation, or even
one year, to the next. The social, political, and psychological *stakes* of historical memory can be
high. The "public" that consumes history is vast, and the marketplace turbulent. Like it
or not, we live in an era in which the impulse to teach the young to have an open *sense* of
history is not enough; that sensibility will be challenged. The pragmatic, questioning sense
of history will encounter social memory – in the classroom, at the international negotiating
table, at the movies, and in the streets. This dilemma desperately calls for trained historians
seeking evidence, demanding verification, offering reasoned explanations of events. But the
truth is that historians, and their cousins in related disciplines, are only playing one part in this
drama. As Natalie Zemon Davis and Randolph Starn, among others, have cautioned,
"whenever memory is invoked we should be asking: by whom, where, in which context, against
what?"[2]

As the 1990 PBS film series "The Civil War," by Ken Burns, demonstrated once again, one
of the most vexing questions in the formation of American historical memory has been to
understand the meaning and memory of the Civil War. The Civil War itself has long been the
object of widespread nostalgia and the subject of durable mythmaking in both North and
South. In the final episode of the film series scant attention is paid to the complicated story of
Reconstruction. The consequences of this American *Iliad* are only briefly assessed as viewers
(likely quite taken by an artistically brilliant and haunting film) are ushered from the surrender
at Appomattox through some fleeting discussion of Reconstruction politics, past Ulysses
S. Grant's final prophecy of an "era of great harmony," to Joseph E. Johnston's bareheaded
encounter with pneumonia and quick death after attending the funeral in 1891 of his former

battlefield rival, William Tecumseh Sherman, and finally to that irresistible footage of the old veterans at the 1913 and 1938 Gettysburg Blue–Gray reunions. Along the way, the narrative is punctuated by the Mississippi writer Shelby Foote informing us that the war "made *us* an *is*" (a reference to how the United States "is" rather than "are" became a common expression) and by historian Barbara Fields reminding us of William Faulkner's claim that history is "not a *was* but an *is*." The film does leave one with a sense that the Civil War was an event with lasting significance for the entire world, that the past and the present inform, even flow into, one another, and that legacies have power over us. But it is a point made as much with feeling, with music and sentiment, as it is with historical analysis. The "Blue" and the "Gray" – men out of a distant past, who were once such familiar images at American train stations and on town greens – became television images for the first time. They charmed millions of late-twentieth-century viewers, their very presence at those picturesque reunions declaring that the nation had survived all the carnage in the previous episodes. They looked at *us* reassuringly as narrator David McCullough announces: "the war was over."[3]

"The Civil War" is epic history converted into superb television. The series always moves and instructs its varied audiences; it leaves indelible sounds and images in the hearts and minds of viewers, and it teaches that the Civil War was a terrible passage through which Americans emerged forever changed. Among the broad populace of history enthusiasts, and in American and international classrooms, that film series is now the base of popular memory about the Civil War. I have used this film series with many American students, as well as with German students at the University of Munich. The reactions of German students were especially interesting. They typically asked questions like: why are there so many sunsets and moonrises in this film? Why is it so "sentimental"? Some actually brought in their own personal collections of Civil War ballad music or Negro spirituals. One student said "The Battle Hymn of the Republic" had always been one of his favorite songs along with those of Elvis Presley and Jimi Hendrix. But another German student asked me whether Americans had ever considered comparing the devastation and sense of loss in their Civil War with that of the Thirty Years' War in Europe? To the latter question, a stretched analogy, I had to answer that most Americans have never heard of the Thirty Years' War. Sometimes, perspective is all. Burns touched many heartstrings, and left some puzzlement among European viewers of his film as well.

But some of these questions go to the heart of another problem: the American tendency toward claims of exceptionalism and consensus in our historical consciousness. At the annual meeting of the Association for the Study of Negro Life and History, in Durham, North Carolina, in October 1961, John Hope Franklin reflected at length on the meaning of Civil War memory. He worried about the persistent American tendency to dissolve the conflict at the base of the war, and to constantly drum it into a "common unifying experience." Franklin characterized the semicentennial commemoration of the war (1911–15) as a time when the nation collectively found it "convenient to remember that slavery had been abolished and to forget that the doctrine of the superiority of the white race was as virulent as ever." Moreover, he characterized the centennial under way in 1961 as a "national circus," and a public cultural outpouring with a "studied lack of appreciation for the implications of the victory at Appomattox."[4] An ever troubled past flowed, indeed, into an ever sovereign present.

On one level, the ending of Burns's remarkable film series offers a vivid reminder of just how much interpretations of the Civil War provide an index of our political culture, of how much the central issues of the war – union and slavery, reunion and racial equality, diversity as the definition of America or as the source of its unraveling – remain for each succeeding generation of Americans to grapple with. However, on another level, the ending of the film offers many

Americans the legacy they find most appealing: the rapid transition from the veteran just returned to his farm, standing on a corn wagon in 1865 (almost an image of a horn of plenty), to the 1913 Gettysburg reunion is the stuff of earnest nostalgia, and it makes good fast-forward history. As Richard Slotkin has written, "Burns evokes as well as anyone the paradoxical and complex emotion of Civil War nostalgia, in which one recognizes the awful tragedy of the war, yet somehow *misses* it." In American collective memory, sectional reconciliation virtually required that some of the deeper tragedies of that conflict be "missed." Such an ending (in Burns's film) becomes transhistorical in American social memory: the time between the real battle of Gettysburg and its fiftieth anniversary reunion is at once a great distance and no distance at all. Time itself can be transcended; and in those mystical exchanges between gracious old veterans on what seem ancient battlefields, one can entertain the notion that American history endures all traumas in its troubled but inexorable path of progress, and that the day may arrive when there will no longer be any need to think historically about long-term consequences. Abraham Lincoln's haunting passage about the "mystic chords of memory, stretching from every battlefield and patriot grave . . . " had, indeed, swelled "the chorus of the Union," and conquered time itself. The pleading poetry in Lincoln's First Inaugural Address in 1861 (from which Burns takes his title for the final episode, "The Better Angels of Our Nature") was delivered, of course, in the midst of crisis and on the brink of war. But the deeper conflicts and contradictions buried in the new "patriot graves" (after the Civil War) could be finely displaced, comfortably forgotten, and truly "mystic" as Joshua Lawrence Chamberlain, the hero of Little Round Top at the battle of Gettysburg (and one of Burns's principal "characters"), describes the 1913 reunion as a "transcendental experience" and a "radiant fellowship of the fallen." American history had "progressed" through Reconstruction, the Gilded Age, the myriad crises of the 1890s, vicious racial violence, unprecedented labor strife, a short foreign war with Spain, massive urbanization and industrialization to be a society divided by a racial apartheid and seething with ethnic pluralism on the eve of World War I. Rarely was there a more confirming context for William Dean Howells's turn-of-the-century assertion that "what the American public always wants is a tragedy with a happy ending."[5]

Explanations of the meaning and memory of the Civil War – whether expressed in fiction, monuments, historiography, the movies, politics, journalism, public schooling, veterans' organizations, the strongly gendered attractions of war-gaming, tourism, or reenactments – have, intentionally or not, provided a means of assessing the elusive question of national self-definition in America. Such constructions of the memory of our most divisive event have also reflected the persistent dilemma of race in public policy, as well as our ongoing challenge to build one political structure that can encompass the interests of the many. By and large, the legions of Americans who transmit a fascination for the Civil War across generations still prefer the drama of the immediate event to discussions of causes and consequences; they continue to be enthralled with the fight as much as, if not more than, with its meanings. This is, of course, partly a measure of human nature, of audiences, and of public tastes for history generally. Burns effectively mixed the broad military struggle with the voices of ordinary people and the perspectives of local communities. The influence of the new social history is altogether apparent in the film. We learn that the Civil War was a ruthless and all-encompassing experience in places like Clarksville, Tennessee, and Deer Isle, Maine. We hear the common soldier's syntax and the war's meaning interpreted from the diaries of ordinary women. Burns put slavery and emancipation at the center of the wartime story; Frederick Douglass's compelling voice commands attention at several turning points in the narrative. Emancipated slaves are real people, and they too help to tell the story. But in the end, the film series is still a narrative about the making and consequences of war (and the horror and destruction are unmistakable), told from headquarters and the perspectives of larger-than-life individuals. The legends of such figures as Robert E. Lee, Stonewall Jackson, Nathan Bedford Forrest, William Tecumseh Sherman, and Lincoln himself are well preserved in Burns's self-conscious attempt at documentary epic. For Burns, as a filmmaker/historian, all of these were, of course, artistic as well as historical choices; at times he simply created what works best on film, with a clear artifice in mind.[6]

For Americans broadly, the Civil War has been a defining event upon which we have often imposed unity and continuity; as a culture, we have preferred its music and pathos to its enduring challenges, the theme of reconciled conflict to resurgent, unresolved legacies. We have displaced complicated consequences by endlessly focusing on the contest itself. We have sometimes lifted ourselves out of historical time, above the details, and rendered the war safe in a kind of Passover offering as we watch the Blue and the Gray veterans shake hands across the little stone walls at Gettysburg. Like stone monuments, monumental films, as well as some monumental books, are sometimes as much about forgetting as they are about remembering. Deeply embedded in an American mythology of mission, and serving as a mother lode of nostalgia for antimodernists and military history buffs, the Civil War remains very difficult to shuck from its shell of sentimentalism. Historian Nina Silber has demonstrated how "a sentimental rubric took hold of the reunion process" during the three decades after the war. Indeed, Silber shows how gender (conceptions of manliness and femininity, and the popular literary ritual of intersectional marriage) provided a principal source of metaphor and imagery through which sectional reconciliation was achieved.[7]

Through scholarship and schooling, much has changed in recent decades regarding the place of the black experience in the era of the Civil War. But in the half century after the conflict, as the sections reconciled, the races increasingly divided. The intersectional wedding that became such a staple of mainstream popular culture had no interracial counterpart in the popular imagination. Quite the opposite was the case. So deeply at the root of the war's causes and consequences, and so powerful a source of division in American social psychology, "race" – and its myriad manipulations in American culture – served as the antithesis of a culture of reconciliation. The memory of slavery, emancipation, and the Fifteenth Amendment never fit well into a culture in which the Old and New South were romanticized and welcomed back to a new nationalism. Persistent discussion of the "Race Problem" (or the "Negro Question"), across the political and ideological spectrum at the turn of the century, meant that American society could not also remember a "Civil War problem," or a "Blue–Gray problem." Interpretations of the Civil War in the broad American culture continue to illustrate what Daniel Aaron meant when he said that, among American writers, the conflict "has not been so much unfelt, as it is unfaced." And, if W. E. B. Du Bois was at all correct in his famous 1903 declaration that "the problem of the twentieth century is the problem of the color line," then we can begin to see how the problem of "reunion" and the problem of "race" were trapped in a tragic, mutual dependence.[8]

The aim of this essay is to suggest in the broadest terms how American culture processed the meaning and memory of the Civil War and Reconstruction down to World War I, with special emphasis on these overlapping themes of reunion and race. In this process, black and white voices spoke both to and completely around each other. In the introduction to the 1991 edition of *Imagined Communities*, Benedict Anderson warns us about the delusion of "shedding" ourselves of the problem of nationalism in the modern world. "The 'end of an era of nationalism,' so long prophesied," writes Anderson, "is not remotely in sight. Indeed, nation-ness is the most universally legitimate value in the political life of our time." Moreover, in his discussion of the function of "memory and forgetting" in the shaping of nationalism, Anderson left this telling comment about the American Civil War: "A vast pedagogical industry works ceaselessly to oblige young Americans to remember/forget the hostilities of 1861–65 as a great 'civil' war between 'brothers' rather than between – as they briefly were – two sovereign nation-states. (We can be sure, however, that if the Confederacy had succeeded in maintaining its independence, this 'civil war' would have been replaced in memory by something quite unbrotherly."[9] There may never be an end to nationalism as we know it, just as there is no end to history. But there are manifest breaks in the process of history, events and commemorations of those events that expose how we use history.

In "The New Negro" (1925), philosopher Alain Locke believed he discerned one of those turning points, both in black self-consciousness and in the nation's race "problem." And the change had everything to do with memory and forgetting. "While the minds of most of us, black and white, have thus burrowed in the *trenches* of the Civil War and Reconstruction," wrote Locke, "the actual march of development has simply *flanked* these positions, necessitating a sudden reorientation of view. We have not been watching in the right direction; set North and South on a sectional axis, we have not noticed the East till the sun has us blinking" (emphasis added). Preoccupied in remembering/forgetting the war as a North–South fight, mired in the increasingly nostalgic details of a heroic war in a lost past, American culture had lost sight of what the fight had been all about. Time would tell whether Locke's optimism about a new generation of blacks' "spiritual coming of age" would be a solution to or an evasion of these problems in American historical memory, whether the blinking of a new era would turn to collective insight.[10] For more than two decades before Locke wrote, the reform fervor of the Progressive era, with its quests for order, honesty, and efficiency, and its impulse against monopolism, compelled Americans to look inward and forward, but they did so in a culture full of sentimentalized remembrance. Moreover, for at least the same twenty years, black thinkers had been fashioning definitions of the "New Negro" for the new century. But what would be the place of "New Negroes" at Blue–Gray reunions in the land of Jim Crow? In a society inexorably looking ahead, the culture of sectional reconciliation would force millions, consciously or not, to avert their eyes.

The chronological reach of this essay is long, and large aspects of the topic will, therefore, have to be left to later explorations. Such aspects include the impact of popular literature (the "plantation school") on Northern readers and editors in the late nineteenth century, the post-Reconstruction generation of black and white writers who wrote directly and indirectly about the legacies of the Civil War and emancipation, the myriad ways sectional politics and the emergence of Jim Crow (in law and life) melded into an uneasy national consensus from the 1880s to World War I, and the cultural nostalgia rooted in the alienation born of rapid industrialization.[11] I have selected two ways to demonstrate the dialectic between race and reunion as the memory of the Civil War evolved in American culture: first, an encounter between two major African American leaders, Alexander Crummell and Frederick Douglass, over how blacks should best remember slavery and the Civil War; and second, the 1913 fiftieth anniversary Blue–Gray reunion at Gettysburg as a ritual of national reconciliation, an event in which race, black participation in the war, indeed the very idea of slavery as cause and emancipation as result of the war might be said to be thunderously conspicuous by their absence.

In 1875, as the march away from radicalism and protection of African American rights threatened to become a full retreat, Frederick Douglass gave a Fourth of July speech in Washington, DC, entitled "The Color Question." Events, both personal and national, had cast a pall over the normally sanguine Douglass, forcing him to reflect in racialized terms on the American Centennial, which was to be celebrated the following year. The nation, Douglass feared, would "lift to the sky its million voices in one grand Centennial hosanna of peace and good will to all the white race . . . from gulf to lakes and from sea to sea." As a black citizen, he dreaded the day when "this great white race has renewed its vows of patriotism and flowed back into its accustomed channels." Douglass looked back upon fifteen years of unparalleled change for his people, worried about the hold of white supremacy on America's historical consciousness, and asked the core question in the nation's struggle over the memory of the Civil War: "If war among the whites brought peace and liberty to the blacks, *what will peace among the whites bring?*"[12] (emphasis added). For more than a century, through cycles of great advancement and periods of cynical reaction in American race relations, Douglass's question in various forms has echoed through our political culture. Answers to Douglass's question have depended, of course, on context – on time, place, one's positioning along the color line, the available sources for scholars, access to power, the medium through which the history is transmitted, and differing revisionist questions and agendas. But always, the answers have emerged from the struggle over the content, meaning, and uses of the past. John Hope Franklin recognized this in a 1979 essay on what he describes as the "enormous influence" of the combination of Thomas Dixon's novel *The Clansman* (1905), D. W. Griffith's film *Birth of a Nation* (1915), and Claude Bowers's popular history *The Tragic Era* (1928), all produced within the first three decades of the twentieth century. Franklin's analysis of how history can be used as "propaganda" in the shaping of a nation's memory of itself echoed Ralph Ellison's poignant comment during the same year (1979). Nothing in our past, said Ellison, like the question of race in the story of the Civil War and Reconstruction had ever caused Americans to be so "notoriously selective in the exercise of historical memory."[13] All practice of historical memory formation is, of course, selective. How some selections become or remain dominant, taking on mythic dimensions, and others do not is the tale to be told.

The 1880s were a pivotal decade in the development of traditions and social memories of the Civil War. The "Lost Cause" in the South, as well as a growing willingness among Northerners to embrace sectional reconciliation, underwent cultural transformation. The situation among black intellectuals was similar; an index of their struggle over how and if to remember slavery and the Civil War era can be found in a debate between Alexander Crummell and Frederick Douglass. Then as now, no single persuasion controlled African American thought; black social memories were often as diverse as were debates within the Grand Army of the Republic (GAR) or among advocates of the Lost Cause tradition. As editors, ministers, community leaders, or writers, black intellectuals in the late nineteenth century were as compelled as anyone else to engage in what became an intraracial debate over the meaning and best uses of the age of emancipation. The contours of such debates were established well before Booker T. Washington and W. E. B. Du Bois came to embody the classic division in black thought over historical consciousness and political strategies.[14]

At Storer College, in Harpers Ferry, West Virginia, on May 30, 1885 (Memorial Day), Alexander Crummell, one of the most accomplished and well-traveled black intellectuals of the nineteenth century, gave a commencement address to the graduates of that black college, which had been founded for freedmen at the end of the Civil War. Crummell, an Episcopal priest, educated at the abolitionist Oneida Institute in Upstate New York and at Cambridge University in England in the 1840s, had spent nearly twenty years as a missionary and an advocate of African nationalism in Liberia (1853–71). Crummell later considered the Storer address, entitled "The Need of New ideas and New Aims for a New Era," to be the most important he ever gave. Although Crummell could not resist acknowledging that Harpers Ferry was a setting "full of the most thrilling memories in the history of our race," his aim was to turn the new generation of blacks, most of whom would have been born during the Civil

War, away from dwelling "morbidly and absorbingly upon the servile past," and toward an embrace of the urgent economic and moral "needs of the present." As a minister and theologian, and as a social conservative, Crummell was concerned not only with racial uplift – his ultimate themes were family, labor, industrial education, and moral values – but with the unburdening of blacks from what he believed was the debilitating, painful memory of slavery. Crummell made a careful distinction between memory and recollection. Memory, he contended, was a passive, unavoidable, often essential part of group consciousness; recollection, on the other hand, was active, a matter of choice and selection, and dangerous in excess. "What I would fain have you guard against," he told the graduates, "is not the memory of slavery, but the constant *recollection* of it." Such recollection, Crummell maintained, would only degrade racial progress in the Gilded Age; for him, unmistakably, "duty lies in the future."[15]

Prominent in the audience that day at Harpers Ferry (probably in the front row or on the stage) was Frederick Douglass, whom Crummell described as his "neighbor" from Washington, DC. According to Crummell's own account, his call to reorient African American consciousness from the past to the future met with Douglass's "emphatic and most earnest protest." Douglass rose to the occasion, as he did so many times in the 1880s on one anniversary or Memorial Day after another, to assert an African-American/abolitionist memory of the Civil War era, which almost always included an abiding reminder of the nature and significance of slavery.[16] No verbatim account of what Douglass said at Harpers Ferry survives; but several other speeches from the 1880s offer a clear picture of what the former abolitionist may have said. Douglass and Crummell shared a sense of the dangers and limitations of social memory, especially for a group that had experienced centuries of slavery. A healthy level of forgetting, said Douglass, was "Nature's plan of relief." But in season and out, Douglass insisted that whatever the psychological need for avoiding the woeful legacy of slavery, it would resist all human effort to suppress it. The history of black Americans, he said many times in the 1880s, could "be traced like that of a wounded man through a crowd by the blood."[17] Better to confront such a history, he believed, than to wait for its resurgence.

Douglass's many postwar speeches about the memory of the conflict typically began with an acknowledgment of the need for healing and living. But then he would forcefully call his audiences to remembrance of the origins and consequences, as well as the sacrifices, of the Civil War. He would often admit that his own personal memory of slavery was best kept sleeping like a "half-forgotten dream." But he despised the politics of forgetting that American culture seemed to necessitate in the 1880s. "We are not here to visit upon the children the sins of the fathers," Douglass told a Memorial Day audience in Rochester, New York, in 1883, "but we are here to remember the causes, the incidents, and the results of the late rebellion." Most of all, Douglass objected to the historical construction that portrayed emancipation as a great national "failure" or "blunder." The argument that slavery had protected and nurtured blacks and that freedom had gradually sent them "falling into a state of barbarism" forced Douglass to argue for an aggressive use of memory. The problem was not merely the rise of the Lost Cause myth of Southern virtue and victimization. The problem was "not confined to the South," declared Douglass in 1888. "It [the theory of black degeneration coupled with historical misrepresentations of emancipation and Reconstruction] has gone forth to the North. It has crossed the ocean. It has gone to Europe, and it has gone as far as the wings of the press, and the power of speech can carry it. There is no measuring the injury inflicted upon the negro by it."[18] Such, Douglass understood, were the stakes of conflicts over rival versions of the past, when combined with sociobiological theories of racial inferiority, and put to the service of the present. Douglass died the year before the *Plessy v. Ferguson* Supreme Court decision. But he had lived long enough to peer across the horizon and see the society America was becoming in the age of Jim Crow. In all discussion of the "race question" in America, Douglass had long understood that the historical was always political.

Even before the most violent outbreaks of lynching and an increasingly radical racism took hold in the South, there was good reason to be worried about the uses of the theory of black degeneration. The theory would eventually be spread widely in popular literature, emerge full-blown in minstrelsy, film, and cartoons, and, most tellingly, it gained many spokesmen in academic high places. Produced by historians, statisticians in the service of insurance companies, and scientists of all manner, a hereditarian and social Darwinist theory of black capacity fueled racial policies of evasion and repression. By the turn of the century, the negrophobia practiced in daily conversations among many ordinary whites was now buttressed by highly developed, academic notions of blacks as a "vanishing race," destined to lose the struggle of natural selection.[19]

In 1900, Dr. Paul B. Barringer, chairman of the medical faculty at the University of Virginia, gave the keynote address at a major symposium (on heredity and the Southern "Negro problem") of the Tri-State Medical Society, in Charleston, South Carolina. Barringer began with a discussion of dog species and habits, and the dangers of "indiscriminate breeding." He then found his central theme, the "habits of a race." Barringer's clinical analysis of his topic demonstrates the structure of thought Douglass and others had good reason to fear. "Let us apply this biological axiom to the human race, taking as our example . . . the Southern Negro," declared the doctor:

> I will show from the study of his racial history (phylogeny) that his late tendency to return to barbarism is as natural as the return of the sow that is washed to her wallowing in the mire. I will show that the degradation under which he was formed and the fifty centuries of historically recorded savagery with which he came to us cannot be permanently influenced by one or two centuries of enforced correction if the correcting force be withdrawn . . . when the correcting force of discipline was removed he, like the released planet, began to fall . . . a motion as certain in its results as the law of gravitation. Fortunately for us experience (history) shows that these savage traits can be held down, and we have seen that if held down long enough, they will be bred out. In this one fact lies the hope of the South.

With these words and more, Barringer demonstrated that for the sheer virulence of white supremacy and racial demagoguery, some academics took no back seat to politicians. Throughout, his speech mixed social with biological prescriptions. He predicted the worst: "unless a brake is placed upon the natural ontogeny of this savage, the South will be uninhabitable for the white." But Barringer preferred to place his hope in "education of trade or industrial type" for blacks. "Then and not till then," he concluded, "will the franchise become for him [blacks] a reality and the Jim Crow car a memory."[20]

Although black intellectuals were by no means immune to notions of "race" as the source of group characteristics and traits – such a conception was pervasive in turn-of-the-century Western thought – they would, as a whole, denounce the Barringers and their ideas. Against such racism, whether in this vicious, biological form or in a calmer, paternalistic mode, older memories of emancipation had to contend with newer memories of segregation and lynch mobs in black communities. Indeed, what African American historical memory faced in the new century was not only a pedagogical and historiographical consensus about the "failure" of Reconstruction that seemed to render further discussion of the Fourteenth and Fifteenth Amendments moot; most bluntly, what the racial equalitarian legacy of the Civil War faced was, as George Fredrickson has shown, the sense of permanence and determinism in white supremacist theory and practice.[21] "Race" theory, whether held passively or advanced aggressively, had everything to do with the way white Americans chose to remember emancipation, or whether they chose to remember it at all. From such spokesmen as Barringer, Douglass's question – what will peace among the whites bring? – received some loud and terrible answers.

Although Douglass and Crummell had great respect for each other, they spoke during their Storer confrontation with different agendas, informed by different experiences and representing different traditions. Crummell had never been a slave; he achieved a classical education, was a missionary of evangelical Christianity, a thinker of conservative instincts, and had spent almost the entire Civil War era in West Africa. He returned to the United States twice during the war to recruit black Americans for possible emigration from America to Liberia, while Douglass worked aggressively as an advocate of the Union cause, demanded emancipation, and recruited approximately one hundred members of the Fifty-fourth Massachusetts black regiment (two of whom were his sons Charles and Lewis). Crummell represented a paradoxical brand of black nationalism, which survived through Marcus Garvey and beyond: a combination of Western, European Christian civilizationism and race pride and purity. Crummell contended that the principal problems faced by American blacks were moral weakness, self-hatred, and industrial primitiveness. In the 1870s, Crummell became the founding pastor of St. Luke's Episcopal Church in Washington, DC, while Douglass became a regular speaker at the middle-class Metropolitan AME Church in the same city.[22]

Douglass, the former slave, had established his fame by writing and speaking about the meaning of slavery; his life's work and his very identity were inextricably linked to the transformations of the Civil War. The past made and inspired Douglass; there was no meaning for him without memory, whatever the consequences of "recollection." He believed he had remade himself from slavery to freedom, and he believed that blacks generally had been regenerated in the Second American Revolution of emancipation and the Civil War. The past had also made Crummell; but his connection to many of the benchmarks of African American social memory had been largely distant, and informed by African nationalism and Christian mission. For Douglass, emancipation and the Civil War were truly *felt* history, a moral and legal foundation upon which to demand citizenship and equality. For Crummell, they were the potentially paralyzing memories to be resisted; they were not the epic to be retold, merely the source of future needs. Crummell sought to redeem Africa, and to inspire moral values in the freedpeople by the example of an elite black leadership. Douglass was devoted to the same values and essentially the same model of leadership; he sought, preeminently, however, to redeem the civil and political rights promised by the verdicts of Fort Wagner and Appomattox. Both men believed that the talented had to uplift the ordinary, although they, certainly in Douglass's case, had fallen out of touch with much of the material plight of Southern freedmen. Crummell had tried to be a founding father of Liberia; Douglass dearly wished to see himself as a founding father of a reinvented American republic. Both were from the same generation, had traveled far, seen great changes, and, at Storer College, were speaking to the postfreedom generation. With different reasons and aims, Crummell and Douglass both sought to teach this new generation how to understand and use the legacy of slavery and the Civil War era, how to preserve yet destroy the past.

The contrast between them could be overdrawn in the pursuit of dualities in African American thought. But such a comparison is suggestive of the recurring dilemma of black intellectuals in American history. Is the black experience in America a racial memory, or is it thoroughly intertwined with a collective, national memory? Is the core image of the black experience in America represented by black institutions, cultural forms, and aesthetics that have flourished by rejecting American nationalism or European cultural forms, or by the black Civil War soldier and the Fourteenth Amendment? By Booker T. Washington's image of the "hand and the fingers," or by Thurgood Marshall standing on the steps of the Supreme Court after winning *Brown v. Board of Education*? In a Garvey-UNIA parade, or in the Selma march? In Malcolm X at a Harlem street rally, or Martin Luther King at the Lincoln Memorial? Can there be a single, core image at all? When does it matter how benchmark African American memories are directly linked to the changing master narratives of American history, and when does it not? Are there not multiple core images of African American historical memory – jagged, diverse, regional, rural, and urban? These kinds of questions are, in part, what keeps African American history at the center of research agendas in the new histories. Dichotomies have sometimes blurred more truth than they have revealed. All such comparisons – among scholars or in larger public uses of memory and history – must, of course, be historicized. However politicized, romanticized, regionalized, or class-based these questions have become in each succeeding generation, the answers have always been contested and complex. Rival memories among black thinkers should be treated as equally dynamic as similar struggles in the larger culture.[23]

As America underwent vast social changes in the late nineteenth century, and fought a foreign war in 1898, so too the memory of the Civil War changed as it was transmitted to new generations. This is a complex story, but one of the principal features of the increasingly sentimentalized road to reunion was the celebration of the veteran, especially at Blue–Gray reunions, which became important aspects of popular culture in an age that loved pageantry, became obsessed with building monuments, and experienced a widespread revival of the martial ideal.[24] A brief focus on the fiftieth anniversary reunion at Gettysburg in 1913 may help illuminate the relationship of race and reunion in Civil War memory.

As early as 1909 the state of Pennsylvania established a commission and began planning for the 1913 celebration. In the end, the states appropriated some $1,750,000 to provide free transportation for veterans from every corner of the country. Pennsylvania alone spent at least $450,000, and the federal government, through Congress and the War Department, appropriated approximately $450,000 to build the "Great Camp" for the "Great Reunion," as it became known. A total of 53,407 veterans attended the reunion, and again as many spectators were estimated to have descended upon the small town of Gettysburg for the July 1–4 festival of reconciliation.[25]

The railroad transportation of any Civil War veteran, living anywhere in the United States, was paid for by public monies. Some one hundred veterans arrived in Gettysburg from California, ten of them Confederates. Vermont sent 669 men, four of them listed as Confederates. Nevada and Wyoming were the only states not accounted for at the reunion, although New Mexico sent only one Union veteran. The whole event was an organizational, logistical, and financial triumph. Not only did a small army of souvenir salesmen flood the streets of the town of Gettysburg, but no fewer than forty-seven railroad companies operating in or through Pennsylvania alone were paid a total of $142,282 for the transportation of veterans. One hundred fifty-five reporters from the national and international press covered the event, which was headlined (along with stunning photographs) in most newspapers during the week of the reunion. Once the old men had arrived in their uniforms, decked out in ribbons, and graced with silver beards, the tent city on the old battlefield became one of the most photogenic spectacles Americans had ever seen. For most observers, the veterans were men out of another time, images from the history beyond memory, icons that stimulated deep feelings, a sense of pride, history, and idle amusement all at once. They were an irresistible medium through which Americans could see their inheritance, and be deflected from it at the same time.[26]

Many reunions had been held and a vast array of monuments constructed at Gettysburg long before 1913. But if social memory on the broadest scale is best forged and transmitted by performed, ritual commemorations, as many anthropologists have argued, then the memory of the Civil War as it stood in the general American culture in the early twentieth century never saw a more fully orchestrated expression than at Gettysburg on the battle's semicentennial. The Great Camp, covering 280 acres, serving 688,000 "cooked meals" prepared by 2,170 cooks, laborers, and bakers using 130,048 pounds of flour, must have warmed the hearts of even the most compulsive advocates of Taylorism. Frederick W. Taylor's *Principles of Scientific Management* had just been published in 1911, and the Taylor Society had been founded in the same year as the Civil War semicentennial began. The forty-seven miles of "avenues" on the battlefield, lighted by 500 electric arc lights, provided a perfect model of military mobilization and mass production. Those thirty-two automatic "bubbling ice water fountains" throughout the veterans' quarters offered a delightful, if hardly conscious, experience with "incorporation." Taylorite advocates of efficiency warmly approved the extraordinary "preparedness" of the Red Cross and the army medical corps in their efforts to provide first-class hospital care for the veterans during the encampment. The average age of veterans at the event was seventy-four, and the Pennsylvania Commission's report celebrated the fact that only nine of the old fellows died during the reunion, a statistic many times lower than the national average for such an age group. Moreover, efficiency enthusiasts could marvel at the ninety elaborate, modern latrines (men's and women's) constructed all over the encampment. The commission's report was careful to include notes on the successful functioning of all latrine mechanisms, cleaning procedures, and estimates of tonnage of waste material. The press was full of celebration of such efficiency. The *Philadelphia Inquirer* marveled at the "more pains-taking care, more scientific preparation and a better discipline than has ever before been known on such an occasion." The camp was "policed in a way," observed the *Inquirer*, "that made it the healthiest place on earth . . . there never was anything better done in our history."[27]

As one would expect, the theme of the reunion from the earliest days of its conception was nationalism, patriotism, and harmony – the great "Peace Jubilee," as the planning commission had announced as early as 1910. Fifty years after Pickett's charge (and the Emancipation Proclamation, which was utterly ignored during the week's ceremonies), Douglass's question received a full-throated answer. I have found only limited reference to the attendance of black veterans at the 1913 reunion. In a book by Walter H. Blake, a New Jersey veteran who compiled a narrative of anecdotes and personal reminiscences of his journey to the event, one finds the claim that "there were colored men on both sides of the lines." The Pennsylvania Commission "had made arrangements only for negroes from the Union side," lamented the New Jersey veteran, "forgetful of the fact that there were many faithful slaves who fought against their own interests in their intense loyalty to their Southern masters." Numerous black men worked as camp laborers, building the tent city and distributing mess kits and blankets (they appear in photographs published by the commission and elsewhere). Nowhere in its detailed, 281-page published report does the Pennsylvania Commission indicate how many black veterans attended the reunion. The commission was explicitly concerned that "*only*" those determined to be "known veteran[s] of the Civil War" by their documented honorable discharges were to receive free transportation. Presumably this included black GAR members; if so, further research will reveal how many, if any, attended as well as how black veterans may have responded to the reunion's tone and purpose. One of Walter Blake's anecdotes of the reunion is what he calls a "very pretty little incident" in which "a giant of an old negro, Samuel

Thompson," was resting under a shade tree. Some Confederate veterans came up to shake hands with "the old darky" and exchange greetings. It is not made clear whether Thompson was a veteran or not. Blake declares this incident another triumph for kindness and concludes without the slightest sense of irony: "no color line here."[28]

The reunion was to be a source of lessons transmitted between generations, as several hundred Boy Scouts of America served the old veterans as aides-de-camp, causing scenes much celebrated in the press. Like any event fraught with so much symbolism, the reunion also became a "site" for contentious politics. Suffragists lobbied the veterans' camp, asking that they shout "votes for women" rather than the refurbished "rebel yell," a scene much derided by some of the press. Most of all, the reunion was a grand opportunity for America's political officialdom, as well as purveyors of popular opinion, to declare the meaning and memory of the Civil War in the present. One does have to wonder if there had ever been an assembly quite like this in the history of the modern world: can we imagine another event commemorated by so many actual participants in so grand a manner, involving such imagery of past, present, and future? Lafayette's tour of America in 1827, the United States Centennial in 1876, and the Columbian Exposition in Chicago in 1893, as well as other world's fairs, come to mind as possible comparisons. But for the transmission of a public, social memory of an epoch, such a platform had rarely existed as that given the state governors and the president of the United States on July 3 and 4, 1913.[29]

On the third day of the reunion the governors of the various states spoke. All, understandably, asserted the themes of sectional harmony and national cohesion. As one would expect, the soldiers' valor was the central idea of such reunion rhetoric. Perhaps William Hodges Mann, the governor of Virginia, struck the most meaningful chord of memory on that occasion: "We are not here to discuss the Genesis of the war," said Mann, "but men who have tried each other in the storm and smoke of battle are here to discuss this great fight, which if it didn't establish a new standard of manhood came up to the highest standard that was ever set. We came here, I say, *not to discuss what caused the war of 1861–65*, but to talk over the events of the battle here as man to man" (emphasis added). The following day, July 4, in the great finale of the reunion staged in a giant tent erected in the middle of the field where Pickett's charge had occurred, the Blue and the Gray gathered to hear what turned out to be a short address by Woodrow Wilson, just recently inaugurated, the first Southern president elected since the Civil War. "We are debtors to those fifty crowded years," announced Wilson, "they have made us all heirs to a mighty heritage." What have the fifty years meant? Wilson asked. The answer struck that mystic chord of memory that most white Americans, North and South, probably desired to hear:

> They have meant peace and union and vigor, and the maturity and might of a great nation. How wholesome and healing the peace has been. We have found one another again as brothers and comrades, in arms, enemies no longer, generous friends rather, our battles long past, the *quarrel forgotten* – except that we shall not forget the splendid valor, the manly devotion of the men then arrayed against one another, now grasping hands and smiling into each other's eyes. How complete the Union has become and how dear to all of us, how unquestioned, how benign and majestic as state after state has been added to this, our great family of free men! (emphasis added)[30]

That great "hosanna" that Douglass had anticipated forty years before had certainly come to fruition. "Thank God for Gettysburg, hosanna!" declared the *Louisville Courier-Journal*. "God bless us everyone, alike the Blue and the Gray, the Gray and the Blue! The world ne'er witnessed such a sight as this. Beholding, can we say happy is the nation that hath no history?" In Ernest Renan's famous essay, "What is a Nation?" (1882), he aptly described a nation as "a large-scale solidarity . . . a daily plebiscite" constantly negotiated between "memories" and "present-day consent," and requiring a great deal of "forgetting." In varieties of irony, the United States in 1913 fit Renan's definition.[31]

The deep causes and consequences of the Civil War – the role of slavery and the challenge of racial equality – in those fifty "crowded years" had been actively suppressed and subtly displaced by the celebration of what Oliver Wendell Holmes, Jr., had termed the "soldier's faith," the celebration of the veterans' manly valor and devotion. Oh what a glorious fight they had come to commemorate; and in the end, everyone was right, no one was wrong, and something so transforming as the Civil War had been rendered a mutual victory of the Blue and the Gray by what Governor Mann called the "splendid movement of reconciliation." And Wilson's great gift for mixing idealism with ambiguity was in perfect form. He gave his own, preacherly, restrained endorsement of the valor of the past. Then, putting on his Progressive's hat, he spoke to the present. "The day of our country's life has but broadened into morning," he declared. "Do not put uniforms by. Put the harness of the present on." Wilson's speech offers a poignant illustration of the significance of presidential rhetoric in the creation of American nationalism.[32]

If, as Garry Wills has argued, Abraham Lincoln, in the brevity of the "Gettysburg Address" in 1863, "revolutionized the revolution," and offered the nation a "refounding" in the principle of *equality* forged out of the crucible of the war, then Woodrow Wilson, in his Gettysburg address fifty years later, offered a subtle and strikingly less revolutionary response. According to Wills, Lincoln had suggested a new constitution at Gettysburg, "giving people a new past to live with that would change their future indefinitely." So did Wilson in 1913. But the new past was one in which all sectional strife was gone, and in which all racial strife was ignored or covered over in claims for Wilson's own brand of Progressivism. He appealed to a social and moral equivalent of war directed not at the old veterans but at the younger generations who "must contend, not with armies, but with principalities and powers and wickedness in high places." He came with "orders," not for the old men in Blue and Gray but for the "host" of the American people, "the great and the small, without class or difference of race or origin . . . our constitutions are their articles of enlistment. The orders of day are the laws upon our statute books." Lincoln's "rebirth of freedom" had become in fifty years Wilson's forward-looking "righteous peace" (Wilson's "New Freedom" program in the 1912 election campaign). The potential in the Second American Revolution had become the "quarrel forgotten" on the statute books of Jim Crow America. Wilson, of course, did not believe he was speaking for or about the ravages of segregation, or other aspects of racial division in America, on his day at Gettysburg. He was acutely aware of his presence at the reunion as a Southerner, and was no doubt still negotiating the uneasy terrain of a minority president, elected by only 42 percent of the popular vote in the turbulent four-way election of 1912. Wilson's Progressivism was antimonopolist, antitariff, and concerned with banking reform and other largely middle-class causes. Although racial issues only rarely occupied him while president, he was instinctively a state rightist.[33] Educated by events, and rising beyond his own constraints, Lincoln had soared above the "honored dead" to try to imagine a new future in America. Wilson soared above the honored veterans and described a present and a future in which white patriotism and nationalism flourished, in which society seemed threatened by disorder, and in which the principle of equality might be said, by neglect and action, to have been living a social death.

The ceremonies at Gettysburg in 1913 represented a public avowal of the deeply laid mythology of the Civil War (some scholars prefer the term *tradition*) that had captured the popular imagination by the early twentieth century.[34] The war was remembered primarily as a tragedy that led to greater unity and national cohesion, and as a soldier's call to sacrifice in order to save a troubled, but essentially good, Union, not as the crisis of a nation deeply divided over slavery, race, competing definitions of labor, liberty, political economy, and the future of the West, issues hardly resolved in 1913.

Press reports and editorials demonstrate just how much this version of Civil War history had become what some theorists have called "structural amnesia" or social "habit memory."[35] The issues of slavery and secession, rejoiced the conservative *Washington Post*, were "no longer discussed argumentatively. They are scarcely mentioned at all, except in connection with the great war to which they led, and by which they were *disposed of for all time*." To the extent that slavery involved a "moral principle," said the *Post*, "no particular part of the people was responsible unless, indeed, the burden of responsibility should be shouldered *by the North for its introduction*" (emphasis added). Echoing many of the governors (North and South) who spoke at the reunion, the "greater victory," declared the *Post*, was that won by the national crusade to reunite the veterans, and not that of the Army of the Potomac in 1863. The *New York Times* hired Helen D. Longstreet (widow of the Confederate general James Longstreet, who had been much maligned by the Lost Cause devotees for his caution at Gettysburg and his Republicanism after the war) to write daily columns about the reunion. She entertained *Times* readers with her dialogues with Southern veterans about the value of Confederate defeat and the beauty of "Old Glory." She also challenged readers to remember the sufferings of women during the Civil War and to consider an intersectional tribute to them as the theme of the next reunion. The nation's historical memory, concluded the *Times*, had become so "balanced" that it could never again be "disturbed" by sectional conflict. The editors of the liberal magazine *The Outlook* were overwhelmed by the spirit of nationalism at the reunion, and declared it a reconciliation of "two conceptions of human right and human freedom." The war, said the *Outlook*, had been fought over differing notions of "idealism": "sovereignty of the state" versus "sovereignty of the nation." Demonstrating to what degree slavery had vanished from understandings of Civil War causation in serious intellectual circles, the *Outlook* announced that "it was slavery that raised the question of State sovereignty; but it was not on behalf of slavery, but on behalf of State sovereignty and all that it implied, that these men fought." So normative was this viewpoint – not to be replaced by a new historiographical consensus for several decades – that the *Outlook's* special correspondent at the reunion, Herbert Francis Sherwood, could conclude that the veterans' "fraternity ... showed that no longer need men preach a reunited land, for there were no separated people." Such was the state of historical consciousness in Jim Crow America. In the larger culture, slavery (and the whole black experience) was read out of the formulas by which Americans found meanings in the Civil War. As in all deep ironies, the *Outlook* was both accurate and oblivious in its interpretation of the reunion; and thus could it conclude without blinking that "both sides" had fought for "the same ideal – the ideal of civil liberty."[36]

The Gettysburg reunion was an event so full of symbolic meaning, and perhaps so photogenic, that it compelled editorial comment from far and wide. The *Times* (London) correspondent reported back to England that the reunion had sent a "great and memorable lesson ... eradicating forever the scars of the civil war in a way that no amount of preaching or political maneuvering could have done." Reporters from every section of the country registered their sense of awe and wonderment at the Gettysburg celebration. "The Reunion fifty years after stands alone in the annals of the world," said the *Cincinnati Enquirer*, "for no similar event has ever taken place." The *San Francisco Examiner*, in an editorial that modeled Lincoln's "Gettysburg Address" in form, declared the "jubilee" to be the "supreme justification of war and battle." Now "we know that the great war had to be fought, that it is well that it was fought," announced the *Examiner*, "a necessary, useful, splendid sacrifice whereby the whole race of men has been unified." Such martial spirit and claims of ritual purging were answered (albeit by a minority voice) in the *Charleston (South Carolina) News and Courier*. The newspaper in the city where secession began urged readers not to glorify the "battle itself," for it was "a frightful and abominable thing." If war "thrills us," declared the *News and Courier*, "we lose a vitally important part of the lesson." But the *Brooklyn Daily Eagle* kept the discussion on a higher plane with a theme that allowed, simultaneously, for a recognition of Northern victory, Southern respect, and faith in American providential destiny:

> Two civilizations met at Gettysburg and fought out the issue between them under the broad, blue sky, in noble, honorable battle. . . . In one, as historians have pointed out, the family was the social unit – the family in the old Roman sense, possibly inclusive of hundreds of slaves. In the other, the individual was the only social unit. Within half a century those two civilizations have become one. Individualism has triumphed. Yet has that triumph been tempered with a fuller recognition than ever before the war, of the charm and dignity and cultivation of what has yielded to the hand of Fate. . . . The ways of Providence are inscrutable.

The Brooklyn editor had neatly wrapped the whole package in nostalgia for the masses. He offered mystic honor to the Lost Cause of patriarchal "family" structure, combined with an uneasy celebration of the triumph of individualism in the age of industrialization, all justified by God's design.[37]

Such homilies about nationalism and peace, though often well-meaning in their context, masked as much as they revealed. One should not diminish the genuine sentiment of the veterans in 1913; the Civil War had left ghastly scars to be healed in the psyches of individual men, as well as in the collective memories of Americans in both sections. The war's impact on the social psychology of Americans of both sections and races had been enormous. Understandably, monuments and reunions had always combined remembrance with healing and, therefore, with forgetting. But it is not stretching the evidence to suggest that white supremacy was a silent master of ceremonies at the Gettysburg reunion. No overt conspiracy need be implied, but commemorative rituals are not merely benign performances; their content and motivation must be explored along with their form. The reunion was a national ritual in which the ghost of slavery might, once and for all, be exorcised, and in which a conflict among whites might be transmogrified into national mythology.

Black newspapers of the era were, understandably, wary and resentful of the celebration of the great "Peace Jubilee." At a time when lynching had developed into a social ritual of its own horrifying kind in the South, and when the American apartheid had become almost fully entrenched, black opinion leaders found the sectional love feast at Gettysburg to be more irony than they could bear. "We are wondering," declared the *Baltimore Afro-American Ledger*, "whether Mr. Lincoln had the slightest idea in his mind that the time would ever come when the people of this country would come to the conclusion that by the 'People' he meant only white people." Black memory of the Civil War seemed at such variance with what had happened at the reunion. The *Afro-American* captured the stakes and the potential results of this test of America's social memory. "Today the South is in the saddle, and with the single exception of slavery, everything it fought for during the days of the Civil War, it has gained by repression of the Negro within its borders. And the North has quietly allowed it to have its own way." The *Afro-American* asserted the loyalty of black soldiers during the war and of black citizens since, and pointed to President Wilson's recent forced segregation of federal government workers. The "blood" of black soldiers and lynched citizens was "crying from the ground" in the South, unheard and strangely unknown at the Blue–Gray reunion. When the assembled at Gettysburg paused to hear Lincoln's lines about that "government of the people," suggested the *Afro-American*, it ought to "recall the fact that at least part of the people of this country are Negroes and at the same time human beings, and civilized human beings at that; struggling towards the light, as God has given them to see the light."[38]

These reactions in the black press are especially telling given one of the most striking ironies of all during that summer of 1913: the Wilson administration's increasingly aggressive program of racial segregation in federal government agencies, which were major employers of black Americans. On the day after Decoration Day the official segregation of black clerks in the Post Office Department began. And on July 12, only a week after Wilson spoke at Gettysburg, orders were issued to create separate lavatories for blacks and whites working at the Treasury Department. These and other segregation policies, stemming in part from the many new white Southerners who had come to Washington with the Wilson administration (some racial radicals and some moderates), caused deep resentment and protest among blacks, led largely by the National Association for the Advancement of Colored People (NAACP). Such policies, and the sense of betrayal they caused among blacks, prompted Booker T. Washington, no friend of the NAACP, to declare that he had "never seen the colored people so discouraged and bitter" as they were in the summer of 1913. That summer the NAACP launched a sometimes successful campaign against segregation practices in the federal government.[39]

The *Washington Bee* was even more forthright than other papers in its criticism of the planned reunion at Gettysburg:

> The occasion is to be called a Reunion! A Reunion of whom? Only the men who fought for the preservation of the Union and the extinction of human slavery? Is it to be an assemblage of those who fought to destroy the Union and perpetuate slavery, and who are now employing every artifice and argument known to deceit and sophistry to propagate a national sentiment in favor of their nefarious contention that emancipation, reconstruction and enfranchisement are a dismal failure?

The *Bee*'s editor, W. Calvin Chase, asserted that the Blue–Gray ritual was not a "reunion" at all, but a "Reception" thrown by the victors for the vanquished. Most significantly, he argued that the event was a national declaration of a version of history and a conception of the legacy of the Civil War. The message of the reunion, wrote Chase, was "an insane and servile acknowledgment that the most precious results of the war are a prodigious, unmitigated failure."[40] Commemorative rituals can inspire decidedly different interpretations; sometimes it depends simply on whether one is on the creating or the receiving end of historical memory. Sometimes it depends simply on whether a construction of social memory is to be used to sustain or dislodge part of the social order.

As with the earlier generation in the 1880s, when Douglass and Crummell conducted their debate, the stakes of social memory in 1913 were roughly the same. An interpretation of national history had become wedded to racial theory; the sections had reconciled, nationalism flourished, some social wounds had healed, and Paul Buck could later confidently write, in his Pulitzer Prize-winning *The Road to Reunion* (1937, still the only major synthetic work written on this subject), of the "leaven of forgiveness" that grew in a generation into the "miracle" of reconciliation, and of a "revolution in sentiment" whereby "all people within the country felt the electrifying thrill of a common purpose." Such a reunion had been possible, Buck argued, because Americans had collectively admitted that the "race problem" was "basically insoluable," and had "taken the first step in learning how to live with it." Gone with the wind, indeed. Peace between North and South, Buck wrote, unwittingly answering Douglass's question, had given the South, and therefore the nation, a "stability of race relations" upon which the "new patriotism" and "new nationalism" could be built. A segregated society required a segregated historical memory and a national mythology that could blunt or contain the conflict at the root of that segregation. Buck sidestepped, or perhaps simply missed, the irony in favor of an unblinking celebration of the path to reunion. Just such a celebration is what one finds in the *Atlanta Constitution*'s coverage of the Gettysburg reunion in 1913. With mystic hyperbole and what may seem to us strange logic, the *Constitution* declared that "as never before in its history the nation is united in demanding that justice and equal rights be given all of its citizens." No doubt, these sentiments reflected genuinely held beliefs among some white Southerners that Jim Crow meant "progress." The *Constitution* gushed about the "drama" and "scale" of the symbolism at the Gettysburg reunion, even its "poetry and its fragrance." But most important was "the thing for which it stands – the world's mightiest republic purged of hate and unworthiness, *seared clean of dross* by the most fiery ordeal in any nation's history"[41] (emphasis added). Such were the fruits of America's segregated mind and its segregated historical consciousness.

Theorists and historians have long argued that myth as history often best serves the ends of social stability and conservatism. That is certainly the case with the development of Civil War mythology in America. But we also know that mythic conceptions or presentations of the past can be innovative as well as conservative, liberating instead of destructive, or the result of sheer romance. Whether we like it or not, history is used this way generation after generation. "Only a horizon ringed with myths," warned Friedrich Nietzsche in 1874, "can unify a culture." As professional historians, we would do well to keep in mind C. Vann Woodward's warning that "the twilight zone that lies between living memory and written history is one of the favorite breeding places of mythology." But great myths have their "resilience, not completely controllable," as Michael Kammen reminds us. This reality is precisely the one W. E. B. Du Bois recognized in the final chapter of his *Black Reconstruction in America* (1935), published just two years before Buck's *Road to Reunion*. Du Bois insisted that history should be an "art using the results of science," and not merely a means of "inflating our national ego." But by focusing on the subject of the Civil War and Reconstruction in the 1930s, he offered a tragic awareness, as well as a trenchant argument, that written history cannot be completely disengaged from social memory. Du Bois echoed the *Atlanta Constitution* editor, admitting that there had been a "searing of the memory" in America, but one of a very different kind. The "searing" Du Bois had in mind was not that of the Civil War itself but that of a white supremacist historiography and a popular memory of the period that had "obliterated" the black experience and the meaning of emancipation by "libel, innuendo, and silence."[42] The stakes in the development of America's historical memory of the Civil War have never been benign. The answers to Douglass's question have never been benign either. "Peace among the whites" brought segregation and the necessity of later reckonings. The Civil War has not yet been disengaged from a mythological social memory, and perhaps it never will be. But likewise, the American reunion cannot be disengaged from black experience and interpretations, nor from the question of race in the collective American memory.

As with other major touchstones of American history, Americans will continue to use the Civil War for ends that serve the present. There are many reasons for this, but one of the most compelling perhaps is the fact that emancipation in America (contrary to the experience of every other country in the century of emancipations) came as a result of total war and social revolution. Revolutions, as we have all learned, can go backward as well as revive again in new, reconstructed forms from one generation to the next. All such questions, of course, must be explained in their contexts. But the Civil War and emancipation may remain in the mythic realm precisely because, in the popular imagination anyway, they represent reconciled discord, a crucible of tragedy and massive change survived in a society that still demands a providential conception of its history. Facing the deepest causes and consequences of the Civil War has always forced us to face the kind of logic Nathan Huggins insisted upon in his final work. "The challenge of the paradox [of race in American history]," wrote Huggins, "is that there can be no white history or black history, nor can there be an integrated history that does not begin to comprehend that slavery and freedom, white and black, are joined at the hip."[43]

Notes

1   John R. Gillis, "Memory and Identity: The History of a Relationship," in *Commemorations: The Politics of National Identity*, ed. John R. Gillis (Princeton, NJ: Princeton Univ. Press, 1994), p. 5.
2   Natalie Zemon Davis and Randolph Starn, Introduction to special issue on "Memory and Counter-Memory," *Representations* 26 (Spring 1989), 2. There are many theoretical works that discuss social memory as a matter of cultural conflict. Some places to start are Maurice Halbwachs, *On Collective Memory*, trans. and intro. Lewis A. Coser (Chicago: Univ. of Chicago Press, 1992); David Thelen, ed., *Memory in American History* (Bloomington: Univ. of Indiana Press, 1991); Michael Kammen, *Mystic Chords of Memory: The Transformation of Tradition in American Culture* (New York: Knopf, 1991), pp. 3–14; Friedrich Nietzsche, *On the Advantage and Disadvantage of History for Life*, intro. Peter Preuss (Indianapolis: Hackett, 1980); Peter Burke, "History as Social Memory," in *Memory: History, Culture, and the Mind*, ed. Thomas Butler (London: Basil Blackwell, 1989), pp. 97–113; Pierre Nora, "Between Memory and History: Les Lieux de Mémoire," *Representations* 26 (Spring 1989), pp. 7–25; Barry Schwartz, "The Social Context of Commemoration: A Study in Collective Memory," *Social Forces* 67 (Dec. 2, 1982), 374–402; Eric Hobsbaum and Terrence Ranger, eds., *The Invention of Tradition* (Cambridge, Eng.: Cambridge Univ. Press, 1983); David Lowenthal, *The Past Is a Foreign Country* (Cambridge, Eng.: Cambridge Univ. Press, 1985), pts. 2 and 3; Charles S. Maier, *The Unmasterable Past: History, Holocaust, and German National Identity* (Cambridge, Mass.: Harvard Univ. Press, 1988); Benedict Anderson, *Imagined Communities: Reflection on the Origin and Spread of Nationalism* (London: Verso, 1991), 187–206; and the many rich essays in Gillis, ed., *Commemorations: The Politics of National Identity*.
3   Episode 9, "The Better Angels of Our Nature," *The Civil War*, produced and directed by Ken Burns (Washington, DC: WETA Television). Fields is quoting from Faulkner's *Absalom, Absalom!*
4   John Hope Franklin, "A Century of Civil War Observances," *Journal of Negro History* 47 (Apr. 1962), 98, 105. On the Civil War Centennial from a black perspective, also see J. A. Rogers, "Civil War Centennial, Myth and Reality," *Freedomways* 3 (Winter 1963), 7–18.
5   Richard Slotkin, " 'What Shall Men Remember?': Recent Work on the Civil War," *American Literary History* 3 (Spring 1991), 13; Chamberlain is quoted in *The Civil War*, episode 9; Howells is quoted in Allan Gurganus, *Oldest Confederate Widow Tells All* (New York: Ivy Books, 1984), epigraph. For a trenchant recent critique of the "master narrative" of American history rooted in the idea of automatic progress, see Nathan Irvin Huggins, "The Deforming Mirror of Truth," introduction to new edition, *Black Odyssey: The African–American Ordeal in Slavery* (New York: Vintage, 1990).
6   For a similar critique of the PBS film series, one that argues effectively that Burns employed an American "family" metaphor as the overall framework, see Bill Farrell, "All in the Family: Ken Burns's The Civil War and Black America," *Transition: An International Review* 58 (1993): 169–73.
7   Nina Silber, *The Romance of Reunion: Northerners and the South, 1865–1900* (Chapel Hill: Univ. of North Carolina Press, 1993), p. 3.
8   Daniel Aaron, *The Unwritten War: American Writers and the Civil War* (New York: Knopf, 1973), p. 328; W. E. B. Du Bois, *The Souls of Black Folk*, Signet edition (1903; reprint, New York: Signet, 1969), pp. 54, 78.

9   Anderson, *Imagined Communities*, pp. 3, 201.

10 Alain Locke, "The New Negro," in *The New Negro*, Atheneum edition, ed. Alain Locke (1925; reprint, New York: Atheneum, 1968), pp. 4, 16.

11 On nostalgia as a psychological and social phenomenon, see Jean Starobinski, "Nostalgia," *Diogenes* 14 (Summer 1966), 80–103; and Renato Rosaldo, "Imperialist Nostalgia," *Representations* 26 (Spring 1989): 107–22.

12 Frederick Douglass, "The Color Question," July 5, 1875, Frederick Douglass Papers, Library of Congress (hereafter LC), reel 15. On this stage of Reconstruction, see William Gillette, *The Retreat from Reconstruction, 1869–1879* (Baton Rouge: Louisiana State Univ. Press, 1979).

13 John Hope Franklin, "The Birth of a Nation: Propaganda as History," reprinted from the *Massachusetts Review*, 1979, in John Hope Franklin, *Race and History: Selected Essays, 1938–1988* (Baton Rouge: Louisiana State Univ. Press, 1989), pp. 10–23; Ralph Ellison, "Going to the Territory," address given at Brown University, Sept. 20, 1979, reprinted in Ralph Ellison, *Going to the Territory* (New York: Vintage, 1986), p. 124. On Dixon's significance, see Joel Williamson, *The Crucible of Race: Black-White Relations in the American South Since Emancipation* (New York: Oxford Univ. Press, 1984), 140–76.

14 On the turn in American cultural attitudes in the 1880s, see Gerald Linderman, *Embattled Courage: The Experience of Combat in the Civil War* (New York: Free Press, 1987), pp. 266–97; Gaines M. Foster, *Ghosts of the Confederacy: Defeat, the Lost Cause, and the Emergence of the New South* (New York: Oxford Univ. Press, 1987), pp. 63–162; Paul M. Gaston, *The New South Creed: A Study in Southern Myth-Making* (New York: Knopf, 1970); Silber, *Romance of Reunion*, pp. 93–123; and Kammen, *Mystic Chords*, pp. 91–116. On the dynamics of black thought, see August Meier, *Negro Thought in America, 1880–1915: Racial Ideologies in the Age of Booker T. Washington* (Ann Arbor: Univ. of Michigan Press, 1970), pp. 3–82.

15 Alexander Crummell, *Africa and America: Addresses and Discourses* (1891; rpt. New York: Atheneum, 1969), pp. iii, 14, 18, 13. I am indebted to Robert Gooding-Williams for bringing Crummell's speech to my attention. On Crummell, see Wilson J. Moses, *Alexander Crummell: A Study of Civilization and Discontent* (New York: Oxford Univ. Press, 1990); and Alfred A. Moss, Jr., *The American Negro Academy: Voice of the Talented Tenth* (Baton Rouge: Louisiana State Univ. Press, 1981), pp. 19–34, 53–62. Crummell was the founder of the American Negro Academy.

16 See David W. Blight, "For Something Beyond the Battlefield: Frederick Douglass and the Memory of the Civil War," *Journal of American History* 75 (Spring 1989); pp. 1156–78; and John David Smith, *An Old Creed for the New South: Proslavery Ideology and Historiography, 1865–1918* (Westport, CT.: Greenwood, 1985), pp. 287–8.

17 Frederick Douglass, "Speech at the Thirty-Third Anniversary of the Jerry Rescue," 1884, Frederick Douglass Papers, LC, reel 16.

18 Frederick Douglass, "Thoughts and Recollections of the Antislavery Conflict," speech undated, but it is at least from the early 1880s; "Decoration Day," speech at Mt. Hope Cemetery, Rochester, NY, May 1883; and "Address Delivered on the 26th Anniversary of Abolition in the District of Columbia," Apr. 16, 1888, Washington, DC, all in Frederick Douglass Papers, LC, reel 15.

19 On white racial thought, see George M. Fredrickson, *The Black Image in the White Mind: The Debate on Afro-American Character and Destiny*, pp. 1817–1914 (New York: Harper & Row, 1971), pp. 228–82; and Williamson, *Crucible of Race*, pp. 111–323.

20 Paul B. Barringer, "The American Negro, His Past and Future" (address delivered Feb. 20, 1900, Charleston, SC; copy in Widener Library, Harvard University). On Barringer, see Williamson, *Crucible of Race*, p. 177; Fredrickson *Black Image in the White Mind*, pp. 252–53; and Smith, *Old Creed for the New South*, p. 286. Barringer was a leader of the University of Virginia faculty from 1890 to 1903, and later a founder of Virginia Polytechnic Institute.

21 Fredrickson, *Black Image in the White Mind*, pp. 320–2. On the role of white supremacy in the development of a historiographical consensus, see Smith, *Old Creed for the New South*, pp. 103–96, 239–77.

22   See Moses, *Crummell*, pp. 226–8; William S. McFeely, *Frederick Douglass* (New York: Norton, 1991), pp. 238–304; and David W. Blight, *Frederick Douglass' Civil War: Keeping Faith in Jubilee* (Baton Rouge: Louisiana State Univ. Press, 1989), pp. 189–245.

23   Other such comparisons of black intellectuals and competing conceptions of memory might involve Booker T. Washington and his various critics, historian George Washington Williams and activist Ida B. Wells-Barnett, A.M.E. Church Bishop Henry McNeal Turner and historian-activist Archibald Grinke. The list could be much longer. On W. E. B. Du Bois in this regard, see David W. Blight, "W. E. B. Du Bois and the Struggle for American Historical Memory," in *History and Memory in Afro-American Culture*, ed. Genevieve Fabre and Robert O'Meally (New York: Oxford Univ. Press, 1994), pp. 45–71.

24   See David Glassberg, *American Historical Pageantry: The Uses of Tradition in the Early Twentieth Century* (Chapel Hill: Univ. of North Carolina Press, 1990); T. J. Jackson Lears, *No Place of Grace: Antimodernism and the Transformation of American Culture, 1880–1920* (New York: Pantheon, 1981), pp. 97–138; Wallace E. Davies, *Patriotism on Parade: The Story of Veterans' and Hereditary Organizations in America, 1783–1900* (Cambridge, MA.: Harvard Univ. Press, 1955); and Kammen, *Mystic Chords*. On the development of patriotism and nationalism, see John Bodnar, *Public Memory, Commemoration and Patriotism in the Twentieth Century* (Princeton, N.J.: Princeton Univ. Press, 1992).

25   *Fiftieth Anniversary of the Battle of Gettysburg: Report of the Pennsylvania Commission*, Dec. 31, 1913 (Harrisburg, PA: n.p., 1915), pp. 39–41. Every state did not participate in providing funds for veteran transportation, especially some in the South and Southwest. On commemorations at Gettysburg over the years, also see Edward Tabor Linenthal, *Sacred Ground: Americans and Their Battlefields* (Urbana: Univ. of Illinois Press, 1991), pp. 89–126; John S. Patterson, "A Patriotic Landscape: Gettysburg, 1863–1913," *Prospects 7* (1982), pp. 315–33.

26   *Fiftieth Anniversary of the Battle of Gettysburg*, pp. 31, 36–7. The Pennsylvania Commission's report contained dozens of photographs, with one compelling scene after another of the spirit of reconciliation as well as of the generational transmission of national memory. In a few of these photographs one sees black laborers and camp workers, constructing the tents, serving as bakers, or passing out blankets and mess kits. Nowhere is there any photograph of a black veteran.

27   Ibid., pp. 6, 39–41, 49–51, 53, 57–8. Paul Connerton, *How Societies Remember* (New York: Cambridge Univ. Press, 1989); and Alan Trachtenberg, *The Incorporation of America: Culture and Society in the Gilded Age* (New York: Hill & Wang, 1982); *Philadelphia Inquirer*, July 6, 1913. An essay might be written on the "scientific management" and efficiency aspects of the Gettysburg reunion alone. For understanding the Gettysburg community's extraordinary preparation for the reunion, I have relied in part on the *Gettysburg Compiler*, March–July, 1913, microfilm copy at the Gettysburg National Military Park.

28   *Fiftieth Anniversary of the Battle of Gettysburg*, pp. 6, 25; Walter H. Blake, *Hand Grips: The Story of the Great Gettysburg Reunion of 1913* (Vineland, NJ.: n.p., 1913), pp. 66–7.

29   For the Boy Scouts and the suffragists at the reunion, see *Washington Post*, June 28, 30, 1913; *New York Times*, July 1, 1913; and *Fiftieth Anniversary of the Battle of Gettysburg*, pp. 49–51. On the notion of "sites" of memory, see Nora, "Between Memory and History."

30   The Mann speech is reprinted in *Fiftieth Anniversary of the Battle of Gettysburg*, 144, pp. 174–6; Wilson's speech in Arthur Link, ed., *The Papers of Woodrow Wilson*, vol. 28 (Princeton, N.J.: Princeton Univ. Press, 1978), 23.

31   *Louisville Courier-Journal*, July 4, 1913; Ernest Renan, "What is a Nation," in *Nation and Narration*, trans. Martin Thom, ed. Homi K. Bhabha (London: Routledge, 1990), pp. II, 19.

32   Oliver Wendell Holmes, "A Soldier's Faith," an address delivered on Memorial Day, May 30, 1895, at a meeting called by the graduating class of Harvard University, in *Speeches of Oliver Wendell Holmes, Jr.* (Boston: Little, Brown, 1934), pp. 56–66; *Fiftieth Anniversary of the Battle of Gettysburg*, p. 176. On the role of language in the creation of nationalisms, see Anderson, *Imagined Communities*, 154.

33   Garry Wills, *Lincoln at Gettysburg: The Words that Remade America* (New York: Simon and Schuster, 1992), pp. 38, 40; Link, ed., *Papers of Woodrow Wilson* 28:24–5. On the Wilson administration and racial segregation, see Henry Blumenthal, "Woodrow Wilson and the Race Question," *Journal of Negro History* 48 (Jan. 1963), 1–21; and Williamson, *Crucible of Race*, pp. 358–95. On the 1912 election and Wilson's Progressivism in relation to race, see Nell Irvin Painter, *Standing at Armageddon: The United States, 1877–1919* (New York: Norton, 1987), pp. 268–72.

34   See Foster, *Ghosts of the Confederacy*, pp. 7–8. Foster avoids the term *myth* in favor of *tradition*. Also see Alan T. Nolan, *Lee Considered: General Robert E. Lee and Civil War History* (Chapel Hill: Univ. of North Carolina Press, 1991). Nolan comfortably uses the term *myth*. Distinctions between these slippery terms are important, but *myth* seems to be an appropriate terminology in this instance. On the idea of myth for historians, there are many good sources, but see Richard Slotkin, *The Fatal Environment: The Myth of the Frontier in the Age of Industrialization, 1800–1890* (New York: Atheneum, 1985), pp. 1–48; Warren I. Susman, *Culture as History: The Transformation of American Society in the Twentieth Century* (New York: Pantheon, 1973), pp. 7–26; and Kammen, *Mystic Chords*, esp. p. 431–71.

35   Burke, "History as Social Memory," p. 106; Connerton, *How Societies Remember*, pp. 22–5, 28–31. Connerton's anthropological analysis of commemorative rituals is provocative and useful, but the content and the form, the meaning and the performance, must be examined with equal vigor. On commemorations, also see Schwartz, "The Social Context of Commemoration," and the many essays in Gillis, ed., *Commemorations*.

36   *Washington Post*, June 30, 1913. The *Post* also took direct aim at Progressive reformers in the context of the nationalism expressed at Gettysburg. *New York Times*, July 1–4, 1913; *The Outlook* 104 (July 12, 1913); 541, 554–5, 610–12.

37   *Times* (London), July 4, 1913; *Cincinnati Enquirer*, July 6, 1913; *San Francisco Examiner*, July 4, 1913; *Charleston News and Courier*, July 1, 1913; *Brooklyn Daily Eagle*, July 2, 1913.

38   *Baltimore Afro-American Ledger*, July 5, 1913.

39   See Williamson, *Crucible of Race*, pp. 364–95. Booker T. Washington, *New York Times*, Aug. 18, 1913, quoted in Blumenthal, "Woodrow Wilson and the Race Question," p. 8. An especially interesting counterattack on Wilson administration segregation policies in 1913 is Oswald Garrison Villard's "Segregation in Baltimore and Washington," an address delivered to the Baltimore branch of the National Association for the Advancement of Colored People, Oct. 20, 1913, copy in Widener Library, Harvard University. Villard had been a friend and supporter of Wilson's, and was then national chairman of the NAACP. The central figure in the NAACP's often successful resistance to Wilson administration segregation schemes was Archibald Grimke, the branch director for Washington, DC. On Grimke's role in the 1913 disputes see Dickson D. Bruce, Jr., *Archibald Grimke: Portrait of a Black Independent* (Baton Rouge: Louisiana State Univ. Press, 1993), pp. 184–200. It is also interesting to note that in the NAACP's monthly, *Crisis*, editor W. E. B. Du Bois made no mention whatsoever of the Gettysburg reunion. Instead, he wrote a celebration of the 54th Massachusetts black regiment including a full-page photograph of the Shaw/54th Memorial in Boston. See *Crisis* 5–8 (July 1913), 122–6.

40   *Washington Bee*, May 24, June 7, 1913.

41   Paul H. Buck, *The Road to Reunion, 1865–1900* (New York: Random House, 1937), pp. 126, 319, 308–9. The term *miracle* was frequently used in reviews of Buck's book as a means of referring to the triumph of sectional reconciliation. Arthur Schlesinger, Sr., also used the term on the jacket of the original edition. Among the many letters Buck received about his book was one from Margaret Mitchell, author of *Gone With the Wind*, which had just won the Pulitzer Prize for literature the year before. "I am sure your wonderful book, 'The Road to Reunion,' wrote Mitchell, "has never had as interested a reader as 1. I am especially sure that no reader took greater pleasure in the Pulitzer award than I. My sincere congratulations to you." Margaret Mitchell Marsh (Mrs. John R. Marsh) to Paul Buck, May 10, 1938, in Buck's "Scrapbook" collection of reviews, commemorating his Pulitzer Prize, Paul Buck Papers, Harvard University Archives. *Atlanta Constitution*, July 2, 1913.

42 Friedrich Nietzsche, *The Birth of Tragedy* (1872; Garden City, NY: Anchor Books, 1956), p. 136; C. Vann Woodward, *The Strange Career of Jim Crow* (New York: Oxford Univ. Press, 1955), p. viii; Kammen, *Mystic Chords*, p. 37; W. E. B. Du Bois, *Black Reconstruction in America, 1860–1880* (New York: Atheneum, 1935), pp. 714, 717, 723, 725. It is worth pointing out here, of course, that 1913 was also the fiftieth anniversary of emancipation, an event much commemorated in black communities, popular culture, pageants, poetry, song, and literature. The US Congress also held hearings in order to plan an official recognition of emancipation. Du Bois testified before a Senate committee on Feb. 2, 1912. See hearings, "Semicentennial Anniversary of Act of Emancipation," Senate Report no. 31, 62d Cong., 2d sess. Du Bois wrote and helped produce, under the auspices of the NAACP, a pageant, "The Star of Ethiopia," which was performed in 1913, 1915, and 1916. See Glassberg, *American Historical Pageantry*, pp. 132–5; and William H. Wiggins, Jr., *O Freedom!: Afro-American Emancipation Celebrations* (Nashville: Univ. of Tennessee Press, 1987), pp. 49–78. Also see Blight, "W. E. B. Du Bois and the Struggle for American Historical Memory."
43 Huggins, "Deforming Mirror of Truth," *Black Odyssey*, p. xliv.

Questions to consider

- What does Blight think is at stake in the ways Americans choose – or, perhaps, don't choose – to remember the Civil War? More specifically, what's at stake in that image of the embrace of former adversaries at Gettysburg in 1913?

- How does Blight use the term "myth" in this essay? How would you describe the relationship between myth and history?

- Can you imagine a society in which the Civil War is not regarded any more important than, say, the War of 1812? What kind of society do you imagine that to be? Would you want to live in it?

Chapter 35

Memory: Primary Sources

The United States Cannot Remain Half-Slave and Half-Free

Frederick Douglass

By the end of the nineteenth century, Frederick Douglass had literally become the face of freedom to millions of Americans of all colors. He certainly had his critics, among them those who felt he stood closely (albeit uncomfortably) with an increasingly complacent and remote Republican establishment. But Douglass's own history as an escaped slave – and, especially, a dignified eloquence that rings across centuries – made him a compelling spokesman for black rights with a broad credibility that exceeded that of heirs like Booker T. Washington and W. E. B. DuBois. In the pantheon of black heroes – in the pantheon of American heroes – he belongs in an inner circle that includes that non-violent warrior of Second Reconstruction, Martin Luther King, Jr.

   The title of this speech, given twenty years after the Emancipation Proclamation took effect, comes from the famous – and at the time, highly controversial – 1858 assertion by Abraham Lincoln that the nation could not survive half-slave and half-free. Surveying the gigantic changes that had taken place in the quarter century since, Douglass nevertheless asserts that the nation is in some ways still half-slave and half-free. But he maintains his faith that this will not continue, and his hope that it will end in a truly integrated society of all people, by all people, and for all people.

Frederick Douglass, "The United States Cannot Remain Half-Slave & Half-Free," (April 16, 1883), in *Frederick Douglass: Selected Speeches and Writings*, ed. P. S. Foner and Y. Taylor (Chicago: Lawrence Hill Books, 2000), pp. 656–68.

Friends and Fellow Citizens:

   I could have wished that some one from among the younger men of Washington, some one with a mind more fruitful, with a voice more eloquent, with an oratorical ambition more lofty, more active, and more stimulating to high endeavor than mine, had been selected by your Committee of Arrangements, to give suitable utterance to the thoughts, feelings, and purposes, which this 21st anniversary of Emancipation in the District of Columbia is fitted to inspire. That such a one could have been easily found among the aspiring and promising young colored men of Washington, I am happy to know and am proud to affirm. They are the legitimate children of the great act we are met to celebrate. They have been reared in the light of its *new* born freedom, qualified by its education, and by the elevating spirit of liberty, to speak the wise and grateful words befitting the occasion. The presence of one such, as your orator to-night, would be a more brilliant illustration of the wisdom and beneficence of the act of Emancipation, than any words of mine, however well chosen and appropriate. I represent the past, they the present. I represent the downfall of slavery, they the glorious triumphs of liberty. I speak of deliverance from bondage, they speak of concessions to liberty and equality. Their mission begins where my mission ends.

Nevertheless, while I would have gladly given place to one of these rising young men, I could not well decline the duty and the honor of appearing here tonight. It may, after all, be well to have something of the past mingled with the present, well that one who has had some share in the conflict should share also in the public joy of the victory.

At the outset, as an old watchman on the walls of liberty, eagerly scanning the social and political horizon, you naturally ask me, What of the night? It is easy to break forth in joy and thanksgiving for Emancipation in the District of Columbia. It is easy to call up the noble sentiments and the startling events which made that grand measure possible. It is easy to trace the footsteps of the Negro in the past, marked as they are all the way along with blood. But the present occasion calls for something more. How stands the Negro to-day? What are the relations subsisting between him and the powerful people among whom he lives, moves, and has his being? What is the outlook, and what is his probable future?

You will readily perceive that I have raised more questions than I shall be able for the present to answer. My general response to these inquiries is a mixed one. The sky of the American Negro is dark, but not rayless; it is stormy, but not cheerless. The grand old party of liberty, union, and progress, which has been his reliance and refuge so long, though less cohesive and strong than it once was, is still a power and has a future. I give you notice, that while there is a Democratic party there will be a Republican party. As the war for the Union recedes into the misty shadows of the past, and the Negro is no longer needed to assault forts and stop rebel bullets, he is in some sense, of less importance. Peace with the old master class has been war to the Negro. As the one has risen, the other has fallen. The reaction has been sudden, marked, and violent. It has swept the Negro from all the legislative halls of the Southern States, and from those of the Congress of the United States. It has, in many cases, driven him from the ballot box and the jury box. The situation has much in it for serious thought, but nothing to cause despair. Above all the frowning clouds that lower about our horizon, there is the steady light of stars, and the thick clouds that now obscure them, will in due season pass away.

In fact, they are already passing away. Time and events which have done so much for us in the past, will, I trust, not do less for us in the future. The moral government of the universe is on our side, and cooperates, with all honest efforts, to lift up the down-trodden and oppressed in all lands, whether the oppressed be white or black.

In whatever else the Negro may have been a failure, he has, in one respect, been a marked and brilliant success. He has managed by one means or another to make himself one of the most prominent and interesting figures that now attract and hold the attention of the world.

Go where you will, you will meet with him. He is alike present in the study of the learned and thoughtful, and in the play house of the gay and thoughtless. We see him pictured at our street corners, and hear him in the songs of our market places. The low and the vulgar curse him, the snob and the flunky affect to despise him, the mean and the cowardly assault him, because they know that his friends are few, and that they can abuse him with impunity, and with the applause of the coarse and brutal crowd. But, despite of it all, the Negro remains like iron or granite, cool, strong, imperturbable and cheerful.

Men of all lands and languages make him a subject of profound thought and study. To the statesman and philosopher he is an object of intense curiosity. Men want to know more of his character, his qualities, his attainments, his mental possibilities, and his probable destiny. Notwithstanding their black faces, the Jubilee singers, with their wild and plaintive music, thrill and charm the most refined and cultivated of the white race, both here and in Europe. Generous and brave men like Andrew Jackson, Benjamin F. Butler, and General Grant, have borne ample testimony to the courage of the Negro, to his gallantry, and to his patriotism. Of the books, pamphlets, and speeches concerning him, there is literally, no end. He is the one inexhaustible topic of conversation at our firesides and in our public halls.

Great, however, as is his advantage at this point, he is not altogether fortunate after all, as to the manner in which his claims are canvassed. His misfortune is that few men are qualified to discuss him candidly and impartially. They either exalt him too high or rate him too low. Americans can consider almost any other question more calmly and fairly than this one. I know of nothing outside of religion which kindles more wrath, causes wider differences, or gives force and effect to fiercer and more irreconcilable antagonisms.

It was so in the time of slavery, and it is so now. Then, the cause was interest, now, the cause is pride and prejudice. Then, the cause was property. He was then worth twenty hundred millions to his owner. He is now worth uncounted millions to himself. While a slave there was a mountain of gold on his breast to keep him down – now that he is free there is a mountain of prejudice to hold him down.

[. . .]

With a knowledge of the events of the last score of years, with a knowledge of the sudden and startling changes which have already come to pass, I am not prepared to say what the future will be.

But I will say that I do not look for colonization either in or out of the United States. Africa is too far off, even if we desired to go there, which we do not. The navy of all the world would not be sufficient to remove our natural increase to that far off country. Removal to any of the territories is out of the question.

We have no business to put ourselves before the bayonets of the white race. We have seen the fate of the Indian. As to extinction, the prospect in that direction has been greatly clouded by the census just taken, in which it is seen that our increase is ten per cent greater than that of the white people of the South.

There is but one destiny, it seems to me, left for us, and that is to make ourselves and be made by others a part of the American people in every sense of the word. Assimilation and not isolation is our true policy and our natural destiny. Unification for us is life: separation is death. We cannot afford to set up for ourselves a separate political party, or adopt for ourselves a political creed apart from the rest of our fellow citizens. Our own interests will be subserved by a generous care for the interests of the Nation at large. All the political, social and literary forces around us tend to unification.

I am the more inclined to accept this solution because I have seen the steps already taken in that direction. The American people have their prejudices, but they have other qualities as well. They easily adapt themselves to inevitable conditions, and all their tendency is to progress, enlightenment and to the universal.

"It's comin' yet for a' that,
    That man to man the world o'er
Shall brothers be for a' that."

Questions to consider

- How does Douglass understand his role in giving this speech?

- What are some of the accomplishments – and problems – facing former slaves 20 years after Emancipation?

- Would you say that "the Negro" has still "managed to make himself one of the most prominent and interesting figures that now attract and hold the attention of the world?" Why?

- How close are we to Frederick Douglass's dream of "assimilation?" How much more has to happen for it to be realized? Do you think it will be?

Index

Note: page numbers and plate numbers in *italics* refer to illustrations.